Developing Java™ Web Services

Architecting and Developing Secure Web Services Using Java

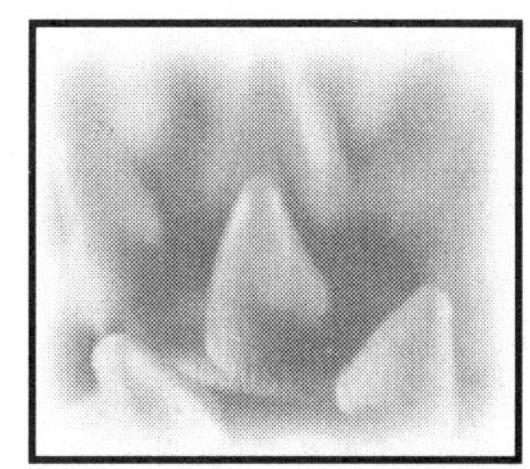

Developing Java™ Web Services

Architecting and Developing Secure Web Services Using Java

Ramesh Nagappan
Robert Skoczylas
Rima Patel Sriganesh

Wiley Publishing, Inc.

Publisher: Robert Ipsen
Editor: Theresa Hudson
Developmental Editors: Scott Amerman and James Russell
Editorial Manager: Kathryn A. Malm
Managing Editor: Angela Smith
Text Design & Composition: Wiley Composition Services

This book is printed on acid-free paper. ♾

For general information on our other products and services please contact our Customer Care Department within the United States at (800) 762-2974, outside the United States at (317) 572-3993 or fax (317) 572-4002.

Wiley also publishes its books in a variety of electronic formats. Some content that appears in print may not be available in electronic versions.

For more information about Wiley products, visit our Web site at www.wiley.com.

Library of Congress Cataloging-in-Publication Data:

ISBN 0-471-23640-3

Printed in the United States of America

10 9 8 7 6 5 4 3 2

Contents

Foreword xiii

Introduction xv

Part One Evolution and Emergence of Web Services 1

Chapter 1 Evolution of Distributed Computing 3

What Is Distributed Computing? 4
The Importance of Distributed Computing 5
Client-Server Applications 6
CORBA 8
Java RMI 10
Microsoft DCOM 13
Message-Oriented Middleware 14
Common Challenges in Distributed Computing 16
The Role of J2EE and XML in Distributed Computing 17
The Emergence of Web Services 20
Summary 20

Chapter 2 Introduction to Web Services 21

What Are Web Services? 22
Motivation and Characteristics 24
Why Use Web Services? 26
Basic Operational Model of Web Services 26
Core Web Services Standards 27
- Extensible Markup Language (XML) 28
- Simple Object Access Protocol (SOAP) 28
- Web Services Definition Language (WSDL) 29
- Universal Description, Discovery, and Integration (UDDI) 29
- ebXML 30

Other Industry Standards Supporting Web Services 31
Web Services Choreography Interface (WSCI) 31
Web Services Flow Language (WSFL) 31
Directory Services Markup Language (DSML) 31
XLANG 32
Business Transaction Protocol (BTP) 32
XML Encryption (XML ENC) 32
XML Key Management System (XKMS) 32
XML Signature (XML DSIG) 33
Extensible Access Control Markup Language (XACML) 33
Security Assertions Markup Language (SAML) 33
Known Challenges in Web Services 34
Web Services Software and Tools 34
BEA Systems Products 34
Cape Clear Products 35
IBM Products 35
IOPSIS Products 35
Oracle Products 35
Sun Products 36
Systinet Products 36
Web Services Strategies from Industry Leaders: An Overview 36
Sun ONE (Sun Open Net Environment) 37
IBM e-Business 37
Microsoft .NET 37
Key Benefits of Web Services 38
Summary 38

Part Two Web Services Architecture and Technologies 39

Chapter 3 Building the Web Services Architecture 41
Web Services Architecture and Its Core Building Blocks 42
Tools of the Trade 46
Simple Object Access Protocol (SOAP) 46
Web Services Description Language (WSDL) 47
Universal Description, Discovery, and Integration (UDDI) 49
ebXML 49
Web Services Communication Models 50
RPC-Based Communication Model 50
Messaging-Based Communication Model 51
Implementing Web Services 52
Developing Web Services-Enabled Applications 54
How to Develop Java-Based Web Services 55
Developing Web Services Using J2EE: An Example 60
Summary 101

Chapter 4 Developing Web Services Using SOAP 103
XML-Based Protocols and SOAP 104
The Emergence of SOAP 105
Understanding SOAP Specifications 106

	Anatomy of a SOAP Message	107
	SOAP Envelope	110
	SOAP Header	111
	SOAP Body	112
	SOAP Fault	112
	SOAP mustUnderstand	115
	SOAP Attachments	116
	SOAP Encoding	118
	Simple Type Values	118
	Polymorphic Accessor	119
	Compound Type Values	120
	Serialization and Deserialization	124
	SOAP Message Exchange Model	124
	SOAP Intermediaries	126
	SOAP Actor	127
	SOAP Communication	128
	SOAP RPC	128
	SOAP Messaging	130
	SOAP Bindings for Transport Protocols	131
	SOAP over HTTP	131
	SOAP over SMTP	134
	Other SOAP Bindings	136
	SOAP Message Exchange Patterns	138
	SOAP Security	140
	SOAP Encryption	140
	SOAP Digital Signature	142
	SOAP Authorization	143
	Building SOAP Web Services	144
	Developing SOAP Web Services Using Java	145
	Developing Web Services Using Apache Axis	146
	Installing Axis for Web Services	147
	Running Axis without Tomcat/Servlet Engine	149
	Axis Infrastructure and Components	149
	Axis Web Services Programming Model	154
	Creating Web Services Using Axis: An Example	160
	Building Axis-Based Infrastructure	161
	Setting Up the ACME Web Services Environment	165
	Implementing the ACME Web Services	173
	Known Limitations of SOAP	199
	Summary	199
Chapter 5	**Description and Discovery of Web Services**	**201**
	Web Services Description Language (WSDL)	202
	WSDL in the World of Web Services	202
	Anatomy of a WSDL Definition Document	204
	WSDL Bindings	211
	WSDL Tools	214

Future of WSDL 221
Limitations of WSDL 222
Universal Description, Discovery, and Integration (UDDI) 222
UDDI Registries 223
Programming with UDDI 226
Inquiry API 235
Publishing API 249
Implementations of UDDI 254
Registering as a Systinet UDDI Registry User 255
Publishing Information to a UDDI Registry 257
Searching Information in a UDDI Registry 260
Deleting Information from a UDDI Registry 264
Limitations of UDDI 269
Summary 269

Chapter 6 Creating .NET Interoperability 271
Means of Ensuring Interoperability 272
Declaring W3C XML Schemas 273
Exposing WSDL 273
Creating SOAP Proxies 273
Testing Interoperability 274
Microsoft .NET Framework: An Overview 274
Common Language Runtime (CLR) 275
.NET Framework Class Library 275
Developing Microsoft .NET Client for Web Services 276
Key Steps in Creating a Web Service Requestor Using the .NET Framework 276
Case Study: Building a .NET Client for Axis Web Services 278
Challenges in Creating Web Services Interoperability 289
Common SOAP/HTTP Transport Issues 290
XML Schema- and XML-Related Issues 290
SOAP/XML Message Discontinuities 290
Version and Compatibility 291
The WS-I Initiative and Its Goals 291
Public Interoperability testing efforts 292
Summary 292

Part Three Exploring Java Web Services Developer Pack 293

Chapter 7 Introduction to the Java Web Services Developer Pack (JWSDP) 295
Java Web Services Developer Pack 296
Java XML Pack 297
Java APIs for XML 297
JavaServer Pages Standard Tag Library 309
Apache Tomcat Container 309
Java WSDP Registry Server 310
ANT Build Tool 310

Downloading the Web Services Pack 310
Summary 311

Chapter 8 XML Processing and Data Binding with Java APIs 313
Extensible Markup Language (XML) Basics 314
XML Syntax 316
Namespaces 322
Validation of XML Documents 324
Java API for XML Processing (JAXP) 337
JAXP 337
Uses for JAXP 338
JAXP API Model 339
JAXP Implementations 342
Processing XML with SAX 342
Processing XML with DOM 353
XSL Stylesheets: An Overview 364
Transforming with XSLT 372
Threading 383
Java Architecture for XML Binding (JAXB) 383
Data Binding Generation 386
Marshalling XML 393
Unmarshalling Java 395
Other Callback Methods 396
Sample Code for XML Binding 396
Summary 399

Chapter 9 XML Messaging Using JAXM and SAAJ 401
The Role of JAXM in Web Services 402
JAXM Application Architecture 403
JAXM Messaging: Interaction Patterns 406
JAXM API Programming Model 407
javax.xml.messaging 407
javax.xml.soap (SAAJ 1.1 APIs) 409
Basic Programming Steps for Using JAXM 413
Using a JAXM Provider 413
Using JAXM without a Provider (Using SOAPConnection) 419
JAXM Deployment Model 425
Deploying JAXM-Based Applications in JWSDP 1.0 425
Configuring JAXM Applications Using a JAXM Provider 427
Configuring a Client 428
Configuring a Provider 428
Developing JAXM-Based Web Services 430
Point-to-Point Messaging Using JAXM (SOAPConnection) 431
Asynchronous Messaging Using the JAXM Provider 439
JAXM Interoperability 450
JAXM in J2EE 1.4 450
Summary 450

Chapter 10	**Building RPC Web Services with JAX-RPC**	**451**
	The Role of JAX-RPC in Web Services	452
	Comparing JAX-RPC with JAXM	454
	JAX-RPC Application Architecture	454
	JAX-RPC APIs and Implementation Model	456
	JAX-RPC-Based Service Implementation	456
	JAX-RPC-Based Client Implementation	464
	JAX-RPC-Supported Java/XML Mappings	471
	Java/WSDL Definition Mappings	474
	Developing JAX-RPC-Based Web Services	476
	Creating a JAX-RPC-Based Service (BookPriceService)	476
	Developing JAX-RPC Clients (BookPriceServiceClient)	484
	JAX-RPC in J2EE 1.4	491
	JAX-RPC Interoperability	491
	Summary	492
Chapter 11	**Java API for XML Registries**	**493**
	Introduction to JAXR	494
	JAXR Architecture	494
	JAXR Architectural Components	494
	JAXR Capabilities and Capability Profiles	496
	The JAXR Programming Model	498
	JAXR Information Model	499
	Classes and Interfaces	499
	Classification of Registry Objects	502
	Association of Registry Objects	508
	JAXR Registry Services API	510
	Connection Management API	510
	Life Cycle Management API	516
	Query Management API	522
	JAXR Support in JWSDP 1.0	532
	Registry Server	532
	Registry Browser	534
	Understanding JAXR by Examples	536
	Publishing Using JAXR	536
	Querying Using JAXR	549
	Deleting Information Using JAXR	556
	Summary	561
Chapter 12	**Using the Java Web Services Developer Pack: Case Study**	**563**
	Case Study Overview	563
	The Roles of Service Provider, Requestor, and Registry	564
	Important Components and Entities	564
	Case Study Architecture	567
	Design of Components	568
	Provider Environment	568
	Designing the Publishing and Discovery Classes	572
	Designing the Service Requestor Environment (computerBuy.com)	575

	Implementation	582
	Developing the Service Environment	582
	Developing the Service Requestor Environment	593
	Setting Up the JWSDP Environment	602
	Service Provider Runtime Infrastructure (acmeprovider.com)	602
	Service Registry Infrastructure	609
	Service Requestor Runtime Infrastructure (computerBuy.com)	610
	Executing a Scenario	612
	Summary	615
Part Four	**Security in Web Services**	**617**
Chapter 13	**Web Services Security**	**619**
	Challenges of Securing Web Services	620
	Technologies behind Securing Web Services	621
	Rapid-Fire Cryptography	621
	XML Encryption	630
	What XML Encryption Is	631
	Implementations of XML Encryption	633
	XML Encryption	633
	Encrypting <Accounts> XML Element	641
	Decrypting the <Accounts> XML Element	643
	Programming Steps for Encryption and Decryption	644
	XML Signatures	650
	Types of XML Signatures	650
	XML Signature Syntax	652
	Canonicalization	655
	Implementations of XML Signature	656
	XML Signature: An Example	657
	XML Key Management Specification (XKMS)	668
	XKMS Components	670
	XKMS Implementations	671
	XML Key Information Service Specification (X-KISS)	671
	XML Key Registration Service Specification (X-KRSS)	677
	Security Assertions Markup Language (SAML)	685
	SAML Implementations	687
	SAML Architecture	689
	Authentication Assertion	691
	Attribute Assertion	693
	Authorization (Decision) Assertion	694
	SAML Bindings and Protocols	696
	Model of Producers and Consumers of SAML Assertions	697
	Single Sign-On Using SAML	698
	XML Access Control Markup Language (XACML)	706
	Architecture of an XML Access Control System	707
	Conclusion	710
	Summary	711

Part Five Web Services Strategies and Solutions **713**

Chapter 14 Introduction to Sun ONE **715**

The Vision behind Sun ONE 715
Delivering Services on Demand (SoD) 718
  Web Applications 718
  Web Services 718
  Web Clients 723
Sun ONE Architecture 724
  Sun ONE Service Layers 724
  Sun ONE Standards and Technologies 725
  Sun ONE Product Stack: Integrated versus Integrate-able 727
Summary 731

Further Reading **733**

Index **741**

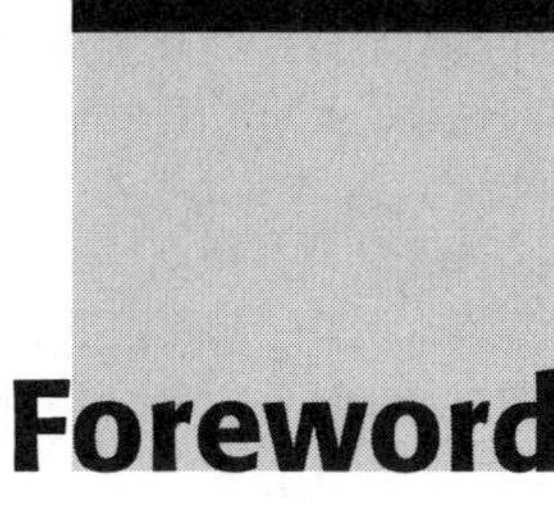

Foreword

In the last decade of computing, we have seen a growing realization that most of the cost of computing comes not from the initial purchase of the hardware, not even from the purchase of the software, but from the cost of responding to change throughout the life of the system. When one part changes, the degree of tight coupling between the elements of the system dictates the "brittleness" or probability that change will be forced elsewhere. When you have to retest the software because the operating system was "upgraded," that's brittleness. When you can't open your word processor documents because the software version is wrong, that's brittleness. When a policy change in the accounting department dictates a software rewrite in the sales department, that's brittleness.

In seeking to eliminate brittleness, there have been three significant steps taken:

- The first was the introduction of Java technology, which separated software from the platform and allowed the creation of business logic that wasn't greatly affected by changes to the underlying server.
- The second was the introduction of Extensible Markup Language (XML), which separated the data from the software and enabled different software systems to share data without being affected by changes to the data structures unless they needed to respond to them.
- The most recent is the introduction of Web services. Web services separate collaborating computer systems connected by networks, enabling them to delegate processing without becoming coupled in a brittle way.

All three of these steps need one another. The maximum protection against brittleness occurs when software written for the Java platform uses agreed XML data formats to supply or consume services, which are connected using Web services technologies such as SOAP and WSDL and perhaps UDDI, if the application calls for it. Systems built with Java technology, XML, and Web services are loosely coupled in all three dimensions and will be the most resilient and flexible in the uncertain future that faces us all.

The conjunction of Java for the software, XML for the data, and Web services for the collaborative processing makes this book especially timely and welcome. The majority of Web services development today is being conducted using products from the extraordinarily rich Java community, and the rapid integration of Web services into Java 2 Enterprise Edition (J2EE) by the Java Community Process (JCP) offers the software developer a comprehensive toolchest. In the pages that follow, you will find the following:

- Discussion of the evolving standards landscape for Web services, including the important developments at ebXML, the XML successor to EDI
- The Java APIs for XML (JAX) standards so skillfully evolved by the JCP to address everything connected to XML and Web services in a vendor-neutral way
- Information about the approaches being taken by all of the important Web services vendors, including a variety of tools
- Practical examples that will help you get started with your own Java Web services implementations
- A discussion of the essentials of Web services security that considers both the needs of identity management and of in-transit data protection
- A valuable case study of a real-world Web services deployment using Java

Web services are such a fundamental idea in the world of connected computing that they will rapidly become part of the everyday fabric of information systems, just as Java technology and XML have already. I commend this book to you as your springboard to the future of how to make the Internet work.

–Simon Phipps (www.webmink.net)
Chief Technology Evangelist at Sun Microsystems, Inc.

Introduction

"The big Web Services story is the end-to-end, side-to-side integration of technology."

James Gosling,
The father of Java Platform

In this age of Internet, the success of the Web-based applications played a vital role in moving our businesses from brick-and-mortar infrastructures to 24 × 7 online businesses running on different systems and locations. As a next evolutionary step, Web services are a new breed of Web-based applications that address the new phenomenon of building a general-purpose platform for creating efficient integration among business processes, applications, enterprises, partners, customers, and so on. Web services are the next evolution phase of distributed computing, based on XML standards and Internet protocols. Web services provide a promising mechanism for communication and collaboration among business applications, which were constructed using various resources, that enables them to work together regardless of their differences in their underlying implementation.

This book is a developer's guide for designing and developing Web services using a Java platform. It bundles together a wealth of knowledge and detailed study materials, focusing on concepts, technologies, and practical techniques for implementing and deploying Web services. It combines the Web services vision of the Java community by providing in-depth coverage of the Java Web Services Developer Pack (JWSDP). In addition, this book also addresses the fundamentals of Web services from the ground up.

Technologies Covered in This Book

The book covers the core Web services standards and technologies for designing and implementing Web services. In particular, it focuses in depth on the following subject areas:

- Web services standards, protocols, and technologies, including SOAP, WSDL, and UDDI
- Web services architecture and exposing J2EE applications as Web services.
- The development of Web services using Java APIs (JAXP, JAXB, JAX-RPC, JAXM, and JAXR) on JWSDP
- Web services security technologies: XML Encryption, XML Signature, Security Assertion Markup Language (SAML), XML Key Management Services (XKMS), and XML Access Control Markup Language (XACML)
- Interoperability with Microsoft .NET
- The real-world implementation of Web services on JWSDP, using a case study
- Introduction to Sun ONE

In addition, the book also provides example illustrations using tools such as Sun Microsystems JWSDP 1.0, BEA WebLogic 7.0, Systinet WASP 4.0, Apache Axis 1.0 Beta 3, IBM XML Security Suite, Exolab CASTOR, and Microsoft .NET framework.

Target Audience

This book is for all Web services enthusiasts, architects, and developers who perceive Java as their platform of choice for Web services development and deployment.

This book presumes that the reader has the basic conceptual and programming knowledge of implementing Web applications using Java and XML.

Organization of the Book

The content of this book is organized into following five parts, with exclusive chapters concentrating on the Web services technologies:

Part One, "Evolution and Emergence of Web Services." Introduces the reader to Web services by taking a evolutionary journey of distributed computing and the emergence of Web services, and then it devotes an exclusive overview on Web services, addressing its motivation, characteristics, industry standards and technologies, strategies and solutions, and its benefits and limitations.

Chapter 1, "Evolution of Distributed Computing." The background of distributed computing and the evolution of Internet-enabled technologies is explored in the first chapter. Here, we will examine the definition and reasons for using distributed computing and the core distributed computing technologies.

Chapter 2, "Introduction to Web Services." This chapter presents an introduction to Web services, especially focusing on the definition of Web services, the standards and technologies that the services use, and the benefits of using these services.

Part Two, "Web Services Architecture and Technologies." This section walks through the different Web services standards and technologies such as SOAP, WSDL, and UDDI with real-world examples. It features an in-depth coverage of the Web services architecture on a J2EE implementation model, with example illustrations showing how to expose enterprise applications to Web services. It also demonstrates an interoperability scenario with non-Java based Web services.

Chapter 3, "Building the Web Services Architecture." This chapter focuses on the Web services architecture, its core building blocks, implementation models, and deployment processes for building Web services-based application solutions. In addition, this chapter illustrates, using an example, the development of a complete Web services solution, exposing J2EE applications as services over the Internet.

Chapter 4, "Developing Web services using SOAP." This chapter provides an in-depth discussion on SOAP and its role in developing Web services. It covers the W3C definition of SOAP's standards, conventions, messages, communication models, and implementation of SOAP-based applications for Web services. In addition, the chapter also includes example illustrations of adopting different SOAP communication models in Web services.

Chapter 5, "Description and Discovery of Web Services." This chapter explains two important Web services specifications: WSDL and UDDI. It provides a detailed explanation on the important aspects of a WSDL specification and examples of using WSDL tools within Web services development. UDDI specification also is covered in great detail, complete with practical examples on working with UDDI registries. This chapter also covers issues with the current WSDL and UDDI technologies.

Chapter 6, "Creating .NET Interoperability." This chapter discusses the Web services interoperability scenarios, challenges, and issues. It also illustrates a full-featured interoperability example that involves Java and Microsoft .NET environments.

Part Three, "Exploring Java Web Services Developer Pack (JWSDP)." This section exclusively focuses on Java APIs for Web services: JAXP, JAXB, JAXM, JAX-RPC, and JAX-R, and their reference implementation on JWSDP. This section provides complete example illustrations and developer essentials for implementing and deploying Java-based Web services on JWSDP. It also includes a special chapter that illustrates a case study demonstrating a real-world Web services implementation using JWSDP.

Chapter 7, "Introduction to the Java Web Services Developer Pack." This chapter introduces the reader to the Java Web Services Developer Pack (JWSDP) 1.0. It covers the Java XML Pack APIs and provides an overview of the runtime environment and tools used for building, deploying, and testing Web services applications.

Chapter 8, "XML Processing and Data Binding with Java APIs." This chapter discusses the Java API for XML Processing (JAXP) and Java Architecture for XML Binding (JAXB). It provides an overview of XML, DTD, and W3C XML Schema and then provides a walkthrough of the various techniques used for processing XML data. The chapter also covers the Simple API for XML (SAX), Document Object Model (DOM), and eXtensible Stylesheet transformations (XSLT). For completeness, it also dedicates a section on data binding using JAXB.

Chapter 9, "XML Messaging Using JAXM and SAAJ." This chapter discusses the Java API for XML messaging (JAXM) and SOAP with Attachment API for Java (SAAJ). It covers the JAXM/SAAJ-based application architecture, an API programming model, and deployment. It also includes example illustrations of using JAXM and SAAJ APIs.

Chapter 10, "Building RPC Web Services with JAX-RPC." This chapter discusses the Java API for XML RPC (Remote procedural call) for developing RPC-based Web services. It also covers the

JAX-RPC application architecture, an API programming model, deployment, and its different client Invocation models. It also includes example illustrations using JAX-RPC and demonstrates the different client invocations.

Chapter 11, "Java API for XML Registries." This chapter provides detailed information on the Java API for XML Registry (JAXR) specification from the Java Community Process (JCP). It also discusses the various aspects of JAXR in terms of its classification support, association support, connection management, life cycle management, and querying capabilities. Also provided with this chapter is the discussion on the various JAXR examples about working with UDDI registries.

Chapter 12, "Using theJava Web Services Developer Pack: Case Study." This chapter focuses on implementing a complete Web services solution using the Java Web Services Developer Pack (JWSDP) 1.0. It puts together all of the JWSDP-based APIs covered in this book to demonstrate a working Web services example.

Part Four, "Security in Web Services." This section covers Web services security concepts and various security standards and technologies. In addition, it illustrates real-world Web services security implementation scenarios on XML Encryption, XML Signature, and SAML-based Single Sign-On.

Chapter 13, "Web Services Security." This chapter provides great details on the issues revolving around Web services security, which is followed by a discussion on each of the five major Web services security technologies: XML Encryption, XML Signature, XML Key Management Services (XKMS) , Security Assertions Markup Language (SAML), and XML Access Control Markup Language (XACML). It also provides good examples of using tools for securing Web services through XML Encryption and XML Signature technologies. In addition, the chapter provides a hypothetical use case study of applying SAML for achieving Single Sign-On.

Part Five, "Web Services Strategies and Solutions." This section introduces the reader to the Sun ONE initiative and provides information on Sun ONE tools and platform servers for implementing Web services.

Chapter 14, "Introduction to Sun ONE." This chapter aims at introducing the Sun ONE platform technologies and products. It also provides some brief information on the Sun ONE product stack, including its tools and platform servers. In addition, it also introduces ebXML technologies.

Companion Web Site

All the source code from the example illustrations found within this book is available for download from the companion Web site, www.wiley.com/compbooks/nagappan.

In addition, this site also includes the following material:

- Errata
- Further reading and references
- Changes and updates

Support and Feedback

The authors would like to receive the reader's feedback. You are encouraged to post questions and/or contact the authors at their prospective email addresses. Contact information can be found at the companion Web site to this book at www.wiley.com/compbooks/nagappan.

Acknowledgments

The authors would like to extend their big thanks to the Wiley publishing team, including Terri Hudson, Kathryn Malm, Scott Amerman, James Russell, and Angela Smith; and the reviewers for their constant help, from beginning to end, in fulfilling this dream work.

Thanks to Simon Phipps for writing the Foreword and sharing his best thoughts on Web services in this book.

Thanks, too, to Dave Martin and Chris Steel for having reviewed this work and sharing their views.

Heartfelt gratitude to our friends at Sun Microsystems for their help and support while accomplishing this work.

Ramesh Nagappan

After six months of hard work, it is an utter surprise for me to see the completion of the project, and it's a great feeling to see the quality of work the way we wanted.

It's quite fun to recall the genesis of this book: Two friends, Sada Rajagopalan and Sameer Tyagi, started gathering ideas for this mammoth project on September 19, 2001, at the John Harvard's Pub in Natick, Massachusetts. Around 10:45 P.M., after most of us had three pitchers of a seasonal flavor and all had shared rip-roaring hilarious talk, Sada, who didn't drink, came up with this idea of writing a book on Java Web services. In the next few days, we created the proposal for this book. Both Sameer and Sada helped us initiating this huge effort and in getting the proposal written; much thanks to them for all their efforts. It's always been great fun calling Sameer in the middle of the night, especially to discuss emerging technologies, as well as known bugs, changes, and issues.

My special thanks goes to Sunil Mathew and my fellow architects at the Sun Java center for their constant encouragement for writing this book. Thanks to the Apache Axis team and my friends at Apache Software Foundation for being helpful, answering my questions, and updating me with changes. Thanks also to the Exolab CASTOR, Systinet WASP, and W3C SOAP discussion groups for answering my questions with insightful responses and initiating valuable discussions.

Finally, the largest share of the credit goes to my loving wife, Joyce, my little buddy Roger, and my parents for all their love and support. Only through their love and support, am I able to accomplish any goal.

Robert Skoczylas

After long, long hours of hard work we are finally done with the chapters and ready to thank and recognize the help of many people who gave us guidance, direction, and support.

Special thanks to Sada Rajagopalan for his contributions to the first chapter of the book. Your amazing motivation got this ball rolling. Thanks!

Big thanks to all the expert contributors of the Java, XML, and Web services mailing lists out there, your feedback adds a great value to this work.

I want to thank all my friends at the Sun Java Center for all their support, especially my manager, Sunil Mathew, for his constant encouragement.

Also, to the many people who have directly or indirectly influenced my career: Albert Rudnicki, Paul Dhanjal, Mario Landreville, Ray Sabourin, Jan Bratkowski, Sameer Tyagi, Tomasz Ratajczak, Carol McDonald, Chris Steel, and Dan Hushon.

Thanks to my parents, Urszula and Jacek, and my brother Slawomir, who always show me the way things need to be done.

Finally, I would like to thank my fiancée, Urszula Masalska, who put up with this project for the last couple of months. Without your patience and encouragement, I wouldn't have had the strength to cross the finish line. Thank you!

Rima Patel Sriganesh

This book has been an exciting roller-coaster ride of my life. When I first started as a reviewer of this book, I never imagined that I would end up being a co-author. All of a sudden when that opportunity came up, I was overwhelmed with joy as well as work. It was during the course of this project that I realized how challenging this work was, not only for me, but also for my husband, who'd happily let go of all the fun moments for the sake of my venture.

In the memory of those fun times we lost, I would like to dedicate my share of this hard work, success, and joy to my dearest and loving husband, Sriganesh, without whom life would not have been so beautiful; and my most wonderful parents, who spent the best years of their lives in turning me into the person that I am today.

My special thanks goes to Max Goff, without whom I would have never got to know this beautiful world of Technology Evangelism.

Also, I would like to thank my fellow Evangelist Carol McDonald for introducing me to my cohorts on this book as well as the rest of the Sun Technology Evangelism group, including my manager, Reginald Hutcherson.

About the Authors

Ramesh Nagappan is an experienced software architect who specializes in Java-, XML-, and CORBA-based distributed computing architectures for Internet-based business applications and Web services. He is an active contributor to popular Java- and XML-based open source applications. Prior to this work, he has co-authored two books on J2EE and EAI. He is also an avid Unix enthusiast. Before he hooked on to Java and CORBA, he worked as a research engineer for developing software solutions for CAD/CAM, fluid dynamics, system simulation, and aerodynamics applications.

Currently he is working for Sun Microsystems as an Enterprise Java Architect with the Sun Java Center in Boston. He lives in the Boston suburb with his wife and son. In his spare time, he enjoys water sports and playing with his son Roger. He graduated from Harvard University, specializing in applied sciences. He can be reached at nramesh@post.harvard.edu.

Robert Skoczylas is an Enterprise Java Architect with the Sun Java Center in Boston, MA. He has many years of experience in Object-Oriented technologies. He has been focused on design and implementation of large-scale enterprise applications using Java and XML technologies. He currently consults and mentors large projects specializing in server side Java-based distributed systems. He is driven by new technologies and loves reading about them. His past experiences include working on Java applications for performance and analysis of cellular networks with Ericsson Research Canada (LMC).

Outside of Java World, Robert enjoys techno beats, playing golf, and any extreme sport that involves a board, including snowboarding, wakeboarding, and windsurfing. Robert holds a Computer Science degree from Concordia University in Montreal, Quebec. He can be reached at robert.skoczylas@sun.com

Rima Patel Sriganesh is a Technology Evangelist presently working for Sun Microsystems, Inc. She specializes in Java, XML, and Integration platforms. Her areas of technology passion include Distributed Computing Models, Trust Computing, Semantic Web, and Grid Computing architectures. She speaks frequently at premiere industry conferences such as JavaOne, Web Services Edge, SIGS 101, and others. She also publishes on Sun's Technology Evangelism portal: www.sun.com/developers/evangcentral.

Rima and her husband live in the Greater Boston area. She most enjoys eating spicy Indian food and reading Gujarati novels. Also, she loves debating world politics and Vedic philosophy when energy permits her. Rima holds a graduate degree in Mathematics. She can be reached at rima.patel@sun.com.

PART

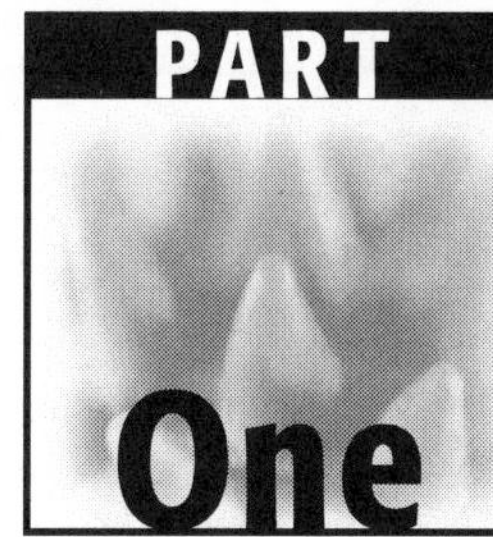

One

Evolution and Emergence of Web Services

CHAPTER 1

Evolution of Distributed Computing

The Internet has revolutionized our business by providing an information highway, which acts as a new form of communication backbone. This new information medium has shifted business from the traditional brick-and-mortar infrastructures to a virtual world where they can serve customers not just the regular eight hours, but round-the-clock and around the world. Additionally, it enhances our organizations with significant benefits in terms of business productivity, cost savings, and customer satisfaction. As a result, modern organizations are compelled to re-evaluate their business models and plan on a business vision to interact with their customers, suppliers, resellers, and partners using an Internet-based technology space. To achieve this goal of obtaining an Internet business presence, organizations are exposing and distributing their business applications over the Internet by going through a series of technological innovations. The key phenomenon of enabling business applications over the Internet is based on a fundamental technology called distributed computing.

Distributed computing has been popular within local area networks for many years, and it took a major step forward by adopting the Internet as its base platform and by supporting its open standard-based technologies. This chapter discusses the background of distributed computing and the evolution of Internet-enabled technologies by focusing on the following:

- The definition of distributed computing
- The importance of distributed computing
- Core distributed computing technologies such as the following:
  - Client/server
  - CORBA
  - Java RMI
  - Microsoft DCOM
  - Message-Oriented Middleware
- Common challenges in distributed computing
- The role of J2EE and XML in distributed computing
- Emergence of Web services and service-oriented architectures

What Is Distributed Computing?

In the early years of computing, mainframe-based applications were considered to be the best-fit solution for executing large-scale data processing applications. With the advent of personal computers (PCs), the concept of software programs running on standalone machines became much more popular in terms of the cost of ownership and the ease of application use. With the number of PC-based application programs running on independent machines growing, the communications between such application programs became extremely complex and added a growing challenge in the aspect of application-to-application interaction. Lately, network computing gained importance, and enabling remote procedure calls (RPCs) over a network protocol called Transmission Control Protocol/Internet Protocol (TCP/IP) turned out to be a widely accepted way for application software communication. Since then, software applications running on a variety of hardware platforms, operating systems, and different networks faced some challenges when required to communicate with each other and share data. This demanding requirement lead to the concept of distributed computing applications.

As a definition, "Distributing Computing is a type of computing in which different components and objects comprising an application can be located on different computers connected to a network" (www.webopedia.com, May 2001). Figure 1.1 shows a distributed computing model that provides an infrastructure enabling invocations of object functions located anywhere on the network. The objects are transparent to the application and provide processing power as if they were local to the application calling them.

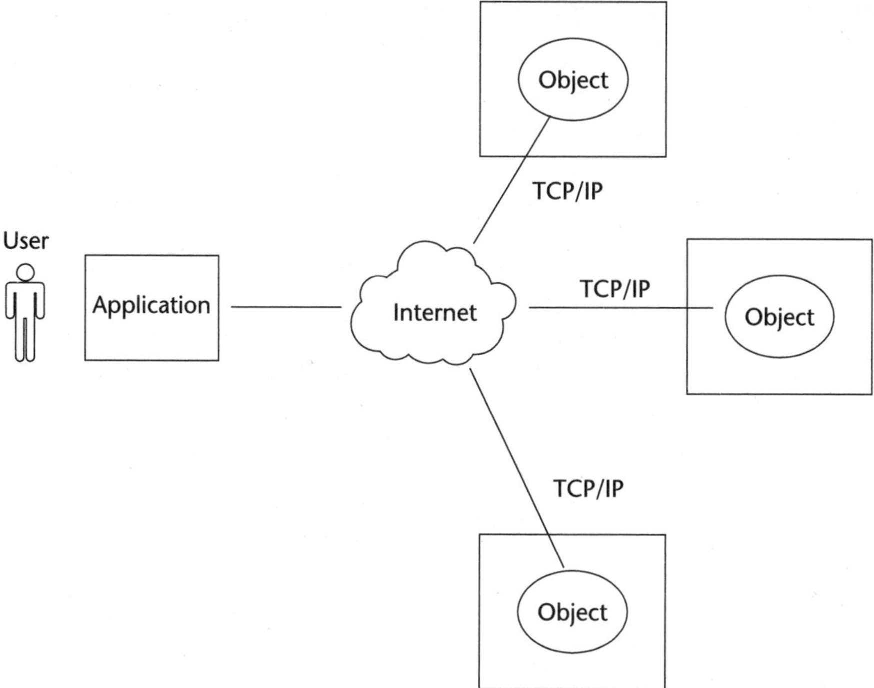

Figure 1.1 Internet-based distributed computing model.

Today, Sun Java RMI (Remote Method Invocation), OMG CORBA (Common Object Request Broker Architecture), Microsoft DCOM (Distributed Component Object Model), and Message-Oriented Middleware (MOM) have emerged as the most common distributed computing technologies. These technologies, although different in their basic architectural design and implementation, address specific problems in their target environments. The following sections discuss the use of distributed computing and also briefly describe the most popular technologies.

The Importance of Distributed Computing

The distributed computing environment provides many significant advantages compared to a traditional standalone application. The following are some of those key advantages:

Higher performance. Applications can execute in parallel and distribute the load across multiple servers.

Collaboration. Multiple applications can be connected through standard distributed computing mechanisms.

Higher reliability and availability. Applications or servers can be clustered in multiple machines.

Scalability. This can be achieved by deploying these reusable distributed components on powerful servers.

Extensibility. This can be achieved through dynamic (re)configuration of applications that are distributed across the network.

Higher productivity and lower development cycle time. By breaking up large problems into smaller ones, these individual components can be developed by smaller development teams in isolation.

Reuse. The distributed components may perform various services that can potentially be used by multiple client applications. It saves repetitive development effort and improves interoperability between components.

Reduced cost. Because this model provides a lot of reuse of once developed components that are accessible over the network, significant cost reductions can be achieved.

Distributed computing also has changed the way traditional network programming is done by providing a shareable object like semantics across networks using programming languages like Java, C, and C++. The following sections briefly discuss core distributed computing technologies such as Client/Server applications, OMG CORBA, Java RMI, Microsoft COM/DCOM, and MOM.

Client-Server Applications

The early years of distributed application architecture were dominated by two-tier business applications. In a two-tier architecture model, the first (upper) tier handles the presentation and business logic of the user application (client), and the second/lower tier handles the application organization and its data storage (server). This approach is commonly called client-server applications architecture. Generally, the server in a client/server application model is a database server that is mainly responsible for the organization and retrieval of data. The application client in this model handles most of the business processing and provides the graphical user interface of the application. It is a very popular design in business applications where the user interface and business logic are tightly coupled with a database server for handling data retrieval and processing. For example, the client-server model has been widely used in enterprise resource planning (ERP), billing, and Inventory application systems where a number of client business applications residing in multiple desktop systems interact with a central database server.

Figure 1.2 shows an architectural model of a typical client server system in which multiple desktop-based business client applications access a central database server.

Some of the common limitations of the client-server application model are as follows:

- Complex business processing at the client side demands robust client systems.
- Security is more difficult to implement because the algorithms and logic reside on the client side making it more vulnerable to hacking.
- Increased network bandwidth is needed to accommodate many calls to the server, which can impose scalability restrictions.
- Maintenance and upgrades of client applications are extremely difficult because each client has to be maintained separately.
- Client-server architecture suits mostly database-oriented standalone applications and does not target robust reusable component-oriented applications.

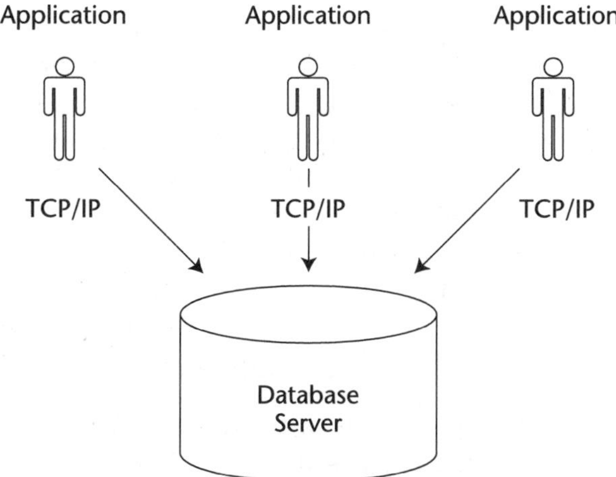

Figure 1.2 An example of a client-server application.

CORBA

The Common Object Request Broker Architecture (CORBA) is an industry wide, open standard initiative, developed by the Object Management Group (OMG) for enabling distributed computing that supports a wide range of application environments. OMG is a nonprofit consortium responsible for the production and maintenance of framework specifications for distributed and interoperable object-oriented systems.

CORBA differs from the traditional client/server model because it provides an object-oriented solution that does not enforce any proprietary protocols or any particular programming language, operating system, or hardware platform. By adopting CORBA, the applications can reside and run on any hardware platform located anywhere on the network, and can be written in any language that has mappings to a neutral interface definition called the Interface Definition Language (IDL). An IDL is a specific interface language designed to expose the services (methods/functions) of a CORBA remote object. CORBA also defines a collection of system-level services for handling low-level application services like life-cycle, persistence, transaction, naming, security, and so forth. Initially, CORBA 1.1 was focused on creating component level, portable object applications without interoperability. The introduction of CORBA 2.0 added interoperability between different ORB vendors by implementing an Internet Inter-ORB Protocol (IIOP). The IIOP defines the ORB backbone, through which other ORBs can bridge and provide interoperation with its associated services.

In a CORBA-based solution, the Object Request Broker (ORB) is an object bus that provides a transparent mechanism for sending requests and receiving responses to and from objects, regardless of the environment and its location. The ORB intercepts the client's call and is responsible for finding its server object that implements the request, passes its parameters, invokes its method, and returns its results to the client. The ORB, as part of its implementation, provides interfaces to the CORBA services, which allows it to build custom-distributed application environments.

Figure 1.3 illustrates the architectural model of CORBA with an example representation of applications written in C, C++, and Java providing IDL bindings.

The CORBA architecture is composed of the following components:

IDL. CORBA uses IDL contracts to specify the application boundaries and to establish interfaces with its clients. The IDL provides a mechanism by which the distributed application component's interfaces, inherited classes, events, attributes, and exceptions can be specified in a standard definition language supported by the CORBA ORB.

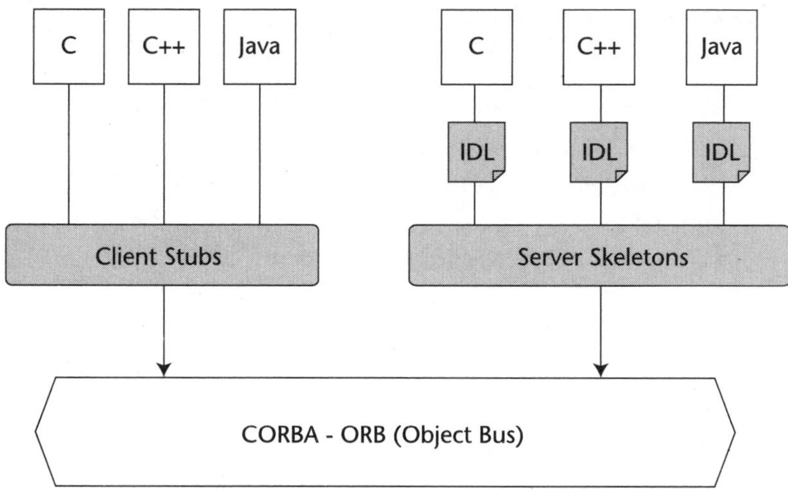

Figure 1.3 An example of the CORBA architectural model.

ORB. It acts as the object bus or the bridge, providing the communication infrastructure to send and receive request/responses from the client and server. It establishes the foundation for the distributed application objects, achieving interoperability in a heterogeneous environment.

Some of the distinct advantages of CORBA over a traditional client/server application model are as follows:

OS and programming-language independence. Interfaces between clients and servers are defined in OMG IDL, thus providing the following advantages to Internet programming: Multi-language and multi-platform application environments, which provide a logical separation between interfaces and implementation.

Legacy and custom application integration. Using CORBA IDL, developers can encapsulate existing and custom applications as callable client applications and use them as objects on the ORB.

Rich distributed object infrastructure. CORBA offers developers a rich set of distributed object services, such as the Lifecycle, Events, Naming, Transactions, and Security services.

Location transparency. CORBA provides location transparency: An object reference is independent of the physical location and application level location. This allows developers to create CORBA-based systems where objects can be moved without modifying the underlying applications.

Network transparency. By using the IIOP protocol, an ORB can interconnect with any ORB located elsewhere on the network.

Remote callback support. CORBA allows objects to receive asynchronous event notification from other objects.

Dynamic invocation interface. CORBA clients can both use static and dynamic methods invocations. They either statically define their method invocations through stubs at compile time, or have the opportunity to discover objects' methods at runtime. With those advantages, some key factors, which affected the success of CORBA evident while implementing CORBA-based distributed applications, are as follows:

High initial investment. CORBA-based applications require huge investments in regard to new training and the deployment of architecture, even for small-scale applications.

Availability of CORBA services. The Object services specified by the OMG are still lacking as implementation products.

Scalability. Due to the tightly coupled nature of the connection-oriented CORBA architecture, very high scalability expected in enterprise applications may not be achieved.

However, most of those disadvantages may be out of date today. The Internet community for the development of Intranet and Extranet applications has acknowledged using CORBA with IIOP and Java as their tools of choice. Sun has already released its JDK 1.4 (Java development kit), which includes a full-featured CORBA implementation and also a limited set of services.

Java RMI

Java RMI was developed by Sun Microsystems as the standard mechanism to enable distributed Java objects-based application development using the Java environment. RMI provides a distributed Java application environment by calling remote Java objects and passing them as arguments or return values. It uses Java object serialization—a lightweight object persistence technique that allows the conversion of objects into streams.

Before RMI, the only way to do inter-process communications in the Java platform was to use the standard Java network libraries. Though the java.net APIs provided sophisticated support for network functionalities, they were not intended to support or solve the distributed computing challenges. Java RMI uses Java Remote Method Protocol (JRMP) as the interprocess communication protocol, enabling Java objects living in different Java Virtual Machines (VMs) to transparently invoke one another's methods. Because these VMs can be running on different computers anywhere on the network, RMI enables object-oriented distributed computing. RMI also uses a reference-counting garbage collection mechanism that keeps track of external live object references to remote objects (live connections) using the virtual machine. When an object is found unreferenced, it is considered to be a weak reference and it will be garbage collected.

In RMI-based application architectures, a registry (rmiregistry)-oriented mechanism provides a simple non-persistent naming lookup service that is used to store the remote object references and to enable lookups from client applications. The RMI infrastructure based on the JRMP acts as the medium between the RMI clients and remote objects. It intercepts client requests, passes invocation arguments, delegates invocation requests to the RMI skeleton, and finally passes the return values of the method execution to the client stub. It also enables callbacks from server objects to client applications so that the asynchronous notifications can be achieved.

Figure 1.4 depicts the architectural model of a Java RMI-based application solution.

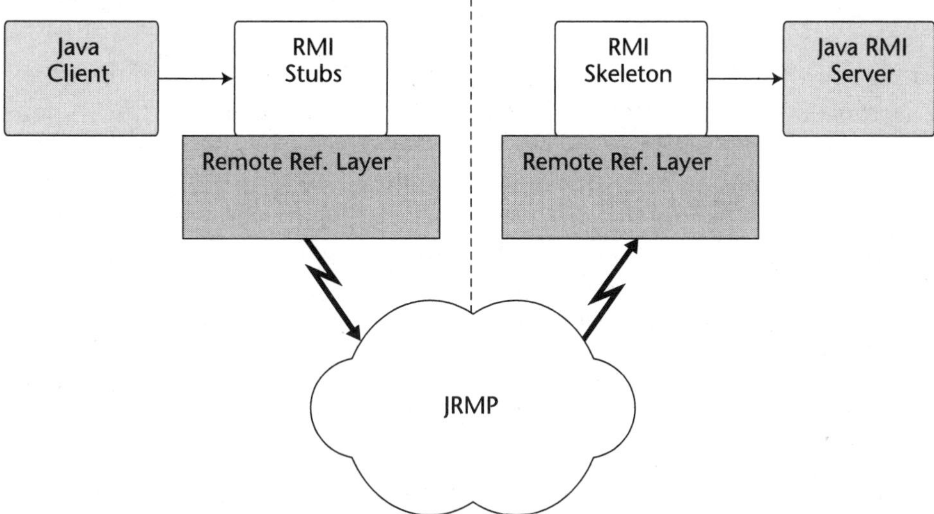

Figure 1.4 A Java RMI architectural model.

The Java RMI architecture is composed of the following components:

RMI client. The RMI client, which can be a Java applet or a stand-alone application, performs the remote method invocations on a server object. It can pass arguments that are primitive data types or serializable objects.

RMI stub. The RMI stub is the client proxy generated by the rmi compiler (*rmic* provided along with Java developer kit—JDK) that encapsulates the network information of the server and performs the delegation of the method invocation to the server. The stub also marshals the method arguments and unmarshals the return values from the method execution.

RMI infrastructure. The RMI infrastructure consists of two layers: the remote reference layer and the transport layer. The remote reference layer separates out the specific remote reference behavior from the client stub. It handles certain reference semantics like connection retries, which are unicast/multicast of the invocation requests. The transport layer actually provides the networking infrastructure, which facilitates the actual data transfer during method invocations, the passing of formal arguments, and the return of back execution results.

RMI skeleton. The RMI skeleton, which also is generated using the RMI compiler (rmic) receives the invocation requests from the stub and processes the arguments (unmarshalling) and delegates them to the RMI server. Upon successful method execution, it marshals the return values and then passes them back to the RMI stub via the RMI infrastructure.

RMI server. The server is the Java remote object that implements the exposed interfaces and executes the client requests. It receives incoming remote method invocations from the respective skeleton, which passes the parameters after unmarshalling. Upon successful method execution, return values are sent back to the skeleton, which passes them back to the client via the RMI infrastructure.

Developing distributed applications in RMI is simpler than developing with Java sockets because there is no need to design a protocol, which is a very complex task by itself. RMI is built over TCP/IP sockets, but the added advantage is that it provides an object-oriented approach for interprocess communications. Java RMI provides the Java programmers with an efficient, transparent communication mechanism that frees them of all the application-level protocols necessary to encode and decode messages for data exchange. RMI enables distributed resource management, best processing power usage, and load balancing in a Java application model. RMI-IIOP (RMI over IIOP) is a protocol that has been developed for enabling RMI applications to interoperate with CORBA components. Although RMI had inherent advantages provided by the distributed object model of the Java platform, it also had some limitations:

- RMI is limited only to the Java platform. It does not provide language independence in its distributed model as targeted by CORBA.
- RMI-based application architectures are tightly coupled because of the connection-oriented nature. Hence, achieving high scalability in such an application model becomes a challenge.
- RMI does not provide any specific session management support. In a typical client/server implementation, the server has to maintain the session and state information of the multiple clients who access it. Maintaining such information within the server application without a standard support is a complex task.

In spite of some of its limitations, RMI and RMI-IIOP has become the core of the J2EE architectural model due to its widespread acceptance in the Java distributed computing paradigm and rich features.

Microsoft DCOM

The Microsoft Component Object Model (COM) provides a way for Windows-based software components to communicate with each other by defining a binary and network standard in a Windows operating environment. COM evolved from OLE (Object Linking and Embedding), which employed a Windows registry-based object organization mechanism. COM provides a distributed application model for ActiveX components.

As a next step, Microsoft developed the Distributed Common Object Model (DCOM) as its answer to the distributed computing problem in the Microsoft Windows platform. DCOM enables COM applications to communicate with each other using an RPC mechanism, which employs a DCOM protocol on the wire.

Figure 1.5 shows an architectural model of DCOM.

DCOM applies a skeleton and stub approach whereby a defined interface that exposes the methods of a COM object can be invoked remotely over a network. The client application will invoke methods on such a remote COM object in the same fashion that it would with a local COM object. The stub encapsulates the network location information of the COM server object and acts as a proxy on the client side. The servers can potentially host multiple COM objects, and when they register themselves against a registry, they become available for all the clients, who then discover them using a lookup mechanism.

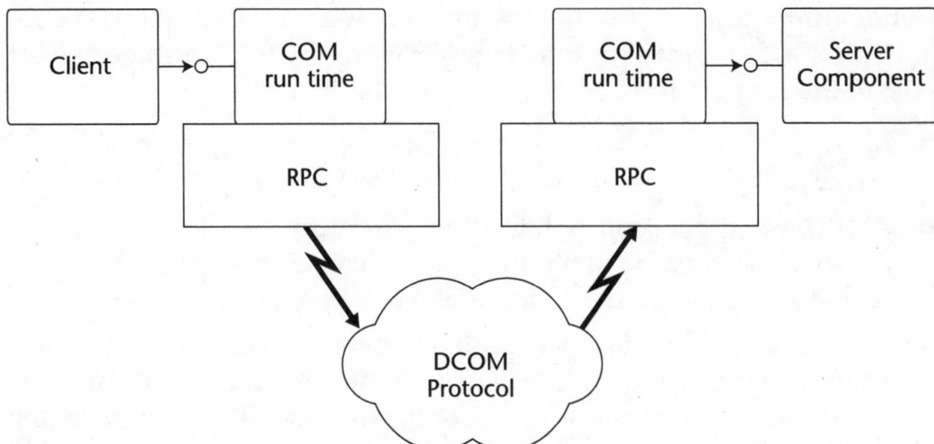

Figure 1.5 Basic architectural model of Microsoft DCOM.

DCOM is quite successful in providing distributed computing support on the Windows platform. But, it is limited to Microsoft application environments. The following are some of the common limitations of DCOM:

- Platform lock-in
- State management
- Scalability
- Complex session management issues

Message-Oriented Middleware

Although CORBA, RMI, and DCOM differ in their basic architecture and approach, they adopted a tightly coupled mechanism of a synchronous communication model (request/response). All these technologies are based upon binary communication protocols and adopt tight integration across their logical tiers, which is susceptible to scalability issues.

Message-Oriented Middleware (MOM) is based upon a loosely coupled asynchronous communication model where the application client does not need to know its application recipients or its method arguments. MOM enables applications to communicate indirectly using a messaging provider queue. The application client sends messages to the message queue (a message holding area), and the receiving application picks up the message from the queue. In this operation model, the application sending messages to another application continues to operate without waiting for the response from that application.

Figure 1.6 illustrates a high-level MOM architecture showing application-to-application connectivity.

In MOM-based architecture, applications interacting with its messaging infrastructure use custom adapters. Client applications communicate with the underlying messaging infrastructure using these adapters for sending and receiving messages. For reliable message delivery, messages can be persisted in a database/file system as well.

Some of the widely known MOM-based technologies are SunONE Message Queue, IBM MQSeries, TIBCO, SonicMQ, and Microsoft Messaging Queue (MSMQ). The Java Platform provides a Java-based messaging API (JMS-Java Message Service), which is developed as part of the Sun Java Community Process (JCP) and also is currently part of the J2EE 1.3 specifications. All the leading MOM vendors like SunONE, TIBCO, IBM, BEA, Talarian, Sonic, Fiorano, and Spiritwave support the JMS specifications.

JMS provides Point-to-Point and Publish/Subscribe messaging models with the following features:

- Complete transactional capabilities
- Reliable message delivery
- Security

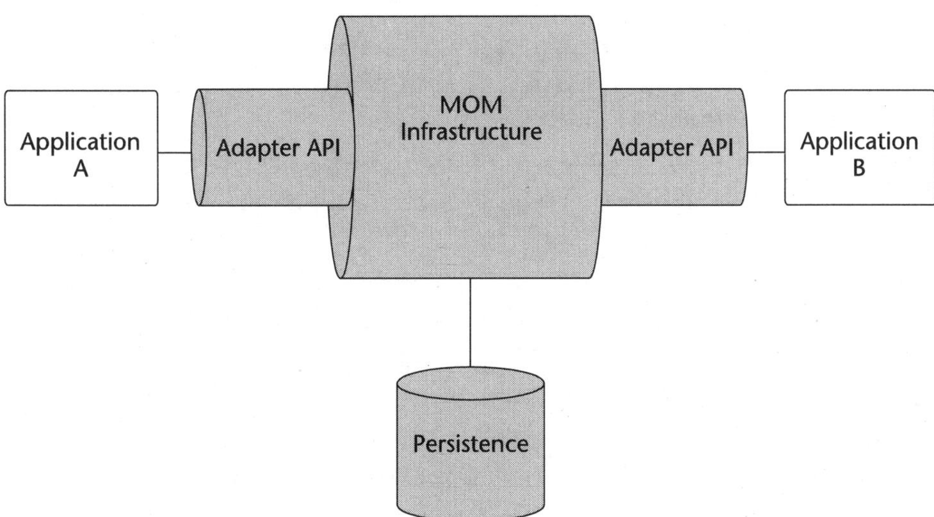

Figure 1.6 A typical MOM-based architectural model.

Some of the common challenges while implementing a MOM-based application environment have been the following:

- Most of the standard MOM implementations have provided native APIs for communication with their core infrastructure. This has affected the portability of applications across such implementations and has led to a specific vendor lock-in.
- The MOM messages used for integrating applications are usually based upon a proprietary message format without any standard compliance.

Adopting a JMS-based communication model enables a standardized way to communicate with a MOM provider without having to lock in to any specific vendor API. It leverages the use of open standards l, thus enhancing the flexibility in connecting together diverse applications.

Common Challenges in Distributed Computing

Distributed computing technologies like CORBA, RMI, and DCOM have been quite successful in integrating applications within a homogenous environment inside a local area network. As the Internet becomes a logical solution that spans and connects the boundaries of businesses, it also demands the interoperability of applications across networks. This section discusses some of the common challenges noticed in the CORBA-, RMI-, and DCOM-based distributed computing solutions:

- Maintenance of various versions of stubs/skeletons in the client and server environments is extremely complex in a heterogeneous network environment.
- Quality of Service (QoS) goals like Scalability, Performance, and Availability in a distributed environment consume a major portion of the application's development time.
- Interoperability of applications implementing different protocols on heterogeneous platforms almost becomes impossible. For example, a DCOM client communicating to an RMI server or an RMI client communicating to a DCOM server.
- Most of these protocols are designed to work well within local networks. They are not very firewall friendly or able to be accessed over the Internet.

The biggest problem with application integration with this tightly coupled approach spearheaded by CORBA, RMI, and DCOM was that it influenced separate sections of the developer community who were already tied to specific platforms. Microsoft Windows platform developers used DCOM, while UNIX developers used CORBA or RMI. There was no big effort in the community to come up with common standards that focused on the interoperability between these diverse protocols, thus ignoring the importance, and hence, the real power of distributed computing. Enough said about the weaknesses, we now are going to discuss what is becoming an alternative technology, which still has all the existing strengths and targets to solve the complexities of current systems.

The Role of J2EE and XML in Distributed Computing

The emergence of the Internet has helped enterprise applications to be easily accessible over the Web without having specific client-side software installations. In the Internet-based enterprise application model, the focus was to move the complex business processing toward centralized servers in the back end.

The first generation of Internet servers was based upon Web servers that hosted static Web pages and provided content to the clients via HTTP (HyperText Transfer Protocol). HTTP is a stateless protocol that connects Web browsers to Web servers, enabling the transportation of HTML content to the user.

With the high popularity and potential of this infrastructure, the push for a more dynamic technology was inevitable. This was the beginning of server-side scripting using technologies like CGI, NSAPI, and ISAPI.

With many organizations moving their businesses to the Internet, a whole new category of business models like business-to-business (B2B) and business-to-consumer (B2C) came into existence.

This evolution lead to the specification of J2EE architecture, which promoted a much more efficient platform for hosting Web-based applications. J2EE provides a programming model based upon Web and business components that are managed by the J2EE application server. The application server consists of many APIs and low-level services available to the components. These low-level services provide security, transactions, connections and instance pooling, and concurrency services, which enable a J2EE developer to focus primarily on business logic rather than plumbing.

The power of Java and its rich collection of APIs provided the perfect solution for developing highly transactional, highly available and scalable enterprise applications. Based on many standardized industry specifications, it provides the interfaces to connect with various back-end legacy and information systems. J2EE also provides excellent client connectivity capabilities, ranging from PDA to Web browsers to Rich Clients (Applets, CORBA applications, and Standard Java Applications).

Figure 1.7 shows various components of the J2EE architecture.

A typical J2EE architecture is physically divided in to three logical tiers, which enables clear separation of the various application components with defined roles and responsibilities. The following is a breakdown of functionalities of those logical tiers:

Presentation tier. The Presentation tier is composed of Web components, which handle HTTP requests/responses, Session management, Device independent content delivery, and the invocation of business tier components.

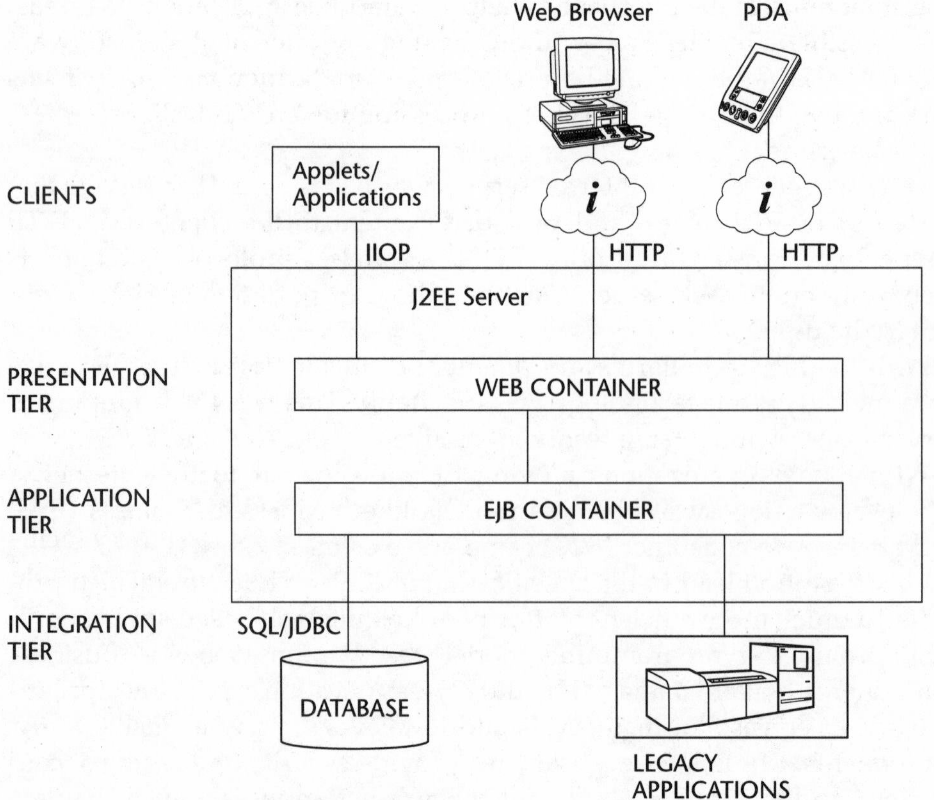

Figure 1.7 J2EE application architecture.

Application tier. The Application tier (also known as the Business tier) deals with the core business logic processing, which may typically deal with workflow and automation. The business components retrieve data from the information systems with well-defined APIs provided by the application server.

Integration tier. The Integration tier deals with connecting and communicating to back-end Enterprise Information Systems (EIS), database applications and legacy applications, or mainframe applications.

With its key functionalities and provisions for partitioning applications into logical tiers, J2EE has been highly adopted as the standard solution for developing and deploying mission critical Web-based applications. The power of J2EE-based applications would be tremendous, if it is enabled to interoperate with other potential J2EE-deployed applications. This enables business components across networks to negotiate among them and interact without human interaction. It also enables the realization of syndication and collaboration of business processes across the Internet by enabling them to share data and component-level processes in real time. This phenomenon is commonly referred to as business-to-business (B2B) communication.

The emergence of the Extensible Markup Language (XML) for defining portable data in a structured and self-describing format is embraced by the industry as a communication medium for electronic data exchange. Using XML as a data exchange mechanism between applications promotes interoperability between applications and also enhances the scalability of the underlying applications. Combining the potential of a J2EE platform and XML offers a standard framework for B2B and inter-application communication across networks.

With J2EE enabling enterprise applications to the Internet and XML acting as a "glue" bridges these discrete J2EE-based applications by facilitating them to interoperate with each other. XML, with its incredible flexibility, also has been widely adopted and accepted as a standard by major vendors in the IT industry, including Sun, IBM, Microsoft, Oracle, and HP. The combination of these technologies offers more promising possibilities in the technology sector for providing a new way of application-to-application communication on the Internet. It also promotes a new form of the distributed computing technology solution referred to as Web services.

The Emergence of Web Services

Today, the adoption of the Internet and enabling Internet-based applications has created a world of discrete business applications, which co-exist in the same technology space but without interacting with each other. The increasing demands of the industry for enabling B2B, application-to-application (A2A), and inter-process application communication has led to a growing requirement for service-oriented architectures. Enabling service-oriented applications facilitates the exposure of business applications as service components enable business applications from other organizations to link with these services for application interaction and data sharing without human intervention. By leveraging this architecture, it also enables interoperability between business applications and processes.

By adopting Web technologies, the service-oriented architecture model facilitates the delivery of services over the Internet by leveraging standard technologies such as XML. It uses platform-neutral standards by exposing the underlying application components and making them available to any application, any platform, or any device, and at any location. Today, this phenomenon is well adopted for implementation and is commonly referred to as Web services. Although this technique enables communication between applications with the addition of service activation technologies and open technology standards, it can be leveraged to publish the services in a register of yellow pages available on the Internet. This will further redefine and transform the way businesses communicate over the Internet. This promising new technology sets the strategic vision of the next generation of virtual business models and the unlimited potential for organizations doing business collaboration and business process management over the Internet.

Summary

In this chapter, we discussed the evolution and the basics of distributed computing technologies and the emergence of Web services that define the next generation of business services models and business process communication over the Internet.

In particular, we looked at the background of distributed computing; the fundamentals of distributed computing techniques; the basics of industry-accepted technologies like CORBA, RMI, DCOM, and MOM; the role of J2EE and XML for enabling distributed computing over the Internet; and the concept of service-oriented architectures and the emergence of Web services.

In the following chapters, we will go into a more detailed introduction to Web services concepts and focus on the various aspects of designing and developing Web services.

CHAPTER

2

Introduction to Web Services

Today, people use the Internet as an everyday service provider for reading headline news, obtaining stock quotes, getting weather reports, shopping online, and paying bills, and also for obtaining a variety of information from different sources. These Web-enabled applications are built using different software applications to generate HTML, and their access is limited only through an Internet browser or by using an application-specific client. This is partially due to the limitations of HTML and the Web server-based technologies, which are primarily focused on presentation and their inability to interact with another application.

The emergence of Web services introduces a new paradigm for enabling the exchange of information across the Internet based on open Internet standards and technologies. Using industry standards, Web services encapsulate applications and publish them as services. These services deliver XML-based data on the wire and expose it for use on the Internet, which can be dynamically located, subscribed, and accessed using a wide range of computing platforms, handheld devices, appliances, and so on. Due to the flexibility of using open standards and protocols, it also facilitates Enterprise Application Integration (EAI), business-to-business (B2B) integration, and application-to-application (A2A) communication across the Internet and corporate intranet. In organizations with heterogeneous applications and distributed application architectures, the introduction of

Web services standardizes the communication mechanism and enables interoperability of applications based on different programming languages residing on different platforms.

This chapter presents an introduction on Web services, especially focusing on the following:

- The definition of Web services
- Motivation and characteristics of Web services
- Web services industry standards and technologies
- Web services strategies and solutions
- Benefits of Web services

Today's leading technology vendors have set their strategies around providing infrastructure solutions for delivering Web services. With the increasing adoption, acceptance, and availability of platforms, languages, application tools, and supporting technology solutions, it is expected that Web services will become a new service industry providing businesses services over the Internet.

What Are Web Services?

Web services are based on the concept of service-oriented architecture (SOA). SOA is the latest evolution of distributed computing, which enables software components, including application functions, objects, and processes from different systems, to be exposed as services.

According to Gartner research (June 15, 2001), "Web services are loosely coupled software components delivered over Internet standard technologies."

In short, Web services are self-describing and modular business applications that expose the business logic as services over the Internet through programmable interfaces and using Internet protocols for the purpose of providing ways to find, subscribe, and invoke those services.

Based on XML standards, Web services can be developed as loosely coupled application components using any programming language, any protocol, or any platform. This facilitates delivering business applications as a service accessible to anyone, anytime, at any location, and using any platform.

Consider the simple example shown in Figure 2.1 where a travel reservation services provider exposes its business applications as Web services supporting a variety of customers and application clients. These business applications are provided by different travel organizations residing at different networks and geographical locations.

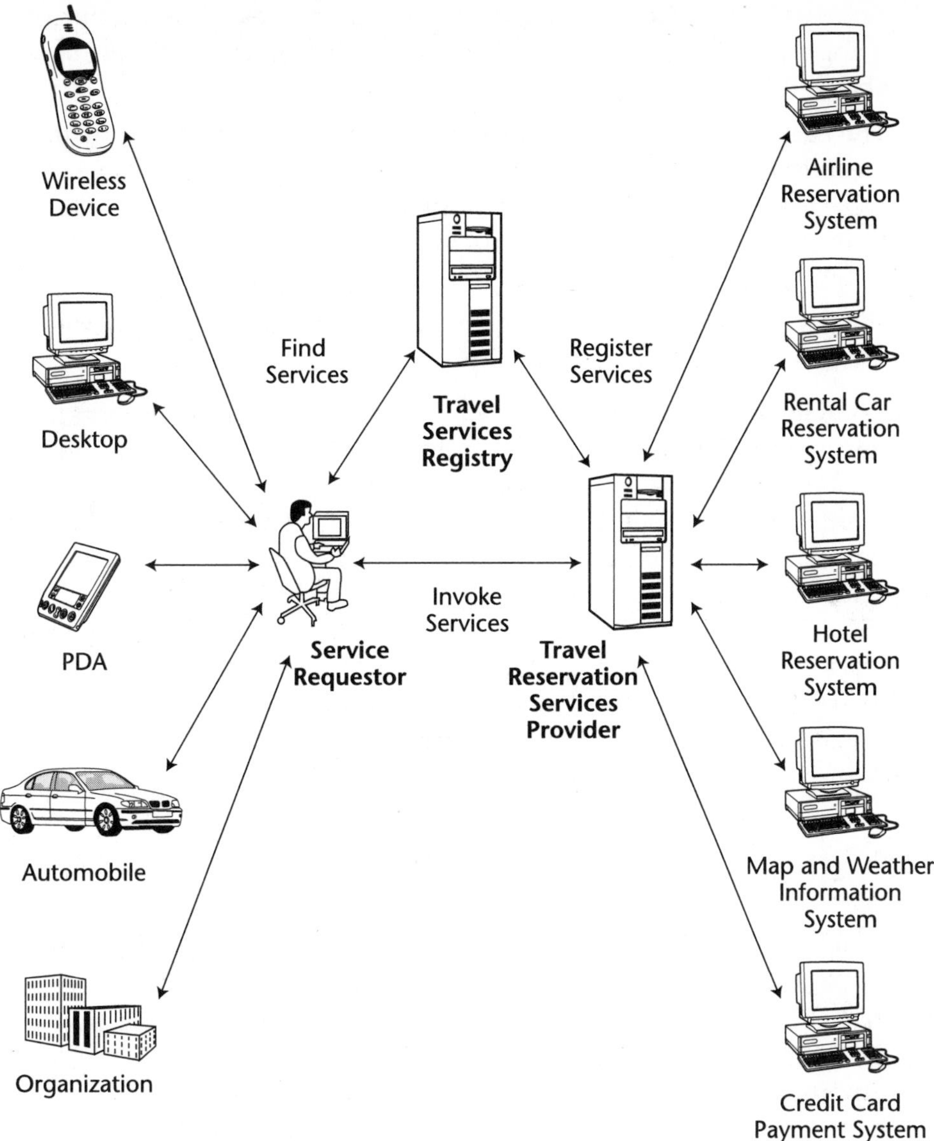

Figure 2.1 An example scenario of Web services.

The following is a typical scenario:

1. The Travel service provider deploys its Web services by exposing the business applications obtained from different travel businesses like airlines, car-rental, hotel accommodation, credit card payment, and so forth.

2. The service provider registers its business services with descriptions using a public or private registry. The registry stores the information about the services exposed by the service provider.
3. The customer discovers the Web services using a search engine or by locating it directly from the registry and then invokes the Web services for performing travel reservations and other functions over the Internet using any platform or device.
4. In the case of large-scale organizations, the business applications consume these Web services for providing travel services to their own employees through the corporate intranet.

The previous example provides a simple scenario of how an organization's business functionalities can be exposed as Web services and invoked by its customers using a wide range of application clients.

As we discussed earlier, Web services are typically implemented based on open standards and technologies specifically leveraging XML. The XML-based standards and technologies, such as Simple Object Access Protocol (SOAP); Universal Description, Discovery, and Integration (UDDI); Web Services Definition Language (WSDL); and Electronic Business XML (ebXML), are commonly used as building blocks for Web services. These technologies are discussed briefly in the section *Core Web Services Standards*, which follows later.

Motivation and Characteristics

Web-based B2B communication has been around for quite some time. These Web-based B2B solutions are usually based on custom and proprietary technologies and are meant for exchanging data and doing transactions over the Web. However, B2B has its own challenges. For example, in B2B communication, connecting new or existing applications and adding new business partners have always been a challenge. Due to this fact, in some cases the scalability of the underlying business applications is affected. Ideally, the business applications and information from a partner organization should be able to interact with the application of the potential partners seamlessly without redefining the system or its resources. To meet these challenges, it is clearly evident that there is a need for standard protocols and data formatting for enabling seamless and scalable B2B applications and services. Web services provide the solution to resolve these issues by adopting open standards. Figure 2.2 shows a typical B2B infrastructure (e-marketplace) using XML for encoding data between applications across the Internet.

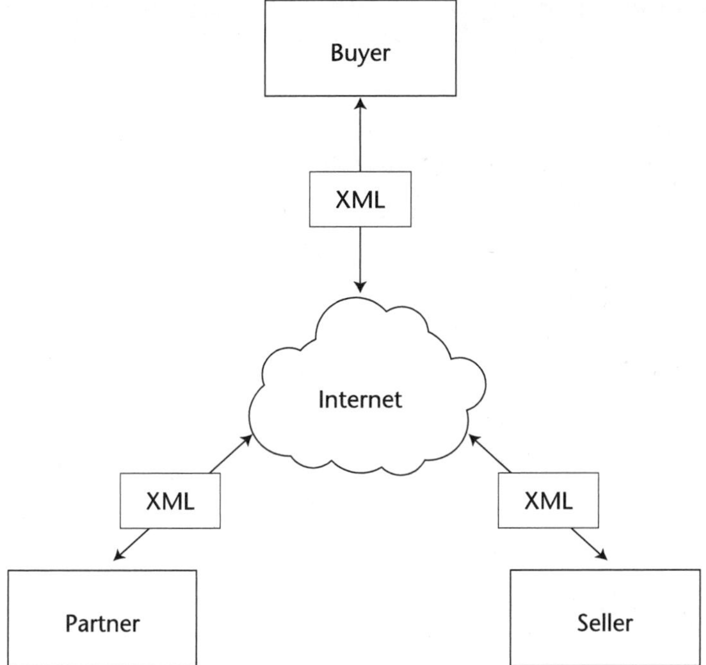

Figure 2.2 Using XML for encoding data in a B2B communication.

Web services enable businesses to communicate, collaborate, and conduct business transactions using a lightweight infrastructure by adopting an XML-based data exchange format and industry standard delivery protocols.

The basic characteristics of a Web services application model are as follows:

- Web services are based on XML messaging, which means that the data exchanged between the Web service provider and the user are defined in XML.
- Web services provide a cross-platform integration of business applications over the Internet.
- To build Web services, developers can use any common programming language, such as Java, C, C++, Perl, Python, C#, and/or Visual Basic, and its existing application components.
- Web services are not meant for handling presentations like HTML context—it is developed to generate XML for uniform accessibility through any software application, any platform, or device.

- Because Web services are based on loosely coupled application components, each component is exposed as a service with its unique functionality.
- Web services use industry-standard protocols like HTTP, and they can be easily accessible through corporate firewalls.
- Web services can be used by many types of clients.
- Web services vary in functionality from a simple request to a complex business transaction involving multiple resources.
- All platforms including J2EE, CORBA, and Microsoft .NET provide extensive support for creating and deploying Web services.
- Web services are dynamically located and invoked from public and private registries based on industry standards such as UDDI and ebXML.

Why Use Web Services?

Traditionally, Web applications enable interaction between an end user and a Web site, while Web services are service-oriented and enable application-to-application communication over the Internet and easy accessibility to heterogeneous applications and devices. The following are the major technical reasons for choosing Web services over Web applications:

- Web services can be invoked through XML-based RPC mechanisms across firewalls.
- Web services provide a cross-platform, cross-language solution based on XML messaging.
- Web services facilitate ease of application integration using a lightweight infrastructure without affecting scalability.
- Web services enable interoperability among heterogeneous applications.

Basic Operational Model of Web Services

Web services operations can be conceptualized as a simple operational model that has a lot in common with a standard communication model (see Figure 2.3). Operations are conceived as involving three distinct roles and relationships that define the Web services providers and users.

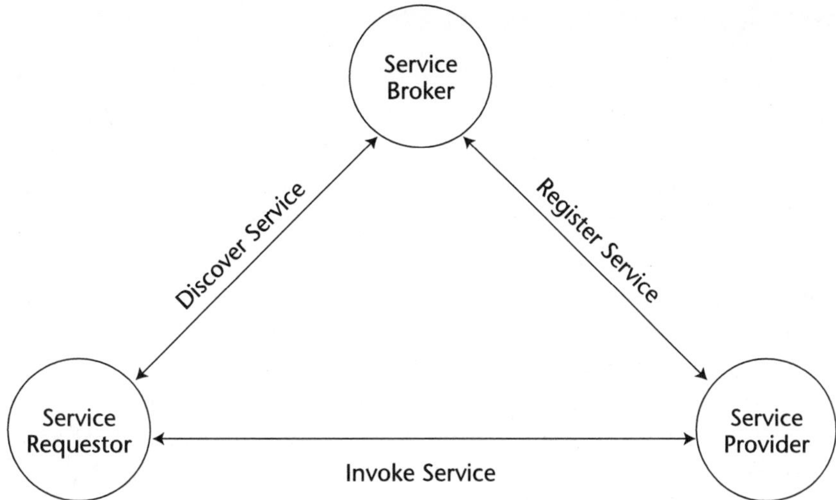

Figure 2.3 Web services operational model, showing roles and relationships.

These roles and relationships are defined as follows:

Service provider. The service provider is responsible for developing and deploying the Web services. The provider also defines the services and publishes them with the service broker.

Service broker. The service broker (also commonly referred to as a service registry) is responsible for service registration and discovery of the Web services. The broker lists the various service types, descriptions, and locations of the services that help the service requesters find and subscribe to the required services.

Service requestor. The service requestor is responsible for the service invocation. The requestor locates the Web service using the service broker, invokes the required services, and executes it from the service provider.

Let's examine more closely some of the open standard technologies such as SOAP, WSDL, UDDI, and ebXML that enable Web services.

Core Web Services Standards

The five core Web services standards and technologies for building and enabling Web services are XML, SOAP, WSDL, UDDI, and ebXML. An overview of each is presented in the following sections.

Extensible Markup Language (XML)

In February 1998, the Worldwide Web Consortium (W3C) officially endorsed the Extensible Markup Language (XML) as a standard data format. XML uses Unicode, and it is structured self-describing neutral data that can be stored as a simple text document for representing complex data and to make it readable. Today, XML is the *de facto* standard for structuring data, content, and data format for electronic documents. It has already been widely accepted as the universal language lingua franca for exchanging information between applications, systems, and devices across the Internet.

In the core of the Web services model, XML plays a vital role as the common wire format in all forms of communication. XML also is the basis for other Web services standards. By learning XML, you will be well prepared to understand and explore Web services. For more information on XML, go to Chapter 8, "XML Processing and Data Binding with Java APIs," or to the official W3C Web site for XML at www.w3c.org/XML/.

Simple Object Access Protocol (SOAP)

Simple Object Access Protocol, or SOAP, is a standard for a lightweight XML-based messaging protocol. It enables an exchange of information between two or more peers and enables them to communicate with each other in a decentralized, distributed application environment. Like XML, SOAP also is independent of the application object model, language, and running platforms or devices. SOAP is endorsed by W3C and key industry vendors like Sun Microsystems, IBM, HP, SAP, Oracle, and Microsoft. These vendors have already announced their support by participating in the W3C XML protocol-working group. The ebXML initiative from UN/CEFACT also has announced its support for SOAP.

In the core of the Web services model, SOAP is used as the messaging protocol for transport with binding on top of various Internet protocols such as HTTP, SMTP, FTP, and so on. SOAP uses XML as the message format, and it uses a set of encoding rules for representing data as messages. Although SOAP is used as a messaging protocol in Web services, it also can operate on a request/response model by exposing the functionality using SOAP/RPC based on remote procedural calls. SOAP also can be used with J2EE-based application frameworks. For more information about SOAP, go to Chapter 4, "Developing Web Services Using SOAP," or to the official W3C Web site for SOAP at www.w3c.org/TR/SOAP/.

Web Services Definition Language (WSDL)

The Web Services Definition Language (WSDL) standard is an XML format for describing the network services and its access information. It defines a binding mechanism used to attach a protocol, data format, an abstract message, or set of endpoints defining the location of services.

In the core of the Web services model, WSDL is used as the metadata language for defining Web services and describes how service providers and requesters communicate with one another. WSDL describes the Web services functionalities offered by the service provider, where the service is located, and how to access the service. Usually the service provider creates Web services by generating WSDL from its exposed business applications. A public/private registry is utilized for storing and publishing the WSDL-based information. For more information about WSDL, go to Chapter 5, "Description and Discovery of Web Services," or the official W3C Web site for WSDL at www.w3c.org/TR/wsdl/.

Universal Description, Discovery, and Integration (UDDI)

Universal Description, Discovery, and Integration, or UDDI, defines the standard interfaces and mechanisms for registries intended for publishing and storing descriptions of network services in terms of XML messages. It is similar to the yellow pages or a telephone directory where businesses list their products and services. Web services brokers use UDDI as a standard for registering the Web service providers. By communicating with the UDDI registries, the service requestors locate services and then invoke them.

In the core Web services model, UDDI provides the registry for Web services to function as a service broker enabling the service providers to populate the registry with service descriptions and service types and the service requestors to query the registry to find and locate the services. It enables Web applications to interact with a UDDI-based registry using SOAP messages. These registries can be either private services within an enterprise or a specific community, or they can be public registries to service the whole global business community of the Internet. The UDDI working group includes leading technology vendors like Sun Microsystems, IBM, HP, SAP, Oracle, and Microsoft. For more information about UDDI, go to Chapter 5, "Description and Discovery of Web Services," or to the official Web site of UDDI at www.uddi.org/.

ebXML

ebXML defines a global electronic marketplace where enterprises find one another and conduct business process collaborations and transactions. It also defines a set of specifications for enterprises to conduct electronic business over the Internet by establishing a common standard for business process specifications, business information modeling, business process collaborations, collaborative partnership profiles, and agreements and messaging. ebXML is an initiative sponsored by the United Nations Center for Trade Facilitation and Electronic Business (UN/CEFACT) and the Organization for the Advancement of Structured Information Standards (OASIS). Popular standards organizations like Open Travel Alliance (OTA), Open Application Group, Inc. (OAGI), Global Commerce Initiative (GCI), Health Level 7 (HL7, a healthcare standards organization), and RosettaNet (an XML standards committee) also have endorsed it.

In the Web services model, ebXML provides a comprehensive framework for the electronic marketplace and B2B process communication by defining standards for business processes, partner profile and agreements, registry and repository services, messaging services, and core components. It complements and extends with other Web services standards like SOAP, WSDL, and UDDI. In particular:

- ebXML Business Process Service Specifications (BPSS) enable business processes to be defined.
- ebXML CPP/CPA enables business partner profiles and agreements to be defined, and it provides business transaction choreography.
- ebXML Messaging Service Handler (MSH) deals with the transport, routing, and packaging of messages, and it also provides reliability and security, a value addition over SOAP.
- ebXML registry defines the registry services, interaction protocols, and message definitions, and ebXML repository acts as storage for shared information. The ebXML registries register with other registries as a federation, which can be discovered through UDDI. This enables UDDI to search for a business listing point to an ebXML Registry/Repository.
- ebXML Core components provide a catalogue of business process components that provide common functionality to the business community. Examples of such components are Procurement, Payment, Inventory, and so on.

For more information about ebXML, go to the official Web site of ebXML standards at www.ebxml.org.

Other Industry Standards Supporting Web Services

Many industry initiatives and standards supporting Web services are currently available and many more will be available in the future. The most prominent initiatives to embrace Web services standards are described in the following sections.

Web Services Choreography Interface (WSCI)

The Web Services Choreography Interface, or WSCI, is an initiative from Sun Microsystems, BEA, Intalio, and SAP that defines the flow of messages exchanged in a particular process of Web services communication. It describes the collective message flow model among Web services by providing a global view of the processes involved during the interactions that occur between Web services communication. This facilitates the bridging of business processes and Web services by enabling Web services to be part of the business processes of an organization or spanning multiple organizations. For more information about WSCI, go to the Sun XML Web site at www.sun.com/software/xml.

Web Services Flow Language (WSFL)

The Web Services Flow Language, or WSFL, is an XML-based language initiative from IBM for describing Web services compositions. These compositions are categorized as flow models and global models. Flow models can be used for modeling business processes or workflows based on Web services, and global models can be used for modeling links between Web services interfaces that enable the interaction of one Web service with an operation to another Web service interface. Using WSFL compositions support a wide range of interaction patterns between the partners participating in a business process, especially hierarchical interactions and peer-to-peer interaction between partners. For more information about WSFL, go to the IBM Web site at www.ibm.com/software/solutions/webservices/pdf/WSFL.pdf.

Directory Services Markup Language (DSML)

The Directory Services Markup Language, or DSML, defines an XML schema for representing directory structural information as an XML document, and it allows the publishing and sharing of directory information via Internet protocols like HTTP, SMTP, and so forth. DSML does not define the attributes for the directory structure or for accessing the information. A

DSML document defines the directory entries or a directory schema or both, and it can be used on top of any industry standard directory protocols like LDAP. DSML defines the standard for exchanging information between different directory services and enables interoperability between them. Bowstreet originally proposed DSML as a standard and later it received support from leading vendors like IBM, Oracle, Sun Microsystems, Microsoft, and so on. For more information about DSML standards, visit www.dsml.org.

XLANG

Similar to WSFL, XLANG defines an XML-based standard specification for defining business process flows in Web services. It also defines a notation for expressing actions and complex operations in Web services. Microsoft developed the XLANG specification and it has been implemented in Microsoft BizTalk server 2000, especially for handling Enterprise Application Integration (EAI) and B2B communication.

Business Transaction Protocol (BTP)

The Business Transaction Protocol (BTP) specification provides a support for Web services-based distributed transactions enabling the underlying transaction managers to provide the flexibility of handling XA-compliant, two-phase commit transaction engines. BTP is an OASIS initiative that facilitates large-scale business-to-business (B2B) deployments enabling distributed transactions in Web services. For more information about BTP, go to the OASIS Web site at www.oasis-open.org/committees /business-transactions/.

XML Encryption (XML ENC)

The XML Encryption, or XML ENC, is an XML-based standard for securing data by encryption using XML representations. In Web services, it secures the exchange of data between the communicating partners. For more information about XML Encryption, refer to Chapter 13, "Web Services Security," or go to the W3C Web site at www.w3.org/Encryption/.

XML Key Management System (XKMS)

The XML Key Management System, or XKMS, is an XML-based standard for integrating public key infrastructure (PKI) and digital certificates used for securing Internet transactions, especially those used in Web services. XKMS consists of two parts: the XML Key Information Service Specification (X-KISS) and the XML Key Registration Service Specification (X-KRSS). The X-KISS specification defines a protocol for a trust service that resolves public key information contained in XML-SIG elements. The X-KRSS describes how public key information is registered. For more information about XKMS, refer to Chapter 13, "Web Services Security," or go to the W3C Web site at www.w3.org/2001/XKMS/.

XML Signature (XML DSIG)

The XML Encryption, or XML DSIG, is an XML-based standard for specifying XML syntax and processing rules for creating and representing digital signatures. In Web services, an XML digital signature helps XML-based transactions by adding authentication, data integrity, and support for non-repudiation to the data during data exchange among the communicating partners. For more information about XML Signature, refer to Chapter 13, "Web Services Security" or go to the W3C Web site at www.w3.org/Signature/.

Extensible Access Control Markup Language (XACML)

The Extensible Access Control Markup Language, or XACML, is an XML-based standard for specifying policies and rules for accessing information over Web-based resources. In Web services, XACML sets the rules and permissions on resources shared among the communicating partners. XACML is one of the security initiatives made by the OASIS security services technical committee. For more information about XACML, refer to Chapter 13, "Web Services Security," or go to the OASIS Web site at www.oasis-open.org/committees/xacml/.

Security Assertions Markup Language (SAML)

The Security Assertions Markup Language, or SAML, defines an XML-based framework for exchanging authentication and authorization information. SAML uses a generic protocol consisting of XML-based request and response message formats, and it can be bound to many communication models and transport protocols. One of the key objectives of SAML is to provide and achieve single sign-on for applications participating in Web services. SAML is an initiative from the security services technical committee of OASIS. For more information about SAML, refer to Chapter 13, "Web

Services Security," or go to the OASIS Web site at www.oasis-open.org/committees/security/.

Known Challenges in Web Services

Web services present some key challenges associated with the mission-critical business requirements. These challenges need to be addressed before the services are fully implemented. Some of the key challenges are as follows:

Distributed transactions. If the environment requires distributed transactions with heterogeneous resources, it should be studied and tested with standard solutions based on BTP, WS-Transactions, and WS-Coordination.

Quality of Service (QoS). In case of a mission-critical solution, the service providers must examine the reliability and performance of the service in peak load and uncertain conditions for high availability. The exposed infrastructure must provide load balancing, and failover and fault tolerance, to resolve these scenarios.

Security. Web services are exposed to the public using http-based protocols. As Web services is publicly available, it must be implemented using authentication and authorization mechanisms and using SSL-enabling encryption of the messages for securing the usage. Adopting open security standards like SAML, XML Encryption, XML Signature, or XACML may be a solution.

Other challenges include the manageability and testing of the Web services deployment, which is subjected to different operating system environments and platforms and managing service descriptions in public/private registries.

Web Services Software and Tools

Let's now take a look at the Web services software and tool vendors offering solutions for developing and deploying Java-based Web services solutions. The following is a list of the most popular software solutions commercially available for implementing Web services.

BEA Systems Products

BEA WebLogic Server 7.0 provides the infrastructure solution for Web services supporting the standards and protocols of Web services. The BEA

WebLogic Integration Server also enables complex Web services to be deployed with transactional integrity, security, and reliability while supporting the emerging ebXML and BTP standards.

In this book, we have provided some example illustrations of using BEA WebLogic Server 7.0 in Chapter 3, "Building the Web Services Architecture." For more information about BEA Systems Products, go to their Web site at www.bea.com.

Cape Clear Products

Cape Clear provides Web services infrastructure and product solutions such as CapeConnect and CapeStudio, which enable the development of Web services solutions based on industry standards such as XML, SOAP, WSDL, and UDDI. Cape Clear also enables business applications from diverse technologies such as Java, EJB, CORBA, and Microsoft .NET. These components can be exposed as Web services over the Internet.

For more information about Cape Clear Systems Products, go to their Web site at www.capeclear.com.

IBM Products

IBM WebSphere Application Server 4.5 provides an infrastructure solution for deploying Web services-based applications. IBM also provides a Web Services Tool Kit (WSTK) bundle (now part of WebSphere Studio) for developers as a runtime environment that creates, publishes, and tests Web services solutions based on open standards such as XML, SOAP, WSDL, and UDDI. It also generates WSDL wrappers for existing applications without any reprogramming. The IBM WSTK is available for download at www.alphaworks.ibm.com/tech/webservicestoolkit.

IOPSIS Products

IOPSIS provides B2Beyond suite iNsight and W2Net, an Integrated Services Development Framework (ISDF), that enables the creation, assembly, deployment, and publication of Web services based on open standards such as XML, SOAP, WSDL, and UDDI. It also provides tools for the deployment of Web Services to popular J2EE-based Web application servers.

Oracle Products

Oracle's Oracle9i Release 2 application server provides the J2EE-based infrastructure solution for Web services supporting Web services standards including SOAP, UDDI, and WSDL. It also has features that define and coordinate business processes using Web services integrating legacy applications and back-end systems.

Sun Products

As part of the Java community process, Sun has already released its Java and XML technology-based APIs and its implementation referred to as JAX Pack for developing and testing Java and open standards-based Web services solutions. In addition, Sun also has released a comprehensive set of technologies specific to Web services that are referred to as the Java Web Services Developer Pack (JWSDP). In this book, we have discussed extensively JWSDP API technologies and provided example illustrations in Chapters 7 to 12.

The suite of products of Sun ONE Application Server 7.0, formerly called iPlanet Application Server 6.0, provide a J2EE- and open standards-based infrastructure for implementing Web services. The Sun ONE suite is a key component of Sun's Open Net Environment (Sun ONE), a comprehensive Web-services software environment for customers and developers interested in migrating to the next generation of Web services.

Systinet Products

Systinet provides Web services infrastructure and product solutions such as WASP Server, WASP Developer, and WASP UDDI, which develops Web services solutions based on industry standards such as XML, SOAP, WSDL, and UDDI. Systinet also enables business applications from diverse technologies such as Java, EJB, CORBA, and Microsoft .NET to be exposed as Web services over the Internet. It enables integration with J2EE-based applications and also supports security frameworks based on GSS API and Kerberos. It also provides the implementation of Java XML API technologies that were especially meant for Web services.

In this book, we have provided example illustrations of using Systinet WASP Server in Chapter 5, "Description and Discovery of Web Services."

Web Services Strategies from Industry Leaders: An Overview

Let's take a brief look at the leading vendor initiatives and strategies focused on the core of the Web services framework, which includes the architecture, platform, and software solutions for developing and deploying Web services. Adopting these frameworks offers a simplified implementation solution, interoperability, and industry standards compliance for enabling Web services. The following are the most popular initiatives for providing the core Web services frameworks that are offered by leading technology vendors in the industry.

Sun ONE (Sun Open Net Environment)

Sun ONE is Sun's open standards-based software vision, architecture, platform, and solution for building and deploying Services on Demand-based solutions that support the development and deployment of Web services. Sun ONE's architecture is based on open standards like SOAP, WSDL, and UDDI and also adopts the Java/J2EE-based solutions as its core runtime technology. The major strength of SunONE is that it does not exhibit any vendor lock-in problems or issues caused by other proprietary solutions. For more information on Sun ONE, refer to Chapter 14, "Introduction to Sun ONE," or refer to the Sun Web site at www.sun.com/software/sunone/.

IBM e-Business

IBM e-business is IBM's conceptual architecture and open standards-based product offering for the development and deployment of Web services. IBM's offering is based on Java/J2EE and Web services standards like SOAP, WSDL, and UDDI, and collectively reflects the set of Web services technologies for Dynamic e-Business. For more information on IBM e-business initiatives, refer to the IBM Web site at www.ibm.com/e-business/index.html.

Microsoft .NET

Microsoft .NET defines the framework and the programming model of the .NET platform for developing and deploying standards-based Web services and all types of applications. The framework defines three layers consisting of the Microsoft operating system, enterprise servers, and .Net building blocks using Visual Studio. The .NET-based Web services interfaces were developed using the .Net building blocks provided by the Microsoft Visual Studio .NET framework supporting standards like SOAP, WSDL, and UDDI. For more information about Microsoft .NET, go to Microsoft's Web site at www.microsoft.com.

Key Benefits of Web Services

The key benefits of implementing Web services are as follows:

- Provides a simple mechanism for applications to become services that are accessible by anyone, anywhere, and from any device.
- Defines service-based application connectivity facilitating EAI, and intra-enterprise and inter-enterprise communication.
- Defines a solution for businesses, which require flexibility and agility in application-to-application communication over the Internet.
- Enables dynamic location and invocation of services through service brokers (registries).
- Enables collaboration with existing applications that are modeled as services to provide aggregated Web services.

Quite clearly, Web services are the next major technology for demonstrating a new way of communication and collaboration.

Summary

In this chapter, we provided an introduction to Web services and the core open standard technologies available today for implementing Web services applications. We also discussed the operational model and characteristics of Web services in business-to-business communication.

In general, we have looked at what Web services are; the core standards, tools, and technologies for enabling Web services; the industry standards that support those services; leading technology vendors; and the uses as well as benefits and challenges of using Web services.

In the next chapter, we will explore the Web services architecture and its core buildings blocks, and then illustrate an example of a J2EE-based Web services application.

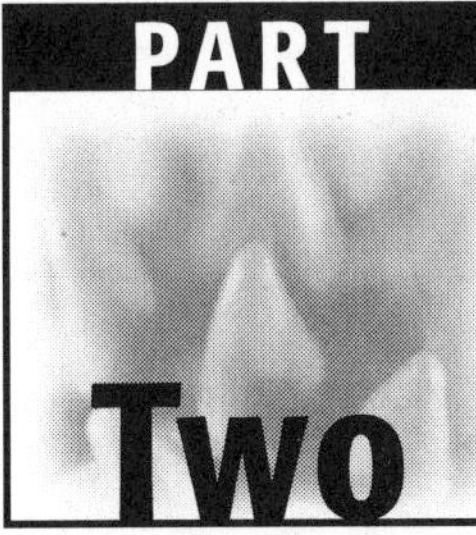

Web Services Architecture and Technologies

CHAPTER

3

Building the Web Services Architecture

This chapter focuses on the Web services architecture: its core building blocks, implementation models, and deployment process for building Web services-based application solutions. In addition, this chapter also illustrates an example demonstrating the development of a complete Web services solution exposing J2EE applications as services over the Internet.

The Web services architecture represents the logical evolution of traditional computer-based applications to services-oriented applications over the Internet. It defines a distributed computing mechanism by adopting a service-oriented architecture (SOA), where all of the applications are encapsulated as services and made available for invocation over a network. These services can be leveraged from different applications and platforms with varying technologies adopting common industry standards and platform-independent and language-neutral Internet protocols for enabling application interoperability, thus making them easily accessible over the Internet. In addition, it provides a mechanism for categorizing and registering the services in a common location by making them available for discovery and collaboration over the Internet or corporate networks. Using Web services architecture and adhering to its standards also exposes existing and legacy applications as Web services, and the clients invoking these services do not require that they are aware of their target system environment and its underlying implementation model.

Over the course of this chapter, we will study all about the Web services architecture and its associated standards and technologies addressing the challenges in implementation. In particular, we will be focusing on the following:

- Understanding the basics of Web services architecture
- Key architectural requirements and constraints
- Building blocks of Web services architecture
- The role of Web services standards and technologies
- Web services communication models
- How to implement Web services
- How to develop a Web services provider environment using J2EE
- How to develop a client service requester environment

Because the key focus of this book is developing Web services using the Java platform, this chapter will illustrate an example of building a Web services solution by exposing a J2EE application deployed in a J2EE application server.

Before moving forward, it is also important to note that during January 2002, W3C started its Web services activity as an ongoing effort to identify the requirements and standards-based technologies for addressing the key aspects of Web services, such as the architecture, protocols, and services description and coordination, and so forth. Today, leading Web services technology vendors, joined together as part of the W3C Web services working group, are working on identifying the requirements and developing full-fledged Web services architecture-based solutions. To find out the status of W3C working group activities on Web services architecture, refer to the W3C URL at www.w3c.org/2002/ws/arch/.

Web Services Architecture and Its Core Building Blocks

In the last chapter, we looked at the basic operational model of a Web services environment with the three roles as service provider, service broker, and service requestor associated with three operational relationships such as registering, discovering, and invoking services.

The basic principles behind the Web services architecture are based on SOA and the Internet protocols. It represents a composable application solution based on standards and standards-based technologies. This ensures that the implementations of Web services applications are compliant to standard specifications, thus enabling interoperability with those compliant applications. Some of the key design requirements of the Web services architecture are the following:

- To provide a universal interface and a consistent solution model to define the application as modular components, thus enabling them as exposable services
- To define a framework with a standards-based infrastructure model and protocols to support services-based applications over the Internet
- To address a variety of service delivery scenarios ranging from e-business (B2C), business-to-business (B2B), peer-to-peer (P2P), and enterprise application integration (EAI)-based application communication
- To enable distributable modular applications as a centralized and decentralized application environment that supports boundary-less application communication for inter-enterprise and intra-enterprise application connectivity
- To enable the publishing of services to one or more public or private directories, thus enabling potential users to locate the published services using standard-based mechanisms that are defined by standards organizations
- To enable the invocation of those services when it is required, subject to authentication, authorization, and other security measures

To handle these requirements, a typical Web service architectural model consists of three key logical components as core building blocks mapping the operational roles and relationships of a Web services environment. Figure 3.1 represents the core building blocks of a typical Web services architecture.

Services container/runtime environment. The services container acts as the Web services runtime environment and hosts the service provider. Typical to a Web application environment, it defines the Web services runtime environment meant for client communication as a container of Web services interfaces by exposing the potential components of the underlying applications. It facilitates the service deployment and services administration. In addition, it also handles the registration of the service description with the service registries. Usually, the Web services platform provider implements the services container. In some circumstances, the Web application servers provide system services and APIs that can be leveraged as the Web services container.

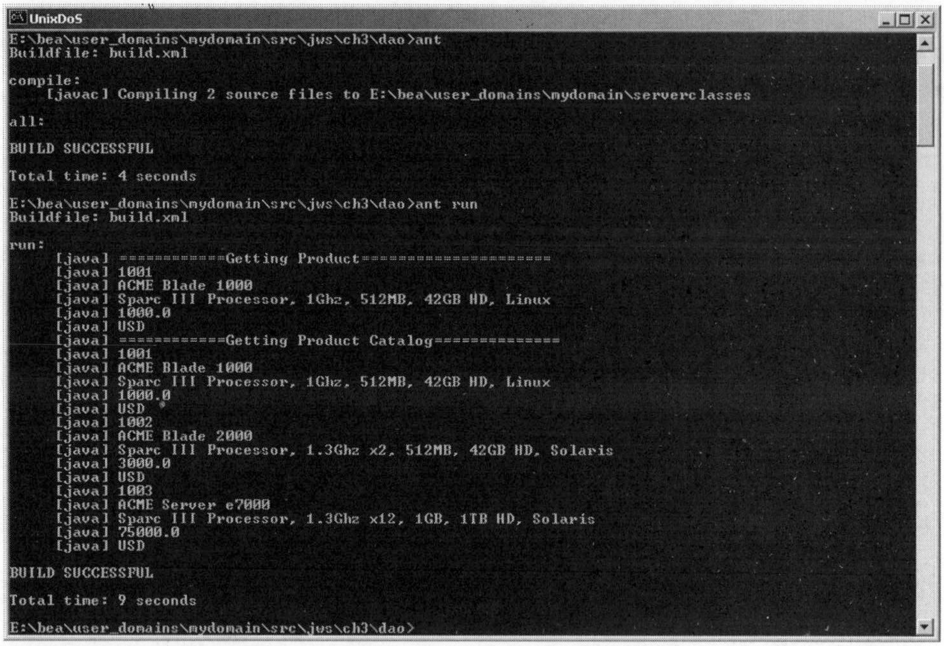

```
UnixDoS
E:\bea\user_domains\mydomain\src\jws\ch3\dao>ant
Buildfile: build.xml

compile:
    [javac] Compiling 2 source files to E:\bea\user_domains\mydomain\serverclasses

all:

BUILD SUCCESSFUL

Total time: 4 seconds

E:\bea\user_domains\mydomain\src\jws\ch3\dao>ant run
Buildfile: build.xml

run:
     [java] ============Getting Product=====================
     [java] 1001
     [java] ACME Blade 1000
     [java] Sparc III Processor, 1Ghz, 512MB, 42GB HD, Linux
     [java] 1000.0
     [java] USD
     [java] ============Getting Product Catalog==============
     [java] 1001
     [java] ACME Blade 1000
     [java] Sparc III Processor, 1Ghz, 512MB, 42GB HD, Linux
     [java] 1000.0
     [java] USD
     [java] 1002
     [java] ACME Blade 2000
     [java] Sparc III Processor, 1.3Ghz x2, 512MB, 42GB HD, Solaris
     [java] 3000.0
     [java] USD
     [java] 1003
     [java] ACME Server e7000
     [java] Sparc III Processor, 1.3Ghz x12, 1GB, 1TB HD, Solaris
     [java] 75000.0
     [java] USD

BUILD SUCCESSFUL

Total time: 9 seconds

E:\bea\user_domains\mydomain\src\jws\ch3\dao>
```

Figure 3.1 Core building blocks of Web services architecture.

Services registry. The services registry hosts the published services and acts as a broker providing a facility to publish and store the description of Web services registered by the service providers. In addition, it defines a common access mechanism for the service requestors for locating the registered services.

Services delivery. It acts as the Web services client runtime environment by looking up the services registries to find the required services and invoking them from the service provider. It is represented as a presentation module for service requestors, by exposing the appropriate interfaces or markups for generating content and delivery to a variety of client applications, devices, platforms, and so forth.

To build the Web services architecture with these logical components, we need to use standardized components and a communication model for describing and invoking the services that are universally understood between the service providers and their potential service requestors. It also requires a standard way to publish the services by the service provider and store them in the service broker. In turn, service requestors can find them.

As we discussed in the previous chapter, today the industry has well embraced the XML-based Web services standards and technologies as its core building blocks of Web services architecture. A typical Web services architecture relies on *de facto* Web services standards commonly referred to nowadays as WUST (WSDL/UDDI/SOAP technologies), so that the technologies relate to one another and communicate with each other. The ebXML specifications build on portions of the WUST technologies and provide a standard for conducting electronic e-business globally and integrating disparate business systems based on a Web services architecture model for eMarketplace. The technical architectural model of ebXML is discussed in Chapter 14, "Introduction to Sun ONE."

Figure 3.2 illustrates the Web services architecture, with its core building blocks working together using its corresponding Web services standards.

Figure 3.2 represents the Web services architecture with the following standards and technologies playing the role as its core building blocks:

SOAP. This provides a standardized way to transmit data and acts as a messaging service for enabling the service invocation calls between the service provider and the service requestor. In ebXML-based architecture, ebXML MS provides reliable messaging between the service provider and service requester.

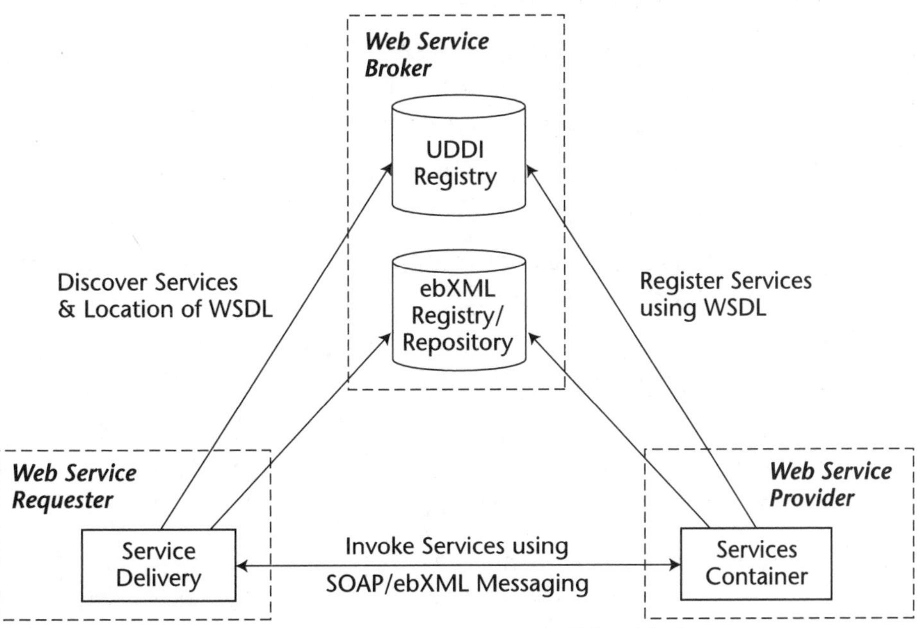

Figure 3.2 Web Services architecture and its core building blocks.

WSDL. This resides in the services container and provides a standardized way to describe the Web services as a service description. In ebXML-based architecture, ebXML CPP/A provides services descriptions including business partner profiles and agreements.

UDDI. This provides a standard mechanism for publishing and discovering registered Web services, and it also acts as the registry and repository to store WSDL-based service descriptions. In ebXML-based architecture, ebXML Registry & Repository provides a facility to store CPP/CPA descriptions for business collaboration.

As we noted, Web services are accessed using standard Internet protocols and XML—the Web services architecture forms the standard infrastructure solution for building distributed applications as services that can be published, discovered, and accessed over the Internet.

Tools of the Trade

Let's take a closer look at the role of those Web services standards and technologies and how they are represented in Web services architecture and its development process.

Simple Object Access Protocol (SOAP)

The Simple Object Access Protocol, or SOAP, plays the role of the messaging protocol for exchanging information between the service provider and the service requestor. It consists of the following:

SOAP Envelope. It describes the message, identifying the contents and the envelope's processing information.

SOAP Transport. It defines the bindings for the underlying transport protocols such as HTTP and SMTP.

SOAP Encoding. It defines a set of encoding rules for mapping the instances of the application-specific data types to XML elements.

SOAP RPC conventions. It defines the representation of the RPC requests and responses. These SOAP requests and responses are marshaled in a data type and passed in to a SOAP body.

Listing 3.1 represents a SOAP message using an HTTP post request for sending a `getBookPrice()` method with `<bookname>` as an argument to obtain a price of a book.

```
POST /StockQuote HTTP/1.1
Host: www.acmeretailer.com
Content-Type: text/xml; charset="utf-8"
Content-Length: 1000
SOAPAction: "getBookPrice"
<SOAP-ENV:Envelope
   xmlns:SOAP-ENV="http://schemas.xmlsoap.org/soap/envelope/"
   xmlns:xsi="http://www.w3c.org/2001/XMLSchema-instance"
   xmlns:xsd="http://www.w3c.org/2001/XMLSchema"
   SOAP-ENV:encodingStyle
            ="http://schemas.xmlsoap.org/soap/encoding/">
     <SOAP-ENV:Body>
     <m:getBookPrice
       xmlns:m="http://www.wiley.com/jws.book.priceList">
     <bookname xsi:type='xsd:string'>
            Developing Java Web services</bookname>
     </m:getBookPrice>
   /SOAP-ENV:Body>
</SOAP-ENV:Envelope>
```

Listing 3.1 SOAP message using HTTP.

At the time of writing, the current version of SOAP is SOAP 1.2 with attachments (SwA) and it is still being worked on in W3C. (For more information on SOAP and developing Web services applications using SOAP, refer to Chapter 4, "Developing Web Services Using SOAP.")

Web Services Description Language (WSDL)

The Web Services Description Language, or WDDL, is an XML schema-based specification for describing Web services as a collection of operations and data input/output parameters as messages. WSDL also defines the communication model with a binding mechanism to attach any transport protocol, data format, or structure to an abstract message, operation, or endpoint.

Listing 3.2 shows a WSDL example that describes a Web service meant for obtaining a price of a book using a `GetBookPrice` operation.

```
<?xml version="1.0"?>
    <definitions name="BookPrice"
       targetNamespace="http://www.wiley.com/bookprice.wsdl"
       xmlns:tns="http://www.wiley.com/bookprice.wsdl"
```

Listing 3.2 A WSDL document describing a Service. *(continues)*

```
        xmlns:xsd="http://www.w3.org/2000/10/XMLSchema"
        xmlns:xsd1="http://www.wiley.com/bookprice.xsd"
        xmlns:soap="http://schemas.xmlsoap.org/wsdl/soap/"
        xmlns="http://schemas.xmlsoap.org/wsdl/">
        <message name="GetBookPriceInput">
       <part name="bookname" element="xsd:string"/>
        </message>
           <message name="GetBookPriceOutput">
           <part name="price" type="xsd:float"/>
           </message>
             <portType name="BookPricePortType">
               <operation name="GetBookPrice">
                  <input message="tns:GetBookPriceInput"/>
                   <output message="tns:GetBookPriceOutput"/>
                   </operation>
               </portType>
         <binding name="BookPriceSoapBinding"
                                 type="tns:BookPricePortType">
                <soap:binding style="rpc"
               transport="http://schemas.xmlsoap.org/soap/http"/>
               <operation name="GetBookPrice">
        <soap:operation
               soapAction="http://www.wiley.com/GetBookPrice"/>
        <input>
               <soap:body use="encoded"
                 namespace="http://www.wiley.com/bookprice"
      encodingStyle="http://schemas.xmlsoap.org/soap/encoding/"/>
         </input>
         <output>
         <soap:body use="encoded"
         namespace="http://www.wiley.com/bookprice"
     encodingStyle="http://schemas.xmlsoap.org/soap/encoding/"/>
      </output>
       </operation>>
        </binding>
        <service name="WileyBookPriceService">
          <documentation>Wiley Book Price Service</documentation>
          <port name="BookPricePort"
                 binding="tns:BookPriceSoapBinding">
         <soap:address
                location="http://www.wiley.com/bookprice"/>
      </port>
   </service>
   </definitions>
```

Listing 3.2 A WSDL document describing a Service. *(continued)*

At the time of writing, the current version of WSDL is WSDL 1.1 and it has been discussed throughout this book. (For more information on WSDL, refer to the section *Describing Web Services Using WSDL* in Chapter 5, "Description and Discovery of Web Services.")

Universal Description, Discovery, and Integration (UDDI)

Universal Description, Discovery, and Integration, or UDDI, defines a mechanism to register and categorize Web services in a general-purpose registry that users communicate to in order to discover and locate registered services. While querying a UDDI registry for a service, the WSDL description describing the service interface will be returned. Using the WSDL description, the developer can construct a SOAP client interface that can communicate with the service provider.

UDDI can be implemented as a public registry to support the requirements of a global community or as a private registry to support an enterprise or a private community.

At the time of this book's writing, the current version of UDDI is UDDI 2.0 and it will be discussed throughout this book. (For more information on UDDI, refer to Chapter 5, "Description and Discovery of Web Services.")

ebXML

ebXML provides a standard framework for building an electronic marketplace by enabling the standardization of business processes, business partner profiles, and partner agreements. In general, ebXML complements other Web services standards like SOAP, WSDL, and UDDI.

The following are major features of ebXML:

- ebXML Messaging Service (MS) is a value-add over SOAP that provides reliability and security mechanisms.
- ebXML BPSS enables business processes to be described.
- ebXML CPP/CPA is a value-add over WSDL that enables business partner profiles and partner agreements to be described.
- ebXML reg/rep provides a registry and repository, while UDDI is just a registry.
- ebXML Core components provide a catalogue of business process components for the business community.

Although ebXML-based Web services are not in the scope of this book, ebXML framework-based components will be discussed throughout the book in all of the chapters where the complementing Web services technologies are presented. For more information on ebXML, refer to the official ebXML Web site at www.ebxml.org.

Web Services Communication Models

In Web services architecture, depending upon the functional requirements, it is possible to implement the models with RPC-based synchronous or messaging-based synchronous/asynchronous communication models. These communication models need to be understood before Web services are designed and implemented.

RPC-Based Communication Model

The RPC-based communication model defines a request/response-based synchronous communication. When the client sends a request, the client waits until a response is sent back from the server before continuing any operation. Typical to implementing CORBA or RMI communication, the RPC-based Web services are tightly coupled and are implemented with remote objects to the client application. Figure 3.3 represents an RPC-based communication model in Web services architecture.

The clients have the capability to provide parameters in method calls to the Web service provider. Then, clients invoke the Web services by sending parameter values to the Web service provider that executes the required methods, and then sends back the return values. Additionally, using RPC-based communication, both the service provider and requestor can register and discover services, respectively.

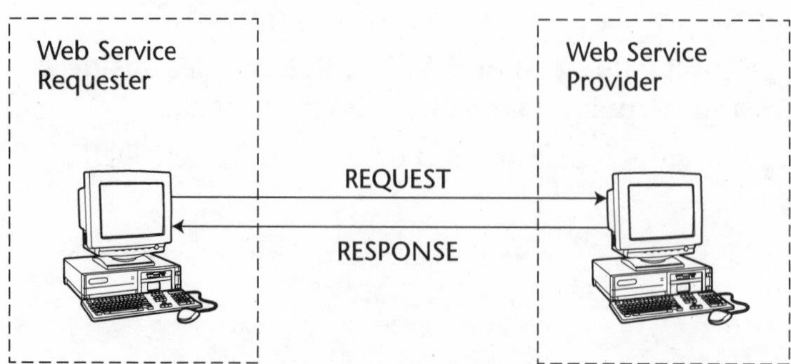

Figure 3.3 RPC-based communication model in Web services.

Messaging-Based Communication Model

The messaging-based communication model defines a loosely coupled and document-driven communication. The service requestor invoking a messaging-based service provider does not wait for a response. Figure 3.4 represents a messaging-based communication model in Web services architecture.

In Figure 3.4, the client service requestor invokes a messaging-based Web service; it typically sends an entire document rather than sending a set of parameters. The service provider receives the document, processes it, and then may or may not return a message. Depending upon the implementation, the client can either send or receive a document asynchronously to and from a messaging-based Web service, but it cannot do both functionalities at an instant. In addition, it also is possible to implement messaging with a synchronous communication model where the client makes the service request to the service provider, and then waits and receives the document from the service provider.

Adopting a communication model also depends upon the Web service provider infrastructure and its compliant protocol for RPC and Messaging. The current version of SOAP 1.2 and ebXML Messaging support these communication models; it is quite important to ensure that the protocols are compliant and supported by the Web services providers. It also is important to satisfy other quality of services (QoS) and environmental requirements like security, reliability, and performance.

Before jumping into the development approaches, let's take a look at the process steps of implementing a Web services model.

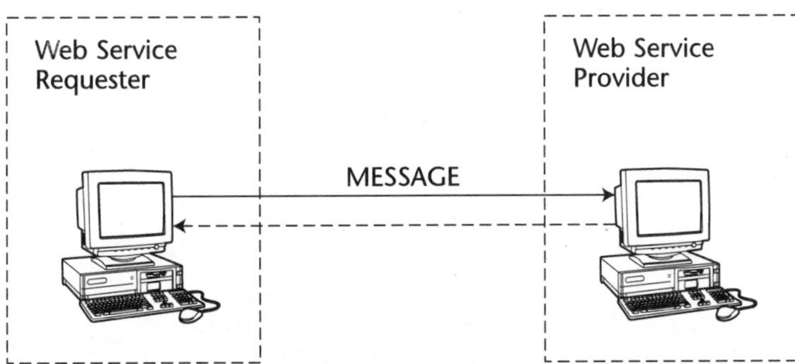

Figure 3.4 Messaging-based communication model.

Implementing Web Services

The process of implementing Web services is quite similar to implementing any distributed application using CORBA or RMI. However, in Web services, all the components are bound dynamically only at its runtime using standard protocols. Figure 3.5 illustrates the process highlights of implementing Web services.

As illustrated in Figure 3.5, the basic steps of implementing Web services are as follows:

1. The service provider creates the Web service typically as SOAP-based service interfaces for exposed business applications. The provider then deploys them in a service container or using a SOAP runtime environment, and then makes them available for invocation over a network. The service provider also describes the Web service as a WSDL-based service description, which defines the clients and the service container with a consistent way of identifying the service location, operations, and its communication model.

2. The service provider then registers the WSDL-based service description with a service broker, which is typically a UDDI registry.

3. The UDDI registry then stores the service description as binding templates and URLs to WSDLs located in the service provider environment.

4. The service requestor then locates the required services by querying the UDDI registry. The service requestor obtains the binding information and the URLs to identify the service provider.

5. Using the binding information, the service requestor then invokes the service provider and then retrieves the WSDL Service description for those registered services. Then, the service requestor creates a client proxy application and establishes communication with the service provider using SOAP.

6. Finally, the service requestor communicates with the service provider and exchanges data or messages by invoking the available services in the service container.

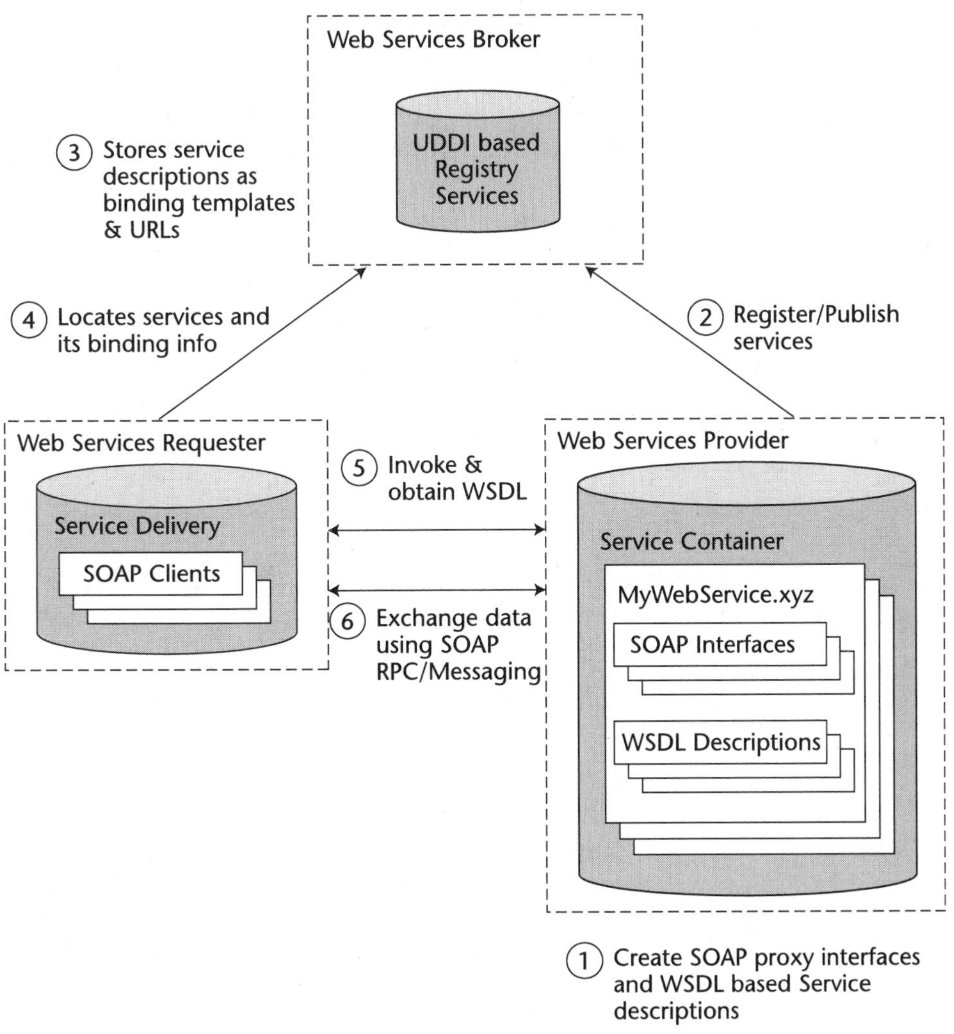

Figure 3.5 Process steps involved in implementing Web services.

In the case of an ebXML-based environment, the steps just shown are the same, except ebXML registry and repository, ebXML Messaging, and ebXML CPP/CPA are used instead of UDDI, SOAP, and WSDL, respectively. The basic steps just shown also do not include the implementation of security and quality of service (QoS) tasks. These subjects are discussed in Chapter 13, "Web Services Security." So far we have explored the Web services architecture and technologies. Let's now move forward to learn how to develop Web services-enabled applications as services using the Web services architecture.

Developing Web Services-Enabled Applications

The design and development process of creating a Web services-enabled application is not different from the typical process of developing a distributed application. In case of Web services, it can be created as a new application or from using an existing application by repurposing them as services.

In a Web services implementation, it also is possible to expose existing/legacy applications as services by encapsulating the core business functionalities of those underlying applications. The underlying applications can be of any application implemented in any programming language and running on any platform.

Figure 3.6 represents a typical Web services implementation model providing service-oriented interfaces supporting a variety of back-end application environments.

The implementation steps generally involved in developing Web services solutions by exposing back-end business applications are as follows:

1. The potential business component of the underlying application will be encapsulated as service-oriented interfaces using SOAP and then exposed as Web services by deploying them in a Web services service container or a SOAP runtime environment. Using those SOAP-based interfaces, the service container handles all the incoming SOAP requests/responses or messaging-based operations and maps them as methods and arguments of the underlying business application.

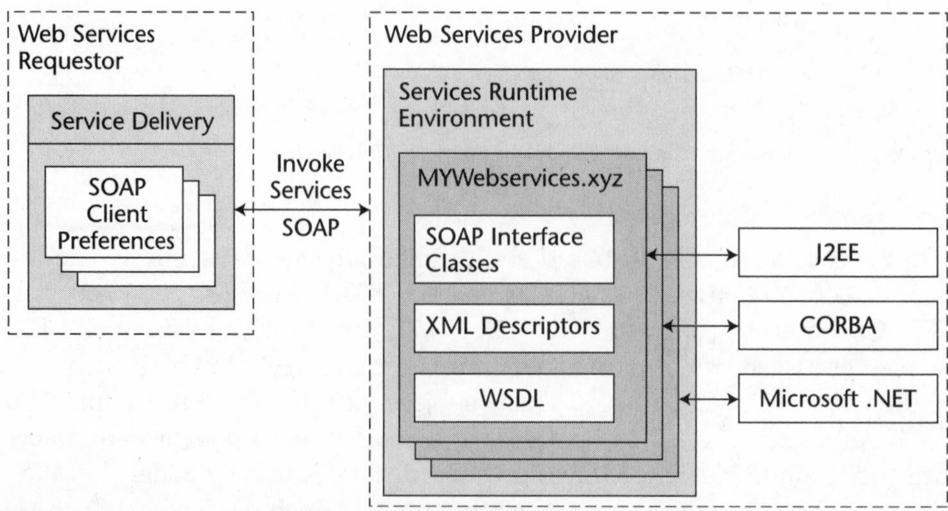

Figure 3.6 Exposing applications through Web services.

2. WSDL-based service descriptions will be generated and then reside in a service container. WSDL defines the communication contract required for invoking the SOAP-based service interfaces. These WSDL-based service descriptions will be published in a UDDI registry as service templates and its location URLs. The interfaces required for publishing in the UDDI registry are usually provided by the Web service container provider.
3. The service requester finds the services using the discovery mechanisms (registry API) and obtains the service description and its provider location URL. It then connects to the service provider to obtain WSDL.
4. To invoke the services exposed by the service provider, the service requestor (service delivery environment) is required to implement SOAP-based client interfaces according to the service description defined in the WSDL.

The Web services container/runtime environment provider generally provides the tools required for creating SOAP-based services interfaces from existing applications and generating WSDL-based service descriptions. Depending upon the Web services runtime environment, some providers also include test environments for UDDI and interfaces for publishing services interfaces.

The previous steps are usually common at all levels of Web services development, irrespective of the target application environment such as J2EE, CORBA, Microsoft .NET, or standalone applications based on Java, C++, Microsoft Visual Basic, and legacy applications based on, the Mainframe environment. As a result, implementing Web services unifies J2EE, CORBA, .NET, and other XML-based applications with interoperability and data sharing.

Because the scope of this book is focused on developing the Web services using the Java platform, let's focus on the key technologies and development processes required. We'll begin with implementing Web services using Java-based applications.

How to Develop Java-Based Web Services

With the overwhelming success of Java in Web and pervasive applications running on a variety of platforms and devices, the Java platform has become the obvious choice for enterprise architects and developers. In addition to the Java platform, today the J2EE-based application environment also has become the preferred solution for running Web services-based solutions.

Web services are generally driven using a Web-enabled application environment for HTTP communication. Because of that fact, in most cases the J2EE-based Web services environment plays a vital role as a service enabler for deploying Java and J2EE components as Web services. In addition, the adoption of a J2EE-based Web services environment carries one significant advantage: the deployment of Web services interfaces by the automatic inheritance of all the characteristics of the J2EE container-based services such as transactions, application security, and back-end application/databases connectivity.

Let's take a closer look at how to build Web services implementation using a J2EE environment.

Building Web Services in the J2EE Environment

The process of building Web services using a J2EE environment involves exposing J2EE components such as servlets and EJBs. In addition, J2EE applications also can access these exposed services using standard protocols.

In a typical implementation, a J2EE-based Web services model defines another way of exposing their business components similar to Web applications and RMI/IIOP-based application connectivity and without changing the architectural model or code of the existing J2EE components. For example, in a J2EE-based application server environment, J2EE components can be exposed for remote access through RMI/IIOP. In the case of a Web service provider using a J2EE environment, in addition to RMI/IIOP, it also is possible to expose those components as a service via WSDL and handle the exposed service by sending and receiving SOAP-based requests/responses or messages.

Today, most Web services platform providers and J2EE application server vendors have released their supporting toolsets for exposing the J2EE components such as EJBs and Servlets as Web services. Typically, these tools provide functionality to generate WSDL-based service descriptions and service interface classes, which send and receive SOAP messages based on the services defined in the WSDL.

The following steps are commonly involved in creating Web services from a J2EE-based application component:

1. Select a Web services platform provider, which provides a consistent platform for building and deploying Web services over the J2EE applications.
2. Define a Web service-enabled application and its behavior.
   a. Select the potential J2EE components (for example, EJBs, Servlets, and JMS applications) that are required to be exposed as services or are using the existing services.

   b. Choose the communication model (RPC-based synchronous or messaging-based asynchronous) depending upon the required behavior of the underlying components (for example, Session or Entity EJBs using RPC-based communication or JMS applications using messaging-based communication).

   c. Ensure that the service uses only built-in/custom data types mapping for XML and Java supported by the Web services container. This applies only to RPC-based communication models.

3. Develop the Web service by writing the interfaces required for accessing the exposed components (for example, EJBs, Servlets, and JMS applications).

   a. Develop the potential J2EE component (for example, EJBs, Servlets, and JMS applications) that are required and deploy them in a J2EE-compliant container. Ensure that the data types used by the components are supported in the XML/Java mappings defined by the provider.

   b. Implement the SOAP message handlers.

4. Assemble the required components into a required structure (defined by the Web services platform provider), additionally creating the deployment descriptors for the services (as defined by the Web services platform provider) and package them as a deployable EAR.

   a. Most Web service platform vendors provide utility tools to generate Web services components (SOAP interfaces) by introspecting the components (especially its methods and values) and mapping them to its supported data types.

   b. Also it is important to note, the upcoming release of the J2EE 1.4 specification is expected to provide a complete J2EE-based Web services platform and would enable the deployment of J2EE components as Web services.

5. Deploy the Web service components in the Web services container and make them available to its remote clients (based on the required protocol bindings such as HTTP and SMTP).

6. Create test clients for invoking the deployed Web services.

7. Register and publish your Web service in a UDDI registry, in case you require enabling the service available by searching public/private UDDI registries for Web services.

These steps are common. They are based on the implementation available from most popular Web services platform vendors. Perhaps in the future, implementation may vary, based on emerging standards.

J2EE and Java Web Services Developer Pack (JWSDP)

Sun Microsystems as part of its Java community process has already released its Java API for Web Services for the developer community as the Java Web Services Developer Pack (JWSDP). It provides a full-fledged solution package for developing and testing Web services using the Java APIs. In addition, leading Web services platform providers like Systinet, CapeClear, and Mind Electric and leading J2EE vendors like BEA, IBM, and Sun iPlanet also released their Web services capabilities, adopting a Java platform and supporting Java APIs for Web services as per JWSDP.

JWSDP 1.0 provides a one-stop Java API solution for building Web services using a Java platform. The key API components include the following:

- Java API for XML Messaging (JAXM)
- Java API for XML Processing (JAXP)
- Java API for XML Registries (JAXR)
- Java API for XML Binding (JAXB)
- Java API for XML-Based RPC (JAX-RPC)
- Java WSDP Registry Server (JWSDP)
- Java Server Pages Standard Tag Library (JSTL)

Leading J2EE application server vendors have announced their support to this effort and also started releasing their JWSDP API implementation. This helps the developers to build Web services by exposing their existing J2EE applications. The JWSDP and its API components are discussed with examples in Part Three of this book, "Exploring Java Web Services Pack." At the time of writing this book, Sun Microsystems and its JCP partners are currently working on a specification: Implementing Enterprise Web Services (JSR 109). This specification essentially addresses how to implement Web services in the J2EE platform defining a standard programming model and J2EE container-based runtime architecture for implementing Web services.

So far we have examined the Web services architecture and the concepts of developing Java-based Web services. In the next section, let's take a look at how to develop Web services by exposing J2EE components deployed in a J2EE application server.

Exposing J2EE Components as Web Services

This section explores the J2EE environment and the Web services techniques available for leveraging J2EE components as Web services. The J2EE environment delivers platform-independent Java component-based applications providing a multi-tiered distributed application model with several advantages like security, scalability, administration tools, portability between vendor implementations, and reliability of deployed applications. In general, it defines the following components residing in different logical tiers:

- JavaServer Pages (JSP) and Java Servlet-based components act as Web components running on the Web/Servlet container of the J2EE server.
- Enterprise JavaBeans (EJB)-based components act as business or persistence components running on the EJB container of the J2EE server.
- JDBC (Java Database connectivity) and J2EE connector architecture-based components act as the integration tier of the J2EE server for integrating database applications and enterprise information systems.

The key differences between J2EE components and traditional Java applications is that J2EE components are assembled and deployed into a J2EE application server in compliance with the J2EE specification. These components are managed by J2EE server system services such as synchronization, multithreading, and connecting pooling. Additionally, the J2EE server implementation also provides capabilities like clustering, transaction coordination, messaging, and database connection pooling. Exposing J2EE components as Web services provides robust Web services-based applications by fully utilizing the potential of J2EE application server-deployed components and standards-based communication provided by the Web services container.

In short, developing Web services from J2EE-based applications requires the implementation of components using J2EE component APIs (such as EJBs and servlets), then packaging and deploying them in a J2EE container environment as target enterprise applications. The components are then hosted in a J2EE-compliant application server. Exposing these J2EE components as Web services also requires a Web services container environment, which enables the creation and deployment of SOAP-based proxy interfaces.

In a typical scenario, exposing a J2EE-based application component as Web services involves the steps in the following list:

STEPS FOR THE SERVICE PROVIDER

1. The potential J2EE component deployed in an application server environment will be encapsulated as a service-oriented interface using SOAP and then deployed in a Web services runtime environment.

2. WSDL-based service descriptions are generated and then reside in the services runtime environment. The service requestor clients create SOAP-based client interfaces using the WSDL-based descriptions.
3. Using registry APIs, WSDLs are used for publishing the services in a public/private UDDI registry.

STEPS FOR THE SERVICE REQUESTOR

1. The service requestor clients create SOAP-based client interfaces using the WSDL-based descriptions exposed by the service provider.
2. The service requestor may choose to use any language for implementing the client interfaces, but it must support the use of SOAP for communication.
3. These client interfaces then are used to invoke the service provider-deployed services.

At this time of writing, most J2EE application server vendors are developing their Web services runtime environment as a service container for a J2EE environment; most of them have already made their beta available. The upcoming release of J2EE 1.4 and EJB 2.1 specifications focuses on Web services.

Now, let's take a look at the full-featured implementation of a real-world example of exposing J2EE components as Web services.

Developing Web Services Using J2EE: An Example

Before we start, let's take a look at the background of this example illustration that is based on a fictitious company named ACME Web Services Company. In this example, we will be implementing the J2EE components using a J2EE application server and will expose them as service interfaces using its service container for the service provider. We also will build the client invocation interfaces using a SOAP provider.

The ACME Web Services Company is a Web-based services provider that sells computer products by delivering XML-based data over the Internet as Web services to its partners and resellers by exposing its business functions. The functions exposed by the service provider are as follows:

- Catalog of computer system products to retail sellers
- Product specific information
- Selling computer systems and products to resellers

The service requesters are partners and resellers who use ACME Web services to obtain catalogs and product information, place orders, obtain invoices, and the like. The service requesters use their own application environment and do SOAP-based service invocation with ACME Web services (see Figure 3.7).

To build and deploy ACME Web services, we chose to use the following infrastructure solutions:

SERVICE PROVIDER SIDE FEATURES

- The ACME Web services provider will use BEA WebLogic 7.0 as its J2EE application server and its Web services runtime environment/container.
- BEA WebLogic 7.0 is a J2EE 1.3-compliant application server with capabilities that enable the creation, assembly, and deployment of Web services from the existing J2EE components. WebLogic Server provides early access implementation of Sun JAX-RPC API that enables the building of RPC-style Web services. It also includes WebLogic Workshop—a development environment (IDE) for developing and testing Web services. The BEA WebLogic 7.0 server is available for download as an evaluation copy for developers at www.bea.com.

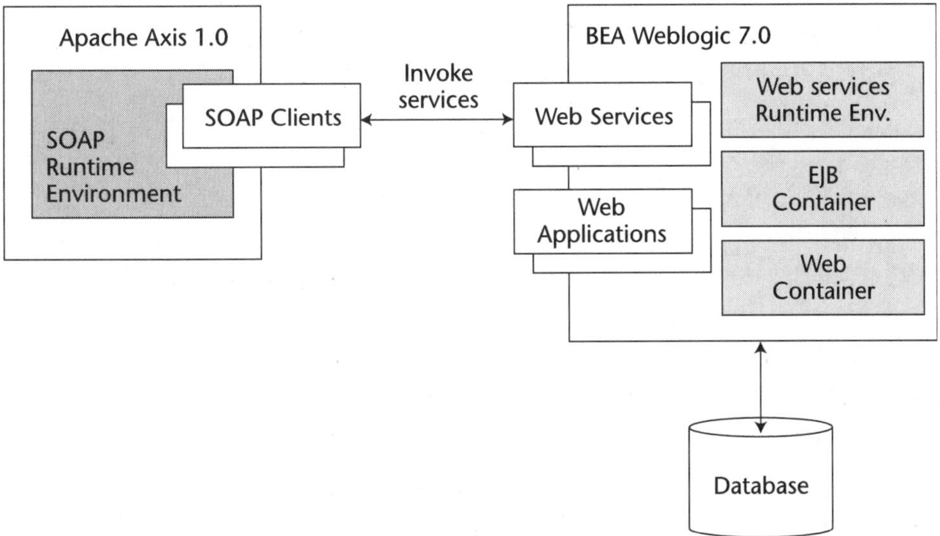

Figure 3.7 Developing Web services using a J2EE environment.

- WebLogic 7.0 provides `servicegen`, a SOAP and WSDL generation utility that enables the creation of SOAP-based service-oriented interfaces from J2EE components. It also provides a client generator utility, `clientgen`, which enables the creation of Java-based clients to invoke Web services. Additionally, it also provides serializer and deserializer classes, which convert XML to Java representations of data, and vice-versa.
- The ACME Web services provider also uses JAXP-compliant XML parser and PointBase as its database for storing and querying information. JAXP and PointBase also are available as part of the BEA WebLogic bundle and no separate download is required. The PointBase database also can be used as an evaluation copy for development purposes. For more information on understanding the PointBase database, refer to the documentation available at www.pointbase.com.

SERVICE REQUESTOR SIDE FEATURES

- Apache Axis 1.0B3 is a SOAP 1.1-compliant implementation with capabilities to enable Java-based SOAP services to be created, assembled, and deployed. More importantly, it also provides a utility for automatic WSDL generation from deployed services and a WSDL2 Java tool for building Java proxies and skeletons from WSDL obtained from service providers.
- The service requestor will use Apache Axis 1.0B3 as its SOAP client environment to invoke the services of an ACME Web services provider.
- Apache Axis is an open-source effort from Apache and is available as a free download from http://xml.apache.org/axis/index.html.

To build and deploy the J2EE components and SOAP interfaces, we create XML-based build scripts using Apache Ant. Apache Ant is a Java-based Makefile utility available as a free download at http://jakarta.apache.org/ant/index.html.

Developing the ACME Web Services Provider

The following tasks are commonly involved in building the complete ACME Web services provider in the BEA WebLogic 7.0 environment:

1. Design the business application understanding the problem, then layout the sequence of events, choose the appropriate design pattern, and then create the conceptual class model for implementation.

2. Install and set up the WebLogic-based J2EE development environment, including the required class libraries in the Java compiler class path.
3. Create the database tables required for the applications.
4. Implement the J2EE components and the required DAO (Data access objects), XML helper classes, and database tables, and so on.
5. Build and test the J2EE component and other classes.
6. Generate the SOAP-based service-oriented interfaces and WSDL-based service descriptions using WebLogic `<servicegen>` and `<clientgen>` utilities.
7. Assemble and deploy components as Web services in the WebLogic server.
8. Create test clients and test the environment.

To test this example, you may download the chapter-specific source code and documentation available at this book's companion Web site at www.wiley.com/compbooks/nagappan. The source code and README for installing and running this example are available as part of chapter-3.zip.

Let's walk through the previous process with more details and demonstrations.

Designing the Application

As mentioned, the ACME Web services provider will host its product catalog application as Web services over the Internet by exposing its associated J2EE components. In particular, we will be looking at the following business functions:

- Getting the complete product catalog listing from the ACME product database
- Getting product details for the given product identifier

To understand the problem and flow of events, look at Figure 3.8. This sequence diagram further illustrates the various sequences of actions performed by a client invoking the ACME Web services and in the WebLogic server.

Based on the previous sequence of events, we choose to use a façade pattern by having a session bean act as a proxy by encapsulating the interactions between the business service components such as `AcmeXMLHelper` and `AcmeDAO`. `AcmeXMLhelper` will handle all the XML construction and `AcmeDAO` will do the database interaction. To find out more information on J2EE design patterns and best practices, refer to the Sun Java site URL at http://java.sun.com/blueprints/patterns/j2ee_patterns/catalog.html.

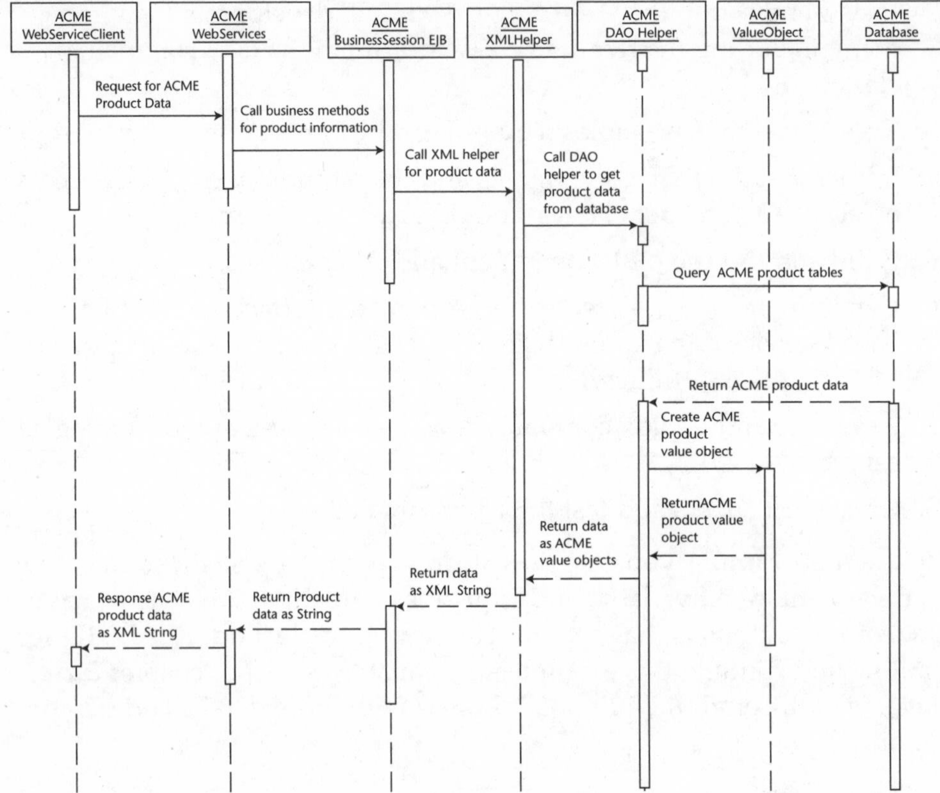

Figure 3.8 Sequence diagram illustrating flow of events.

Figure 3.9 depicts the class diagram of the J2EE components to support the ACME Web services provider.

Now let's take a look at how to set up the development environment and implementation of those J2EE components.

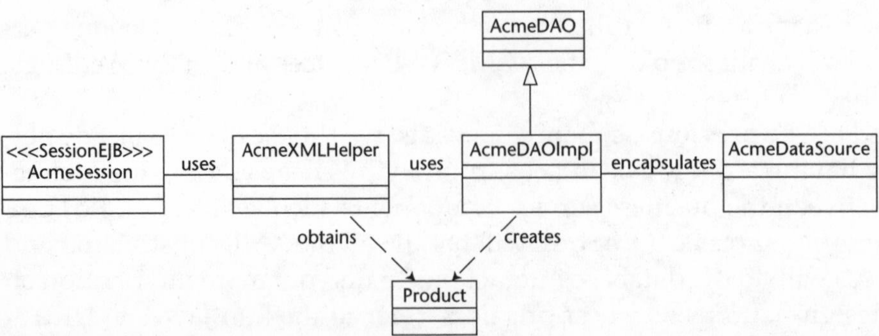

Figure 3.9 Class diagram for the J2EE components.

Setting Up the Development Environment

Ensure that all of the JDK classes, WebLogic libraries (Jars), and database drivers are available in the CLASSPATH. Also ensure that the JDK, WebLogic, and PointBase (database) bin directories are available in the system PATH. To test, start the WebLogic server and ensure that the database server also is started.

Creating the ACME Database Tables

Ensure that all of the JDK, WebLogic libraries (Weblogic JARs), and database drivers are available in the CLASSPATH. Also ensure that the JDK, WebLogic, and PointBase (database) bin directories are available in the system PATH.

1. Create a WebLogic JDBC `DataSource` with JNDI name `JWSPoolDataSource` to provide access to database connection pools required for connecting the PointBase database. This can be accomplished by using a WebLogic console or by editing the `config.xml` file.
2. Use the WebLogic Server Console (for example, http://localhost7001/console), navigate to `JDBC > Tx Data Sources`, create a data source using JNDI name `JWSPoolDataSource`. The data source should have the following attributes:

```
JNDI Name: JWSPoolDataSource
Pool Name: JWSPool
Targets-Server (on the Targets tab:) myserver
```

3. Then navigate to `JDBC > Connection Pools` and create a connection pool named `JWSPool` with the following attributes (in case of PointBase):

```
URL: jdbc:pointbase:server://localhost/demo
Driver Classname:com.pointbase.jdbc.jdbcUniversalDriver
Properties: user=public
Password: (hidden)
Targets-Server (on the Targets tab): myserver
```

4. Restart the WebLogic server and ensure that the database server has been started. The WebLogic server `config.xml` should look like the following:

```
<JDBCConnectionPool
 DriverName="com.pointbase.jdbc.jdbcUniversalDriver"
     Name="JWSPool" Password="yourchoice"
      Properties="user=public" Targets="myserver"
       URL="jdbc:pointbase:server://localhost/demo"/>
       <JDBCTxDataSource JNDIName="JWSPoolDataSource"
       Name="JWSPoolDataSource" PoolName="JWSPool"
        Targets="myserver"/>
```

Table 3.1 Database Table Parameters

COLUMN NAME	COLUMN DATA TYPE
ITEM_NUM	INT
ITEM_NAME	VARCHAR(30)
ITEM_DESC	VARCHAR(255)
ITEM_PRICE	DOUBLE
CURRENCY	VARCHAR(3)

With these steps, the WebLogic data source and database server are ready for use.

1. Now let's create the database table `product_catalog` required for the ACME product catalog. We use the table parameters shown in Table 3.1.
2. To create the `product_catalog` table and to populate the data, you may choose to use the Java code `CreateACMETables.java` (see Listing 3.3).

```
// CreateACMETables.java

  package jws.ch3.db;
  import java.sql.*;
  import java.util.*;
  import javax.naming.*;

  public class CreateACMETables {

  public static void main(String argv[])
                              throws Exception {
  java.sql.Connection conn = null;
  java.sql.Statement stmt  = null;

  try {

  // === Make connection to database ==============
  // Obtain a Datasource connection from JNDI tree.

  Context ctx = null;

  // Put connection properties in to a hashtable.
```

Listing 3.3 `CreateACMETables.java.`

```
    Hashtable ht = new Hashtable();
   ht.put(Context.INITIAL_CONTEXT_FACTORY,
     "weblogic.jndi.WLInitialContextFactory");
    ht.put(Context.PROVIDER_URL, "t3://localhost:7001");

    // Get a context for the JNDI look up
   ctx = new InitialContext(ht);
      javax.sql.DataSource ds
         = (javax.sql.DataSource)
               ctx.lookup ("JWSPoolDataSource");
    conn = ds.getConnection();
    System.out.println("Making connection...\n");

    // execute SQL statements.

    stmt = conn.createStatement();

   try {
      stmt.execute("drop table product_catalog");
       System.out.println("Table
                        product_catalog dropped.");
         } catch (SQLException e) {
            System.out.println("Table product_catalog
                         doesn't need to be dropped.");
     }

  stmt.execute("create table product_catalog
              (item_num int, item_name
                varchar(30), item_desc varchar(255),
                item_price double,
                currency varchar(3))");
  System.out.println("Table product_catalog created.");

     int numrows = stmt.executeUpdate("insert into
                    product_catalog values (1001,
                    'ACME Blade 1000', 'Ultra Sparc III
                     Processor, 1Ghz, 512MB, 42GB HD,
                      Linux',  1000.00, 'USD')");

   System.out.println("Number of rows inserted = "
                                          + numrows);

    numrows = stmt.executeUpdate("insert into
               product_catalog values (1002,
                 'ACME Blade 2000', 'Sparc III
                  Processor, 1.3Ghz x2, 512MB, 42GB HD,
                      Solaris',  3000.00, 'USD')");

   System.out.println("Number of rows inserted = "
```

Listing 3.3 CreateACMETables.java. *(continues)*

```
                                                + numrows);

          numrows = stmt.executeUpdate("insert into
                     product_catalog values (1003, 'ACME Server
                     e7000', 'Sparc III Processor, 1.3Ghz x12,
                      1GB, 1TB HD, Solaris',  75000.00,
                       'USD')");

         System.out.println("Number of rows inserted = "
                                          + numrows);

          stmt.execute("select * from product_catalog");

          ResultSet rs = stmt.getResultSet();

          System.out.println("Querying data ...");

        while (rs.next()) {

          System.out.println("Product No:
               " + rs.getString("item_num")
                 + "  Product Name: "
                 + rs.getString("item_name")
                 + "  Product Desc: "
                 +  rs.getString("item_desc")
                 + "  Price: " +  rs.getString("item_price")
                 + "  Currency: " +  rs.getString("currency") );
         }
        } catch (Exception e) {
           System.out.println("Exception was thrown: "
                                        + e.getMessage());
        } finally {
          try {
           if (stmt != null)
                 stmt.close();
                 if (conn != null)
                         conn.close();
           } catch (SQLException sqle) {
               System.out.println("SQLException
                                        during close(): "
                                       + sqle.getMessage());
        }
       }
     }
}
```

Listing 3.3 `CreateACMETables.java`. *(continued)*

To compile and run the previous classes, ensure that the WebLogic JAR and PointBase drivers are available in the CLASSPATH. Then navigate to the source directory and run the Ant build script (`build.xml`). The `build.xml` file for compiling and testing the previous classes is shown in Listing 3.4.

```
<project name="acme_tables" default="all" basedir=".">
     <property file="../../../../mydomain.properties"/>
    <property name="build.compiler" value="${JAVAC}"/>
    <!-- set global properties for this build -->
      <property name="source" value="."/>
          <target name="all" depends="compile"/>

<!-- Compile 'CreateACMETables' class into
                the clientclasses directory -->
 <target name="compile">
     <javac srcdir="${source}"
          destdir="${CLIENT_CLASSES}"
          includes="CreateACMETables.java" />
    </target>

<!-- Run the ACME Tables Creation -->
  <target name="run">
  <java classname="jws.ch3.db.CreateACMETables"
                fork="yes" failonerror="true">
  <classpath>
    <pathelement path="${CLASSPATH}"/>
  </classpath>
  </java>
  </target>
</project>
```

Listing 3.4 Ant script for creating ACME business tables.

Run the Ant utility in the source directory. The compiled classes will be saved in the respective destinations defined in the `build.xml` file.

Now, to execute the `CreateACMETables`, you may execute the Ant utility with `run` as an argument. The successful execution of the program creates the `product_catalog` tables in the PointBase database and inserts `Product` records in to the table.

If everything works successfully, you will get the output shown in Figure 3.10.

```
E:\bea\user_domains\mydomain\src\jws\ch3\db>ant
Buildfile: build.xml

compile:
    [javac] Compiling 1 source file to E:\bea\user_domains\mydomain\clientclasses

all:

BUILD SUCCESSFUL

Total time: 20 seconds

E:\bea\user_domains\mydomain\src\jws\ch3\db>ant run
Buildfile: build.xml

run:
     [java] Making connection...
     [java]
     [java] Table product_catalog dropped.
     [java] Table product_catalog created.
     [java] Number of rows inserted = 1
     [java] Number of rows inserted = 1
     [java] Number of rows inserted = 1
     [java] Querying data ...
     [java] Product No: 1001  Product Name: ACME Blade 1000  Product Desc: Sparc III Processor, 1Ghz
, 512MB, 42GB HD, Linux  Price: 1000  Currency: USD
     [java] Product No: 1002  Product Name: ACME Blade 2000  Product Desc: Sparc III Processor, 1.3G
hz x2, 512MB, 42GB HD, Solaris  Price: 3000  Currency: USD
     [java] Product No: 1003  Product Name: ACME Server e7000  Product Desc: Sparc III Processor, 1.
3Ghz x12, 1GB, 1TB HD, Solaris  Price: 75000  Currency: USD

BUILD SUCCESSFUL

Total time: 10 seconds

E:\bea\user_domains\mydomain\src\jws\ch3\db>
```

Figure 3.10 Output showing creation of ACME business tables.

Implementing the J2EE Components

Based on the class diagram, the J2EE components required for implementing the ACME Web service are as follows:

AcmeDAO A DAO class enables access to the data source and abstracts the underlying data access implementation for the product catalog business clients.

AcmeXMLHelper This class gathers the data and constructs an XML document as a string for use by the business clients (AcmeSessionBean).

AcmeSessionBean This acts as a proxy by encapsulating the interactions with back-end service components.

Building the DAO Classes

To implement the `AcmeDAO`, we need to define the `AcmeDAO` as an interface class and `AcmeDAOImpl` implements the `AcmeDAO`. The source code implementation for the `AcmeDAO` interface is shown in Listing 3.5.

```
            // AcmeDAO.java

            package jws.ch3.dao;

            import java.util.Collection;
            import jws.ch3.exceptions.AcmeDAOException;
            import jws.ch3.model.Product;

            /**
            * AcmeDAO.java is an interface and it is
            * implemented by AcmeDAOImpl.java
            */

            public interface AcmeDAO {

              public Product getProduct(int productID)
                                       throws AcmeDAOException;

             public Iterator getProductCatalog()
                                 throws AcmeDAOException;
 }
```

Listing 3.5 `AcmeDAO.java.`

The source code implementation for `AcmeDAOImpl.java` is shown in Listing 3.6.

```
          // AcmeDAOImpl.java

           package jws.ch3.dao;

           import java.sql.Connection;
           import java.sql.ResultSet;
           import java.sql.SQLException;
           import java.sql.Statement;
           import java.sql.PreparedStatement;
           import java.util.*;
           import javax.naming.Context;
           import javax.naming.InitialContext;
```

Listing 3.6 `AcmeDAOImpl.java.` ***(continues)***

```
import javax.sql.DataSource;
import javax.naming.NamingException;

import jws.ch3.model.Product;
import jws.ch3.exceptions.AcmeDAOException;

/**
 * This class implements AcmeDAO for PointBase DBs.
 * This class encapsulates all the SQL calls
 * and maps the relational data stored in the database
 */

 public class AcmeDAOImpl implements AcmeDAO {

 // data access methods

   protected static DataSource getDataSource()
                            throws AcmeDAOException {

  try {

       // ======= Make connection to database ======
       // Obtain Datasource connection from JNDI tree.

       Context ctx = null;

      // Put connection properties in  a hashtable.

       Hashtable ht = new Hashtable();
       ht.put(Context.INITIAL_CONTEXT_FACTORY,
     "weblogic.jndi.WLInitialContextFactory");
       ht.put(Context.PROVIDER_URL,
                    "t3://localhost:7001");

      // Get a context for the JNDI look up
         ctx = new InitialContext(ht);
         javax.sql.DataSource ds
                = (javax.sql.DataSource)
                    ctx.lookup ("JWSPoolDataSource");

          return ds;

        }
          catch (NamingException ne) {
           throw new AcmeDAOException
               ("NamingException while looking up
                     DB context : "+ ne.getMessage());
        }
       }
```

Listing 3.6 AcmeDAOImpl.java.

```
        // Business methods

    public Product getProduct(int productID)
                        throws AcmeDAOException {

            Connection c = null;
            PreparedStatement ps = null;
            ResultSet rs = null;
            Product ret = null;

        try {
              c = getDataSource().getConnection();

            ps = c.prepareStatement("select item_num,
                   item_name, item_desc, item_price,
                    currency "
                   + "from product_catalog "
                   + "where item_num = ? ",
                     ResultSet.TYPE_SCROLL_INSENSITIVE,
                     ResultSet.CONCUR_READ_ONLY);
                     ps.setInt(1, productID);
              rs = ps.executeQuery();
               if (rs.first()) {
                 ret = new Product(rs.getInt(1),
                                   rs.getString(2),
                                     rs.getString(3),
                                    rs.getDouble(4),
                                    rs.getString(5));
          }
               rs.close();
               ps.close();

               c.close();
               return ret;
          }
           catch (SQLException se) {
                 throw new AcmeDAOException("
                  SQLException: " + se.getMessage());
           }
         }

         public Iterator getProductCatalog()
                           throws AcmeDAOException {

            Connection c = null;
            PreparedStatement ps = null;
            ResultSet rs = null;
            Product prod = null;
```

Listing 3.6 AcmeDAOImpl.java. *(continues)*

```
            try {
            c = getDataSource().getConnection();

              ps = c.prepareStatement("select
                          item_num, item_name, item_desc,
                             item_price, currency "
                      + "from product_catalog ",
                         ResultSet.TYPE_SCROLL_INSENSITIVE,
                           ResultSet.CONCUR_READ_ONLY);
                rs = ps.executeQuery();
                ArrayList prodList = new ArrayList();
                  while (rs.next()) {
                  prod = new Product(rs.getInt(1),
                                       rs.getString(2),
                                       rs.getString(3),
                                       rs.getDouble(4),
                                       rs.getString(5));
                                      prodList.add(prod);
          }
            rs.close();
            ps.close();
            c.close();
              return prodList.iterator();
            }
            catch (SQLException se) {
                    throw new AcmeDAOException("
                            SQLException: "
                                  + se.getMessage());
          }
       }

    public static void main(String[] arg) {
        AcmeDAOImpl adi = new  AcmeDAOImpl();
         Product prod = adi.getProduct(1001);
         prod.print();

         Iterator itr = adi.getProductCatalog();
          while(itr.hasNext())
           {
             Product p = (Product)itr.next();
              p.print();
            }
          }
      }
```

Listing 3.6 AcmeDAOImpl.java.

We also need to implement the value object `Product` and exception classes for the `AcmeDAO` and the source code for the value object `Product.java`. The implementation is shown in Listing 3.7.

```
// Product.java
package jws.ch3.model;

import java.util.*;
import java.io.*;


/**
 * This class acts as the value object for Product
*  and it defines the accessor methods
*/

public class Product {

    private int productID;
    private String productName;
    private String productDesc;
    private double productPrice;
    private String currency;


    public Product(int prodID, String prodName,
           String prodDesc, double prodPrice, String curr) {
           productID = prodID;
           productName = prodName;
           productDesc = prodDesc;
           productPrice = prodPrice;
           currency = curr;
    }

   public int getProductID() {
     return productID;
    }
     public String getProductName() {
        return productName;
    }

    public String getProductDesc() {
       return productDesc;
    }
```

Listing 3.7 `Product.java`. *(continues)*

```
    public double getProductPrice() {
     return productPrice;
     }

    public String getCurrency() {
     return currency;
    }

    public void setProductID(int aProductID) {
        productID=aProductID;
    }

    public void setProductName(String aProductName) {
        productName=aProductName;
    }

    public void setProductDesc(String aProductDesc) {
         productDesc=aProductDesc;
    }

    public void setProductPrice(double aProductPrice) {
     productPrice=aProductPrice;
    }

   public void setCurrency(String aCurrency) {
     currency=aCurrency;
    }

    public void print()   {
       System.out.println(productID);
       System.out.println(productName);
       System.out.println(productDesc);
       System.out.println(productPrice);
       System.out.println(currency);
     }
}
```

Listing 3.7 `Product.java`. *(continued)*

And the source code for the DAO Exceptions `AcmeDAOException.java` is shown in Listing 3.8.

```
 // AcmeDAOException.java

package jws.ch3.exceptions;
```

Listing 3.8 `AcmeDAOException.java`.

```
/**
 * AcmeDAOException is an exception that extends the standard
 * RunTimeException Exception. This is thrown by the DAOs
 * of the catalog
 * component when there is some irrecoverable error
 * (like SQLException)
 */

public class AcmeDAOException extends RuntimeException {

public AcmeDAOException (String str) {
        super(str);
    }

public AcmeDAOException () {
        super();
    }
}
```

Listing 3.8 `AcmeDAOException.java.` *(continued)*

To compile and run the previous classes, ensure that the WebLogic JAR and PointBase drivers are available in the CLASSPATH. Then navigate to the source directory and run the Ant build script (`build.xml`). The `build.xml` for compiling and testing the previous classes is shown in Listing 3.9.

```
<project name="acme_dao" default="all" basedir=".">

  <property file="../../../../mydomain.properties"/>
  <property name="build.compiler" value="${JAVAC}"/>

  <!-- set global properties for this build -->
  <property name="source" value="."/>

  <target name="all" depends="compile"/>

  <!-- Compile DAO class into the serverclasses directory -->
  <target name="compile">
    <javac srcdir="${source}"
      destdir="${SERVER_CLASSES}"
      includes="AcmeDAO.java, AcmeDAOImpl.java"
    />
  </target>
```

Listing 3.9 Ant build script for ACME DAO classes. *(continues)*

```
        <!-- Run ACME DAO Test -->
    <target name="run">
    <java classname="jws.ch3.dao.AcmeDAOImpl"
         fork="yes"   failonerror="true">
      <classpath>
        <pathelement path="${CLASSPATH}"/>
      </classpath>
    </java>
    </target>
  </project>
```

Listing 3.9 Ant build script for ACME DAO classes. *(continued)*

Now to execute the AcmeDAO classes, you may execute the Ant utility with run as an argument. The successful execution of the program queries the product_catalog tables from the PointBase database and inserts Product records in to the table.

If everything works successfully, you will get the output shown in Figure 3.11.

```
UnixDoS
E:\bea\user_domains\mydomain\src\jws\ch3\dao>ant
Buildfile: build.xml

compile:
    [javac] Compiling 2 source files to E:\bea\user_domains\mydomain\serverclasses

all:

BUILD SUCCESSFUL

Total time: 4 seconds

E:\bea\user_domains\mydomain\src\jws\ch3\dao>ant run
Buildfile: build.xml

run:
     [java] ===========Getting Product===================
     [java] 1001
     [java] ACME Blade 1000
     [java] Sparc III Processor, 1Ghz, 512MB, 42GB HD, Linux
     [java] 1000.0
     [java] USD
     [java] ===========Getting Product Catalog=============
     [java] 1001
     [java] ACME Blade 1000
     [java] Sparc III Processor, 1Ghz, 512MB, 42GB HD, Linux
     [java] 1000.0
     [java] USD
     [java] 1002
     [java] ACME Blade 2000
     [java] Sparc III Processor, 1.3Ghz x2, 512MB, 42GB HD, Solaris
     [java] 3000.0
     [java] USD
     [java] 1003
     [java] ACME Server e7000
     [java] Sparc III Processor, 1.3Ghz x12, 1GB, 1TB HD, Solaris
     [java] 75000.0
     [java] USD

BUILD SUCCESSFUL

Total time: 9 seconds

E:\bea\user_domains\mydomain\src\jws\ch3\dao>
```

Figure 3.11 Output showing execution of the ACME DAO classes.

Building the XML Helper Classes

To implement the AcmeXMLHelper classes, we need to define the XML elements as constants in an AcmeConsts class, and the AcmeXMLHelper is the class implementation that provides methods for constructing XML mapping for the DAO data objects.

The source code for AcmeConsts.java is shown in Listing 3.10.

```
//AcmeConsts.java

package jws.ch3.xmlhelper;

public class AcmeConsts {

    public static final String ProductCatalog="ProductCatalog";
    public static final String LineItem="LineItem";
    public static final String ItemNumber="ItemNumber";
    public static final String ItemName="ItemName";
    public static final String ItemDesc="ItemDesc";
    public static final String ItemPrice="ItemPrice";
    public static final String Currency="Currency";

  }
```

Listing 3.10 AcmeConsts.java.

The source code for the AcmeXMLHelper.java is shown in Listing 3.11.

```
// AcmeXMLHelper.java

package jws.ch3.xmlhelper;
import java.io.*;
import java.util.*;

import org.w3c.dom.*;
import javax.xml.parsers.*;
import javax.xml.transform.*;
import javax.xml.transform.stream.*;
import javax.xml.transform.dom.DOMSource;
import jws.ch3.model.Product;
import jws.ch3.dao.*;

/**
```

Listing 3.11 AcmeXMLHelper.java. *(continues)*

```
 * XML & XML String object mapping the DAO methods
 */

public class AcmeXMLHelper {

    private Document doc;
    private Element root;

    // Helper methods

   // Create the XML document
     private void createXMLDocument(String rootTagName) {

      DocumentBuilderFactory factory =
              DocumentBuilderFactory.newInstance();

       try {
        factory.setNamespaceAware(true);
        DocumentBuilder builder = factory.newDocumentBuilder();
        doc = builder.newDocument();
        root = doc.createElementNS("ProductCatalog.xsd",
                                        rootTagName);
        doc.appendChild(root);
       } catch (ParserConfigurationException e) {
          e.printStackTrace();
         }
        }

      // Create the ProductCatalog XML document

       private void createProductCatalogXML() {
           createXMLDocument(AcmeConsts.ProductCatalog);
             AcmeDAOImpl adi = new  AcmeDAOImpl();
                 Iterator itr = adi.getProductCatalog();
               while (itr.hasNext()) {
                 Product p = (Product)itr.next();
                   createLineItemNode(root, p);
             }
          }

       // Create the Product XML document

        private void createProductXML(int productID) {
            createXMLDocument(AcmeConsts.ProductCatalog);
            AcmeDAOImpl adi = new  AcmeDAOImpl();
            Product prod = adi.getProduct(productID);
             createLineItemNode(root, prod);
        }
```

Listing 3.11 AcmeXMLHelper.java.

```
        // Method to obtain Product Catalog as XML

        public Document getProductCatalogDocument() {
             createProductCatalogXML();
             return doc;
}


    // Method to obtain Product Catalog XML as String

        public String getProductCatalogXMLasString()
                          throws TransformerException{
            createProductCatalogXML();
            return transformDOMtoString(doc);
        }

     // Method to obtain Product as XML

     public Document getProductDocument(int productID) {
         createProductXML(productID);
         return doc;
       }

     // Method to obtain Product XML as String

      public String getProductXMLasString(int productID)
                                throws TransformerException{
         createProductXML(productID);
         return transformDOMtoString(doc);
       }

     // Method to convert XML document as String

       private String transformDOMtoString(Document xDoc)
                                throws TransformerException {
          try{
             // Use a Transformer for String output
              TransformerFactory tFactory
                     = TransformerFactory.newInstance();
              Transformer transformer =
                               tFactory.newTransformer();

               DOMSource source = new DOMSource(xDoc);
               StringWriter sw = new StringWriter();
               transformer.transform(source,
                                  new StreamResult(sw));
           return sw.toString();
            } catch (TransformerConfigurationException tce) {
```

Listing 3.11 AcmeXMLHelper.java. *(continues)*

```
                throw new TransformerException(
                  tce.getMessageAndLocation());
        } catch (TransformerException te) {
                throw new TransformerException(
                   te.getMessageAndLocation());
      }
      }

     // Methods to create Product XML adding the Line items

      private void createLineItemNode(Node parent, Product p) {
     try {
            Element liElem =
                   doc.createElement(AcmeConsts.LineItem);
              parent.appendChild(liElem);

            //Make <ItemNumber> element and add it
            Element elem =
              doc.createElement(AcmeConsts.ItemNumber);
              elem.appendChild(doc.createTextNode(
                    String.valueOf(p.getProductID()) ));
               liElem.appendChild(elem);

           //  Make <ItemName> element and add it
                elem = doc.createElement(AcmeConsts.ItemName);
                elem.appendChild(doc.createTextNode(
                                         p.getProductName() ));
                liElem.appendChild(elem);

             //  Make <ItemDesc> element and add it
                elem = doc.createElement(AcmeConsts.ItemDesc);
                elem.appendChild(doc.createTextNode(
                                  p.getProductDesc() ));
                liElem.appendChild(elem);

             //  Make <ItemPrice> element and add it

                 elem =
                    doc.createElement(AcmeConsts.ItemPrice);
                 elem.appendChild(doc.createTextNode (
                       String.valueOf(p.getProductPrice())));
                 liElem.appendChild(elem);

              //  Make <Currency> element and add it
                elem = doc.createElement(AcmeConsts.Currency);
                elem.appendChild(doc.createTextNode(
                                           p.getCurrency() ));
                liElem.appendChild(elem);
```

Listing 3.11 AcmeXMLHelper.java.

```
                    } catch (Exception e) {
                        e.printStackTrace();
                    }
                }

// Main method for testing
        public static void main(String[] arg) {
            try {
                AcmeXMLHelper ax = new  AcmeXMLHelper();
                System.out.println(ax.getProductCatalogXMLasString());
                System.out.println("-------------------------");
                System.out.println(ax.getProductXMLasString(1001));
              } catch (Exception e) {
                e.printStackTrace();
              }
            }
        }
```

Listing 3.11 `AcmeXMLHelper.java`. *(continued)*

To compile and run the `AcmeXMLHelper` classes, ensure that the WebLogic JARs (includes a JAXP compliant XML parser) are available in the CLASSPATH. Then navigate to the source directory and run the Ant build script (`build.xml`). The `build.xml` for compiling and testing the `AcmeXMLHelper` classes is shown in Listing 3.12.

```
<project name="acme_xmlhelper" default="all" basedir=".">

  <property file="../../../../mydomain.properties"/>
  <property name="build.compiler" value="${JAVAC}"/>

  <!-- set global properties for this build -->
  <property name="source" value="."/>

  <target name="all" depends="compile"/>

  <!-- Compile ACME XML helper classes In serverclasses dir -->
  <target name="compile">
    <javac srcdir="${source}"
      destdir="${SERVER_CLASSES}"
      includes="AcmeXMLHelper.java, AcmeConsts.java"
    />
    </target>
```

Listing 3.12 `build.xml` for compiling and testing the `AcmeXMLHelper` classes. *(continues)*

```
        <!-- Run ACME XML Helper Test -->
        <target name="run">
        <java classname="jws.ch3.xmlhelper.AcmeXMLHelper"
                              fork="yes"    failonerror="true">
        <classpath>
          <pathelement path="${CLASSPATH}"/>
        </classpath>
      </java>
      </target>
    </project>
```

Listing 3.12 `build.xml` for compiling and testing the `AcmeXMLHelper` classes. *(continued)*

Now to execute the `AcmeXMLHelper` classes, you may execute the Ant utility with `run` as an argument. The successful execution of the program queries the `'product_catalog` tables from the PointBase database and inserts `Product` records in to the table.

If everything works successfully, you will get the output shown in Figure 3.12.

```
UnixDoS
E:\bea\user_domains\mydomain\src\jws\ch3\xmlhelper>ant
Buildfile: build.xml

compile:
    [javac] Compiling 2 source files to E:\bea\user_domains\mydomain\serverclasses

all:

BUILD SUCCESSFUL

Total time: 9 seconds

E:\bea\user_domains\mydomain\src\jws\ch3\xmlhelper>ant run
Buildfile: build.xml

run:
     [java] ====== Printing Product Catalog XML as String ============
     [java] <?xml version="1.0" encoding="UTF-8"?>
     [java] <ProductCatalog><LineItem><ItemNumber>1001</ItemNumber><ItemName>ACME Blade 1000</ItemNa
me><ItemDesc>Sparc III Processor, 1Ghz, 512MB, 42GB HD, Linux</ItemDesc><ItemPrice>1000.0</ItemPrice
><Currency>USD</Currency></LineItem><LineItem><ItemNumber>1002</ItemNumber><ItemName>ACME Blade 2000
</ItemName><ItemDesc>Sparc III Processor, 1.3Ghz x2, 512MB, 42GB HD, Solaris</ItemDesc><ItemPrice>30
00.0</ItemPrice><Currency>USD</Currency></LineItem><LineItem><ItemNumber>1003</ItemNumber><ItemName>
ACME Server e7000</ItemName><ItemDesc>Sparc III Processor, 1.3Ghz x12, 1GB, 1TB HD, Solaris</ItemDes
c><ItemPrice>75000.0</ItemPrice><Currency>USD</Currency></LineItem></ProductCatalog>
     [java] ====== Printing Product Catalog XML as String ============
     [java] <?xml version="1.0" encoding="UTF-8"?>
     [java] <ProductCatalog><LineItem><ItemNumber>1001</ItemNumber><ItemName>ACME Blade 1000</ItemNa
me><ItemDesc>Sparc III Processor, 1Ghz, 512MB, 42GB HD, Linux</ItemDesc><ItemPrice>1000.0</ItemPrice
><Currency>USD</Currency></LineItem></ProductCatalog>

BUILD SUCCESSFUL

Total time: 9 seconds

E:\bea\user_domains\mydomain\src\jws\ch3\xmlhelper>
```

Figure 3.12 Testing the ACME XML helper Classes.

Building the Session Bean

Finally, we need to implement the stateless session bean to act as the session façade for all of the business service classes. Like any other EJB, it contains the home interface `AcmeSessionHome`, a remote interface `AcmeSession`, and the bean implementation class `AcmeSessionBean`.

The `AcmeSessionHome` interface simply defines a `create()` method to return a reference to the `AcmeSession` remote interface. The source code for the `AcmeSessionHome` interface is shown in Listing 3.13.

```
//AcmeSessionHome.java

package jws.ch3.ejb;

import javax.ejb.CreateException;
import java.rmi.RemoteException;
import javax.ejb.EJBHome;

/** The Home interface for Acme Session Bean*/

 public interface AcmeSessionHome extends EJBHome {
     public AcmeSession create() throws CreateException,
                                          RemoteException;
}
```

Listing 3.13 `AcmeSessionHome.java.`

`AcmeSession` defines the remote interface for the Acme Web service with two business methods. The source code for the `AcmeSession` interface is shown in Listing 3.14.

```
//AcmeSession.java
package jws.ch3.ejb;

import java.rmi.RemoteException;
import javax.ejb.EJBObject;

/**
 * This is the remote interface for the ACME Session EJB.
```

Listing 3.14 `AcmeSession.java.` *(continues)*

```
 * It provides a session facade as an ejb-tier implementation
 * for all ACME functions
 */

public interface AcmeSession extends EJBObject {

   public String getProductCatalog()  throws RemoteException;
   public String getProduct(int productID)
                                      throws RemoteException;

}
```

Listing 3.14 AcmeSession.java. ***(continued)***

And finally the bean class `AcmeSessionBean.java` implementing the business methods is defined by the remote interface. The source code for the `AcmeSessionBean` class is shown in Listing 3.15.

```
// AcmeSessionBean.java

package jws.ch3.ejb;

import javax.ejb.SessionBean;
import javax.ejb.SessionContext;
import javax.ejb.EJBException;
import javax.naming.InitialContext;
import javax.naming.NamingException;

import jws.ch3.xmlhelper.AcmeXMLHelper;

/**
 * Session Bean implementation for ACME business methods
 * - Acts as a Session Facade which encapsulates the
 * ACME XML Helper and DAO
 */

  public class AcmeSessionBean implements SessionBean {

  private static final boolean VERBOSE = true;
  private SessionContext ctx;

  public void ejbCreate() {
         tracelog ("AcmeSessionBean: ejbCreate called");
   }
```

Listing 3.15 AcmeSessionBean.java.

```
    public void ejbActivate() {
        tracelog("AcmeSessionBean: ejbActivate called");
}

    public void ejbRemove() {
        tracelog("AcmeSessionBean: ejbRemove called");
    }

    public void ejbPassivate() {
        tracelog("AcmeSessionBean: ejbPassivate called");
        }

    public void setSessionContext(SessionContext ctx) {
        tracelog("AcmeSessionBean: setSessionContext called");
        this.ctx = ctx;
    }


    // Returns Product as XML based String

    public String getProduct(int productID) {
      try {
          AcmeXMLHelper axh = new AcmeXMLHelper();
          tracelog("getProduct called");
          return axh.getProductXMLasString(productID);
        } catch (Exception e) {
            throw new EJBException(e.getMessage());
        }
      }

    // Returns ProductCatalog as an XML String

      public String getProductCatalog() {
        try {
          AcmeXMLHelper axh = new AcmeXMLHelper();
          tracelog("getProductCatalog called");
          return axh.getProductCatalogXMLasString();
          } catch (Exception se) {
              throw new EJBException(se.getMessage());
          }
        }

    // Logging the EJB Calls
          private void tracelog(String ts) {
                if (VERBOSE) System.out.println(ts);
          }
}
```

Listing 3.15 AcmeSessionBean.java. *(continued)*

Now let's create the deployment descriptors for the EJB such as `ejb-jar.xml` and `weblogic-ejb-jar.xml` to define its internal dependencies and the assembly information. We will use the EJB name as `ACMEWebService` and its JNDI name as `jws-ch3-statelessejb-AcmeSessionHome`.

The deployment descriptor `ejb-jar.xml` is shown in Listing 3.16.

```
<?xml version="1.0"?>
<!DOCTYPE ejb-jar PUBLIC
 '-//Sun Microsystems, Inc.//DTD Enterprise JavaBeans 2.0//EN'
 'http://java.sun.com/dtd/ejb-jar_2_0.dtd'>
 <ejb-jar>
  <enterprise-beans>
    <session>
      <ejb-name>ACMEWebservice</ejb-name>
      <home>jws.ch3.ejb.AcmeSessionHome</home>
      <remote>jws.ch3.ejb.AcmeSession</remote>
      <ejb-class>jws.ch3.ejb.AcmeSessionBean</ejb-class>
      <session-type>Stateless</session-type>
      <transaction-type>Container</transaction-type>
      </session>
  </enterprise-beans>
  <assembly-descriptor>
    <container-transaction>
      <method>
        <ejb-name>ACMEWebservice</ejb-name>
      <method-name>*</method-name>
      </method>
      <trans-attribute>Required</trans-attribute>
    </container-transaction>
  </assembly-descriptor>
</ejb-jar>
```

Listing 3.16 Deployment descriptor for AcmeSessionBean (`ejb-jar.xml`).

The WebLogic-specific deployment descriptor `webLogic-ejb-jar.xml` is shown in Listing 3.17.

```
<?xml version="1.0"?>
<!DOCTYPE WebLogic-ejb-jar PUBLIC
'-//BEA Systems, Inc.//DTD WebLogic 7.0.0 EJB//EN'
'http://www.bea.com/servers/wls700/dtd/Weblogic700-ejb-jar.dtd'>
```

Listing 3.17 WebLogic-specific deployment descriptor `webLogic-ejb-jar.xml`.

```
<weblogic-ejb-jar>
  <weblogic-enterprise-bean>
    <ejb-name>ACMEWebservice</ejb-name>
    <jndi-name>jws-ch3-statelessejb-AcmeSessionHome</jndi-name>
  </weblogic-enterprise-bean>
    </weblogic-ejb-jar>
```

Listing 3.17 WebLogic-specific deployment descriptor `webLogic-ejb-jar.xml`. *(continued)*

To compile the EJB, we need to create the Ant build script (`build.xml`). The `build.xml` for compiling, assembling, and deploying the EJB is shown in Listing 3.18.

```
<project name="ejb-build" default="all" basedir=".">

 <!-- set global properties for this build -->
 <property environment="env"/>
 <property file="../../../../mydomain.properties"/>
 <property name="build.compiler" value="${JAVAC}"/>
 <property name="source" value="."/>
 <property name="build" value="${source}/build"/>
 <property name="dist" value="${source}/dist"/>

 <target name="all" depends="clean, init,
              compile_ejb, jar_ejb, ejbc,
              ear_app, compile_client"/>

 <target name="init">
   <!-- Create the time stamp -->
   <tstamp/>
   <!-- Create the build directory structure used
         by compile and copy the deployment descriptor
             into it-->
   <mkdir dir="${build}"/>
   <mkdir dir="${build}/META-INF"/>
   <mkdir dir="${dist}"/>
   <copy todir="${build}/META-INF">
     <fileset dir="${source}">
       <include name="ejb-jar.xml"/>
       <include name="weblogic-ejb-jar.xml"/>
     </fileset>
     </copy>
 </target>
```

Listing 3.18 Build.xml for compiling, assembling, and deploying the EJB. *(continues)*

```
  <!-- Compile ejb classes into the build directory
                               (jar preparation) -->
  <target name="compile_ejb">
    <javac srcdir="${source}" destdir="${build}"
      includes="AcmeSession.java,
        AcmeSessionHome.java, AcmeSessionBean.java"/>
  </target>

  <!-- Make a standard ejb jar file,
          including XML deployment descriptors -->
  <target name="jar_ejb" depends="compile_ejb">
    <jar jarfile="${dist}/jws-ch3-statelessejb.jar"
      basedir="${build}">
    </jar>
  </target>

  <!-- Run ejbc to create the deployable jar file -->
  <target name="ejbc" depends="jar_ejb">
    <java classname="weblogic.ejbc"
              fork="yes" failonerror="yes">
      <sysproperty key="weblogic.home"
               value="${WL_HOME}/server"/>
      <arg line="-compiler javac
           ${dist}/jws-ch3-statelessejb.jar
               ${dist}/jws-ch3-statelessejb.jar"/>
      <classpath>
        <pathelement path="${CLASSPATH}"/>
      </classpath>
    </java>
  </target>

  <!-- Put the ejb into an ear, to be
           deployed from the ${APPLICATIONS} dir -->
  <target name="ear_app" depends="jar_ejb">
    <ear earfile="${APPLICATIONS}/
               jws-ch3-statelessejb.ear"
                appxml="${source}/application.xml">
      <fileset dir="${dist}"
               includes="jws-ch3-statelessejb.jar"/>
    </ear>
  </target>
  <target name="clean">
    <delete dir="${build}"/>
    <delete dir="${dist}"/>
  </target>
<project>
```

Listing 3.18 Build.xml for compiling, assembling, and deploying the EJB. *(continued)*

Now to compile the AcmeSession EJB classes, you may execute the Ant utility. The successful execution of the program assembles the EAR file and deploys it in to the server and then displays "BUILD SUCCESSFUL."

Generating the Web Services

After the successful creation of EJB, let's include the WebLogic servicegen and clientgen utilities as Ant tasks to generate the Web service interfaces and client jar files for Web services clients.

In the WebLogic 7.0 environment, using the servicegen utility requires an EJB jar file as input. It automatically generates the 'JAX-RPC based' service-oriented interfaces, user-defined data type components (serializer and deserializer classes), and the web-services.xml deployment descriptor, and then packages them as a deployable EAR file by introspecting the input EJB.

Thus, by creating a servicegen Ant task in the build.xml, it is possible to generate all the service classes required for exposing an EJB as a Web service. Listing 3.19 is an Ant task for generating the service classes for AcmeSession EJB. For the deployed components, we will be using ACMEWebService as the name of the Web service, and its URI and the names for EAR, JAR, and WAR are webservices_acmes.ear, acmes_ejb.jar, and acme_service.war, respectively.

```
<target name="build-ear" depends="build-ejb">
 <delete dir="${build}" />
 <mkdir dir="${build}" />
 <copy todir="${build}" file="${dist}/acme_ejb.jar"/>
 <servicegen
     destEar="${build}/webservices_acme.ear"
     warName="acme_service.war">
     <service
        ejbJar="${build}/acme_ejb.jar"
         targetNamespace=
          "http://localhost:7001/acme_services/ACMEWebService"
           serviceName="ACMEWebService"
           serviceURI="/ACMEWebService"
           generateTypes="True"
           expandMethods="True" >
           <client
             packageName="jws.ch3.ejb"
             clientJarName="${client_file}"/>
     </service>
   </servicegen>
 </target>
```

Listing 3.19 Ant task for generating the service classes from AcmeSession EJB.

Similar to the `servicegen` utility, WebLogic 7.0 also provides a `clientgen` utility that creates a client JAR file containing the client specific stubs (JAX-RPC based), and serializer and deserializer classes used for invoking the Web service deployed as an EAR file in the WebLogic server. This helps the testing of the Web services deployed in the WebLogic server.

Adding a `clientgen` Ant task generates the required client stub classes required for invoking the Web services. Listing 3.20 is an Ant task for generating the client classes required for invoking `ACMEWebService`.

```
<target name="build-client" depends="build-ear">
   <clientgen
     ear="${build}/webservices_acme.ear"
     warName="acme_service.war"
     packageName="jws.ch3.ejb"
     clientJar="acme_client.jar" />
</target>
```

Listing 3.20 Ant task for generating the client classes required for invoking ACMEWebService.

It also is important to create a client to test the Web service, and all that it requires is to know the name of the Web service and signatures of its operations. To find the signature of the Web service operations, un-JAR the Web service-specific client JAR file `acme_client.jar`. The files `ACMEWebService_Impl.java` and `ACMEWebServicePort.java` contain the implementation of the Web service operations `getProductCatalog()` and `getProduct(int productID)`, and `ACMEWebService` refers to the name of the Web service.

To build a static client, no imports are required, just make sure that `'acme_client.jar'` is available in the CLASSPATH. Listing 3.21 is the complete source code of `ACMEWebServiceClient.java`.

```
package jws.ch3.ejb;

public class ACMEWebServiceClient {

  public static void main(String[] args) throws Exception {

    // Parse the argument list
    ACMEWebServiceClient client = new ACMEWebServiceClient();
    String wsdl = (args.length > 0? args[0] : null);
    client.example(wsdl);
```

Listing 3.21 Complete source code of `ACMEWebServiceClient.java`.

```
    }

    public void example(String wsdlURI) throws Exception {

      // Set properties for JAX-RPC service factory
      System.setProperty( "javax.xml.rpc.ServiceFactory",
        "weblogic.webservice.core.rpc.ServiceFactoryImpl");

      if (wsdlURI == null) {
        System.out.println("WSDL location not available");
      } else {
         ACMEWebService_Impl awsI =
                  new ACMEWebService_Impl(wsdlURI);

         ACMEWebServicePort aws = awsI.getACMEWebServicePort();
         System.out.println("==Getting Product info
                                  for ProductID 1001==");
         System.out.println(aws.getProduct(1001));
         System.out.println("==Getting
                                     Product Catalog==");
         System.out.println(aws.getProductCatalog());
    }
  }
```

Listing 3.21 Complete source code of `ACMEWebServiceClient.java`. *(continued)*

Now let's include the compilation of the `ACMEWebServiceClient.java` in the `build.xml` (see Listing 3.22).

```
   <target name="build-client" depends="build-ear">
      <clientgen
       ear="${build}/${ear_file}"
       warName="${war_file}"
       packageName="jws.ch3.ejb"
       clientJar="${client_file}" />
     <javac srcdir="." includes="ACMEWebServiceClient.java"
                                             fork ="true"
       destdir="${CLIENT_CLASSES}" >
       <classpath>
         <pathelement path="${client_file}"/>
         <pathelement path="${java.class.path}"/>
       </classpath>
     </javac>
   </target>
```

Listing 3.22 `ACMEWebServiceClient.java` in the `build.xml`.

With all of these steps, we have now completed all of the required processes for creating the ACME Web services provider.

To compile and run the previous classes, ensure that the WebLogic JARs and other required packages are available in the CLASSPATH. Then, navigate to the source directory and run the Ant utility.

Upon successful completion, you will find the output shown in Figure 3.13.

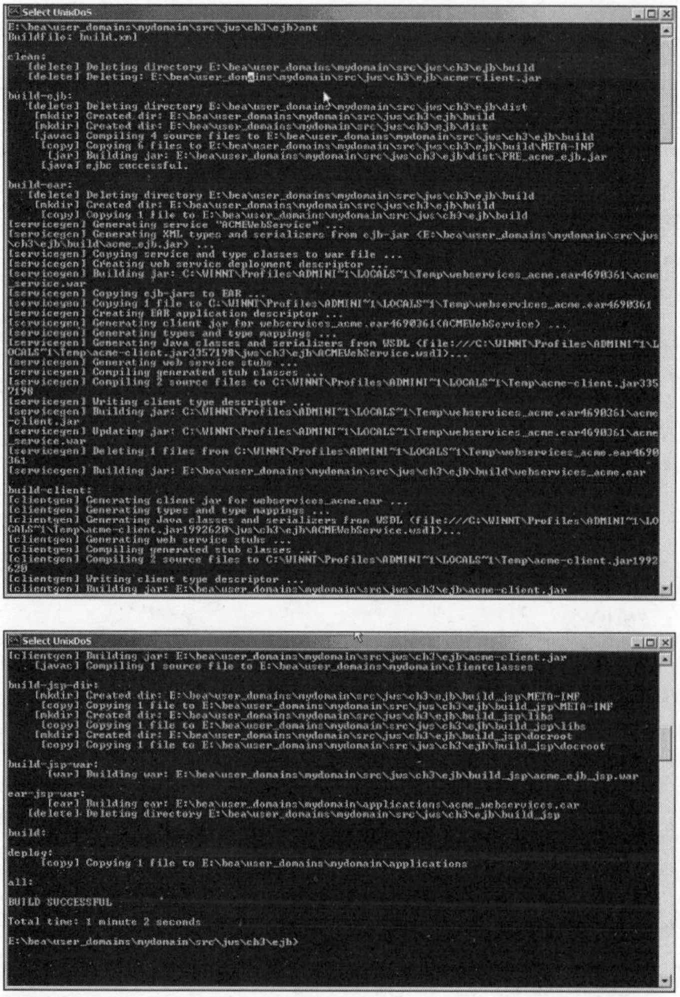

```
E:\bea\user_domains\mydomain\src\jws\ch3\ejb>ant
Buildfile: build.xml

clean:
   [delete] Deleting directory E:\bea\user_domains\mydomain\src\jws\ch3\ejb\build
   [delete] Deleting: E:\bea\user_domains\mydomain\src\jws\ch3\ejb\acme-client.jar

build-ejb:
   [delete] Deleting directory E:\bea\user_domains\mydomain\src\jws\ch3\ejb\dist
    [mkdir] Created dir: E:\bea\user_domains\mydomain\src\jws\ch3\ejb\build
    [mkdir] Created dir: E:\bea\user_domains\mydomain\src\jws\ch3\ejb\dist
    [javac] Compiling 4 source files to E:\bea\user_domains\mydomain\src\jws\ch3\ejb\build
     [copy] Copying 6 files to E:\bea\user_domains\mydomain\src\jws\ch3\ejb\build\META-INF
      [jar] Building jar: E:\bea\user_domains\mydomain\src\jws\ch3\ejb\dist\PRE_acme_ejb.jar
     [java] ejbc successful.

build-ear:
   [delete] Deleting directory E:\bea\user_domains\mydomain\src\jws\ch3\ejb\build
    [mkdir] Created dir: E:\bea\user_domains\mydomain\src\jws\ch3\ejb\build
     [copy] Copying 1 file to E:\bea\user_domains\mydomain\src\jws\ch3\ejb\build
[servicegen] Generating service "ACMEWebService" ...
[servicegen] Generating XML types and serializers from ejb-jar (E:\bea\user_domains\mydomain\src\jws
\ch3\ejb\build\acme_ejb.jar) ...
[servicegen] Copying service and type classes to war file ...
[servicegen] Creating web service deployment descriptor ...
[servicegen] Building jar: C:\WINNT\Profiles\ADMINI~1\LOCALS~1\Temp\webservices_acme.ear4690361\acme
_service.war
[servicegen] Copying ejb-jars to EAR ...
[servicegen] Copying 1 file to C:\WINNT\Profiles\ADMINI~1\LOCALS~1\Temp\webservices_acme.ear4690361
[servicegen] Creating EAR application descriptor ...
[servicegen] Generating client jar for webservices_acme.ear4690361(ACMEWebService) ...
[servicegen] Generating types and type mappings ...
[servicegen] Generating Java classes and serializers from WSDL (file:///C:\WINNT\Profiles\ADMINI~1\L
OCALS~1\Temp\acme-client.jar3357198\jws\ch3\ejb\ACMEWebService.wsdl)...
[servicegen] Generating web service stubs ...
[servicegen] Compiling generated stub classes ...
[servicegen] Compiling 2 source files to C:\WINNT\Profiles\ADMINI~1\LOCALS~1\Temp\acme-client.jar335
7198
[servicegen] Writing client type descriptor ...
[servicegen] Building jar: C:\WINNT\Profiles\ADMINI~1\LOCALS~1\Temp\webservices_acme.ear4690361\acme
-client.jar
[servicegen] Updating jar: C:\WINNT\Profiles\ADMINI~1\LOCALS~1\Temp\webservices_acme.ear4690361\acme
_service.war
[servicegen] Deleting 1 files from C:\WINNT\Profiles\ADMINI~1\LOCALS~1\Temp\webservices_acme.ear4690
361
[servicegen] Building jar: E:\bea\user_domains\mydomain\src\jws\ch3\ejb\build\webservices_acme.ear

build-client:
[clientgen] Generating client jar for webservices_acme.ear ...
[clientgen] Generating types and type mappings ...
[clientgen] Generating Java classes and serializers from WSDL (file:///C:\WINNT\Profiles\ADMINI~1\LO
CALS~1\Temp\acme-client.jar1992620\jws\ch3\ejb\ACMEWebService.wsdl)...
[clientgen] Generating web service stubs ...
[clientgen] Compiling generated stub classes ...
[clientgen] Compiling 2 source files to C:\WINNT\Profiles\ADMINI~1\LOCALS~1\Temp\acme-client.jar1992
620
[clientgen] Writing client type descriptor ...
[clientgen] Building jar: E:\bea\user_domains\mydomain\src\jws\ch3\ejb\acme-client.jar
```

```
[clientgen] Building jar: E:\bea\user_domains\mydomain\src\jws\ch3\ejb\acme-client.jar
    [javac] Compiling 1 source file to E:\bea\user_domains\mydomain\clientclasses

build-jsp-dir:
    [mkdir] Created dir: E:\bea\user_domains\mydomain\src\jws\ch3\ejb\build_jsp\META-INF
     [copy] Copying 1 file to E:\bea\user_domains\mydomain\src\jws\ch3\ejb\build_jsp\META-INF
    [mkdir] Created dir: E:\bea\user_domains\mydomain\src\jws\ch3\ejb\build_jsp\libs
     [copy] Copying 1 file to E:\bea\user_domains\mydomain\src\jws\ch3\ejb\build_jsp\libs
    [mkdir] Created dir: E:\bea\user_domains\mydomain\src\jws\ch3\ejb\build_jsp\docroot
     [copy] Copying 1 file to E:\bea\user_domains\mydomain\src\jws\ch3\ejb\build_jsp\docroot

build-jsp-war:
      [war] Building war: E:\bea\user_domains\mydomain\src\jws\ch3\ejb\build_jsp\acme_ejb_jsp.war

ear-jsp-war:
      [ear] Building ear: E:\bea\user_domains\mydomain\applications\acme_webservices.ear
   [delete] Deleting directory E:\bea\user_domains\mydomain\src\jws\ch3\ejb\build_jsp

build:

deploy:
     [copy] Copying 1 file to E:\bea\user_domains\mydomain\applications

all:

BUILD SUCCESSFUL

Total time: 1 minute 2 seconds

E:\bea\user_domains\mydomain\src\jws\ch3\ejb>
```

Figure 3.13 Packaging and deployment of the ACME service provider.

Testing the ACME Web Services Provider

So far we have looked at building the components and generating the service classes for the ACME Web services provider. From now on, let's test the service classes using the static client and WebLogic server-provided utilities.

To execute the static client `AcmeWebServiceClient` class, you may execute the Ant utility with `run` as an argument. The successful execution of the program invokes the ACMEWebService and then fetches the `Product Catalog` as an XML base string.

If everything works successfully, you will get the output shown in Figure 3.14.

As part of every Web service deployment, the WebLogic 7.0 server automatically generates home pages for all of the deployed Web services. Through this home page, it does the following:

- Tests the invoke operations to ensure the operations are working correctly
- Displays SOAP request and response messages based on the invocation
- Displays the WSDL describing the service and operations provided by the Web service
- Downloads the deployed Web service-specific client JAR file containing the JAX-RPC stub interfaces and classes required for invoking the Web service from an application

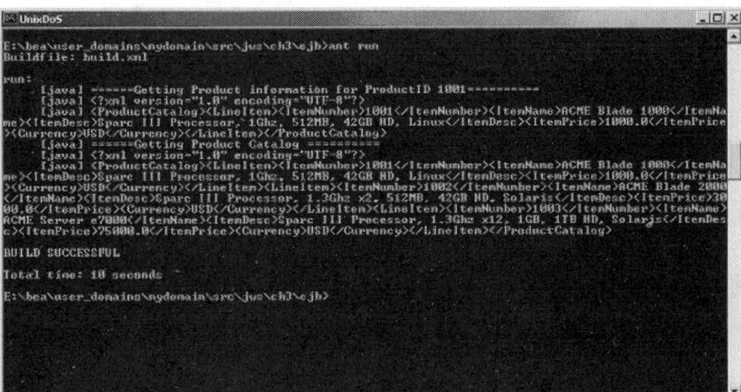

Figure 3.14 Output showing the test invoking the service provider.

The WebLogic Web Services home page URLs for invoking the Web serviced and for displaying the WSDL are as follows:

- http://host:port/war_name/service_uri
- http://host:port/war_name/service_uri/?WSDL

`host` refers to the WebLogic Server host, `port` refers to the server `listening port`, `war_name` refers to the name of the Web application WAR file, and `service_uri` refers to the name of the Web service.

In our case, the URL to invoke the ACME Web services home page will be as follows:

```
http://localhost7001/acme_service/ACMEWebService
```

You may choose to use `localhost` or your `hostname`. If everything works successfully, you will get the output shown in Figure 3.15.

You will also notice the WebLogic home page of ACME Web services, displaying the following supported operations:

- getProductCatalog
- getProduct

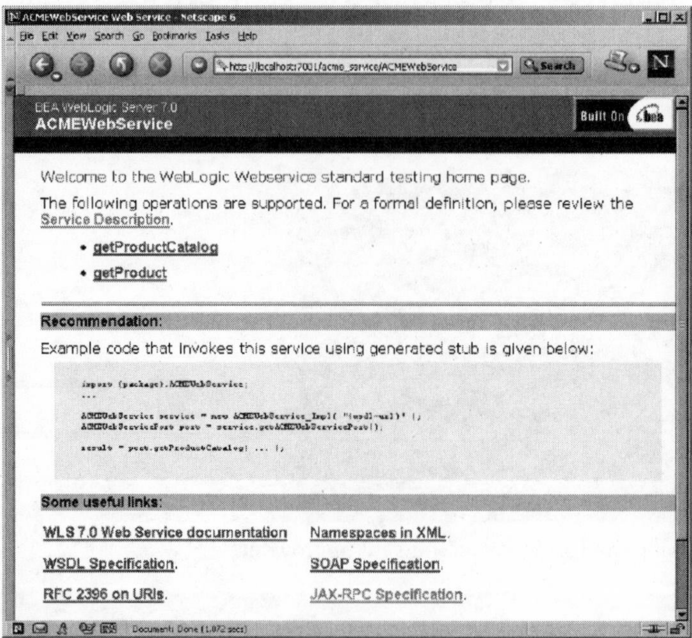

Figure 3.15 Output showing successful deployment of ACMEWebService.

To test the operations, just click on the operation links. To invoke the `getProductCatalog` operation, click on the link.

Then click on the `Invoke` button to display the results. The results page shows the SOAP request and response messages and the data exchanged as XML.

Upon successful execution, the browser will display the output shown in Figure 3.16.

And, the final test is to display the WSDL-based service description describing the service and operations provided by the Web service provider. To display the WSDL-based service description, just execute the following URL using your local http browser:

```
http://localhost:7001/acme_service/ ACMEWebService?WSDL
```

The browser will display the complete WSDL for the ACME Web service in an XML format. The browser then will display the output shown in Figure 3.17.

This concludes the design, implementation, and testing of the ACME Web service provider using a J2EE-based application environment.

Now let's take a look at developing the service requester environment to provide service delivery.

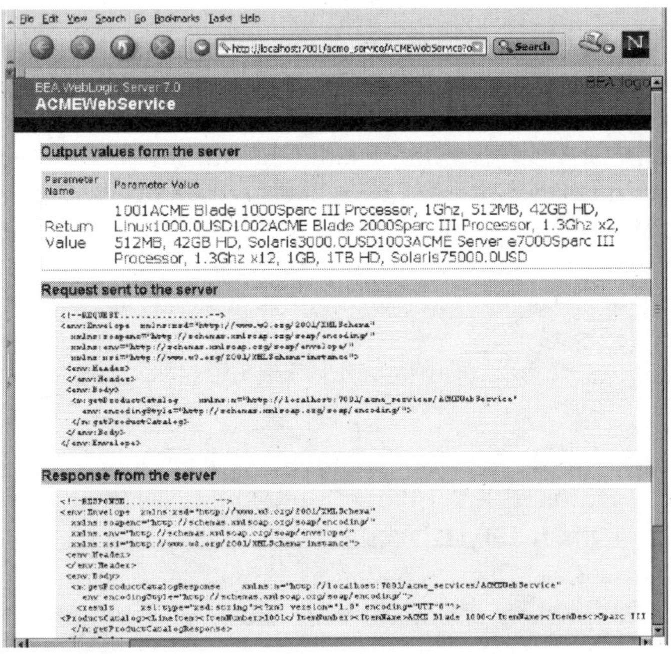

Figure 3.16 Output showing the SOAP request and response messages.

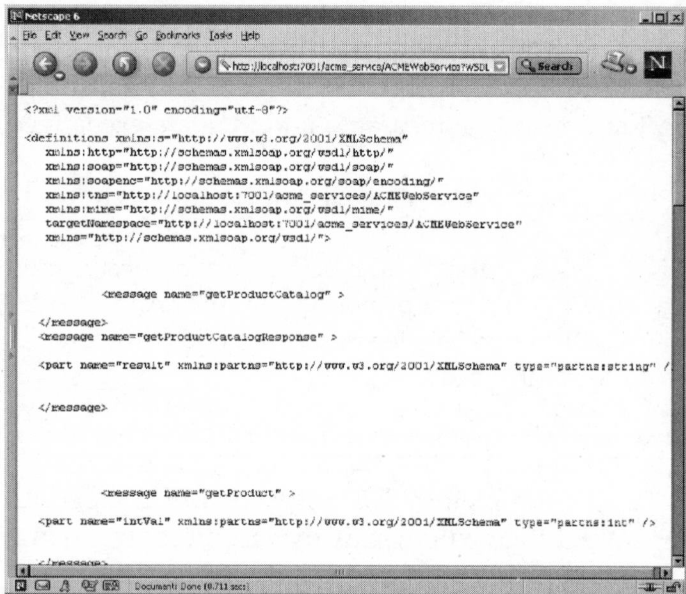

Figure 3.17 WSDL emitted from an ACME service provider.

Developing the ACME Web Service Requestor

To build the ACME Web service requestor, it is a requirement to create SOAP-based client interfaces using the WSDL-based descriptions exposed by the ACME Web service provider (WebLogic environment). Although it is not mandatory to choose any programming language for implementing the client interfaces, it must support the use of SOAP for communication.

As discussed earlier, we will be using Apache Axis 1.0B3 to build the ACME service requestor client environment. Axis provides a `WSDL2Java` tool to build Java-based proxies and skeletons for services with WSDL descriptions.

To create the service requestor clients as Java proxies, the following tasks are involved:

1. Install and set up the Apache Axis development environment. Ensure that Axis class libraries and other optional libraries (that is, Apache Xerces, Xalan) are in the Java compiler class path.
2. Create a test client directory and run the `org.apache.axis.wsdl.WSDL2Java` utility by providing an ACME Web services WSDL URI as an argument; this will generate the Java-based client bindings.

3. Using an Ant script, compile the generated source files along with a stub client, which invokes the services from the ACME Web services.
4. Test the client execution.

Let's take a closer look at the details of demonstrating the previous steps.

Setting up the Axis Environment

Install the Apache Axis download and create a shell/batch script to set up the CLASSPATH environment, including all the provided Axis libraries.

Generating the Java Proxies

Create a directory named `ACMEClient` and run the `WSDL2Java` utility with the WSDL URI of `ACMEWebService` as an argument.

For example, you may execute the following command line:

```
java org.apache.axis.wsdl.WSDL2Java \
http://nramesh:7001/acme_service/ACMEWebService?WSDL
```

This will generate a package named `localhost` that includes a list of client stub classes as follows:

```
ACMEWebService.java
ACMEWebServiceLocator.java
ACMEWebServicePort.java
ACMEWebServiceSoapBindingStub.java
```

Upon successful completion, you typically will find the output shown in Figure 3.18.

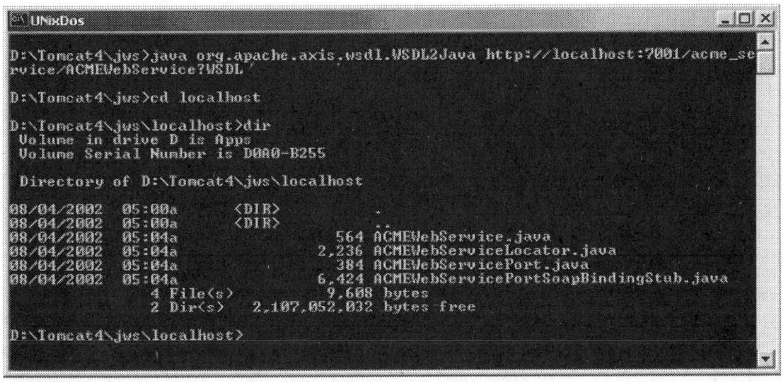

```
UNixDos
D:\Tomcat4\jws>java org.apache.axis.wsdl.WSDL2Java http://localhost:7001/acme_se
rvice/ACMEWebService?WSDL

D:\Tomcat4\jws>cd localhost

D:\Tomcat4\jws\localhost>dir
 Volume in drive D is Apps
 Volume Serial Number is D0A0-B255

 Directory of D:\Tomcat4\jws\localhost

08/04/2002  05:00a      <DIR>          .
08/04/2002  05:00a      <DIR>          ..
08/04/2002  05:04a                 564 ACMEWebService.java
08/04/2002  05:04a               2,236 ACMEWebServiceLocator.java
08/04/2002  05:04a                 384 ACMEWebServicePort.java
08/04/2002  05:04a               6,424 ACMEWebServicePortSoapBindingStub.java
               4 File(s)          9,608 bytes
               2 Dir(s)   2,107,052,032 bytes free

D:\Tomcat4\jws\localhost>
```

Figure 3.18 Output showing the client side stubs generated by an Axis WSDL2Java utility.

Creating the Java Clients

Using the generated stub classes, implement a Java client for ACME Web services. A typical implementation will be as follows:

- Use `ACMEWebServicelocator` to locate the service.
- Use `ACMEWebServicePort` to obtain the service port.
- Invoke the operations using the obtained port.

Listing 3.23 is the `AxisWebServiceClient.java` source code using the generated stub classes.

```
// AxisWebServiceClient.java

package localhost;
import localhost.*;

public class AxisWebServiceClient  {

public static void main(String [] args) throws Exception {

// Locate the service
 ACMEWebServiceLocator service
               = new ACMEWebServiceLocator();

// Obtain the service port
   ACMEWebServicePortType port =
                    service.getACMEWebServicePort();

// Invoke the operations
 String catalog = port.getProductCatalog();
 String product = port.getProduct(1001);
 System.out.println("=====Get Product Catalog ====");
 System.out.println(catalog);
 System.out.println("= Get Product info for
                                product ID 1001 =");
 System.out.println("=====");
 System.out.println(product);
}
}
```

Listing 3.23 `AxisWebServiceClient.java` **using the generated stub classes.**

To execute `AxisWebServiceClient`, compile using `javac *.java` and execute the client running `java localhost.AxisWebService-Client`. Upon successful completion, the system will display the output shown in Figure 3.19.

```
UNixDos
D:\Tomcat4\jws>java localhost.AxisWebServicesClient
=======Get Product Catalog ========
<?xml version="1.0" encoding="UTF-8"?>
<ProductCatalog><LineItem><ItemNumber>1001</ItemNumber><ItemName>ACME Blade 1000
</ItemName><ItemDesc>Sparc III Processor, 1Ghz, 512MB, 42GB HD, Linux</ItemDesc>
<ItemPrice>1000.0</ItemPrice><Currency>USD</Currency></LineItem><LineItem><ItemN
umber>1002</ItemNumber><ItemName>ACME Blade 2000</ItemName><ItemDesc>Sparc III P
rocessor, 1.3Ghz x2, 512MB, 42GB HD, Solaris</ItemDesc><ItemPrice>3000.0</ItemPr
ice><Currency>USD</Currency></LineItem><LineItem><ItemNumber>1003</ItemNumber><I
temName>ACME Server e7000</ItemName><ItemDesc>Sparc III Processor, 1.3Ghz x12, 1
GB, 1TB HD, Solaris</ItemDesc><ItemPrice>75000.0</ItemPrice><Currency>USD</Curre
ncy></LineItem></ProductCatalog>
= Get Product info for product ID 1001 ==
=====
<?xml version="1.0" encoding="UTF-8"?>
<ProductCatalog><LineItem><ItemNumber>1001</ItemNumber><ItemName>ACME Blade 1000
</ItemName><ItemDesc>Sparc III Processor, 1Ghz, 512MB, 42GB HD, Linux</ItemDesc>
<ItemPrice>1000.0</ItemPrice><Currency>USD</Currency></LineItem></ProductCatalog
>

D:\Tomcat4\jws>_
```

Figure 3.19 Output showing successful invocation of ACMEWebService.

This concludes the implementation and testing of the ACME service requester environment using Apache Axis.

The complete source code and instructions for executing the previous example are available as part of the source code bundle as Chapter3.zip and they can be downloaded from this book's companion Web site at www.wiley.com/compbooks/nagappan.

In this section, we have illustrated a complete example of implementing Web services by exposing J2EE components deployed in a J2EE application server and accessing those services using a SOAP-based client environment.

Summary

This chapter has thoroughly studied building Web services architecture and implementing J2EE-based Web services. It also has examined the different strategies and architectural models of developing Web services.

In general, we have looked at such varied topics as Web service architecture and its characteristics, the core building blocks of Web services, standards and technologies available for implementing Web services, Web services communication models, how to develop Web services-enabled applications, how to develop Web services from J2EE applications, and a complete illustration of developing J2EE-based Web services.

In the following chapter, we will extensively discuss understanding SOAP and how to develop Web services applications using SOAP.

CHAPTER

4

Developing Web Services Using SOAP

This chapter presents an in-depth discussion on the core fundamentals of Simple Object Access Protocol (SOAP) and the role of SOAP in developing Web services architecture and its implementation. This chapter covers the W3C definition of SOAP standards, conventions, messages, SOAP communication models, and implementation of SOAP-based applications for Web services. In addition, this chapter illustrates an example of developing a Web services solution using a SOAP implementation.

With the emergence of Web services, SOAP has become the *de facto* communication protocol standard for creating and invoking applications exposed over a network. SOAP is similar to traditional binary protocols like IIOP (CORBA) or JRMP (RMI), but instead of using a binary data representation, it adopts text-based data representation using XML.

Using XML notation, SOAP defines a lightweight wire protocol and encoding format to represent data types, programming languages, and databases. SOAP can use a variety of Internet standard protocols (such as HTTP and SMTP) as its message transport, and it provides conventions for representing communication models like remote procedural calls (RPCs) and document-driven messaging. This enables inter-application communication in a distributed environment and interoperability between heterogeneous applications over the networks. With its widespread acceptance by leading IT vendors and Web developers, SOAP is gaining popularity and adoption in most popular business applications for enabling them as Web services. It is important to note that SOAP is an ongoing W3C effort in which leading IT vendors are participating in order to come to a consensus on such important tasks associated with XML-based protocols and to define their key requirements and usage scenarios.

In this chapter, we will explore the fundamentals of SOAP, implementation details, and how to develop Web services using SOAP-based technologies. In particular, we will be focusing on the following:

- Background of SOAP and XML-based protocols
- Anatomy of a SOAP message
- SOAP encoding
- SOAP message exchange models
- SOAP communication
- SOAP bindings for transport protocols
- SOAP security
- Java APIs for developing SOAP applications
- Development of a Web services application using a SOAP server
- Limitations of SOAP

Because the key focus of this book is developing Web services using the Java platform, it will illustrate a Java API-based example using a SOAP implementation for developing Web services. At the time of this book's writing, SOAP 1.1 has been released as a public specification and SOAP 1.2 is available as a W3C working draft. For consistency and better understanding, the chapter discusses both versions of SOAP and its features.

To find out the current status of SOAP from the W3C Working Group activities, refer to the W3C Web site at www.23.org/2002/ws/.

XML-Based Protocols and SOAP

In the last chapter, we discussed typical Web services architecture and looked at how the service provider and service requestor communicate with each other using an XML-based wire protocol (such as SOAP). XML-based protocols have been used in the industry for a while now—some even before the W3C SOAP effort began—however, some of these protocols did not get accepted by the industry for various reasons. Some of the popular XML-based protocols are the following:

XMI (XML Metadata Interchange). XMI was developed by OMG to explore technological synergy between XML and OMG technologies such as UML and CORBA. XMI defines an open information interchange model for CORBA and object-based technologies in a standardized way, enabling them to interoperate using XML and providing the ability to exchange programming data over the Internet. To find more information on XMI, refer to the OMG Web site at http://cgi.omg.org/news/pr99/xmi_overview.html.

XML RPC (XML - Remote Procedure Call). XML-RPC was originally developed by Userland Inc. It is an RPC-based communication protocol that runs over the Internet using HTTP as its transport protocol. It encodes RPC call parameters and return values in XML. The parameters can consist of numbers, scalars, strings, dates, lists, and complex records. To find more information on XML-RPC, refer to the XML-RPC Web site at www.xmlrpc.com/spec.

WDDX (Web Distributed Data Exchange). Allaire (Macromedia, Inc.) originally developed WDDX. It defines an XML-based data exchange model between applications leveraging data syndication and B2B collaboration. It consists of XML data using document type definitions (DTDs) and a set of modules for programming languages to use WDDX and to transfer data. Additionally, it also uses standard protocols such as HTTP, SMTP, and FTP for transport. To find more information on WDDX, refer to the WDDX Web site at www.openwddx.org/.

JABBER. JABBER was developed by the JABBER Software Foundation (JSF), a non-profit organization promoting XML-based protocols for Internet-based instant messaging and presence. To find out more information on JABBER, refer to the JABBER Web site at www.jabber.org.

The Emergence of SOAP

SOAP initially was developed by DevelopMentor, Inc., as a platform-independent protocol for accessing services, objects between applications, and servers using HTTP-based communication. SOAP used an XML-based vocabulary for representing RPC calls and its parameters and return values. In 1999, the SOAP 1.0 specification was made publicly available as a joint effort supported by vendors like RogueWave, IONA, ObjectSpace, Digital Creations, UserLand, Microsoft, and DevelopMentor. Later, the SOAP 1.1 specification was released as a W3C Note, with additional contributions from IBM and the Lotus Corporation supporting a wide range of systems and communication models like RPC and Messaging.

Nowadays, the current version of SOAP 1.2 is part of the W3C XML Protocol Working Group effort led by vendors such as Sun Microsystems, IBM, HP, BEA, Microsoft, and Oracle. At the time of this book's writing, SOAP 1.2 is available as a public W3C working draft. To find out the current status of the SOAP specifications produced by the XML Protocol Working Group, refer to the W3C Web site at www.w3c.org.

Understanding SOAP Specifications

The SOAP 1.1 specifications define the following:

- Syntax and semantics for representing XML documents as structured SOAP messages
- Encoding standards for representing data in SOAP messages
- A communication model for exchanging SOAP messages
- Bindings for the underlying transport protocols such as SOAP transport
- Conventions for sending and receiving messages using RPC and messaging

Note that SOAP is not a programming language or a business application component for building business applications. SOAP is intended for use as a portable communication protocol to deliver SOAP messages, which have to be created and processed by an application.

In general, SOAP is simple and extensible by design, but unlike other distributed computing protocols, the following features are not supported by SOAP:

- Garbage collection
- Object by reference
- Object activation
- Message batching

SOAP and ebXML are complementary to each other. In fact, SOAP is leveraged by an ebXML Messaging service as a communication protocol with an extension that provides added security and reliability for handling business transactions in e-business and B2B frameworks.

More importantly, SOAP adopts XML syntax and standards like XML Schema and namespaces as part of its message structure. To understand the concepts of XML notations, XML Schema, and namespaces, refer to Chapter 8, "XML Processing and Data Binding with Java APIs."

Now, let's take a closer look at the SOAP messages, standards, conventions, and other related technologies, and how they are represented in a development process.

Anatomy of a SOAP Message

SOAP defines the structure of an XML document, rules, and mechanisms that can be used to enable communication between applications. It does not mandate a single programming language or a platform, nor does it define its own language or platform.

Before we go exploring the SOAP features, let's walk through an existing SOAP message and understand the XML syntax, semantic rules, and conventions. The example shown in Listing 4.1 is a SOAP request/response message for obtaining book price information from a book catalog service provider. The SOAP request accepts a string parameter as the name of the book and returns a float as the price of the book as a SOAP response.

In the scenario in Listing 4.1, the SOAP message is embedded in an HTTP request for getting the book price information from www.wiley.com for the book *Developing Java Web Services*.

```
POST /BookPrice HTTP/1.1
Host: catalog.acmeco.com
Content-Type: text/xml; charset="utf-8"
Content-Length: 640
SOAPAction: "GetBookPrice"

<SOAP-ENV:Envelope
 xmlns:SOAP ENV="http://schemas.xmlsoap.org/soap/envelope/"
 xmlns:xsi="http://www.w3c.org/2001/XMLSchema-instance"
 xmlns:xsd="http://www.w3c.org/2001/XMLSchema"
 SOAP-ENV:encodingStyle
          ="http://schemas.xmlsoap.org/soap/encoding/">

<SOAP-ENV:Header>
 <person:mail
     xmlns:person="http://acmeco.com/Header/">xyz@acmeco.com
  </person:mail>
 </SOAP-ENV:Header>

 <SOAP-ENV:Body>
   <m:GetBookPrice
       xmlns:m="http://www.wiley.com/jws.book.priceList">
   <bookname xsi:type='xsd:string'>
            Developing Java Web Services</bookname>
   </m:GetBookPrice>
  </SOAP-ENV:Body>
</SOAP-ENV: Envelope>
```

Listing 4.1 SOAP request message.

Listing 4.2 shows the SOAP message embedded in an HTTP response returning the price of the book.

```
HTTP/1.1 200 OK
Content-Type: text/xml; charset="utf-8"
Content-Length: 640

<SOAP-ENV:Envelope
       xmlns:SOAP-ENV=http://schemas.xmlsoap.org/soap/envelope/
       xmlns:xsi="http://www.w3c.org/2001/XMLSchema-instance"
       xmlns:xsd="http://www.w3c.org/2001/XMLSchema"
     SOAP-ENV:
     encodingStyle="http://schemas.xmlsoap.org/soap/encoding/"/>
     <SOAP-ENV:Header>
         <wiley:Transaction
              xmlns:wiley="http://jws.wiley.com/2002/booktx"
              SOAP-ENV:mustUnderstand="1"> 5
         </wiley:Transaction>
     </SOAP-ENV:Header>
     <SOAP-ENV:Body>
         <m:GetBookPriceResponse xmlns:m="
                http://www.wiley.com/jws.book.priceList">
         <Price>50.00</Price>
         </m:GetBookPriceResponse>
     </SOAP-ENV:Body>
</SOAP-ENV:Envelope>
```

Listing 4.2 SOAP response message.

In Listing 4.2, you might have noticed that the SOAP message contains a SOAP Envelope `SOAP-ENV:Envelope` as its primary `root` element, and it relies on defined "XML Namespaces" commonly identified with a keyword `xmlns` and specific prefixes to identify the elements and its encoding rules. All the elements in the message are associated with `SOAP-ENV`-defined namespaces.

Note that a SOAP application should incorporate and use the relevant SOAP namespaces for defining its elements and attributes of its sending messages; likewise, it must be able to process the receiving messages with those specified namespaces. These namespaces must be in a qualified W3C XML Schema, which facilitates the SOAP message with groupings of elements using prefixes to avoid name collisions.

Usually a SOAP message requires defining two basic namespaces: SOAP Envelope and SOAP Encoding. The following list their forms in both versions 1.1 and 1.2 of SOAP.

SOAP ENVELOPE

- http://schemas.xmlsoap.org/soap/envelope/ (SOAP 1.1)
- http://www.w3.org/2001/06/soap-envelope (SOAP 1.2)

SOAP ENCODING

- http://schemas.xmlsoap.org/soap/encoding/ (SOAP 1.1)
- http://www.w3.org/2001/06/soap-encoding (SOAP 1.2)

Additionally, SOAP also can use attributes and values defined in W3C XML Schema instances or XML Schemas and can use the elements based on custom XML conforming to W3C XML Schema specifications. SOAP does not support or use DTD-based element or attribute declarations. To understand the fundamentals of XML namespaces, refer to Chapter 8, "XML Processing and Data Binding with Java APIs."

Typical to the previous example message, the structural format of a SOAP message (as per SOAP version 1.1 with attachments) contains the following elements:

- Envelope
- Header (optional)
- Body
- Attachments (optional)

Figure 4.1 represents the structure of a SOAP message with attachments. Typically, a SOAP message is represented by a SOAP envelope with zero or more attachments. The SOAP message envelope contains the header and body of the message, and the SOAP message attachments enable the message to contain data, which include XML and non-XML data (like text/binary files). In fact, a SOAP message package is constructed using the MIME Multipart/Related structure approaches to separate and identify the different parts of the message.

Now, let's explore the details and characteristics of the parts of a SOAP message.

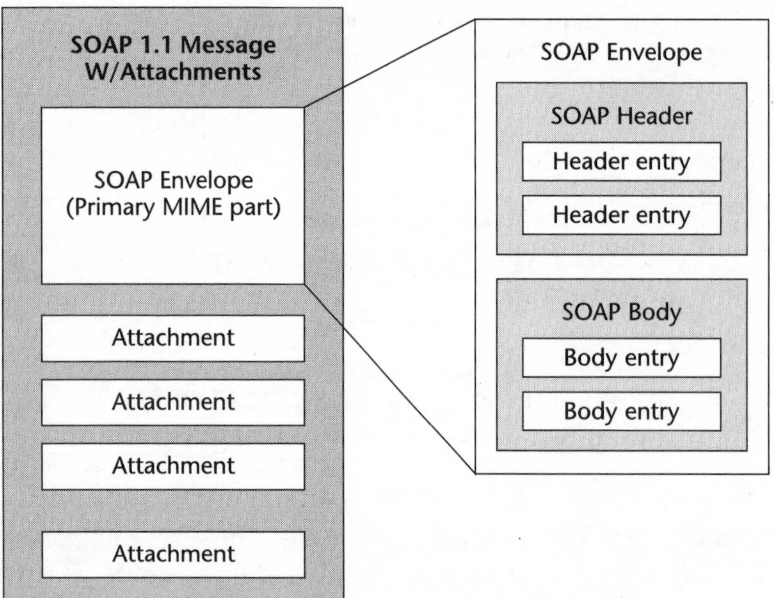

Figure 4.1 Structure of a SOAP message with attachments.

SOAP Envelope

The SOAP envelope is the primary container of a SOAP message's structure and is the mandatory element of a SOAP message. It is represented as the root element of the message as `Envelope`. As we discussed earlier, it is usually declared as an element using the XML namespace http://schemas.xmlsoap.org/soap/envelope/. As per SOAP 1.1 specifications, SOAP messages that do not follow this namespace declaration are not processed and are considered to be invalid. Encoding styles also can be defined using a namespace under `Envelope` to represent the data types used in the message. Listing 4.3 shows the SOAP envelope element in a SOAP message.

```
<SOAP-ENV:Envelope
        xmlns:SOAP-ENV=http://schemas.xmlsoap.org/soap/envelope/
   xmlns:xsi="http://www.w3c.org/2001/XMLSchema-instance"
        xmlns:xsd="http://www.w3.org/2001/XMLSchema"
    SOAP-ENV:
    encodingStyle="http://schemas.xmlsoap.org/soap/encoding/"/>

<!--SOAP Header elements - -/>
```

Listing 4.3 SOAP `Envelope` element.

```
<!--SOAP Body element - -/>

</SOAP-ENV:Envelope>
```

Listing 4.3 SOAP `Envelope` element. *(continued)*

SOAP Header

The SOAP header is represented as the first immediate child element of a SOAP envelope, and it has to be namespace qualified. In addition, it also may contain zero or more optional child elements, which are referred to as SOAP header entries. The SOAP `encodingStyle` attribute will be used to define the encoding of the data types used in header element entries. The SOAP `actor` attribute and SOAP `mustUnderstand` attribute can be used to indicate the target SOAP application node (Sender/Receiver/Intermediary) and to process the `Header` entries. Listing 4.4 shows the sample representation of a SOAP header element in a SOAP message.

```
<SOAP-ENV:Header>
     <wiley:Transaction
       xmlns:wiley="http://jws.wiley.com/2002/booktx"
                            SOAP-ENV:mustUnderstand="1">
                            <keyValue> 5 </keyValue>
      </wiley:Transaction>
</SOAP-ENV:Header>
```

Listing 4.4 SOAP `Header` element.

In Listing 4.4, the SOAP header represents a transaction semantics entry using the SOAP `mustUnderstand` attribute. The `mustUnderstand` attribute is set to "1", which ensures that the receiver (URI) of this message must process it. We will look into the `mustUnderstand` attributes in the next section.

SOAP headers also provide mechanisms to extend a SOAP message for adding features and defining high-level functionalities such as security, transactions, priority, and auditing. These mechanisms are discussed in Chapter 13, "Web Services Security."

SOAP Body

A SOAP envelope contains a SOAP body as its child element, and it may contain one or more optional SOAP body block entries. The `Body` represents the mandatory processing information or the payload intended for the receiver of the message. The SOAP 1.1 specification mandates that there must be one or more optional SOAP `Body` entries in a message. A `Body` block of a SOAP message can contain any of the following:

- RPC method and its parameters
- Target application (receiver) specific data
- SOAP fault for reporting errors and status information

Listing 4.5 illustrates a SOAP body representing an RPC call for getting the book price information from www.wiley.com for the book name *Developing Java Web Services*.

```
<SOAP-ENV:Body>
   <m:GetBookPrice
    xmlns:m="http://www.wiley.com/jws.book.priceList/">
         <bookname xsi:type='xsd:string'>
              Developing Java Web services</bookname>
         </m:GetBookPrice>
  </SOAP-ENV:Body>
```

Listing 4.5 SOAP `Body` element.

Like other elements, the `Body` element also must have a qualified namespace and be associated with an `encodingStyle` attribute to provide the encoding conventions for the payload. In general, the SOAP Body can contain information defining an RPC call, business documents in XML, and any XML data required to be part of the message during communication.

SOAP Fault

In a SOAP message, the SOAP `Fault` element is used to handle errors and to find out status information. This element provides the error and/or status information. It can be used within a `Body` element or as a `Body` entry.

It provides the following elements to define the error and status of the SOAP message in a readable description, showing the source of the information and its details:

Faultcode. The `faultcode` element defines the algorithmic mechanism for the SOAP application to identify the fault. It contains standard values for identifying the error or status of the SOAP application. The namespace identifiers for these `faultcode` values are defined in http://schemas.xmlsoap.org/soap/envelope/. The following `faultcode` element values are defined in the SOAP 1.1 specification:

VersionMismatch This value indicates that an invalid namespace is defined in the SOAP envelope or an unsupported version of a SOAP message.

MustUnderstand This value is returned if the SOAP receiver node cannot handle and recognize the SOAP header block when the `MustUnderstand` attribute is set to 1. The `MustUnderstand` values can be set to 0 for false and 1 for true.

Client This `faultcode` is indicated when a problem originates from the receiving client. The possible problems could vary from an incorrect SOAP message, a missing element, or incorrect namespace definition.

Server This `faultcode` indicates that a problem has been encountered during processing on the server side of the application, and that the application could not process further because the issue is specific to the content of the SOAP message.

Faultstring. The `faultstring` element provides a readable description of the SOAP fault exhibited by the SOAP application.

Faultactor. The `faultactor` element provides the information about the ultimate SOAP actor (Sender/Receiver/Intermediary) in the message who is responsible for the SOAP fault at the particular destination of a message.

Detail. The `detail` element provides the application-specific error or status information related to the defined `Body` block.

Let's take a look at the common examples of SOAP fault scenarios.

How a SOAP Fault Is Represented in a SOAP Message

Listing 4.6 shows how a SOAP `Fault` is represented in a SOAP message.

```
<SOAP-ENV:Envelope xmlns:SOAP-ENV
                  ="http://schemas.xmlsoap.org/soap/envelope/"
   SOAP-ENV:encodingStyle=

     "http://schemas.xmlsoap.org/soap/encoding/">
     <SOAP-ENV:Body>
             <SOAP-ENV:Fault>
             <faultcode>SOAP-ENV:MustUnderstand</faultcode>
             <faultstring>Header element missing</faultstring>
<faultactor>http://jws.wiley.com/GetBookPrice</faultactor>
             <detail>
           <wiley:error
xmlns:wiley="http://jws.wiley.com/GetBookPrice">
               <problem>The Book name parameter missing.</problem>
                     </wiley:error>
                   </detail>
             </SOAP-ENV:Fault>
     </SOAP_ENV:Body>
   </SOAP-ENV:Envelope>
```

Listing 4.6 SOAP `Fault` in a SOAP message.

SOAP Fault Is Caused Due to Server Failure

Listing 4.7 shows how a SOAP `Fault` is caused due to server failure.

```
<SOAP-ENV:Fault>
  <faultcode> SOAP-ENV:Server</faultcode>
  <faultstring> Server OS Internal failure - Reboot server</faultstring>
  <faultactor>http://abzdnet.net/net/keysoap.asp</faultactor>
</SOAP-ENV:Fault>
```

Listing 4.7 SOAP `Fault` due to server failure.

Listing 4.8 shows how a SOAP `Fault` is caused due to client failure.

```
<SOAP-ENV:Fault>
   <faultcode>Client</faultcode>
   <faultstring>Invalid Request</faultstring>
   <faultactor>http://jws.wiley.com/GetCatalog</faultactor>
</SOAP-ENV:Fault>
```

Listing 4.8 SOAP `Fault` due to client failure.

SOAP mustUnderstand

The SOAP `mustUnderstand` attribute indicates that the processing of a SOAP header block is mandatory or optional at the target SOAP node. The following example is a SOAP request using `mustUnderstand` and the response message from the server.

Listing 4.9 shows the request message where the SOAP message defines the header block with a `mustUnderstand` attribute of 1.

```
<SOAP-ENV:Header>
     <wiley:Catalog
       xmlns:wiley="http://jws.wiley.com/2002/bookList"
                             SOAP-ENV:mustUnderstand="1">
      </wiley:Catalog>
</SOAP-ENV: Header>
```

Listing 4.9 SOAP `mustUnderstand` attribute.

Listing 4.10 is an example response message from the server when the server could not understand the header block where the `mustUnderstand` is set to 1. Listing 4.10 is the server-generated fault message detailing the issues with the header blocks using `misUnderstood` and `qname` (faulting SOAP nodes) and providing a complete SOAP fault.

```
<SOAP-ENV:Envelope xmlns:SOAP-ENV
                ="http://www.w3.org/2001/06/soap-envelope/"
   SOAP-ENV:encodingStyle=
              "http://www.w3.org/2001/06/soap-encoding/"
          xmlns:fx="http://www.w3.org/2001/06/soap-faults/">
<SOAP-ENV:Header>
<fx:misUnderstood qname="wiley:Catalog"
       xmlns:wiley="http://jws.wiley.com/2002/bookList/" />
</SOAP-ENV:Header>
           <SOAP-ENV:Body>
             <SOAP-ENV:Fault>
             <faultcode>SOAP-ENV:mustUnderstand</faultcode>
             <faultstring>Could not understand
                         Header element</faultstring>
                <SOAP-ENV:Fault>
            </SOAP_ENV:Body>
 </SOAP-ENV:Envelope>
```

Listing 4.10 SOAP response using SOAP `mustUnderstand`.

So far, we have discussed the basic structure and elements of a SOAP message. Now, let's take a look at how to represent application-specific data in a SOAP message.

SOAP Attachments

As per SOAP 1.1 with the attachment specification, a SOAP message contains the primary SOAP envelope in an XML format and SOAP attachments in any data format that can be ASCII or binary (such as XML or non-text). SOAP attachments are not part of the SOAP envelope but are related to the message.

As the SOAP message is constructed using a MIME multipart/related structure, the SOAP attachment part of the message is contained to a MIME boundary (defined in the Context-Type header). Each MIME part in the structure of the SOAP message is referenced using either Content-ID or Content-Location as labels for the part. Both the SOAP header and body of the SOAP message also can refer to these labels in the message. Each attachment of the message is identified with a Content-ID (typically an `href` attribute using a URL scheme) or Content-Location (a URI reference associated to the attachment).

Listing 4.11 uses "WileyCoverPage.gif" as an attachment and illustrates the use of the Content-ID (CID) reference in the body of the SOAP 1.1 message using absolute URI-referencing entities labeled for using Content-Location headers.

```
MIME-Version: 1.0
Content-Type: Multipart/Related; boundary=MIME_boundary; type=text/xml;
   start="<http://jws.wiley.com/coverpagedetails.xml>"
Content-Description: SOAP message description.

--MIME_boundary--
Content-Type: text/xml; charset=UTF-8
Content-Transfer-Encoding: 8bit
Content-ID: <http://jws.wiley.com/coverpagedetails.xml>
Content-Location: http://jws.wiley.com/coverpagedetails.xml

<?xml version='1.0' ?>
<SOAP-ENV:Envelope
xmlns:SOAP-ENV="http://schemas.xmlsoap.org/soap/envelope/">
<SOAP-ENV:Body>
<!-- SOAP BODY - ->
<theCoverPage href="http://jws.wiley.com/DevelopingWebServices.gif"/>
<!-- SOAP BODY - ->
</SOAP-ENV:Body>
</SOAP-ENV:Envelope>

--MIME_boundary--
Content-Type: image/gif
Content-Transfer-Encoding: binary
Content-ID: <http://jws.wiley.com/DevelopingWebServices.gif>
Content-Location: http://jws.wiley.com/DevelopingWebServices.gif

<!--...binary GIF image... - ->
--MIME_boundary--
```

Listing 4.11 SOAP attachment in a MIME structure.

Although the SOAP 1.1 specification addressed the SOAP attachments based on `MIME Multipart/related`, the W3C Working Group also is evaluating the support of `MIME Application/Multiplexed`-based attachments that facilitate the attachment binary data of the message can be interleaved from the XML contents of the message. To find out more information on the latest specification of SOAP attachments, refer to www.w3.org/TR/SOAP-attachments.

SOAP Encoding

SOAP 1.1 specifications stated that SOAP-based applications can represent their data either as literals or as encoded values defined by the "XML Schema, Part -2" specification (see www.w3.org/TR/xmlschema-2/). Literals refer to message contents that are encoded according to the W3C XML Schema. Encoded values refer to the messages encoded based on SOAP encoding styles specified in SOAP Section 5 of the SOAP 1.1 specification. The namespace identifiers for these SOAP encoding styles are defined in http://schemas.xmlsoap.org/soap/encoding/ (SOAP 1.1) and http://www.w3.org/2001/06/soap-encoding (SOAP 1.2).

The SOAP encoding defines a set of rules for expressing its data types. It is a generalized set of data types that are represented by the programming languages, databases, and semi-structured data required for an application. SOAP encoding also defines serialization rules for its data model using an `encodingStyle` attribute under the `SOAP-ENV` namespace that specifies the serialization rules for a specific element or a group of elements.

SOAP encoding supports both simple- and compound-type values.

Simple Type Values

The definition of simple type values is based on the "W3C XML Schema, Part -2: Datatypes" specification. Examples are primitive data types such as string, integer, decimal, and derived simple data types including enumeration and arrays. The following examples are a SOAP representation of primitive data types:

```
<int>98765</int>
<decimal> 98675.43</decimal>
<string> Java Rules </string>
```

The derived simple data types are built from simple data types and are expressed in the W3C XML Schema.

Enumeration

Enumeration defines a set of names specific to a base type. Listing 4.12 is an example of an enumeration data type expressed in a W3C XML Schema.

```
<xs:schema xmlns:xs="http://www.w3.org/2001/XMLSchema"
                          elementFormDefault="qualified">
   <xs:element name="ProductType">
        <xs:simpleType base="xsd:string">
             <xs:enumeration value="Hardware">
             <xs:enumeration value="Software">
        </xs:simpleType>
   </xs:element>
</xs:schema>
```

Listing 4.12 Enumeration data type.

Array of Bytes

Listing 4.13 is an example of an array data type of an array of binary data that is represented as text using base64 algorithms and expressed using a W3C XML Schema.

```
<myfigure xmlns:xsi="http://www.w3.org/2001/XMLSchema-instance"
        xmlns:enc=" http://schemas.xmlsoap.org/soap/encoding">
        xsi:type="enc:base64">
        sD334G5vDy9898r32323</myfigure>
```

Listing 4.13 An array.

Polymorphic Accessor

The polymorphic accessor enables programming languages to access data types during runtime. SOAP provides a polymorphic accessor instance by defining an `xsi: type` attribute that represents the type of the value.

The following is an example of a polymorphic accessor named `price` with a value type of `"xsd:float"` represented as follows:

```
<price xsi:type="xsd:float">1000.99</price>
```

And, the XML instance of the `price` data type will be as follows:

```
<price>1000.99</price>
```

Compound Type Values

Compound value types are based on composite structural patterns that represent member values as structure or array types. The following sections list the main types of compound type values.

Structure Types

Listing 4.14 is an XML Schema of the `Structure` data type representing the "Shipping address" with subelements like "Street," "City," and "State."

```
<xs:element name="ShippingAddress"
            xmlns:xs="http://www.w3.org/2001/XMLSchema" >
     <xs:complexType>
          <xs:sequence>
              <xs:element ref="Street"type="xsd:string"/>
              <xs:element ref="City" type="xsd:string"/>
              <xs:element ref="State" type="xsd:string"/>
              <xs:element ref="Zip" type="xsd:string"/>
              <xs:element ref="Country" type="xsd:string"/>
          </xs:sequence>
     </xs:complexType>
</xs:element>
```

Listing 4.14 Structure data type.

And, the XML instance of the `ShippingAddress` data type is shown in Listing 4.15.

```
<e:ShippingAddress>
 <Street>1 Network Drive</Street>
 <City>Burlington</City>
 <State>MA</State>
 <Zip>01803</Zip>
 <Country>USA</Country>
</e:ShippingAddress>
```

Listing 4.15 Resulting XML instance of a structure data type.

The structure also can contain both simple and complex data type values that can reference each other (see Listing 4.16). The structure uses the "href" attribute to reference the value of the matching element.

```
<e:Product>
 <product>Sun Blade 1000</product>
 <type>Hardware</type>
 <address href="#Shipping"/>
 <address href="#Payment"/>
<e:/Product>
<e:Address id="Shipping">
 <Street>1 Network Drive</Street>
 <City>Burlington</City>
 <State>MA</State>
 <Zip>01803</Zip>
 <Country>USA</Country>
</e:Address>
<e:Address id="Payment">
 <Street>5 Sunnyvale Drive</Street>
 <City>Menlopark</City>
 <State>CA</State>
 <Zip>21803</Zip>
 <Country>USA</Country>
</e:Address>
```

Listing 4.16 Structure data type using simple and complex types.

Array Types

Listing 4.17 is an XML Schema of an `Array` data type representing `MyPortfolio` — a list of portfolio stock symbols.

```
<xs:schema xmlns:xs="http://www.w3.org/2001/XMLSchema"
   xmlns:enc="http://schemas.xmlsoap.org/soap/encoding" >
<xs:import
   namespace="http://schemas.xmlsoap.org/soap/encoding" >
<xs:element name="MyPortfolio" type="enc:Array"/>
</xs:schema>
```

Listing 4.17 Compound array types.

The XML instance of the `MyPortfolio` data type is shown in Listing 4.18.

```
<MyPortfolio xmlns:xs="http://www.w3.org/2001/XMLSchema"
          xmlns:enc=" http://schemas.xmlsoap.org/soap/encoding"
          enc:arrayType="xs:string[5]">
 <symbol>SUNW</symbol>
 <symbol>IBM</symbol>
 <symbol>HP</symbol>
 <symbol>RHAT</symbol>
 <symbol>ORCL</symbol>
</MyPortfolio>
```

Listing 4.18 Resulting XML instance of a compound array type.

Multiple References in Arrays

SOAP encoding also enables arrays to have other arrays as member values. This is accomplished by having the `id` and `href` attributes to reference the values. Listing 4.19 shows an example of an XML instance that has arrays as member values.

```
 <MyProducts xmlns:xs="http://www.w3.org/2001/XMLSchema"
          xmlns:enc="
          http://schemas.xmlsoap.org/soap/encoding"
          enc:arrayType="xs:string[][3]">
 <item href="#product-hw"/>
 <item href="#product-sw"/>
 <item href="#product-sv"/>
<SOAP-ENC:Array id="product-hw"
                    SOAP-ENC:arrayType="xsd:string[3]">
 <item>SUN Blade 1000</item>
 <item>SUN Ultra 100</item>
 <item>SUN Enterprise 15000</item>
  </SOAP-ENC:Array>
   <SOAP-ENC:Array id="product-sw"
                    SOAP-ENC:arrayType="xsd:string[2]">
 <item>Sun Java VM</item>
 <item>Sun Solaris OS</item>
 </SOAP-ENC:Array>
   <SOAP-ENC:Array id="product-sv"
```

Listing 4.19 Multiple references in arrays.

```
                    SOAP-ENC:arrayType="xsd:string[2]">
 <item>Sun Java Center services</item>
<item>Sun Java Web Services</item>
 </SOAP-ENC:Array>
```

Listing 4.19 Multiple references in arrays. *(continued)*

Partially Transmitted Arrays

Partially transmitted arrays are defined using a `SOAP-ENC:offset`, which enables the offset position to be indicated from the first element (counted as zero-origin), which is used as an offset of all the elements that will be transmitted. Listing 4.20 is an array of size [6]; using `SOAP-ENC:offset="4"` transmits the fifth and sixth elements of a given array of numbers (0,1,2,3,4,5).

```
<SOAP-ENC:Array SOAP-ENC:arrayType="xsd:string[6]"
                                SOAP-ENC:offset="[2]">
    <item> No: 2</item>
    <item> No: 3</item>
    <item> No: 4</item>
    <item> No: 5</item>
 </SOAP-ENC:Array>
```

Listing 4.20 Partially transmitted arrays.

Sparse Arrays

Sparse arrays are defined using a `SOAP-ENC:position`, which enables the position of an attribute to be indicated with an array and returns its value instead of listing every entry in the array. Listing 4.21 shows an example of using a sparse array in an array.

```
<SOAP-ENC:Array SOAP-ENC:arrayType="xsd:int[10]">
   <SOAP-ENC:int SOAP-ENC:position="[0]">0</SOAP-ENC:int>
   <SOAP-ENC:int SOAP-ENC:position="[10]">9</SOAP-ENC:int>
</SOAP-ENC:Array>
```

Listing 4.21 Sparse arrays.

This summarizes the SOAP encoding defined in the SOAP 1.1 specification. Now, let's take a look at how to handle the custom encoding requirements specific to applications.

Serialization and Deserialization

In SOAP messages, all data and application-specific data types are represented as XML, and it is quite important to note that there is no generic mechanism to serialize application-specific data types to XML. SOAP implementation provides application-specific encoding for application programming languages (such as Java and C++). It also enables developers to define custom application-specific encoding, especially to handle the data representation required and its data types adopting data types defined by the "W3C XML Schema, Part -2" specification (see www.w3.org/TR/xmlschema-2/). This is usually implemented as application- or programming language-specific serialization and deserialization mechanisms that represent application-specific data as XML and XML as application-specific data.

Most SOAP implementations provide their own serialization and deserialization mechanisms and a predefined XML Schema supporting the SOAP encoding rules and mapping application-specific data types. These serializers and deserializers supporting SOAP encoding rules provide the encoding and decoding of data on runtime by mapping XML elements to target application objects and vice versa. It leverages interoperability between disparate applications using SOAP messages.

We will study the serializers and deserializers of a SOAP implementation in the example illustration using Apache Axis discussed in the section titled *Axis Infrastructure and Components*. So far we discussed the structure of a SOAP message and the representation of its data types. Now, let's take a look at how to exchange SOAP messages using SOAP communication.

SOAP Message Exchange Model

Basically, SOAP is a stateless protocol by nature and provides a composable one-way messaging framework for transferring XML between SOAP applications which are referred to as SOAP nodes. These SOAP nodes represent the logical entities of a SOAP message path to perform message routing or processing. In a SOAP message, SOAP nodes are usually represented with an endpoint URI as the next destination in the message. In a SOAP message, a SOAP node can be any of the following:

SOAP sender. The one who generates and sends the message.

SOAP receiver. The one who ultimately receives and processes the message with a SOAP response, message, or fault.

SOAP intermediary. The one who can play the role of a SOAP sender or SOAP receiver. In a SOAP message exchange model, there can be zero or more SOAP intermediaries between the SOAP sender and receiver to provide a distributed processing mechanism for SOAP messages.

Figure 4.2 represents a basic SOAP message exchange model with different SOAP nodes.

In a SOAP message exchange model, the SOAP message passes from the initiator to the final destination by passing through zero to many intermediaries. In a SOAP messaging path, the SOAP intermediaries represent certain functionalities and provide routing to the next message destination. It is important to note that SOAP does not define the actual SOAP senders, intermediaries, and receivers of the SOAP message along its message path or its order of destination. However, SOAP can indicate which part of the message is meant for processing at a SOAP node. Thus, it defines a decentralized message-exchanging model that enables a distributed processing in the message route with a message chain.

Figure 4.3 represents an example of a complete message exchange model with a sender, receiver, and its intermediaries. In the previous example, the message originates from Sender A to Receiver D via Intermediaries B and C as a request chain, and then as a response chain the message originates from Receiver D to Sender A via Intermediary E.

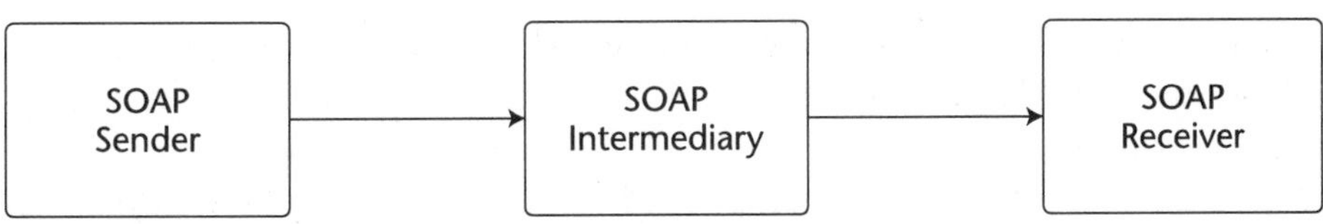

Figure 4.2 Basic SOAP message exchange model.

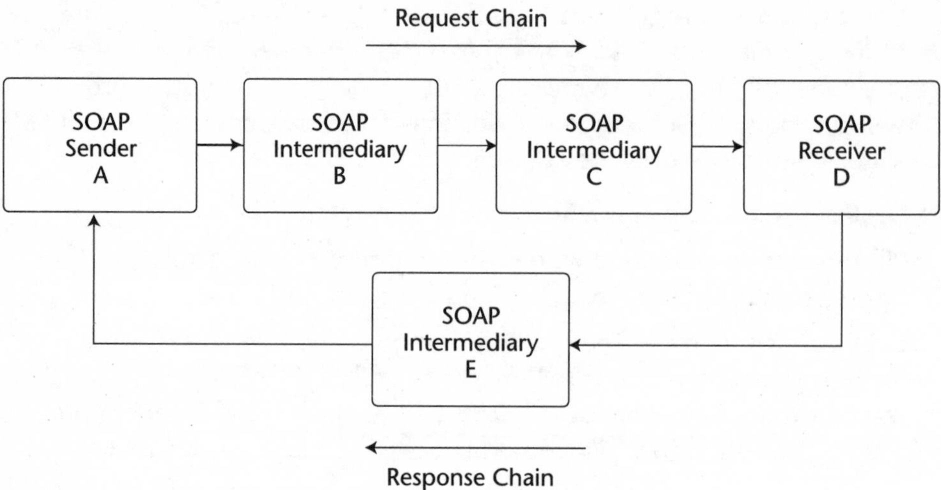

Figure 4.3 SOAP message exchange model with intermediaries.

SOAP Intermediaries

SOAP defines intermediaries as nodes for providing message processing and protocol routing characteristics between sending and receiving applications. Intermediary nodes reside in between the sending and receiving nodes and process parts of the message defined in the SOAP header. The two types of intermediaries are as follows:

Forwarding intermediaries. This type processes the message by describing and constructing the semantics and rules in the SOAP header blocks of the forwarded message.

Active intermediaries. This type handles additional processing by modifying the outbound message for the potential recipient SOAP nodes with a set of functionalities.

In general, SOAP intermediaries enable a distributed processing model to exist within the SOAP message exchange model. By using SOAP intermediaries, features can be incorporated like store and forward, intelligent routing, transactions, security, and logging, as well as other value additions to SOAP applications.

SOAP Actor

In a SOAP message to represent a target SOAP node, the SOAP `actor` global attribute with a URI value can be used in the `Header` element. SOAP defines an `actor` with a URI value, which identifies the name of the SOAP receiver node as an ultimate destination. Listing 4.22 is an example of a SOAP `actor` attribute.

```
<SOAP-ENV:Envelope xmlns:SOAP-
ENV="http://schemas.xml.org/soap/envelope/"
    SOAP-ENV:encodingStyle="http://schemas.xml.org/soap/encoding/"/>
<SOAP-ENV:Header>
<b:Name xmlns:t="http://www.wiley.com/BookService/"
         SOAP-ENV:actor="http://www.wiley.com/jws/"
         SOAP-ENV :mustUnderstand="1">
          WebServices</b:Name >
</SOAP-ENV:Header>
<SOAP:Body> <m:NewBook xmlns:m="http://www.wiley.com/Books">
<BookName>Developing Java Web services</BookName>
</m:NewBook>
</SOAP:Body>
</SOAP:Envelope>
```

Listing 4.22 SOAP `actor` attribute.

Additionally, SOAP defines the `actor` with a special URI http://schemas.xmlsoap.org/soap/actor/next, which indicates a hop-by-hop communication using the header element where the SOAP message is routed via one to many intermediaries before its final destination. Listing 4.23 is an example of a SOAP message that is forwarded via two SOAP intermediaries before the final receiving node.

```
<SOAP-ENV:Header>
      <zz:path xmlns:zz="http://schemas.xmlsoap.org/rp/"
         SOAP-ENV:actor="http://schemas.xmlsoap.org/soap/actor/next"
         SOAP-ENV:mustUnderstand="1">
      <zz:action></zz:action>
```

Listing 4.23 SOAP message forwarded via SOAP intermediaries. *(continues)*

```
      <zz:to>http://www.wiley.com/soap/servlet/rpcrouter</zz:to>
      <zz:fwd>
       <zz:via>http://javabooks.congo.com/std/multihop/</zz:via>
       <zz:via>http://linux.wiley.com/javawebservices/</zz:via>
      </zz:fwd>
      </zz:path>
   </SOAP-ENV:Header>
```

Listing 4.23 SOAP message forwarded via SOAP intermediaries. *(continued)*

So far, we have looked at the SOAP message exchange model and the different roles involved in a SOAP message path. Now, let's take a look at the SOAP communication and the supported message flow patterns.

SOAP Communication

SOAP is designed to communicate between applications independent of the underlying platforms and programming languages. To enable communication between SOAP nodes, SOAP supports the following two types of communication models:

SOAP RPC. It defines a remote procedural call-based synchronous communication where the SOAP nodes send and receive messages using request and response methods and exchange parameters and then return the values.

SOAP Messaging. It defines a document-driven communication where SOAP nodes send and receive XML-based documents using synchronous and asynchronous messaging.

Now, let's explore the details of both the communication model and how it is represented in the SOAP messages.

SOAP RPC

The SOAP RPC representation defines a tightly coupled communication model based on requests and responses. Using RPC conventions, the SOAP message is represented by method names with zero or more parameters and return values. Each SOAP request message represents a call method to a remote object in a SOAP server and each method call will have zero or more parameters. Similarly, the SOAP response message will return the results as return values with zero or more out parameters. In both

SOAP RPC requests and responses, the method calls are serialized into XML-based data types defined by the SOAP encoding rules.

Listing 4.24 is an example of a SOAP RPC request making a method call `GetBookPrice` for obtaining a book price from a SOAP server namespace `http://www.wiley.com/jws.book.priceList` using a `"book-name"` parameter of `"Developing Java Web Services"`.

```
<SOAP-ENV:Envelope
   xmlns:SOAP-ENV="http://schemas.xmlsoap.org/soap/envelope/"
    xmlns:xsi="http://www.w3c.org/2001/XMLSchema-instance"
     xmlns:xsd="http://www.w3c.org/2001/XMLSchema"
     SOAP-ENV:encodingStyle
             ="http://schemas.xmlsoap.org/soap/encoding/">
   <SOAP-ENV:Header>
   </SOAP-ENV:Header>
   <SOAP-ENV:Body>
          <m:GetBookPrice
             xmlns:m="http://www.wiley.com/jws.book.priceList">
          <bookname xsi:type='xsd:string'>
                        Developing Java Web services</bookname>
           </m:GetBookPrice>
       </SOAP-ENV:Body>
</SOAP-ENV: Envelope>
```

Listing 4.24 SOAP request using RPC-based communication.

The SOAP message in Listing 4.25 represents the SOAP RPC response after processing the SOAP request, which returns the result of the `GetBookPrice` method from the SOAP server namespace `http://www.wiley.com/jws.book.priceList` using a `"Price"` parameter with `"$50"` as its value.

```
<SOAP-ENV:Envelope
     xmlns:SOAP-ENV=http://schemas.xmlsoap.org/soap/envelope/
     xmlns:xsi="http://www.w3c.org/2001/XMLSchema-instance"
     xmlns:xsd="http://www.w3c.org/2001/XMLSchema"
     SOAP-ENV:encodingStyle
             ="http://schemas.xmlsoap.org/soap/encoding/"/>
     <SOAP-ENV:Body>
          <m:GetBookPriceResponse xmlns:m="
                http://www.wiley.com/jws.book.priceList">
             <Price>50.00</Price>
```

Listing 4.25 SOAP response message using RPC-based communication. *(continues)*

```
        </m:GetBookPriceResponse>
</SOAP-ENV:Body>
</SOAP-ENV:Envelope>
```

Listing 4.25 SOAP response message using RPC-based communication. *(continued)*

The communication model in Listing 4.25 is similar to a traditional CORBA- or RMI-based communication model, except the serialized data types are represented by XML and derived from SOAP encoding rules.

SOAP Messaging

SOAP Messaging represents a loosely coupled communication model based on message notification and the exchange of XML documents. The SOAP message body is represented by XML documents or literals encoded according to a specific W3C XML schema, and it is produced and consumed by sending or receiving SOAP node(s). The SOAP sender node sends a message with an XML document as its body message and the SOAP receiver node processes it.

Listing 4.26 represents a SOAP message and a SOAP messaging-based communication. The message contains a header block `InventoryNotice` and the body `product`, both of which are application-defined and not defined by SOAP. The header contains information required by the receiver node and the body contains the actual message to be delivered.

```
<env:Envelope xmlns:env="http://www.w3.org/2001/12/soap-envelope">
 <env:Header>
  <n:InventoryNotice xmlns:n="http://jws.wiley.com/Inventory">
   <n:productcode>J6876896896</n:productcode>
  </n: InventoryNotice>
 </env:Header>
 <env:Body>
  <m:product xmlns:m="http://jws.wiley.com/product">
   <m:name>Developing Java Web Services</m:name>
   <m:quantity>25000</n:quantity>
   <m:date>2002-07-01T14:00:00-05:00</n:date>
  </m:product>
 </env:Body>
</env:Envelope>
```

Listing 4.26 SOAP message using messaging-based communication.

So far, we have looked at SOAP messages, conventions, encoding rules, and its communication model. Now, let's take a look at its bindings to the transport protocols required for its messaging environment.

SOAP Bindings for Transport Protocols

In the last section, we looked at SOAP communication and how the SOAP messages are represented using RPC- and messaging-based communication approaches. But, interestingly, the SOAP specifications do not specify and mandate any underlying protocol for its communication as it chooses to bind with a variety of transport protocols between the SOAP nodes. According to the SOAP specifications for binding the framework, the SOAP bindings define the requirements for sending and receiving messages using a transport protocol between the SOAP nodes. These bindings also define the syntactic and semantic rules for processing the incoming/outgoing SOAP messages and a supporting set of message exchanging patterns. This enables SOAP to be used in a variety of applications and on OS platforms using a variety of protocols.

Although SOAP can potentially be used over a variety of transport protocols, initially the SOAP 1.0 specification mandated the use of HTTP as its transport protocol; the later specifications opened their support for other Internet-based protocols like SMTP and FTP. Lately, major SOAP vendors have made their implementations available using popular transport protocol bindings like POP3, BEEP, JMS, Custom Message-Oriented-Middleware, and proprietary protocols using TCP/IP sockets. SOAP uses these protocol bindings as a mechanism for carrying the URI of the SOAP nodes. Typically in an HTTP request, the URI indicates the endpoint of the SOAP resource where the invocation is being made.

Now, let's explore the SOAP bindings for HTTP and SMTP and understand how the SOAP messages are represented in these transport protocols during communication.

SOAP over HTTP

The use of HTTP as a transport protocol for SOAP communication becomes a natural fit for SOAP/RPC. This enables a decentralized SOAP environment to exist by using the HTTP request/response-based communication over the Internet or an intranet by sending SOAP request parameters in an HTTP request and receiving SOAP response parameters in an HTTP response. Using SOAP over HTTP does not require overriding any existing syntactic and semantic rules of HTTP, but it maps the syntax and semantics of HTTP.

By adopting SOAP over HTTP, SOAP messages can be sent through the default HTTP port 80 without requiring and opening other firewall ports. The only constraint while using SOAP over HTTP is the requirement to use the special header tag for defining the MIME type as `Content-Type: text/xml`.

Example of an HTTP-Based SOAP Request

Listing 4.27 is an example of an HTTP-based SOAP request for obtaining the book price from http://jws.wiley.com/GetBookPrice using `bookname` as its parameter.

```
POST /GetBookPrice HTTP/1.1
User Agent: Mozilla/4.0 (Linux)
Host: nramesh:8080
Content-Type: text/xml; charset="utf-8"
Content-length: 546
SOAPAction: "/GetBookPrice"

<?xml version="1.0"?>

   <SOAP-ENV:Envelope
     SOAP-ENV:encodingStyle=
              "http://schemas.xmlsoap.org/soap/encoding/"
       xmlns:SOAP-ENC="http://schemas.xmlsoap.org/soap/encoding/"
       xmlns:SOAP-ENV="http://schemas.xmlsoap.org/soap/envelope/"
       xmlns:xsd="http://www.w3.org/2001/XMLSchema"
       xmlns:xsi="http://www.w3.org/2001/XMLSchema-instance">
     <SOAP-ENV:Body>
        <m:getBookPrice xmlns:m="http://jws.wiley.com/">
            <bookname xsi:type="xsd:string">
                      Developing Java Web Services</bookname>
        </m:getBookPrice>
     </SOAP-ENV:Body>
   </SOAP-ENV:Envelope>
```

Listing 4.27 SOAP request message using HTTP.

Example of an HTTP-Based SOAP Response

Listing 4.28 is an example of an HTTP-based SOAP response returning the results as the book price from http://jws.wiley.com/GetBookPrice.

```
HTTP/1.1 200 OK
Connection: close
Content-Length: 524
Content-Type: text/xml; charset="utf-8"
Date: Fri, 3 May 2002 05:05:04 GMT
Server: Apache/1.3.0

<?xml version="1.0"?>
<SOAP-ENV:Envelope
     SOAP-ENV:encodingStyle="
          http://schemas.xmlsoap.org/soap/encoding/"
     xmlns:SOAP-ENC="http://schemas.xmlsoap.org/soap/encoding/"
     xmlns:SOAP-ENV="http://schemas.xmlsoap.org/soap/envelope/"
     xmlns:xsd="http://www.w3.org/2001/XMLSchema"
     xmlns:xsi="http://www.w3.org/2001/XMLSchema-instance">
     <SOAP-ENV:Body>
        <m:getBookPriceResponse
         xmlns:m="http://jws.wiley.com/GetBookPrice">
         <Result xsi:type="xsd:string">USD 50.00</Result>
        </m:getBookPriceResponse>
     </SOAP-ENV:Body>
</SOAP-ENV:Envelope>
```

Listing 4.28 SOAP response message using HTTP.

In case of errors while processing the SOAP request, the SOAP application will send a response message with `HTTP 500 "Internal Server Error"` and include a `SOAP Fault` indicating the SOAP processing error.

The SOAP 1.1 specifications define the usage of HTTP as its primary transport protocol for communication. SOAP 1.1 specifications also define the usage of the HTTP extension framework—an extension of the HTTP protocol for adding message extensions, encoding, HTTP-derived protocols, and so on.

Using a SOAP/HTTP Extension Framework

How the HTTP extension framework is used as a transport binding depends upon the SOAP communication requirements defined by the SOAP nodes. It is similar to HTTP with additional mandatory declarations in the header using an "M-" prefix for all HTTP methods (that is, M-GET, M-POST, and so forth).

Listing 4.29 is a sample header using an HTTP extension framework-based SOAP request.

```
M-POST /GetBookPrice HTTP/1.1
Man: "http://schemas.xmlsoap.org/soap/envelope/";
Content-Type: text/xml; charset="utf-8"
Content-Length: xxxx
SOAPAction: "http://jws.wiley.com/BookPrice#WebServices"

<SOAP-ENV:Envelope>
</SOAP-ENV:Envelope>
```

Listing 4.29 SOAP request message using an HTTP extension framework.

Listing 4.30 shows the response header using the HTTP extension framework.

```
HTTP/1.1 200 OK
Ext:
Content-Type: text/xml; charset="utf-8"
Content-Length: xxxx

<SOAP-ENV:Envelope>
</SOAP-ENV:Envelope>
```

Listing 4.30 SOAP response message using an HTTP extension framework.

In case of errors, the servers force a response message. If the extension declarations do not match the resource, then it responds with a 510 (Not Extended) HTTP status-code. If one or more mandatory extension declarations are present and other following declarations are not true, then it responds with a 505 (HTTP Version Not Supported) HTTP status-code.

SOAP over SMTP

The use of SOAP over the Simple Mail Transport Protocol (SMTP) permits SOAP messages to be enabled with asynchronous communication and supports one-way notifications and document-driven messaging requirements.

It also helps SOAP messaging where request/response messaging is not a good fit and also where HTTP semantics do not apply naturally.

The SOAP 1.1 specifications define the usage of SMTP as a protocol binding for SOAP applications, especially where the HTTP-based request/response is not possible and where document-driven messaging is applicable. In case SOAP over SMTP is used to perform request/response scenarios, it is handled using message correlation techniques by providing unique Message-Id and Reply-To headers. This means that the SOAP message will send the request with a Message-Id in the header and the response SOAP message will contain an In-Reply-To header containing the originator's Message-Id.

Listing 4.31 shows an example of a SOAP request message using SOAP over SMTP for obtaining the status information of a purchase order.

```
To: <webservices@wiley.com>
From: <nramesh@post.harvard.edu>
Reply-To: <nramesh@post.harvard.edu>
Date: Tue, 03 May 2002 02:21:00 -0200
Message-Id: <1E23B5F132D3EF3C44BCB54532167C5@post.harvard.edu>
MIME-Version: 1.0
Content-Type: text/xml; charset=utf-8
Content-Transfer-Encoding: QUOTED-PRINTABLE

<?xml version="1.0" encoding="UTF-8"?>
<SOAP-ENV:Envelope
SOAP-ENV:encodingStyle=
     "http://schemas.xmlsoap.org/soap/encoding/"
     xmlns:SOAP-ENC="http://schemas.xmlsoap.org/soap/encoding/"
     xmlns:SOAP-ENV="http://schemas.xmlsoap.org/soap/envelope/"
     xmlns:xsd="http://www.w3.org/2001/XMLSchema"
     xmlns:xsi="http://www.w3.org/2001/XMLSchema-instance">
  <SOAP-ENV:Body>
    <m:getStatusInfo xmlns:m="http://jws.wiley.com/">
      <PurchaseOrderNo>JWS739794-04</PurchaseOrderNo>
    </m:getStatusInfo>
  </SOAP-ENV:Body>
</SOAP-ENV:Envelope>
```

Listing 4.31 SOAP request message using SMTP.

The response message returning the results will be as shown in Listing 4.32.

Most SOAP implementations providing the SOAP messaging-based communication model use SMTP to transport SOAP documents between the SOAP nodes.

```
To: <nramesh@post.harvard.edu>
From: <webservices@wiley.com>
Date: Tue, 03 May 2002 02:31:00 -0210
In-Reply-To: <1E23B5F132D3EF3C44BCB54532167C5@post.harvard.edu>
Message-Id: <1E23B5F132D3EF3C44BCB54532167C5@wiley.com>
MIME-Version: 1.0
Content-Type: TEXT/XML; charset=utf-8
Content-Transfer-Encoding: QUOTED-PRINTABLE

<?xml version="1.0" encoding="UTF-8"?>
<SOAP-ENV:Envelope
   SOAP-ENV:encodingStyle=
              "http://schemas.xmlsoap.org/soap/encoding/"
    xmlns:SOAP-ENC="http://schemas.xmlsoap.org/soap/encoding/"
    xmlns:SOAP-ENV="http://schemas.xmlsoap.org/soap/envelope/"
    xmlns:xsd="http://www.w3.org/2001/XMLSchema"
    xmlns:xsi="http://www.w3.org/2001/XMLSchema-instance">
  <SOAP-ENV:Body>
     <m:getStatusResponse xmlns:m="http://jws.wiley.com/">
        <status>Product Shipment scheduled - Fedex ID
                  866689689689</status>
     </m:getStatusResponse>
  </SOAP-ENV:Body>
</SOAP-ENV:Envelope>
```

Listing 4.32 SOAP response message using SMTP.

Note that SMTP may not provide guaranteed message delivery in cases of limitations of message size of the receiving SOAP nodes. Therefore, the SOAP sender nodes may require using custom-delivery receipts and reading the receipts for the email messages they send. The SOAP application developers can use the Internet email messaging servers as the provider to send SOAP messages as email text or attachments. And, it becomes the application developer's responsibility to parse through the email contents and to process the contents of the messages. Some common problems are the result of partial email messages and missing attachments.

Other SOAP Bindings

As already noted, SOAP does not mandate any protocol-specific requirements and it can be used with any transport protocols. Using it has a distinct advantage for enabling application integration, interapplication communication, and interoperability. Lately, SOAP application vendors have released their implementations providing support for the SOAP bindings, especially for the most popular industry standard protocols such as HTTP/S, JMS, and BEEP.

Now, let's take a brief look at those popular SOAP bindings for industry protocols and their features.

SOAP over HTTP/SSL

In addition to using SOAP over HTTP, the SOAP messages can take advantage of using Secure Socket Layer (SSL) for security and other HTTP-based protocol features. SSL enables encrypted data to be securely transmitted between the HTTP client and the server with the use of encryption algorithms. Using SSL with SOAP messages enables the encryption of messages with greater security and confidentiality between the SOAP nodes. It also is possible to add MAC (Media access control) addresses of network card interfaces in the transmitted messages.

Using HTTP/SSL requires certificates on both the sending and receiving SOAP nodes. As SOAP does not define security or reliability mechanisms as part of its messages, most SOAP implementations use HTTP/SSL as its transport protocol for secure communication.

SOAP over JMS

To enable SOAP messages to communicate with J2EE-based components and messaging applications, most SOAP vendors provide SOAP messaging over JMS (Java Messaging Service) with JMS-compliant MOM providers such as Sun One MQ, Sonic MQ, Websphere MQSeries, and so on. This allows SOAP-based asynchronous messaging and enables the SOAP messages to achieve reliability and guaranteed message delivery using a JMS provider.

In this case, the JMS destination queues are represented in the SOAP messages as target destinations. The SOAP nodes use the JMS queue for sending and receiving SOAP requests and SOAP responses. The JMS provider then would implement methods to handle the SOAP message as a payload.

SOAP over BEEP

Blocks Extensible Exchange Protocol (BEEP) defines a generic application transport protocol framework for connection-oriented, asynchronous messaging that enables peer-to-peer, client-server, or server-to-server messaging.

SOAP over BEEP enables the use of BEEP as a protocol framework that enables SOAP developers to focus on the aspects of the SOAP applications instead of finding a way to establish communication. This means that BEEP takes care of the communication protocol. BEEP, as a protocol, governs the connections, authentication, and sending and receiving of messages at the level of TCP/IP. At the time of this book's writing, the SOAP over BEEP specification is available as an IETF (Internet Engineering Task Force) working draft that can be obtained from http://beepcore.org/beepcore/beep-soap.jsp.

So far, we have looked at SOAP communication and protocols. Let's now take a look at the different messaging patterns supported by them.

SOAP Message Exchange Patterns

Based on the underlying transport protocol, to enhance the communication and message path model between the SOAP nodes, SOAP chooses an interaction pattern depending upon the communication model. Although it depends upon SOAP implementation, SOAP messages may support the following messaging exchange patterns to define the message path and transmission of messages between SOAP nodes, including intermediaries. It is important to note that these patterns are introduced as part of SOAP 1.2 specifications.

The most common SOAP messaging patterns are as follows:

One-way message. In this pattern, the SOAP client application sends SOAP messages to its SOAP server without any response being returned (see Figure 4.4). It is typically found in email messages.

Request/response exchange. In this pattern, the SOAP client sends a request message that results in a response message from the SOAP server to the client (see Figure 4.5).

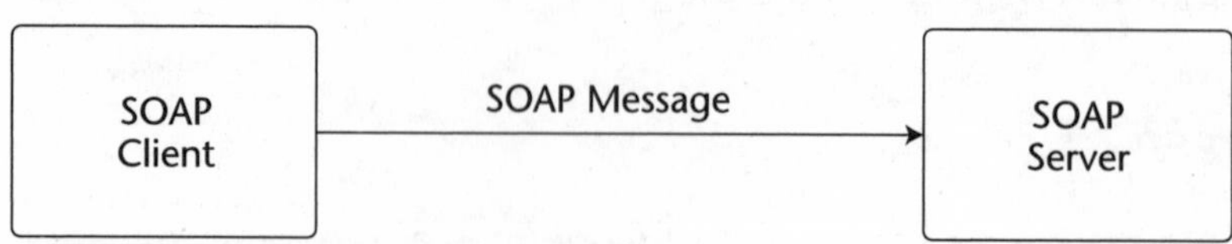

Figure 4.4 One-way message pattern.

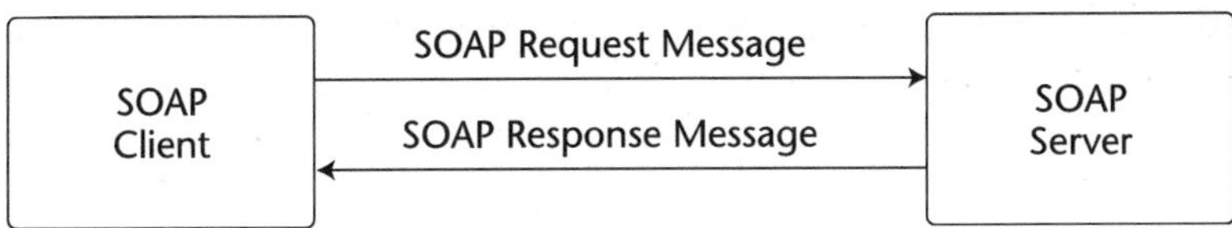

Figure 4.5 Request/Response pattern.

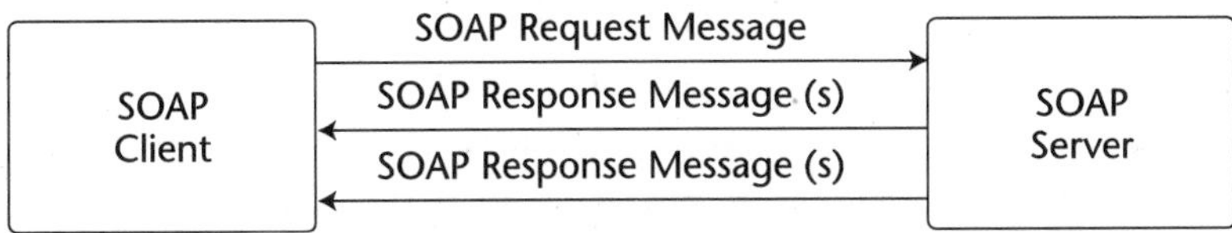

Figure 4.6 Request/N*Response pattern.

Request/N*Response pattern. It is similar to a request/response pattern, except the SOAP client sends a request that results in zero to many response messages from the SOAP server to the client (see Figure 4.6).

Notification pattern. In this pattern, the SOAP server sends messages to the SOAP client like an event notification, without regard to a response (see Figure 4.7).

Solicit-response pattern. In this pattern, the SOAP server sends a request message to the SOAP client like a status checking or an audit and the client sends out a response message (see Figure 4.8).

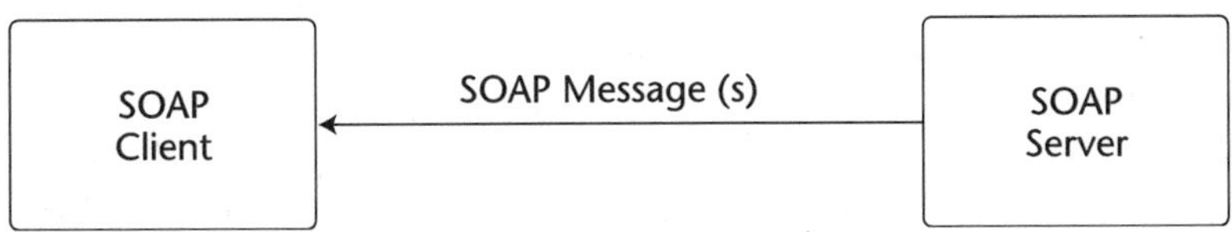

Figure 4.7 Notification pattern.

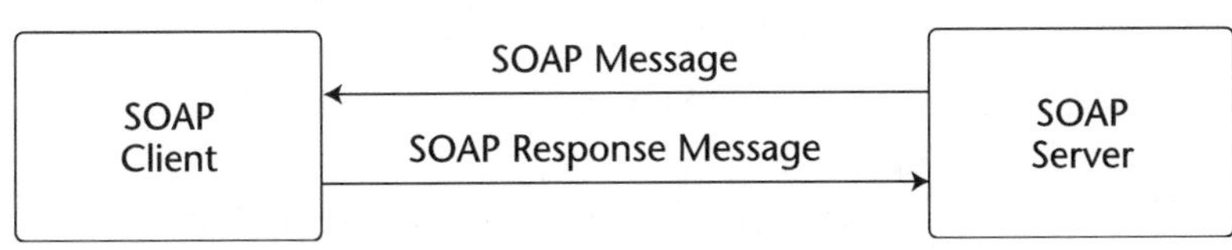

Figure 4.8 Solicit-response pattern.

Note that the previous patterns can be implemented based on the transport protocols and their supporting communication models.

SOAP Security

Security in SOAP messages plays a vital role in access control, encryption, and data integrity during communication. In general, SOAP messages do not carry or define any specific security mechanisms. However, using the SOAP headers provides a way to define and add features enabling the implementation of application-specific security in a form of XML-based metadata. The metadata information can be application-specific information incorporating message security with associated security algorithms like encryption and digital signatures. More importantly, SOAP supports various transport protocols for communication, thus it also is possible to incorporate transport protocol-supported security mechanisms like SSL/TLS for SOAP messages.

The first release of SOAP specifications (SOAP 1.0) did not specify any security-related mechanisms; the following versions of W3C SOAP 1.1 draft specifications were considering enabling security by providing support for implementation of the XML-based security features. At the time of this book's writing, the W3C SOAP Security Extensions specifications were available as a Note to define encryption, authorization, and digital signatures in SOAP messages. But all of the security-related elements are identified using a single namespace identifier using the prefix `SOAP-SEC` and with an associated URI using http://schemas.xmlsoap.org/soap/security/. It also defines the three security element tags `<SOAP-SEC:Encryption>`, `<SOAP-SEC:Signature>`, and `<SOAP-SEC:Authorization>`. Use of these security tags enables the incorporation of encryption, digital signatures, and authorization in SOAP messages.

The following section takes a look at how to represent these security tags in a SOAP message.

SOAP Encryption

The use of XML-based encryption in SOAP permits secure communication and access control to be implemented by encrypting any element in the SOAP envelope. The W3C XML Encryption WG (XENC) defines the mechanisms of XML encryption in the SOAP messages. In SOAP communication, encryption can be done at the SOAP sender node or at any of the intermediaries in the message path.

Listing 4.33 is a sample representation of a SOAP message using XML encryption for encrypting its data elements.

```
<SOAP-ENV:Envelope
    xmlns:SOAP-ENV="http://schemas.xmlsoap.org/soap/envelope/">
   <SOAP-ENV:Header>
   <SOAP-SEC:Encryption
     xmlns:SOAP-SEC="http://schemas.xmlsoap.org/soap/security/"
       SOAP-ENV:actor="some-URI"
       SOAP-ENV:mustUnderstand="1">
       <SOAP-SEC:EncryptedData>
         <SOAP-SEC:EncryptedDataReference URI="#encrypted-
                                                  element"/>
       </SOAP-SEC:EncryptedData>
       <xenc:EncryptedKey xmlns:xenc=
                        "http://www.w3.org/2001/04/xmlenc#"
               Id="myKey"
               CarriedKeyName="Symmetric Key"
               Recipient="Bill Allen">
       <xenc:EncryptionMethod
       Algorithm="http://www.w3.org/2001/04/xmlenc#rsa-1_5"/>
       <ds:KeyInfo xmlns:ds=
                       "http://www.w3.org/2000/09/xmldsig#">
          <ds:KeyName>Bill Allen's RSA Key</ds:KeyName>
       </ds:KeyInfo>
       <xenc:CipherData>
           <xenc:CipherValue>ENCRYPTED KEY</xenc:CipherValue>
       </xenc:CipherData>
       <xenc:ReferenceList>
           <xenc:DataReference URI="#encrypted-element"/>
       </xenc:ReferenceList>
       </xenc:EncryptedKey>
     </SOAP-SEC:Encryption>
   </SOAP-ENV:Header>
   <SOAP-ENV:Body>
.. </SOAP-ENV:Body>
</SOAP-ENV:Envelope>
```

Listing 4.33 SOAP message using XML encryption.

Listing 4.33 illustrates a SOAP message with a `<SOAP-SEC:Encryption>` header entry to encrypt data referred to in the SOAP header. It uses a symmetric key for encrypting the body element referred to in the `<xenc:EncryptedData>` element. The `<xenc:EncryptedData>` element in the header entry provides the reference to the `<xenc:EncryptedData>` element and the symmetric key is defined in the

<xenc:EncryptedKey> element. On the SOAP receiver node, the receiver decrypts each encrypted element by associating a DecryptionInfoURI, which indicates <xenc:DecryptionInfo> for providing information on how to decrypt it. To find out more information on the syntax and processing rules of representing XML-based encryption, refer to www.w3.org/TR/xmlenc-core/.

SOAP Digital Signature

The use of an XML-based digital signature in SOAP messages provides message authentication, integrity, and non-repudiation of data during communication. The SOAP sender node that originates the message applies an XML-based digital signature to the SOAP body and the receiver node validates the signature.

Listing 4.34 is a sample representation of a SOAP message using XML digital signatures.

```
<SOAP-ENV:Envelope
  xmlns:SOAP-ENV="http://schemas.xmlsoap.org/soap/envelope/">
  <SOAP-ENV:Header>
    <SOAP-SEC:Signature
      xmlns:SOAP-SEC="http://schemas.xmlsoap.org/soap/security/"
      SOAP-ENV:actor="Some-URI"
      SOAP-ENV:mustUnderstand="1">
      <ds:Signature Id="TestSignature"
           xmlns:ds="http://www.w3.org/2000/02/xmldsig#">
        <ds:SignedInfo>
          <ds:CanonicalizationMethod
            Algorithm="http://www.w3.org/TR/2000/CR-xml-c14n-
                                                  20001026">
          </ds:CanonicalizationMethod>
          <ds:SignatureMethod
           Algorithm="http://www.w3.org/2000/09/xmldsig#hmac-sha1"/>
           <ds:Reference URI="#Body">
            <ds:Transforms>
              <ds:Transform Algorithm
                  ="http://www.w3.org/TR/2000/CR-xml-c14n-20001026"/>
            </ds:Transforms>
            <ds:DigestMethod Algorithm
                    ="http://www.w3.org/2000/09/xmldsig#sha1"/>
              <ds:DigestValue>vAKDSiy987rplkju8ds:DigestValue>
              </ds:Reference>
        </ds:SignedInfo>
      <ds:SignatureValue>JHJH2374e<ds:SignatureValue>
    </ds:Signature>
    </SOAP-SEC:Signature>
```

Listing 4.34 SOAP message using XML digital signatures.

```
  </SOAP-ENV:Header>
  <SOAP-ENV:Body>
..
  </SOAP-ENV:Body>
</SOAP-ENV:Envelope>
```

Listing 4.34 SOAP message using XML digital signatures. *(continued)*

Listing 4.34 illustrates a SOAP message with a <SOAP-SEC: Signature> entry applying an XML-based digital signature for signing data included in the SOAP envelope. It uses `<ds:CanonicalizationMethod>`, `<ds:SignatureMethod>`, and `<ds:Reference>` elements for defining the algorithm methods and signing information. The `<ds:CanonicalizationMethod>` refers to the algorithm for canonicalizing the `SignedInfo` element digested before the signature. The `SignatureMethod` defines the algorithm for converting the canonicalized `SignedInfo` as a `SignatureValue`. To find more information on the syntax and processing rules of representing XML-based digital signatures, refer to www.w3.org/TR/xmldsig-core/.

SOAP Authorization

Using XML-based authorization in SOAP messages enables the authorization of the SOAP messages using certificates from the originating SOAP sender nodes. SOAP authorization applies an XML-based digital certificate from an independent authorization authority to the SOAP message from the sender.

Listing 4.35 is a sample representation of a SOAP message using an XML-based authorization.

```
<SOAP-ENV:Envelope
  xmlns:SOAP-ENV="http://schemas.xmlsoap.org/soap/envelope/">
  <SOAP-ENV:Header>
    <SOAP-SEC:Authorization
      xmlns:SOAP-SEC="http://schemas.xmlsoap.org/soap/security/"
      SOAP-ENV:actor=" actor-URI"
      SOAP-ENV:mustUnderstand="1">
      <AttributeCert xmlns=
           "http://schemas.xmlsoap.org/soap/security/AttributeCert">
         An encoded certificate inserted here as
         encrypted using actor's public key.
      </AttributeCert>
```

Listing 4.35 SOAP message using an XML-based authorization. *(continues)*

```
</SOAP-SEC:Authorization>
    </SOAP-ENV:Header>
    <SOAP-ENV:Body>
    </SOAP-ENV:Body>
</SOAP-ENV:Envelope>
```

Listing 4.35 SOAP message using an XML-based authorization. *(continued)*

Listing 4.35 illustrates a SOAP message with a `<SOAP-SEC: Authorization>` entry in the SOAP header applying an XML-based authorization to authorize the SOAP message. It uses an `<AttributeCert >` element to define the certificate from an independent authorization authority. And, it can be encrypted using the receiver node or an actor's public key. On the SOAP receiving node, the actor uses its private key to retrieve the certificate.

As we noted earlier, at the time of writing this chapter, the W3C SOAP security specifications were released as a Note that is subject to change without notice. To understand the core concepts of security and implementing security in Web services security, refer to Chapter 13, "Web Services Security."

Building SOAP Web Services

We all are aware that SOAP provides an XML-based communication protocol solution for bridging disparate applications in a distributed environment using XML-based messaging or by remotely invoking methods.

From a Web services point of view, it defines and provides the following:

- A standardized way to transmit data using Internet-based protocols and a common-wire format (XML) between the Web service provider and its requestors.
- An extensible solution model using an XML-based framework enabling the Web service providers and requestors to interoperate with each other in a loosely coupled fashion and without knowing the underlying application architecture (such as programming languages and operating systems). This enables the creation of Web services over existing applications without modifying the underlying applications.

In a Web services implementation model, SOAP can be implemented as a client, as a server application, or both, as follows:

- A SOAP-based client application plays the role of a Web services requestor, which typically handles an XML-based request/response, a message containing a XML document, parameters required to invoke a remote method, or the calling of a SOAP server application. A SOAP client can be a Web server or a traditional application running a SOAP-based proxy, which send SOAP requests or SOAP messages using HTTP or any other supporting protocol.
- A SOAP server application plays the role of a Web services provider, which processes the SOAP requests and messages from calling SOAP-based clients. The SOAP server application interacts with its encapsulated applications to process the requests or messages and then sends a response to the calling SOAP client. SOAP server applications also can act as SOAP intermediaries, which allows the extensibility of the application to enable the processing and forwarding of messages through a series of SOAP nodes or a final destination. In case of acting SOAP intermediaries, the SOAP server application typically works as a SOAP client application to the final destination of the message.

To understand the key challenges in the implementation of Web services using SOAP, let's take a look at how SOAP applications can be implemented using Java and then deployed in a Java-based Web services runtime environment.

Developing SOAP Web Services Using Java

SOAP does not mandate a single programming model nor does it define programming language-specific bindings for its implementation. It is up to the provider to choose a language and to define the implementation of its language-specific bindings. In this context, to use Java as a language for developing SOAP applications requires its Java implementation for SOAP-specific bindings. As of today, there are many SOAP application vendors that have made Java-based SOAP implementations for developing Web applications to Web services.

In general, the use of Java for developing SOAP applications enables scalable and portable applications to be built that also can interoperate with heterogeneous applications residing on different platforms by resolving the platform-specific incompatibilities and other issues. Additionally, having SOAP-based applications that adopt a J2EE-based infrastructure and component framework allows the inheritance of the characteristics of J2EE container-based services such as transactions, application security, and back-end application/databases connectivity. The release of the Java Web Services Developer Pack (JWSDP) also provides a full-fledged API solution for developing SOAP-based Web services. A long list of open source communities, Web services platform providers, and J2EE vendors also have released their SOAP implementations adopting Java platform and Java-based APIs.

To study and explore the features of a Java-based SOAP implementation, we chose to use Apache Axis, a Java-based toolkit from Apache Software foundation for developing SOAP-based Web services. Axis also supports the JAX-RPC, JAXM, SAAJ, and SOAP 1.2 specifications in its forthcoming implementations. Axis follows its predecessor efforts of Apache SOAP. Apache refers to Axis as the next generation of Apache SOAP implementation that provides a complete solution kit for Web services, which is more than sending and receiving SOAP messages. The Axis toolkit is available for download at http://xml.apache.org/axis.

Developing Web Services Using Apache Axis

Apache Axis is an open-source implementation that provides a Java-based SOAP implementation for developing Web services. To implement Web services, it facilitates a SOAP runtime environment and Java-based API framework for implementing the core components of Web services adopting compliant standards and protocols.

As a packaged solution, the Apache Axis environment provides the following:

- A SOAP-compliant runtime environment that can be used as a standalone SOAP server or as a plug-in component in a compliant Java servlet engine (such as Tomcat, iPlanet, and Weblogic)
- An API library and runtime environment for developing SOAP RPC and SOAP messaging-based applications and services
- A transport-independent means for adopting a variety of transport protocols (such as HTTP, SMTP, and FTP)
- Automatic serialization and deserialization for Java objects to and from XML in SOAP messages
- Support for exposing EJBs as Web services, especially the methods of stateless session EJBs

- Tools for creating WSDL from Java classes and vice-versa
- Tools for deploying, monitoring, and testing the Web services

Axis also provides full-fledged implementation support for Sun JWSDP 1.0 APIs, especially JAX-RPC and SAAJ. At the time of this book's writing, Axis 1.0B3 provides limited implementation support of JAX-RPC 1.0 and SAAJ 1.1 specifications. To find out the current status of the Axis implementation and its availability for download, go to Apache's XML Web site at http://xml.apache.org/axis/.

Installing Axis for Web Services

The process of installing Axis for building a Web services environment is quite simple. Axis can be installed as part of a Java servlet engine or as a J2EE-compliant application server, or it also can run as an independent server. Because our focus is creating Web services using Axis, we require Axis installation using a Java servlet engine. For our illustration, we will be using the Apache Tomcat 4.0.3 servlet engine available for download from http://jakarta.apache.org/tomcat/index.html.

Now, let's take a look at the steps involved in installing Axis within an Apache Tomcat server environment:

1. Download the Apache Axis tool kit (current release) from http://xml.apache.org/axis/. Unzip (Windows) or untar (UNIX) the package to your local system directory (for example, d:\xml-axis) and set an environment variable as AXIS_HOME.
2. Download Apache Tomcat 4.0.3 (or current release) from http://jakarta.apache.org/builds/jakarta-tomcat-4.0/release/ and then install it to your local system directory (that is, d:\tomcat4) and set an environment variable as TOMCAT_HOME. After installation, start the Tomcat server and ensure that it is working by locating http://localhost:8080/index.html with your browser. The browser will display the screen shown in Figure 4.9.
3. Navigate to your Axis installation home directory and copy the axis folder from AXIS_HOME\webapps\ to TOMCAT_HOME\webapps\ to deploy the Axis libraries as an Axis servlet.
4. To deploy the Axis libraries as a servlet in the Tomcat container, create a context in the Tomcat server configuration by editing TOMCAT_HOME/conf/server.conf with the following lines:

```
<Context path="/axis" docBase="axis" debug="0"
        reloadable="true" crossContext="true">
</Context>
```

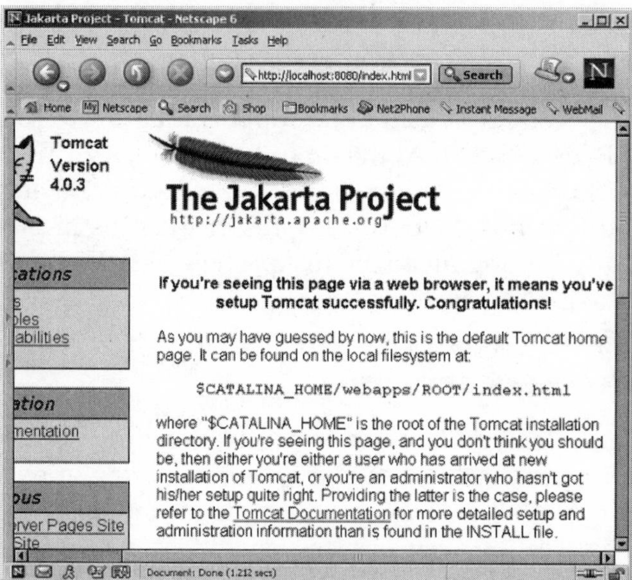

Figure 4.9 Browser showing successful installation of the Apache Tomcat environment.

5. Add axis-specific supporting class libraries (JARs) in the Tomcat environment. The required supporting class libraries include the following:
   - Apache Xerces parser for Java (Xerces2) with JAXP 1.1 support, which is available for download a http://xml.apache.org/xerces2-j/index.html. Unzip the download and copy the `xerces.jar file` to TOMCAT_HOME\webapps\axis\WEB-INF\lib.
   - If your application requires database connectivity or other application access, ensure that you copy all of the JDBC drivers and required class libraries to TOMCAT_HOME\webapps\axis\WEB-INF\lib.
   - As part of the kit, Axis provides class libraries for JAXRPC and JAXM as jaxrpc.jar and saaj.jar. In the case of using JAX-RPC and JAXM/SAAJ libraries, ensure that these JAR files are copied to TOMCAT_HOME\common\lib.
6. To test the Axis Web services environment, start the Tomcat server. Then, use your Web browser and open the followings URLs:

- To confirm installation: http:localhost:8080/axis/index.html
- To validate the Axis environment: http://localhost:8080/axis/happyaxis.jsp
- To list the available Axis services: http://localhost:8080/axis/servlet/AxisServlet

7. To compile and test applications, create a run script (.bat or .sh) to ensure that the CLASSPATH in the development environment includes the following:

```
AXIS_HOME/lib/axis.jar
AXIS_HOME/lib/jaxrpc.jar
AXIS_HOME/lib/saaj.jar
AXIS_HOME/lib/commons-logging.jar
AXIS_HOME/lib/log4j-1.2.4.jar
AXIS_HOME/lib/xmlsec.jar
AXIS_HOME/lib/tt-bytecode.jar
AXIS_HOME/lib/wsdl4j.jar
AXIS_HOME/xerces.jar
AXIS_HOME/<DATABASE/OTHER_LIBRARIES.jar>
DEVELOPMENT_HOME/
```

Running Axis without Tomcat/Servlet Engine

The Axis toolkit also provides a server environment to test Axis-deployed applications, which enables the services to be run and tested without having a Web server or a J2EE environment. To start an Axis server, run your AXIS CLASSPATH script and then execute the following:

```
java org.apache.axis.transport.http.SimpleAxisServer <port>
```

Although it helps to run and test applications in a developer environment, it is better to run the Axis environment from a Web server or a J2EE container. Before creating services, let's take a closer look at the Axis infrastructure and components.

Axis Infrastructure and Components

In general, the Axis infrastructure consists of the following components as modular subsystems functioning together as a server or client, depending upon whether the Web services environment is a service provider or service requestor.

Axis Engine

The Axis engine acts as the SOAP runtime environment for processing the inbound and outbound messages by looking up the SOAPAction headers for transport (that is, http.SOAPAction). To process messages, the Axis engine facilitates a series of handlers as chains to invoke and process the messages. The messages are passed to the handler for invocation as `MessageContext` objects.

Handlers and Chains

The Axis engine provides both client- and server-side message processors as client-side handlers and server-side handlers. The Axis engine processes messages using a series of request handlers, and after the invocation of a target service it returns as a series of response handlers. Axis defines the group of handlers that contain similar responsibilities combined together as chains. Axis provides a set of request and response chains grouped to process messages on the message path and especially to support transport, global request/response, and messaging. Axis provides service handlers to facilitate RPC- and messaging-based Web services, depending upon the type of the deployed services in the server environment.

The key characteristics of the Axis service handlers for RPC- and messaging-based Web services are as follows:

In the RPC style of Web services, the service handler `org.apache.axis.providers.java.RPCProvider` identifies the required method for invocation and then executes it by providing the parameters obtained as part of the SOAP request message. It uses serialization and deserialization of Java objects to XML and vice versa during the service request and response.

In the messaging (document-style) type of services, the service handler `org.apache.axis.providers.java.MsgProvider` calls the method and passes the XML document obtained from the SOAP message.

Note that with the RPC-style services, the service handler processes the messages using serialization and deserialization to convert XML into Java objects and vice versa. With messaging-style services, the XML data are handed over to the target method for processing. During processing, the service handlers also throw SOAP faults as AxisFault exceptions.

Figure 4.10 illustrates the server-side infrastructure representing the Axis engine with the handlers and chains.

Figure 4.11 illustrates the client-side infrastructure representing the Axis engine with the handlers and chains.

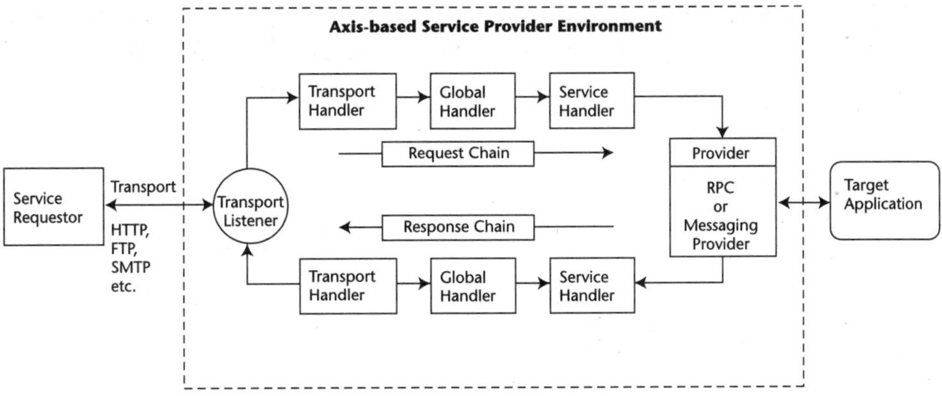

Figure 4.10 Axis-based service provider infrastructure.

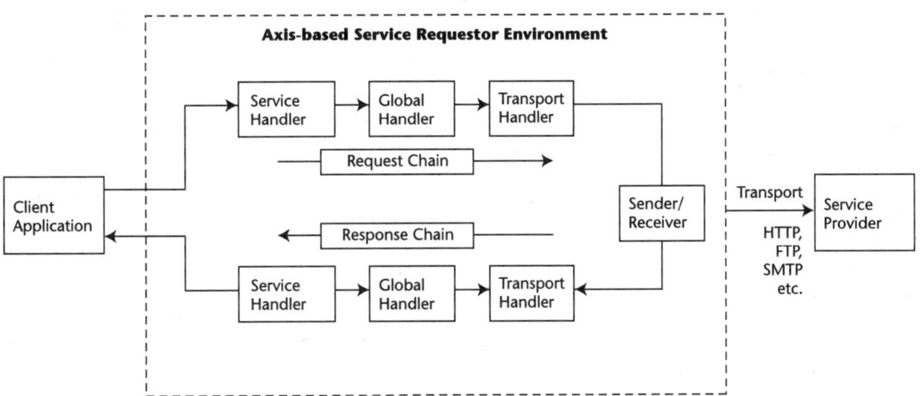

Figure 4.11 Axis-based service requestor infrastructure.

Axis Administration

The Axis administration provides the administration and configuration information for the Axis engine to enable the runtime service chains and other SOAP services. It allows the environment of the Axis engine to be configured with a Web service deployment descriptor (WSDD) file. The WSDD file defines the supported transports, global configuration of the axis engine as handlers, and the deployed services. It is usually represented as server-config.wsdd. To obtain information about the Axis engine installation and its supported transports, services, handlers, and so on, run the following command:

```
java org.apache.axis.client.AdminClient list
```

It will bring up the listing that includes an Axis administration service deployed as AdminService. Axis also allows remote administration, which can be configured by setting an enableRemoteAdmin parameter as true.

We will take a closer look at configuring other administration and deployment tasks in the section, "Creating Web Services Using Axis: An Example," later in this chapter.

Serializers and Deserializers

Axis supports SOAP encoding to convert objects and their values between the native programming language and XML representations. To support SOAP encoding, Axis provides serializing and deserializing mechanisms, which enable the conversion of the Java primitives and objects to XML-based representations and vice versa, without writing any specific code. In the case of Java Beans, Axis requires the Java classes to be mapped with a W3C XML Schema type using a `<beanMapping>` tag in the WSDD file. If bean mapping is not flexible, Axis allows the definition of custom serialization using a `<typeMapping>` tag. In this case, the developer has to implement the serializers and deserializers factory classes to convert the object to XML and vice versa supporting SOAP encoding specifications. An example mapping in an Axis `WSDD` file is shown as follows:

```
 <typeMapping qname="ns:BookCatalog"
        xmlns:ns="http://jws.wiley.com/Book.xsd"
        languageSpecificType="java:jws.wiley.CustomObject"
        serializer="com.jws.wiley.CustomSerializer"
        deserializer="com.jws.wiley.CustomDeserializer"
encodingStyle="http://schemas.xmlsoap.org/soap/encoding/"/>
```

Tools for Emitting WSDL

Axis supports WSDL to describe Web services as service descriptions representing the location of services, supported data types, supported messaging styles and patterns, and so on. Axis facilitates WSDL support with the following three options:

- If an Axis-based service provider deployed its Web services using a Web server, then the service requestor may obtain the WSDL by appending ?WSDL to the end of the service URL. This would generate the WSDL describing the deployed service at the service provider. For example:

  ```
  http://jws.wiley.com/axis/services/AcmeCatalogService?WSDL
  ```

- The WSDL2Java utility enables the creation of Java-based artifacts such as stubs, skeletons, and its associated data types from WSDL. This helps the service requestors to build Java proxy clients from the WSDL generated by the service provider.

  ```
  java org.apache.axis.wsdl.WSDL2Java <PROVIDER-WSDL-URL>
  ```

- The Java2WSDL utility enables the generation of WSDL from Java classes, which helps developers to create and describe a Web service from a Java interface.

  ```
  java org.apache.axis.wsdl.Java2WSDL -o myService.wsdl
                         -l <Service_url_location>
                         -n <Namespace URL>
                         -p "java.class"
  ```

Axis TCP Monitor

Axis provides `tcpmon`, a TCP monitor utility that allows viewing, logging, and debugging of the SOAP request and responses. It helps the Axis-based Web services environment to monitor the SOAP requests and responses in real time and also allows the testing of the SOAP requests by editing and resubmitting them.

Use of the `tcpmon` utility requires a client listening port, a target SOAP server host, and its port. The Axis client application should choose a local client port through which the `tcpmon` can listen to the connections then route them by tunneling to the target SOAP server host and using its port. The `tcpmon` logs all the SOAP request and response traffic and displays it in the GUI window.

To view the `tcpmon` utility, you may run the following command with options:

```
java org.apache.axis.utils.tcpmon
      <listeningport>
             <targetservername>
                       <targetserverport>
```

For instance, to create a `tcpmon` session for a client sending requests to a listening port 9999 and the target Axis server running on `localhost` using port 8080, the command line option will be as follows:

```
java org.apache.axis.utils.tcpmon 9999 localhost 8080
```

This will display the Axis `tcpmon` utility, a GUI window as shown in Figure 4.12.

The requests also can be modified and then resent. This enables the behavior to be studied and the response message to be viewed without changing the client application.

You also may execute the `tcpmon` command without options, which would show up in an Administration window where those options could be filled in. The `tcpmon` utility enables all of the requests and responses in XML to be saved as a text file.

Axis Web Services Programming Model

To create a Web service in an Axis environment, implementation of the following is required:

1. Create the service provider (server application)
2. Create the service requestor (client applications)

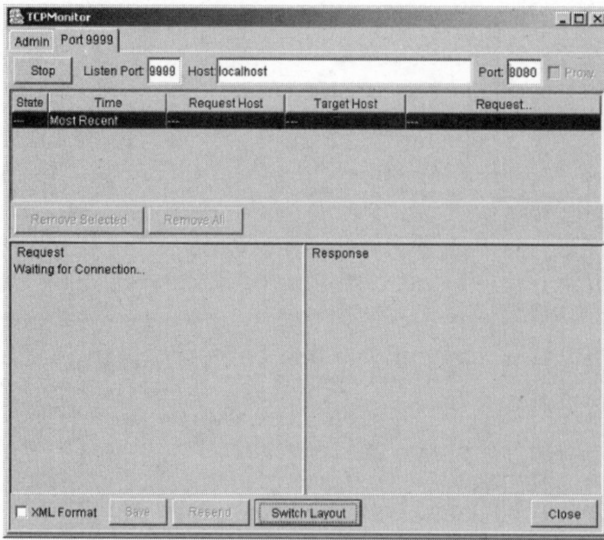

Figure 4.12 Axis TCP Monitor utility for viewing SOAP messages.

Let's take a look at the key concepts involved in implementing the Web service provider and requestors using an Axis environment.

Creating the Service

Axis allows a service to be created from an existing Java-based Web application just by identifying the methods required to be exposed and deploying them in the Axis server.

1. In an RPC-based communication model, a service client invokes the exposed method and a response is returned. In this process, the Axis server engine transforms the Java objects to XML and vice versa, using automatic serializer and deserializer mechanisms during communication. The following example is a simple service example, which accepts a string parameter and invokes a method `justSayHello` and returns a `String` parameter:

```
public class HelloAxis {
   public String justSayHello(String s) {
         return "Hello " + s ", Welcome to Axis !!!";
   }
}
```

2. In a messaging-based communication model, the client sends an XML document and the server application receives the XML as a W3C `Document` object for processing. It is not mandatory for the service to send a response back to the client. In case of sending a response, the service returns a W3C `Document` object as a body of the SOAP response message. The following snippet is a method that receives a purchase order XML as a W3C document for processing. Upon successful processing, it sends out a response message as a W3C document with the shipping notice, otherwise it sends out a product availability status notice.

```
public Document sendPODocument (Document poXML)
                                       throws Exception {

  // process purchase order
  boolean processPO = submitPurchaseOrder(poXML);

  if (processPO) {
     //TRUE: create Shipping notice
     Document doc = getShippingDoc(poXML);
  }
  else
```

```
        // FALSE: create product availability status
        Document doc = getAvailabilityStatus(poXML);
        return doc;
    }
```

Creating the Service Requestor

Axis allows service clients to be created in two different ways:

1. Having the required values for locating and invoking the service provider, such as SOAP, endpoint of the service, methods, parameters, and so on
2. Using a WSDL-based service description exposed by the service provider

Now, let's take a look at the programming steps involved in creating the service client with all of the required parameters and how to invoke the service exposed by the provider.

Creating a Normal Service Requestor Client

In case of an RPC-based communication model, the key programming steps involved for creating a service client are as follows:

1. Import Axis packages, the most important ones of which are the following:

   ```
   import org.apache.axis.AxisFault;
   import org.apache.axis.client.Call;
   import org.apache.axis.client.Service;
   import org.apache.axis.encoding.XMLType;
   import javax.xml.rpc.ParameterMode;
   import javax.xml.namespace.QName;
   ```

2. Define the endpoint of the service:

   ```
   String endpoint =
           "http://localhost:8080/axis/services/HelloService";
   ```

3. Create a service:

   ```
   Service service = new Service();
   ```

4. Create a SOAP request call:

   ```
   Call call = (Call) service.createCall();
   ```

5. Set the target endpoint of the provider location:

   ```
   call.setTargetEndpointAddress( endpoint );
   ```

6. Set the service operation name and its methods:

```
call.setOperationName(
                 new QName("HelloService", "sayHello") );
```

7. Set the parameters required for the operation. The parameters must provide the equivalent mapping of a W3C XML Schema:

```
call.addParameter( "myName",
                  MLType.XSD_STRING, ParameterMode.IN );
```

8. Set the return type parameters from the SOAP response. The parameters must provide the equivalent mapping of a W3C XML Schema:

```
call.setReturnType( XMLType.XSD_STRING );
```

9. Invoke the service by sending the request and retrieve the results. The invoke() method returns a Java object with parameters of the method and it is required to cast the return values as a Java object:

```
Object responseObj = call.invoke( new Object[]
                      {new Integer(myName)} );
```

In case of a messaging-based communication model, the key programming steps involved for creating the service client are as follows:

1. Import the Axis packages, the most important ones of which are the following:

```
import org.apache.axis.client.Service;
import org.apache.axis.client.Call;
import org.apache.axis.message.*;
import org.apache.axis.*;
import java.net.URL;
import org.apache.axis.utils.XMLUtils;
import org.w3c.dom.*;
```

2. Define the endpoint of the service:

```
String endpoint =
          "http://localhost:8080/axis/services/HelloMSG";
```

3. Read the XML document as an input stream or string:

```
InputStream is =
        ClassLoader.getSystemResourceAsStream("hello.xml");
```

4. Create a new service:

```
Service  service = new Service();
```

5. Create a SOAP request call using the service:

```
Call call = (Call) service.createCall();
```

6. Set the target endpoint of the provider location:

```
call.setTargetEndpointAddress( endpoint );
```

7. Create a SOAP envelope with an XML payload:

```
SOAPEnvelope env = new SOAPEnvelope(is);
```

8. Send the SOAP envelope with an XML payload to the destination:

```
call.invoke(env);
```

9. In case of obtaining a response message, the response message also will be a W3C document as well:

```
SOAPEnvelope elems = (SOAPEnvelope)call.invoke(env);
```

Creating the Service Requestor Client from WSDL

Axis provides a WSDL2Java utility for building Java proxies and skeletons from WSDL obtained from service providers. To create Java proxy classes from a WSDL, you would run the following command:

```
java org.apache.axis.wsdl.WSDL2Java <Provider-WSDL-URL>
```

It also is possible to create service clients dynamically using dynamic invocation interfaces provided by JAX-RPC. This is discussed further in Chapter 10, "Building RPC Web Services with JAX-RPC."

To understand how to create Axis service clients from WSDL, refer to the full-featured example in Chapter 3, "Building the Web Services Architecture."

Axis Deployment Model

Axis facilitates easy deployment and undeployment of services using XML-based Web services deployment descriptors (WSDDs). It enables deploying and undeploying services and also Axis-specific resources like handlers and chains using an administration utility 'AdminClient' provided as part of the Axis toolkit.

To deploy a service, ensure that the AXIS CLASSPATH is set and run the following command:

```
java org.apache.axis.client.AdminClient deploy.wsdd
```

The deploy.wsdd refers to the deployment descriptor defining the service, classes, methods, provider (RPC or Messaging), and its namespaces.

Listing 4.36 is a sample WSDD to deploy a service in an Axis environment.

```
<deployment name="test"
   xmlns="http://xml.apache.org/axis/wsdd/"
    xmlns:java="http://xml.apache.org/axis/wsdd/providers/java"
   xmlns:xsd="http://www.w3.org/2000/10/XMLSchema"
   xmlns:xsi="http://www.w3.org/2000/10/XMLSchema-instance">

    <service name="HelloService" provider="java:RPC">
      <parameter name="className"
                 value="jws.ch4.helloservice.HelloService"/>
      <parameter name="allowedMethods" value="justSayHello"/>
   </service>
</deployment>
```

Listing 4.36 Web services deployment descriptor (WSDD) for deploying a service.

The previous WSDD defines `HelloService` using a provider with an RPC-based communication model by exposing its class `jws.ch4.helloservice.HelloService` and its method `justSayHello`. The deployment name `test` is an identifier and the namespaces define the W3C XML schemas associated with the implementation.

Similarly, to undeploy a service, ensure that the AXIS CLASSPATH is set and then run the following command:

```
java org.apache.axis.client.AdminClient undeploy.wsdd
```

The `undeploy.wsdd` defines the service required to undeploy from the Axis runtime environment. Listing 4.37 is a sample `WSDD` defining the services to be undeployed:

```
<undeployment name="test"
          xmlns="http://xml.apache.org/axis/wsdd/"
  xmlns:java="http://xml.apache.org/axis/wsdd/providers/java"
  xmlns:xsd="http://www.w3.org/2000/10/XMLSchema"
  xmlns:xsi="http://www.w3.org/2000/10/XMLSchema-instance">
  <service name=" HelloService "/>
</undeployment>
```

Listing 4.37 Web services deployment descriptor (WSDD) for undeploying a service.

Additionally, to find out the list of services deployed in the Axis environment, run the following command:

```
java org.apache.axis.client.AdminClient list
```

This command will list all the services deployed in an Axis environment. It also is possible to deploy and undeploy the services in an Axis environment by editing the `server-config.xml` file located at AXIS_HOME directory.

Deploying Axis Services Using JWS Files (.jws)

Axis allows the deployment of Web services using Java classes with .jws extensions. It is quite typical to the Java server pages (JSP) deployed in a servlet engine. By placing Java classes (source files) with .jws extensions in the Web applications directory (that is, TOMCAT_HOME/webapps/axis/) during runtime, Axis runtime automatically compiles and deploys the classes with all of the methods as deployed services. In this case, it does not require WSDD-deployment descriptors.

Creating Web Services Using Axis: An Example

In this section, we build on the case study example done in Chapter 3, "Building the Web Services Architecture," featuring the 'ACME Web Services Company' with additional functionalities. Basically, the ACME Web Services Company is a Web-based services provider that sells computer products by delivering XML-based data over the Internet as Web services to its partners and resellers by exposing its business functions.

This case study illustration discusses the following functions exposed as services from the ACME Web Services provider:

- Getting the product information
- Submitting the purchase order

The service requesters invoke ACME Web Services to obtain product information and then to submit a purchase order for a selected product. The service requesters use an Axis-based application environment to do SOAP-based service invocation with ACME Web services.

We will be creating Apache Axis-based Web service components for the service provider, and for the client service requestor we will implement client service components using an Axis client engine-based client invocation. It adopts a SOAP RPC and SOAP messaging-based communication model to cater the specific functional scenarios.

Building an Axis-Based Infrastructure

To build and deploy ACME Web services in the Axis environment, we chose to use the following infrastructure solutions:

ON THE SERVICE PROVIDER SIDE

- The ACME Web services provider will use Apache Tomcat as its Servlet engine/Web server, including the Axis-based SOAP runtime environment.
- It also will use PointBase as its database for querying product catalog information and storing its purchase orders. The PointBase database also can be used as an evaluation copy for development purposes. For more information on understanding the PointBase database, refer to the documentation available at http://www.pointbase.com/.

ON THE SERVICE REQUESTOR SIDE

- The service requester will use Apache Axis as its SOAP client environment to invoke the services of the ACME Web services provider.

To build and deploy the components and SOAP interfaces, we created XML-based build scripts using Apache Ant. Apache Ant is a Java-based Makefile utility available as a free download at http://jakarta.apache.org/ant/index.html.

Figure 4.13 represents the Axis-based Web services infrastructure for building ACME Web services.

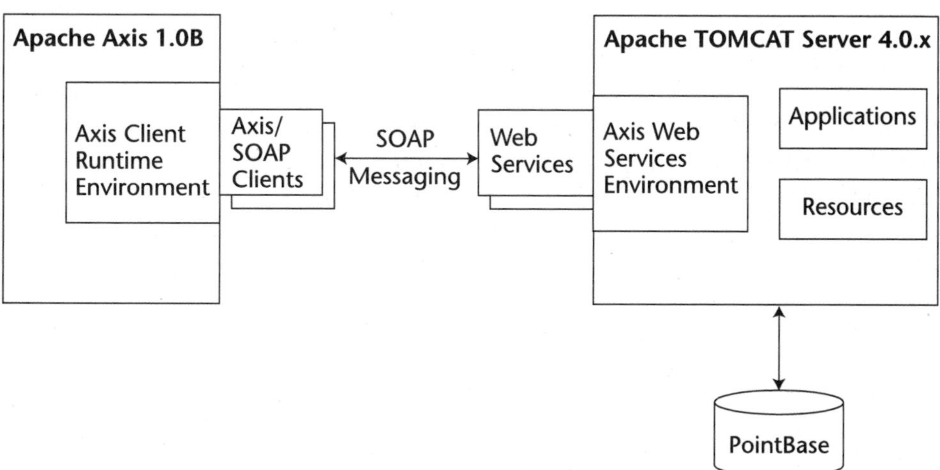

Figure 4.13 Axis-based infrastructure for ACME Web services.

To try out this example, you may download the chapter-specific source code and documentation made available at http://www.wiley.com/compbooks/nagappan. The source code and README for installing and running this example are available as part of chapter-4.zip.

Understanding the Application Design

As we discussed earlier, the ACME Web services provider will host its application as services over the Internet by exposing its underlying business components. In particular, we will be implementing the following scenarios of the ACME business functions as services:

Scenario 1 (RPC model). Get the complete product information for a particular product ID from the ACME product database. This will be handled using SOAP RPC-based communication, where the service requestor client sends a product ID and gets the product information as it response.

Scenario 2 (Messaging model). Submit a purchase order to the ACME PO database. This will be handled using SOAP messaging-based communication, where the service requestor sends as purchase order as an XML document to the service provider, and the service provider processes the message and then writes it to a database. In return, the service provider then sends a document containing a response message, mentioning the success or failure of the process.

To understand the problem and flow of events, the sequence diagrams shown in Figure 4.14 and Figure 4.15 illustrate the various sequences of actions performed by a client invoking the ACME Web services deployed in the Axis-based Web services environment.

Based on the previous sequence of events, we chose to use a façade pattern (GoF) using an AcmeXMLHelper class to act as a proxy by encapsulating the business functionalities, which also include database interaction, XML construction, XML parsing operations, and so on. More specifically, the AcmeXMLhelper will handle all of the XML construction tasks, and AcmeDAO will handle the database interaction.

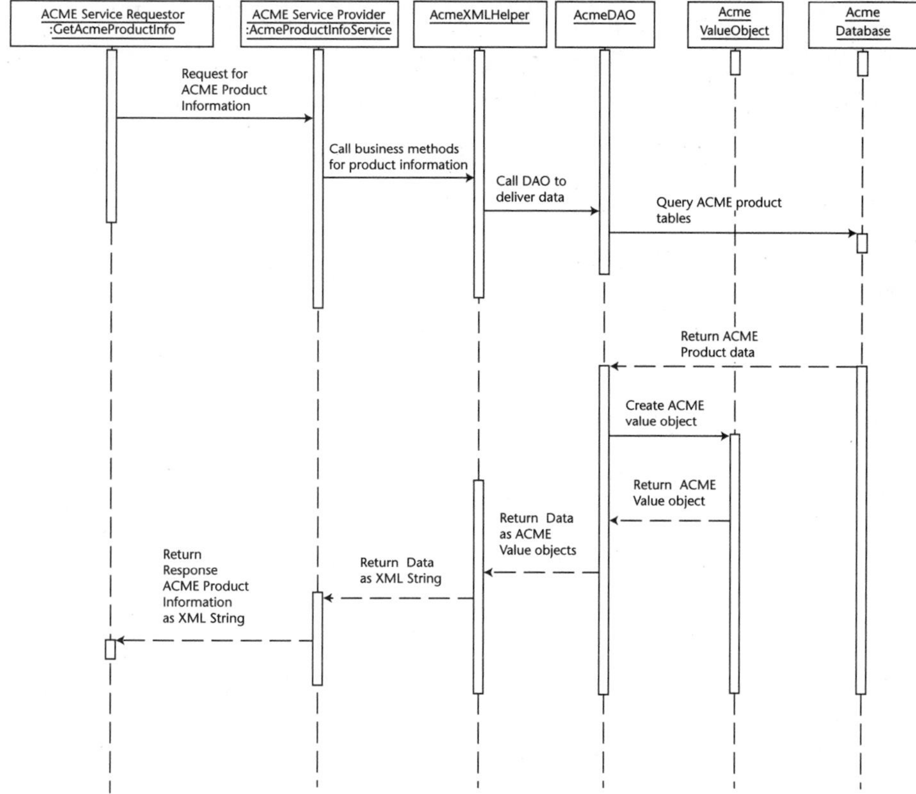

Figure 4.14 Sequence diagram for ACME Web services (RPC scenario).

The following Figures 4.16 and 4.17 depict the class diagram of the server-side components that support the ACME Web service provider for RPC and Messaging scenarios.

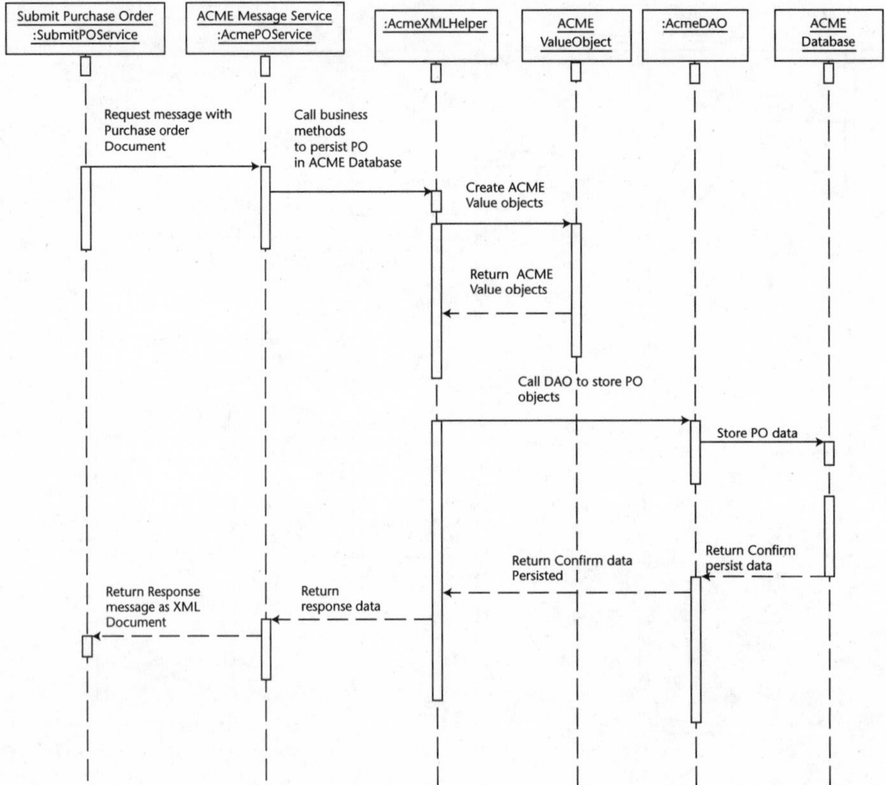

Figure 4.15 Sequence diagram for ACME Web services (Messaging scenario).

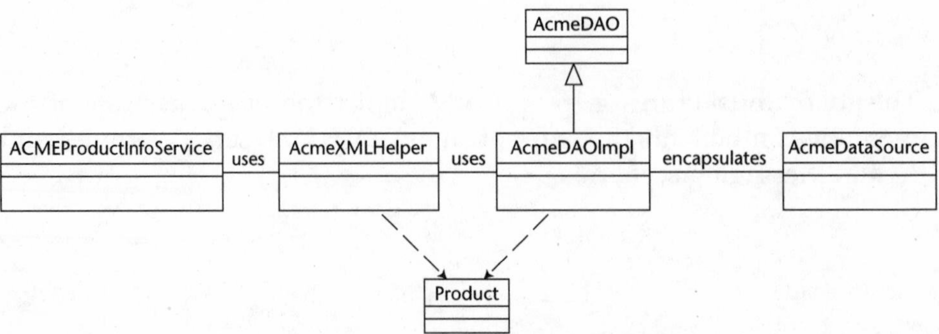

Figure 4.16 Class diagram for the service provider (RPC scenario).

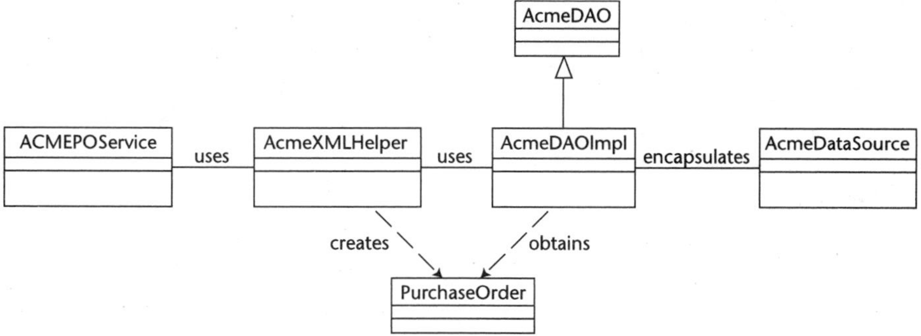

Figure 4.17 Class diagram for the service provider (Messaging scenario).

Now, let's take a look at how to set up the development environment and implementation of those service components.

Setting Up the ACME Web Services Environment

Specific tasks are involved in setting up the development environment for creating ACME Web services. They are described in the following sections.

Creating the Service Provider Environment

1. Download the Apache Axis toolkit (current release) from http://xml.apache.org/axis/. Unzip or untar the package to your local system directory (that is, d:\xml-axis) and set an environment variable as AXIS_HOME to its home directory.
2. Download Apache Tomcat 4.0.3 (or current release) from http://jakarta.apache.org/builds/jakarta-tomcat-4.0/release/ and then install it to your local system directory (that is, d:\tomcat4) and set an environment variable as TOMCAT_HOME. After installation, start the Tomcat server and ensure that it is working by typing this http://localhost:8080/index.html in your browser.
3. Navigate to your Axis installation home directory and copy the Axis folder from AXIS_HOME\webapps\to TOMCAT_HOME\webapps\ in order to deploy the Axis libraries as an Axis servlet.

4. To deploy the Axis libraries as a servlet in the Tomcat container, create a context in the Tomcat server configuration by editing TOMCAT_HOME/conf/server.conf with the following lines:

```
<Context path="/axis" docBase="axis" debug="0"
           reloadable="true" crossContext="true">
</Context>
```

5. Download the Apache Xerces parser for Java (Xerces2) and Apache Xalan with JAXP 1.1 support from http://xml.apache.org/. Unzip the download and copy the `xerces.jar and xalan.jar` files to TOMCAT_HOME\webapps\axis\WEB-INF\lib.
6. Download the PointBase database server from www.pointbase.com. Install the download to your local system directory (that is, d:\pointbase). Start the server, running `startserver.bat`, available at the `PointBase` tools directory (that is, d:\pointbase \tools\server\startserver.bat).
7. Make sure that you copy all of the PointBase drivers (pserver42.jar and pbclient42.jar) to TOMCAT_HOME\webapps\axis\WEB-INF\lib.
8. Additionally, copy the PointBase drivers and JAX-RPC and JAXM libraries to TOMCAT_HOME\common\lib. As part of the kit, Axis provides class libraries for JAXRPC and JAXM as `jaxrpc.jar` and `jaxm.jar`. You also will need to download the JDBC 2.0 optional package from http://java.sun.com/products/jdbc. Copy the JDBC 2.0 extension drivers from this optional package to TOMCAT _HOME\common\lib.
9. By performing these steps, the Axis environment setup is complete. To test the Axis Web services environment, start the Tomcat server. Then, use your Web browser and open http://localhost:8080/axis/index .html. The browser will display the screen shown in Figure 4.18.

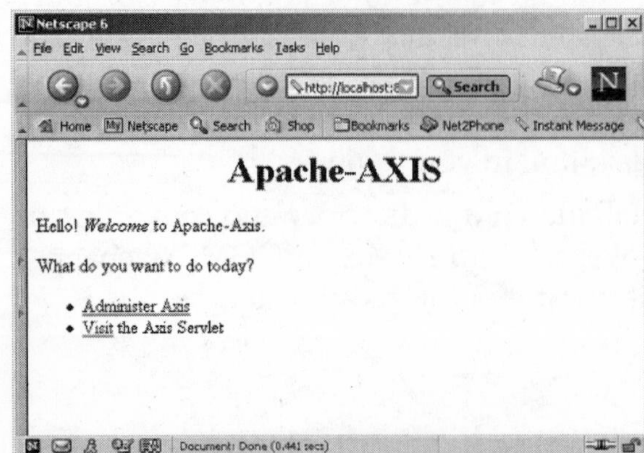

Figure 4.18 Browser displaying the Axis environment setup.

10. To compile and test the applications, create a run script (.bat or .sh) to ensure that the CLASSPATH in the environment includes the following:

```
TOMCAT_HOME\webapps\axis\WEB-INF\lib\axis.jar
TOMCAT_HOME\webapps\axis\WEB-INF\lib\jaxrpc.jar
TOMCAT_HOME\webapps\axis\WEB-INF\lib\saaj.jar
TOMCAT_HOME\webapps\axis\WEB-INF\lib\commons-logging.jar
TOMCAT_HOME\webapps\axis\WEB-INF\lib\tt-bytecode.jar
TOMCAT_HOME\webapps\axis\WEB-INF\lib\xmlsec.jar
TOMCAT_HOME\webapps\axis\WEB-INF\lib\wsdl4j.jar
TOMCAT_HOME\webapps\axis\WEB-INF\lib\xerces.jar
TOMCAT_HOME\webapps\axis\WEB-INF\lib\xalan.jar
TOMCAT_HOME\webapps\axis\WEB-INF\lib\log4j-1.2.4.jar
TOMCAT_HOME\webapps\axis\WEB-INF\lib\pbclient42.jar
TOMCAT_HOME\webapps\axis\WEB-INF\lib\pbserver42.jar
TOMCAT_HOME\common\lib\jdbc2_0-stdext.jar
YOUR_DEVELOPMENT_HOME\.
```

11. Now, let's create the ACME business specific database tables. The following tables are required for storing and querying the product catalog data and to save purchase order information including buyer information and ordered items.

    a. To store and query ACME product information, we create a table by the name of `product_catalog` using the following parameters:

COLUMN NAME	COLUMN DATA TYPE
ITEM_NUM	INT
ITEM_NAME	VARCHAR(30)
ITEM_DESC	VARCHAR(255)
ITEM_PRICE	DOUBLE
CURRENCY	VARCHAR(3)
ITEM_TYPE	VARCHAR(3)

    b. To store and query ACME buyer information, we create a table by the name of `purchase_order_header` using the following parameters:

COLUMN NAME	COLUMN DATA TYPE
PO_NUM	INT
PO_DATE	VARCHAR(10)
BUYER_NO	VARCHAR(10)
BUYER_NAME	VARCHAR(55)
STREET_ADDR	VARCHAR(150)
CITY	VARCHAR(100)
STATE	VARCHAR(100)
ZIP	VARCHAR(10)
COUNTRY	VARCHAR(10)
PAYMENT_TYPE	VARCHAR(255)
PAYMENT_NUMBER	VARCHAR(30)
TOTAL_AMOUNT	DOUBLE

c. To store and query ACME order information, we create a table by the name of `purchase_order_line` using the following parameters:

COLUMN NAME	COLUMN DATA TYPE
PO_NUM	INT
LINE_NUM	INT
PRODUCT_NO	INT
QTY	INT
UNIT_PRICE	DOUBLE

To create the `product_catalog`, `purchase_order_header`, and `purchase_order_line` tables and to populate the data, you may choose to use the Java code `'CreateACMETables.java'` shown in Listing 4.38.

```
package jws.ch4.db;
import java.sql.*;
import javax.sql.*;
import javax.naming.*;
import java.util.*;

public class CreateACMETables {

 public static void main(String argv[]) throws Exception {

   java.sql.Connection con = null;
   java.sql.Statement stmt  = null;

   try {

    // Make driver connection to database
    String driver = "com.pointbase.jdbc.jdbcUniversalDriver";
    Class.forName(driver);

    String URL = "jdbc:pointbase:server://localhost/sample";
    con = DriverManager.getConnection(URL, "public",
                                               "public");

    System.out.println("Making connection...\n");

    // execute SQL statements
    stmt = con.createStatement();

    try {
      stmt.execute("drop table product_catalog");
      System.out.println("Table product_catalog dropped.");
      stmt.execute("drop table purchase_order_header");
      System.out.println("Table po_header dropped.");
      stmt.execute("drop table purchase_order_line");
      System.out.println("Table po_line dropped.");
    } catch (SQLException e) {
        System.out.println("Tables already exists and
                             doesn't need to be dropped.");
    }

    stmt.execute("create table product_catalog
                   (item_num int, item_name varchar(30),
                   item_desc varchar(255), item_price
                    double, currency varchar(3))");
    System.out.println("Table product_catalog created.");

    stmt.execute("create table
```

Listing 4.38 `CreateACMETables.java`. ***(continues)***

```
                         purchase_order_header (po_num int,
                         po_date varchar(10),
                         buyer_no varchar(10),
                         buyer_name varchar(55),
                         street_addr varchar(150),
                         city varchar(100),
                         state varchar(100), zip varchar(10),
                         country varchar(10),
                         payment_type varchar(10),
                         payment_number varchar(30),
                         total_amount double)");
      System.out.println("Table product_purchase_order_header
                                                  created.");

      stmt.execute("create table
                   purchase_order_line (po_num int,
                   line_num int,
                   product_no int,
                   qty int,
                   unit_price double)");
      System.out.println("Table product_purchase_order_line
                                                   created.");

      // Insert dummy data for Product Catalog
      int numrows = stmt.executeUpdate("insert into
                         product_catalog values (1001,
                        'ACME Blade 1000',
                        'Sparc III Processor,
                         1Ghz, 512MB, 42GB HD,
                         Linux',  1000.00, 'USD')");

      System.out.println "Number of rows inserted = " +
                                                 numrows);

      numrows = stmt.executeUpdate
                ("insert into product_catalog values
                (1002, 'ACME Blade 2000', 'Sparc III Processor,
                 1.3Ghz x2, 512MB, 42GB HD, Solaris',  3000.00,
                 'USD')");
      System.out.println
                 ("Number of rows inserted = " + numrows);
    } catch (Exception e) {
       System.out.println("Exception was thrown: "
                                   + e.getMessage());
    } finally {
```

Listing 4.38 CreateACMETables.java.

```
            try {
               if (stmt != null)
                  stmt.close();
               if (con != null)
                  con.close();
            } catch (SQLException sqle) {
                System.out.println("SQLException during close(): "
                                                 + sqle.getMessage());
            }
        }
    }
}
```

Listing 4.38 `CreateACMETables.java`. *(continued)*

To create the ACME business tables, start the PointBase server, ensure that the CLASSPATH is set, then compile `CreateACMETables.java`, and run them preferably using an Ant script. The successful execution of the program creates the `product_catalog`, `purchase_order_header`, and `purchase_order_line` tables in the PointBase database and inserts `Product` records in to the `product_catalog` table.

If everything works successfully, you will get the output shown in Figure 4.19.

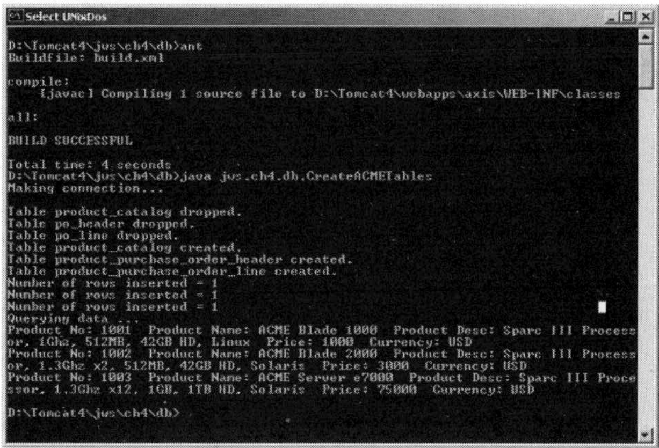

Figure 4.19 Output showing the compiling and running of `CreateACMETables`.

In order to access the database from the Axis environment, we must declare a datasource resource reference in the Tomcat Web application deployment descriptor located at TOMCAT_HOME \webapps\axis\WEB-INF\web.xml. We use a JNDI name, `jdbc/AcmeDB`, to access the resource.

```
<resource-ref>
   <res-ref-name>jdbc/AcmeDB</res-ref-name>
   <res-type>javax.sql.DataSource</res-type>
   <res-auth>Container</res-auth>
</resource-ref>
```

The JNDI name `jdbc/AcmeDB` will be used by AcmeDAO to access the data sources.

Now, configure the resource in the Tomcat server configuration by providing the resource and resource parameters entries found in Tomcat's configuration file located at TOMCAT_HOME\conf\ server.xml, as shown in Listing 4.39.

```
<Context path="/axis" docBase="axis" debug="0"
            reloadable="true" crossContext="true">
   <Logger
        className="org.apache.catalina.logger.FileLogger"
        prefix="localhost_jws_log." suffix=".txt"
        timestamp="true"/>
        <Resource name="jdbc/AcmeDB" reloadable="true"
                  auth="Container"
                  type="javax.sql.DataSource"/>
        <ResourceParams name="jdbc/AcmeDB">
          <parameter>
            <name>user</name>
            <value>public</value>
          </parameter>
          <parameter>
            <name>password</name>
            <value>public</value>
          </parameter>
          <parameter>
            <name>driverClassName</name>
            <value>com.pointbase.jdbc.jdbcUniversalDriver
            </value>
          </parameter>
          <parameter>
            <name>driverName</name>
            <value>
```

Listing 4.39 Tomcat resource configuration (`server.xml`).

```
                jdbc:pointbase:server://localhost/sample
            </value>
        </parameter>
    </ResourceParams>
</Context>
```

Listing 4.39 Tomcat resource configuration (`server.xml`). *(continued)*

Restart the Tomcat server and ensure that the PointBase database server has been started. This concludes the Axis configuration requirements for the service provider environment.

Creating the Service Requestor Environment

1. Download the Apache Axis tool kit (current release) from http://xml.apache.org/axis/. Unzip or untar the package to your local system directory (that is, d:\xml-axis-client) and set an environment variable as AXIS_CLIENT_HOME to its home directory.
2. To compile and test the client applications, create a run script (.bat or .sh) to ensure that the client CLASSPATH environment includes the following:

```
AXIS_CLIENT_HOME\lib\axis.jar
AXIS_CLIENT_HOME\lib\jaxrpc.jar
AXIS_CLIENT_HOME\lib\commons-logging.jar
AXIS_CLIENT_HOME\lib\log4j-core.jar
AXIS_CLIENT_HOME\lib\tt-bytecode.jar
AXIS_CLIENT_HOME\lib\wsdl4j.jar
AXIS_CLIENT_HOME\lib\xerces.jar
```

The previous steps conclude the Axis configuration requirements for the service requestor environment. Now, let's explore the implementation of the ACME business scenarios using the Axis Web services environment.

Implementing the ACME Web Services

As we discussed earlier in the section titled *Understanding the Application Design,* we will be implementing the following two scenarios for the ACME Web services provider:

Scenario 1. Getting product information using ACME Web services.

Scenario 2. Submitting a purchase order using ACME Web services.

Creating RPC-Based Web Services (Scenario 1)

To implement this scenario, we will be reusing the components that we built in Chapter 3, "Building the Web Services Architecture," and we will deploy them in an Axis environment. The components are as follows:

- `AcmeDAO`, a DAO class that provides access to the data source and abstracts the underlying data access implementation for the product catalog
- `AcmeXMLHelper`, a class that gathers the data and constructs an XML document as a string for use by the business clients

To find out the programming steps and the source code implementation of the previous classes, refer to Chapter 3, particularly the section titled *Developing Web Services Using J2EE: An Example.*

Using the previous business classes as part of the application, we will be creating `ACMEProductInfoService` and `GetAcmeProductInfo` classes, which act as service providers and service requestors, respectively, using the Axis environment.

- The `ACMEProductInfoService` class uses the `AcmeXMLHelper` and `AcmeDAO` as helper classes for XML processing and database interaction. The `ACMEProductInfoService` class will be then deployed in the Axis environment as a service. This service will be invoked as requests and responses using the `GetAcmeProductInfo` application—a service requestor client using the Axis client engine.
- The `GetAcmeProductInfo` class acts as the service requestor using the Axis client environment. During communication with the service provider, it sends a SOAP request with a `Product ID` parameter and fetches a SOAP response with the complete product information as a string.

Now, let's take a closer look at the implementation and walk through the programming steps involved in building the service provider and service requestor.

Implementing the Service Provider (ACMEProductInfoService.java)

The source code implementation for the `ACMEProductInfoService` class is shown in Listing 4.40.

```
package jws.ch4.acmerpcservice;

import jws.ch4.xmlhelper.*;
import java.io.*;
import java.util.*;

public class AcmeProductInfoService {

   String pc;

   // Helper method for getting the ProductInfo
   public String getProduct(int productID)
                                    throws Exception {

      AcmeXMLHelper axh;

      try {
        // Instantiate the AcmeXMLHelper
        axh = new AcmeXMLHelper();

        // Call the Get Product method
        ProductID pc =
                 axh.getProductXMLasString(productID);

      } catch (Exception te) {
          te.printStackTrace();
      }
      // Return ProductInfo XML as String
      return pc;
   }
}
```

Listing 4.40 `AcmeProductInfoService.java.`

To compile and run the previous class, ensure that the CLASSPATH is set for the service provider environment. Then, navigate to the source directory and run the Ant build script. After successful compilation, deploy the `ACMEProductInfoService.class` as a service in the Axis environment. The deployment descriptor (WSDD) for deploying the `ACMEProductInfoService.class` as a service is as shown in Listing 4.41.

```
<deployment name="test"
 xmlns="http://xml.apache.org/axis/wsdd/"
 xmlns:java="http://xml.apache.org/axis/wsdd/providers/java"
 xmlns:xsd="http://www.w3.org/2000/10/XMLSchema"
 xmlns:xsi="http://www.w3.org/2000/10/XMLSchema-instance">
 <service name="acmerpcservice" provider="java:RPC">
   <parameter name="className"
     value="jws.ch4.acmerpcservice.AcmeProductInfoService"/>
   <parameter name="allowedMethods" value="*"/>
 </service>
</deployment>
```

Listing 4.41 Web service deployment descriptor (`wsdd.xml`) for AcmeProductInfoService.

If everything works successfully, you will get the output shown in Figure 4.20.

Implementing the Service Requestor (GetACMEProductInfo.java)

The source code implementation for `GetACMEProductInfo.java` is shown in Listing 4.42.

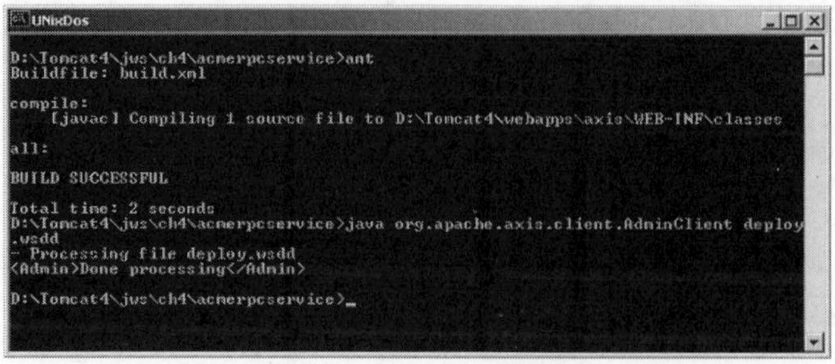

```
UNixDos

D:\Tomcat4\jws\ch4\acmerpcservice>ant
Buildfile: build.xml

compile:
    [javac] Compiling 1 source file to D:\Tomcat4\webapps\axis\WEB-INF\classes

all:

BUILD SUCCESSFUL

Total time: 2 seconds
D:\Tomcat4\jws\ch4\acmerpcservice>java org.apache.axis.client.AdminClient deploy
.wsdd
- Processing file deploy.wsdd
<Admin>Done processing</Admin>

D:\Tomcat4\jws\ch4\acmerpcservice>_
```

Figure 4.20 Output showing the packaging and deployment of AcmeProductInfoService.

```
package client;
import org.apache.axis.AxisFault;
import org.apache.axis.client.Call;
import org.apache.axis.client.Service;
import org.apache.axis.encoding.XMLType;
import javax.xml.rpc.ParameterMode;
import javax.xml.namespace.QName;
import java.net.URL;

public class GetAcmeProductInfo {

 // 'getProduct' method - Creates the Client
 //  SOAP request for obtaining product Info
 //  from the service provider

 public String getProduct(int productID) throws Exception {
   String endpoint =
        "http://localhost:8080/axis/services/acmerpcservice";

   // Create a new Service request
   Service  service = new Service();

   // Create the SOAP request message
   Call call = (Call) service.createCall();

   // Set the provider location
   call.setTargetEndpointAddress( endpoint );

   // Set the service name and methods
   call.setOperationName(
            new QName("acmeservice", "getProduct") );

   // Set the input parameters of the SOAP request
   call.addParameter( "productID",
                        XMLType.XSD_INT, ParameterMode.IN );

   // Set the return parameters of the SOAP response
   call.setReturnType( XMLType.XSD_STRING );

   // Invoke the service by sending the
 // request and retrieve the results
```

Listing 4.42 GetACMEProductInfo.java. *(continues)*

```
        // from the response
        Object responseObj = call.invoke(
                    new Object[] {new Integer(productID)} );

        // Retrieve the values from the response object
        String respString = (String) responseObj;

        return respString;
      }

      // Main Method
      public static void main(String args[]) {
           if (args.length != 1) {
               System.err.println(
                      "Usage: GetAcmeProductInfo <productID>" );
               System.exit(1);
           }

           String inp = args[0];
           int product = Integer.valueOf(inp).intValue();
           try {
              GetAcmeProductInfo gq = new GetAcmeProductInfo();
              String val = gq.getProduct(product);
              System.out.println("ACME Product Info: " + val);
           }
           catch( Exception e ) {
              // Trapping the SOAP Fault
              if ( e instanceof AxisFault ) {
                System.err.println(
                         ((AxisFault)e).dumpToString()  );
              } else
                  e.printStackTrace();
              }
           }
      }

     }
```

Listing 4.42 `GetACMEProductInfo.java`. *(continued)*

Ensure that the CLASSPATH is set for the service requestor environment and compile the source code. Upon successful compilation, the ACME Web services for getting the product information is ready for testing and use.

Testing the Services

To test the services, ensure that the environment is ready and try out following:

1. Ensure that the Tomcat server and PointBase database server is up and running. Also ensure that the `AcmeProductInfoService` is deployed. To find out the list of deployed services, you may try the following command:

   ```
   java org.apache.axis.client.AdminClient list
   ```

2. To test out and to invoke the `AcmeProductInfoService`, set the CLASSPATH to the service requestor environment and run the following command:

   ```
   java client.GetAcmeProductInfo 1001
   ```

   If everything works successfully, you will get the output shown in Figure 4.21.

Using the TCP monitor will show the SOAP request and responses. To start TCP monitor, run the following command:

```
java org.apache.axis.utils.tcpmon 9999 localhost 8080
```

This command assumes that the client listening port is 9999, and that the target server name is `localhost` running Tomcat using port 8080. Using the previous command, start the `tcpmon` utility. Set the client calling port as 9999 in `GetAcmeProductInfo.java` and then recompile it. Now, rerun the service client application.

The successful execution of the SOAP requests and responses will display the screen shown in Figure 4.22.

This summarizes the example scenario of creating SOAP RPC-based Web services using the Axis environment.

```
UNixDos
D:\Tomcat4\jws>javac -d . GetAcmeProductInfo.java

D:\Tomcat4\jws>java client.GetAcmeProductInfo 1001
ACME Product Info: <?xml version="1.0" encoding="UTF-8"?>
<ProductCatalog><LineItem><ItemNumber>1001</ItemNumber><ItemName>ACME Blade 1000
</ItemName><ItemDesc>Sparc III Processor, 1Ghz, 512MB, 42GB HD, Linux</ItemDesc>
<ItemPrice>1000.0</ItemPrice><Currency>USD</Currency></LineItem></ProductCatalog
>

D:\Tomcat4\jws>_
```

Figure 4.21 Output showing the service requestor invoking the service.

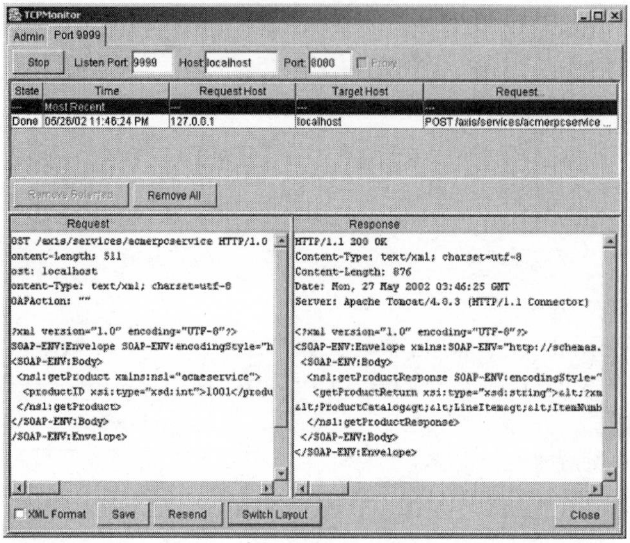

Figure 4.22 `tcpmon` showing the SOAP requests and responses.

Creating Messaging-Based Web Services (Scenario 2)

To implement this scenario, we build on the components discussed in Chapter 3, "Building the Web Services Architecture," by adding new business methods and then deploying them in the Axis environment.

Implementing the Business Methods

The following additional business methods are required for submitting the purchase order XML in the ACME database:

AcmeDAO. A DAO class abstracts the underlying data access implementation and enables the purchase order information to be stored to the database. The `AcmeDAO` uses the following value object classes `POHeader`, `PurchaseOrder`, and `POLine`, which represent the business objects buyer information and product order.

The source code for the value object `POHeader.java` is shown in Listing 4.43.

```
//POHeader.java
package jws.ch4.model;

import java.util.*;
import java.io.*;
```

Listing 4.43 `POHeader.java`.

```
// Value object representing the Buyer information
public class POHeader {

  private int poNumber;
  private String poDate;
  private String poBuyerNo;
  private String poBuyerName;
  private String shipToAddressStreet;
  private String shipToCity;
  private String shipToState;
  private String shipToZip;
  private String shipToCountry;
  private String paymentType;
  private String paymentNumber;
  private double totalPrice;

  // Accessor methods
  public void setPONumber(int ponum)  {
       poNumber = ponum;
  }

  public int getPONumber() {
      return poNumber;
  }

  public void setPODate(String podate) {
       poDate = podate;
  }

  public String getPODate() {
       return poDate;
  }

  public void setBuyerNumber(String buyerno) {
       poBuyerNo = buyerno;
  }

  public String getBuyerNumber() {
       return poBuyerNo;
  }

  public void setBuyerName(String buyername) {
       poBuyerName = buyername;
  }

  public String getBuyerName() {
       return poBuyerName;
  }
```

Listing 4.43 `POHeader.java`. *(continues)*

```
public void setShipToStreet(String shiptoaddr) {
     shipToAddressStreet = shiptoaddr;
}

public String getShipToStreet() {
     return shipToAddressStreet;
}

public void setShipToCity(String shiptocity) {
    shipToCity = shiptocity;
}

public String getShipToCity() {
    return shipToCity;
}

public void setShipToState(String shiptostate) {
    shipToState = shiptostate;
}

public String getShipToState()  {
    return shipToState;
}

public void setShipToZipcode(String shiptozip) {
     shipToZip = shiptozip;
}

public String getShipToZipcode() {
     return shipToZip;
}

public void setShipToCountry(String shiptocountry) {
     shipToCountry = shiptocountry;
}

public String getShipToCountry() {
     return shipToCountry;
}

public void setPaymentType(String paymenttype) {
      paymentType = paymenttype;
}

public String getPaymentType() {
```

Listing 4.43 POHeader.java.

```
        return paymentType;
    }

    public void setPaymentNumber(String paymentnumber) {
        paymentNumber = paymentnumber;
    }

    public String getPaymentNumber() {
        return paymentNumber;
    }

    public void setTotalPrice(double price) {
        totalPrice = price;
    }

    public double getTotalPrice() {
        return totalPrice;
    }
}
```

Listing 4.43 `POHeader.java`. *(continued)*

The source code for the value object `PurchaseOrder.java` is shown in Listing 4.44.

```
package jws.ch4.model;
import java.util.*;
import java.io.*;

public class PurchaseOrder {
    private POHeader poHeader = new POHeader();
    private ArrayList poLines = new ArrayList();

    public void setPOHeader(POHeader hdr) {
        poHeader = hdr;
    }

    public POHeader getPOHeader() {
        return poHeader;
    }

    public void setPOLines(ArrayList lines) {
```

Listing 4.44 `PurchaseOrder.java`. *(continues)*

```
            poLines = lines;
        }

        public ArrayList getPOLines() {
            return poLines;
        }
    }
```

Listing 4.44 `PurchaseOrder.java`. *(continued)*

The source code for the value object `POLines.java` representing the product order information is shown in Listing 4.45.

```
package jws.ch4.model;
    import java.util.*;
    import java.io.*;

    // Value object representing
    // the line Items (Product ordered)

    public class POLine {
       private int poNumber;
       private int poProductNo;
       private int poLineNo;
       private int poProductQty;
       private double poUnitPrice;

       // Accessor methods
       public void setPONumber(int ponum) {
          poNumber = ponum;
       }

       public int getPONumber() {
          return poNumber;
       }

       public void setProductNumber(int prodNo) {
          poProductNo = prodNo;
       }

       public int getProductNumber() {
```

Listing 4.45 `POLines.java`.

```
        return poProductNo;
    }

    public void setLineNumber(int lineNo) {
        poLineNo = lineNo;
    }

    public int getLineNumber() {
        return poLineNo;
    }

    public void setProductQty(int prodQty) {
        poProductQty = prodQty;
    }

    public int getProductQty() {
        return poProductQty;
    }

    public void setUnitPrice(double unitPrice) {
        poUnitPrice = unitPrice;
    }

    public double getUnitPrice() {
        return poUnitPrice;
    }
}
```

Listing 4.45 `POLines.java`. *(continued)*

The methods shown in Listing 4.46 are used by the DAO to insert the business objects (`POHeader`, `PurchaseOrder`, and `POLine`) in the database.

```
// Insert the purchase order
public boolean insertPurchaseOrder(PurchaseOrder poObj)
                                        throws AcmeDAOException {

   Connection c = null;
   PreparedStatement ps = null;
   ResultSet rs = null;
```

Listing 4.46 DAO methods for inserting data (`AcmeDAO.java`). *(continues)*

```
POHeader poHdr = poObj.getPOHeader();
ArrayList poLineList = poObj.getPOLines();

//Make Database connection and Insert data
try {
  c = getDataSource().getConnection();

  ps = c.prepareStatement("insert into
                  purchase_order_header (po_num, po_date,
                  buyer_no, buyer_name, street_addr, city,
                  state, zip, country, payment_type,
                  payment_number, total_amount)"
            + "values (?, ?, ?, ?, ?, ?, ?, ?, ?, ?, ?, ?) ",
             ResultSet.TYPE_SCROLL_INSENSITIVE,
             ResultSet.CONCUR_READ_ONLY);

  ps.setInt(1,    poHdr.getPONumber());
  ps.setString(2, poHdr.getPODate());
  ps.setString(3, poHdr.getBuyerNumber());
  ps.setString(4, poHdr.getBuyerName());
  ps.setString(5, poHdr.getShipToStreet());
  ps.setString(6, poHdr.getShipToCity());
  ps.setString(7, poHdr.getShipToState());
  ps.setString(8, poHdr.getShipToZipcode());
  ps.setString(9, poHdr.getShipToCountry());
  ps.setString(10, poHdr.getPaymentType());
  ps.setString(11, poHdr.getPaymentNumber());
  ps.setDouble(12, poHdr.getTotalPrice());

  boolean bSuccess = false;
  if (ps.executeUpdate() > 0) {
     Iterator itr = poLineList.iterator();
     bSuccess = true;
     while (itr.hasNext()) {
       POLine poLine = (POLine)itr.next();
       if (! insertPOLine(poLine)) {
          bSuccess = false;
          break;
       }
     }
  }
  ps.close();
  c.close();
  return bSuccess;
} catch (SQLException se) {
     throw new AcmeDAOException("SQLException: "
                                          + se.getMessage());
```

Listing 4.46 DAO methods for inserting data (AcmeDAO.java).

```
    }
  }


  //Insert the product order
  public boolean insertPOLine(POLine line)
                                    throws AcmeDAOException {

    Connection c = null;
    PreparedStatement ps = null;
    ResultSet rs = null;

    //Make connection and Insert data
    try {
      c = getDataSource().getConnection();
      ps = c.prepareStatement("insert into
                              purchase_order_line (
                              po_num, line_num,
                              product_no, qty, unit_price)"
                              + "values (?, ?, ?, ?, ?) ",
                              ResultSet.TYPE_SCROLL_INSENSITIVE,
                              ResultSet.CONCUR_READ_ONLY);

      ps.setInt(1, line.getPONumber());
      ps.setInt(2, line.getLineNumber());
      ps.setInt(3, line.getProductNumber());
      ps.setInt(4, line.getProductQty());
      ps.setDouble(5, line.getUnitPrice());

      boolean bSuccess = false;
      if (ps.executeUpdate() > 0) {
        bSuccess = true;
      }
      ps.close();
      c.close();
      return bSuccess;

    } catch (SQLException se) { throw new
          AcmeDAOException("SQLException: "+ se.getMessage());
    }
  }
```

Listing 4.46 DAO methods for inserting data (`AcmeDAO.java`). *(continued)*

AcmeXMLHelper. This class takes the Purchase order XML as a string from the application and constructs Java objects for use with

AcmeDAO. We will be adding the methods shown in Listing 4.47 to convert the string (XML data) to business objects (POHeader, PurchaseOrder, POLine) for persisting in the ACME database.

```
public boolean createPurchaseOrder(String POXML)
                                          throws XMLException {
      Document poDoc = null;

      boolean bRetValue = false;

      // Obtain an instance of DocumentBuilderFactory
      //  and get an Instance of DocumentBuilder

      try {
         DocumentBuilderFactory factory =
                           DocumentBuilderFactory.newInstance();
         DocumentBuilder builder =
                           factory.newDocumentBuilder();
         InputSource isStr;

         // Use the DocumentBuilder to parse
         // XML string and contruct a DOM

         try {
             StringReader xml = new StringReader(POXML);
             isStr = new InputSource(xml);
             poDoc = builder.parse(isStr);
         } catch (Exception ee) {
             System.out.println("parse exception....");
             ee.printStackTrace();
         }

         if (poDoc == null)
            return false;
         else
            System.out.println("poDoc not null....");

         // Get the root element In the DOM tree
         Element poRoot = poDoc.getDocumentElement();

         if (poRoot == null) {
            System.out.println("Root element is null")
         } else
            System.out.println("Root element is NOT null");

         // Instantiate PurchaseOrder and POHeader objects
         PurchaseOrder poObj = new PurchaseOrder();
```

Listing 4.47 XML helper methods for AcmePOService (AcmeXMLHelper.java)

```
POHeader poHdr = new POHeader();

// Get the necessary XML Node value
// one by one and the set the POHeader
// object attributes

int poNumber =
        Integer.valueOf(getNodeValue
       (poRoot,"PurchaseOrderNumber")).intValue();
poHdr.setPONumber(poNumber);
System.out.println(poNumber);
poHdr.setPODate(getNodeValue(poRoot,"Date"));
poHdr.setBuyerNumber(getNodeValue(poRoot,"BuyerNumber"));
poHdr.setBuyerName(getNodeValue(poRoot,"BuyerName"));

NodeList nodes =
   ((Element)poRoot).getElementsByTagName("ShipToAddress");

if (nodes.getLength() < 0) {
      throw new Exception("getElementsByTagName
              for ShipToAddress does not return any node");
}

Node shipNode = nodes.item(0);
poHdr.setShipToStreet(getNodeValue(shipNode,"Street"));
poHdr.setShipToCity(getNodeValue(shipNode,"City"));
poHdr.setShipToState(getNodeValue(shipNode,"State"));
poHdr.setShipToZipcode(getNodeValue(shipNode,"Zip"));

poHdr.setShipToCountry(getNodeValue(shipNode,"Country"));
nodes =
    ((Element)poRoot).getElementsByTagName("PaymentInfo");

if (nodes.getLength() < 0) {
    throw new Exception("getElementsByTagName for
                    PaymentInfo does not return any node");
}

Node paymentNode = nodes.item(0);
poHdr.setPaymentType(getNodeValue(paymentNode,"Type"));
poHdr.setPaymentNumber
         (getNodeValue(paymentNode,"Number"));
poHdr.setTotalPrice(Double.valueOf
      (getNodeValue(poRoot,"TotalAmount")).doubleValue());

poObj.setPOHeader(poHdr);

// Print success message
```

Listing 4.47 XML helper methods for AcmePOService (`AcmeXMLHelper.java`). *(continues)*

```
            System.out.println("PO Header submission successful...");

            // Get Line Item details In the DOM tree
            // as a arraylist of POLine objects

            ArrayList poLineList =
                          createPOLines(poDoc, poRoot, poNumber);

            // Set the POLine list In the PurchaseOrder object
            poObj.setPOLines(poLineList);
            System.out.println("LineItems submission successful.");

            AcmeDAOImpl adi = new  AcmeDAOImpl();
            bRetValue = adi.insertPurchaseOrder(poObj);
            System.out.println("PO submission successful...");

         } catch (Exception e) {
              throw new XMLException(e.toString());
         }
         return bRetValue;
    }

    public ArrayList createPOLines(Document poDoc,
              Element poRoot, int PONumber) throws XMLException {

         ArrayList poLineList = new ArrayList();

         // Get the necessary XML Node value
         // one by one and the set the POLine  object attributes

         try {
           NodeList cNodes = poDoc.getElementsByTagName("LineItem");
           int count = cNodes.getLength();
           if (count > 0) {
              for (int i = 0; i < count; i++) {
                 Node line = cNodes.item(i);
                 POLine poLine = new POLine();
                 poLine.setPONumber(PONumber);

                 poLine.setProductNumber(Integer.valueOf(getNodeValue
                            (line, i, "ProductNumber")).intValue());
                 poLine.setLineNumber(i+1);
                 poLine.setProductQty(Integer.valueOf
                        (getNodeValue(line, i, "Quantity")).intValue());
                 poLine.setUnitPrice(Double.valueOf
                   (getNodeValue(line, i, "UnitPrice")).doubleValue());
                 poLineList.add(poLine);
```

Listing 4.47 XML helper methods for AcmePOService (`AcmeXMLHelper.java`).

```
                }
            }
        } catch (Exception e) {
                throw new XMLException(e.toString());
        }
        return poLineList;
    }
```

Listing 4.47 XML helper methods for AcmePOService (`AcmeXMLHelper.java`). *(continued)*

Now compile the classes and ensure that these classes are available as part of your Tomcat webapps directory specific to the Axis environment.

Implementing the Service

Using the previous business classes as part of the application, we will be creating `ACMEPOService` and `SubmitPOService` classes, which act as service providers and service requestors, respectively, using the Axis environment.

- The `ACMEPOService` class is the service provider application deployed in the Axis environment as a service. It uses `AcmeXML-Helper` and `AcmeDAO` as helper classes for processing the purchase order XML and to persist the PO data in the ACME database. This service will receive W3C documents as XML messages from the `SubmitPOService` application—a service requestor client using the Axis client engine.
- The `SubmitPOService` class acts as the service requestor using the Axis client environment. During communication with the service provider, it sends a purchase order as an XML message (W3C Document) and then it receives a response message as an XML message from the service provider.

Now, let's take a closer look at the implementation and walk through the programming steps involved in building the service provider and the service requestor.

Implementing the Service Provider (ACMEPOService.java)

The source code implementation for the `ACMEPOService` class is shown in Listing 4.48.

```
package jws.ch4.acmemsgservice;

import org.w3c.dom.*;
import org.apache.axis.*;
import java.io.*;
import java.util.*;
import javax.xml.parsers.*;
import jws.ch4.xmlhelper.*;
import jws.ch4.dao.*;
import jws.ch4.model.*;
import jws.ch4.exceptions.*;
import org.apache.xml.serialize.*;
import org.apache.xerces.dom.*;
import org.apache.axis.client.*;
import org.apache.axis.message.*;
import org.apache.axis.utils.XMLUtils;
import org.w3c.dom.Element;

public class AcmePOService {

  String pc;
  String poxml;

  // Helper method for submitting the Purchase Order
  public Document submitAcmePO(Document podoc) {
    AcmeXMLHelper axh;
    AcmeDAOImpl dao;
    Document doc = null;

    try {
     axh = new AcmeXMLHelper();

     // Convert W3C document to String
     poxml = getXMLString(podoc);

     // Submit the purchase order
     boolean bSubmit = axh.createPurchaseOrder(poxml);

     if (bSubmit) {
         pc = "Submitted Purchase Order successfully";
     }
     else
```

Listing 4.48 AcmePOService.java.

```
                pc = "Failed to submit Purchase Order";

            // Creating a W3C document for response message

            DOMImplementationImpl domImpl
= new DOMImplementationImpl();

            doc = domImpl.createDocument(null, "POStatus", null);

            Element root = doc.getDocumentElement();
            Element e = doc.createElement("status");
            e.appendChild(doc.createTextNode(pc));
            root.appendChild(e);
            doc.appendChild(root);
           } catch (Exception te) {
              te.printStackTrace();
           }

           // Return the response message
           return doc;
        }

        // Helper method for converting W3C document to String
        private String getXMLString(Document doc)
                                               throws XMLException {
        try {
            StringWriter XMLStrWriter = new StringWriter();
            XMLSerializer serializer = new XMLSerializer();
            serializer.setOutputCharStream (XMLStrWriter);
            OutputFormat fmt = new OutputFormat (doc);
            fmt.setIndenting(true);
            serializer.setOutputFormat (fmt);
            serializer.serialize(doc);
            String s = XMLStrWriter.toString();
            System.out.println("getXMLString: "+s);
            return s;
        }
        catch (Exception e) {
                throw new XMLException(e.toString());
        }
    }
}
```

Listing 4.48 `AcmePOService.java`. *(continued)*

To compile and run the previous class, ensure that the CLASSPATH is set for the service provider environment. Then, navigate to the source directory and run the Ant build script. After successful compilation, deploy `ACMEPOoService.class` as a service in the Axis environment. The deployment descriptor (WSDD) for deploying `ACMEPOService.class` as a service is shown in Listing 4.49.

```
<deployment name="test" xmlns="http://xml.apache.org/axis/wsdd/"
      xmlns:java="http://xml.apache.org/axis/wsdd/providers/java"
      xmlns:xsd="http://www.w3.org/2000/10/XMLSchema"
      xmlns:xsi="http://www.w3.org/2000/10/XMLSchema-instance">

      <service name="acmemsgservice" provider="java:MSG">
        <parameter name="className"
            value="jws.ch4.acmemsgservice.AcmePOService"/>
        <parameter name="allowedMethods" value="submitAcmePO"/>
      </service>
 </deployment>
```

Listing 4.49 Web service deployment descriptor (`wsdd.xml`) for AcmePOService.

If everything works successfully, you will get the output shown in Figure 4.23.

Implementing the Service Requestor (SubmitPOService.java)

The source code implementation for `SubmitPOService.java` is shown in Listing 4.50.

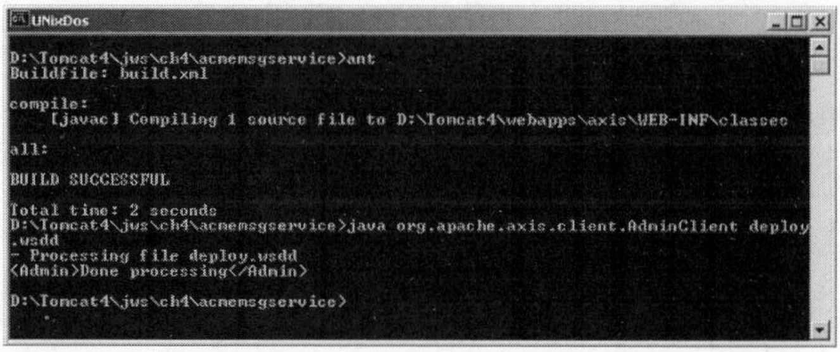

```
D:\Tomcat4\jws\ch4\acmemsgservice>ant
Buildfile: build.xml

compile:
    [javac] Compiling 1 source file to D:\Tomcat4\webapps\axis\WEB-INF\classes

all:

BUILD SUCCESSFUL

Total time: 2 seconds
D:\Tomcat4\jws\ch4\acmemsgservice>java org.apache.axis.client.AdminClient deploy
.wsdd
- Processing file deploy.wsdd
<Admin>Done processing</Admin>

D:\Tomcat4\jws\ch4\acmemsgservice>
```

Figure 4.23 Output showing the packaging and deployment of AcmePOService.

```
package client;

import java.io.*;
import java.util.Vector;

import org.apache.axis.client.Service;
import org.apache.axis.client.Call;
import org.apache.axis.message.*;
import org.apache.axis.*;
import java.net.URL;
import org.apache.axis.utils.XMLUtils;
import org.w3c.dom.Element;

public class SubmitPOService {

  String str;

  public String execute() throws Exception {

    try{

        // Define the SOAP endpoint
        String endpoint =
         "http://localhost:8080/axis/services/acmemsgservice";

         // Read the PurchaseOrder.xml
         InputStream is =
             ClassLoader.getSystemResourceAsStream
                          ("PurchaseOrder.xml");

         // Create a service
         Service  service = new Service();

         // Create a Service request call to the server
         Call call = (Call) service.createCall();

         // Set the SOAP endpoint for the request call
          call.setTargetEndpointAddress(endpoint);

         // Create SOAP envelope with the
         //PO document as payload
         SOAPEnvelope env = new SOAPEnvelope(is);

         // Send the PO document to the destination
```

Listing 4.50 `SubmitPOService.java`. *(continues)*

```
                // and wait for the response message.
                // The response message will be a document as well.

                SOAPEnvelope elems = (SOAPEnvelope)call.invoke(env);

                //Retrieve the SOAP body element
                //from the SOAP envelope.
                SOAPBodyElement elem = elems.getFirstBody();

                // Get the XML element from the SOAPBodyElement
                Element  e  = elem.getAsDOM();

                // Convert the XMLElement to String
                str = XMLUtils.ElementToString(e);
            }
            catch(Exception e){
                    e.printStackTrace();
            }

            // Return the response message as String
            return( str );
        }

        public static void main(String[] args) throws Exception {

            String res = (new SubmitPOService()).execute();
                // Print the response message
            System.out.println(res);
        }
    }
```

Listing 4.50 `SubmitPOService.java`. ***(continued)***

Ensure that the CLASSPATH is set for the service requestor environment and compile the source code. Upon successful compilation, the ACME Web services for getting the product information is ready for testing and use.

Testing the Services

To test the scenario, use the ACME purchase order (XML file) sample shown in Listing 4.51. Ensure that this file exists in the CLASSPATH.

```
<PurchaseOrder>
   <Header>
      <PurchaseOrderNumber>212</PurchaseOrderNumber>
         <Date>02/22/2002</Date>
         <BuyerNumber>0002232</BuyerNumber>
         <BuyerName>Roger Marrison</BuyerName>
          <ShipToAddress>
             <Street>233 St-John Blvd</Street>
             <City>Boston</City>
             <State>MA</State>
             <Zip>03054</Zip>
             <Country>USA</Country>
          </ShipToAddress>
        <TotalAmount>870.00</TotalAmount>
       <PaymentInfo>
       <Type>Visa</Type>
       <Number>03239898989890</Number>
       </PaymentInfo>
   </Header>
   <LineItem>
        <ProductNumber>22112</ProductNumber>
        <Quantity>250</Quantity>
        <UnitPrice>10.00</UnitPrice>
   </LineItem>
</PurchaseOrder>
```

Listing 4.51 Acme purchase order (XML file).

1. To test the services, ensure that the Tomcat and PointBase database servers are up and running. Also, ensure that `AcmePOService` is deployed. To find out the list of deployed services, you may try the following command:

   ```
   java org.apache.axis.client.AdminClient list
   ```

2. To test out and invoke `AcmePOService`, set the CLASSPATH to the service requestor environment and run the following command:

   ```
   java client.submitPOService
   ```

   If everything works successfully, you will get the output shown in Figure 4.24.

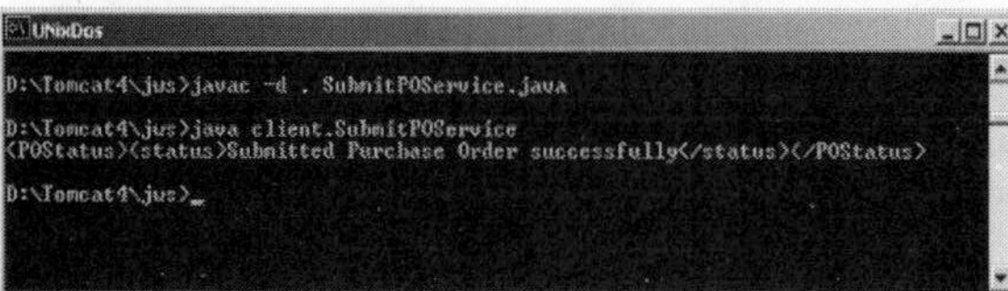

Figure 4.24 Output showing the successful submission of a purchase order with AcmePOService.

Use the TCP monitor to display the SOAP message sent and received. To start TCP monitor, run the following command:

```
java org.apache.axis.utils.tcpmon 9999 localhost 8080
```

The previous command assumes that the client listening port is 9999 and the target server name is `localhost` running the Tomcat server using port 8080. Using the previous command, start the `tcpmon` utility. Set the client calling port as 9999 in the `SubmitPOService.java` and then recompile it. Now, rerun the service client application.

Upon successful execution of `SubmitPOService`, the TCP monitor will display the output shown in Figure 4.25.

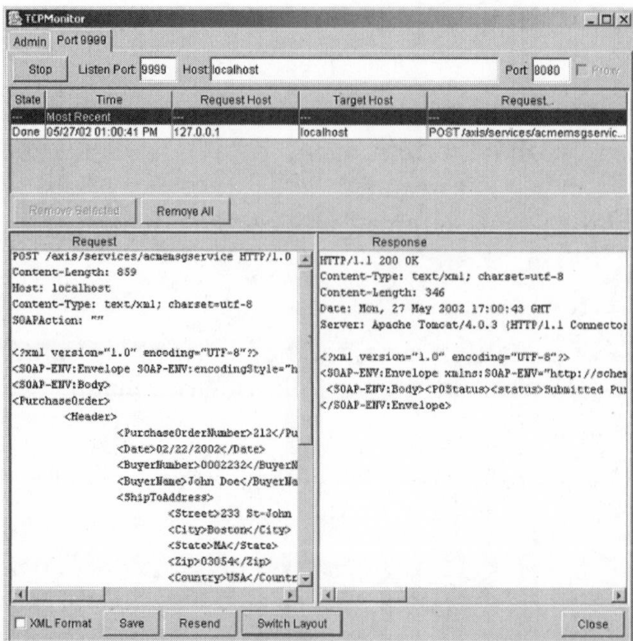

Figure 4.25 TCP monitor showing the SOAP messages with AcmePOService.

This concludes our case study example on creating SOAP RPC and messaging-based Web services using Apache Axis.

So far, we have discussed SOAP specifications and the role of SOAP in Web services, and we studied how we can use SOAP implementation for developing Web services.

Now, let's take a look at the some of the known limitations of SOAP.

Known Limitations of SOAP

Although the SOAP specifications define a promising communication model for Web services, the following limitations exist that are not currently addressed by the SOAP specifications:

1. The specification does not address message reliability, secure message delivery, transactional support, and its communication requirements of a SOAP implementation.
2. The specification does not address issues like object activation and object lifecycle management.
3. The specification discusses HTTP as the primary transport protocol but does not discuss the usage of other transport protocols.
4. The specification does not address how to handle SOAP messages out of a SOAP implementation.

Note that the limitations of SOAP have been currently well addressed by the ebXML framework as part of the ebXML messaging service, which complements SOAP and other Web services standards.

Summary

In this chapter, we have had a detailed discussion on the fundamentals of SOAP and its role in developing Web services. We have looked at how SOAP provides an XML-based communication protocol and a consistent mechanism for RPC and messaging between applications, components, objects, and systems across networks. We demonstrated a Web services-based application using a SOAP implementation and studied how SOAP provides the communication for Web services.

In general, we focused on the background and fundamentals of SOAP and XML messaging, SOAP encoding, transport protocols and security, and developing SOAP and Web services applications.

In the next chapter, we will discuss how to describe and publish Web services using WSDL and UDDI.

CHAPTER

5

Description and Discovery of Web Services

In Chapter 4, "Developing Web Services Using SOAP," we saw how to develop and deploy Web services that use the Simple Object Access Protocol, or SOAP. But there is more to Web services than just SOAP support. A Web service can further its capabilities by supporting a description of its interfaces so that its potential users can study it and determine whether the Web service supports the behavior that they need. Also, an organization that develops Web services can register these Web services at a location that is well known, so that its potential users can *discover* them.

This chapter covers such description and discovery aspects of a Web service. Detailed information is provided on two mainstream technologies that are used today for describing and discovering Web services: the Web Services Description Language (WSDL) and Universal Description, Discovery, and Integration (UDDI). Furthermore, examples demonstrate how to use these technologies in the real world.

The following are key topics covered in this chapter:

- Web Services Description Language (WSDL)
  - WSDL in the World of Web services
  - Anatomy of a WSDL definition document
  - WSDL bindings
  - WSDL tools

- Universal Description, Discovery, and Integration (UDDI)
- Programming with UDDI
- Inquiry APIs
- Publishing APIs
- Implementations of UDDI
- Registering as a Systinet UDDI Registry user
- Publishing information to a UDDI registry
- Searching information in a UDDI registry
- Deleting information from a UDDI registry

Web Services Description Language (WSDL)

Microsoft, IBM, and Ariba released the first version of the WSDL specification jointly, in September 2000, briefly after announcing a UDDI specification along with 36 other companies. This version of WSDL was based on two precedent description languages: Network Accessible Services Specification Language (NASSL) and (SOAP Contract Language SCL), from IBM and Microsoft, respectively. Later on in March 2001, the same companies joined by a few others submitted the WSDL 1.1 specification to W3C. Thus, currently the WSDL specification is in works at W3C. Officially, it is a W3C Note that forms the basis of the upcoming WSDL 1.2 specification from W3C. This chapter goes into detail in understanding WSDL 1.1.

JSR 110 (Java API for WSDL) is currently in the works in the Java Community Process (JCP). When released, it will provide an API for manipulating WSDL documents instead of directly interacting with the XML syntax of WSDL. This would avoid manipulating the WSDL documents with the help of low level APIs such as JAXP. JWSDL would be much easier and faster to use, simplifying things further for a developer. More information on JWSDL can be obtained from the JCP Web site at www.jcp.org/jsr/detail/110.jsp.

WSDL in the World of Web Services

WSDL, as we know, is a description language for Web services. So what does this exactly mean? This means that WSDL represents information about the interface and semantics of how to invoke or call a Web service. A WSDL definition contains four important pieces of information about the Web service:

- Interface information describing all the publicly available functions
- Data type information for the incoming (request) and outgoing (response) messages to these functions
- Binding information about the protocol to be used for invoking the specified Web service
- Address information for locating the specified Web service

Once we develop a Web service, we create its WSDL definition. We can create this definition either manually or by using a tool. Many tools are available for generating a WSDL definition from existing Java classes, J2EE components (such as Servlets/EJBs), or from scratch. Once the WSDL definition is created, a link to it is published in a Web services registry (based on UDDI, for instance), so that the potential user(s) of this Web service can follow this link and find out the location of the Web service, the function calls that it supports, and how to invoke these calls. Finally, the user(s) would use this information to formulate a SOAP request or any other type of request based on the binding protocol supported, in order to invoke the function on a Web service.

Web Service Life Cycle

Figure 5.1 illustrates the steps of the Web service life cycle.

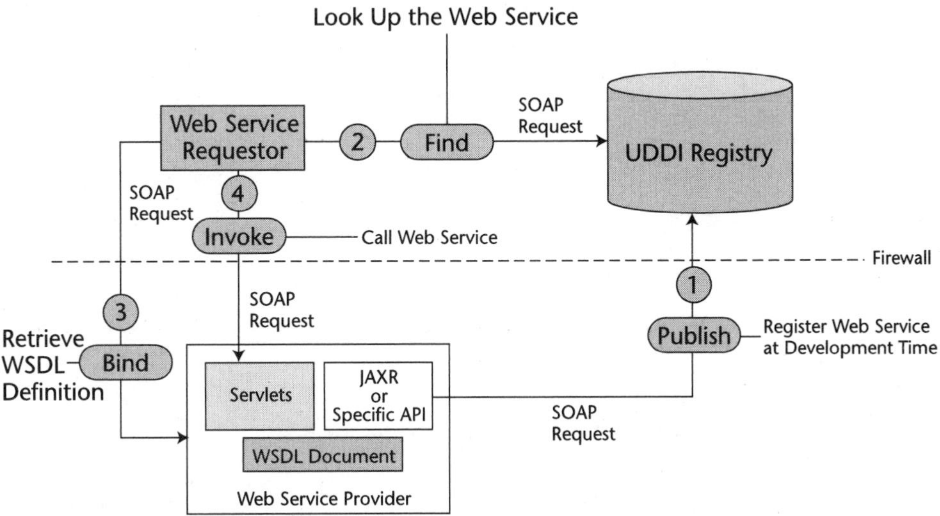

Figure 5.1 Web service life cycle.

In Figure 5.1, all of the communication over the wire takes place on SOAP. The following list explains the steps depicted in Figure 5.1:

- Step 1 illustrates a service provider publishing its Web service to a UDDI registry. This is when the service provider would create a WSDL definition and publish a link to this definition along with the rest of the Web service information to a UDDI registry.
- Step 2 illustrates an interested service user locating the Web service and finally obtaining information about invoking the Web service from the published WSDL definition. This step involves downloading a WSDL definition to the service user system and deserializing WSDL to a Java class (or any other language). This Java interface serves as a proxy to the actual Web service. It consists of the binding information of the Web service.
- Step 3 shows the service user binding at runtime to the Web service. In this step, the service user's application would make use of the Java interface representing WSDL as a proxy, in order to bind to the Web service.
- Step 4 finally shows the service user invoking the Web service based on the service invocation information it extracted from the Web service WSDL definition. This is when the service user's application would make use of the Java interface representing WSDL as a proxy, in order to invoke the methods/functions exposed by the Web service.

Language and Platform Independency of WSDL

WSDL is capable of describing Web services that are implemented using any language and deployed on any platform. Thus, WSDL contributes toward enabling interoperability in the Web service architecture. In other words, as long as a WSDL definition can be understood and consumed by the service user, the service user systems can obtain all of the information necessary to invoke a Web service potentially developed and deployed using a completely different set of platform tools and servers.

Now, let's see what a typical WSDL document looks like and understand its structural elements.

Anatomy of a WSDL Definition Document

A WSDL definition document consists of the following seven key structural elements:

<definitions>. A WSDL document is a set of definitions. These definitions are defined inside the <definitions> element, which is the root element in a WSDL document. It defines the name of the Web service and also declares the namespaces that are used throughout the rest of the WSDL document.

<types>. This element defines all of the data types that would be used to describe the messages that are exchanged between the Web service and the service user. WSDL does not mandate the use of a specific typing system. However, as per the WSDL specification, XML Schema is the default typing system.

XML Schema was discussed in Chapter 4, "Developing Web Services Using SOAP," in the context of SOAP encoding.

<message>. This element represents a logical definition of the data being transmitted between the Web service and the service user. This element describes a one-way message, which may represent a request or response sent to or from the Web service. It contains zero or more message `<part>` elements, which basically refer to the request parameters or response return values.

<portType>. This element defines the abstract definition of the operations supported by a Web service, by combining various request and response messages defined by `<message>` elements. Each operation refers to an input message and an output message.

<binding>. This element specifies a concrete protocol and data format used for representing the operations and messages defined by a particular `<portType>`, on the wire.

<port>. This element specifies an address for binding to the Web service.

<service>. This element aggregates a set of related `<port>` elements, each which uniquely specify the binding information of the Web service. A `<service>` consisting of multiple `<port>` elements essentially represents the capability of the service to be invoked over multiple bindings. More information on WSDL bindings is discussed in the next section.

We will further examine each of these elements later. First, let's take a look at Listing 5.1, which shows a WSDL document describing a weather information Web service, `WeatherInfoService`. This WSDL definition is present in the `WeatherInfo.wsdl` file.

```
<?xml version="1.0"?>

<definitions name="WeatherInfo"
targetNamespace="http://myweather.com/weatherinfo.wsdl"
xmlns:tns="http://myweather.com/weatherinfo.wsdl"
xmlns:xsd1="http://myweather.com/weatherinfo.xsd"
xmlns:soap="http://schemas.xmlsoap.org/wsdl/soap/"
xmlns="http://schemas.xmlsoap.org/wsdl/">

     <types>
          <schema targetNamespace=
          "http://myweather.com/weatherinfo.xsd" xmlns=
          "http://www.w3.org/2000/10/XMLSchema">
               <element name="WeatherInfoRequest">
                    <complexType>
                         <all>
                              <element name="Country"
                              type="string"/>

                              <element name="Zip"
                              type="string"/>

                              <element name="Instant"
                              type="string"/>
                         </all>
                    </complexType>
               </element>

               <element name="WeatherInfo">
                    <complexType>
                         <all>
                              <element name="FTemp"
                              type="float"/>

                              <element name="Humidity"
                              type="float"/>
                         </all>
                    </complexType>
               </element>
          </schema>
     </types>

     <message name="GetWeatherInfoInput">
          <part name="WeatherInfoRequestSpec"
          element="xsd1:WeatherInfoRequest"/>
     </message>

     <message name="GetWeatherInfoOutput">
          <part name="WeatherInfo"
```

Listing 5.1 WeatherInfo.wsdl.

```
        element="xsd1:WeatherInfo"/>
    </message>


    <portType name="WeatherInfoPortType">
        <operation name="GetWeatherInfo">
            <input message="tns:GetWeatherInfoInput"/>
            <output message="tns:GetWeatherInfoOutput"/>
        </operation>



    </portType>

    <binding name="WeatherInfoSoapBinding"
    type="tns:WeatherInfoPortType">

        <soap:binding style="document"
        transport="http://schemas.xmlsoap.org/soap/http"/>

        <operation name="GetWeatherInfo">

            <soap:operation soapAction=
            "http://myweather.com/GetWeatherInfo"/>

            <input>
                <soap:body use="literal"/>
            </input>

            <output>
                <soap:body use="literal"/>
            </output>
        </operation>
    </binding>

    <service name="WeatherInfoService">

        <documentation>
            Provides Weather Information
        </documentation>

        <port name="WeatherInfoPort"
        binding="tns:WeatherInfoSoapBinding">
            <soap:address location=
            "http://myweather.com/provideweatherinfo"/>
        </port>
    </service>
</definitions>
```

Listing 5.1 WeatherInfo.wsdl. *(continued)*

Now, let's understand how exactly `WeatherInfo.wsdl` describes the `WeatherInfoService` Web service.

<definitions> Element

The `<definitions>` element specifies the name of the document in which this WSDL definition is stored, which is `WeatherInfo` in our case.

This element specifies namespaces that would be used in the rest of the WSDL document. The following are the two important namespaces that the `<definitions>` element defines:

WSDL instance specific namespace. The `targetNamespace` attribute of the `<definitions>` element lets the WSDL document make references to itself as an XML Schema namespace. Note however that it is not required for the WSDL document to actually exist at the address specified by the `targetNamespace` attribute. This attribute is just a mechanism to refer to our WSDL definition in a unique way.

Default namespace for a WSDL document. The default namespace is specified by `xmlns="http://schemas.xmlsoap.org/wsdl/"`. The default namespace indicates that all of the elements in this WSDL definition without a namespace prefix, such as `<types>`, `<message>`, and `<portType>`, are part of this namespace.

<message> Element

WeatherInfo.wsdl defines two `<message>` elements.

The first `<message>` definition named `GetWeatherInfoInput` will be used later to define the input message of the `GetWeatherInfo` operation. The second `<message>` definition named `GetWeatherInfoOutput` will be used later to define the output message of the `GetWeatherInfo` operation. This binding of `<message>` definitions to an actual operation is defined in the `<portType>` element.

Again, each of these `<message>` definitions consists of a `<part>` element. In case of the `GetWeatherInfoInput` message, `<part>` essentially specifies the name, that is, `WeatherInfoRequestSpec`, and type, that is, `WeatherInfoRequest`, of the request parameter to `GetWeatherInfo` operation. Whereas, in case of the `GetWeatherInfoOutput` message, `<part>` refers to the name and type of the return value sent within the response of the `GetWeatherInfo` operation. Note that both `WeatherInfoRequest` and `WeatherInfo`, which were referred to by the `type` attribute of `<part>` element also were defined by the preceding `<types>` element.

Also in cases where operations take multiple arguments or return multiple values, the `<message>` element can define multiple `<part>` elements.

<portType> Element

The `<portType>` element in `WeatherInfo.wsdl` defines a single operation named `GetWeatherInfo` by combining the `<input>` message as defined by the `GetWeatherInfoInput` `<message>` element and the `<output>` message as defined by the `GetWeatherInfoOutput` `<message>` element.

Note the use of `WeatherInfo.wsdl` as a target namespace by the `<input>` and `<output>` elements.

Four types of operations are supported by WSDL:

One-way operation. One-way operation represents a service that just receives the message, and thus a one-way operation is typically defined by a single `<input>` message element.

Request-response operation. A request-response operation represents a service that receives a request message and sends a response message. Typically, a request-response operation is defined by one `<input>` message followed by one `<output>` message. An optional `<fault>` element also can be included in the definition of a request-response operation to specify the abstract message format for any error messages that may be output as a result of the operation.

The `GetWeatherInfo` operation follows the request-response transmission pattern.

Solicit-response operation. A solicit-response operation represents a service that sends a request message and that receives the response message. Such operations are therefore defined by one `<output>` message, followed by an `<input>` message. A solicit-response operation also can include a `<fault>` element in order to specify the format of any error messages resulting from the operation.

Notification operation. This operation represents a service that sends a message, hence this kind of operation is represented by a single `<output>` element.

Figure 5.2 provides the pictorial representation of the previous four transmission types.

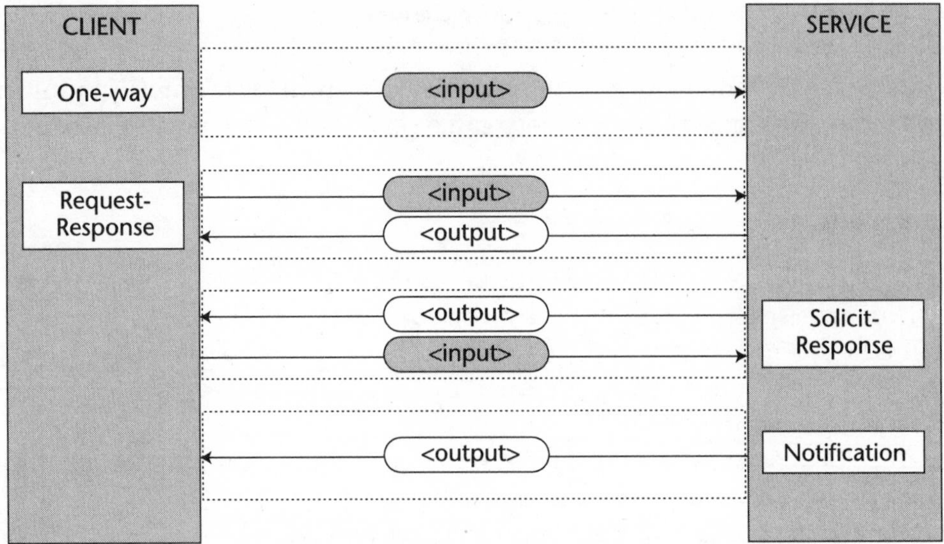

Figure 5.2 WSDL operation types.

<binding> Element

A binding defines the message format and protocol details for operations and messages defined by a particular `<portType>`. There may be any number of bindings for a given `<portType>`. The `type` attribute of the `<binding>` element refers to the `<portType>` that it binds to, which is `WeatherInfoPortType` in our case. Our `WeatherInfoService` specifies a SOAP binding, as is defined in the WSDL 1.1 specification. The WSDL 1.1 SOAP binding is discussed in detail in a later section titled *SOAP Binding*.

<service> Element

The `<service>` element specifies the location of the service. Because our `WeatherInfoService` is bound to SOAP, we use the `<soap:address>` element and specify the service URL as `http://myweather.com/provideweatherinfo/`.

Now, let's take a look at the support for various bindings in the WSDL 1.1 specification.

WSDL Bindings

In WSDL, the term binding refers to the process of associating protocol or data format information with an abstract entity such as `<message>`, `<operation>`, or `<portType>`. In this section, we examine the support for bindings in the WSDL 1.1 specification. Let's begin with the WSDL binding extensions.

WSDL Binding Extensions

WSDL allows user-defined elements, also known as *Extensibility Elements*, under various elements defined by a default WSDL namespace. These elements are commonly used to specify some technology-specific binding, although they can be used for other purposes as well. Extensibility elements, when used to specify a technology-specific binding, are known as *WSDL Binding Extensions*.

Extensibility elements provide a powerful mechanism for extending WSDL because they enable support for network and message protocols to be revised without having to revise the WSDL specification.

The base specification of WSDL defines three WSDL binding extensions, which are as follows:

- SOAP binding
- HTTP GET & POST binding
- MIME binding

We will take a look at the most commonly used WSDL binding extension, the SOAP binding, in a later section titled *SOAP Binding*.

WSDL Binding Support for Operations

All four types of operations supported by WSDL—one-way, request-response, solicit-response, and notification—represent an abstract notion only. Binding describes the concrete correlation to these abstract notions. Binding determines how the messages are actually sent, for instance, within a single communication (for example, an HTTP request/response) or as two independent communications (for example, two HTTP requests). Thus, binding for a specific operation type must be defined in order to successfully carry out that type of operation. Note that although the WSDL structure supports the bindings for these four operations, the WSDL specification defines bindings for only one-way and request-response operations. Hence, in order to use WSDL to describe services that support solicit-response and/or notification types of operations, the communication protocol of the Web service must define the WSDL binding extensions, thus enabling the use of these operations.

Let's now take a look at SOAP binding as defined by the WSDL 1.1 specification.

SOAP Binding

WSDL 1.1 defines a binding for SOAP 1.1 endpoints. This binding provides the following SOAP protocol specific information:

- An indication that the binding is bound to the SOAP 1.1 protocol
- A way of specifying an address for a SOAP endpoint
- The URI for the SOAP action HTTP header for the HTTP binding of SOAP
- A list of definitions of headers that are transmitted as part of the SOAP envelope

Let's examine the SOAP binding of the request-response RPC operation over HTTP as defined in the `WeatherInfo.wsdl` file shown earlier (see the section titled *Anatomy of a WSDL Definition Document*).

<soap:binding>

The `<soap:binding>` element is defined in `WeatherInfo.wsdl` as follows:

```
<soap:binding style="document"
transport="http://schemas.xmlsoap.org/soap/http"/>
```

The `<soap:binding>` element says that the binding is bound to the SOAP protocol format, that is, envelope, header, and body. However, this element does not give any information about the format or encoding of the message. This element must be present whenever describing services that have a SOAP binding.

The `style` attribute indicates whether the operations supported by this binding are RPC-oriented or document-oriented. In RPC-oriented communication, the messages contain parameter and return values, whereas in document-oriented communication, the messages contain document(s). This information about the style of communication can be useful because it helps in selecting the programming model for communicating with the

Web service. For example, if a Web service is described to support RPC, we can choose a JAX-RPC programming model to communicate with it, or if a Web service is described to support document-style communication, we can appropriately choose a JAXM programming model.

The `transport` attribute specifies the transport binding for the SOAP protocol. The URI value of `http://schemas.xmlsoap.org/soap/http` corresponds to the HTTP binding as defined in the SOAP specification. Similarly, respective URIs can be used to indicate other types of transports such as SMTP or FTP.

<soap:operation>

The `<soap:operation>` element is defined in `WeatherInfo.wsdl` as follows:

```
<soap:operation soapAction=
"http://myweather.com/GetWeatherInfo"/>
```

The `<soap:operation>` element defines the information with regard to communication style and the SOAP action header at that specific operation level.

The semantics of the `style` attribute remains the same as that for a `<soap:binding>` element.

The `soapAction` attribute specifies the value of a SOAP action header in the form of a URI. The usage of the SOAP action header was discussed in Chapter 4, "Developing Web Services Using SOAP."

<soap:body>

The `<soap:body>` element is defined in `WeatherInfo.wsdl` as follows:

```
<soap:body use="literal"/>
```

This element defines how the message `<part>` elements appear inside the SOAP body element. Based on the style of communication, RPC-oriented or document-oriented, the `<Body>` element of the SOAP message is constructed.

The `use` attribute indicates whether the message `<part>` elements are encoded using some encoding rules or whether the `<part>` elements already define the concrete schema of the message.

If the value of the `use` attribute is "`encoded`", then each message `<part>` refers to an abstract type defined through the `type` attribute. These abstract types are then used to produce a concrete definition of the message by applying the encoding specified by an `encodingStyle` attribute.

Consider the following example:

```
<output>
     <soap:body
     encodingStyle="http://schemas.xmlsoap.org/soap/encoding/"
     namespace="urn:acmens:acmeservice"
     use="encoded"/>
</output>
```

The `<soap:body>` element in this code depicts a SOAP binding wherein the body of the output SOAP message consists of abstract `<part>` elements that are used to produce the concrete definition of the message by applying the `encodingStyle` as defined in `http://schemas.xmlsoap.org/soap/encoding/`.

<soap:address>

The `<soap:address>` element is defined as follows in `WeatherInfo.wsdl`:

```
<soap:address location=
"http://myweather.com/provideweatherinfo"/>
```

The `<soap:address>` element specifies an address for the given service port.

WSDL Tools

WSDL tools typically provide functionality in terms of the following:

WSDL generation. Generating WSDL from an existing service component—for example, a J2EE component or a Java Bean component or from scratch.

WSDL compilation. A typical WSDL compiler would generate the necessary data structures and a skeleton for the implementation of the service. The generated implementation skeleton contains all the methods (operations) that are described in the given WSDL definition.

WSDL proxy generation. This functionality can read a WSDL and produce a specific language binding (for example, Java or Perl) consisting of all the code required to bind the Web service and to invoke the Web service functions at runtime. This functionality is typically used at the client end.

Many WSDL tools provide support for these three functionalities. Table 5.1 lists some of the famous ones in the Java Web Services space.

Table 5.1 WSDL Tools

TOOL	DOWNLOAD FROM ...
Sun ONE Studio 4	wwws.sun.com/software/sundev/jde/index.html
Systinet WASP	www.systinet.com/wasp
The Mind Electric GLUE	www.themindelectric.com/glue/index.html
IBM Web Services Toolkit	www.alphaworks.ibm.com/tech/webservicestoolkit/
BEA WebLogic Workshop	www.bea.com/products/weblogic/workshop /easystart/index.shtml
Apache Axis	http://xml.apache.org/axis

In the following section, we examine the WSDL tools provided by the Systinet WASP platform.

Support for WSDL in Systinet WASP 4.0

Systinet WASP provides two tools for working with WSDL: Java2WSDL and WSDL Compiler. Both of these tools accomplish two different types of functionalities related to WSDL:

Generating WSDL from a Java class that is a potential candidate for a Web service. This functionality is taken care of by the Java2WSDL tool.

Generating Java code from an existing WSDL. This functionality is taken care of by the WSDL Compiler.

We will check out both these tools in the following two sections.

Generating WSDL from a Java Class

In situations in which an implementation of the Web service has already been created first, the Java2WSDL tool can be used to generate WSDL. This tool provides a lot of options for generating WSDL from an existing Java implementation.

To understand the functioning of this tool, consider the following Java class:

```
package jws.ch5;

public class WeatherInfoJavaService
{
     public float GetWeatherInfo (String sCountry, String sZip,
```

```
        String sInstance)
        {
            // Talk to some backend services to get hold
            // of the weather information

            // Return the weather information;
            // a manipulated value for now.
            return 65.0f;
        }

        public void SetWeatherInfo (String sCountry, String sZip,
        String sInstance, String sTemperature)
        {
            // Update the backend weather databases
            // with this information
        }
    }
```

As can be seen from the previous listing, this class provides `get` and `set` methods. The main job of this class is to manage information related to weather. Note that this is a very simplistic version of such a weather information service.

For example, we want to expose this class as a Web service. In which case, we also decide to provide the description of the interface of this Web service as a WSDL. Our Web service supports SOAP-based communication, and hence, a SOAP binding as well. Thus, this fact also should be considered while generating WSDL using the Java2WSDL tool.

Once the WSDL has been generated, it can be registered in a registry such as UDDI accompanied by the business- and other service-related information. So when the prospective Web service users find the Web service, they can obtain the WSDL description corresponding to this Web service and start using it.

The following command line instruction shows the usage of the Java2WSDL tool such that it would generate a `WeatherInfo.wsdl` from the `WeatherInfoJavaService` class:

```
> Java2WSDL jws.ch5.WeatherInfoJavaService --package-mapping
"jws.ch5=http://www.myweather.com/WeatherInfo" --output-file-mapping
"http://www.myweather.com/WeatherInfo=
WeatherInfo.wsdl" —output-directory jws/ch5
```

This command would generate `WeatherInfo.wsdl` and place it in the `%DEMO_DIR%/jws/ch5` directory. Table 5.2 gives the explanation of the arguments used in the previous command.

Table 5.2 Java2WSDL Command Line Options

Package mapping	Whenever a Java class is processed by a Java2WSDL tool, it assumes that the package namespace is the target namespace as well. Hence, in order to provide a new mapping of package name to the WSDL namespace, this argument must be provided.
Outputfile mapping	By default, the Java2WSDL tool would generate a WSDL document named as the package namespace, preceded by "`Definitions_`". Thus, in order to give a new name to the WSDL definition document, we can use this argument.
Output directory	This argument specifies the directory where the output WSDL definition would be stored. The default is the current directory.

The Java2WSDL tool supports many more arguments than what are shown in Table 5.2. To find detailed information on these arguments and the Java2WSDL tool in general, please visit the Systinet Web site at www.systinet.com/doc/wasp_jserver/tools/java2WSDL.html.

The output `WeatherInfo.wsdl` generated by the Java2WSDL tool is shown in Listing 5.2.

```
<?xml version='1.0'?>
<wsdl:definitions name='jws.ch5.WeatherInfoJavaService'
targetNamespace='http://www.myweather.com/WeatherInfo'
xmlns:wsdl='http://schemas.xmlsoap.org/wsdl/'
xmlns:tns='http://www.myweather.com/WeatherInfo'
xmlns:ns0='http://systinet.com/xsd/SchemaTypes/'
xmlns:soap='http://schemas.xmlsoap.org/wsdl/soap/'
xmlns:map='http://systinet.com/mapping/'>

     <wsdl:types>
          <xsd:schema elementFormDefault="qualified"
          targetNamespace=
          "http://systinet.com/xsd/SchemaTypes/"
          xmlns:tns="http://systinet.com/xsd/SchemaTypes/"
          xmlns:xsd="http://www.w3.org/2001/XMLSchema">

               <xsd:element name="sCountry" nillable="true"
```

Listing 5.2 WeatherInfo.wsdl generated by the Java2WSDL tool. *(continues)*

```
            type="xsd:string"/>

            <xsd:element name="sZip" nillable="true"
            type="xsd:string"/>

            <xsd:element name="sInstance" nillable="true"
            type="xsd:string"/>





            <xsd:element name="float_res"
            type="xsd:float"/>

            <xsd:element name="sTemperature"
            nillable="true" type="xsd:string"/>
        </xsd:schema>
    </wsdl:types>

    <wsdl:message name=
    'WeatherInfoJavaService_GetWeatherInfo_1_Request'>
        <wsdl:part name='sCountry' element='ns0:sCountry'/>
        <wsdl:part name='sZip' element='ns0:sZip'/>
        <wsdl:part name='sInstance' element='ns0:sInstance'/>
    </wsdl:message>

    <wsdl:message name=
    'WeatherInfoJavaService_GetWeatherInfo_Response'>
        <wsdl:part name='response' element='ns0:float_res'/>
    </wsdl:message>

    <wsdl:message name
    ='WeatherInfoJavaService_SetWeatherInfo_Response'/>

    <wsdl:message name=
    'WeatherInfoJavaService_SetWeatherInfo_1_Request'>
        <wsdl:part name='sCountry' element='ns0:sCountry'/>
        <wsdl:part name='sZip' element='ns0:sZip'/>
        <wsdl:part name='sInstance' element='ns0:sInstance'/>
        <wsdl:part name='sTemperature'
        element='ns0:sTemperature'/>
    </wsdl:message>

    <wsdl:portType name='WeatherInfoJavaService'>
        <wsdl:operation name='GetWeatherInfo'
        parameterOrder='sCountry sZip sInstance'>
            <wsdl:input message=
```

Listing 5.2 WeatherInfo.wsdl generated by the Java2WSDL tool.

```
        'tns:WeatherInfoJavaService_GetWeatherInfo_1_Request'/>

        <wsdl:output message=
        'tns:WeatherInfoJavaService_GetWeatherInfo_Response'/>

    </wsdl:operation>

    <wsdl:operation name='SetWeatherInfo'
    parameterOrder='sCountry sZip sInstance
    sTemperature'>

        <wsdl:input message=
        'tns:WeatherInfoJavaService_SetWeatherInfo_1_Request'/>

        <wsdl:output message=
        'tns:WeatherInfoJavaService_SetWeatherInfo_Response'/>
    </wsdl:operation>
</wsdl:portType>

<wsdl:binding name='WeatherInfoJavaService'
type='tns:WeatherInfoJavaService'>

    <soap:binding transport=
    'http://schemas.xmlsoap.org/soap/http'
    style='document'/>

    <wsdl:operation name='GetWeatherInfo'>
    <map:java-operation name=
    'GetWeatherInfo' signature='KExq...'/>

    <soap:operation soapAction='_10'
    style='document'/>

        <wsdl:input>
            <soap:body use='literal'
            namespace='http://www.myweather.com/
            WeatherInfoWeatherInfoJavaService'/>
        </wsdl:input>

        <wsdl:output>
            <soap:body use='literal' namespace=
            'http://www.myweather.com/
            WeatherInfoWeatherInfoJavaService'/>
        </wsdl:output>
    </wsdl:operation>

    <wsdl:operation name='SetWeatherInfo'>
        <map:java-operation name='SetWeatherInfo'
        signature='KExq...'/>
```

Listing 5.2 WeatherInfo.wsdl generated by the Java2WSDL tool. *(continues)*

```
                <soap:operation soapAction='_11'
                style='document'/>

                <wsdl:input>
                     <soap:body use='literal' namespace=
                     'http://www.myweather.com/
                     WeatherInfoWeatherInfoJavaService'/>
                </wsdl:input>

                <wsdl:output>
                     <soap:body use='literal' namespace=
                     'http://www.myweather.com/
                     WeatherInfoWeatherInfoJavaService'/>
                </wsdl:output>
           </wsdl:operation>
      </wsdl:binding>

      <wsdl:service name='JavaService'>
           <wsdl:port name='WeatherInfoJavaService'
           binding='tns:WeatherInfoJavaService'>

                <soap:address location=
                'urn:unknown-location-uri'/>
           </wsdl:port>
      </wsdl:service>
 </wsdl:definitions>
```

Listing 5.2 WeatherInfo.wsdl generated by the Java2WSDL tool. *(continued)*

Generating Java Code from an Existing WSDL

In situations in which WSDL definitions are created before actually implementing a Web service, the WSDLCompiler tool of WASP can be used to generate the skeleton of a Java interface. A Java class consisting of the actual method implementations then can implement this generated Java interface.

The usage of the WSDLCompiler tool is as follows:

```
> WSDLCompiler WeatherInfo.wsdl
```

In this case, a Java interface with the name `WeatherInfoJavaService` is created as shown in Listing 5.3.

```
/**

  */
public interface WeatherInfoJavaService {/
    /**

      */
    float GetWeatherInfo(java.lang.String sCountry, java.lang.String
sZip, java.lang.String sInstance);

    /**

      */
    void SetWeatherInfo(java.lang.String sCountry, java.lang.String
sZip, java.lang.String sInstance, java.lang.String sTemperature);

}

/*
 * Generated by WSDLCompiler, (c) 2002, Systinet Corp.
 *                           http://www.systinet.com
 */
```

Listing 5.3 WeatherInfoJavaService Java class generated by the WSDLCompiler tool.

This tool also has various options that enable fine-tuning of the generation of the Java interface. Also, WSDLCompiler supports the generation of Java Bean components from WSDL definitions. To find further information about this tool, visit www.systinet.com/doc/wasp_jserver/tools/wsdlCompiler.html.

Note that tools such as Apache Axis also provide support for generating messaging implementation classes from WSDL.

Future of WSDL

As mentioned earlier, WSDL 1.2 is presently a work in progress under the Web Services Description Working Group at W3C. W3C released the draft specifications of WSDL 1.2 in July 2002. The WSDL 1.2 specification consists of two documents: *Web Services Description Language Version 1.2* and *Web Services Description Language Version 1.2 Bindings*. The former defines the core language that can be used to describe Web services based on an abstract model of what the service offers. The latter describes how to use WSDL for describing services that use SOAP 1.2, MIME, or HTTP 1.1 bindings.

The following lists some of the important enhancements of WSDL 1.2 over WSDL 1.1:

- WSDL 1.2 provides support for W3C Recommendations, including XML Schemas and XML Information Set.
- WSDL 1.2 removes non-interoperable features from WSDL 1.1.
- WSDL 1.2 clearly defines HTTP 1.1 binding.

To obtain further information on WSDL 1.2, visit www.w3.org/2002/ws/desc/.

Limitations of WSDL

WSDL 1.1 has an obvious limitation: its incapability of being able to describe complex business Web services, which typically are constituted by orchestrating multiple finer-grained Web services. This drawback is due to the lack of support for workflow descriptions in WSDL. To overcome these limitations of WSDL, standards such as ebXML Collaborative Protocol Profile/Collaborative Protocol Agreement (CCP/A), Business Process Specification Schema (BPSS), and Web Services Choreography Interface (WSCI) can be leveraged. An EbXML set of technologies can be used to build business Web services. To find more information on EbXML technical architecture, refer to Chapter 14, "Introduction to Sun ONE." A WSCI specification can be downloaded from wwws.sun.com/software/xml/developers/wsci/. Also Chapter 2, "Introduction to Web Services," provides a brief introduction to WSCI.

Apart from these, there are some low-level issues with WSDL 1.1 specification in terms of the clarity of specification. To get a complete listing of WSDL 1.1 issues, visit wsdl.soapware.org/.

We will now begin our journey with UDDI.

Universal Description, Discovery, and Integration (UDDI)

As already discussed, UDDI technology is the core and one of the building blocks of Web services apart from SOAP and WSDL. UDDI enables the businesses providing services (in electronic form or in any other medium) to register information to enable the discovery of their services and business profile by prospective customers and/or partners. Similarly, it enables businesses to discover other businesses for expanding potential business partnerships. Thus, UDDI presents businesses with an opportunity to step into new markets and services. It powers all kinds of businesses, large, medium, or small, to accelerate their business presence in this global market.

UDDI initially started as a joint effort from IBM, Microsoft, and Ariba. Since then, a number of companies joined the UDDI community. As of this book's writing, the UDDI project community is looking forward to releasing version 3.0 of the UDDI specification. This chapter covers version 2.0 of the UDDI specification because it is widely implemented and adopted as of this writing. To find more information on the UDDI effort, visit the UDDI official Web site at www.uddi.org.

UDDI Registries

An implementation of the UDDI specification is termed as a *UDDI registry*. *UDDI registry services* are a set of software services that provide access to the UDDI registry. Meanwhile, registry services can perform a plethora of other activities such as authenticating and authorizing registry requests, logging registry requests, load-balancing requests, and so on.

Public and Private UDDI Registries

A UDDI registry can be operated in two modes: public mode and private mode. A *public UDDI registry* is available for everyone to publish/query the business and service information on the Internet. Such public registries can be a logical single system built upon multiple UDDI registry nodes that have their data synchronized through replication. Thus, all the UDDI registry node operators would each host a copy of the content and accessing any node would provide the same information and quality of service as any other operator node. Such global grouping of UDDI registry nodes is known as a *UDDI Business Registry,* or UBR. Content can be added into a UBR from any node, however, content can be modified or deleted only at a node at which it was inserted.

A *private UDDI registry* is operated by a single organization or a group of collaborating organizations to share the information that would be available only to the participating bodies. Private UDDI registries can impose additional security controls to protect the integrity of the registry data and to prevent access by unauthorized users. Note that a private node also can participate in information replication.

A UDDI registry in itself is a Web service. A Web service consumer queries the UDDI registry using the SOAP API defined by UDDI specification. Also, the UDDI specification publishes a WSDL description of the UDDI registry service.

The UDDI project community members operate a UBR. This registry is available to everyone for free publishing/querying of businesses and services information. To find more information on this publicly operated UDDI registry, visit the UDDI Web site at www.uddi.org.

Interacting with a UDDI Registry

Typically, vendors implementing a UDDI registry provide two ways of interacting with a UDDI Registry Service.

- A graphical user interface (GUI), for interacting with a UDDI registry. These GUIs also can be browser-based. The following is a list of public UDDI registries, operated by various companies such as Microsoft, IBM, Hewlett Packard, and so on, that provide a browser-based interface to these registries:
  - https://uddi.rte.microsoft.com/search/frames.aspx
  - https://www-3.ibm.com/services/uddi/v2beta/protect/registry.html
  - https://uddi.hp.com/uddi/index.jsp
  - http://udditest.sap.com/
  - http://www.systinet.com/uddi/web

Figure 5.3 shows a browser-based GUI provided by Systinet in order to interact with its publicly hosted UDDI registry. This screenshot depicts the interface provided for searching businesses registered with the Systinet registry.

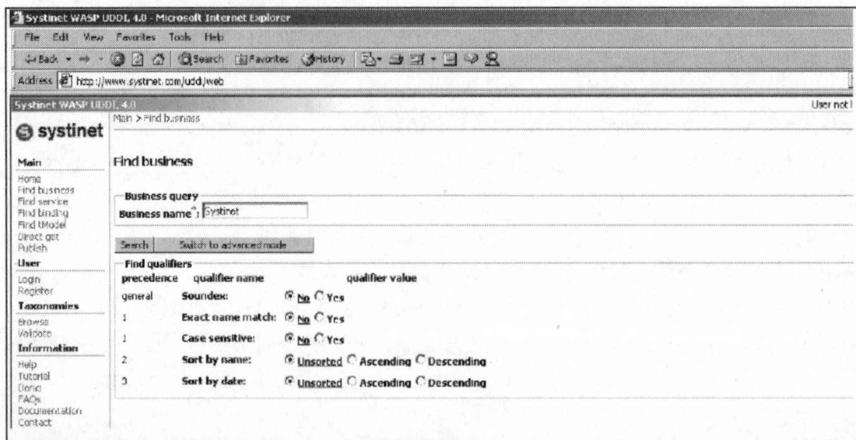

Figure 5.3 Web-based GUI to UDDI registry.

- A programmatic interface for communicating with the UDDI registry. These programmatic interfaces are based on SOAP, because the UDDI registry supports SOAP as the communication protocol.
  - Most of the vendors providing the UDDI registry implementations support both of these types of access to the registry.

Uses of UDDI Registry

Businesses can use a UDDI registry at three levels:

White pages level. Businesses that intend to register just the very basic information about their company, such as company name, address, contact information, unique identifiers such as D-U-N-S numbers or Tax IDs, or Web services use UDDI as white pages.

Yellow pages level. Businesses that intend to classify their information based on categorizations (also known as classification schemes or taxonomies) make use of the UDDI registry as yellow pages.

Green pages level. Businesses that publish the technical information describing the behavior and supported functions on their Web services make use of the UDDI registry as green pages.

Note that the UDDI specification does not explicitly make references to these different types of usage levels of the UDDI registry. The categorization of these levels is rather implicit.

UDDI Specifications

All versions of the UDDI specifications can be obtained from the UDDI organization at their Web site at http://uddi.org/specification.html. The UDDI 2.0 specification set includes the following documents:

UDDI replication. The document describes the data replication process of the UDDI registries. Also, it describes the programmatic interfaces supported by UDDI for achieving replication between UDDI registries operated by different operators.

UDDI operators. This document provides information on the operational behavior that should be followed by UDDI node operators. For example, the document defines guidelines that node operators can follow in order to manage the data of the UDDI registry node. Such guidelines include the following:

- Node operators' responsibility for durable recording and backup of all data.

- Checking the validity of information provided by businesses during registration, such as email addresses.
- Checking the integrity of data in the UDDI registry after it has been modified. For example, if a business has been deleted from the registry, then the operator should ensure that the services corresponding to this business also are deleted.

Note that private UDDI node operators are not required to follow the guidelines mentioned in this document.

UDDI programmer's API. This document describes the programming interfaces supported by a UDDI registry in terms of SOAP messages. This document is targeted towards programmers who want to write software that would interact with a UDDI registry operated at a public or private level, using SOAP.

UDDI data structures. This document outlines the details of the XML structures that are associated with the SOAP messages used to communicate with the UDDI registries. These SOAP messages are well defined by the UDDI programmer's API specification and are used to perform the inquiry and publishing functions on the UDDI registry.

To begin with, let's take a look at how to retrieve, search, and publish information to a UDDI registry in the next section.

Programming with UDDI

This section introduces the APIs used for communicating with a UDDI registry. Also, important data structures and categorization support of UDDI are discussed.

UDDI Programming API

The UDDI specification defines two XML-based programming APIs for communicating with the UDDI registry node: inquiry API and publishing API. The following sections describe each of these.

Inquiry API

The inquiry API consists of XML messages defined using a UDDI Schema, which can be used to locate information about a business, such as the services a business offers and the technical specification of those services (such as a link to a WSDL document describing the interface of the service, the binding of the service and the URL where the service is running, and so on). A UDDI programmer would use these inquiry APIs to retrieve information stored in the registry. To retrieve information, a registry user does not need to be authenticated.

The following is a list of inquiry API functions that can be used for finding information in a UDDI registry:

- <find_business>
- <find_relatedBusinesses>
- <find_service>
- <find_binding>
- <find_tModel>

To get further detailed information from the UDDI registry, the following inquiry API functions are available:

- <get_businessDetail>
- <get_businessDetailExt>
- <get_serviceDetail>
- <get_bindingDetail>
- <get_tModelDetail>

Publishing API

The publishing API consists of functions represented by a UDDI Schema, which defines XML messages that can be used to create, update, and delete the information present in a UDDI registry. Note that in order to publish to a UDDI registry, the registry user needs to be authenticated.

The following is a list of publishing API functions that can be used for adding/modifying information to a UDDI registry:

- <save_business>
- <set_publisherAssertions>
- <add_publisherAssertions>
- <save_service>
- <save_binding>
- <save_tModel>

The following is a list of publishing API functions that can be used for deleting information from a UDDI registry:

- <delete_business>
- <delete_publisherAssertions>

- <delete_service>
- <delete_binding>
- <delete_tModel>

Apart from the functions just mentioned, the publishing API also defines functions that deal with the authentication of the registry users, which is required in order to successfully execute the rest of the functions of this API:

- <get_authToken>
- <discard_authToken>

We will discuss each of the aforementioned APIs in detail in the sections titled *Inquiry API* and *Publishing API,* which follow.

The XML messages constituting the UDDI programmer APIs are defined using a UDDI XML Schema. These XML messages are wrapped in a SOAP message and then sent to the UDDI registry. In other words, all of the XML messages are enveloped within a SOAP <body> element and then sent as an HTTP POST request to the UDDI registry. The UDDI registry then processes these SOAP messages and gets hold of the actual API function represented by the XML message, which further instructs the registry services to provide either publishing or querying services.

A UDDI registry node typically enables access to both inquiry and publishing functionalities through different access point URLs. Table 5.3 lists the URLs for publicly operated UDDI registry nodes.

As we can see from Table 5.3, all of the URLs corresponding to the publishing access points support HTTPS, because publishing operations need authenticated access.

Table 5.3 Access Point URLs

OPERATOR	INQUIRY URL	PUBLISHING URL
Microsoft	http://uddi.microsoft.com/inquire	https://uddi.microsoft.com /publish
IBM	http://www-3.ibm.com/services /uddi/inquiryapi	https://www-3.ibm.com /services/uddi/protect /publishapi
HP	http://uddi.hp.com/inquire	https://uddi.hp.com/publish
SAP	http://udditest.sap.com/uddi /api/inquiry	https://udditest.sap.com /uddi/api/publish

Note that all the UDDI invocations follow a synchronous request/response mechanism and are stateless in nature. This statelessness has a significant impact on the authentication of a registry user to the UDDI registry, which is required when performing a publishing operation on the registry. Because of the stateless nature of the UDDI programming API, each time a registry user uses a publishing programming API, the security credentials of the identity associated with the registry user also are passed with each UDDI invocation.

UDDI Data Structures

The information managed by a UDDI registry is represented as XML data structures also known as UDDI data structures. The UDDI data structures specification document defines the meaning of these data structures and the relationship between them. Ultimately, it is these data structures with which a UDDI client needs to work. A UDDI client makes use of these, in conjunction with the XML messages of programming APIs, to manipulate a specific type of information in a registry. Similarly, response to a search operation received from the UDDI registry also would consist of these data structures. Hence, the UDDI data structures are more or less input and output parameters for the UDDI programming API.

The following are the five primary UDDI data structures defined in the specification:

- `<businessEntity>`
- `<publisherAssertion>`
- `<businessService>`
- `<bindingTemplate>`
- `<tModel>`

Note that all of these data structures except `<publisherAssertion>` are identified and referenced through a 128-bit globally unique identifier also known as UUID. These UUIDs can later be used as keys to access the specific data within the registry.

Now, let's take a look at each of these one by one.

<businessEntity>

The `<businessEntity>` data structure represents the primary information about a business, such as contact information, categorization of the business according to a specific taxonomy or classification scheme, identifiers, relationships to other business entities, and descriptions about that particular business. The categorizations are discussed in a later section titled *Support for Categorization in UDDI Registries*.

<publisherAssertion>

A business registered in a UDDI registry can have active business relationships with other businesses. This relationship can be of any form, for example, a relationship of business partners or a business-to-customer relationship. Such relationships are represented by a `<publisherAssertion>` data structure in a UDDI Registry. The `<publisherAssertion>` structure is used to establish a relationship between two `<businessEntity>` structures.

A very interesting aspect about relationships in a UDDI registry is its ability to not make the relationship visible to the public unless and until both of the parties establishing this association assert for the same. This means that if a `<businessEntity>` structure representing Company A asserts its relationship with a `<businessEntity>` structure representing Company B through a `<publisherAssertion>` structure, a UDDI registry would not make this relationship public until Company B has created another similar `<publisherAssertion>` structure. This provision is supported by the UDDI registries in order to ensure that a company can claim a business relationship with another company, only if the other partner also asserts for the same relationship.

<businessService>

The `<businessService>` data structure represents the service of a business. These services can be Web services or any other type of service. For example, the `<businessService>` data structure may represent a service that is offered over the telephone, such as a telephone banking service. The `<businessService>` data structure is merely a logical representation of services that a business has to offer.

A `<businessEntity>` structure contains one or more `<businessService>` structures. The same `<businessService>` structure also can be used by multiple `<businessEntity>` structures. For example, if a business has two departments—say, manufacturing and sales— that are each published to a UDDI registry as a `<businessEntity>` structure, then both of them can use the same `<businessService>` structure representing another business service—say, legal counseling.

<bindingTemplate>

The `<bindingTemplate>` structure consists of pointers to technical descriptions and access URLs of the service. Each `<businessService>`

structure can contain one or more <bindingTemplate> structures. So, for example, if the <businessService> structure represents a Web service, then its <bindingTemplate> would refer to a PDF document providing the technical description of this Web service and the URL at which the Web service can be accessed. Also, the <bindingTemplate> structure can provide an optional description of the Web service.

Note that the <bindingTemplate> structure does not provide the details of the service specification, such as the interface of a service. That information is provided by the <tModel> structures, and <bindingTemplate> simply refers to one or more of such <tModel> structures.

<tModel>

The <tModel> structure provides a description of a particular specification or behavior of the service. The <tModel> structure does not contain the service specification directly; instead, it contains a link to the service specification, which is managed elsewhere. The <tModel> thus defines the interaction pattern in order to use the service. For example, a business may provide a Web service whose WSDL interface may be referenced through a link from within the <tModel> structure.

Thus, <tModel> defines the lowest-level and most concrete piece of information about the services offered by a business. A UDDI client typically gets hold of the service specification pointed out by the <tModel> structure in order to use a publicly available Web service registered by a particular business.

The linking between these five core data structures of UDDI is depicted in Figure 5.4.

Apart from these five primary data structures, two other structures exist that represent the category and identification information of the primary data structures: <identifierBag> and <categoryBag>. Let's take a look at each of them now.

<identifierBag>

The <identifierBag> structure enables <businessEntity> or <tModel> structures to include information about the common forms of identification such as D-U-N-S numbers and tax IDs. This data can be used to signify the identity of <businessEntity>, or it can be used to signify the identity of the publishing party. Including such identification information is optional. However, when a published <businessEntity> or <tModel> carries such common forms of identification, it greatly enhances the search behaviors exposed via inquiry API functions.

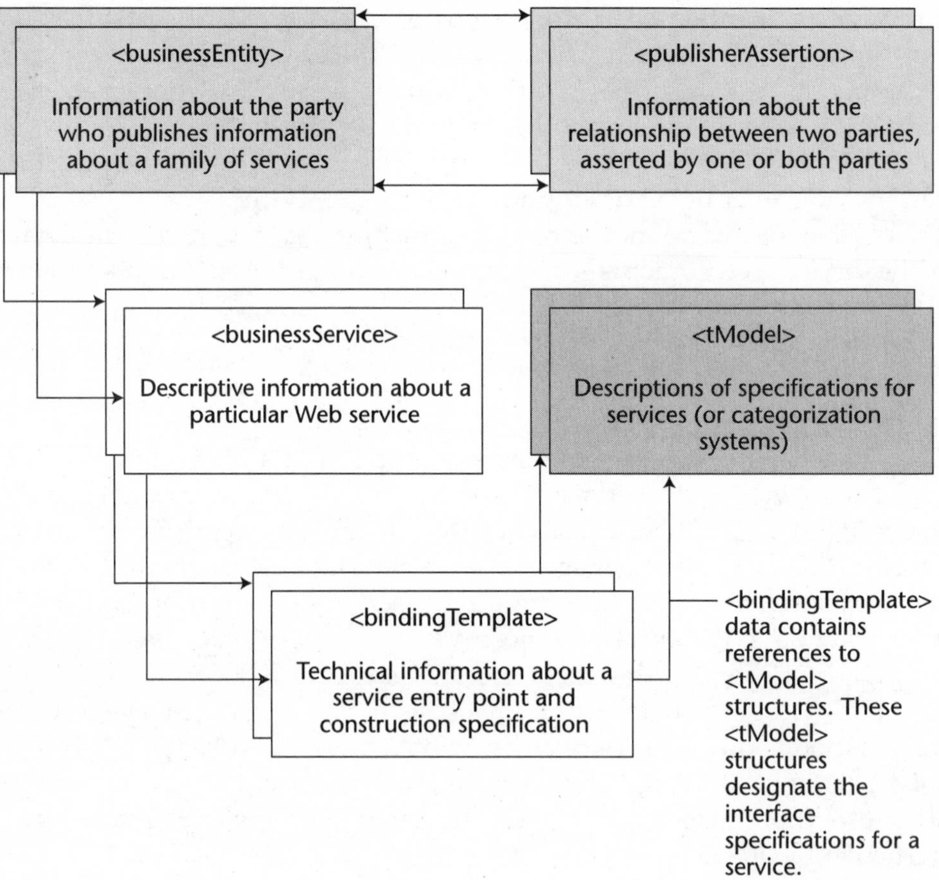

Figure 5.4 Primary UDDI data structures.

<categoryBag>

The `<categoryBag>` structure enables `<businessEntity>`, `<businessService>`, and `<tModel>` structures to be categorized according to any categorization system, such as an industry categorization system or a geography categorization system. Categorizing the data structures mentioned previously is optional. However, when these data structures are published along with their categorization information, it greatly enhances the search behaviors exposed via inquiry API functions. The categorization support in a UDDI registry is discussed in the following section.

Support for Categorization in UDDI Registries

Categorization—also known as classification in JAXR terminology—is considered to be the prominent functionality of any registry. Categorization enables the data to be classified with the help of various categorization systems (also known as taxonomies or classification schemes), such as an industry categorization system or a geography categorization system. For example, a business can be classified as being located in the United States with the help of a standard geography categorization system such as ISO-3166.

Categorizing data aids in searching for a particular piece of data. For example, searching for a software organization whose name begins with the letter M is much easier when that data is categorized as being located in Redmond, Washington, than when it is not. Searching by the letter M for an organization that does not have a geographical categorization returns a much broader set of results, thus making it much more difficult to discover the business in which one is interested. Hence, categorization is especially useful in the *discovery* of information managed by a UDDI registry.

UDDI registries have built-in support for three industry standard categorization systems. Also, the registry specification enables support for an open-ended categorization system that can be used in specific ways by a UDDI registry node operator. In UDDI, the categorization system is represented by a `<tModel>` structure. These `<tModel>` structures have a unique name across all the UDDI registry node operators; however, the `<tModel>` UUID may change between the node operators.

UDDI-Supported Categorization Systems

The UDDI supported categorization systems and their `<tModel>` names are shown in Table 5.4.

Checked and Unchecked Categorization System

UDDI version 2.0 included the capability of validating the categorization of a particular UDDI data structure. Depending upon whether an organization chooses to use the validation service of a UDDI registry, one of the two types of categorization systems will be supported:

Checked categorization system. Checked categorization systems are used when the publisher of a categorization system wishes to ensure that the categorization code values registered represent accurate and validated information. The categorization code values represented by UDDI structure `<categoryBag>` would be checked for valid values during a `<save_business>`, `<save_service>`, or `<save_tModel>` API call.

Table 5.4. UDDI-Supported Categorization Systems and Their <tModel> Names

CATEGORIZATION SYSTEM	<TMODEL> NAME	DESCRIPTION
NAICS	`ntis-gov:naics:1997`	This is a standard industry and services categorization system. NAICS abbreviates to the North American Industry Classification System. This system is the most elaborate and comprehensive industry classification scheme defined so far. Further information on this categorization system can be obtained from www.census.gov/epcd/www/naics.html.
UNSPSC	`unspcs-org:unspsc:3-1`	This standard industry and services categorization system abbreviates to the Universal Standard Products and Services Classification. This was the first such industry classification scheme defined for electronic businesses. Further information on this categorization system can be obtained from www.unspsc.org.
ISO 3166	`iso-ch:3166:1999`	This is the standard geography-based categorization system. Further information can be found at www.din.de/gremien/nas/nabd/iso3166ma.
Operator Specific	`uddi-org:general_keywords`	This categorization system is operator specific. This is an open-ended categorization system that is not predefined. As a result, it can consist of any category entries that may be defined specifically for that UDDI registry node.

UDDI version 2 also enables third parties registering new categorization systems to control the categorization validation process. In such case, the third party would implement a Web service, in the same manner as UDDI does, that exposes a single XML API function named `<validate_values>`.

Unchecked categorization system. Unchecked categorization systems are used for categorization without the need for a UDDI to perform validation of categorization code values. Businesses can choose to make their categorization system available for categorization as an unchecked categorization system. Registering a new <tModel> structure and categorizing that <tModel> as a categorization system would register it as an unchecked categorization system.

Now, let's take a look at the available programming APIs for searching information in a UDDI registry.

Inquiry API

This section will cover all of the XML messages that perform the functionality of inquiring certain information from a UDDI registry. Inquiry API constitutes of two types of functions:

- Functions that return zero or more homogeneous data structures containing abbreviated information
- Functions that return zero or more homogeneous data structures containing detailed information

To begin with, we will take a look at the API functions, which return abbreviated information in response.

Find_xx Inquiry API Functions

The find_xx functions follow the *browse pattern*. The browse pattern typically involves starting with some broad information, performing a search, finding general result sets, and then selecting more specific information for drill-down purposes.

The find_xx calls form the search capabilities such that the summary of matched results are returned in the response message. Hence, a UDDI client would get the overview information about the registered data by using find_xx inquiry API calls. Once the client gets hold of the key for one of the primary UDDI data structures, it then can use get_xx inquiry API functions to get further details.

<find_business>

The <find_business> API function represented by an XML message is used to locate information about one or more businesses. Given a regular expression, business category, business identifier, or <tModel> as criteria, this message retrieves zero or more <businessInfo> structures contained within a single <businessList> structure.

The syntax for this API is as follows:

```
<find_business [maxRows="nn"] generic="2.0"
xmlns="urn:uddi-org:api_v2">
      [<findQualifiers/>]
      [<name/> [<name/>]...]
      [<discoveryURLs/>]
      [<identifierBag/>]
      [<categoryBag/>]
      [<tModelBag/>]
</find_business>
```

Arguments to this function are listed in Table 5.5.

Table 5.5 <find_business> Function Arguments

ARGUMENT	DESCRIPTION
maxRows	This argument specifies the maximum number of results that can be returned.
findQualifiers	This argument represents a collection of search qualifiers that form the criteria of the given operation. The search qualifiers are discussed in more detail in a later section.
name	This argument can be a partial or full name of the business being searched. The name pattern can make use of the wildcard character % as well. Up to five name values can be specified in the argument. In cases when multiple name values are passed, the match occurs on a logical OR basis. The returned `<businessList>` contains `<businessInfo>` structures for businesses whose name matches the name value(s) passed in a lexical (leftmost in left to right languages) fashion.
IdentifierBag	This argument contains a list of business identifier references. The returned `<businessList>` contains `<businessInfo>` structures matching any of the identifiers passed (logical OR).
categoryBag	This is a list of category references. The returned `<businessList>` contains `<businessInfo>` structures matching all of the categories passed (logical AND).

Table 5.5 *(Continued)*

ARGUMENT	DESCRIPTION
tModelBag	This argument enables searching for businesses that have bindings exposing a specific *fingerprint* within the <tModelInstanceDetails> structure. The returned <businessList> structure contains <businessInfo> consisting of a <businessEntity> structure, which in turn contains <bindingTemplate> referencing <tModel> structures that match all the <tModel> keys passed in this argument (logical AND).
discoveryURLs	This argument contains a list of URLs to be matched against the <discoveryURL> data associated with any registered <businessEntity> structures.

The following code shows the <find_business> XML message that is sent within the request SOAP message to the UDDI registry. This function call basically suggests that the UDDI registry returns information on the businesses that lexically match 'ACM':

```
<uddi:find_business generic="2.0" maxRows="10">
     <uddi:name>
          ACM
     </uddi:name>
</uddi:find_business>
```

The complete SOAP message response, containing the <businessList> structure returned from the registry, is shown in Listing 5.4.

```
<?xml version="1.0" encoding="UTF-8"?>
<SOAP-ENV:Envelope xmlns:SOAP-ENV=
"http://schemas.xmlsoap.org/soap/envelope/">
     <SOAP-ENV:Body>
          <businessList xmlns="urn:uddi-org:api_v2"
          generic="2.0" operator="SYSTINET">
               <businessInfos>
                    <businessInfo businessKey=
                    "uuid:23453aef-af35-6a3f-c34a-
                    bf798dab965a">
```

Listing 5.4 Response to <find_business> function. *(continues)*

```
                              <name xml:lang="en">
                                   ACME Computer Services
                              </name>
                              <description xml:lang="en">
                                   Provides professional services
                                   in the areas of computer software
                              </description>

                              <serviceInfos>
                                   <serviceInfo

                                   serviceKey=
                                   "uuid:1245sdef-af35-6a3f-c34a-
                                   bf798dab965a"

                                   businessKey="uuid:523f3aef-
                                   af35-6a3f-c34a-bf798dab965a">
                                        <name xml:lang="en">
                                             Billing Services
                                        </name>
                                   </serviceInfo>
                              </serviceInfos>
                         </businessInfo>
                    </businessInfos>
               </businessList>
          </SOAP-ENV:Body>
     </SOAP-ENV:Envelope>
```

Listing 5.4 Response to <find_business> function. *(continued)*

Thus, as can be seen from the response in Listing 5.4, the <businessList> structure contains information about each matching business and summaries of the <businessServices> exposed by the individual businesses. If <tModelBag> were used in the search, the resulting <serviceInfo> structures would only reflect data for the <businessServices> that contain the matching <bindingTemplate>.

If any error occurred in processing this API call, a <disposition Report> structure would be returned to the caller in the SOAP Fault.

<find_relatedBusinesses>

Given the UUID of a <businessEntity>, this message returns a list of UUIDs contained within a <relatedBusinessesList> structure. The <relatedBusinessesList> structure would consist of <related

BusinessInfo> structures consisting of information about the businesses that have a relationship with this business.

The syntax for this API is as follows:

```
<find_relatedBusinesses generic="2.0" xmlns="urn:uddi-org:api_v2">
     [<findQualifiers/>]
     <businessKey/>
     [keyedReference/>
</find_relatedBusinesses>
```

Arguments for this function are listed in Table 5.6. Note that the <findQualifiers> argument has been discussed before and hence is not discussed again.

The following code shows the <find_relatedBusinesses> XML message that is sent within the request SOAP message to the UDDI registry. This function call suggests that the UDDI registry return the businesses that are related to the <businessEntity> specified by the UUID '23453aef-af35-6a3f-c34a-bf798dab965a':

```
<uddi:find_relatedBusinesses generic="2.0">
     <uddi:businessKey>
          23453aef-af35-6a3f-c34a-bf798dab965a
     </uddi:name>
</uddi:find_relatedBusinesses>
```

Table 5.6 <find_relatedBusinesses> Function Arguments

ARGUMENT	DESCRIPTION
businessKey	This is a UUID that is used to specify a particular <businessEntity> to use as the focal point of the search. This is a mandatory argument, and it must be used to specify an existing <businessEntity> in the registry. The results would include the businesses that are related in some way to the <businessEntity> whose key has been specified by this argument.
keyedReference	This is a single, optional <keyedReference> element that is used to specify that only businesses related to the focal point in a specific way should be included in the results. The <keyedReference> structure is used to classify a data structure in a UDDI registry. The usage of the <keyedReference> structure is shown later.

The following code shows the partial SOAP message response, containing the <relatedBusinessesList> structure, returned from the registry:

```
<relatedBusinessesList generic="2.0" operator="SYSTINET"
xmlns="urn:uddi-org:api_v2">
     <businessKey>
          23453aef-af35-6a3f-c34a-bf798dab965a
     </businessKey>

     <relatedBusinessInfos>
          <relatedBusinessInfo>
               <businessKey>
                    22443aef-ac35-2f3f-c34a-ca4423bb931c
               </businessKey>

               <name>
                    XYZ Corporation
               </name>

               <description>
                    Outsourced HR Services provider
               </description>

               <sharedRelationships>
                    <keyedReference tModelKey="uuid:..."
                    keyName="XYZ Provides HR Services to ACME
                    Computer Services"
                    keyValue="1">
               </sharedRelationships>
          </relatedBusinessInfo>

     </relatedBusinessInfos>
</relatedBusinessesList>
```

<find_service>

Given the UUID of a <businessEntity> structure, the name of the service, the <tModel> of a specification, or the service category, this message returns a summary of matching services represented by <serviceInfo> structures contained within a <serviceList> structure.

The following code shows the syntax for this API:

```
<find_service businessKey=uuid_key" [maxRows="nn"] generic="2.0"
xmlns="urn:uddi-org:api_v2">
     [<findQualifiers/>]
     [<name/>[<name/>]...]
     [<categoryBag/>]
     [<tModelBag/>]
</find_service>
```

Semantics of the arguments to this API function have already been discussed earlier in the "*<find_business>*" and "*<find_relatedBusinesses>*" sections and hence are not covered again to avoid redundancy.

The following code shows the `<find_service>` XML message that is sent within the request SOAP message to the UDDI registry. This function call suggests that the UDDI registry return a list of services that match to the name pattern 'Bill' specified by the `<name>` element.

```
<uddi:find_service generic="2.0">
     <findQualifiers>
          <findQualifier>
               caseSensitiveMatch
          </findQualifier>
     </findQualifiers>
     <uddi:name>
          Bill
     </uddi:name>
</uddi:find_service>
```

Also, note how this query makes use of `<findQualifiers>` consisting of an enumerated value `'caseSensitiveMatch'` to instruct a case-sensitive matching. Find qualifiers are discussed in detail in a later section.

The following code shows the partial SOAP message response, containing a `<serviceList>` structure, returned from the registry:

```
<serviceList generic="2.0" operator="SYSTINET"
xmlns="urn:uddi-org:api_v2">
     <serviceInfos>
          <serviceInfo
          serviceKey=
          "uuid:1245sdef-af35-6a3f-c34a-bf798dab965a"
          businessKey=
          "uuid:23453aef-af35-6a3f-c34a-bf798dab965a">
               <name>
                    Billing Services
               </name>
          </serviceInfo>
     </ServiceInfos>
</serviceList>
```

<find_binding>

Given the UUID of a `<businessService>` structure, the `<find_binding>` message returns a `<bindingDetail>` structure containing zero or more `<bindingTemplate>` structures matching the criteria specified by the argument list.

The syntax for this API is as follows:

```
<find_binding serviceKey=uuid_key" [maxRows="nn"] generic="2.0"
xmlns="urn:uddi-org:api_v2">
     [<findQualifiers/>]
     [<tModelBag/>]
</find_binding>
```

Semantics of the arguments to this API function have been discussed earlier and hence will not be covered again.

The following code shows the `<find_binding>` XML message that is sent within the request SOAP message to the UDDI registry. This function call suggests that the UDDI registry return a list of `<bindingTemplate>` structures that belong to the service whose key is `'1245sdef-af35-6a3f-c34a-bf798dab965a'`.

```
<uddi:find_binding serviceKey=
"uuid:1245sdef-af35-6a3f-c34a-bf798dab965a" generic="2.0">
     <findQualifiers>
          <findQualifier>
               sortByNameAsc
          </findQualifier>
     </findQualifiers>
</uddi:find_binding>
```

Also, note this query makes use of `<findQualifiers>` carrying an enumerated value of `'sortByNameAsc'` to instruct the sorting of returned results by names of the `<tModel>` structures, in an ascending order. Find qualifiers are discussed in the *Search Qualifiers* section.

The partial SOAP message response, containing a `<serviceList>` structure returned from the registry, is as follows:

```
<bindingDetail generic="2.0" operator="SYSTINET"
xmlns="urn:uddi-org:api_v2">

     <bindingTemplate
     bindingKey="uuid:acd5sdef-1235-6a3f-c34a-bf798dab124a"
     serviceKey="uuid:1245sdef-af35-6a3f-c34a-bf798dab965a">

          <accessPoint URLType="http">
               http://www.acmecomputerservices.com/
               billingservices_entry/
          </accessPoint>

          <tModelInstanceDetails>
```

```
                <tModelInstanceInfo tModelKey=
                "uuid:acd5sdef-1235-6a3f-c34a-bf798dab124b">

                     <description>
                          Provides SOAP Interface. Described
                          by BillingServices_WSDL.wsdl.
                     </description>

                </tModelInstanceInfo>
           </tModelInstanceDetails>
      </bindingTemplate>
 </bindingDetail>
```

<find_tModel>

Given a name, a category, or an identifier, this message returns abbreviated information of all the matching <tModel> structures contained in a <tModelList> structure.

The syntax for this API is as follows:

```
<find_tModel [maxRows="nn"] generic="2.0"
xmlns="urn:uddi-org:api_v2">
     [<findQualifiers/>]
     [<name/>]
     [<identifierBag/>]
     [<categoryBag/>]
</find_tModel>
```

Semantics of the arguments to this API function have already been discussed earlier and hence are not covered again in order to avoid redundancy.

The following code shows the <find_tModel> XML message that is sent within the request SOAP message to the UDDI registry. This function call suggests that the UDDI registry return a list of <tModel> structures that match to the name pattern 'WSDL'.

```
<uddi:find_tModel generic="2.0">
     <name>
          WSDL
     </name>
</uddi:find_tModel>
```

The partial SOAP message response, containing a <tModelList> structure, returned from the registry is as follows:

```
<tModelList generic="2.0" operator="SYSTINET"
xmlns="urn:uddi-org:api_v2">
     <tModelInfos>
          <tModelInfo tModelKey=
          "uuid:acd5sdef-1235-6a3f-c34a-bf798dab124b">
               <name>
                    SOAP_WSDL_BillingServices
               </name>
          </tModelInfo>
     </tModelInfos>
</tModelList>
```

Get_xx Inquiry API Functions

The get_xx functions follow the *drill-down pattern*. This pattern typically involves getting more specific and detailed information about an entity based on a unique key corresponding to the entity.

The get_xx calls form the search capabilities wherein once the UDDI client has a UUID key for any of the primary UDDI data structures of `<businessEntity>`, `<businessService>`, `<bindingTemplate>`, and `<tModel>`, it can use that key to get access to the full registered details of that particular structure. The client then can access the details of these structures by passing a relevant key type to one of the get_xx Inquiry API function calls.

All of these get_xx functions are quite straightforward. These functions require a valid UUID for the data structure whose details need to be drilled down.

Table 5.7 lists these four get_xx functions and an explanation of their semantics. Also listed in the table are the response structures returned by the UDDI registry in response to each of these calls.

Table 5.7 get_xx Functions

GET_XX FUNCTION	RETURNED STRUCTURE	DESCRIPTION
<get_businessDetail>	<businessDetail>	This message returns a <businessDetail> structure consisting of one or more <businessEntity> structures matching the UUID(s) passed as an argument to this function call.

Table 5.7 *(Continued)*

GET_XX FUNCTION	RETURNED STRUCTURE	DESCRIPTION
<get_serviceDetail>	<serviceDetail>	This message returns a <serviceDetail> structure containing one or more <businessService> structures matching the UUID(s) passed as an argument to this function call.
<get_bindingDetail>	<bindingDetail>	If the integrity of <bindingTemplate> is not intact, for example if the document referred to by the <tModel> referenced by <bindingTemplate> has been moved or deleted, this function call should be used to get hold of the new <bindingDetail> structure.
<get_tModelDetail>	<tModelDetail>	This message returns a <tModelDetail> structure consisting of one or more <tModel> data structures matching the UUID(s) passed as an argument to this function call.

In order to understand the nature of get_xx functions, let's examine the working of the <get_businessDetail> function call.

The following code shows the <get_businessDetail> XML message that is sent within the request SOAP message to the UDDI registry. This function call suggests that the UDDI registry return the registered details for business corresponding to the key '23453aef-af35-6a3f-c34a-bf798dab965a'.

```
<uddi:get_businessDetail generic="2.0">
     <businessKey>
          23453aef-af35-6a3f-c34a-bf798dab965a
     </businessKey>
</uddi:find_tModel>
```

The partial SOAP message response, containing a <businessDetail> structure, returned from the registry is as follows:

```
<businessDetail generic="2.0" operator="SYSTINET"
xmlns="urn:uddi-org:api_v2">

     <businessEntity authorizedName = "John Smith"
     businessKey="uuid:23453aef-af35-6a3f-c34a-bf798dab965a"
     operator="SYSTINET">

          <discoveryURLs>
               <discoverURL useType="businessEntity">
                    http://www.systinet.com/wasp/uddi/
                    discovery?businessKey=
                    23453aef-af35-6a3f-c34a-bf798dab965a
               </discoveryURL>
          </discoveryURLs>

          <name>
               ACME Computer Services
          </name>

          <description xml:lang="en">
               Provides professional services in the areas of
               computer software
          </description>

          <contacts>
               <contact useType="information">

                    <description xml:lang="en">
                         For sales related information
                    </description>

                    <personName>
                         Joe Smith
                    </personName>

                    <address>
                         1, Computer Drive, Burlington,
                         MA 01803 USA
                    </address>
               </contact>
          </contacts>

          <businessServices>
               ...
          </businessServices>
     </businessEntity>
</businessDetail>
```

The <businessServices> structure in the previous listing is expanded as follows:

```
<businessService
businessKey="23453aef-af35-6a3f-c34a-bf798dab965a"
serviceKey="1245sdef-af35-6a3f-c34a-bf798dab965a">
     <name xml:lang="en">
          Billing Services
     </name>

     <description xml:lang="en">
          Billing Services
     </description>

     <bindingTemplates>
          <bindingTemplate bindingKey=
          "uuid:acd5sdef-1235-6a3f-c34a-bf798dab124a"
          serviceKey="1245sdef-af35-6a3f-c34a-bf798dab965a ">

               <description xml:lang="en">
                    Here is where you should be visiting to
                    get started with using billing services
                    provided by us.
               </description>

               <accessPoint URLType="http">
                    http://www.acmecomputerservices.com/
                    billingservices_entry/
               </accessPoint>

               <tModelInstanceDetails>
                    <tModelInstanceInfo tModelKey=
                    "uuid:acd5sdef-1235-6a3f-c34a-
                    bf798dab124b">

                         <description xml:lang="en">
                              Provides SOAP Interface.
                              Described by
                              BillingServices_WSDL.wsdl.
                         </description>

                         <instanceDetails>
                              <overviewDoc>
                                   <description
                                   xml:lang="en">
                                        Describes how to use
                                        this service
                                   </description>

                                   <overviewURL>
```

```
                                    http://www.acmecomputer
                                    services.com/billing_
                                    services_description/
                                </overviewURL>
                            </overviewDoc>
                        </instanceDetails>
                    </tModelInstanceInfo>
                </tModelInstanceDetails>
            </bindingTemplate>
        </bindingTemplates>

        <categoryBag>
            <keyedReference keyName=
            "Custom Computer Programming Services "
            keyValue="541511"
            tModelKey=
            "uuid:C0B9FE13-179F-413D-8A5B-5004DB8E5BB2"/>

            <keyedReference keyName="United States"
            keyValue="US"
            tModelKey=
            "uuid:4e49a8d6-d5a2-4fc2-93a0-0411d8d19e88"/>
        </categoryBag>
    </businessService>
```

Thus, this business is classified by two categories:

The standard industry categorization system (NAICS). The first `<keyedReference>` structure under `<categoryBag>` suggests that ACME Computer Services is a "Custom Computer Programming Services" company.

The standard geography categorization system (ISO-3166). The second `<keyedReference>` structure under `<categoryBag>` in the previous listing suggests that ACME Computer Services is geographically related to "United States".

The next section talks about search qualifiers, one of the arguments to most of the inquiry API functions.

Search Qualifiers

Most of the inquiry API functions accept `<findQualifiers>` as arguments. The `<findQualifiers>` structure consists of search qualifiers expressed by a `<findQualifier>` data structure. The UDDI Programmer's API specification document pre-defines search qualifiers as an enumeration.

Table 5.8 shows some of the most frequently used search qualifiers, represented by their enumerated values, and explains their semantics.

Table 5.8 The Most Frequently Used Search Qualifiers

ENUMERATED SEARCH QUALIFIER	DESCRIPTION
exactNameMatch	When this search qualifier is specified, only the entries that exactly match the name pattern passed in the <name> argument would be returned in the result.
caseSensitiveMatch	This search qualifier signifies that case sensitive matching between entries has been searched and the entry has been specified by the <name> argument.
sortByNameAsc	This is the default sort qualifier, if no other conflicting sort qualifier is specified.
sortByNameDesc	This signifies that the result returned by a find_xx or get_xx Inquiry API call should be sorted based on the name field in descending alphabetic sort order.
sortByDateAsc	This is the default sort qualifier, if no other conflicting sort qualifier is specified. Also, the sort qualifiers involving a date are secondary in precedence to the sortByName qualifiers. This causes the sortByName elements to be sorted within name by date, oldest to newest.
sortByDateDesc	Also, because the sort qualifiers involving dates are secondary in precedence to the sortByName qualifiers, this causes sortByName elements to be sorted within name by date, newest to oldest.

With this, now we will proceed to the publishing API of the UDDI registry.

Publishing API

This section will cover all of the XML messages that perform the functionality of adding/modifying/deleting information from a UDDI registry. As mentioned earlier, publishing to a UDDI registry requires an authenticated access. UDDI specification does not define authentication mechanisms, and hence, authentication is dependent upon the implementations of UDDI. Also, a URL different from an inquiry URL usually handles publishing-related API calls. Typically, HTTPS is used for carrying publishing call request/response information.

Table 5.9 lists the publishing API functions as well as their semantics. The table also lists the structure that is returned in response to each of these function calls.

Table 5.9 Publishing API Functions

PUBLISHING API FUNCTION	RETURNED STRUCTURE	DESCRIPTION
<get_authToken>	<authToken>	The UDDI registry node will return an authentication token in response to this message in an <authToken> structure. This message consists of a login ID and password corresponding to a registry user that the UDDI registry would use for authentication purposes. *Note*: A valid authentication token is required in order to execute *any* function in the publishing API.
<discard_authToken>	<dispositionReport>	The message informs a UDDI registry node to discard the active authentication session associated with this user, essentially resulting into a logoff operation. This message should be sent to the UDDI registry node after the execution of publishing operations has been completed. UDDI errors are communicated to the client as SOAP fault messages. The UDDI data structure <dispositionReport> maps to the <detail> structural element of the SOAP fault message. Thus, <dispositionReport> is used in all the cases where errors need to be communicated. However, UDDI also uses this structure to communicate successes in non-error situations. The <dispositionReport> message is always returned in response to delete_xx or <discard_authToken> messages.

PUBLISHING API FUNCTION	RETURNED STRUCTURE	DESCRIPTION
`<save_business>`	`<businessDetail>`	This message consists of `<businessEntity>` structure(s) corresponding to the one or more business instances that need to be added/modified to the UDDI registry. Changes to an existing `<businessEntity>` structure can impact existing references to `<publisherAssertion>`, `<businessService>`, or `<bindingTemplate>` structures. The registry response consists of the `<businessDetail>` structure containing the full details of the business that has just been added/modified.
`<delete_business>`	`<dispositionReport>`	This message suggests that the UDDI registry delete businesses corresponding to the keys specified within the `<delete_business>` message. Deleting businesses would cause the deletion of any contained `<businessService>` as well as `<bindingTemplate>` structures. Also any `<publisherAssertion>` structures created with the UUID of this business would be deleted from the registry.
`<save_service>`	`<serviceDetail>`	This message consists of `<businessService>` structure(s) corresponding to the service(s) that need to be added/modified to the UDDI registry. Changes to an existing `<businessService>` structure can impact existing references to `<bindingTemplate>` structures. The registry response consists of the `<serviceDetail>` structure containing the full details of the service(s) that have just been added/modified.

(continues)

Table 5.9 Publishing API Functions *(continued)*

PUBLISHING API FUNCTION	RETURNED STRUCTURE	DESCRIPTION
<delete_service>	<dispositionReport>	This message informs the registry to delete the service(s) instances corresponding to the UUID key(s) specified within the <delete_service> message.
<save_binding>	<bindingDetail>	The registry response to this message consists of the <bindingDetail> structure containing the full details of the binding(s) that have just been added/modified.
<delete_binding>	<dispositionReport>	This message informs the registry to delete one or more <bindingTemplate> instances corresponding to the UUID key(s) specified within the <delete_binding> message.
<save_tModel>	<tModelDetail>	The registry response to this message consists of the <tModelDetail> structure containing the full details of the <tModel> instances that have just been added/modified.
<delete_tModel>	<dispositionReport>	The reason for not completely destroying <tModel> instances is to enable organizations still using that specific <tModel> structure to get basic details about it.
<get_publisherAssertions>	<publisherAssertions>	This message returns a list of <publisherAssertion> structures that were published by this registry user.
<add_publisherAssertions>	<dispositionReport>	This message *adds* the <publisherAssertion> structures contained within this message to the list of existing <publisherAssertion> instances associated with this registry user.

PUBLISHING API FUNCTION	RETURNED STRUCTURE	DESCRIPTION
<set_publisherAssertions>	<publisherAssertions>	This returns a <publisherAssertions> structure as part of the response, containing a collection of the replacing <publisherAssertion> structures.
<get_assertionStatusReport>	<assertionStatusReport>	This is a query function that returns a list of all the <publisherAssertion> instances, created by this registry user or others, as part of the structure <assertionStatusReport>, which involves the <businessEntity> instance published by this registry user.
<get_registeredInfo>	<registeredInfo>	The message returns a list of all the <businessEntity> and <tModel> documents that are managed (owned) by this registry user.

Implementations of UDDI

The UDDI specification enjoys tremendous amounts of vendor support. There are a lot of offerings in the UDDI space. Vendors provide UDDI support in two ways:

UDDI client. Almost all of the vendors participating in the UDDI space provide UDDI client support. A UDDI client basically provides APIs required for working with the UDDI registry. These APIs can be in a variety of languages such as Java, C++, Python, and so on. Note that most of the vendors, as of this writing, provide proprietary implementations of Java APIs for UDDI. JSR-093 JAXR is an effort to provide a standard Java API for communicating with UDDI registries. Because the JAXR specification has just recently been finalized, vendors should now be able to start providing support for JAXR in their API implementations. The JAXR specification is covered in more detail in Chapter 11, "Java API for XML Registries." The examples covered in this chapter do not make use of JAXR APIs.

UDDI registry server implementation. Many implementations of the UDDI registry server are available now. Apart from the public registries hosted by Microsoft, HP, IBM, and Systinet, several vendors also provide implementations of private UDDI registries.

Table 5.10 is a partial listing of the UDDI implementations.

Table 5.10 UDDI Implementations

IMPLEMENTATION	DOWNLOAD FROM . . .
Java Web Services Developer Pack (JWSDP)*	java.sun.com/xml/download.html
Systinet WASP**	www.systinet.com/wasp
The Mind Electric GLUE	www.themindelectric.com/glue/index.html
IBM Web Services Toolkit	www.alphaworks.ibm.com/tech/webservicestoolkit/
BEA WebLogic Workshop	www.bea.com/products/weblogic/workshop/easystart/index.shtml

* JWSDP provides an implementation of private UDDI registry implemented on the Tomcat and Xindice databases. Chapter 11, "Java API for XML Registries," uses the JWSDP UDDI Registry Server for examples.

** UDDI examples in this chapter are developed using Systinet WASP UDDI APIs.

UDDI Support in Systinet WASP 4.0

The Systinet WASP 4.0 platform includes extensive support for the UDDI registry. WASP provides an implementation of the UDDI version 2.0 registry. Also, WASP provides a client API to work with the UDDI registry.

In the following three examples, we will examine how to work with the UDDI registry on the Systinet WASP 4.0 platform:

`SubmitBusiness (SubmitBusiness.java)`. This example shows how to submit business information to the UDDI registry.

`SearchBusiness (SearchBusiness.java)`. This example shows how to look up the business information using name patterns.

`DeleteBusiness (DeleteBusiness.java)`. This example demonstrates the deletion of business information from a UDDI registry.

The examples are discussed in detail in the following sections: *Publishing Information to a UDDI Registry, Searching Information in a UDDI Registry,* and *Deleting Information from a UDDI Registry*. Note that all of these three examples along with their source code and readme.txt consisting of setup instructions can be downloaded from Wiley's Web site at www.wiley.com/compbooks/nagappan.

Note that we will run these examples against the public UDDI registry that is hosted by Systinet at www.systinet.com/uddi/web. The following are the inquiry and publishing URLs supported by Systinet's public registry:

- www.systinet.com/wasp/uddi/inquiry
- www.systinet.com:443/wasp/uddi/publishing

In order to work with the Systinet UDDI client APIs, ensure that the following JAR files are in the CLASSPATH:

`uddiclient.jar`. This archive implements UDDI Versions 1 and 2 inquiry and publishing. It can be found under `$WASP_HOME/dist`.

`wasp.jar`. This archive can be found under `$WASP_HOME/lib`.

In order to execute `SubmitBusiness` and `DeleteBusiness`, which make use of the UDDI publishing API, we first need to register as a user of the UDDI registry. Registration of the user is covered in the next section.

Registering as a Systinet UDDI Registry User

Anyone can easily register as a Systinet registry user. Figure 5.5 shows the browser interface supported by Systinet for registering a user.

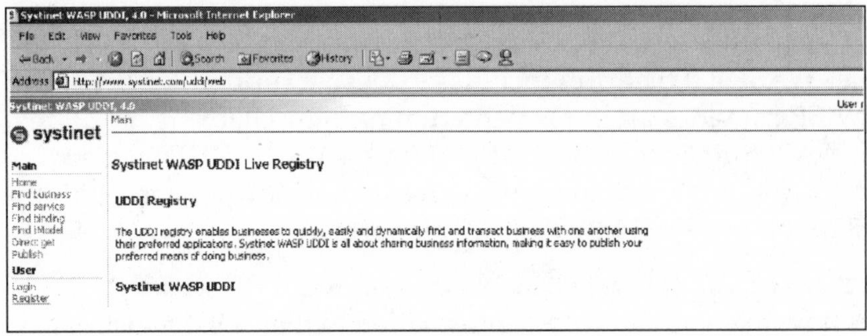

Figure 5.5 Browser interface for registering a user.

Figure 5.6 shows registering a user with login ID: `registry_user` and password: `registry_user`.

Our examples will make use of this account, in order to authenticate to the UDDI registry. Hence, before trying to run the examples, please ensure that this account does exist in the Systinet public UDDI registry. If it does not, create a new account with the same credentials. If you are unable to create the account with the same credentials, then create an account with different credentials followed by changing the hard-coded login ID and password to the new account login ID and password, in `SubmitBusiness.java` and `DeleteBusiness.java`, and re-compiling them.

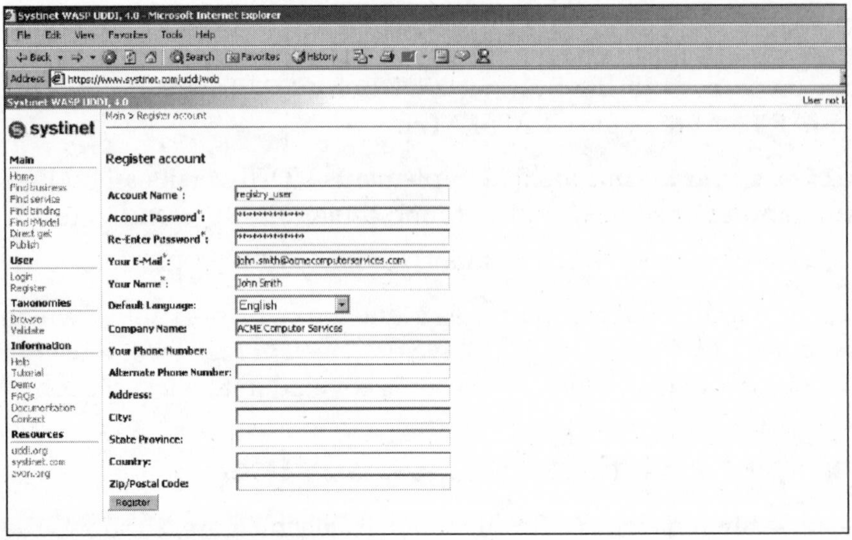

Figure 5.6 Registering a user.

Now, let 's proceed with submitting new business information to the UDDI registry.

Publishing Information to a UDDI Registry

`SubmitBusiness.java` shows us how to publish a business named *ACME Computer Services* along with its description. In the coming sections, we will examine the source code of `SubmitBusiness.java`, followed by its compilation and execution.

Programming Steps for Publishing

The entire publishing logic is provided by the `doSubmit()` method of the `jws.ch5.SubmitBusiness` class, and hence, its implementation is of most interest to us. The following are the steps of `doSubmit()`:

1. Construct the `UDDIApiPublishing` object. This is the object that we will use to actually publish to the registry.
2. Get hold of the authentication token from the registry with the help of the `get_authToken()` API call on the `UDDIApiPublishing` object. Once we have the authentication token, we should be able to publish to the registry.
3. Create the `BusinessEntity` structure and populate it with the name and description of the business to submit. Note that we do not have to create the key for this business because the registry, upon submitting the business information, would generate it.
4. Now, get hold of the `SaveBusiness` object. This object represents a collection of businesses that we wish to submit at a time. Hence, we will need to add the `BusinessEntity` object that we just created to the `SaveBusiness` object using the `addBusinessEntity()` method.
5. Now, publish the business information through a `save_business()` call on `UDDIApiPublishing` object. This method call takes the `SaveBusiness` object as an argument and returns the `BusinessDetail` object upon completion.
6. After the publishing operation has been executed, discard the authentication token. Finally, check whether the publishing operation was successful or not.

SubmitBusiness.java Source Code

Listing 5.5 shows the complete code listing of `SubmitBusiness.java`.

```
package jws.ch5;

import org.idoox.uddi.client.api.v2.*;
import org.idoox.uddi.client.api.v2.request.publishing.*;
import org.idoox.uddi.client.structure.v2.business.*;
import org.idoox.uddi.client.structure.v2.base.*;
import org.idoox.uddi.client.api.v2.response.*;
import org.idoox.uddi.*;

public class SubmitBusiness
{
     public static void main(String args[]) throws Exception
     {
          // Call the method in order to submit new business to
          // the public registry hosted by Systinet.

          doSubmit();
     }

     public static void doSubmit() throws Exception
     {
          String sBusinessName = "ACME Computer Services";
          String sBusinessDescription = "Provides professional
          services in the areas of Computer Software";

          System.out.println("Saving business with the
          following details:");

          System.out.println("Name: " + sBusinessName);

          System.out.println("Description: " +
          sBusinessDescription);

          // Get hold of the UDDI Publishing API
          // Note our usage of Publishing URL for the Systinet
          // UDDI Registry

          UDDIApiPublishing objUDDIApiPublishing =
          UDDILookup.getPublishing("https://www.systinet.com:443
          /wasp/uddi/publishing/");

          // First we get hold of Authentication token from the
          // Registry so that we can publish to the UDDI
          // Registry. Note that registered a user in Systinet
          // Public Registry with registry_user ID and
```

Listing 5.5 SubmitBusiness.java.

```
// registry_user password.

AuthToken objAuthToken  = objUDDIApiPublishing.
get_authToken (new GetAuthToken(new
UserID("registry_user"), new Cred("registry_user")));

// Create the BusinessEntity Structure
BusinessEntity objBusinessEntity =
new BusinessEntity();

// Set the empty businessKey since we are creating a
// new business
objBusinessEntity.setBusinessKey
 (new BusinessKey(""));

// Set the name of the business
objBusinessEntity.addName(new Name(sBusinessName));

// Set the description of the business
objBusinessEntity.addDescription
 (new Description(sBusinessDescription));

// Get hold of the SaveBusiness interface
SaveBusiness objSaveBusiness = new SaveBusiness();

// Set the Authentication Information on SaveBusiness
objSaveBusiness.setAuthInfo
(objAuthToken.getAuthInfo());

// Now add the BusinessEntity to save to the
// SaveBusiness interface
objSaveBusiness.addBusinessEntity(objBusinessEntity);

// Finally publish the SaveBusiness object to the
// registry
BusinessDetail objBusinessDetail =
objUDDIApiPublishing.save_business(objSaveBusiness);

// Discard the Authentication token now
objUDDIApiPublishing.discard_authToken
 (new DiscardAuthToken(objAuthToken.getAuthInfo()));

// See if the Business has been published
// successfully
if (objBusinessDetail==null)
{
     System.err.println("\nUnsuccessful in
     submitting the new business information to
     registry.");
```

Listing 5.5 SubmitBusiness.java. *(continues)*

```
            }
            else
            {
                System.err.println("\nSuccessful in submitting
                the new business information to registry.");
            }
            return;
        }
    }
```

Listing 5.5 SubmitBusiness.java. *(continued)*

Compiling and Executing SubmitBusiness.java

The following command line instruction compiles `SubmitBusiness.java`:

```
> javac jws/ch5/SubmitBusiness.java
```

The following command line instruction executes `SubmitBusiness.java`:

```
> java -classpath %CLASSPATH%;. jws.ch5.SubmitBusiness
```

Figure 5.7 shows the output of this execution.

You can verify the creation of this new business by visiting the Systinet public registry or by executing `SearchBusiness`.

Searching Information in a UDDI Registry

`SearchBusiness.java` shows us how to search for businesses based on the name pattern provided by the user. In the coming sections, we will examine the source code of `SearchBusiness.java`, followed by its compilation and execution.

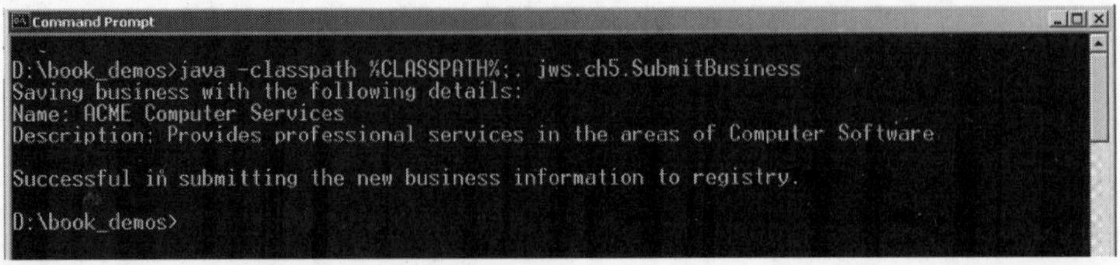

```
Command Prompt

D:\book_demos>java -classpath %CLASSPATH%;. jws.ch5.SubmitBusiness
Saving business with the following details:
Name: ACME Computer Services
Description: Provides professional services in the areas of Computer Software

Successful in submitting the new business information to registry.

D:\book_demos>
```

Figure 5.7 Executing SubmitBusiness.java.

Programming Steps for Searching

The entire querying logic is provided by the doSearch() method of the jws.ch5.SearchBusiness class, and hence, its implementation is of most interest to us. The following are the steps to implementing a doSearch():

1. Construct the FindBusiness object. This object represents the criteria for the search operation. Hence, we will need to add our criteria, that is, the name pattern that the user supplied, using the addName() method on this object.
2. Construct the UDDIApiInquiry object that we would use for placing the inquiry call.
3. Finally, invoke the business inquiry operation through the find _business() method on the UDDIApiInquiry object. This method returns a BusinessList object containing the BusinessInfo structures.
4. Now, check whether the businesses are found matching the given criteria. If there are matching businesses, we need to traverse through their BusinessInfo structures and get hold of the name and key UUID of the business.

SearchBusiness.java Source Code

Listing 5.6 is the complete code listing of SearchBusiness.java.

```
package jws.ch5;

import org.idoox.uddi.client.api.v2.request.inquiry.*;
import org.idoox.uddi.client.structure.v2.tmodel.*;
import org.idoox.uddi.client.structure.v2.base.*;

import org.idoox.uddi.client.api.v2.response.*;
import org.idoox.uddi.client.structure.v2.business.*;
import org.idoox.uddi.client.api.v2.*;

import org.idoox.uddi.*;

public class SearchBusiness
{
     public static void main(String args[]) throws Exception
     {
          if (args.length != 1)
          {
```

Listing 5.6 SearchBusiness.java. *(continues)*

```
            printUsage();
        }
        else
        {
            String sNameOfBusiness =  args[0];

            // Invoke the search operation
            doSearch(sNameOfBusiness);
        }
    }

    private static void printUsage()
    {
        System.err.println("\nUsage: java
        jws.ch5.SearchBusiness <BusinessNamePattern>");

        System.err.println("\nwhere <BusinessNamePattern>
        represents name of the business you want to
        search.");
    }

    public static void doSearch(String sNameOfBusiness) throws
    Exception
    {
        // Create a FindBusiness object
        FindBusiness objFindBusiness = new FindBusiness();

        // Send the find criteria
        objFindBusiness.addName(new Name(sNameOfBusiness));

        // Set the maximum number of rows to return
        objFindBusiness.setMaxRows(new MaxRows("10"));

        // Get hold  of UDDILookup object to place the query
        UDDIApiInquiry objUDDIApiInquiry =
        UDDILookup.getInquiry("http://www.systinet.com:80/
        wasp/uddi/inquiry/");

        // Invoke the query on the UDDI Inquiry API
        BusinessList objBusinessList=
        objUDDIApiInquiry.find_business(objFindBusiness);

        // Check whether anything was found matching the
```

Listing 5.6 SearchBusiness.java.

```
            // criteria
            if (objBusinessList==null)
            {
                System.err.println("No businesses were found
                matching the criteria.");
            }
            else
            {
                // Get hold of the BusinessInfo objects,
                // contained by BusinessList
                BusinessInfos objBusinessInfos =
                objBusinessList.getBusinessInfos();

                System.out.println("\n" +
                objBusinessInfos.size() + " businesses found
                matching the criteria...\n");

                BusinessInfo objBusinessInfo =
                objBusinessInfos.getFirst();

                BusinessKey objBusinessKey;

                if (objBusinessInfo != null)
                {
                    objBusinessKey=objBusinessInfo.
                    getBusinessKey();

                    // Traverse through the results.
                    while (objBusinessInfo!=null)
                    {
                        System.out.println("Business Name =
                        " + objBusinessInfo.getNames().
                        getFirst().getValue());

                        System.out.println("Business UUID = " +
                        objBusinessInfo.getBusinessKey());

                        System.out.println("---------------
                        ------------------------------");

                        // Next BusinessInfo
                        objBusinessInfo =
                        objBusinessInfos.getNext();
                    }
                }
            }
        }
    }
```

Listing 5.6 SearchBusiness.java. *(continued)*

Compiling and Executing SearchBusiness.java

The following command line instruction compiles `SearchBusiness.java`:

```
> javac jws/ch5/SearchBusiness.java
```

The following command line instruction executes `SearchBusiness.java` in order to search for businesses with names starting with a 'A':

```
> java -classpath %CLASSPATH%;. jws.ch5.SearchBusiness A
```

Figure 5.8 shows the output of this execution.

As can be seen from the output in Figure 5.8, ACME Computer Services is one of the businesses that matched our search criteria.

Deleting Information from a UDDI Registry

`DeleteBusiness.java` demonstrates how to delete a business from the UDDI registry based on its key UUID, which is passed by the user as a command line argument. You can get hold of the business key either by browsing the Systinet registry on the Web or by executing `SearchBusiness`. In the coming sections, we will examine the source code of `DeleteBusiness.java`, followed by its compilation and execution.

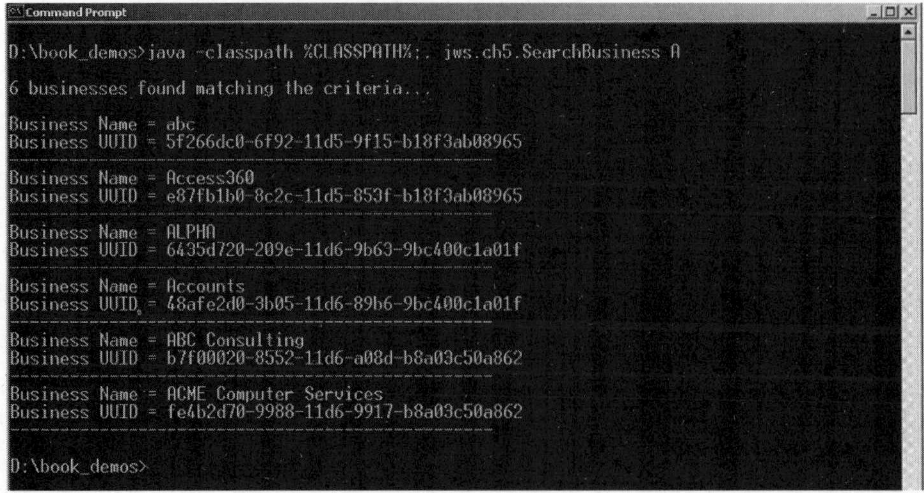

Figure 5.8 Executing SearchBusiness.java.

Programming Steps for Deleting

The deletion logic is provided by the `doDelete()` method of the `jws.ch5.DeleteBusiness` class, and hence, its implementation is of most interest to us. The following are the steps to implementing `doDelete()`:

1. Construct the `UDDIApiPublishing` object. This is the object that we would use to actually delete information from the registry.
2. Get hold of the authentication token from the registry with the help of the `get_authToken()` API call on the `UDDIApiPublishing` object. Once we have a valid authentication token, we should be able to delete from the registry.
3. Now, get hold of the `DeleteBusiness` object. This object represents a collection of businesses that we wish to delete at a time. Hence, we will need to add businesses referenced through `BusinessKey` to this object, using the `addBusinessKey()` method on `DeleteBusiness`.
4. Now, delete the business information through the `delete_business()` call on the `UDDIApiPublishing` object. This method call takes the `DeleteBusiness` object as an argument and returns the `DispositonReport` object upon completion.
5. Check the `DispositionReport` object to see if this operation was a success or a failure.

DeleteBusiness.java Source Code

Listing 5.7 is the complete code listing of `DeleteBusiness.java`.

```
package jws.ch5;

import org.idoox.uddi.*;
import org.idoox.uddi.client.api.v2.*;
import org.idoox.uddi.client.api.v2.request.publishing.*;
import org.idoox.uddi.client.api.v2.response.*;
import org.idoox.uddi.client.structure.v2.business.*;

public class DeleteBusiness
{
    public static void main(String args[]) throws Exception
```

Listing 5.7 DeleteBusiness.java. *(continues)*

```
{
     if (args.length != 1)
     {
          printUsage();
     }
     else
     {
          BusinessKey objBusinessKey =
          new BusinessKey (args[0]);

          doDelete(objBusinessKey);
     }
}

private static void printUsage()
{
     System.err.println("\nUsage: java
     jws.ch5.DeleteBusiness <BusinessKey>");

     System.err.println("\nwhere <BusinessKey> is a string
     representation of UUID corresponding to Business you
     want to delete.");
}

public static void doDelete(BusinessKey objBusinessKey)
throws Exception
{
     System.out.println("\nDeleting Business with Key: ");
     System.out.println(objBusinessKey.toString());

     UDDIApiPublishing objUDDIApiPublishing =
     UDDILookup.getPublishing("
     https://www.systinet.com:443/wasp/uddi/publishing/");

     // First we get hold of Authentication token from the
     // Registry so that we can delete
     // business from the UDDI Registry. Note that
     // registered a user in Systinet Publich Registry
     // with registry_user ID and registry_user password.

     AuthToken objAuthToken = objUDDIApiPublishing.
     get_authToken(new GetAuthToken(
     new UserID("registry_user"),
     new Cred("registry_user")));

     // Now get hold of the DeleteBusiness structure
     org.idoox.uddi.client.api.v2.request.
     publishing.DeleteBusiness objDeleteBusiness =
```

Listing 5.7 DeleteBusiness.java.

```
new org.idoox.uddi.client.api.v2.request.
publishing.DeleteBusiness();

// Set the login information on DeleteBusiness
objDeleteBusiness.setAuthInfo
(objAuthToken.getAuthInfo());

// Add business to delete to the DeleteBusiness
// Structure
objDeleteBusiness.addBusinessKey(objBusinessKey);




// Call Publishing API method delete_business
DispositionReport objDispositionReport =
objUDDIApiPublishing.delete_business
(objDeleteBusiness);

// Discard the Authentication token now
objUDDIApiPublishing.discard_authToken
(new DiscardAuthToken(objAuthToken.getAuthInfo()));

// Check to see if the delete operation was
// successful
if (objDispositionReport == null)
{
     System.err.println("Unsuccessful in deleting
     the business information from the registry.");
}
else
{
     if (objDispositionReport.
     resultIs(UDDIErrorCodes.E_SUCCESS))
     {
          System.out.println("\nSuccessful in
          deleting the business information from the
          registry.");
     }
     else
     {
          System.out.println("\nUnsuccessful in
          deleting the business information due to
          following reason(s):");

          System.out.println(
```

Listing 5.7 DeleteBusiness.java. *(continues)*

```
                        objDispositionReport.toXML());
                    }
                }
            }
        }
```

Listing 5.7 DeleteBusiness.java. *(continued)*

Compiling and Executing SearchBusiness.java

The following command line instruction compiles `DeleteBusiness.java`:

```
> javac jws/ch5/DeleteBusiness.java
```

The following command line instruction executes `DeleteBusiness.java` in order to delete the ACME Computer Services business corresponding to the key `'fe4b2d70-9988-11d6-9917-b8a03c50a862'`.

```
> java -classpath %CLASSPATH%;. jws.ch5.DeleteBusiness
fe4b2d70-9988-11d6-9917-b8a03c50a862
```

Figure 5.9 shows the output of this execution.

Deletion of ACME Computer Services can be verified either by visiting the Systinet public registry or by executing `SearchBusiness`.

```
Select Command Prompt

D:\book_demos>java -classpath %CLASSPATH%;. jws.ch5.DeleteBusiness fe4b2d70-9988-11d6-9917
-b8a03c50a862

Deleting Business with Key:
fe4b2d70-9988-11d6-9917-b8a03c50a862

Successful in deleting the business information from the registry.

D:\book_demos>
```

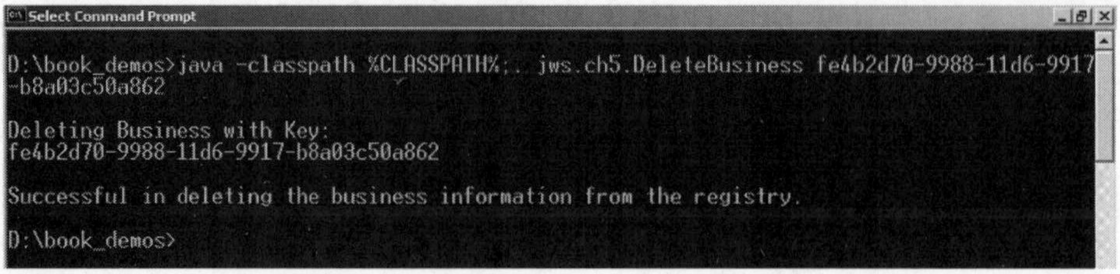

Figure 5.9 Executing DeleteBusiness.java.

Limitations of UDDI

UDDI is an evolving standard. Currently, the most deployed version of UDDI (2.0) is limiting in terms of the information model that it supports, especially when compared to other registry specifications such as ebXML Registry/Repository. UDDI provides support for storing only the basic data structures, such as businesses, users, services, and service technical descriptions. However, storing information about business Web services requires more than just the basic support. For example, potential users of business Web services should be able to publish/query extensive business-oriented information, such as the business process models that a particular business Web service relies upon. This is possible only if the target registry provides a data structure representing the business process model. Thus, an information model is an important feature for any registry. Registry information model, are further discussed in Chapter 11, "Java API for XML Registries."

Also, UDDI is just a registry as opposed to ebXML Registry/Repository, which is, as the name suggests, a registry as well as repository. The basic difference between a registry and repository is that a registry holds just the metadata of the objects submitted, whereas a repository actually stores the submitted objects.

Summary

In this chapter we discussed in detail how to describe and discover Web services. In this regard, we discussed two very important technologies in the Web services space: WSDL and UDDI. We also discussed how to use WSDL and UDDI for describing, publishing, and discovering Web services using various tools in this chapter. In the next chapter, "Creating .NET Interoperability," we will see how to achieve interoperability between Java Web services and .NET Web services.

CHAPTER

6

Creating .NET Interoperability

This chapter discusses the basics of Web services interoperability and illustrates an interoperable Web services scenario using Java and Microsoft .NET-based application environments. As discussed in previous chapters, one of the goals of Web services is to solve the interoperability problem by adopting industry standard protocols and data formats, which enable transparent application-to-application communication and data exchange between applications, systems, networks, and devices. Examples have been given using Web services technologies like XML, SOAP, WSDL, and UDDI and have demonstrated how to create service-oriented applications that communicate and interoperate with one another over a network.

Although Web services promote interoperability, creating and testing interoperability between Web services becomes a real challenge when differences and limitations exist among implementations, especially because of application-specific dependencies and characteristics such as transport protocols, data types, XML processing, and compatibility. In real-world scenarios involving business partner collaborations, the Web service provider needs to take particular care to define standard interoperability mechanisms and communication protocol for the partner applications, enabling them to build their own service clients. This enables partner applications using different systems to easily interact with the Web service provider and conduct seamless transactions with them.

This chapter provides an overview of Web services interoperability and demonstrates a practical interoperability scenario involving a Java-based Web services and Microsoft .NET Framework. It also discusses the key challenges and issues affecting interoperability in Web services. In particular, we will be focusing on the following:

- Understanding interoperability in Web services
- Creating Web services interoperability between J2EE and .NET
- An overview of the Microsoft .NET Framework
- Developing a .NET Client for Java-based Web services
- Common interoperability challenges and issues
- Emergence of the Web Service Interoperability Organization (WS-1) and its goals

Because the scope of this book is limited to developing Java-based Web services, this chapter discusses only the required basics and the process steps for developing .NET-based Web services requestor clients to enable interoperability with Java-based Web services providers. To study more about Microsoft .NET, refer to the Microsoft Web site at http://msdn.microsoft.com/net.

Means of Ensuring Interoperability

In a Web services environment, the Simple Object Access Protocol, or SOAP, is the *de facto* standard communication protocol. (For more on SOAP, see the section titled *Simple Object Access Protocol* in Chapter 4, "Developing Web Services Using SOAP.") This protocol provides conventions for representing data and application interaction models like remote procedural calls (RPCs) and messaging. This facilitates inter-application communication and seamless data sharing among applications residing on a network, regardless of their native language implementation, operating systems, hardware platforms, and the like. In turn, it also enables the development of compatible Web services by leveraging interoperability among business applications running across a wide range of systems and devices.

Interoperability in Web services becomes a real challenge when a service requestor finds problems while invoking a method in the service provider environment or when it does not understand a message sent by the service provider. This is usually caused by prerequisites and factors exposed by the service provider or service requestor environments, and it is mostly caused by the dependencies of the underlying SOAP runtime provider implementation. Thus, it becomes essential for Web services offered by a service provider to ensure that the services are usable by a variety of service requestor clients to the best possible accommodation of both conforming and non-conforming SOAP implementations. Different ways exist to ensure service requestor interoperability with the service providers. The following sections discuss the major ones.

Declaring W3C XML Schemas

Defining W3C XML Schema Definitions (XSD) and target namespaces for all the application data types and having a supporting SOAP implementation for both the service provider and service requestor resolves almost all interoperability issues specific to the data types. This helps to create compliant SOAP proxy-based clients for the service requestors with all the defined data types by providing automatic encoding and mapping for the service provider-dispensed XSD data types.

Exposing WSDL

Most Web services platforms and SOAP implementations provide this as an automatic mechanism by delivering WSDL for all its exposed services. The exposed WSDL defines the service provider information and service specific parameters required by a service requestor for invoking the services, which enables the building service clients to interact with the service provider, thus ensuring interoperability based on the WSDL. The service clients also can be dynamically generated from a service provider's WSDL lookup. In such cases, the SOAP client runtime implementation must provide those dynamic invocation services.

Creating SOAP Proxies

For a Web service, the client SOAP proxies can be created manually or can be generated dynamically based on the WSDL-provided details of the service provider. In the automatic generation of SOAP proxies, sometimes they may throw SOAP faults during service invocation and may require some modifications in the SOAP headers or the encoded RPC calls. In most cases, this problem occurs due to non-conforming WSDL and SOAP implementation in the infrastructure of the service provider or requestor.

Testing Interoperability

To ensure that interoperability between the service provider and requestor exists, the underlying SOAP implementations also can be tested. In that case, the SOAP implementations of the service provider and the requestor must agree and conform to the following SOAP-specific dependencies:

- The defined SOAP transport protocol bindings (like http)
- The supported version of SOAP (like SOAP 1.1 or SOAP 1.2)
- The version of WSDL from the service provider and its ability to support by the service requestor client
- The version of W3C XML Schema supported by the SOAP message, especially the SOAP envelope and its body elements

Most Web services platforms and SOAP implementation providers test their products among SOAP implementations using a standard test suite. This suite can be used to ensure interoperability with other SOAP implementations for conformance testing.

To explore the concepts, let's experiment with an interoperability scenario using a Java-based Web services implementation to interact with a Microsoft-based service client implementation. To try out this scenario, we have chosen to use Apache Axis as the Java-based Web services provider and the Microsoft .NET Framework as the client Web services requestor.

The development and deployment of a Web services requestor is done in a unique part of the Microsoft .NET platform. Like any other Web services platform providers, the Microsoft .NET Framework typically supports industry-standard protocols and technologies, including XML, SOAP, WSDL, and UDDI. The following section examines the basics of the .NET Framework and its core components.

Microsoft .NET Framework: An Overview

Microsoft .NET is part of the Microsoft .NET platform—Microsoft's strategy for developing distributed applications through XML Web services. The Microsoft .NET Framework provides a full-fledged development environment for developing XML Web services in a Microsoft Windows–based environment. It facilitates a runtime infrastructure and APIs for developing Web services applications using a variety of object-oriented programming languages such as C#, Visual Basic, and so forth. The .NET Framework provides the infrastructure for defining the overall .NET platform. Microsoft provides .NET compilers that generate a new code referred to as Microsoft

Intermediate Language (MSIL). MSIL is a CPU-independent code instruction, which is able to run on any system supporting its native machine language. The .NET compilers provided by Microsoft are as follows:

- VB.NET (Visual Basic for .NET)
- C++ .NET (Visual C++ for .NET)
- ASP.NET (Microsoft ASP for .NET)
- C# .NET (New language for .NET)
- JScript (Jscript for .NET)

The Microsoft .NET Framework consists of two core components, which are described in the following sections.

Common Language Runtime (CLR)

The Common Language Runtime, or CLR, provides a managed runtime environment (.NET Engine) for the .NET Framework. CLR enables applications to install and execute code, and it provides services such as memory management, including garbage collection, threading, exception handling, deployment support, application runtime security, versioning, and so on.

CLR provides a set of JIT (just-in-time) compilers, which compile MSIL to produce native code specific to the target system. CLR defines a set of rules as Common Type System (CTS) and Common Language System (CLS) that specifies the .NET-supported languages required to use for developing compilers supporting a .NET platform. This enables the compiler vendors to develop .NET-compliant compilers and to perform cross-language integration. Cross language integration enables .NET-compliant languages to run and interact with one another in a .NET environment.

.NET Framework Class Library

The .NET Framework class library acts as the base class library of the .NET Framework. It provides a collection of classes and a type system as foundation classes for .NET to facilitate CLR. It is included as part of the .NET Framework SDK. The class libraries are reusable object-oriented classes that support .NET programming tasks like establishing database connectivity, data collection, file access, and so on. The class libraries also support the rapid development of software applications such as the following:

- Console applications
- Windows GUI applications

- Windows services
- ASP .NET applications
- .NET XML Web services
- .NET Scripting applications
- .NET Client applications

The .NET class libraries can work with any CLS-compliant language and can use CLR. At the time of this book's writing, the supported languages include Microsoft Visual Studio .NET, C#, and ASP.NET.

Microsoft initially released their .NET Framework to support a Windows-based environment only, although Microsoft will be making .NET available in other platforms. For more information on the Microsoft .NET Framework, go to the Web site: http://msdn.microsoft.com/netframework/. To download the Microsoft .NET Framework SDK, go to the Web site: http://msdn .microsoft.com/net/.

To fully understand the interoperability scenario between Java-based Web services and the Microsoft .NET client environment, you need to understand the process model of developing Microsoft .NET clients.

Developing Microsoft .NET Client for Web Services

Typical to any other Web services requestor environment, the .NET based clients also embrace Web services standards and protocols to communicate with any Web services providers. This enables .NET client applications running on Windows platforms to access Web services exposed from other platforms, as long they are compliant with Web services standards.

To develop Microsoft .NET clients for invoking Web services, the .NET Framework SDK provides toolsets for generating SOAP proxies and for implementing the .NET clients. A .NET Framework SDK installation provides the proxy generators (`wsdl.exe`) for accessing WSDL and the generating proxy classes and compilers (`csc.exe`) for compiling the proxy classes. It also enables clients to be created using any .NET-supported language, such as C# or Visual Basic.

Key Steps in Creating a Web Service Requestor Using the .NET Framework

The key steps involved in creating a Web services client using the .NET Framework are provided in the following sections.

Obtaining the WSDL of a Web Service

The first step in creating a Web services client is to locate the service provider and obtain its WSDL, which describes the exposed Web services defining its message type, operation, port type, binding, and so on.

Generating a Proxy for the Web Service

The .NET Framework SDK provides the WSDL.exe utility, which generates proxy client classes for a Web service exposed using WSDL. To create a .NET-based Web services proxy client class, you may run the following from your Windows command prompt (in a single line):

```
wsdl.exe /l:CS
        /protocol:SOAP
        http://nramesh:8080/axis/AcmeService?WSDL
        /out:AcmeService.cs
```

In the above command, the `/l:CS` option specifies the preferred language as C#, the `/protocol:SOAP` option specifies the protocol as SOAP, the URL refers to the WSDL location of the service provider, and `/out:AcmeService.cs` refers to the name of the proxy class (`AcmeService.cs`). The previous command creates an `AcmeService.cs` as a proxy class source. To create proxy code in Visual Basic, the command would be as follows:

```
wsdl.exe /l:vb
        /protocol:SOAP
        http://nramesh:8080/axis/AcmeService?WSDL
        /out:AcmeService.vb
```

Compiling the SOAP Proxy as a Dynamic Link Library (DLL)

The .NET Framework SDK provides `csc.exe`, a C# compiler, which enables you to build an assembly DLL from the C# proxy source code. To compile the C# proxy client class, you may run the following from your Windows command prompt (in a single line):

```
csc.exe /target:library
       /r:System.Web.Services.dll
       /r:System.Xml.dll
       AcmeService.cs
       /out:AcmeService.dll
```

The command creates a DLL library file to support a proxy class for the client. In the previous command, the option `/target:library` indicates the DLL library, `/r:` specifies the required libraries, `AcmeService.cs` refers to the name of the source file, and the `/out:AcmeService.dll` option indicates the output library file.

Creating a .NET Client Using Proxy Classes

The next step involves creating a .NET client, which uses the instance of the proxy to the Web service to invoke the methods with parameters to get results. You may choose any .NET language (Visual Basic, C#, and so on) to create the client application.

Compiling the Client Application

The next step is to compile the client application including the proxy DLL. To compile the client application, you may run the following from your Windows command prompt (in a single line):

```
csc.exe /target:exe
        /r:AcmeService.dll
        AcmeClient.cs
        /out:AcmeClient.exe
```

This command creates `AcmeClient.exe`, an executable .NET client application file, to invoke the target service provider. In the command, the `/target:exe` option indicates the executable, `/r:` specifies the required libraries, `AcmeClient.cs` refers to the name of the client source file, and the `/out:AcmeClient.exe` option indicates the output executable file.

Executing the Client from a Windows Environment

The final step is running the executable `AcmeClient.exe` file in a Windows environment which will invoke the service provider application and execute the required methods.

This summarizes the steps involved in creating a .NET service client for a Web services provider. Now let's take a look at a real-world case study example of how to create interoperable Web services with a Java-based Web services provider and .NET-based service requestor.

Case Study: Building a .NET Client for Axis Web Services

In this section, we build on the case study example reusing the components used in the previous chapter (Chapter 4, "Developing Web Services Using

SOAP," featuring *ACME Web Services Company*. It discusses getting the Acme products catalog service exposed by the ACME Web services provider:

For the service provider, we will be creating Apache Axis-based Web service components using Java for the service provider and for the client service requestor we will implement .NET-based client components using the .NET Framework. To cater the Acme product catalog service scenario, we will be using an RPC-based communication model between the Apache Axis-based Web services and the .NET-based service requestor. We will be reusing the ACME business specific components as discussed in Chapter 3, "Building the Web Services Architecture." The ACME components to handle this scenario are as follows:

- `AcmeDAO`. A DAO class that provides access to the data source and abstracts the underlying data access implementation for the product catalog
- `AcmeXMLHelper`. A class that gathers the data and constructs an XML document as a string for use by the business clients

To find out the programming steps and the source code implementation of the previous classes, refer to Chapter 3, particularly the section titled *Developing Web Services Using J2EE: An Example.*

To try out the example, you may download the chapter-specific code and documentation made available at www.wiley.com/compbooks/nagappan. Source code and README text for installing and running this example are available as part of Chapter-6.zip.

Building the Infrastructure

To build and deploy ACME Web services in the Axis environment, we chose to use the following infrastructure solutions:

ON THE SERVICE PROVIDER SIDE

- ACME Web services provider will use Apache Tomcat as its servlet engine/Web server, including Axis-based SOAP runtime environment
- Will use PointBase as its database for querying product catalog information

ON THE SERVICE REQUESTOR SIDE

- Service requestor will use the .NET Framework as its SOAP client environment to invoke the services of the ACME Web services provider

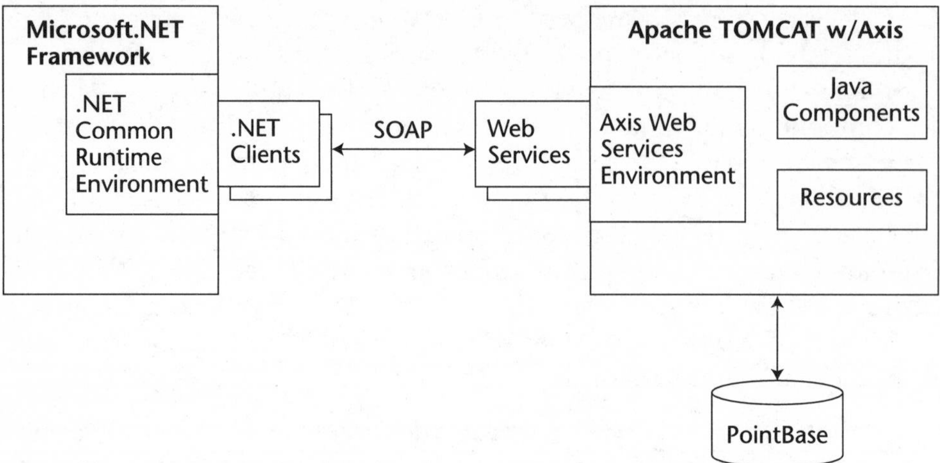

Figure 6.1 Apache Axis and Microsoft .NET-based Web services infrastructure.

Figure 6.1 represents the Web services infrastructure involving Apache Axis and the Microsoft .NET Framework.

To understand the problem and flow of events, the sequence diagram in Figure 6.2 illustrates the various sequences of actions performed by a .NET client invoking the ACME Web services deployed in the Axis-based Web services environment.

Based on the previous sequence of events, we have chosen to use an `AcmeXMLHelper` class to act as a proxy by encapsulating the business functionalities, which include database interaction, XML construction, XML parsing operations, and so forth. More specifically, the `AcmeXMLHelper` class will handle all of the XML construction tasks and `AcmeDAO` will handle the database interaction.

Figure 6.3 depicts the class diagram of the server-side components to support the ACME Web service provider using the Apache Axis infrastructure.

To try out this example, download the chapter-specific source code and documentation available at www.wiley.com/compbooks/nagappan. The source code and README text for installing and running this example are available as part of chapter-6.zip.

Now, let's take a look at how to set up the development environment and implementation of those service components.

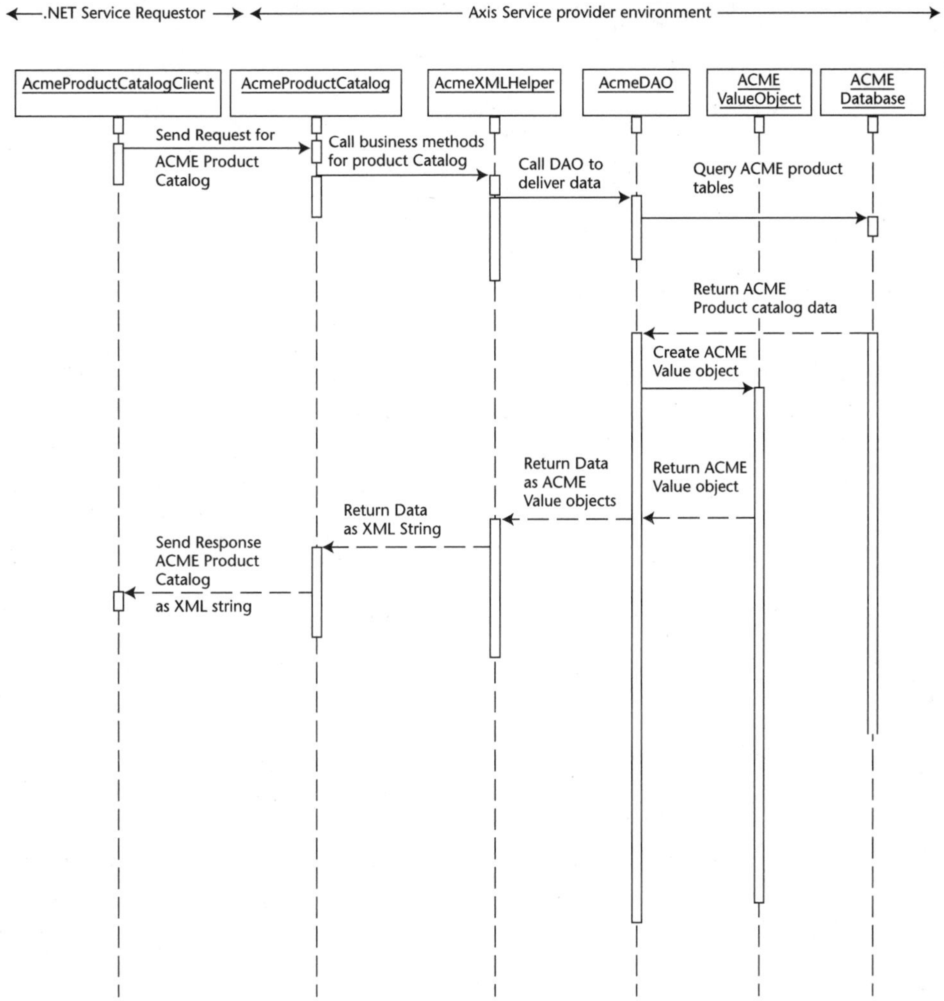

.NET Service Requestor
Axis Service provider environment
AcmeProductCatalogClient
AcmeProductCatalog
AcmeXMLHelper
AcmeDAO
ACME ValueObject
ACME Database
Send Request for ACME Product Catalog
Call business methods for product Catalog
Call DAO to deliver data
Query ACME product tables
Return ACME Product catalog data
Create ACME Value object
Return Data as ACME Value objects
Return ACME Value object
Return Data as XML String
Send Response ACME Product Catalog as XML string

Figure 6.2 Sequence diagram representing the scenario.

AcmeDAO
ACMEProductCatalog
uses
AcmeXMLHelper
uses
AcmeDAOImpl
encapsulates
AcmeDataSource
Product

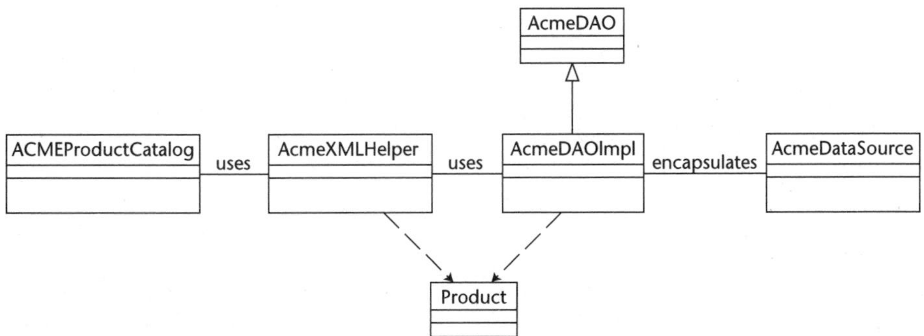

Figure 6.3 Class diagram illustrating the service provider components.

Setting Up the Environment

To set up the development environment for creating ACME Web services, perform the following tasks:

1. Create the service provider environment.
   a. Refer to Chapter 4, "Developing Web Services Using SOAP," in the section titled *Setting Up the Axis Web Services Environment*, and follow Steps 1 to 11.
2. Create the service requestor environment.
   a. Download the Microsoft .NET Framework SDK (current release) from http://msdn.microsoft.com/net and install the application to your local directory. The installation process will update your system path, and all of the .NET Framework utilities will be ready to use.
   b. Create a working directory (for example, `d:\msdotnetclient`) to create and test the .NET client applications.

These steps conclude the configuration requirements for the service provider and requestor environment. Now, let's explore the implementation of the ACME business scenarios by using them.

Creating the Service Provider (Axis Environment)

As was mentioned earlier, to implement the service provider environment, we will be reusing the components that we built in Chapter 3, "Building the Web Services Architecture," and deploying them in Axis environment. The components are as follows:

`AcmeDAO`. A DAO class that provides access to the data source and abstracts the underlying data access implementation for the product catalog.

`AcmeXMLHelper`. A class that gathers the data and constructs an XML document as a string for use by the business clients.

To find out the programming steps and the source code implementation of the previous classes (`AcmeDAO` and `AcmeXMLHelper`), refer to Chapter 3, "Building the Web Services Architecture," particularly the section titled *Developing Web Services Using J2EE: An Example.*

As we discussed in Chapter 4, Axis enables Web services to be deployed using Java classes with .jws extensions. It is quite typical to the Java Server Pages (JSP) deployed in a servlet engine. By placing Java classes with .jws extensions in the Web applications directory (that is, TOMCAT_HOME /webapps/axis/) during runtime, the runtime of Axis automatically compiles and deploys the classes with all of the methods as services.

We will be creating the Acme product catalog service as ACMEProduct Catalog.jws, which will be acting as the service provider in the Axis environment.

The ACMEProductCatalog.jws class uses AcmeXMLHelper and AcmeDAO as helper classes for XML processing and database interaction. The ACMEProductCatalog.jws then will be deployed in the Axis environment as an Axis JWS service.

Now, let's take a closer look at the implementation and walk through the code of ACMEProductCatalog.jws .

Implementing the Service Provider (ACMEProductCatalog.jws)

The source code implementation for ACMEProductCatalog.jws is shown in Listing 6.1.

```
// AcmeProductCatalog.jws

import jws.ch4.xmlhelper.AcmeXMLHelper;

public class AcmeProductCatalog {

String pc;

// Helper function: To obtain Product Catalog it calls
// AcmeXMLhelper method

  public String getProductCatalog() throws Exception {


      AcmeXMLHelper axh;


      try {
          // Instantiate the AcmeXMLhelper
          axh = new AcmeXMLHelper();

          // Call method
          pc = axh.getProductCatalogXMLasString();
      } catch (Exception e) {
          e.printStackTrace();
      }
     // Return the response string
     return pc;
  }
}
```

Listing 6.1 ACMEProductCatalog.jws.

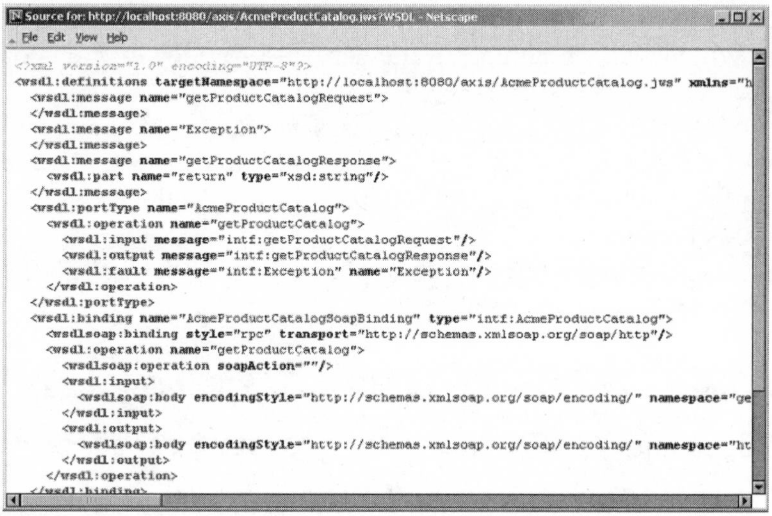

```
Source for: http://localhost:8080/axis/AcmeProductCatalog.jws?WSDL - Netscape
File Edit View Help
<?xml version="1.0" encoding="UTF-8"?>
<wsdl:definitions targetNamespace="http://localhost:8080/axis/AcmeProductCatalog.jws" xmlns="h
  <wsdl:message name="getProductCatalogRequest">
  </wsdl:message>
  <wsdl:message name="Exception">
  </wsdl:message>
  <wsdl:message name="getProductCatalogResponse">
    <wsdl:part name="return" type="xsd:string"/>
  </wsdl:message>
  <wsdl:portType name="AcmeProductCatalog">
    <wsdl:operation name="getProductCatalog">
      <wsdl:input message="intf:getProductCatalogRequest"/>
      <wsdl:output message="intf:getProductCatalogResponse"/>
      <wsdl:fault message="intf:Exception" name="Exception"/>
    </wsdl:operation>
  </wsdl:portType>
  <wsdl:binding name="AcmeProductCatalogSoapBinding" type="intf:AcmeProductCatalog">
    <wsdlsoap:binding style="rpc" transport="http://schemas.xmlsoap.org/soap/http"/>
    <wsdl:operation name="getProductCatalog">
      <wsdlsoap:operation soapAction=""/>
      <wsdl:input>
        <wsdlsoap:body encodingStyle="http://schemas.xmlsoap.org/soap/encoding/" namespace="ge
      </wsdl:input>
      <wsdl:output>
        <wsdlsoap:body encodingStyle="http://schemas.xmlsoap.org/soap/encoding/" namespace="ht
      </wsdl:output>
    </wsdl:operation>
  </wsdl:binding>
```

Figure 6.4 WSDL output for `ACMEProductCatalog.jws`.

To deploy `AcmeProductCatalog.jws`, just copy the source file in your Apache Axis Web applications directory (that is, TOMCAT_HOME /webapps/axis/). If your Tomcat server is not running, then start your Tomcat server. The Apache Axis environment will automatically deploy them as a service and emit the ACME product catalog service details as WSDL. To access the WSDL, use your Web browser and then try out the following URL:

```
http://localhost:8080/axis/AcmeProductCatalog.jws?WSDL
```

If everything works successfully, you will get the output shown in Figure 6.4.

This summarizes the service provider environment using Apache Axis.

Creating the Service Requestor (.NET Environment)

The following steps are involved using the .NET Framework to access the ACME product catalog service requestor.

Obtaining the WSDL of Acme Product Catalog Service

The first step is to locate the ACME service provider and obtain its WSDL. It will be available to the service requestor as an URL. In our case, it will be as follows:

```
http://localhost:8080/axis/AcmeProductCatalog.jws?WSDL
```

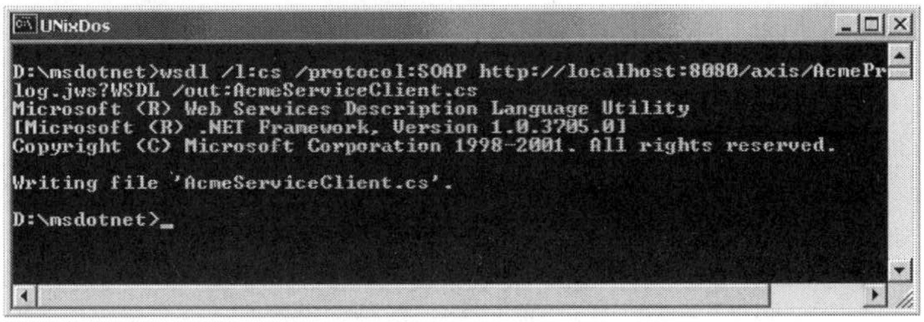

Figure 6.5 Creation of the Proxy C# class.

Generating a Proxy for the Web Service

The next step is to use the WSDL.exe utility to generate proxy client classes from the ACME service provider WSDL. To create the proxy client classes, run the following command from your Windows command prompt (in a single line):

```
wsdl.exe /l:CS
    /protocol:SOAP
    http://localhost:8080/axis/AcmeProductCatalog?WSDL
        /out:AcmeServiceClient.cs
```

This command creates `AcmeServiceClient.cs` as a proxy class for the ACME product catalog service, as shown in Figure 6.5.

Listing 6.2 shows the generated C# source code.

```
//
// This source code was auto-generated by wsdl, Version=1.0.3705.0.
//
using System.Diagnostics;
using System.Xml.Serialization;
using System;
using System.Web.Services.Protocols;
using System.ComponentModel;
using System.Web.Services;


[System.Diagnostics.DebuggerStepThroughAttribute()]
[System.ComponentModel.DesignerCategoryAttribute("code")]
[System.Web.Services.WebServiceBindingAttribute(
                         Name="AcmeProductCatalogSoapBinding",
```

Listing 6.2 Generated C# source code. *(continues)*

```
Namespace="http://localhost:8080/axis/AcmeProductCatalog.jws")]
public class AcmeProductCatalogService :
System.Web.Services.Protocols.SoapHttpClientProtocol {

    public AcmeProductCatalogService() {
    this.Url =
            "http://localhost:8080/axis/AcmeProductCatalog.jws";
    }


    [System.Web.Services.Protocols.SoapRpcMethodAttribute
                ("", RequestNamespace="getProductCatalog",
            ResponseNamespace=
        "http://localhost:8080/axis/AcmeProductCatalog.jws")]
    [return:
       System.Xml.Serialization.SoapElementAttribute("return")]
    public string getProductCatalog() {
        object[] results = this.Invoke
                ("getProductCatalog", new object[0]);
        return ((string)(results[0]));
    }

    public System.IAsyncResult BegingetProductCatalog
          (System.AsyncCallback callback, object asyncState) {
        return this.BeginInvoke("getProductCatalog",
                        new object[0], callback, asyncState);
    }

    public string EndgetProductCatalog
                       (System.IAsyncResult asyncResult) {
        object[] results = this.EndInvoke(asyncResult);
        return ((string)(results[0]));
    }
}
```

Listing 6.2 Generated C# source code. *(continued)*

Compiling the SOAP Proxy as a DLL

The next step is to use the .NET C# compiler `csc.exe` to build an assembly DLL from the generated proxy source code. To compile the `AcmeServiceClient.cs`, run the following command from your Windows command prompt (in a single line):

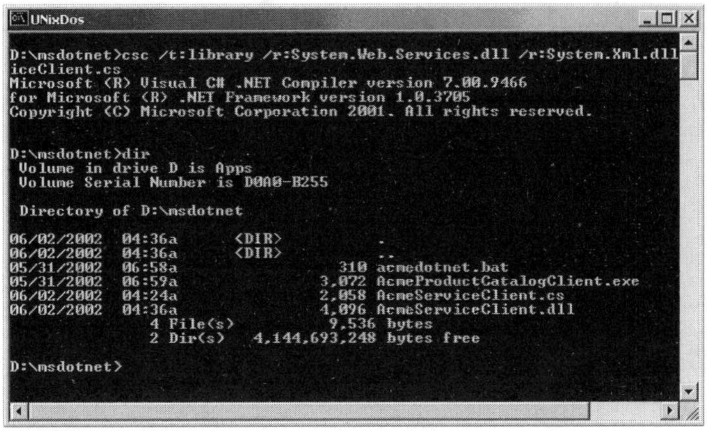

```
UNixDos

D:\msdotnet>csc /t:library /r:System.Web.Services.dll /r:System.Xml.dll
iceClient.cs
Microsoft (R) Visual C# .NET Compiler version 7.00.9466
for Microsoft (R) .NET Framework version 1.0.3705
Copyright (C) Microsoft Corporation 2001. All rights reserved.


D:\msdotnet>dir
 Volume in drive D is Apps
 Volume Serial Number is D0A0-B255

 Directory of D:\msdotnet

06/02/2002  04:36a      <DIR>          .
06/02/2002  04:36a      <DIR>          ..
05/31/2002  06:58a                 310 acmedotnet.bat
05/31/2002  06:59a               3,072 AcmeProductCatalogClient.exe
06/02/2002  04:24a               2,058 AcmeServiceClient.cs
06/02/2002  04:36a               4,096 AcmeServiceClient.dll
               4 File(s)          9,536 bytes
               2 Dir(s)   4,144,693,248 bytes free

D:\msdotnet>
```

Figure 6.6 Creation of a DLL library for the proxy class.

```
csc.exe /t:library
        /r:System.Web.Services.dll
        /r:System.Xml.dll
        AcmeServiceClient.cs
```

This command creates a DLL library file which acts as a proxy stub class for the client, as shown in Figure 6.6.

Creating a .NET Client Application

Next, create a .NET client application using the instances of proxy classes and its methods. (The available proxy instances and the service methods can be read from the proxy source code.) The .NET client application source code `AcmeServiceClientApp.cs` using C# code is shown in Listing 6.3.

```
using System;
namespace AcmeServiceClient {
  public class AcmeServiceClientApp {

    public AcmeServiceClientApp() {
    }
```

Listing 6.3 .NET client application source code, `AcmeServiceClientApp.cs`. *(continues)*

```
    public static void Main () {

      // Create a proxy instance
      AcmeProductCatalogService server
                = new AcmeProductCatalogService();

      // Invoke getProductCatalog method and
      // get the XML as String
      string catalog = server.getProductCatalog ();

      // Print the Acme Product Catalog
      Console.WriteLine ("The ACME Product Catalog :"+catalog);
    }
  }
}
```

Listing 6.3 .NET client application source code, `AcmeServiceClientApp.cs`. *(continued)*

Compiling the Client Application

The next step is to create an executable client application and to compile the client source code `AcmeServiceClientApp.cs`. To compile the client application, run the following command from your Windows command prompt (in a single line):

```
csc.exe /r:AcmeServiceClient.dll
       /t:exe
       /out:AcmeServiceClientApp.exe
       AcmeServiceClientApp.cs
```

This command creates `AcmeServiceClientApp.exe`, which is an executable .NET client application file that invokes the ACME service provider, as shown in Figure 6.7.

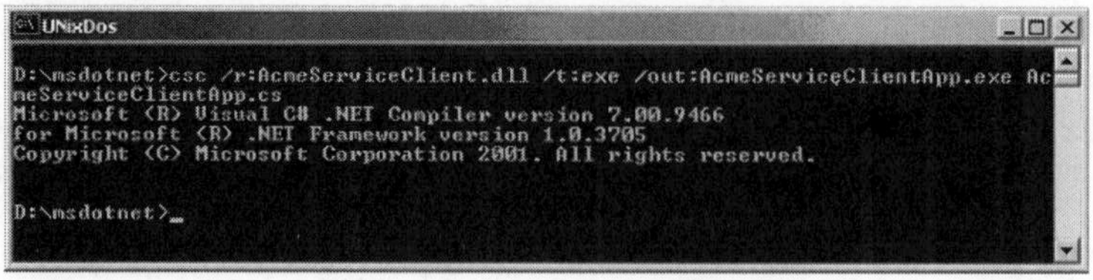

Figure 6.7 The compilation of a client application.

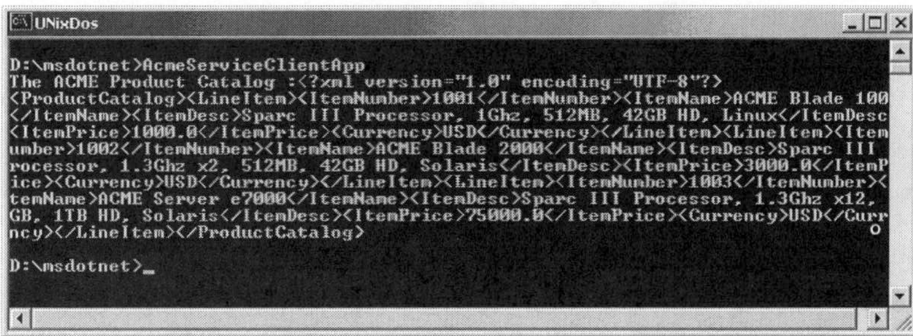

Figure 6.8 Invocation of service from an ACME service provider.

Execute and Test the .NET Client from a Windows Environment

Finally, to invoke the ACME product catalog from the ACME service provider (Axis environment), run the .NET client application `AcmeServiceClientApp.exe` from the command prompt.

If everything works successfully, you will get the output shown in Figure 6.8.

This summarizes our Web service interoperability example scenario involving Apache Axis-based Java Web services and the Microsoft .NET Framework.

Challenges in Creating Web Services Interoperability

As of today, more than 50 Web services platforms, including SOAP implementations, are available to provide Web services support for a variety of languages, APIs, applications, and systems. But not all of the services exposed from these SOAP implementations are guaranteed to interoperate and run across disparate applications and systems. Most interoperability problems occur in RPC-based Web services because of the type mapping issues between the service provider and requestor, which are due to the lack of type mapping support in SOAP processing. In messaging-based Web services, this is not the case, as the SOAP body is represented with an XML document.

The challenges that affect interoperability in Web services will be examined in the following sections.

Common SOAP/HTTP Transport Issues

At the core of Web services, the transport protocols establish the communication and enable the services to send and receive messages. In case of using HTTP protocol, if the service provider requires a SOAPAction with a null value, most HTTP clients may not be able to provide a SOAPAction with a null value. The possible solutions are to fix the service client APIs and to ensure that certain service provider implementations require SOAPAction with a null value. To solve these problems, test the client to see if they can handle those scenarios.

XML Schema- and XML-Related Issues

XML schema validation handling causes a lot of interoperability issues among SOAP implementations. So defining data types using XMS schema definitions must occur in both the service client and provider implementations.

Some SOAP implementations specify the encoding of data as UTF-8 and UTF-16 in the Content-Type header as

```
Content-Type: text/xml; charset=utf-8
```

And some implementations do not specify the charset in the `Content-Type` header, which causes some SOAP implementations to be unable to process messages. To correct this problem, ensure that the SOAP implementation and its encoding standards are compliant with the W3C specifications.

SOAP/XML Message Discontinuities

Message discontinuities cause a major problem between a SOAP implementation in fulfilling the request and response between the service client and service provider. To overcome these issues, ensure that the application is aware of the message discontinuities and throw SOAPFaults in the case of missing elements in the SOAPBody of the request message.

Version and Compatibility

The version of the supported XMLSchema, and the SOAP and WSDL specifications, and its compatibility between SOAP implementations affect interoperability. To ensure that these issues are handled, the Web services platform providers and its SOAP implementations must be tested for the compatible versions of XML Schema definitions and the SOAP and WSDL specifications.

The emergence of the WS-I initiative, which is examined in the next section, will address these issues as part of its goals.

The WS-I Initiative and Its Goals

The Web Services Interoperability Organization, or WS-I, started as an industry initiative by IBM and Microsoft, along with a handful of Web services platform and application vendors. The ultimate goal of WS-I is to promote interoperability in Web services implementations across platforms, applications, programming languages, and devices. At the time of this book's writing, WS-I is in the very early stage of defining its goals and planning its deliverables.

As part of its deliverable plan, WS-I is planning to introduce the concept of WS-I profiles to address the interoperability issues on compatibility problems due to specification versions, dependencies, and requirements. The concept of the WS-I profiles focuses on the Web services applications interoperability to conform their compliance on specifications and its support to profiles.

For example, the basic WS-I profile addresses the specifications listed in Table 6.1.

Table 6.1 WS-I Basic Profile

SPECIFICATIONS	VERSION
XML Schema	XML Schema 1.0
SOAP	SOAP 1.1
WSDL	WSDL 1.1
UDDI	UDDI 1.0

At the time of this book's writing, WS-I is working on developing WS-I profiles on the evolving Web services specifications and its associated W3C standards. Also note that WS-I is still premature, as it still lacks participation from some of the leading vendors on Web services platforms and systems.

Public Interoperability Testing Efforts

In addition to WS-I, an open interoperability testing effort is going on through "WHITE MESA" a public organization that defines the testing strategy for SOAP/WSDL tools interoperability and then maintains Web services interoperability test information for leading vendor implementations. White Mesa demonstrates interoperability by running tests among SOAP/Web services implementations particularly for WSDL, SOAP Data types, and SOAP implementation for both RPC and document-style Web services. The White Mesa tests most popular vendor implementations and its tools for WSDL interoperability scenarios, especially the following:

- Generating WSDL documents for exposing services
- Consuming WSDL documents for service requestor and to generate proxies

To find out White Mesa interoperability results for Sun JWSDP 1.0, refer to http://soapinterop.java.sun.com/soapbuilders/round3.html. For more information on White Mesa interoperability tests, refer to www.whitemesa.net.

Summary

This chapter has discussed the core concepts of Web services interoperability and the key challenges in developing interoperable Web services. An interoperable Web services application scenario also was demonstrated between a Java-based Web services and a Microsoft .NET Framework based service requestor.

In general, this chapter has focused on the fundamentals of Web services interoperability, the development of interoperable Web services between Java and .NET, and the challenges in Web service interoperability.

The following chapter introduces the Java Web Services Developer Pack (JWSDP 1.0).

PART

Three

Exploring Java Web Services Developer Pack

CHAPTER

7

Introduction to the Java Web Services Developer Pack (JWSDP)

As discussed in earlier chapters, XML is a cross platform neutral-data format and Java is a cross platform programming language. These technologies provide a perfect solution for developing network independent and extensible applications; they enable interoperability, portability, and flexibility. They also provide a standard solution for integrating heterogeneous applications and systems ranging from cell phones to large-scale enterprise applications. An application can be written in Java and ported to various supported platforms (hence, the "Write Once, Run Anywhere" mantra trademarked for Java by Sun Microsystems). In addition, XML also has the capability to talk to Java as well as non-Java applications running on diverse platforms.

With the overwhelming success of XML and Java in enterprise applications, the use of XML has required the development of parsers and other supporting technologies to process the XML data. Many XML-based technologies have been developed over the last few years using vendor-specific APIs that require specific vendor implementation knowledge. The introduction of the Java XML APIs provides standard interfaces that are independent of any vendor-specific implementation. For example, in using a JAXP-compliant parser, this standardization provides better support for maintaining application code and enables the application provider to exchange the underlying implementation of the parser. This change does not require any modification in the application code because the method calls are the same due to compliance of the two parsers.

This chapter presents an introduction to Sun Microsystems' Java XML APIs and runtime environments, which together make up a software toolkit for developing Web services. This API toolkit, which is commonly referred to as the *Java Web Services Developer Pack (JWSDP),* provides Java developers with a one-stop API solution for the development of Java Web service applications.

This chapter provides an introduction to JWSDP focusing on the following topics:

- The core components of JWSDP
- Java XML APIs for Web services and their features
- The infrastructure for running Web service applications using JWSDP
  - Java XML Pack
  - Apache Tomcat container
  - JWSDP Registry Server
  - JavaServer Pages Standard Tag libraries
  - ANT Build tool

Java Web Services Developer Pack

A Web service cannot be executed as a standalone program. It is usually a component, which resides in a container that manages the life cycle of these components by providing low-level services, such as security, transaction support, session management, and so forth. JWSDP includes a Web container for hosting applications or services created using servlets and Java Server Pages (JSPs).

Java Web Services Developer Pack (JWSDP) brings together a set of Java APIs for XML-based Java applications by supporting key XML standards such as SAX, DOM, XSLT, SOAP, WSDL, UDDI, and ebXML. These APIs and their reference implementations are bundled together with a set of runtime tools to form a JWSDP to provide a build, deploy, and test environment for Web services applications and components. The pack includes the following toolset:

- Java XML Pack
- JavaServer Pages Standard Tag Libraries

- Apache Tomcat container
- Java WSDP Registry Server
- ANT Build Tool

Java XML Pack

Java XML Pack is an architectural solution toolkit that is intended to ease software development by providing a set of high-level APIs and reference implementations that abstract the complexities behind XML processing. These APIs also enrich the development of XML applications with a modular and simple set of interfaces leading to superior code quality and increased developer productivity. With the rapid emergence of new technologies such as Web services, pervasive computing, and enterprise computing, these APIs become a standard supporting an API solution to cater Java- and XML-enabled applications.

Java XML Pack is very beneficial for Web services development because it leverages most of the aspects of XML-related processing in a typical Web service environment. At the time of this book's publication, the Sun Web services pack contains the following Java XML APIs:

- Java API for XML Processing (JAXP)
- Java API for XML Registries (JAXR)
- Java API for XML-based RPC (JAX-RPC)
- SOAP with Attachments API for Java (SAAJ)
- Java API for XML Messaging (JAXM)

With the overwhelming success of Java and J2EE in enterprise applications, it is likely that the API solutions provided by the Java XML pack and Web services pack will soon emerge as an industry-wide solution for providing and building robust XML-based Web services.

Java APIs for XML

The Java APIs for XML provide a set of Java classes and interfaces for working with the processing of XML data. They are categorized as follows:

Document-oriented APIs. These APIs enable the processing of XML documents that contain XML data (for example, parsing a purchase order defined in XML). Document-oriented APIs are generally used for interpreting data stored in an XML format. The Java XML Pack includes the following document-oriented APIs:

- Java API for XML Processing (JAXP)
- Java Architecture for XML Binding (JAXB)

Procedure-oriented APIs. These APIs facilitate the sending and receiving of XML documents using network services (for example, sending a SOAP message in a B2B communication). Procedure-oriented APIs are generally used for interfacing between Web services applications. The Java XML Pack includes the following APIs:

- Java API for XML Processing (JAXP)
- Java API for XML Messaging (JAXM)
- SOAP with Attachments API for Java (SAAJ)
- Java API for XML Registries (JAXR)
- Java API for XML-based RPC (JAX-RPC)

The following sections briefly describe each of these APIs.

Java API for XML Parsing (JAXP)

Java API for XML Parsing (JAXP) is used for the parsing and transformation of XML documents. *Parsing* is the process of interpreting the content of a structured XML document. *XML transformation* consists of applying a template to the XML data in order to produce a document in a desired format. JAXP version 1.1 supports the following three different standards for XML processing:

FOR PARSING:

- Simple API for XML (SAX)
- Document Object Model (DOM) API

FOR TRANSFORMATIONS:

- Extensible Stylesheet Language Transformation (XSLT) API

JAXP also provides a pluggable interface independent of any particular XML processor implementation. JAXP is an abstraction that enables the exchange of any compliant XML parser. The following sections describe the processing standards supported by these APIs in more detail.

Simple API for XML (SAX)

The Simple Access for XML (SAX) API is a public domain based on an event-driven processing model where data elements are interpreted on a sequential basis and events are triggered based on selected constructs. SAX is similar to the AWT 1.1 Event Delegation Model, where UI components generate events based on user input, and event listeners perform actions when these events are triggered. The biggest advantage of SAX is that it does not load any XML documents into memory, therefore it is considered to be very fast and lightweight. SAX supports validation by using Document Type Definition (DTD) but does not enforce the use of it. By having validation, a document is checked for conformance against the DTD. It uses a sequential read-only approach and does not support random access to XML elements. Figure 7.1 shows an XML document being processed by a JAXP-compliant parser with some events triggered by the elements encountered in the document. These events are the callback methods implemented in the application handler class.

SAX was developed by an XML working group called XML-DEV, which is managed by OASIS. The list is used for implementation and development discussions using SAX. For more information about XML-DEV mailing list initiatives, refer to www.xml.org/xml/xmldev.shtml.

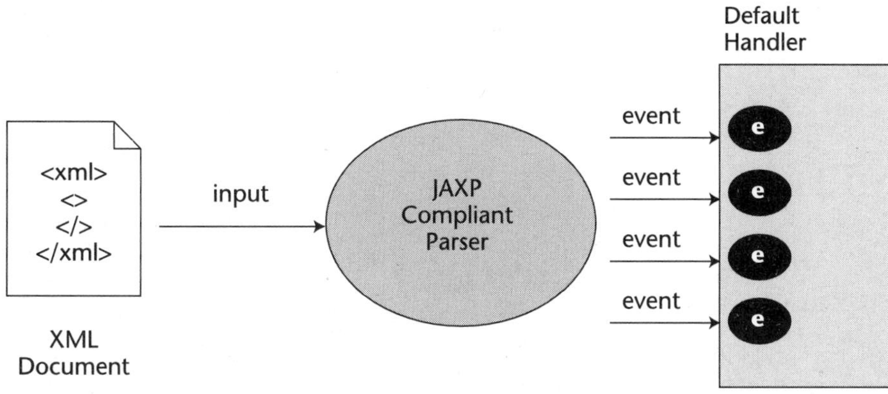

Figure 7.1 JAXP using the SAX processing model.

Document Object Model (DOM)

The Document Object Model (DOM) API was defined and is maintained by the W3C working group (www.w3org/TR/WD-DOM/): "As per W3C definition the Document Object Model is a platform- and language-neutral interface that will allow programs and scripts to dynamically access and update the content, structure, and style of documents."

The DOM processing model consists of reading the entire XML document into memory and building a tree representation of the structured data, as shown in Figure 7.2. This model can require a substantial amount of memory when the XML document is large. By having the data in memory, DOM introduces the capability of manipulating the XML data by inserting, editing, or deleting tree elements. Unlike the SAX API, DOM supports random access to any node in the tree. It also supports validation by using DTD, but it does not enforce the use of validation.

Extensible Stylesheet Language Transformation (XSLT)

Extensible Stylesheet Language Transformation (XSLT) is an XML processing standard used with eXtensible Stylesheet Language (XSL) for XML-based document transformation. XSLT is a process by which XSL templates are applied to XML documents to create new documents in desired formats (XML, HTML, PDF, WML, and so forth). XSL provides the syntax and semantics for specifying formatting and XSLT is the processor that performs the formatting task.

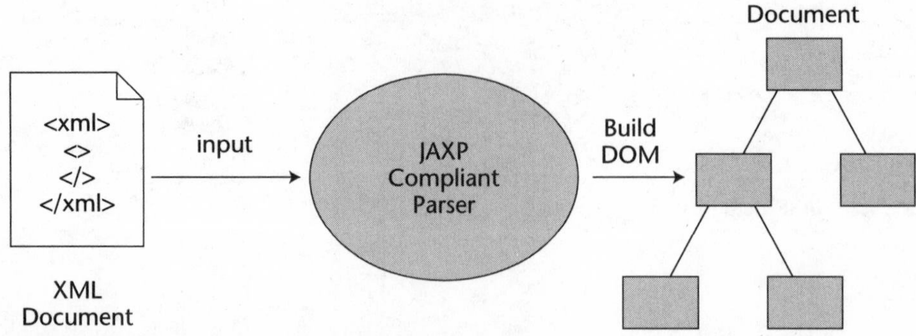

Figure 7.2 JAXP using the DOM processing model.

XSLT is often used for the purpose of generating various output formats for applications that enable access to heterogeneous client types (such as Web browsers, cell phones, Java applications, and so on). XSLT also is used to format one XML representation to another; this is typical in a B2B type environment. Figure 7.3 illustrates a scenario where an application hosts a component that is able to generate various types of output based on the requesting client's type.

JAXP Pluggable Interface

JAXP provides a pluggable layer that enables application developers to change parser implementations without affecting the application logic. With JAXP, one JAXP-compliant parser can be exchanged for another seamlessly, without much effort. JAXP provides a set of standard interfaces that encapsulate the details behind the parser interactions. These interfaces act as abstractions that prevent the developer from working with XML directly. The abstractions are implementations of the SAX and DOM parsing standards and the XSLT transformation standard.

Figure 7.4 shows the high-level blocks that compose the JAXP model. In order for a parser and transformer to be compliant, they must follow the JAXP specification. The freedom to choose any parser is very important: This flexibility enables application developers to choose a parser provider that best suits the requirements of the service.

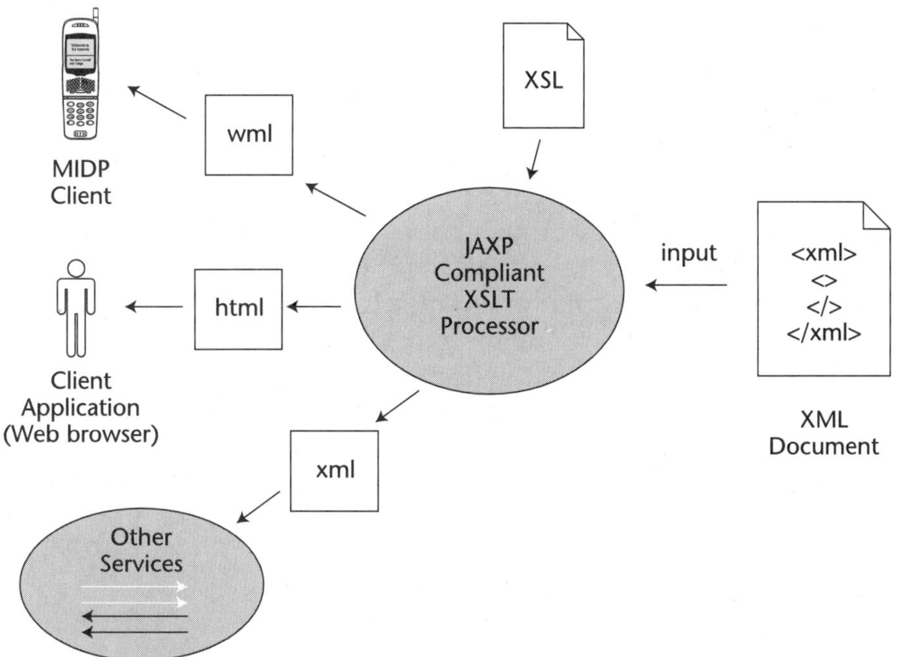

Figure 7.3 Using JAXP for XSLT transformation.

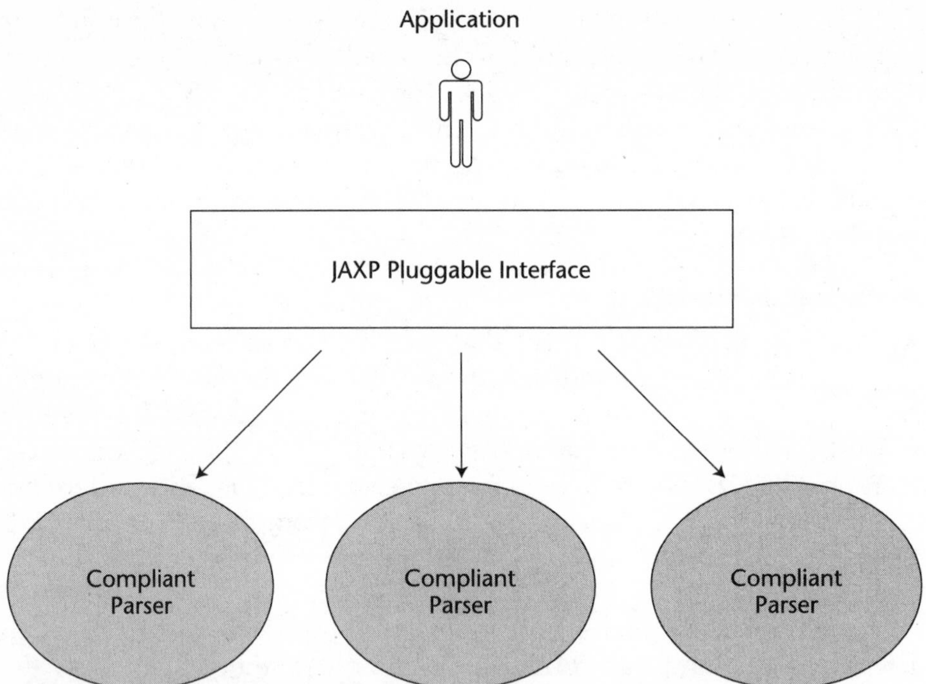

Figure 7.4 JAXP pluggable interface.

For more information on JAXP, refer to Chapter 8 "XML Processing and Data Binding with Java APIs."

Java Architecture for XML Binding (JAXB)

The XML Binding technology provides application developers with a way to generate Java objects based on XML definitions. The Java Architecture for XML Binding (JAXB), formerly known as JCP project Adelard, is a high-level API that abstracts the binding semantics via classes and interfaces. JAXB takes the developer away from the manual steps of parsing and processing the data. It provides the necessary utilities that enable developers to work with the XML data in the form of Java objects. In other words, it provides the means for the developers to generate Java object models based on XML definitions and vice versa.

JAXP REFERENCE IMPLEMENTATIONS

The current release of JAXP (1.1) is packaged with reference implementations of the API specifications. The parser implementation is based on the Crimson codebase, which originates from Sun Project X parser. JAXP is a Sun Microsystems initiative to make the API available to the public for redistribution in commercial products. This parser codebase is currently maintained by the Apache Software Foundation and has moved to a different codebase called Xerces 2. Industry leaders such as Sun, IBM, BEA, and iPlanet have accepted JAXP as a standard API. The XSLT processor is called Xalan and is an implementation of the W3C Recommendation for XSL Transformations (XSLT).

At the time of this publication, JAXP v1.1 conforms to the following standards:

- **XML 1.0 Second Edition**
- **XML Namespaces 1.0**
- **SAX 2.0**
- **SAX2 Extensions version 1.0**
- **DOM Level 2 Core Recommendation**
- **XSLT 1.0**

For more information on the current release of JAXP, refer to the following site:

http://java.sun.com/xml/jaxp/

JAXB architecture provides services such as a schema compiler, binding framework, and a binding language or a runtime API (interfaces and classes) that provide the following services:

Marshalling. The process of converting a Java object tree into an XML document.

Unmarshalling. The process of converting an XML document into a Java object tree.

Validation. The process where an XML document is checked for conformance with a DTD schema.

When building a Java object tree, each object in the tree refers to an element in the XML document. The object in the tree is an instance of a class that was generated by the compiler, based on the DTD and a binding schema. Figure 7.5 shows the life cycle of a Java binding process.

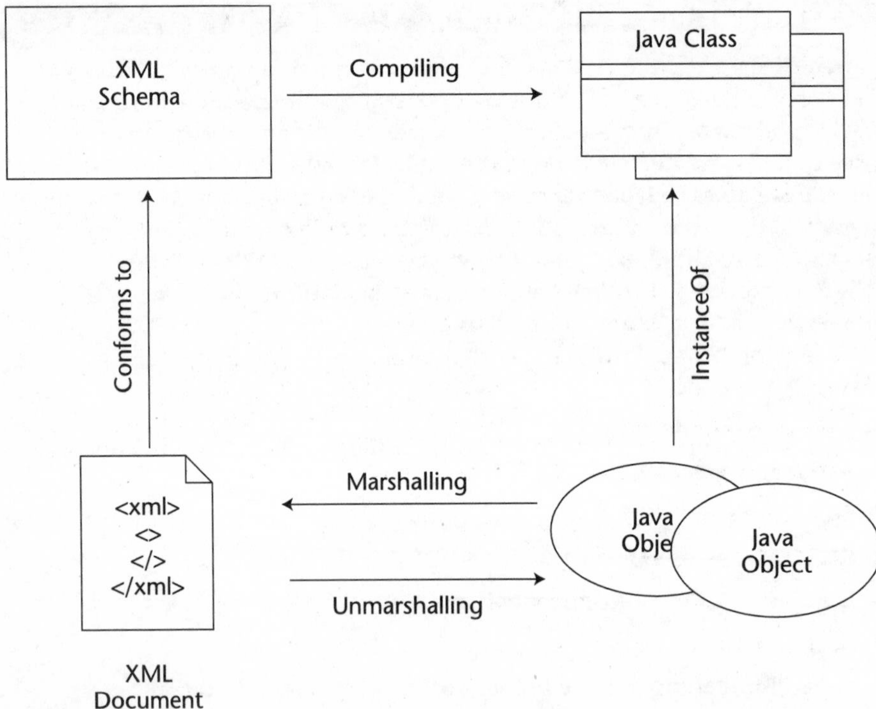

Figure 7.5 Java binding process.

JAXB provides a schema compiler, which follows an XML schema and defines what elements to extract from an XML document. JAXB then compiles the XML schema by generating a Java class. An instance of a Java object can be instantiated manually from the Java class or by unmarshalling the XML document.

In the current release of JWSDP, JAXB is not included due to functionality limitations with validation, W3C schema, and XML namespaces. For more information on JAXB, refer to Chapter 8.

Java API for XML Messaging (JAXM)

The Java API for XML Messaging (JAXM) is designed to be used as a lightweight XML messaging API for application-to-application (A2A) integration and B2B communication, especially Web services environments. It enables the transfer of business-level documents between two parties involved in a transaction. It also enables loosely coupled services to interact with each other using SOAP messaging protocol (specifically, SOAP 1.1 and SOAP with attachments). Through its API, JAXM enables the development of SOAP-compliant messages by making Java API calls. The underlying message delivery infrastructure (message provider) is independent of the JAXM. It is therefore possible to have asynchronous providers that provide services such as reliable message delivery or synchronous providers using a simple request/response model. The specification requires that JAXM supports the following five messaging interaction patterns: Asynchronous inquiry, Asynchronous update with acknowledgement, Synchronous Update, Synchronous Inquiry, and Fire and Forget. For details on these interaction patterns, refer to Chapter 9, "XML Messaging Using JAXM and SAAJ."

The JAXM specification does not enforce any particular messaging protocol standard; it currently focuses around SOAP and SOAP extensions such as ebXML. The JAXM specification also does not mandate the use of any particular communication protocols; the current support focuses around industry standards such as HTTP, SMTP, and FTP.

JAXM clients can be either message provider-driven or non-managed. The API can be used by non-managed clients (standalone applications) for building SOAP-compliant XML messages and for sending them directly to the final destination. In a non-managed environment, the client and its destination can communicate only in a point-to-point fashion. Message providers handle the transmission and routing of messages from the sender to receiver(s), as shown in Figure 7.6. By using message providers, asynchronous communication can be achieved where the underlying architecture is based upon a Java Messaging Service (JMS) implementation. For more information on JMS, refer to http://java.sun.com/products/jms/. The JAXM specification does not mandate the use of any particular messaging architecture. The provider architecture is completely transparent to the JAXM sender or receiver.

In a message provider environment, a sender builds a SOAP-compliant message by using a JAXM API. The sender then sends a message by going through its provider, at which point the message is then transmitted over the network and is forwarded to the receiver's provider. The receiver then gets the message and processes it using the JAXM API. Figure 7.6 illustrates a simple JAXM messaging example of sending and receiving SOAP messages using HTTP.

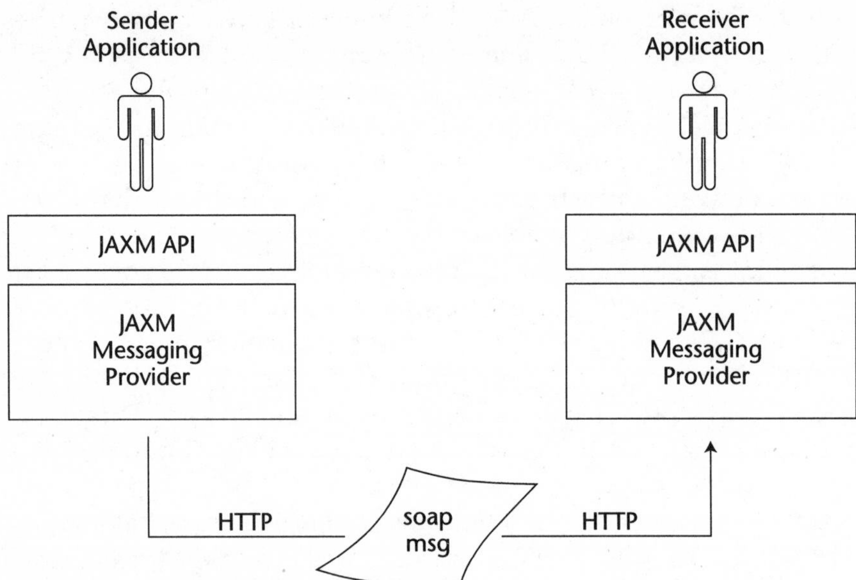

Figure 7.6 JAXM messaging over HTTP.

Because there are other APIs (such as JAX-RPC) that use the SOAP package from JAXM, the specification of JAXM was separated and a new specification called SOAP Attachments API for Java (SAAJ) was formed. This API specification only consists of the java.xml.soap package originally designed for JAXM.

For more information on the current releases, refer to Chapter 9.

Java API for XML Remote Procedure Calls (JAX-RPC)

Java API for XML RPC (JAX-RPC) provides a set of high-level Java APIs for XML-based RPCs and makes the XML-RPC model easy to understand and implement. Because JAX-RPC is based around XML messaging, it is platform independent and can be used in a heterogeneous distributed environment without being limited by a specific platform or technology (unlike its complementary standards such as RMI or CORBA). See Chapter 1, "Evolution of Distributed Computing," for an overview of RMI and CORBA.

JAX-RPC enables XML-based Java applications to interoperate using RPC. The RPC mechanism enables a client to make remote procedure calls that are communicated to a remote server. An XML-based RPC is a remote procedure call encoded using an XML protocol, such as SOAP 1.1. The SOAP message is encoded with an RPC definition to send complex structures and commands to remote servers. The JAX-RPC specification is protocol neutral, but it does require the support of HTTP 1.1 for SOAP messaging. The API facilitates the development of Web services using RPC protocols by encapsulating the plumbing of marshalling and unmarshalling SOAP messages. JAX-RPC supports several modes of interaction: synchronous request-response, one-way RPC, and non-blocking RPC invocation.

Figure 7.7 illustrates a simple JAX-RPC example of Web services. The following are the steps taken in the example:

1. A client looks up a service definition in a UDDI registry. The information is stored using WSDL.
2. The service information is retrieved from the registry to determine the functionality that is offered to the client by the service.
3. The client then encodes a SOAP message and sends it to the server.
4. The JAX-RPC runtime environment parses the request and makes a call to the service using the JAX-RPC API.
5. After the result is computed, it is encoded and returned as a SOAP response.

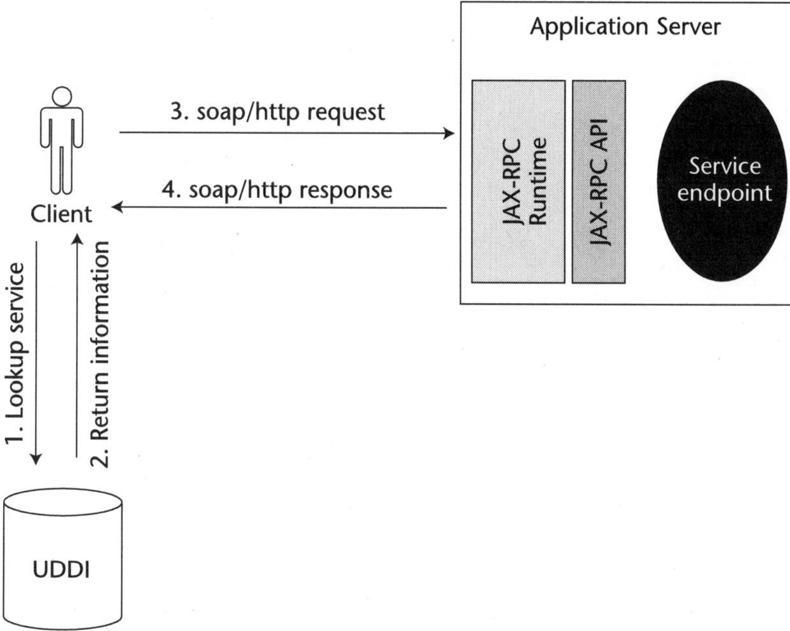

Figure 7.7 Web Services example using JAX-RPC.

For more information on JAX-RPC, refer to Chapter 10, "Building RPC Web services with JAX-RPC."

Java API for XML Registries (JAXR)

Registries are external entities that are accessed by various sources to find out information about particular business services. They hold information such as the name of the business and the services offered by the business. A registry can be public by being exposed to any other application on the network, or it can be private by being exposed to a local network. Client applications use the information provided by these registries to make calls to the services.

Registry providers have the responsibility to provide the implementation of the registry specifications. A JAXR provider acts as a wrapper to the registry provider: that is, it encapsulates all of the plumbing information a developer does not need to worry about by exposing only those interfaces that are needed by the application (JAXR client). JAXR clients can use generic or specific business-type APIs to access the registry.

Java API for XML Registries (JAXR) facilitates access to diverse business registries and repositories, such as UDDI and ebXML. It enables applications to register with a registry or to look for Web services offered by other businesses. Figure 7.8 shows an example scenario of using a JAXR API to enable uniform access to various types of registries.

For more information on the current release of JAXR, refer to Chapter 11, "Java API for XML Registries."

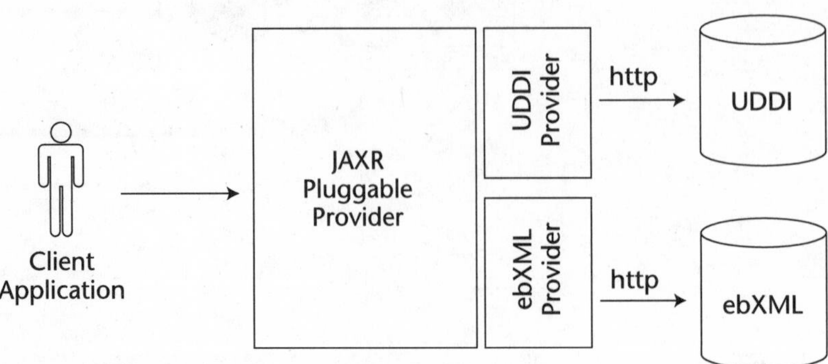

Figure 7.8 Accessing service registries with JAXR.

JavaServer Pages Standard Tag Library

JavaServer Pages Standard Tag Library (JSTL) is an initiative to standardize on a single set of reusable taglibs that expose functionality to solve common problems faced in Web application development. The idea is to implement one standard solution instead of many different proprietary ones. By doing this, developers will only have to learn one set of functions to perform their work instead of many different taglibs which, in the end, perform the same functionality. The JSTL implementation is vendor neutral, which means that it will run in most Web containers that conform to the required Java specifications. Having this kind of specification enables vendors to implement different strategies for their Web containers.

The current implementation of JSTL tags supports functionality for the following:

Core tags. Provide support for conditional processing, iteration over collections, and expression language support.

XML tags. Provide support for XML processing, including the parsing and transformation of XML documents.

Internationalisation tags. Provide support for I18N and localized formatting.

SQL tags. Provide support for database access.

Chapter 12, "Using the Java Web Services Developer Pack: Case Study," provides some examples on how to use JSTL tag libraries. For more information on JSTL, refer to the JSTL home page at: http://java.sun.com/products/jsp/jstl/.

This ends the coverage of the Java XML APIs and standard tag libraries that are part of the JWSDP. The following section will talk about the infrastructure, runtime environment, and tools that aid in the development of Web services.

Apache Tomcat Container

Apache Tomcat is an open-source implementation of a Web container under the Apache Software Foundation. The container conforms to the latest specifications and provides runtime services for hosting and executing servlets and JSPs.

For more information on Tomcat, refer to http://jakarta.apache.org/tomcat/index.html.

Java WSDP Registry Server

JWSDP Registry Server is an implementation of the UDDI version 2.0. The JWSDP Registry Server serves the purpose of testing applications written using Java API for XML Registries (JAXR).

For more information about the Registry Server, UDDI, and JAXR, refer to the following sources:

- Registry Server: Java Sun's Web site at http://java.sun.com/webservices/docs/1.0/tutorial/doc/RegistryServer.html#67421
- UDDI: See Chapter 5
- JAXR: See Chapter 11

ANT Build Tool

Apache ANT is a build tool similar to make and gnumake. It has gained a lot of attention and acceptance from the community for building and deploying Java code. ANT uses XML for specifying the various tasks that must be executed in the build process. It provides many defined tasks that can be used by the developer while compiling, building, or deploying the application code. ANT is extensible because it enables a new task to be implemented and used in the build process. A task is a Java class that implements a specific functionality and conforms to a specific interface. For example, if the developer wants to achieve class files in a jar, she would call the jar task to accomplish this step. The jar task is part of the core set of tasks available with ANT.

For more information on the ANT build tool, refer to http://jakarta.apache.org/ant/index.html.

Downloading the Web Services Pack

JWSDP is available at the Sun Java site. Full documentation, which explains the functionality of each Java XML API included in the pack, also is available for downloading. In addition, the Web services tutorial also is for downloading. This tutorial takes the developer through each API with examples, and it provides instructions on how to set up the JWSDP environment and how to deploy and test Web service applications.

A separate download of the Java XML Pack software bundle is available at http://java.sun.com/xml/javaxmlpack.html. This pack only includes the APIs available in JWSDP, and it does not provide a runtime environment to test Web service applications. JWSDP is available at http://java.sun.com/webservices/webservicespack.html, and it includes the Java XML APIs and a runtime environment.

These development packs are released by Sun on a quarterly basis, thus ensuring support for emerging XML standards and the most recent specifications.

Summary

In this chapter, we introduced the JAVA XML Pack APIs and the Java Web Services Developer Pack (JWSDP) runtime environment for developing and running Web services applications.

This introduction provided a walk-through on document- and procedure-oriented API solutions for XML processing and the importance of JAVA XML Pack in Web services.

In the following chapters, we will take a closer look at these APIs with best practices and real-world example illustrations. Chapter 12, "Using Java Web Services Developer Pack: Case Study," focuses on JWSDP and provides a case study example using various APIs from the pack.

CHAPTER

8

XML Processing and Data Binding with Java APIs

Java and XML are known to be a perfect fit for building portable business applications, where Java provides the portability of code that can be executed on various platforms and XML provides the portability of data that can be processed on diverse platforms. These two technologies can be ported from one platform to another without any effort, and in addition, Java applications can talk to non-Java applications by using XML as the communication protocol. The first generation of Java XML APIs dealt with the parsing of XML covering industry standards like SAX and DOM. By high demand from the developer community, other standards followed such as XML transformations and XML data binding. These emerging XML technologies are a key solution in the Web services arena, where parsing is used for processing XML messages and binding provides an object view of the XML data.

This chapter provides an overview of Java API for XML processing and data binding, focusing on the following:

- Overview of XML and its complementing standards
- Simple API for XML
- Document Object Model (DOM)
- The JAXP processing model and its features

- Using JAXP in Web services development
- Using Java XML binding

The specification of Java API for XML processing is currently at version 1.2 and provides support for XML parsing and XML transformation. Also, the specification for XML data binding API is at version 1.0. These two specifications are very important because they set the fundamentals for XML processing and are essential in understanding the processing as well as benefits of using XML. Before describing the APIs, let's look at the basics of XML.

Extensible Markup Language (XML) Basics

XML is an ASCII-based structured meta-data language that has been widely adopted in the industry. Currently, it is adopted in many areas such as security (for example, SAML and XACML), meta data (for example, XML Schema and TopicMaps), and presentation (for example, XHTML and XSLT).

XML was created in 1996 and embodied by the W3C group since early 1998. It is a derivative of the well-known SGML markup language, which has been around for a long time but has not gotten as much acceptance as XML due to its complexity. XML was created as an extensible way to represent data. It is considered extensible because it does not define a standard and well-defined set of tags (such as HTML) but rather provides the capability to create custom tags. It has the flexibility to define complex data structures in a modular way, thus promoting clarity and consistency.

HTML has tags <>, also referred to as markup, that have a specific meaning. When interpreted by a browser, the HTML tags have a particular presentation-oriented function within the document. For example, the tag `<Body>` marks the beginning of a page. Anything that is put inside the `<Body>` tag is rendered by the browser and displayed on the Web page. The `<Body>` tag also contains a closing tag, which is represented by the `</Body>` tag. In XML, the same set of tags could have hundreds of different meanings. For example, consider an XML file that describes the characteristics of a person. The Person tag contains a Body tag that will contain the weight and height of a person. The following is an XML representation of such a description:

```
<?xml version="1.0" ?>
 <Friends>
  <Person>
   <Name>Jane Doe</Name>
   <Age>21</Age>
   <Body>
```

```
      <Weight Unit="lbs">126</Weight>
      <Height Unit="inches">62</Height>
    </Body>
  </Person>
  <Person>
    <Name>John Doe</Name>
    <Age>26</Age>
    <Body>
      <Weight Unit="kg">80</Weight>
      <Height Unit="meters">1.67</Height>
    </Body>
  </Person>
</Friends>
```

The document starts with a prolog, which is a processing instruction statement identifying the XML document and the version of the document. The XML structure represents data about two people, each identified with the `<person>` tag. Within the person tag, there is a description of the body characteristics of each person such as weight and height. Body characteristics can have different types of measuring units such as kilograms (kg) or pounds (lbs). This is a representation of hierarchical data where the `<Name>`, `<Age>`, and `<Body>` tags are enclosed within the scope of the `<Person>` tag. This makes XML very extensible, where the creator of the XML determines what meaning and content the markup must have.

XML is currently being used in various areas of enterprise computing. One area that all J2EE developers are familiar with is the area of the deployment descriptors, which is used for the configuration of the J2EE components hosted in an application server. Some application servers use XML for storing their setup, configuration, and deployment information. XML also is known to be a perfect solution for integration with legacy systems, because it is a platform and vendor-neutral solution.

Note that XML as a meta language, in most circumstances, is very easy to understand. It only uses ASCII encoding, thus making it readable with simple text editors. By looking at the previous example, one could easily interpret what is meant by the XML structure. To put things into perspective, the following is an equivalent comma-delimited data file representing the equivalent data:

```
Rima P, 18,100, 54
Urszula M, 21, 126, 62
Slawomir S, 45, 80, 1.55
Robert S, 26, 90, 1.67
```

In this particular scenario, commas are used to delimit the data, which was a very frequently used option prior to the standardization of XML. Just by looking at this sample, you will be hard pressed to determine what each entry means. There is no explanation of the data in an intuitive way. Also, the mixing of units into one single file is impossible, because there is no indication of the type of unit being used. Even though it's possible to use these types of data files, they are extremely difficult to maintain because they are very difficult to understand and validate. In fact, they can cause a maintenance nightmare.

XML provides a structured and well-defined syntax that enables data to be defined in a uniform way. This syntax is not very hard to learn, but understanding the different concepts is important. By understanding all of these concepts, a developer will be able to use various tools that will aid in XML development.

Before starting with the API discussion, let's look at the very basics of XML.

XML Syntax

This section will discuss some terminology associated with XML that describes XML-specific syntax and what it means.

XML Naming Conventions

Naming has to be respected for the XML document to be well formed. Blank spaces are not permitted in XML names. A name must start with an alphabetical letter (A to Z or a to z) or an underscore (_). It then can be followed with more letters, digits [0 to 9], underscores, hyphens (-), periods (.), and colons (:). Although a colon is permitted, it is mostly used when a document uses namespaces (see the section titled *Namespaces* that follows). Names are also case-sensitive in an XML document, therefore `<product>` and `<Product>` are considered to be two different elements. It is up to the developer to choose whether the structure is only in lowercase, uppercase, or mixed. For example, the following XML structure would not be valid due to the case mixing of the product:

```
<product>
  <id>1234</id>
  <price>19.99</price>
</Product>
```

The following is the correct product representation because both of the product elements are of the same case:

```
<product>
  <id>1234</id>
  <price>19.99</price>
</product>
```

Prolog

Prolog is the declaration statement that identifies the document as an XML document. It is the first line in an XML file. It identifies the version of the XML specification used, the encoding being used, and whether it is standalone. The prolog is not necessary, but it is a good practice to use it in declarations for internationalization and future extensions set by the W3C. The version attribute is mandatory where the other two are optional. The following is a sample of a prolog:

```
<?xml version="1.0" ?>
```

or

```
<?xml version="1.0" encoding="ISO-8859-1" standalone="yes" ?>
```

Some additional and optional attributes can be provided, including the following:

Encoding. Identifies the character set used for encoding the data.

Standalone. Identifies whether the source accesses external data sources.

Root

A root is the topmost element in an XML document. For a document to be syntactically correct, it must contain only one root element.

The following is not a correct XML document because it does not contain a single root element:

```
<?xml version="1.0"?>
<person1>
  <name>john</name>
</person1>
<person2>
  <name>jane</name>
</person2>
```

The following is a correct version of the same document with the employee element as the root.

```
<?xml version="1.0"?>
<Employee>
 <Person1>
   <Name>john</Name>
 </Person1>
```

```
  <Person2>
    <Name>jane</Name>
  </Person2>
<Employees>
```

Processing Instructions

Processing instructions (PIs) are used for providing information to the XML processing application. Things like scripts could be embedded in XML documents for extra processing. A prolog is considered to be a processing instruction but is reserved for XML standards. Processing instructions usually are used in special applications to perform special tasks.

The following is an example of a processing instruction:

```
<?target instructions?>
```

where the following are indicated:

target. It is the name of the application that will be performing the processing.

instruction. String containing information that is passed to the target application. An example of a PI that is seen in the majority of XML documents is the prolog:

```
<?xml version="1.0" ?>
```

Comments

Comments are used for documenting parts of an XML structure. Comments are defined using the same syntax as HTML. The following is an example of a comment:

```
<!— this is a comment —>
```

Tags

A tag is the element markup identified by the angle brackets. Each tag must have a start tag and a close tag. An XML file that contains a closing tag for every tag in a nested form is considered to be a well-formed file. A tag is considered to be an empty tag if it stands by itself without any attributes. An empty tag serves the purpose of an identifier in a XML structure.

For example,

```
<LineItem Product_No="210020" Quantity="4000"/>
```

can be equivalently represented as

```
<LineItem>
  <Product_No>210020</Product_No>
  <Quantity>4000</Quantity>
</LineItem>
```

The first example shows how the attributes can be used in a tag. This also is an example of an empty tag where no data is present. It simply defines the name and age and closes itself with the slash (/).

A number of things need to be kept in mind when an XML structure is designed. For example, when data is very large, it makes more sense to use elements rather then attributes for clarity. Data that contains various HTML or formatting tags also should be defined as an element. On the other hand, if the data is short and does not change very often, defining it as an attribute might be the right approach to take.

Elements

An element is the data delimited by a start tag and an end tag. It is the building block used for creating XML documents. An XML document essentially is composed of many elements. The topmost element is called the root element. All elements that are directly under the root are referred to as child elements of the root element. In the following code, the root element is the `Catalog` element and the child elements of the root elements are the `CatalogId`, `Product`, and `EuroProducts` elements. These three elements are considered to be siblings in relation to one another, and the root element is considered to be an ancestor of the three siblings. This tree structure can span multiple levels, nesting much deeper than we are able to show in the following simple example code:

```
<!-- Catalog Is a Start or Root element -->
<Catalog>
 <CatalogId Id='123456' />
  <!--Product element contains children elements -->
  <Product>
   <!-- Id element contains character data -->
   <Id>1234</Id>
   <!-- Price contains attribute currency -->
    <Price currency='USD'>199.99</Price>
```

```
    </Product>
    <!-- Empty element -->
    <EuroProducts/>
  <!-- Closing element -->
  </Catalog>
```

Attributes

Attributes provide additional information about an element. They have a key and value pair that identifies the different attribute. Many attributes can exist in one element. If attributes are used, the XML document can have a reduced number of tags, as shown in the following code:

```
<Price currency="USD">12.99</Price>
<Price currency="CND">21.99</Price>
```

In the code, the `Price` attribute specifies the currency type for the enclosed data. Attributes also apply to all of the elements that are nested within the element holding the attribute. The following example shows how the currency attribute applies to different scotch brands:

```
<Price currency="CND">
   <Scotch>
     <Name>Lagavulin</Name>
     <Value>49.99</Value>
   </Scotch>
   <Scotch>
     <Name>Talisker</Name>
     <Value>54.99</Name>
   </Scotch>
</Price>
<Price currency="USD">
   <Scotch>
      <Name>Cardhu</Name>
      <Value>29.99</Value>
   </Scotch>
</Price>
```

The *Lagavulin* and *Talisker* brands have CND currency, where the *Cardhu* brand holds the USD price.

Entities

Entities are variables used to define common text or shortcuts to text. Table 8.1 shows the common ones used in XML specification. For example, the less-than sign (<) can be interpreted as the beginning of a tag; it is therefore important to make use of entities in these situations. Entities are interpreted and expanded at parsing time.

Table 8.1 Entities Supported in XML Specification

ENTITY	CHARACTER
<	<
>	>
&	&
"	"
'	'

The following is a sample of an XML structure representing a purchase order; it includes most of the concepts discussed in this section:

```
<!-- Prolog -->
<?xml version="1.0"?>
<!- Root element -->
<PurchaseOrder>
   <Header>
      <PO_Number>2123536673005</PO_Number>
      <Date>02/22/2002</Date>
      <Customer_No>0002232</Customer_No>
     <!-- This Is the shipping address -->
      <Address>
       <Street1>233 St-John Blvd</Street1>
       <Street2>Building A42</Street2>
       <City>Boston</City>
       <State>MA</State>
       <Zip>03054</Zip>
       <Country>USA</Country>
      </Address>
     <!-- This Is the payment Information -->
      <PaymentInfo>
       <Type>Visa</Type>
      <Number>0323235664664564</Number>
      <Expires>02/2004</Expires>
      <Owner>John Doe</Owner>
      </PaymentInfo>
   </Header>
   <!-- The following section contains a list of -->
   <!-- ordered Items -->
   <Products/>
   <LineItem type="Software">
      <Product_No>21112</Product_No>
      <Quantity>250</Quantity>
   </LineItem>
   <LineItem type="Software">
```

```
        <Product_No>343432</Product_No>
        <Quantity>1000</Quantity>
    </LineItem>
    <LineItem type="Hardware">
        <Product_No>210020</Product_No>
        <Quantity>4000</Quantity>
    </LineItem>
</PurchaseOrder>
```

This XML structure is a representation of a purchase order. It starts with the XML prolog, followed by the root element of the structure called `PurchaseOrder`. `PurchaseOrder` has child elements, starting with `Header`, which contain the buyer information followed by many `LineItem` elements that contain the product number and quantity of the ordered products. Between the `Header` and first `LineItem` is an empty tag called `Products`. This empty tag serves as a delimeter between the header and the line items. Each `LineItem` contains the type of product that it represents. For example, Product_No 21112 is of type software.

Namespaces

Namespaces in an XML document are used to prevent naming collisions within same or different XML documents. The namespace syntax enables a prefix definition and an associated URI/URL to exist. By specifying the URL, the namespace becomes a unique identifier. A URL is usually combined with a prefix to make the different elements distinguishable from each other. The URL does not refer to any particular file or directory on the Web, it simply acts as a unique association or label for the defined namespace. The XML namespaces specification indicates that each XML element is in a namespace. If the namespaces are not explicitly defined, the XML elements are considered to reside in a *default namespace*.

Consider the following example XML structure where the `<Name>` tag is found in two distinct places:

```
Buyer.xml
<!-- This Is a fragment of the xml file -->
<Buyer>
 <Name>Urszula M</Name>
 <email>urszulam@acme.com</email>
</Buyer>
<!-- This Is a fragment of the xml file -->
<Product>

 <Id>090902343</Id>
 <Name>Foo</Name>
</Product>
```

This is a simple example, which calls for namespace support to avoid conflicts when both documents are used together. The most common conflicts arise when multiple XML documents use identical tags that have different meanings. <Name> is a child of both the product and buyer elements. The parser must understand to which <Name> tag the application is referring. Having said that, the syntax using namespaces specification will convert the <Name> tags into something less ambiguous, such as <Person:Name> and <Item:Name>. Namespaces can be found in XML-related documents, schema documents, and XSL stylesheets. The following sample shows the distinction of both tags:

```
<!-- Buyer.xml provides Information about the buyer -->
<PersonInfo:Buyer xmlns:PersonInfo=
"http://www.acme-computers.com/warehouse/personinfo/">
  <PersonInfo:Name>Robert S</Name>
  <PersonInfo:email>roberts@acme.com</email>
</PersonInfo:Buyer>

<!-- Catalog.xml listing of all Items available for sale -->
<Catalog:Product xmlns:Catalog=
 "http://www.acme-computers.com/warehouse/catalog/"
  xmlns="http://www.acme-computers.com/warehouse/default/">
  <!-- uses default namespace -->
  <Header>
    <LastUpdated>05/20/2001</LastUpdated>
  </Header>
  <Catalog:Item>
    <Catalog:Id>090902343</Catalog:Id>
    <Catalog:Name>Futsji</Catalog:Name>
  </Catalog:Item>
  <Catalog:Item>
    <Catalog:Id>123242343</Catalog:Id>
    <Catalog:Name>Sony</Catalog:Name>
  </Catalog:Item>
</Catalog:Product>
```

Element collision is prevented by placing prefixes in front of each XML element. The Header element of the catalog XML document does not use the `Catalog` namespace, instead, it uses the default namespace without any prefixes.

Validation of XML Documents

Before the parser processes a document, it is checked for well-formedness. A well-formed document is a document in which every tag has an equivalent closing tag meaning; it conforms to the XML specification. A document that is well formed may not necessarily be valid. A valid document is a document that conforms to certain constraints defined in a schema definition. Validity is used for checking whether a document conforms to certain standards agreed upon by collaborating parties (for example, two businesses conducting the exchange of computer parts). These two businesses must provide the data in such a way that they both understand what is represented and what is meant by it.

The following example demonstrates a structure that is not well formed:

```
<!-- Not well-formed document -->
<?xml version="1.0"?>
<Employees>
  <Person>Jane</Person>
  <Age>21
  </Employee>
</Age>
```

In the previous example, the `Age` and `Employee` elements are not properly nested. The order in which the paired tags are opened and closed is very important for a document to be considered well formed.

This error is corrected in the following example, in which the two elements are properly nested:

```
<!-- Well-formed document -->
<?xml version="1.0"?>
<Employee>
  <Person>Jane</Person>
  <Age>21</Age>
</Employee>
```

Well-formedness is very important because it enables the parser to process the XML document in a more efficient way.

In order for validity to be checked, a definition document must be provided to define what the document is allowed to have as tags and attributes and the type of elements that should be present within a particular tag.

Consider a simple example in which the `Product` element contains a type defining the type of product that a company is offering. The company offers two types of products (hardware or software). Suppose that its `Product` element is defined as follows:

```
<Product type="hardware">
  <Name>Generic Mouse</Name>
  <Price>19.99</Price>
```

```
</Product>
<Product type="service">
  <Name>Upgrade Services</Name>
  <Price>100.00</Price>
</Product>
```

In the previous code, a new type called service is introduced. In this case, this document would not be considered valid, because the receiving party would not know what the additional type means.

The following sections describe the different standards used for creating XML schemas for validating XML documents. Document Type Definitions (DTDs) were among the first specifications for validating XML data. The newest generation of validation standards is based on the XML Schema Definition, which is a more complete feature set that enables developers to define restrictions using XML syntax.

Document Type Definition

A Document Type Definition (DTD)—commonly known as a DOCTYPE—is a document containing the element restrictions an XML data document must follow in order to be considered *valid*. A DTD can be defined within the XML document or saved in an external file with a .dtd extension.

XML elements are declared with an element declaration using the following syntax:

```
<!ELEMENT element-name (element-content)>
```

Element-name is the XML element definition. Element-content defines the type of element. It defines whether the element is a data type or a compound type consisting of other elements and data. Various element types can be defined in an element, among which are the following:

EMPTY. Empty tag.

#CDATA. Character data; should not be parsed by the XML parser.

#PCDATA. Parsed character data; parsed by the XML parser. If elements are declared in `#PCDATA`, then these elements also must be defined.

ANY. Any content.

If a DTD is defined inside the XML, the declaration is included in the `DOCTYPE` construct. The following examples show how to define DTDs in both internal and external ways. These examples demonstrate how to define an element `Product` with children sequences of `Id` and `Price`:

```
<?xml version="1.0"?>
<!DOCTYPE Product [
 <!ELEMENT Product (Id,Price)>
 <!ELEMENT Id (#PCDATA)>
 <!ELEMENT Price (#PCDATA)>
]>
<Product>
 <Id>3124090231</Id>
 <Price>49.99</Price>
</Product>
```

The following example is an equivalent DTD, but it is defined in an external file called `Product.dtd`:

```
<?xml version="1.0"?>
  <!ELEMENT Product (Id, Price)>
  <!ELEMENT Id (#PCDATA)>
  <!ELEMENT Price (#PCDATA)>
```

The XML file size is reduced to the following:

```
<?xml version="1.0"?>
<!DOCTYPE Product SYSTEM "product.dtd">
<Product>
  <Id>3124090231</Id>
  <Price>49.99</Price>
</Product>
```

It also is possible to control the occurrence of the children within an element. See Table 8.2 for a list of the most common occurrence controls and a description of what they do.

Table 8.2 DTD Element Occurrence Controls

ELEMENT DEFINITION	ATTRIBUTE	DESCRIPTION
`<!ELEMENT Product (Price)>`	None	The Product element may only contain one instance of the child element.
`<!ELEMENT Product (Price*)>`	*	The Product element can contain multiple child elements.

Table 8.2 *(Continued)*

ELEMENT DEFINITION	ATTRIBUTE	DESCRIPTION
`<!ELEMENT Product (Price+)>`	+	The Product element can contain one or more instances of the child elements.
`<!ELEMENT Product (Price?)>`	?	The Product element can contain zero or one instance of the child element.

DTD attributes are used in cases where XML elements contain attributes that need validation. The syntax for a single attribute is as follows:

```
<!ATTLIST element-name attribute-name CDATA "default-value">
<!ATTLIST Product type CDATA "hardware">
```

The syntax for a multi-attribute element is as follows:

```
<!ATTLIST element-name attribute-name (enum1|enum2... ) "default-value">
<!ELEMENT Product (#PCDATA)>
<!ATTLIST Product type(hardware|software|services) "hardware">
```

The following XML code respects the definitions of the enumerated attribute values defined previously. `Product` could be of the type hardware, software, or services. The default value, if not provided in the attribute list definition, is hardware because this is the first entry in the enumeration.

```
<Product type="hardware">
  <Id>34254030546</Id>
</Product>
<Product type="software">
  <Id>99321254030122</Id>
</Product>
```

In the case where text is reused multiple times, entities can be used to define a variable once and then be reused throughout the document thereafter.

`Entity` can be used for internal definitions, as follows:

```
<!ENTITY entity-name "entity-value">
<!ENTITY companyname "ABC Sports">
```

Entities also can be used for external definitions, as follows:

```
<!ENTITY entity-name SYSTEM "URI/URL">
<!ENTITY companyname SYSTEM "http://www.myxml.com/entities/myentity.xml ">
```

The XML data is the same whether or not an internal or external entity source is used.

```
<Information>&companyname;</Information>
```

DTD has been the first and only constraint language for validating XML documents. It has solved many problems that developers were facing. In the current wave of technological evolutions, DTDs are not able to handle some requirements with ease.

For example, one disadvantage of the DTD is that it is hard to read and does not use XML as the definition format. DTDs are not very good at expressing sophisticated constraints on elements, such as the number of maximum and minimum occurrences of a particular element. DTDs do not have the capability to reuse previously defined structures. They also do not have support for type inheritance, subtyping, and abstract declarations.

A more flexible standard that covers most of the limitations of DTDs is XML Schema. This standard is becoming more popular as the definition format, because it is easier to understand and maintain.

XML Schema

XML Schema is currently a W3C recommendation (www.w3.org/XML/Schema). XML Schema is hierarchical and enables type, structure, and relationship definitions to exist as well as field validations within elements. XML Schema is harder to learn and create than DTDs but solves the major limitations of DTDs. The schema definition is written in XML, which seems like a natural fit in the XML world with great tool support for creating and editing XML documents. XML Schema is not part of the XML 1.0 specification, which means that valid XML documents only apply to documents that are validated by DTDs using the `DOCTYPE` declaration.

Comparing DTD to XML Schema

The following demonstrates the difference between a DTD and an XML Schema definition for the same XML file:

```
<Product>123456</Product>
<Price>49.99</Price>
```

The DTD for the previous XML code is as follows:

```
<?xml version="1.0"?>
<!DOCTYPE Product [
     <!ELEMENT Product (Id,Price)>
     <!ELEMENT Price (#PCDATA)>
]>
```

The XML Schema for the same XML code is as follows:

```
<!-- This Is the xml schema for the XML above -->
<element name='Product' type='string'/>
<element name='Price' type='string'/>
```

XML Schema Declaration Using Namespace

The schema declarations begin the same way a regular XML document begins, with a prolog. It starts with `<schema>` as the root element. It then includes references to an XML Schema namespace declaration. Namespace declarations are needed in this case because the document being operated upon references specific elements from the schema. The schema elements provide the semantics for constraining elements in the other namespace of the XML document being processed. The following is a fragment of an XML Schema declaration:

```
<?xml version="1.0" ?>
<schema targetNamespace="http://www.acme.com/warehouse/catalog"
        xmlns="http://www.w3.org/2001/XMLSchema"
        xmlns:Catalog="http://www.acme.com/warehouse/catalog">

<element name='Product' type='string'/>
<element name='Price' type='string'/>
```

The root element `<schema>` contains a `targetNamespace` attribute, which specifies the target that the schema will constrain. The previous example shows that two different namespaces are defined. One is the default namespace (unqualified) used by the XML Schema and the second (qualified) is the target document defined using the `Catalog` prefix. There are no general rules for choosing a namespace as the default. There are suggestions to make the default namespace the same as the `targetNamespace`. There is not an optimal solution to this problem; which default namespace is optimal truly depends upon whether the schema will be extended, whether it will import different schemas, and any number of other things.

Using Multiple Schemas

There could be a case where the XML document refers to names of elements found in multiple namespaces that are defined in multiple schemas. In that case, the location of the XML schemas must be specified using the schemaLocation attribute. The following example shows a fragment of an XML document:

```
<?xml version="1.0" ?>
<Catalog:Product xmlns:Catalog="http://www.acme.com/warehouse/catalog/"
xmlns:Buyer="http://www.acme.com/warehouse/buyers/"
xmlns:xsi="http://www.w3.org/2001/XMLSchema-instance"
xsi:schemaLocation="http://www.acme.com/warehouse/catalog
                    http://www.acme.com/schema/catalogs.xsd
                    http://www.acme.com/warehouse/buyers
                    http://www.acme.com/schema/customers.xsd">
  <!-- uses default namespace -->
  <Buyer:Name>
    John Doe
  </Buyer:Name>
  <Catalog:Item>
    <Catalog:Id>090902343</Catalog:Id>
    <Catalog:Name>Futsji</Catalog:Name>
  </Catalog:Item>
 </Catalog:Product>
```

Another way to use multiple schemas is to import one schema into another, which is achieved in the following code:

```
<schema targetNamespace="http://www.acme.com/warehouse/catalog"
        xmlns="http://www.w3.org/2001/XMLSchema"
        xmlns:Catalog="http://www.acme.com/warehouse/catalog"
        xmlns:Buyer="http://www.acme.com/warehouse/buyers">

<import namespace="http://www.acme.com/warehouse/buyers"
        schemaLocation=="http://www.acme.com/schema/customer.xsd"/>
```

The import element is used to specify the namespace along with the URI location of the schema definition.

Now that we have the root element defined, the rest should be straightforward. A schema definition is composed of elements and attributes that describe the content of the XML document.

Elements

XML schema elements provide definitions for the content of an XML data document. A name and a type represent an element. The type sets a restriction to which the XML document elements must conform. Element types

Table 8.3 XML Schema Data Types

TYPE	DESCRIPTION
`String`	Character string
`Binary`	Binary data
`Boolean`	Logic value (true or false)
`Decimal`	Positive or negative integer value
`Double`	64-bit floating point value
`Float`	32-bit floating point value
`Uri`	Uniform resource Indicator
`TimeInstant`	Date and time stamp
`TimeDuration`	Duration of time
`RecurringInstant`	A recurrence of time occurring over a timeDuration

come in two different forms: primitive or complex. Primitive or simple element types are defined by the XML Schema specification. Table 8.3 lists most of the data types supported by the XML Schema specification.

Simple data types cannot contain other elements or any other attributes. The schema element, using simple data types, is defined using the following syntax:

```
<element name="[name of element]" type="[type of element] [option(s)]>
```

For example:

```
<element name="Price" type="decimal" />
```

`Name` is used to identify the XML element that the schema is constraining. `type` refers to the type of data that is expected to be stored between the elements. There also are other possibilities of various options, such as the occurrence of an element in the XML document.

Similarly to DTDs, XML Schema provides an equivalent to (+,*,?) attributes, which are called `minOccurs` and `maxOccurs`. Revisiting the syntax, we get

```
<element name="[name of element]"
       type="[type of element]"
```

```
  minOccurs="[Min occurences]"
  maxOccurs="[Max occurences]"
>
```

When unspecified, both options default to 1, meaning that one occurrence exists per definition. On the other hand, if a finite occurrence number is not defined, a wildcard (*) character is used. For example, the following is a definition for the `LineItem` element, which has to occur at least many times and has no `maxOccurs` limit:

```
<element name=LineItem type=complexType minOccurs=1>
```

Complex or user-defined elements are used to define elements that consist of other elements and attributes. The syntax used for complex types is represented in the following order:

```
<complexType name="[name of type]">
  <[Element specification] />
  <[Element specification] />
  ...
</complexType>
```

For example, a `Product` contains a name, description, and price, and is considered to be a complex type, as shown in the following fragment:

```
<Product>
  <Name>Product A</Product>
  <Description>
This Is a description for Product A
  </Description>
  <Price>20.99</Price>
</Product>

<complexType name="ProductType">
  <element name="Name"        type="string" />
  <element name="Description" type="string" />
  <element name="Price"       type="decimal" />

</complexType>
```

In this hierarchical structure of elements, the lowest level of elements is considered to be a simple type, the rest are all complex types. The nesting of elements could be very deep; schema does not impose any restrictions on this. For example, a `PurchaseOrder` is composed of `POID`, `Buyer`, and `Product`. The `POID` (Purchase Order ID) is an integer and is considered to be a simple type. `Buyer` and `Product` are user-defined types that contain more embedded elements. The purchase order requires one POID, one buyer, and many products, which can be accomplished by setting `minOccurs` and `maxOccurs` on the elements. One last restriction is that the product description appears zero or one times. This is realized by setting the description element to `maxOccurs="0"`. The following is an example of this scenario:

```
<schema targetNamespace="http://www.acme.com/warehouse/po"
  xmlns="http://www.w3.org/2001/XMLSchema"
  xmlns:PO="http://www.acme.com/warehouse/po"
  xmlns:Catalog="http://www.acme.com/warehouse/catalog"
  xmlns:Buyer="http://www.acme.com/warehouse/buyers"
>

<element name="PurchaseOrder" type="PO:PurchaseOrderType">
<complexType name="PurchaseOrderType">
  <element name="PurchaseOrderNumber" type="Integer" />
  <element name="PurchaseDate" type="string"/>
  <element name="BuyerID" type="Integer"/>
  <element name="BuyerName" type="string"/>
  <element name="Order" type="PO:OrderType"/>
</complexType>

<complexType name="OrderType">
  <element name="LineItem" type="LineItemType" />
</complexType>

<complexType name="LineItemType">
  <element name="ProductNumber" type="decimal" />
  <element name="Quantity" type="decimal"/>
</complexType>
```

The types used in the previous example are called explicit types. Explicit types are defined in such a way that they can be reused in the same or different document. There also are cases where the element contains a type, which is unique to a specific element definition and will not be reused anywhere else. This is referred to as an *implicit type* or a *nameless type*. Implicit type enables the definition of a user-defined type within an element. The following example demonstrates the use of an implicit type. The `BuyerInfo` type cannot be reused anywhere else in this XML document except in the definition of `PurchaseOrderType`, which is shown in the following fragment of code:

```
<complexType name="PurchaseOrderType">
  <element name="POID" type="Integer" />
  <element name="BuyerInfo">
   <complexType>
     <element name="BuyerName" type="string" />
     <element name="BuyerPhone" type="string" />
```

```
    </complexType>
  </element>
</complexType>
```

In addition, there is a notion of local and global definitions for elements, which are shown in the following example.

This example demonstrates an instance of a local definition because the elements of `Name`, `Description`, and `Price` belong to the `ProductType` element.

```
<element name="Product" type="ProductType" />
<complexType name="ProductType">
  <element name="Name" type="string" />
  <element name="Description" type="string" />
  <element name="Price" type="decimal" />
</complexType>
```

The following example uses global definitions, where `Name`, `Description`, and `Price` can be reused in other elements throughout the document:

```
<element name="Name" type="string" />
<element name="Description" type="string" />
<element name="Price" type="decimal" />
<element name="Product" type="ProductType" />

<complexType name="ProductType">
  <element ref="Name" />
  <element ref="Description" />
  <element ref="Price" />
</complexType>
```

The use of global and local definitions is really a matter of taste. Some of the best practices suggest making the declarations local if the elements are specific to the element being defined. Otherwise, if the elements can be reused throughout the document, then make the declarations global.

Figure 8.1 demonstrates how one XML Schema Definition file can be composed of many different schema files. In this case, XML Schema is used as the default to provide a set of simple data types that can be used to define certain elements in an XML document. In addition, the Catalog schema is used to provide more extensible user-defined types used within the XML document.

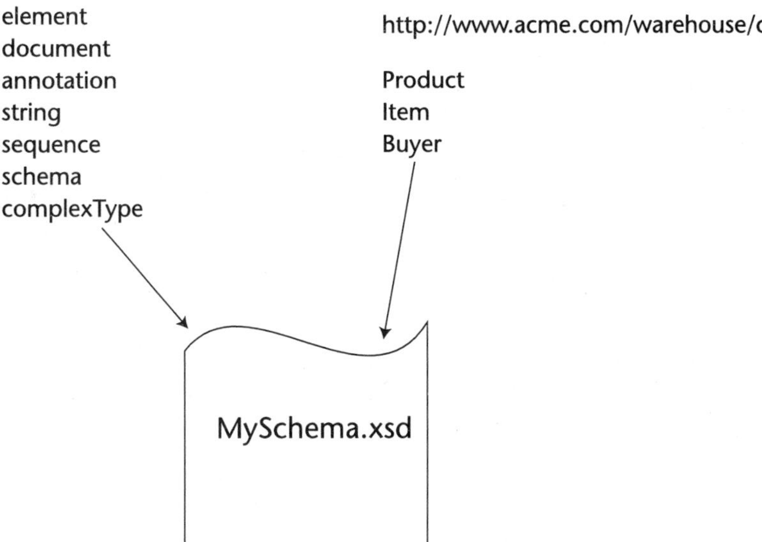

Figure 8.1 XML Schema definition.

Previous sections of this chapter have discussed empty tags. These empty tags also can be constrained by the XML Schema definitions. This is accomplished by defining an element name containing a `complexType` of type `empty`, as follows:

```
<element name="SomeFlag">
  <complexType content="empty" />
</element>
```

Attributes

Attributes are used to provide additional information to an XML data element. For example, the element `Price` can have an attribute identifying the currency of the price, as shown in the following:

```
<Price currency="USD">20.99</Price>
```

XML schemas can be used to enforce constraints on element attributes. The syntax for attribute definitions is as follows:

```
<attribute name="[name of attribute]"
           type="[type of attribute]"
           [Option(s)]
>
```

If an attribute definition for the Product element were provided, the following would be the result:

```
<complexType name="ProductType">
  <element name="Name" type="string" />
  <element name="Description" type="string" minOccurs="0" />
  <element name="Price">
    <complexType content="decimal">
      <attribute name="currency" type="string" />
    </complexType>
  </element>
</complexType>
```

Simple types cannot have attributes; therefore they must be defined as a complexType because of the attribute addition. The attribute for Price is currency, which identifies the kind of currency of the price. The power of this definition can be extended by adding an option for making the attribute mandatory, thus providing a default currency or restricting the attribute to a list of possible currencies.

To make an attribute mandatory, use the minOccurs option by setting it to "1". The minOccurs option defaults to "0" because it is not always required:

```
<attribute name="currency" type="string" minOccurs="1" />
```

To add a default value for an attribute, use the "default" option:

```
<attribute name="currency" type="string" default="USD" />
```

To add a list of restricted values for an attribute, use an enumeration option:

```
<attribute name="currency" default="USD" />
  <simpleType base="string">
    <enumeration value="USD" />
    <enumeration value="CND" />
    <enumeration value="ERO" />
  </simpleType>
</attribute>
```

XML Schema is more powerful and more intuitive than DTDs, but it does not solve all of the problems. There are still limitations that cannot be solved with this standard alone. Instead, other technologies must be added and combined to solve more complex problems revolving around data restrictions and validations. For example, imagine an element, which has the following restrictions: The <Price> element of a Product is smaller or equal to the <TotalPrice> element of a Purchase Order. Additional XML schema languages must be used to solve this problem. There are many different standards and tools that solve problems that DTDs and XML schemas cannot handle, such as the following languages:

- TREX
- Schematron
- SOX
- XDR
- RELAX

In the following sections, XML validation will be used to constrain XML data. We will see how to use XML validation with JAXP parsing and XML data binding using Castor. Parsing of the data is an essential mechanism used for interpreting the tags and elements that compose an XML data structure. There have been many vendor implementations that enable the parsing of XML, but one major factor was lacking: the standardization of XML processing. This is how Java APIs for XML processing and binding were born—these standards also are known as JAXP and JAXB. These two standards provide a standardized and vendor-neutral approach for XML processing. The following sections describe the two standards by going through the APIs and examples.

Java API for XML Processing (JAXP)

Now that we have seen an overview of XML, we can begin looking at the various APIs available for the processing of XML. The process in which the XML is being interpreted is called parsing and the process where various templates are applied to XML to produce a different output is called transformation. The API that embraces both of these processes is called Java API for XML Processing, or JAXP. We give an overview of JAXP in Chapter 7, "Introduction to the Java Web Services Developer Pack (JWSDP)." JAXP also is an integral part of JWSDP and it facilitates the role of XML processing in Java Web services.

JAXP

In the last couple of years, XML parsing has been standardized to two distinct processing models: Simple API for XML (SAX) and Document Object Model (DOM). These two standards address different parsing needs by providing APIs that enable developers to work with XML data. Many vendors have implemented their own specific parsers that address the two most common parsing models of SAX and DOM. This led to API standardization complexities where applications using one specific vendor were using specific method calls to perform equivalent parsing tasks. In the case where the parsers needed to be swapped, developers had to rewrite the parsing code to adapt to the new specific vendor standard.

To address these complexities, in late 1999, Sun Microsystems came up with a draft of the Java API for XML Parsing (JAXP) 1.0 specification. The purpose of the specification was to provide a standard high-level API layer for abstracting lower-level details of XML parsing. The first version of JAXP (1.0) supported SAX 1.0 and DOM Level 1 parsing specifications. The feature set focused around parsing, which was a limitation that many have complained about because it did not provide support for any XML transformation processing. The latest version of JAXP 1.1 supports SAX 2.0, SAX 2 extensions, and DOM level 2. It also includes transformation support based on the eXtensible Stylesheet Language Transformations (XSLT) specification. The purpose behind JAXP is to provide an abstraction so that parsing using SAX or DOM looks the same no matter what type of SAX or DOM parser is being used by the application. This abstraction is referred to as pluggable interface.

Uses for JAXP

JAXP provides a pluggability layer, which enables application developers to change parser implementations without affecting the application logic. One JAXP-compliant parser can be exchanged for another parser seamlessly, without much effort. JAXP provides a set of standard interfaces that encapsulate the details behind parser interactions. These interfaces act as abstractions that prevent the developer from working with XML directly. These abstractions are implementations of the SAX and DOM parsing standards and the XSLT transformation standard.

Figure 8.2 shows the high-level blocks that compose the JAXP model. In order for a parser and transformer to be compliant, it must follow the JAXP specification. The flexibility of having the freedom to choose any parser is very important. It enables an application developer to choose a parser provider that best suits the requirements of the service.

In addition to the pluggability layer, JAXP is made simple. The APIs are very straightforward and the learning curve is much smaller than learning a new proprietary API. The following section steps through the API for parsing and transforming XML documents.

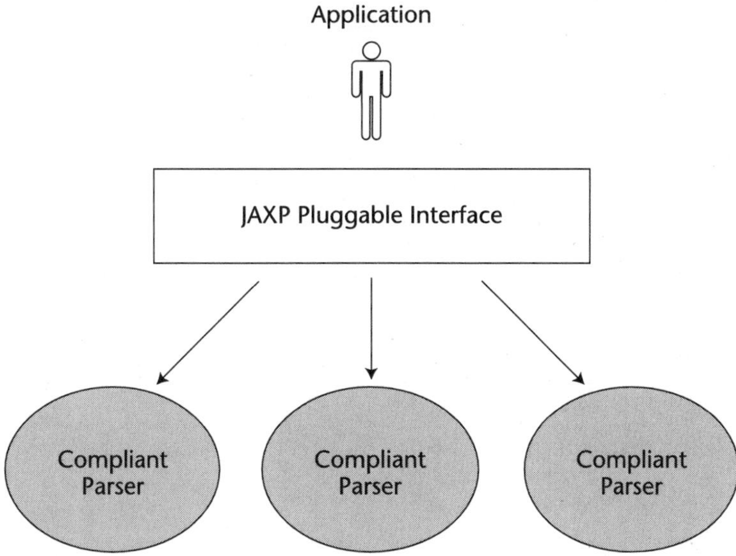

Figure 8.2 JAXP pluggable interface.

JAXP API Model

The JAXP API model is quite easy to understand and simple to use. The parsing classes and interfaces are packaged under the `javax.xml.parsers` package and sit on top of existing SAX or DOM APIs. Transformation classes and interfaces are packaged in `javax.xml.transform` and provide utilities for performing XSLT transformations. Something really important to understand about JAXP is that it ships with Sun's Crimson parser, which is the reference implementation of the JAXP parser. The parser implementation is packaged in `parser.jar` with package name `com.sun.xml.parser`, which is *not* part of the JAXP specifications. Developers have the tendency to refer to the `com.sun.xml.parser` package as JAXP. The use of this package also misuses the concept of JAXP by bypassing the high-level interfaces by calling the parser API directly.

Table 8.4 is a listing of classes and interfaces of the JAXP package (`javax.xml.parsers.*` and `javax.xml.transform.*`).

Table 8.4 Classes and Interfaces of JAXP Package

NAME	USE	CLASS OR INTERFACE NAME
SAX Parser Factory	Instantiating the SAX Parser	`javax.xml.parsers.SAXParserFactory`
SAXParser	JAXP Implementation used for parsing XML	`javax.xml.parsers.SAXParser`
Document Builder Factory	Instantiating DOM Builder	`avax.xml.parsers.DocumentBuilderFactory`
Document Builder	Creating the DOM element tree	`javax.xml.parsers.DocumentBuilder`
Parser Configuration	Exception class used for handling configuration errors	`javax.xml.parsers.ParserConfigurationException`
Factory Configuration Error	Exception class used for handling factory configuration errors	`javax.xml.parsers.FactoryConfigurationError`
Transformer Factory	Used for Instantiating the Transformer class	`javax.xml.transform.TransformerFactory`
Transformer	Transformer class used for XSL transformations	`javax.xml.transform.Transformer`
Transformer Factory Configuration Error	Error class used for catching Factory configuration errors	`javax.xml.transform.TransformerFactoryConfigurationError`

Table 8.4 *(Continued)*

NAME	USE	CLASS OR INTERFACE NAME
Stream Source	Input stream used for XSL transformations	`javax.xml.transform.stream.StreamSource`
Stream Result	Result stream used for XSL transformations	`javax.xml.transform.stream.StreamResult`
DOM Source	DOM tree source	`javax.xml.transform.dom.DOMSource`
DOM Result	DOM tree result	`javax.xml.transform.dom.DOMResult`
DOM Locator	DOM locator	`javax.xml.transform.dom.DOMLocator`
SAX Source	SAX Source	`javax.xml.transform.sax.SAXSource`
SAX Result	SAX Result	`javax.xml.transform.sax.SAXResult`

The factory class is the fundamental pattern of JAXP. It provides the transparent instantiation of the parser implementation. In reality, this is the mechanism that promotes the pluggability approach by enabling the developers to define the factory implementation as a parameter passed to the Java virtual machine. The definition of the factory class can be done in many ways (for example, using `SAXParserFactory`):

System Property	java -Djavax.xml.parsers.SAXParserFactory
Property file	$JAVA_HOME/jre/lib/jaxp.properties
JAR Service Provider	META-INF/services/javax.xml.parsers.SAX ParserFactory
Default	Use the platform default as the last fallback

The same configuration settings apply to `DocumentBuilderFactory` and `TransformerFactory` classes.

JAXP Implementations

Many implementations of JAXP 1.1 currently exist, including Sun Crimson, Apache Xerces, XML parser from IBM, and Oracle. For this chapter and throughout the book, we will use the Apache Xerces 2 XML parser and Xalan 2 Transformer, which are JAXP 1.1-compliant implementations.

A new change found in the new Java Development Toolkit (JDK) 1.4 is the addition of JAXP APIs and reference implementations. The reference implementations include Crimson for XML parsing and Xalan for XML transformations. The Endorsed Standards Override Mechanism must be used in order to override the JAXP implementation classes found in the JDK 1.4 with other JAXP compliant ones. For more information on how the mechanism works, refer to http://java.sun.com/j2se/1.4/docs/guide/standards/.

The following sections discuss the API and the different standards that it supports.

Processing XML with SAX

The Simple Access for XML (SAX) API is based on an event-driven processing model where the data elements are interpreted on a sequential basis and callbacks are called based on selected constructs. It is similar to the AWT 1.1 Event Delegation Model, where UI components generate events based on user input and where event listeners perform actions when these events are triggered. SAX's biggest advantage is that it does not load any XML documents into memory; therefore it is considered to be very fast and lightweight. SAX supports validation but does not enforce the use of it. By having validation, a document is checked for conformance against a schema document (DTD or XML Schema). It uses a sequential read-only approach and does not support random access to the XML elements.

There are several ways to process XML data using SAX APIs. One way of doing it is to use a JAXP (`javax.xml.parsers.*`) API, which abstracts many low-level SAX specific calls or uses the SAX (`org.xml.sax.*`) API directly. Using the SAX API directly is more difficult because it requires more steps to perform equivalent functionality that is encapsulated in the JAXP API. In this section, we will focus around the JAXP specifics and will not cover vendor-specific SAX APIs in great detail because this topic spans a very large area.

SAX as a processing model is very simple (see Figure 8.3). The basics consist of the following three steps:

1. Implement a class that extends the `DefaultHandler` and holds callback methods for every type of construct found in XML that contains implementation based on your needs.
2. Instantiate a new SAX Parser class. The Parser reads the XML source file and triggers a callback implemented in the `DefaultHandler` class.
3. Read the XML source sequentially. With the sequential reading, it is not possible to randomly access elements in the structure. The rest depends upon your implementation residing in the `Handler` class.

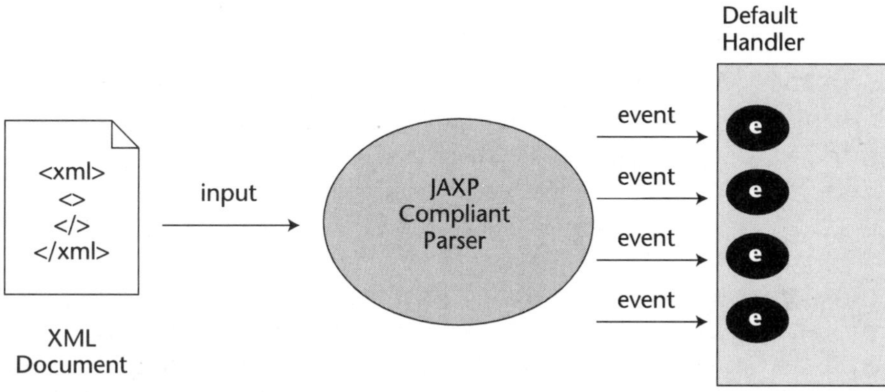

Figure 8.3 JAXP using the SAX processing model.

The following sections describe JAXP-specific SAX processing. These steps consist of the following:

1. Getting `Factory` and `Parser` classes to perform XML parsing
2. Setting options such as namespaces, validation, and features
3. Creating a `DefaultHandler` implementation class

Getting a Factory and Parser

The JAXP `SAXParser` class is responsible for parsing the XML data, and the implementation of the `org.xml.sax.DefaultHandler` handles all of the callbacks for specific tags. In order for an application to obtain an instance of the parser, it must get an instance of the `SAXParserFactory`. It then gets a `SAXParser` upon which it can call parse methods.

How to Get a SAX Parser

The following is a step-by-step demonstration on how to create a SAX parser.

1. Instantiate the implemented `Handler` class. JAXP1.1 requires that the handler extend from `DefaultHandler` class as opposed to `HandlerBase`, which was an implementation used in JAXP 1.0:

   ```
   DefaultHandler handler = new MyImplOfHandler();
   ```

2. Obtain a factory class using the SAXParserFactory's static `newInstance()` method.

   ```
   SAXParserFactory factory =
                       SAXParserFactory.newInstance();
   ```

3. Obtain the SAX parser class from the factory by calling the `newSAXParser()` static method:

   ```
   SAXParser parser = factory.newSAXParser() ;
   ```

4. Parse the XML data by calling the parse method on `SAXParser` and passing in the XML input as the first parameter and the `Default-Handler` implementation as the second. See `SAXParser javadoc` for different options available in the parse method.

   ```
   parser.parse("PurchaseOrder.xml", handler);
   ```

The factory class used in the second step is provided as a system property, jar service, or platform default. This type of implementation is referred to as the JAXP pluggability layer, because it is very generic the way the factory class is retrieved. Parser vendors can be swapped without much effort as long as they comply to the JAXP 1.1 specification. If the property is not found at runtime, a `FactoryConfigurationError` is thrown with a message describing the origin and cause of the problem. The parser factory can additionally be configured to instantiate validating and/or namespace-aware parsers. A `ParserConfigurationException` is thrown when the parser is not returned properly.

Configuration of the Factory

The following code shows how to define a factory class by using a key/value pair set as a system property. This line can be placed in a configuration file (`java.util.Properties`) or simply passed as an argument to the Java call. The most common implementations known to developers are the Sun Crimson reference implementation and Apache Xerces. The following is an example of setting Xerces 2 and Crimson JAXP `SAXParserFactory`.

APACHE XERCES 2

```
javax.xml.parsers.SAXParserFactory=org.apache.xerces.jaxp.SAXParser
FactoryImpl
```

SUN REFERENCE IMPLEMENTATION (CRIMSON)

```
javax.xml.parsers.SAXParserFactory=com.sun.xml.parser.SAXParserFactory
Impl
```

Setting Namespaces

A parser that is namespace aware is a parser that can handle naming collisions. This is important when multiple documents are used with the same application.

To configure the parser to be namespace aware, perform the following steps:

```
/** Set to namespace aware parsers */
factory.setNameSpaceAware(true);
```

To verify if the parser supports namespaces, perform the following steps:

```
If (parser.isNamespaceAware()) {
 System.out.println("Parser supports namespaces");
} else {
 System.out.println("Parser does not support namespaces");
}
```

Setting Validation

Validation is based on providing a validation document that imposes certain constraints on the XML data. Many standards provide validating capabilities based on DTDs and W3C XML schemas.

To configure the parser to be a validation-aware parser, perform the following steps:

```
/** Set to validating parsers */
factory.setValidating(true);
```

The factory class will try to look for a validation-capable parser. If the parser is not available, a factory configuration exception is thrown.

To verify whether a parser supports validation, the following method is available from the parser class:

```
If (parser.isValidating()) {
 System.out.println("Parser supports validation.");
} else {
 System.out.println("Parser does not support validation.");
}
```

Setting Features

SAX 2.0 enables a more flexible configuration option to exist through a method called `setFeature()`. This method is called on the factory class just like `setNamespaceAware()` and `setValidating()`. This option sets various features implemented by the vendors to be configured in a parser. For example, setting a schema validation on/off would have the following syntax:

```
Factory.setFeature("http://www.acme.com/xml/schema", true);
```

The `getFeature()` method enables the application to verify whether a particular feature is set by returning a boolean.

Creating a Default Handler

JAXP 1.1 supports SAX 2.0, which promotes the extension from `Default Handler` rather than from `HandlerBase` like in SAX 1.0. The parser's parse method provides backward compatibility by exposing methods that take both `DefaultHandler` and `HandlerBase`. The following sample shows a sample handler that extends from the `DefaultHandler`. Because the SAX parser consists of a sequential reading of XML documentation, callback methods from the handler class will be invoked for every occurrence of a document, element, and character. The developer has full control over the action that can take place while the XML document is read. The following code lists the methods that need to be implemented when extending from `DefaultHandler`:

```
public class MySAXExampleHandler extends DefaultHandler {

    public MySAXExampleHandler() {
    }

    public void startDocument() throws SAXException {
    }

    public void endDocument() throws SAXException {
    }

    public void characters(char buf [],
                           int offset,
                           int len)
                           throws SAXException {
    }

    public void startElement(String namespaceURI,
                             String localName,
                             String rawName,
                             Attributes attrs)
                             throws SAXException {
    }

    public void endElement(String namespaceURI,
String localName,
String rawName)
                           throws SAXException {

    }
```

In this code, the following callback methods are called:

`startDocument()`. This method is called only once at the start of the XML document.

`endDocument()`. This method is called when the parser reaches the end of the XML document.

`characters()`. This method is called for character data residing inside an element.

`startElement()`. This method is called every time a new opening tag of an element is encountered (for example, `<element>`).

`endElement()`. This method is called when an element ends (for example, `</element>`).

In the SAX sample code section, the default handler will be implemented to read and output the XML to the terminal.

Using SAX Parser

Data can be parsed with SAX in many different ways. The JAXP-compliant parser is obtained from the factory class and is called `SAXParser`. This parser is an implementation that is provided by many vendors. Because it conforms to the specification, it can be easily exchanged. Obtaining the parser object is pretty straightforward. Developers must instantiate the factory class, and from the factory class they must instantiate a new parser class:

```
SAXParserFactory saxFactory = SAXParserFactory.newInstance();
javax.xml.parsers.SAXParser saxParser =
                                  saxFactory.newSAXParser();
```

While getting an instance of the factory and parser, there are a couple of things that can go wrong. The factory configuration can be wrong, and an exception will be thrown to indicate this problem. The exception is called `FactoryConfigurationException`, and it must be caught during the instantiation of the factory object. The second area where the application can fail is while the parser object is instantiated. In this case, the `Parser-ConfigurationException` must be caught while the factory instantiates a new parser. The following is a listing of more complete code:

```
try {
  SAXParserFactory saxFactory = SAXParserFactory.newInstance();
  javax.xml.parsers.SAXParser saxParser =
                                saxFactory.newSAXParser();
} catch (FactoryConfigurationError fce) {
    // handle exception here
} catch (ParserConfigurationException pce) {
    // handle exception here
}
```

The next step, once the parser is obtained, is to call the `parse()` method by passing the XML data to be parsed and a `Handler` class to handle the data that is being passed. The following are possibilities in which the parser can be used:

```
/** Passing file as a parameter */
saxParser.parse(new File(someFileString), mySAXExampleHanlder);

/** Passing a URI as a String parameter */
saxParser.parse("http://www.acme.com/xml/PurchaseOrder.xml",
                mySAXExampleHandler);

/** Parsing Input stream as a parameter */
saxParser.parse(someInputStream, mySAXExampleHanlder);
```

There are options with `HandlerBase` in the `parse()` method, but these are SAX 1.0 implementations. The current JAXP version implements those for backward compatibility, but you should use `DefaultHandler` when JAXP 1.1 is used.

Data also can be parsed with non-JAXP parsers such as the underlying `org.xml.sax.Parser`, but these approaches aren't vendor-neutral and will be omitted in this book. SAX 2.0 introduced the `XMLReader`, which is essentially a parser class that is wrapped by the `SAXParser` implementation. `XMLReader` is obtained by calling `getXMLReader()` from the `XMLParser`. Because low-level SAX parsing is not in the scope of this book, it will not be covered in more detail.

Reading and Writing XML

Reading and writing XML documents with SAX requires a parsing handler class (extended from `DefaultHandler`) to be implemented. This handler class provides logic coded in the callback methods defined by the programmer. The parser then processes the input stream and invokes the handler's callback methods to perform the actual work (see Figure 8.4). The parse method accepts various input parameters, including `java.io.InputStream`, `org.xml.sax.InputSource`, `java.io.File`, and `java.lang.String`. The second parameter is the implementation of the `DefaultHandler` class.

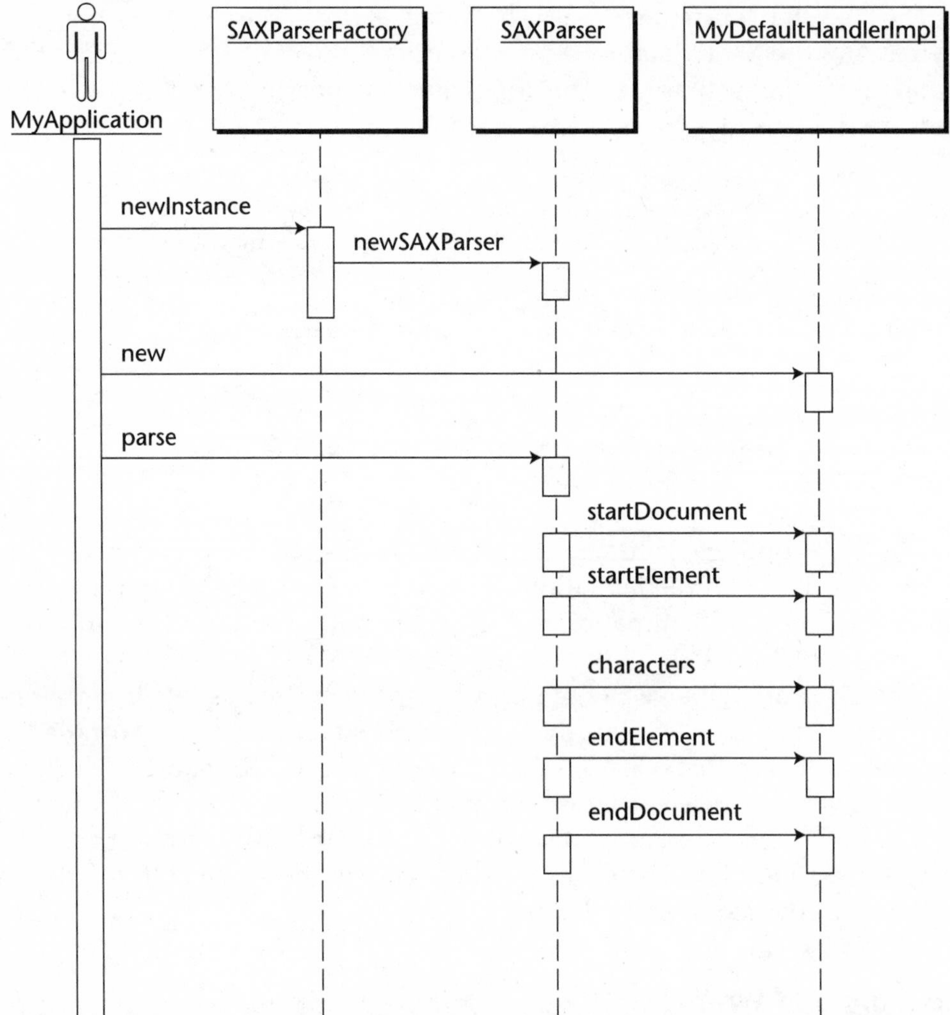

Figure 8.4 Sequence diagram showing JAXP parsing using SAX.

Sample SAX Source Code

The following is a sample `Handler` class and an implementation class, which uses the SAX approach to parse an XML file and to output the whole file into the console (system out).

Before running the code, compile the java files using the ANT script provided with the examples. To run, execute the following command:

```
java -classpath d:\xerces-1_4_4\xerces.jar;. -
Djavax.xml.parsers.SAXParserFactory=org.apache.xerces.jaxp.SAXParserFact
oryImpl jws.ch08.sax.MySAXExample
```

Listing 8.1 is a code listing for `MySAXExampleHandler.java`.

```
package jws.ch08.sax;

import org.xml.sax.*;
import org.xml.sax.helpers.*;
import org.xml.sax.ext.*;

public class MySAXExampleHandler extends DefaultHandler {
 public MySAXExampleHandler() {
 }

 public void startDocument() throws SAXException {
   System.out.println("START DOCUMENT");
   System.out.println("<?xml version='1.0'?>");
 }

 public void endDocument () throws SAXException {
   System.out.println("END DOCUMENT");
 }

 public void characters (char buf [],
                         int offset,
                         int len)
                         throws SAXException {
   String s = new String(buf, offset, len);
   System.out.println (s);
 }

 public void startElement(String namespaceURI,
                          String localName,
                          String rawName,
                          Attributes attrs)
                          throws SAXException {

   System.out.print("<"+localName);
   int length = attrs.getLength();
   for (int i=0; i < length; i++) {
    System.out.print(" "+attrs.getLocalName(i)+
                     "="+attrs.getValue(i));
   }
   System.out.println(">");
 }
```

Listing 8.1 `MySAXExampleHandler.` *(continues)*

```
  public void endElement(String namespaceURI,
                         String localName,
                         String rawName)
                         throws SAXException {
    System.out.println ("</"+localName+">");
  }
 }
```

Listing 8.1 `MySAXExampleHandler`. *(continued)*

Listing 8.2 shows a code listing for `MySAXExample.java`.

```
package jws.ch08.sax;

import javax.xml.parsers.*;

class MySAXExample {

 public MySAXExample () {
 }

 public static void main (String [] args) {
  try {
    SAXParserFactory factory =
                     SAXParserFactory.newInstance();
    SAXParser parser = factory.newSAXParser();
    parser.parse("PurchaseOrder.xml",
                 new MySAXExampleHandler()) ;
   } catch (FactoryConfigurationError fce) {
      System.out.println("FactoryConfigurationError occurred : "+fce);
   } catch (ParserConfigurationException pce) {
      System.out.println("ParserConfigurationException occurred :
                         "+pce);
   } catch (Exception e) {
      System.out.println("Exception occurred : "+e);
   }
  }
 }
```

Listing 8.2 `MySAXExample.java`.

Listing 8.3 is a partial result output of the classes implemented previously. The SAX implementation class reads the XML document and outputs the same XML in the console. When it starts the parsing and reaches the beginning of the XML document, it prints out *START DOCUMENT*. At the end of the document, it prints *END DOCUMENT.*

```
START DOCUMENT
<?xml version='1.0'?>
<PurchaseOrder>
<Header>
<PurchaseOrderNumber>
2123536673005
</PurchaseOrderNumber>
<Date>
02/22/2002
</Date>
<BuyerNumber>
0002232
</BuyerNumber>
<BuyerName>
John Doe
</BuyerName>
...

<LineItem type=SW>
<ProductNumber>
33333
</ProductNumber>
<Quantity>
145
</Quantity>
</LineItem>
</Order>
</PurchaseOrder>
END DOCUMENT
```

Listing 8.3 Sample SAX parsing output.

Processing XML with DOM

The Document Object Model (DOM) API was defined and is maintained by the W3C working group. The W3C definition (www.w3.org/TR/WD-DOM/) states that "the Document Object Model is a platform- and language-neutral interface that will allow programs and scripts to dynamically access and update the content, structure and style of documents."

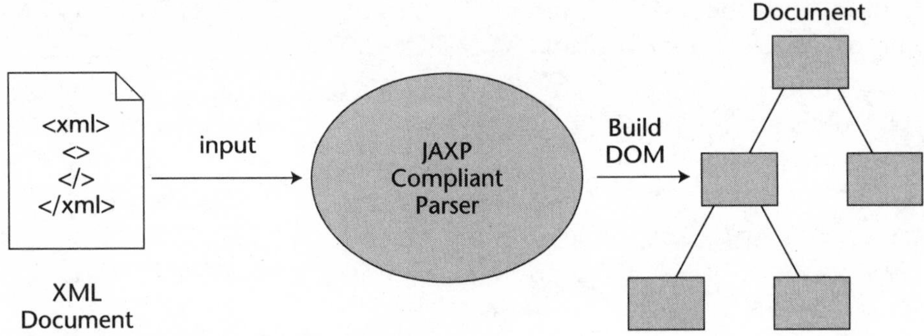

Figure 8.5 JAXP using DOM processing model.

The DOM processing model consists of reading the entire XML document into memory and building a tree representation of the structured data (see Figure 8.5). This process can require a substantial amount of memory when the XML document is large. By having the data in memory, DOM introduces the capability of manipulating the XML data by inserting, editing, or deleting tree elements. Unlike the SAX, it supports random access to any node in the tree. DOM supports validation by using DTD or a W3C XML Schema, but it does not enforce the use of validation.

The DOM processing model is more complete than the SAX alternative. It is considered more intensive on the resources, because it loads the entire XML document into memory. The basic steps for using DOM processing are as follows:

1. Instantiate a new `Builder` class. The Builder class is responsible for reading the XML data and transforming it into a tree representation.
2. Create the Document object once the data is transformed.
3. Use the Document object to access nodes representing elements from the XML document.

The XML source is read entirely into memory and is represented by the `Document` object. This enables the application to access any node randomly, which is something that SAX cannot do. One disadvantage of DOM is that it can be inefficient when large data is read into memory.

The following sections describe JAXP-specific SAX processing. These steps consist of the following:

- Getting a `Factory` and `Builder` class
- Setting namespaces, validation, and features

- Obtaining a Document object representing the XML element tree
- Traversing through the DOM node tree

Getting a Factory and Builder Class

DOM provides a document builder class for parsing XML data. The DOM model is slightly different from SAX, however, because in most implementations it does rely on the SAX model for reading the XML into memory. This is not something that is mandated by the JAXP 1.1 specification, but it makes sense to leverage to existing capabilities of the API to build the document object model. The process of processing XML is very similar to that of SAX with a few class name changes. The following is an example showing the steps for getting a Document (org.w3.dom.Document) object, which consists of an in-memory tree structure composed of nodes. The nodes are representations of XML elements and attributes read from the XML input document.

1. Obtain a new instance of the DOM Factory class by calling the DocumentBuilderFactory class's newInstance() static method:

   ```
   DocumentBuilderFactory factory=
                               DocumentBuilderFactory.newInstance();
   ```

2. Instantiate a new document builder class, once the factory is obtained, by calling the newDocumentBuilder() static method:

   ```
   DocumentBuilder builder =
                                DocumentBuilder.newDocumentBuilder();
   ```

   The document builder is used for loading the XML data into memory and for creating the Document object representation of the XML data.

3. Parse, using the Builder class, which contains a parse method that accepts an input stream representing the XML data:

   ```
           Document document =
   builder.parse(http://www.acme.com/warehouse/PurchaseOrder.xml);
   ```

The result of the parse method returns a Document object that is used for accessing nodes of the tree representing the XML data.

The configuration of the factory class is exactly the same as the SAX configuration, except for the class names. The following is an example of the java system property option for a DocumentBuilderFactory class:

```
-Djavax.xml.parsers.DocumenBuilderFactory=
org.apache.xerces.jaxp.DocumentBuilderFactoryImpl
```

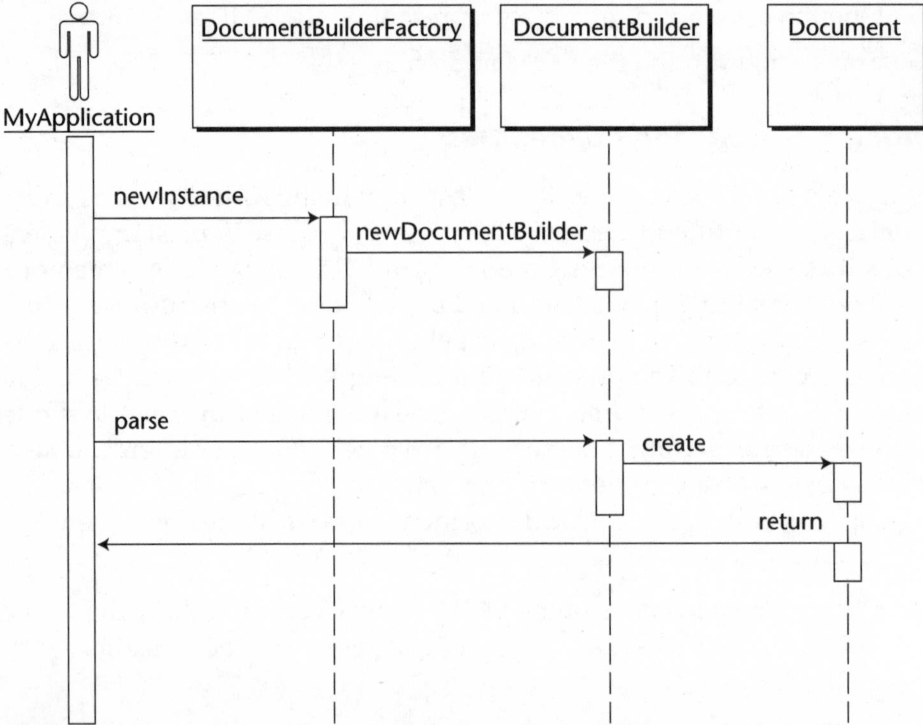

Figure 8.6 Sequence diagram showing JAXP parsing using DOM.

Figure 8.6 shows the different steps that are required in order to parse an XML document into a DOM structure. It uses the steps explained previously to produce a `Document` object that represents the parsed XML data.

Using Namespaces

A parser that is namespace-aware is a parser that is able to handle naming collisions. This is important when multiple documents are used with the same application.

To configure the parser to be namespace-aware, the factory class must be configured. To configure the factory class, perform the following steps:

```
/** Set to namespace aware parsers */
factory.setNameSpaceAware(true);
```

Once configured, the factory class will return a parser that is namespace-aware. The application can always perform checks by calling `isNamespaceAware()` on the `DocumentBuilder` class to verify whether namespaces are supported by the parser:

```
If (builder.isNamespaceAware()) {
  // Builder provides namespace support
} else {
  // Builder does not support namespace support
}
```

Using Validation

Validation is based on providing a validation document that imposes certain constraints on the XML data. Many standards provide validating capabilities, including DTDs and W3C XML Schemas.

To configure the parser to have validation turned on, the factory class must be configured to return validation-aware parsers only. To configure the factory class to do so, perform the following steps:

```
/** Set to validating parsers */
factory.setValidating(true);
```

Once configured, the factory class will return a parser that is validation capable. The application can always perform checks by calling `isValidating()` on the `DocumentBuilder` class to verify whether validation is supported by the parser:

```
If (builder.isValidating()) {
  // Builder is validation capable
} else {
  // Builder is not validation capable
}
```

If the factory class is configured to be namespace-aware or validating, it will try to locate a parser that supports these settings. If it cannot return a correct parser that supports the configurations, it will throw a `ParserConfigurationException`.

Using DocumentBuilder

The document builder is analogous to the `SAXParser` class and is used for parsing XML data. `DocumentBuilder` is used for building the `Document` object (`org.w3c.xml.Document`). This `Document` object is the object graph, which consists of nodes representing the elements and attributes contained in the parsed XML input. In order to obtain the `Document` object, the builder must parse the input XML by using one of the methods shown in Table 8.5.

Table 8.5 Methods for Parsing Input XML

METHOD	PURPOSE
builder.parse (java.io.File file)	Passing file Input as a parameter
builder.parse(java.lang.String uri)	Passing a string URI as a parameter
builder.parse(java.io.InputStream input)	Passing `InputStream` as a parameter
builder.parse(org.xml.sax.InputSource input)	Passing InputSource as a parameter

The following is a snippet of code for obtaining a `Document` object:

```
try {
  DocumentBuilderFactory factory =
                       DocumentBuilderFactory.newInstance();
  DocumentBuilder builder = factory.newDocumentBuilder();

  if (builder.isNamespaceAware()) {
     System.out.println("Builder is namespace aware");
  } else {
     System.out.println("Builder is not namespace aware");
  }

  if (builder.isValidating()) {
     System.out.println("Builder is validation capable");
  } else {
     System.out.println("Builder is not validation capable");
  }

  Document document =
          builder.parse(new File("PurchaseOrder.xml"));

} catch (ParserConfigurationException pce) {
    System.out.println("ParserConfigurationException occured:"+pce);
} catch (FactoryConfigurationError fce) {
    System.out.println("FactoryConfigurationError occured:"+fce);
} catch (FileNotFoundException fnfe) {
    System.out.println("FileNotFoundException occured:"+fnfe);
}
```

While getting an instance of the factory and builder objects, there is the possibility of the same exceptions being thrown as in SAX. The factory configuration can be wrong in this case—an exception is thrown to indicate this problem. The exception is called `FactoryConfigurationException`, and it is required that it be caught during the instantiation of the factory object. The second area where the application can fail is while instantiating the builder object. In this case, the `ParserConfigurationException` is required to be caught while the factory instantiates a new document builder. The following sections outline some of the important concepts when dealing with DOM trees. These sections cover some aspects that will help you understand the naming of each element or node within a tree.

Traversal of a DOM Tree

A DOM tree is composed of nodes. A node is the most essential object of the DOM tree; it is the representation of the XML data structure. When a parser processes the XML input, it produces a `Document` object. This `Document` object extends the node interface. The following are names of properties provided for each type of node in a Document tree. These properties help in the traversal of the tree.

`NodeName` The name of the XML element that this node represents.

`NodeValue` Text value that resides between the start and close element.

`NodeType` A code representing the type of object (for example, element, attribute, text, and so on . . .).

`ParentNode` The parent of the current node (if any).

`ChildNode` List of children of the current node.

`FirstChild` Current node's first child.

`LastChild` Current node's last child.

`PreviousSibling` The node immediately preceding the current node.

`NextSibling` The node immediately following the current node.

`Attributes` List of attributes of the current node (if any).

Sample Source Code

The following (MyDOMExample) is an implementation class that uses the DOM builder for reading the XML input into memory and then prints out the contents to the console.

Before running the code, compile the Java files using the ANT script provided with the examples. To run the code, execute the following command:

```
java -classpath D:\jaxp-1.1\crimson.jar;D:\jaxp-1.1\jaxp.jar;. -
Djavax.xml.parsers.DocumentBuilderFactory=org.apache.crimson.jaxp.Docume
ntBuilderFactoryImpl jws.ch08.dom.MyDOMExample
```

Listing 8.4 is a code listing for MyDOMExample.java.

```
package jws.ch08.dom;

import javax.xml.parsers.*;
import java.io.*;
import org.w3c.dom.*;

class MyDOMExample {

    private int indent = 0;
    private final String basicIndent = "  ";

    public MyDOMExample () {}

    private void printlnCommon(Node n) {
     String val = n.getNamespaceURI();
     if (val != null) {
      System.out.print(" uri=\"" + val + "\"");
     }

     val = n.getPrefix();
     if (val != null) {
      System.out.print(" pre=\"" + val + "\"");
     }

     val = n.getLocalName();
     if (val != null) {
      System.out.print(" local=\"" + val + "\"");
     }

     val = n.getNodeValue();
     if (val != null) {
      if (!val.trim().equals("")) {
       System.out.print(" nodeValue=\"" +
                        n.getNodeValue() + "\"");
```

Listing 8.4 MyDOMExample.java.

```
}
      }
      System.out.println();
    }

    private void outputIndentation() {
      for (int i = 0; i < indent; i++) {
        System.out.print(basicIndent);
      }
    }

    private void printDocTree(Node n) {
      outputIndentation();

      int type = n.getNodeType();
      // verify what type of node we are dealing with
      switch (type) {
        case Node.DOCUMENT_TYPE_NODE:
          printlnCommon(n);
          NamedNodeMap nodeMap =
                      ((DocumentType)n).getEntities();
          indent += 2;
          for (int i = 0; i < nodeMap.getLength(); i++) {
            Entity entity = (Entity)nodeMap.item(i);
            printDocTree(entity);
          }
          indent -= 2;
          break;
        case Node.ELEMENT_NODE:
          printlnCommon(n);
          // verify for more nodes
          NamedNodeMap atts = n.getAttributes();
          indent += 2;
          for (int i = 0; i < atts.getLength(); i++) {
            Node att = atts.item(i);
            printDocTree(att);
          }
          indent -= 2;
          break;
         default:
          printlnCommon(n);
          break;
      }

      // Print children if any
      indent++;
      for (Node child = n.getFirstChild(); child != null;
        child = child.getNextSibling()) {
        printDocTree(child);
```

Listing 8.4 MyDOMExample.java. *(continues)*

```
      }
      indent--;
    }

    public static void main (String [] args) {
      try {
        DocumentBuilderFactory factory =
                      DocumentBuilderFactory.newInstance();
        DocumentBuilder builder = factory.newDocumentBuilder();

        if (builder.isNamespaceAware()) {
          System.out.println("Builder is namespace aware");
        } else {
          System.out.println("Builder is not namespace aware");
        }

        if (builder.isValidating()) {
          System.out.println("Builder is validation capable");
        } else {
          System.out.println("Builder is not validation capable");
        }

        Document document =
                builder.parse(new File("PurchaseOrder.xml"));
        new MyDOMExample().printDocTree(document);
      } catch (ParserConfigurationException pce) {
          System.out.println("ParserConfigurationException occurred :
                              "+pce);
      } catch (FactoryConfigurationError fce) {
          System.out.println("FactoryConfigurationError occurred :
                              "+fce);
      } catch (FileNotFoundException fnfe) {
          System.out.println("FileNotFoundException occurred : "+fnfe);
      } catch (Exception e) {
          System.out.println("Exception occurred : "+e);
      }
    }
}
```

Listing 8.4 `MyDOMExample.java`. ***(continued)***

Listing 8.5 is a sample output for the DOM example. It prints the XML data file to the console and prints the type of node that is being processed.

```
local="PurchaseOrder"
 local="Header"
  local="PurchaseOrderNumber"
```

Listing 8.5 Sample DOM output.

```
   nodeValue="2123536673005"
  local="Date"
   nodeValue="02/22/2002"
  local="BuyerNumber"
   nodeValue="0002232"
  local="BuyerName"
   nodeValue="John Doe"
  local="BuyerAddress"
   local="Street"
    nodeValue="233 St-John Blvd"
   local="City"
    nodeValue="Boston"
   local="State"
    nodeValue="MA"
   local="Zip"
    nodeValue="03054"
   local="Country"
    nodeValue="USA"
  local="ShippingAddress"
   local="Street"
    nodeValue="233 St-John Blvd"
   local="City"
    nodeValue="Boston"
   local="State"
    nodeValue="MA"
   local="Zip"
    nodeValue="03054"
   local="Country"
    nodeValue="USA"
  local="PaymentInfo"
   local="Type"
    nodeValue="Visa"
   local="Number"
    nodeValue="0323235664664564"
   local="Expires"
    nodeValue="02/2004"
   local="Owner"
    nodeValue="John Doe"
 local="Order"
  local="LineItem"
   local="type" nodeValue="SW"
    local="ProductNumber"
     nodeValue="221112"
    local="Quantity"
     nodeValue="250"
  local="LineItem"
   local="type" nodeValue="HW"
    local="ProductNumber"
     nodeValue="343432"
```

Listing 8.5 Sample DOM output. *(continues)*

```
    local="Quantity"
     nodeValue="12"
  local="LineItem"
   local="type" nodeValue="HW"
    local="ProductNumber"
     nodeValue="210020"
    local="Quantity"
     nodeValue="145"
  local="LineItem"
   local="type" nodeValue="SW"
    local="ProductNumber"
     nodeValue="33333"
    local="Quantity"
     nodeValue="145"
```

Listing 8.5 Sample DOM output. *(continued)*

The following section is the new addition to JAXP 1.1. It deals with XML transformations and is referred to as Extensible Stylesheet Language Transformations (XSLT). Before we dive into this fascinating technology, we will look at an overview of the Extensible Stylesheet Language (XSL), which is the building block used for XSLT.

XSL Stylesheets: An Overview

A stylesheet is used to apply a set of rules to transform input in order to produce a desired output format. By nature, XML does not focus on formatting, instead it provides data to the business logic. Stylesheets such as cascading style sheets (CSSs) or Extensible Stylesheet Language (XSL) are used for defining the way input will be formatted to take on a new output form.

Cascading style sheets are mostly used for HTML formatting, where they define the fonts, margins, colors, and so on. CSSs do have a very limited capability when it comes to transformations. XSL is a standard that has a more sophisticated model and provides richer capabilities for XML transforming.

The XSL constructs comply with the XML specification and therefore must be well formed and valid before they are used. This means that the syntax of XSL is restricted to ensure that the processing constructs are correct.

Conceptually, XSL deals with tree structures of data, where the processing instructions indicate what elements should be processed. Templates are used to match the root and leaf elements of the XML document. A large amount of data can be processed at a time, thus making searching and processing really efficient. For example, we can have thousands of `<LineItem>` elements under the `<Order>` element. If you select the `<Order>` element and apply a template to it, then the `<LineItem>` elements also can be affected by the selection. This makes XSL processing really efficient, because a large amount of data is processed at one time. The traversal of the tree is achieved by using the XPath standard. This standard provides the foundation for XSLT processing, where expression patterns are defined using XPath.

XPath is a standard that provides the mechanism for accessing the elements of an XML document. XPath expressions are important in XSLT because they enable stylesheet instructions to flexibly identify the parts of the input document to be transformed.

The specification itself is complex. While including extensive coverage would be impossible in this section, enough material is presented for you to understand the fundamentals of XSLT processing. These fundamentals enable you to traverse an XML document and select the set of elements that need to be included or excluded from the processing.

When anyone is operating on an XML document, the most common approach is to use relative paths to the element or attribute that is being worked on. When selecting a node to use as a starting point in our traversal, we identify what is called an axis. An axis is the path of the tree that is being used for the transformation.

Figure 8.7 shows a path traversed during the transformation. It starts at the root node and traverses only the order containing `LineItems`.

In the following paragraphs, some examples of XPath expressions are given. Consider the following XML:

```
<PurchaseOder>
  <Header>
    <BuyderName>Robert</BuyerName>
  </Header>
  <Order>
    <LineItem type=SW>Item A</LineItem>
    <LineItem type=HW>Item B</LineItem>
    <LineItem type=SW>Item c</LineItem>
  </Order>
</PurchaseOrder>
```

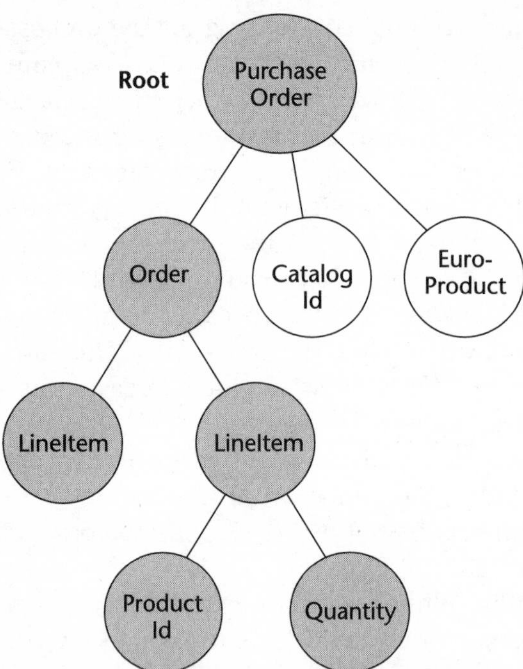

Figure 8.7 Sample axis path used for transformation.

The following XPath expressions are used to access elements and attributes of the previous XML expression:

```
<!-- Order is an element that can be accessed from the current element
(PurchaseOrder) -->
<xsl:value-of select="Order" />

<!-- Match the LineItem element that is nested in the Order element -->
<xsl:value-of select="Order/LineItem" />

<!-- Match LineItem using the absolute path starting from the root
element -->
<xsl:value-of select="/PurchaseOrder/Order/LineItem" />

<!-- Match the 'type' attribute of the current element -->
<xsl:value-of select="@type" />

<!-- Match the 'type' element of LineItem element while being at the
root element -->
<xsl:value-of select="/PurchaseOrder/Order/LineItem/@type" />
```

After evaluating XML using the XPath syntax, we get an element or a set of elements as a result. This also is referred to as a node or node set, because it represents the structured tree-like data. The resulting node set can be operated using additional XPath functionality. The following is the syntax that will help you understand the powerful yet complex mechanism for retrieving XML data for XML transformations. Because XSL is defined using XML, it must contain the following constructs in order to be considered valid:

- XML Declaration
- XSL root element: `<xsl:stylesheet> </xsl:stylesheet>`
- Declaration of used namespaces

XML Declaration

An XSL stylesheet uses the following standard XML declaration:

```
<?xml version="1.0" ?>
```

XSL Root Element

Because XSL stylesheets are defined in XML, they must contain a root element. This root element is defined by the following:

```
<xsl:stylesheet ...>
...
</xsl:stylesheet>
```

XSL Namespaces

The root element defines the namespaces used within the template and it also provides the version number, which is required. For example,

```
<xsl:stylesheet xmlns:xsl="http://www.w3.org/2002/XSL/Transform"
version="1.0">

</xsl:stylesheet>
```

The namespace www.we.org/2002/XSL/Transform recognizes XSL-specific elements. A namespace used for any transformation-related work is prefixed with "`xsl:`". For example,

```
<xsl:template match="PurchaseOrder" />
...
</xsl:template>
```

A document may refer to a stylesheet using the following processing instruction:

```
<?xml-stylesheet type="text/xsl" href="order.xsl"?>
```

XSL Syntax

Many operations can be used to process the data in XML, including locating a particular element, iterating through a document, the conditional processing of elements, sorting, and numbering. In the following text, we look closely at the following topics:

- Templates used for locating parts of a document
- Conditional processing, which is done only when certain criteria are examined
- Looping used for iterating through results
- Sorting used for displaying the output in some logical order

Templates

Templates are mostly used for locating one or more elements of an XML document. Using a template consists of using various rules that have specific requirements or conditions, which also are referred to as patterns. The template matching is defined by specific XPath expressions. To locate a particular element within a document, the Match attribute is used with an XPath expression that will match to zero or more elements in the document. The following is an example that will match the root element (`PurchaseOrder`) of our sample XML document:

```
<xsl:template match="PurchaseOrder">
 /* The content in this block is written to the output.
</xsl:template>
```

In this example, we matched the `PurchaseOrder` element, which is the first element in our path. At this stage of processing, we have matched the portion of the document that we would like to process, and the template has that portion of the XML hierarchy loaded into its memory. This hierarchy is an immutable structure that is used for XSL processing. This means that if you select an element, the process simply selects it but does not remove it. Also, if some elements of the hierarchy should become excluded, there must be a set of templates that tell the processor to ignore them. The most basic way to achieve access to elements is to use relative path expressions. Therefore, in relation to where we stand within the document, we can access various sections by simply specifying the paths to them. For instance, having

```
<xsl:template match="Order\LineItem">
```

as the first matching entry of the template would not take us there, because according to the root, the relative path to `LineItem` would be `PurchaseOrder\Order\LineItem`.

The apply-templates construct tells the processor to match the elements defined in the select attribute or if nothing is specified to match any element relative to the current path with any template defined within the XSL stylesheet:

```
/* apply pattern on selected nodes, the default node Is *all* */
<xsl:apply-templates select="node set expression" ... />
```

If a particular element must be fetched, it sometimes may be overkill to create a template for it. To retrieve particular elements, the `xsl:value-of` construct is used. For instance, getting the buyer ID number from the purchase order would look like the following:

```
<xsl:template match="PurchaseOrder\Header">
   Buyer Number Is : <xsl:value-of select="BuyerNumber"/>
</xsl:template>
```

In the case where we want to ignore an element, a simple solution is to create a template for that element with no action. This is a case where some information needs to be ignored, for instance, if we don't want to transform sensitive information, such as a credit card number or personal information of the buyer. This would result in the following template:

```
<xsl:template match="PurchaseOrder\Header\PaymentInfo">
```

Of course, this isn't the only solution for this sort of processing. We also could use conditional processing, which will be covered in the following section.

An example of conditional processing would look like the following:

```
<xsl:template math="PurchaseOder">
  <H1><xsl:apply-templates select="header"/></h1>
</xsl:template>

<xsl:template match="PurchaseOrder\Header\PaymentInfo">
```

Apart from locating or matching elements in a document, we can perform a lot of other tasks by applying certain rules, which will traverse the XML tree and apply the expected changes under certain conditions.

Conditional Processing

We can have conditional constructs that will apply to an XML document under certain conditions. A good example is one used in the previous section where personal information should not be transformed. In order to ignore the particular elements, we constructed an empty template. While it was a working solution, this example is not as clean as the one proposed in this section. Taking the same example, let's build a condition that will not select the `"PurchaseOrder\Header\PaymentInfo"` element and anything within it. This is accomplished by using the `not( )` node function provided by XPath. The following is the syntax when using the `not()` function:

```
<xsl:apply-templates select="*[not(some expression)]" />
```

Our example would look like the following:

```
<xsl:template match="PurchaseOrder\Header">
     <xsl:apply-templates select="*[not(self:Paymentinfo)]" />
</xsl:template>
```

The self-parameter in the expression indicates what the frame of reference is. This lets the processor know that anything after the self-element is a child of the element.

Other conditional constructs can evaluate expressions based on expressions similar to if-then statements. One of these constructs is the `xsl:if` construct, which returns nodes that conform (evaluate to TRUE) to the expression. For example,

```
/* If expression is TRUE evaluate the template */
<xsl:if test="expression"> ... </...>
```

The test attribute contains the pattern that is evaluated to determine whether the condition is processed or not. In our example, we will separate the hardware (HW) and software (SW) type items:

```
<xsl:template math="PurchaseOrder\Order\LineItem">
   <xsl:if test="@type='SW'">
      Software Product # :<xsl:value-of select="ProductNumber">
   </xsl:if>
</xsl:template>
```

The @ sign indicates that we are referring to an attribute rather than an element, and the single quotes around the SW string refers us to a static string. Another way to process conditional code is to use the `xsl:choose` construct. This construct behaves as an if-then-else type statement, where `<xsl:when ...>` evaluates the conditions, and if those fail then it executes `<xsl:otherwise>`. The `<xsl:when ...>` statement can occur many times within the `xsl:choose` construct, as shown as follows:

```
/* Apply a template to the conditions that evaluate to TRUE */
<xsl:choose>
     <xsl:when test="expression"> ...</xsl:when>
     [<xsl:when test="expression"> ...</xsl:when>]
     ...
     <xsl:otherwise> ...</xsl:otherwise>
</xsl:choose>
```

The following code is an example of an XSL stylesheet. It takes in the `PurchaseOrder xml` file as input and sorts the `LineItems` according to their type: hardware, software, or unknown in the case of an unknown type:

```
<xsl:template math="PurchaseOrder\Order\LineItem">
 <xsl:choose>
   <xsl:when test="@type='SW'">
     Software Product # :<xsl:value-of select="ProductNumber">
   </xsl:when>
   <xsl:when test="@type='HW'">
    Hardware Product # :<xsl:value-of select="ProductNumber">
   </xsl:when>
   <xsl:otherwise>
    Unknown Product # :<xsl:value-of select="ProductNumber">
   </xsl:otherwise>
  </xsl:choose>
</xsl:template>
```

Looping

Sometimes looping is needed when traversing a tree. XSL provides these constructs to facilitate the definition of repeating occurrences. The `xsl:for-each` construct is one of the constructs used for looping. In our example, we will iterate over the order and print out all of the product numbers:

```
<xsl:template math="PurchaseOrder\Order">
  <xsl:for-each select="LineItem">
```

```
    Product # :<xsl:value-of select="ProductNumber">
  </xsl:for-each>
</xsl:template>
```

Although this can be produced with templates, it is much clearer to use the `for-loop` construct.

Sorting

Sorting may be essential when formatting output based on a certain criteria, such as ascending or descending numbers or names. When sorting `<xsl:apply-templates ...>`, `<xsl:for-each ...>` constructs are used when evaluating the XML input. The following is a sorting construct that is used for sorting elements retrieved by templates (`xsl:apply-templates` or `xsl:for-each`) in its body:

```
<xsl:sort select="expression" ..../>
```

The constructs have additional parameters that can be provided:

- `order="ascending|descending"`
- `data-type="text|number"`
- `case-order="upper-first|lower-first"`
- `lang="..."`

The following example takes the product number and sorts it in ascending order based on the `ProductNumber`:

```
<xsl:template math="PurchaseOrder\Order">
  <xsl:apply-template select="LineItem">
    Product # : <xsl:sort select="ProductNumber"/>
  </xsl:apply-template>
</xsl:template>
```

The following section will use some of the important constructs discussed in this section and apply transformation to an XML document.

Transforming with XSLT

Extensible Stylesheet Language Transformation (XSLT) is an XML processing standard used with XSL for XML-based document transformation. This is the process by which XSL templates are applied to XML documents in order to create new documents in desired formats (for example, XML, HTML, PDF, and WML). XSL provides the syntax and semantics for specifying formatting, and XSLT is the processor that performs the formatting task.

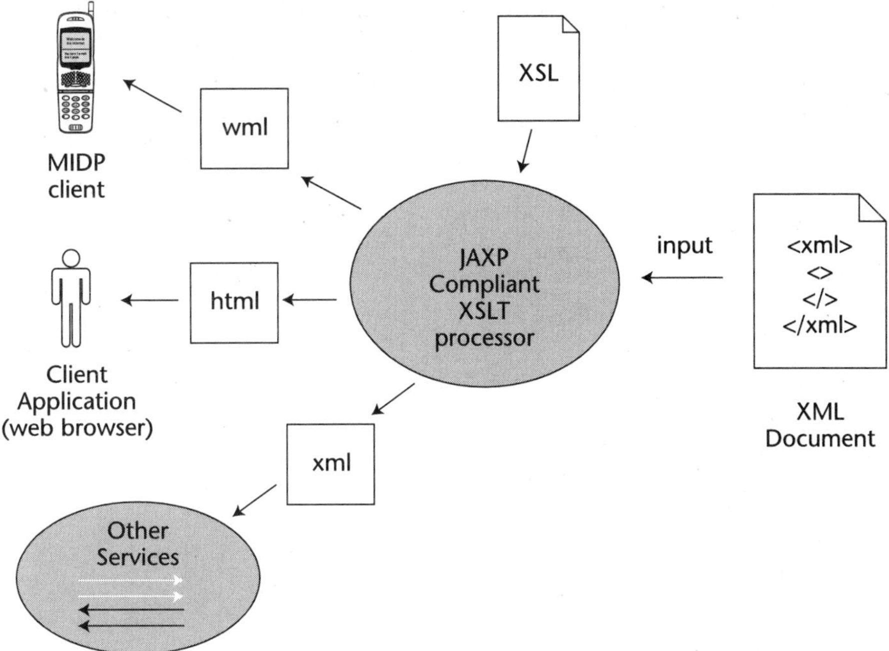

Figure 8.8 Use of JAXP for XSLT transformation.

XSLT is often used for the purpose of generating various output formats for an application that enables access to heterogeneous client types (such as Web browsers, cell phones, and Java applications). It also is used to format one XML representation to another—this is typical in a B2B-type environment. Figure 8.8 depicts a scenario in which an application hosts a component that is able to generate various types of output based on the client type.

XSLT is supported in JAXP 1.1. This was achieved by incorporating Transformations for XML (TRaX) to provide a vendor-neutral solution for XML transformations. The various implementations of XSL processors drastically changed from one vendor to the next and a need for a standard solution was inevitable. The JAXP specification supports most of the XML transformations and is discussed in the next sections.

Processing Model

The processing model of XSLT consists of various rules defined by templates. A rule is defined as a combination of a template and pattern. The output is obtained by passing an input XML source (for example, InputStream, InputSource, File, or URL) to the processor. A node is processed by locating a template rule that contains the matching pattern. Once located, the template is instantiated and a result is created. This process continues until traversed recursively through the data. When many nodes are processed, the end result is known as the node list, which is a concatenation of all the node results. The following is a snippet of a template rule definition in an XSL stylesheet file:

```
<xsl:template match="some pattern">
     template
</xsl:template>
```

Patterns are sets of XPath expressions (location paths) that are used for evaluating node sets. A node matches a defined pattern when the node is a result from an evaluation of the expression, with respect to some context. A node is an additional attribute to the `xsl:template` construct, which enables an element to be processed many times in different ways.

The steps required for transformation follow these logical steps:

1. Obtain a transformation factory class used for instantiating a transformer class. This step is not much different from the previous SAX or DOM factory classes.
2. Once the factory class is instantiated, create a new transformer class by passing it the stylesheet for formatting the output.
3. Use the transformer class for transforming the data by specifying the XML input source and the output source where the results will be sent.

The XSL stylesheet is defined in a separate file with `extension *.xsl`. This stylesheet is passed when the transformer class is instantiated. Once the transformer class is obtained, the transformation can take place. We input the input source and output source when calling the transform method.

The following sections describe the JAXP-specific XSLT processing steps. These steps consist of the following:

- Getting a factory and transformer class
- Transforming the XML

Getting the Factory and Transformer Class

Working with XSLT is similar to working with the parsers. The class responsible for performing the transformation is called the `Transform` class, and it can only be obtained through a factory class (see Figure 8.9). The factory class is called `TransformerFactory` and is instantiated by calling its static method newInstance(). Once the factory class is instantiated, the newTransformer() method is called to get an instance of the transformer. The newTransformer() method takes a StreamSource as a parameter, which is the XSL template that will be applied to the XML input.

The steps for instantiating the class are as follows:

1. As with SAX and DOM, use the factory class for instantiating a transformer implementation class:

```
TransformerFactory factory =
                     TransformerFactory.newInstance();
```

2. Use the transformer class for applying the stylesheet to the input XML data. When getting a new instance, the stylesheet is passed as a parameter to the newTransformer() method:

```
Transformer transformer =
     factory.newTransformer(new StreamSource("order.xsl"));
```

3. The transformer then calls the transform method to invoke the transformation process. The parameters required in the transform method are input stream and output result:

```
transformer.transform(new StreamSource("PurchaseOrder.xml"),
                         new StreamResult(System.out));
```

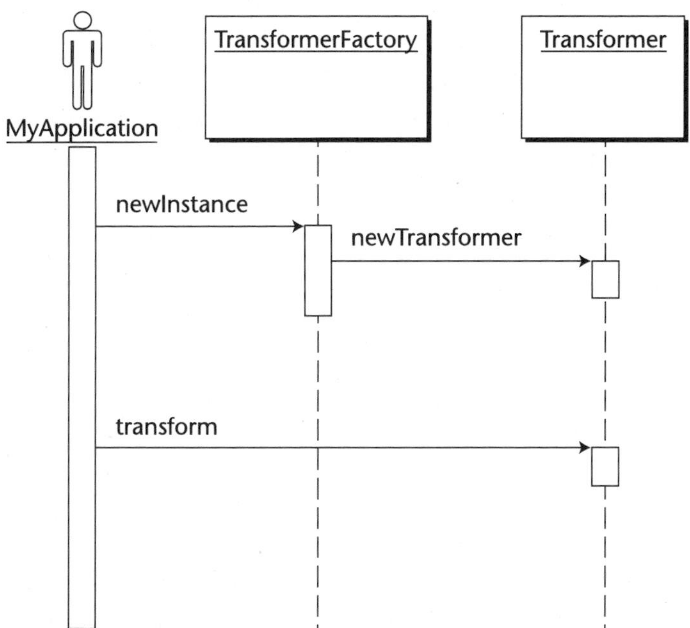

Figure 8.9 Sequence diagram showing a JAXP transformation with XSLT.

The factory implementation class can be supplied as a Java system property using the following syntax:

```
javax.xml.transform.TransformerFactory=org.apache.xalan.processor
.TransformerFactoryImpl
```

Many options can be set on the factory class that affect the instance of the transformer. Some of these options are vendor-specific, such as attributes that can be passed to the transformer. Another more JAXP-related option would be the setting for the `javax.xml.transform.ErrorListener` interface for catching transformation-related errors. The `ErrorListener` interface defines a list of methods:

```
public void warning (TransformerException exception)
                     throws TransformerException;
public void error (TransformerException exception)
                   throws TransformerException;
public void fatalError (TransformerException exception)
                        throws TransformerException;
```

To use the `ErrorListener` interface, an implementation must be provided that implements the various error levels. This implementation of `ErrorListener` then is passed to the factory with a setter method called `setErrorListener()`:

```
factory.setErrorListener(new MyErrorListener());
```

Another useful option is to set the URI to handle URIs found in XML in order for them to be properly handled (for example, constructs such as `xsl:import` or `xsl:output`). The `URIResolver` interface defines one method:

```
public Source resolve (String href, String base) throws
TransformerException;
```

The implementation of the `URIResolver` interface can be set on the factory class with a method called `setURIResolver()`.

Transforming XML

Transforming XML consists of creating a new transformer instance by passing it an XSL template. The template defines the logic that needs to be applied to the XML input. In our example, a purchase order (`PurchaseOrder.xml`) is sent to the ACME Web Service retailer who processes the purchase order to determine what items were ordered. Based on the type of item ordered, the retailer creates new orders (`SWOrder.xml` and `HWOrder.xml`) that are sent to the appropriate warehouse. The following is a snippet of the code that instantiates the transformer:

```
TransformerFactory factory = TransformerFactory.newInstance();
factory.setErrorListener(new MyErrorListener());
Transformer transformer =
        factory.newTransformer(new StreamSource("order.xsl"));
```

The instantiation of a new transformer takes in a source stream representing the stylesheet for transforming XML. The source stream is the mechanism responsible for locating the stylesheet. The specification provides the implementation of the following classes as input sources:

`javax.xml.transform.stream.StreamSource`. Reads the input from I/O devices. The constructor accepts `InputStream`, `Reader`, and `String`.

`javax.xml.transform.dom.DOMSource`. Reads the input from a DOM tree (`org.w3c.dom.Node`).

`javax.xml.transform.sax.SAXSource`. Reads the input from SAX input source events (`org.xml.sax.InputSource` or `org.xml.sax.XMLReader`).

In the case where multiple stylesheets are applied to a single or multiple XML input, multiple transformers need to be instantiated for each stylesheet. Different types can be provided as input streams, such as URL, XML streams, DOM trees, SAX events, or custom data types. As for the output, it contains just as many possibilities with various combinations. The developer does not have to provide the same type of output as the input. It can be a variety of combinations that make this process very flexible and extensible. The following are some of the output classes provided by the specification:

`javax.xml.transform.stream.StreamResult`. Writes to an I/O device. The writer, `OutputStream`, is one of the available parameters.

`javax.xml.transform.dom.DOMResult`. Writes to a `Document` object (`org.w3c.dom.Document`).

`javax.xml.transform.sax.SAXResult`. Writes using `ContentHandler` callback methods.

XSLT Sample Code

Our sample scenario will use the PurchaseOrder XML input and will produce two resulting outputs. The resulting outputs will be orders that are sent to two different warehouses. Each warehouse specializes in different types of products: software or hardware. The idea behind this service is to provide a transformation capability to take the original order and split it into two different orders, depending upon the product's type. We will generate software and hardware XML orders that will be sent to the respective warehouse. Listing 8.6 is the PurchaseOrder.xml file.

```
<?xml version="1.0"?>
<PurchaseOrder>
  <Header>
    <PurchaseOrderNumber>2123536673005</PurchaseOrderNumber>
    <Date>02/22/2002</Date>
    <BuyerNumber>0002232</BuyerNumber>
  </Header>
  <!-- type indicates whether the item is a Software or Hardware
       product -->
  <Order>
    <LineItem type='SW'>
      <ProductNumber>221112</ProductNumber>
      <Quantity>250</Quantity>
    </LineItem>
    <LineItem type='HW'>
      <ProductNumber>343432</ProductNumber>
      <Quantity>12</Quantity>
    </LineItem>
    <LineItem type='HW'>
      <ProductNumber>210020</ProductNumber>
      <Quantity>145</Quantity>
    </LineItem>
    <LineItem type='SW'>
      <ProductNumber>33333</ProductNumber>
      <Quantity>145</Quantity>
    </LineItem>
  </Order>
</PurchaseOrder>
```

Listing 8.6 PurchaseOrder.xml.

The following are the two XSL stylesheets for the software and hardware orders. They take in the PurchaseOrder and transform it to Software-Order.xml and HardwareOrder.xml. In order to produce two types of outputs, the sample client uses two different stylesheets for producing two different outputs.

Listing 8.7 is the `hw-order.xsl` stylesheet.

```
<?xml version="1.0"?>
<xsl:stylesheet xmlns:xsl="http://www.w3.org/1999/XSL/Transform"
version="1.0">
<xsl:output method="xml" indent="no"/>
 <!-- Header is needed in all warehouses -->
 <xsl:template match="PurchaseOrder">
  <HardwareOrder>
    <xsl:apply-templates select="*"/>
  </HardwareOrder>
 </xsl:template>
 <xsl:template match="Header">
  <ShippingInfo>
    <xsl:apply-templates select="ShippingAddress"/>
  </ShippingInfo>
 </xsl:template>

 <xsl:template match="Order">
  <OrderInfo>
    <xsl:apply-templates select="*" />
  </OrderInfo>
 </xsl:template>

<!-- Software and Hardware orders go to different warehouse locations. -
->
 <xsl:template match="LineItem">
  <xsl:if test="@type='HW'">
    <ProductNo>
      <xsl:value-of select="ProductNumber"/>
    </ProductNo>
    <ProductQty>
      <xsl:value-of select="Quantity"/>
    </ProductQty>
  </xsl:if>
 </xsl:template>
</xsl:stylesheet>
```

Listing 8.7 `hw-order.xsl` stylesheet.

Listing 8.8 shows the `sw-order.xsl` stylesheet.

```
<?xml version="1.0"?>
<xsl:stylesheet xmlns:xsl="http://www.w3.org/1999/XSL/Transform"
version="1.0">
 <xsl:output method="xml" indent="no"/>
```

Listing 8.8 sw-order.xsl. *(continues)*

```
<!-- Header is needed in all warehouses -->
<xsl:template match="PurchaseOrder">
  <SoftwareOrder>
    <xsl:apply-templates select="*"/>
  </SoftwareOrder>
</xsl:template>
<xsl:template match="Header">
  <ShippingInfo>
    <xsl:apply-templates select="ShippingAddress"/>
  </ShippingInfo>
</xsl:template>
<xsl:template match="Order">
  <OrderInfo>
    <xsl:apply-templates select="*" />
  </OrderInfo>
</xsl:template>
<!-- Software and Hardware orders go to different warehouse locations. -
->
<xsl:template match="LineItem">
  <xsl:if test="@type='SW'">
    <ProductNo>
      <xsl:value-of select="ProductNumber"/>
    </ProductNo>
    <ProductQty>
      <xsl:value-of select="Quantity"/>
    </ProductQty>
  </xsl:if>
</xsl:template>
</xsl:stylesheet>
```

Listing 8.8 `sw-order.xsl`. *(continued)*

Listing 8.9 is a sample test class `MyXSLTExample.java` that performs the transformation and generates the output to the console for demonstration.

```
package jws.ch08.xslt;

import javax.xml.parsers.*;

import org.w3c.dom.*;
import org.xml.sax.*;
import java.io.*;
import javax.xml.transform.*;
import javax.xml.transform.stream.*;
```

Listing 8.9 `MyXSLTExample.java`.

```
import javax.xml.transform.dom.*;

class MyXSLTExample {

 public MyXSLTExample () {}
 public static void main (String [] args) {

  System.out.println("Transforming .... ");
  try {
   TransformerFactory tFactory = TransformerFactory.newInstance();
   tFactory.setErrorListener(new MyErrorListener());
   if (tFactory.getFeature(DOMSource.FEATURE) &&
       tFactory.getFeature(DOMResult.FEATURE)) {
    //Instantiate a DocumentBuilderFactory.
    DocumentBuilderFactory dFactory =
                           DocumentBuilderFactory.newInstance();
    // And setNamespaceAware, which is required when parsing xsl files
    dFactory.setNamespaceAware(true);
    //Use the DocumentBuilderFactory to create a DocumentBuilder.
    DocumentBuilder dBuilder = dFactory.newDocumentBuilder();
    //Use the DocumentBuilder to parse the Software XSL stylesheet.
    Document xslSWDoc = dBuilder.parse("sw-order.xsl");
    //Use the DocumentBuilder to parse the Hardware XSL stylesheet.
    Document xslHWDoc = dBuilder.parse("hw-order.xsl");
    // Use the DOM Document to define a DOMSource object.
    DOMSource xslDomSWSource = new DOMSource(xslSWDoc);
    // Use the DOM Document to define a DOMSource object.
    DOMSource xslDomHWSource = new DOMSource(xslHWDoc);
    // Set the systemId: note this is actually a URL, not a local
    // filename
    xslDomSWSource.setSystemId("sw-order.xsl");
    // Set the systemId: note this is actually a URL, not a local
    // filename
    xslDomHWSource.setSystemId("hw-order.xsl");

    // Process the stylesheet DOMSource and generate a Transformer.
    Transformer swTransformer =
                tFactory.newTransformer(xslDomSWSource);

    // Process the stylesheet DOMSource and generate a Transformer.
    Transformer hwTransformer =
                tFactory.newTransformer(xslDomHWSource);

    //Use the DocumentBuilder to parse the XML input.
    Document xmlDoc = dBuilder.parse("PurchaseOrder.xml");

    // Use the DOM Document to define a DOMSource object.
    DOMSource xmlDomSource = new DOMSource(xmlDoc);
```

Listing 8.9 MyXSLTExample.java. *(continues)*

```
    // Set the base URI for the DOMSource so any relative URIs it
    // contains can be resolved.
    xmlDomSource.setSystemId("PurchaseOrder.xml");

    // write to System.out
    System.out.println("\n--- Software Order ---\n");
    swTransformer.transform(xmlDomSource,
                            new StreamResult(System.out));
    System.out.println("\n--- Hardware Order ---\n");
    hwTransformer.transform(xmlDomSource,
                            new StreamResult(System.out));
   } else {
      System.out.println("Transformer does not support DOM source and
result!");
   }
  } catch (TransformerConfigurationException tce) {
     System.out.println("TransformerConfigurationException occurred :
"+tce);
  } catch (ParserConfigurationException pce) {
     System.out.println("ParserConfigurationexception occurred : "+pce);
  } catch (TransformerException te) {
     System.out.println("TransformerException occurred : "+te);
  } catch (SAXException se) {
     System.out.println("SAXException occurred : "+se);
  } catch (IOException ioe) {
     System.out.println("IOException occurred : "+ioe);
  }
 }
}
```

Listing 8.9 `MyXSLTExample.java`. ***(continued)***

The output of the XSLT transformation sample is shown in Listing 8.10. It uses two distrinct XSL stylesheets, `sw-order.xsl` and `hw-order.xsl`, to separate the software and hardware orders, respectively. The output shows a shipping address in both the orders and the `Line Items`.

```
------------- Software Order ----------------

<?xml version="1.0" encoding="UTF-8"?>
<SoftwareOrder>
```

Listing 8.10 Output of an XSLT transformation sample.

```
  <ShippingInfo>
          233 St-John Blvd
          Boston

          MA
          03054
          USA
  </ShippingInfo>
  <OrderInfo>
    <ProductNo>221112</ProductNo>
    <ProductQty>250</ProductQty>
    <ProductNo>33333</ProductNo>
    <ProductQty>145</ProductQty>
  </OrderInfo>
</SoftwareOrder>


-------------- Hardware Order -----------------
<?xml version="1.0" encoding="UTF-8"?>
<HardwareOrder>
  <ShippingInfo>
          233 St-John Blvd
          Boston
          MA
          03054
          USA
  </ShippingInfo>
  <OrderInfo>
    <ProductNo>343432</ProductNo>
    <ProductQty>12</ProductQty>
    <ProductNo>210020</ProductNo>
    <ProductQty>145</ProductQty>
  </OrderInfo>
</HardwareOrder>
```

Listing 8.10 Output of an XSLT transformation sample. *(continued)*

Threading

The JAXP specification does not mandate that the processor implementations provide thread safety. The common practice is to instantiate one processor instance per thread to avoid any synchronization issues. In the case where one instance is used by many threads, the application developer must provide the correct synchronized blocks so that the execution does not corrupt the data or produce unexpected results.

Java Architecture for XML Binding (JAXB)

The XML binding technology provides application developers with a way to generate Java objects based on XML definitions and XML definitions based on Java objects. The Java Architecture for XML Binding (JAXB), formerly known as JCP project Adelard, is a high-level specification that defines an abstraction for binding semantics via classes and interfaces. XML data binding provides a way for applications to work with objects rather than complex data trees.

Converting XML to Java can be achieved by using parsing (with JAXP) and then constructing Java objects. The idea behind using a standard such as JAXB is to provide ease of use and performance enhancement. When developers are faced with the design and implementation of such solutions, in many cases they find themselves locked to their homegrown solutions with unnecessary complexities. This is potentially a maintenance nightmare where applications do not scale very well due to poor design decisions. A binding specification aims at taking all that away from the developer by implementing the various techniques in the parser where the classes are generated. It provides a standardized way to validate documents by defining the XML schema and data type mapping definitions to enforce correctness.

The current reference implementation of the JAXB 1.0 specification from Sun is limited to using DTDs as the schema language. This is a limitation that has a significant impact on today's industry requirements especially for Web services. This limitation is solved by XML schema support in the next version of JAXB. In this chapter, we will take a look at a JAXB-like Java/XML data binding framework named CASTOR. CASTOR is an open source project from Exolab (castor.exolab.org). It provides a Java/XML data binding framework with W3C XML schema support. CASTOR is available for download from the Exolab Web site at http://castor.exolab.org/.

XML binding using CASTOR is done with the following steps:

1. Create a W3C XML schema defining the data structure, data types, and semantics of the XML data instance used in the application. In a Java class, it corresponds to a class variable or a property using accessor methods.
2. Using a CASTOR source code generator, transform the XML Schema to bind Java objects.

3. Using the CASTOR implementation enables the binding Java objects to be transformed into XML instances (marshalling), and the XML instances then can be transformed into binding Java objects (unmarshalling) dynamically.

The binding runtime APIs then are used for converting XML data into Java objects and vice versa (see Figure 8.10). The Java objects then can be operated on as regular Java objects; creating and appending objects or deleting them is performed using standard Java semantics. This makes the work transparent of the XML hierarchy and much easier to work with.

- CASTOR provides a code generator, `org.exolab.castor.builder.SourceGenerator`, for generating Java binding objects from an XML Schema.
- CASTOR provides a full-fledged Java object and XML attribute mapping, which enables you to cast the data in the XML format to the proper Java type and vice-versa. The complete list of supported Java object types and XML Schema attributes are available at http://castor.exolab.org/xml-mapping.html.

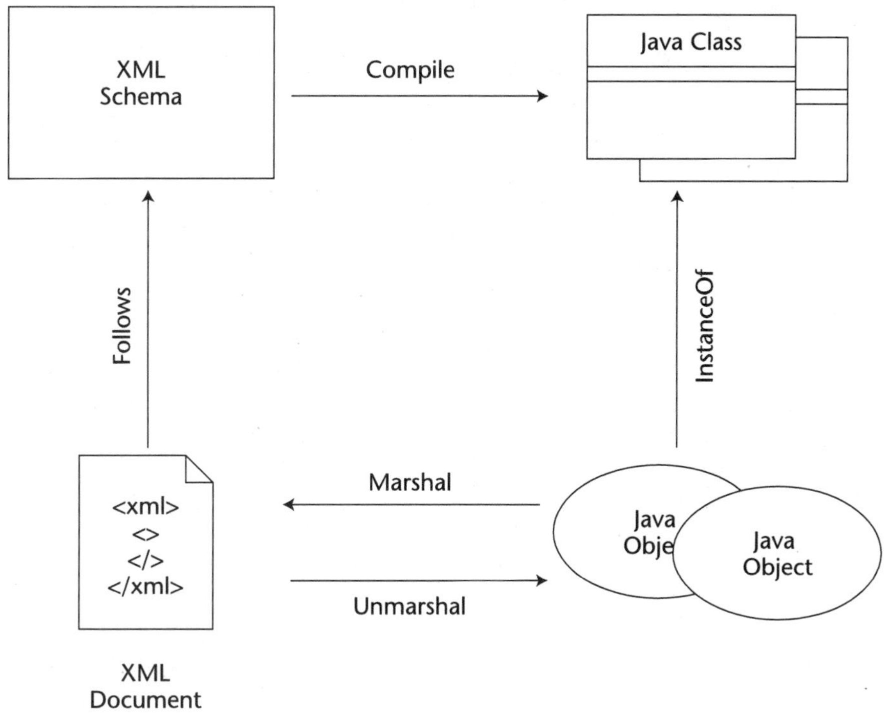

Figure 8.10 XML binding life cycle.

The following section will walk you through an example taking a modified version of our `PurchaseOrder.xml` and using binding techniques to generate domain objects representing data stored in the XML input. The data-binding runtime used for this will be the CASTOR implementation, which provides support for an XML Schema unlike a JAXB reference implementation, which is limited to DTDs. Due to this limitation (as of this book's writing), the specification is going through a major revision. It will soon provide a much richer feature set aligned more with the current needs.

Data Binding Generation

In order to create Java classes, an XML data schema must be created. For our example, we will use the following Purchase Order XML data file (see Listing 8.11) and generate a validation W3C XML Schema.

```
<?xml version="1.0"?>
<PurchaseOrder>
  <Header>
   <PurchaseOrderNumber>2123536673005</PurchaseOrderNumber>
   <Date>02/22/2002</Date>
   <BuyerNumber>0002232</BuyerNumber>
   <BuyerName>John Doe</BuyerName>
   <BuyerAddress>
     <Street>233 St-John Blvd</Street>
     <City>Boston</City>
     <State>MA</State>
     <Zip>03054</Zip>
     <Country>USA</Country>
   </BuyerAddress>
   <ShippingAddress>
     <Street>233 St-John Blvd</Street>
     <City>Boston</City>
     <State>MA</State>
     <Zip>03054</Zip>
     <Country>USA</Country>
   </ShippingAddress>
```

Listing 8.11 `PurchaseOrder.xml` file.

```
    <PaymentInfo>
     <Type>Visa</Type>
     <Number>0323235664664564</Number>
     <Expires>02/2004</Expires>
     <Owner>John Doe</Owner>
    </PaymentInfo>
   </Header>
   <!-- type indicates whether the item is a Software or Hardware product
  -->
   <Order>
     <LineItem type='SW'>
       <ProductNumber>221112</ProductNumber>
       <Quantity>250</Quantity>
     </LineItem>
     <LineItem type='HW'>
       <ProductNumber>343432</ProductNumber>
       <Quantity>12</Quantity>
     </LineItem>
     <LineItem type='HW'>

       <ProductNumber>210020</ProductNumber>
       <Quantity>145</Quantity>
     </LineItem>

     <LineItem type='SW'>
       <ProductNumber>33333</ProductNumber>
       <Quantity>145</Quantity>
     </LineItem>
   </Order>
 </PurchaseOrder>
```

Listing 8.11 `PurchaseOrder.xml` file. *(continued)*

Once the XML input is defined, we can create an XML Schema file to be used for generating the supporting data binding classes. This can be accomplished manually or by using the functionality provided by an XML-based IDE (for example, XML Spy, Breeze XML, Oracle XDK, or Jbuilder). Figure 8.11 is a screenshot of the XML Spy 4.2 screen that enables us to generate the XML Schema for our input file.

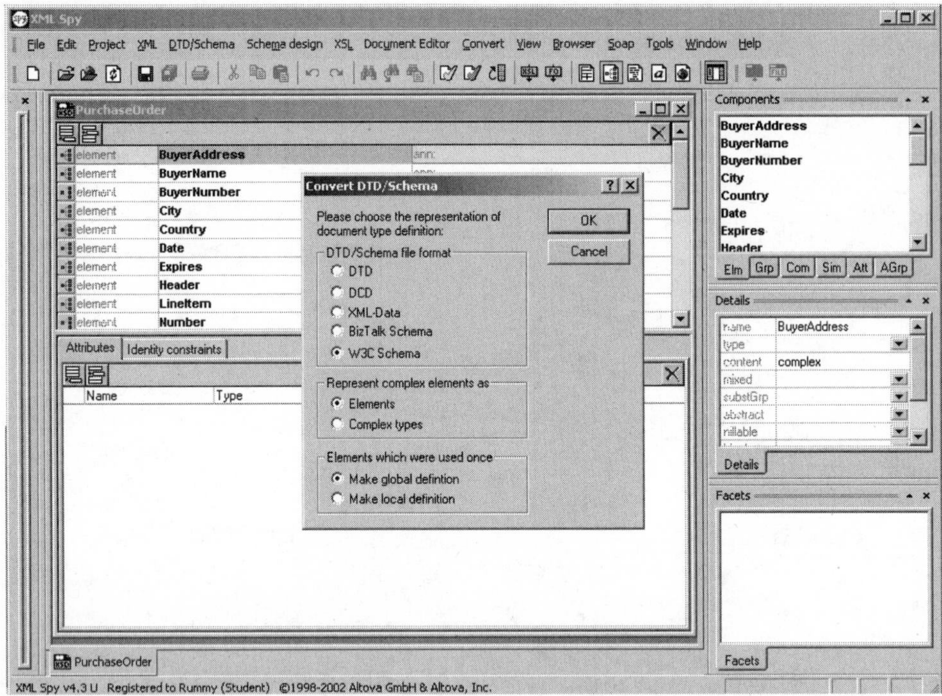

Figure 8.11 XML Schema generation using XML Spy 4.2.

Listing 8.12 shows the purchase order `PurchaseOrder.xsd` XML Schema generated from the `PurchaseOrder.xml` input.

```
<?xml version="1.0" encoding="UTF-8"?>
<xs:schema xmlns:xs="http://www.w3.org/2001/XMLSchema"
elementFormDefault="qualified">
  <xs:element name="BuyerAddress">
    <xs:complexType>
      <xs:sequence>
        <xs:element ref="Street"/>
        <xs:element ref="City"/>
        <xs:element ref="State"/>
        <xs:element ref="Zip"/>
        <xs:element ref="Country"/>
      </xs:sequence>
    </xs:complexType>
```

Listing 8.12 `'PurchaseOrder.xsd'` XML Schema generated from the `PurchaseOrder.xml` input.

```
    </xs:element>
  <xs:element name="BuyerName" type="xs:string"/>
  <xs:element name="BuyerNumber" type="xs:short"/>
  <xs:element name="City" type="xs:string"/>
  <xs:element name="Country" type="xs:string"/>
  <xs:element name="Date" type="xs:string"/>
  <xs:element name="Expires" type="xs:string"/>
  <xs:element name="Header">
    <xs:complexType>
      <xs:sequence>
        <xs:element ref="PurchaseOrderNumber"/>
        <xs:element ref="Date"/>
        <xs:element ref="BuyerNumber"/>
        <xs:element ref="BuyerName"/>
        <xs:element ref="BuyerAddress"/>
        <xs:element ref="ShippingAddress"/>
        <xs:element ref="PaymentInfo"/>
      </xs:sequence>
    </xs:complexType>
  </xs:element>
  <xs:element name="LineItem">
    <xs:complexType>
      <xs:sequence>
        <xs:element ref="ProductNumber"/>
        <xs:element ref="Quantity"/>
      </xs:sequence>
      <xs:attribute name="type" use="required">
        <xs:simpleType>
          <xs:restriction base="xs:NMTOKEN">
          </xs:restriction>
        </xs:simpleType>
      <xs:attribute>
    </xs:complexType>
  </xs:element>
  <xs:element name="Number" type="xs:long"/>
  <xs:element name="Order">
  <xs:complexType>
    <xs:sequence>
      <xs:element ref="LineItem" maxOccurs="unbounded"/>
    </xs:sequence>
  </xs:complexType>
  </xs:element>
  <xs:element name="Owner" type="xs:string"/>
  <xs:element name="PaymentInfo">
    <xs:complexType>
      <xs:sequence>
       <xs:element ref="Type"/>
```

Listing 8.12 `'PurchaseOrder.xsd'` XML Schema generated from the `Purchase Order.xml input.` *(continues)*

```
          <xs:element ref="Number"/>
          <xs:element ref="Expires"/>
          <xs:element ref="Owner"/>
        </xs:sequence>
      </xs:complexType>
  </xs:element>
  <xs:element name="ProductNumber">
    <xs:simpleType>
      <xs:restriction base="xs:int">
      </xs:restriction>
    </xs:simpleType>
  </xs:element>
  <xs:element name="PurchaseOrder">
    <xs:complexType>
      <xs:sequence>
        <xs:element ref="Header"/>
        <xs:element ref="Order"/>
      </xs:sequence>
    </xs:complexType>
  </xs:element>
  <xs:element name="PurchaseOrderNumber" type="xs:long"/>
  <xs:element name="Quantity">
    <xs:simpleType>
      <xs:restriction base="xs:short">
      </xs:restriction>
    </xs:simpleType>
    </xs:element>
    <xs:element name="ShippingAddress">
     <xs:complexType>
       <xs:sequence>
          <xs:element ref="Street"/>
          <xs:element ref="City"/>
          <xs:element ref="State"/>

          <xs:element ref="Zip"/>
          <xs:element ref="Country"/>
       </xs:sequence>
     </xs:complexType>
     </xs:element>
     <xs:element name="State" type="xs:string"/>
     <xs:element name="Street" type="xs:string"/>
     <xs:element name="Type" type="xs:string"/>
     <xs:element name="Zip" type="xs:short"/>
</xs:schema>
```

Listing 8.12 `'PurchaseOrder.xsd'` XML Schema generated from the `PurchaseOrder.xml` input. ***(continued)***

Now that we have an XML Schema definition, we can generate a set of supporting Java classes. The following is an example:

```
java org.exolab.castor.builder.SourceGenerator -i PurchaseOrder.xsd
-package jws.ch08.castor
```

This code will generate a set of Java binding object source files and Java mapping descriptors from the XML Schema, `PurchaseOrder.xsd`, and it will place them in the `jws.ch08.castor.*` package. This package contains the accessor methods, which also include the `'marshal'` and `'unmarshal'` methods required for transforming an XML instance to Java objects and vice-versa.

The source code generator also provides the ability to use the following types of collections when generating source code:

- **Java 1.1 (default).** `Java.util.Vector`.
- **Java 1.2.** Use the option types -j2. The collection type is `java.util.Collection`.

The generated classes reflect the definition of the XML Schema. After running the schema compiler (`org.exolab.castor.builder.SourceGenerator`), we get the following classes:

- `PurchaseOrder.java`
- `Header.java`
- `BuyerAddress.java`
- `ShippingAddress.java`
- `PaymentInfo.java`
- `Order.java`
- `LineItem.java`

These classes contain the getter and setter methods for all of the attributes defined in the schema. In addition to these accessor methods, there are callback methods that contain the logic to create XML from Java or Java from XML. These terms are referred to as marshalling and unmarshalling, respectively. The idea here is to work with the Java classes and not XML. The `PurchaseOrder` class contains references to `Header` and `Order` classes. The `Order` class is composed of one or many `LineItems`, which compose the `Order`. The `Header` contains information about the buyer, such as buyer's address (`BuyerAddress`), shipping address (`ShippingAddress`), and payment information (PaymentInfo). Figure 8.12 is a class diagram that shows the relationship between all of the classes involved in building a PurchaseOrder.

The following is a list of the methods generated for Purchase-Order.java. The first part of the class consists of the accessor methods for the Header and Order objects.

```
public class PurchaseOrder implements java.io.Serializable {
    private Header _header;
    private Order _order;

    public PurchaseOrder()
    public Header getHeader()
    public Order getOrder()
    public void setHeader(Header header)
    public void setOrder(Order order)
```

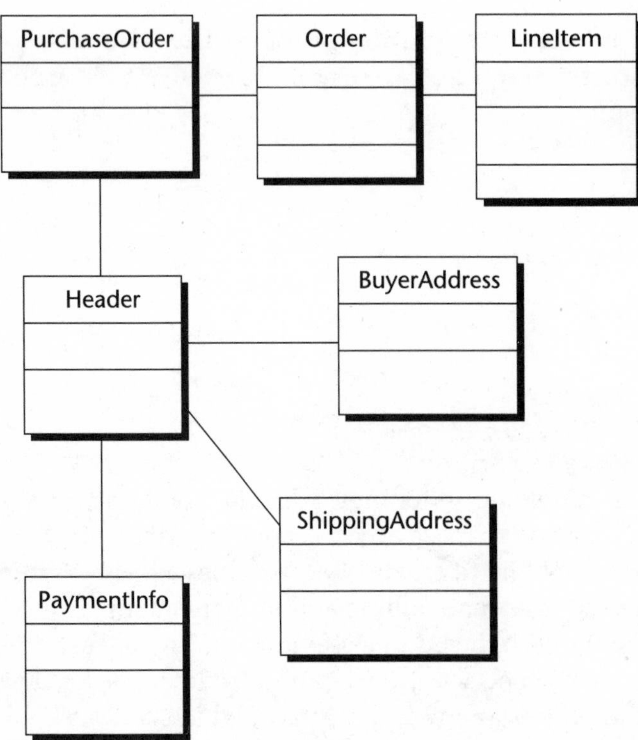

Figure 8.12 Purchase order class diagram.

The rest of the methods are callbacks for binding specific tasks:

```
public boolean isValid()
public void marshal(java.io.Writer out)
            throws MarshalException, ValidationException
public void marshal(org.xml.sax.DocumentHandler handler)
            throws MarshalException, ValidationException

public static PurchaseOrder unmarshal(java.io.Reader reader)
              throws MarshalException, ValidationException

public void validate()throws ValidationException
```

Marshalling XML

When the JAXB provider (CASTOR) is used, the Java object can be dynamically transformed to an XML file. This transformation is based on the binding mapping of the XML Schema, which determines how the given object's property has to be transformed to an XML element (for example, the element or attribute). This process is called marshalling. The following is an extract from the client test program that makes a call to the `PurchaseOrder` marshal method to read an XML input and to transform it to an object representation.

```
PurchaseOrder purchaseOrder;
purchaseOrder= PurchaseOrder.marshal(new
                        FileWriter("UpdatePurchaseOrder.xml"));
```

Now that the object is created, we can add or remove components. If we want to add a new `LineItem` object to the graph, it is very simple:

1. Create a `LineItem` object.
2. Set the attributes (`ProductNumber` or `Quantity`).
3. Get a reference to the `Order` object stored in `PurchaseOrder`.
4. Add the `LineItem` to the `Order` by calling its setter method.
5. Add the `Order` back to the `PurchaseOrder` and voila!
6. The following code shows how to add a `LineItem` to the purchase order:

   ```
   /* create the new line Item */
   LineItem item = new LineItem();
   ```

```
item.setProductNumber("123456");
item.setQuantity("200");
/* SW or HW */
item.setType("SW");

/* get a reference to order object */
Order order = PurchaseOrder.getOrder();
/* set the new line Item */
Order.setLineItem(Item);
/* set the updated oder */
PurchaseOrder.setOrder(order);
```

To remove an `Object` from the graph is just as easy. Suppose we want to remove the `LineItem` with a product number of "33333". Here are the steps to do so:

1. Create a `LineItem` object.
2. Set the attributes (`ProductNumber` or `Quantity`).
3. Get a reference to the `Order` object stored in `PurchaseOrder`.
4. Call `removeLineItem()` passing the `LineItem` that we want to delete.
5. The following is the code that removes the `LineItem` from the purchase order:

```
/*Create the line Item to remove */
LineItem item = new LineItem();
item.setProductNumber("33333");
item.setQuantity("145");
item.setType("SW");

/* get order from purchase order */
Order order = PurchaseOrder.getOrder();

/* remove the line Item from list */
Order.removeLineItem(Item);

/* set the updated order */
PurchaseOrder.setOrder(order);
```

We can now save the new changes back to the same or different file. This process is called unmarshalling and is examined in the following section.

Unmarshalling Java

The XML instance created by an application can be dynamically transformed to a Java object based on the mapping XML schema, which determines how a given XML element/attribute is transformed into the Java object model. This is performed by the Java introspection to determine the function form `getXxxYyy()` or `setXxxYyy(<type> z)`. The accessor then is associated with an XML element/attribute named 'xxx-yyy', which is based on the mapping XML schema. This process is referred to as unmarshalling.

In order to unmarshal the XML data into a Java class graph, we must use the callback method provided in the `PurchaseOrder` class:

```
PurchaseOrder purchaseOrder;
purchaseOrder = PurchaseOrder.unmarshal(new
                           FileReader("PurchaseOrder.xml"));
```

If we take the example where a new `LineItem` was added and then unmarshaled, the `PurchaseOrder` that we would get is shown in the following output:

```
<Order>
    <LineItem type='SW'>
       <ProductNumber>221112</ProductNumber>
       <Quantity>250</Quantity>
    </LineItem>
    <LineItem type='HW'>
       <ProductNumber>343432</ProductNumber>
       <Quantity>12</Quantity>
    </LineItem>
    <LineItem type='HW'>
       <ProductNumber>210020</ProductNumber>
       <Quantity>145</Quantity>
    </LineItem>
    <LineItem type='SW'>
       <ProductNumber>33333</ProductNumber>
       <Quantity>145</Quantity>
    </LineItem>
    <LineItem type='SW'>
       <ProductNumber>123456</ProductNumber>
       <Quantity>200</Quantity>
    </LineItem>
</Order>
```

Other Callback Methods

Additional methods are generated by the binding compiler to provide further functionality. Validation is something that occurs before the data objects are written to the output source (that is, the XML file). The binding compiler generates `validate()` and `isValid()` methods. The `isValidate(")` method is a wrapper of validate but returns `true` or `false`. The `validate` method itself throws a `ValidateException` if the new data graph does not conform to the XML schema.

This covers the surface of XML binding and should be sufficient for performing most of the binding operations. The most challenging part in binding is to generate a correct XML Schema definition. Once this is achieved, the rest is magic. Most of the operation is handled by the runtime of the binding provider. This is a significant improvement over doing it manually, where fewer method calls are needed, thus resulting in a much cleaner code. The code in the following section is the complete list of code used in this section.

Sample Code for XML Binding

The source code shown in Listing 8.13 uses the `PurchaseOrder.xml` and `PurchaseOrder.xsd` files used in previous examples.

The sample data-binding client code unmarshals the XML input source into a Java object representation. The code then traverses the `Object` and prints out all the `LineItem` objects of the `Order`. Finally, it adds a new `LineItem` object to the vector and marshals the object back to an XML format, saving it as `MyPurchaseOrder.xml`.

```
package jws.ch08.castor;

import java.io.*;
import org.exolab.castor.xml.ClassDescriptorResolver;import
org.exolab.castor.xml.Unmarshaller;
import org.exolab.castor.xml.Marshaller;
import org.exolab.castor.xml.MarshalException;
import org.exolab.castor.xml.util.ClassDescriptorResolverImpl;

import java.beans.PropertyChangeEvent;
import java.beans.PropertyChangeListener;
import org.exolab.castor.types.Duration;
```

Listing 8.13 ProductOrderClient.java.

```
import org.exolab.castor.types.Date;
import org.exolab.castor.types.Time;

public class PurchaseOrderClient implements PropertyChangeListener {

 public void propertyChange(PropertyChangeEvent event) {
   System.out.println("PropertyChange: " + event.getPropertyName());
 } //-- propertyChange

 public static void main(String[] args) {
  try {
   System.out.println("Unmarshalling Purchase Order");
   PurchaseOrder purchaseOrder = null;
   purchaseOrder = PurchaseOrder.unmarshal(new
   FileReader("PurchaseOrder.xml"));
   System.out.println();
   System.out.println("unmarshalled...performing tests...");
   System.out.println();
   System.out.println("Getting Header ...");
   Header header = purchaseOrder.getHeader();
   System.out.println("Getting Buyer Address ...");
   BuyerAddress buyerAddress = header.getBuyerAddress();
   System.out.println("Getting Shipping Address ...");
   ShippingAddress shipAddress = hader.getShippingAddress();
   System.out.println("Getting Order ...");
   Order order = purchaseOrder.getOrder();

   LineItem [] itemList = order.getLineItem();
   for (int i=0; i<itemList.length; i++) {
    //-- Display unmarshalled address to the screen
    System.out.println("Purchase Order - Unmarshalling from XML to
JavaObject");
    System.out.println("-----------------");
    System.out.println();

    System.out.println("Order Type");
    System.out.println("" + itemList[i].getType());

    System.out.println("Product Number");
    System.out.println(""+

    itemList[i].getProductNumber());

    System.out.println("Quantity:");
    System.out.println("" + itemList[i].getQuantity());
```

Listing 8.13 `ProductOrderClient.java`. *(continues)*

```
    }

    System.out.println("==UnMarshalling complete==");
    System.out.println("Add a new Item ...");
    LineItem newItem = new LineItem();
    newItem.setProductNumber(98234);
    newItem.setQuantity((short)666);
    newItem.setType("HW");

    System.out.println("Set item in order");
    int index = order.getLineItemCount();
    System.out.println("Count before:"+index);
    order.addLineItem(newItem);

    System.out.println("Count before:"+
                        order.getLineItemCount());

    System.out.println("Set order in purchase order");
    purchaseOrder.setOrder(order);


    System.out.println("\n\n=Marshalling PrescriberMessage Java object
to XML =");
    purchaseOrder.marshal(new FileWriter("MyPurchaseOrder.xml"));

   } catch (Exception e) {
        e.printStackTrace();
   }
  }
 }
```

Listing 8.13 `ProductOrderClient.java`. *(continued)*

The client generates the output shown in Listing 8.14. This code displays the contents of an `Order` and adds a new `Order` saving it to `MyPurchaseOrder.xml`.

```
Getting Header ...
Getting Buyer Address ...
Getting Shipping Address ...
Getting Order ...
Purchase Order - Unmarshalling from XML to JavaObject
-----------------------------------------------------
Order Type
   SW
Pruduct Number
   221112
```

Listing 8.14 A sample binding output.

```
Quantity:
   250
Purchase Order - Unmarshalling from XML to JavaObject
---------------------------------------------------------
Order Type
   HW
Pruduct Number
   343432
Quantity:
   12
Purchase Order - Unmarshalling from XML to JavaObject
---------------------------------------------------------
Order Type
   HW
Pruduct Number
   210020
Quantity:
   145
Purchase Order - Unmarshalling from XML to JavaObject
---------------------------------------------------------
Order Type
   SW
Pruduct Number
   33333
Quantity:
   145
==================UnMarshalling complete============
Add a new Item ...
Set item in order
Count before adding the item: 4
Count after adding item : 5
Set order in purchase order
```

Listing 8.14 A sample binding output. *(continued)*

Summary

You now should have a better understanding of Java APIs for XML processing and binding. These APIs provide the functionality that is essential in developing Java Web services.

In this chapter, we addressed Java APIs for XML processing and binding. We covered such varied topics as XML and XSL basics, JAXP and its APIs, how to process XML data with SAX and DOM, how to parse and transform XML documents using the JAXP API, and data binding between Java and XML using CASTOR.

CHAPTER

9

XML Messaging Using JAXM and SAAJ

This chapter discusses the Java API for XML messaging (JAXM) and SOAP with Attachment API for Java (SAAJ). Both JAXM and SAAJ enable XML-based messaging for B2B and Web services applications supporting a wide range of industry standards, including SOAP and ebXML.

JAXM is an integral part of the JWSDP, which provides synchronous and asynchronous messaging capabilities in the Web services environment and enables the exchanging of XML documents over the intranet or Internet. JAXM provides a messaging infrastructure and standard API mechanisms for building, sending, and receiving XML messages. In addition to JAXM, JWSDP provides SAAJ, which facilitates the sending and receiving of XML documents as SOAP-messages without a JAXM provider infrastructure and the handling of SOAP-based HTTP requests/responses. Initially, SAAJ was part of the JAXM 1.0 API bundle, and from JAXM 1.1 this package is referred to as SAAJ 1.1 APIs.

Both the JAXM and SAAJ APIs are fully compliant with SOAP 1.1 specifications and SOAP 1.1 with attachments, which helps Java Web services developers write JAXM- or SAAJ-based XML messaging applications with minimal effort and little understanding of SOAP messaging. In a business context using JAXM or SAAJ, the XML documents exchanged can be product information, purchase orders, invoices, order confirmations, or whatever.

This chapter provides in-depth coverage of the JAXM- and SAAJ-based API mechanisms and illustrates its usage scenarios for developing and deploying Web services applications. In particular, we will be focusing on the following:

- The role of JAXM in Web services
- JAXM application architecture
- JAXM APIs and its programming model
- SAAJ APIs and its programming model
- Understanding JAXM implementation scenarios
- JAXM deployment model
- Developing JAXM-based XML messaging applications
- Using JAXM provider and without provider scenarios

At the time of this book's writing, JAXM 1.1 and SAAJ 1.1 are the most recent specifications. The reference implementation and API libraries for JAXM and SAAJ are available for downloading as part of JWSDP 1.0 at http://java.sun.com/xml/download.html.

Both JAXM and SAAJ are developed by Sun Microsystems as part of its Java Community Process (JCP) backed by J2EE vendors and most Java-based Web services platforms. In the upcoming J2EE 1.4 specifications, it is expected that JAXM and SAAJ will be available as part of the J2EE server implementations to support Web services. In this chapter, we will be using JWSDP Reference Implementation (RI) for discussion and also to illustrate the case study examples.

The Role of JAXM in Web Services

JAXM is an API framework based on the messaging protocols defined by the SOAP 1.1 specifications and SOAP attachments. JAXM uses a standard messaging provider infrastructure and Java-based APIs to facilitate the sending and receiving of XML-based messages asynchronously in a Web services environment and supporting Web services standards and protocols. The core features of JAXM are as follows:

- Has portable XML messaging applications
- Has synchronous (request/response) and asynchronous (one-way) messaging
- Transmits and routes messages to many providers

- Ensures message delivery through reliable messaging
- Supports standard Internet protocols, such as HTTP, SMTP, and FTP

When using JAXM without a provider infrastructure, the messages can be sent and received as requests and responses through a SOAP connection using the SAAJ 1.1 APIs provided with JWSDP 1.0.

JAXM provides the notion of *messaging profiles,* which enable messaging protocols to be implemented over SOAP messaging. A JAXM-based application client must use a messaging profile to identify its underlying transport bindings, message structure, and semantics. This establishes an agreement between the JAXM client and its JAXM messaging provider.

JAXM-based applications (senders and receivers) can be deployed in Java servlet 2.2- or J2EE 1.3-compliant server providers. JAXM runs as an asynchronous application and executes methods upon receiving messages from the provider. JAXM applications running without providers can run as standalone clients, exchanging messages as requests and responses with another JAXM/SOAP 1.1-compliant application.

In a Web services scenario, the JAXM messaging infrastructure acts like a SOAP intermediary to route messages between destinations. The Web services requestor application sends messages to its JAXM messaging provider, which then routes the messages to the Web service provider's JAXM messaging provider. The Web services provider receives the message and then executes the appropriate methods as required by the service requestor or it may reroute the message to its next intermediate destination or its final destination.

JAXM Application Architecture

Figure 9.1 represents a JAXM-based application architecture and its core elements.

A typical JAXM application architecture consists of the following elements:

JAXM clients. JAXM clients are JAXM-based application components that send and receive JAXM messages. The JAXM clients (senders and receivers) can run using a JAXM provider or without a provider. JAXM clients using a provider connection can send and receive messages asynchronously as one-way transmissions. A JAXM client also can take advantage of the provider-offered features like message reliability and ensured delivery. In the case of using JAXM without a provider, the JAXM client can send and receive messages as requests and responses over a SOAP connection. In general, a JAXM receiver client does not require a JAXM provider.

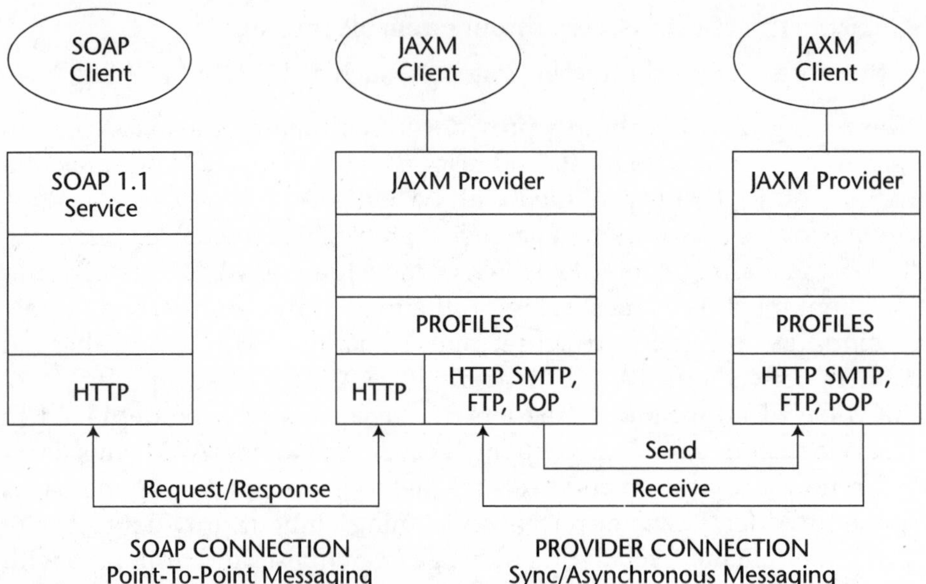

Figure 9.1 A JAXM-based application architecture.

JAXM messages. JAXM messages are XML documents based on SOAP standards and conventions that define the basic message format during a JAXM communication. The SAAJ 1.1 API provides the low-level Java APIs for constructing SOAP 1.1-compliant XML messages (with or without attachments). To understand the basic structure of a SOAP 1.1 message, refer to Chapter 4, "Developing Web Services Using SOAP," in the section *Anatomy of a SOAP Message*.

JAXM connections. JAXM connections are a set of pre-configured JAXM client connections to a JAXM provider or a SOAP implementation. The JAXM clients send and receive messages using these connections. A JAXM connection using a provider is quite similar to a connection to a message-oriented middleware. In the case of connections without a JAXM provider, it works quite similar to a peer-to-peer communication model where the destination is referring to a SOAP endpoint.

JAXM profiles. JAXM messaging profiles provide the flexibility to use messaging protocols implemented over SOAP messaging. In a client application, the profile defines the underlying transport bindings, message header definitions, and semantics specific to SOAP messages. The JAXM client using a JAXM provider is required to

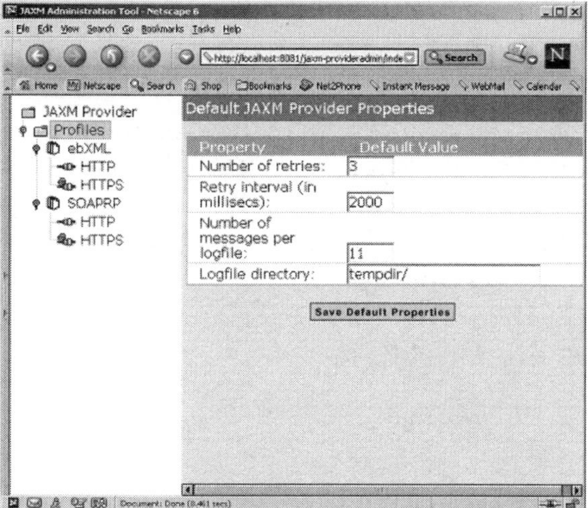

Figure 9.2 A JAXM provider administration console.

use a messaging profile, which is usually provided as a URL referring to an XML schema that defines the message structure. For instance, the profile for the ebXML Message Service (MS) specification can be found at http://www.ebxml.org/project_teams/transport/messageHeader.xsd. The JAXM 1.1 reference implementation provided with JWSDP 1.0 supplies messaging profiles for SOAP-RP and ebXML.

JAXM administration console. The JAXM administration console enables the configuration of JAXM provider-specific properties such as a number of retries for message delivery, retry intervals, logging, and so forth. (See Figure 9-2.) The console also enables the configuration of application endpoint mappings with the provider. In a JWSDP 1.0 default installation (JAXM 1.1 Reference implementation), the JAXM administration console can be accessed through a Web browser at http://localhost:8081/jaxm-provideradmin/index.jsp.

JAXM provider. The JAXM provider is a JAXM-compliant messaging infrastructure that implements the JAXM API interfaces and classes. It facilitates the transmission and routing of JAXM messages. When there is a transmission failure, the provider takes the responsibility of resending it. The provider also facilitates other reliability requirements like message persistence, acknowledgement, and so on. The JAXM infrastructure providers are required to be in compliance with SOAP 1.1 specifications and its supported transport protocol bindings, which enables messaging interoperability with non-JAXM clients with SOAP 1.1 compliance. A provider can be set up and configured as part of a Java servlet 2.2-compliant Web container or a J2EE 1.3-compliant application server. To send and receive messages, the JAXM client establishes a connection with the provider. The provider tracks the sending and receiving of messages, ensuring guaranteed message delivery as defined by the underlying messaging protocol. The JAXM provider uses profiles to support the messaging protocols implemented over SOAP 1.1. The JAXM 1.1 RI currently provides messaging profiles for SOAP-RP and ebXML.

JAXM Messaging: Interaction Patterns

As per the JAXM 1.1 specifications, all JAXM provider implementations must provide and facilitate the following message interaction patterns:

Asynchronous inquiry. In this pattern, a message producer application sends a message and does not wait for a response from the message consumer. The message consumer processes the message and returns a response as a new operation. That is, the process of both sending and receiving the messages occurs in two separate operations.

Asynchronous update with acknowledgment. The message consumer acknowledges the receipt of the message to the provider or its message sender. This acknowledgment depends upon the implementation of the provider.

Synchronous inquiry. Synchronous inquiries are typical to request/response-based communication: The message sender waits for a response after sending a message to the receiver using the same connection.

Synchronous update. Like the asynchronous update, in a synchronous update after sending the initial request, the message's sender waits for a response as an acknowledgement that the message was sent.

Fire and forget. The message sender does not wait or anticipate a response from the message receiver.

Now, let's explore the previous JAXM features and how they are represented in the JAXM programming model.

JAXM API Programming Model

The JAXM 1.1 API defines a single package structure with a set of interfaces and classes to support the JAXM clients intending to do messaging with a JAXM provider or directly to a SOAP service:

```
javax.xml.messaging
```

JAXM also depends upon the `javax.xml.soap` package provided by the SAAJ 1.1 API. SAAJ 1.1 provides the high-level abstraction factory classes for constructing and handling SOAP 1.1-compliant messages with or without attachments.

javax.xml.messaging

This package provides a set of interfaces and classes for creating JAXM clients. JAXM clients can send and receive messages as asynchronous or synchronous one-way transmissions with a JAXM provider- or SOAP-based service. The JAXM API interfaces and classes are discussed in the following text.

Interfaces

`javax.xml.messaging.OneWayListener`. An asynchronous messaging listener interface for the JAXM client components intended to be the asynchronous consumers of JAXM messages. JAXM clients can implement this interface and use an `onMessage()` method to consume messages. The `onMessage()` method is invoked when the message arrives at the destination endpoint of the JAXM provider. `OneWayListener` can be implemented as a servlet by extending a JAXM servlet interface and deploying Java servlet 2.2-compliant servlet containers (like Apache Tomcat or J2EE 1.3-compliant application servers). It also can be implemented as a `MessageDrivenBean` in the future J2EE environment because the upcoming J2EE 1.4-compliant application server is expected to support it.

```
public class ConsumerServlet extends JAXMServlet
                              implements OnewayListener {
      public void onMessage(SOAPMessage msg) {
        //Implement your business logic here
      }
}
```

`javax.xml.messaging.ReqRespListener.` Provides a synchronous messaging listener interface for the JAXM client components to consume JAXM messages as http-based requests and responses. In this case, the client sending the request `javax.xml.soap.SOAPConnection` via a call method waits for a response from the receiver. The receiver receives the `ReqRespListener` interface and uses an `onMessage()` method to receive and send a response back to the sender. When using the `OneWayListener`, the `ReqRespListener` interface can be implemented as a servlet by extending a JAXM servlet interface and deploying Java Servlet 2.2-compliant servlet containers (like Apache Tomcat or J2EE 1.3-compliant application servers). But in this case, the JAXM provider connection is not required because the request/responses, using a SOAP connection, are directly bound to HTTP.

```
public class ConsumerServlet extends JAXMServlet
                                 implements ReqRespListener {
      public void onMessage(SOAPMessage msg) {
        //Implement your business logic here
      }
}
```

`javax.xml.messaging.ProviderConnection.` Creates a client connection to a JAXM provider. The connection is obtained from a `ProviderConnectionFactory` object that defines a set of preconfigured connections to a JAXM provider. The JAXM client does a JNDI lookup of a `ProviderConnectionFactory` and then uses a `createConnection()` method to obtain a connection to the JAXM provider.

```
Context myCtx = new InitialContext();
ProviderConnectionFactory pcf =
 (ProviderConnectionFactory)
                        myCtx.lookup("SunOneProvider");
ProviderConnection pcon = pcf.createConnection();
```

`javax.xml.messaging.ProviderMetaData.` Provides the details of the JAXM provider to which the client has a connection.

Classes

`javax.xml.messaging.JAXMServlet.` A utility class for implementing a JAXM client as an HTTP servlet. It also facilitates sending and receiving JAXM messages synchronously or asynchronously using HTTP.

javax.xml.messaging.Endpoint. An object that represents an application's endpoint, which represents the actual destination of messages and is identified using a URI. It is a messaging provider that identified with a destination, which has to be configured to be an endpoint.

javax.xml.messaging.URLEndpoint. Represents a URL as a special endpoint for JAXM client applications that communicate directly with another SOAP-based application without using a JAXM provider.

Exceptions

javax.xml.messaging.JAXMException. Throws an exception while a JAXM exception occurs. The exception details the reasons such as failure to obtain provider connection, message header issues, and so on.

javax.xml.soap (SAAJ 1.1 APIs)

The JAXM APIs depend upon this package for creating and handling SOAP messages and its attachments. In addition to creating and handling SOAP messages, this package also provides a SOAP client view for enabling point-to-point or request/response messaging with any SOAP 1.1-compliant service. The SAAJ API interfaces and classes are discussed in the following text.

Interfaces

javax.xml.soap.SOAPEnvelope. The container of the `SOAPHeader` and `SOAPBody` object entries. It also is part of a `SOAPPart` object. The client can access the `SOAPHeader` and `SOAPBody` objects by using its setter or getter methods for creating or retrieving elements.

```
SOAPPart soapPart = message.getSOAPPart();
SOAPEnvelope soapEnv = soapPart.getEnvelope();
SOAPHeader soapHeader = soapEnv.getHeader();
SOAPBody soapBody = soapEnv.getBody();
```

javax.xml.soap.SOAPBody. Represents the contents of the SOAP body element in a SOAP message.

javax.xml.soap.SOAPBodyElement. Represents the contents in a SOAPBody object. The SOAPBodyElement object can be added to a SOAPBody object with a SOAPBody method (addBodyElement(elementName).

```
SOAPBodyElement
     soapBodyElement = soapBody.addBodyElement(bookName);
```

javax.xml.soap.SOAPHeader. Represents the contents of the SOAPHeader element. A SOAPHeader object can be created using the SOAPEnvelope method addHeader().

```
SOAPHeader soapHeader = soapEnv.addHeader();
```

javax.xml.soap.SOAPHeaderElement. Represents the contents in the SOAPHeader part of the SOAP envelope. The SOAPHeader-Element object can be created using addHeaderElement, which adds a header element to the SOAPHeader object.

```
SOAPHeaderElement soapHeaderElem
        = soapHeader.addHeaderElement(elementName);
```

javax.xml.soap.SOAPConstants. Defines a number of constants specific to the SOAP 1.1 protocol, such as namespace, URI identifier for SOAP encoding, and so on.

javax.xml.soap.SOAPElement. Represents the contents of a SOAPBody object, SOAPHeader object, SOAPFault object, and the content in a SOAPEnvelope object, and so forth. It acts as the base class\representation for all of the SOAP objects as per the SOAP 1.1 specifications.

javax.xml.soap.SOAPFault. Contains the error/status information of a SOAP message. It provides the getter and setter methods for getting the SOAP fault information contained in a SOAPFault object and for setting the fault code, the fault actor, and fault string. The contents of a SOAPFault object can be defined with the SOAPFaultElement object using the SOAPElement method addTextNode(String).

javax.xml.soap.Detail. Is the part of a SOAPFault object that provides detailed error information. It also is a container for the DetailEntry objects that contain application-specific error or status information.

javax.xml.soap.DetailEntry. Represents the contents of a Detail object that provides details for a SOAPFault object.

javax.xml.soap.Name. A representation of an XML name that declares namespace-qualified names and obtains the prefix associated with the namespace. An example of an application-specific namespace declaration of an element is shown as follows:

```
<wiley:GetBookPrice
        xmlns:wiley="http://jws.wiley.com/JavaWebservices">
```

where `<wiley:GetBookPrice>` refers to the qualified name, `wiley` refers to the prefix, `GetBookPrice` refers to the name, and `http://jws.wiley.com/JavaWebservices` refers to its namespace URI.

To create an application-specific XML name object in a `SOAPEnvelope`, see the following sample code snippet:

```
Name nameObj = soapEnvelope.createName
         ("GetBookPrice", "wiley",
                  "http://jws.wiley.com/JavaWebservices");
```

javax.xml.soap.Node. Represents the DOM representation of a node in an XML document and provides methods for manipulating a DOM tree—like adding, setting the values of a node, and removing a node from the tree.

javax.xml.soap.Text. Represents the value of node as a text object.

Classes

javax.xml.soap.MessageFactory. Provides a factory class for creating `SOAPMessage` objects. The SOAP message object can be created by obtaining an instance of the `MessageFactory` class:

```
MessageFactory msgFactory = MessageFactory.newInstance();
SOAPMessage soapMsg = msgFactory.createMessage();
```

In the case of using a JAXM provider connection, the SOAP message objects can be created using a messaging profile:

```
MessageFactory msgFactory
        = providerConn.createMessageFactory(ProfileURI);
SOAPMessage soapMsg = msgFactory.createMessage();
```

where `ProfileURI` refers to the URI of the XML schema of the messaging profile.

javax.xml.soap.SOAPConnection. Using the `SOAPConnection` object, a SOAP client can send and receive messages as requests and responses. To create a `SOAPConnection`, the client can obtain an instance of `SOAPConnectionFactory` and then use the factory to create a connection:

```
SOAPConnectionFactory scf =
SOAPConnectionFactory.newInstance();
SOAPConnection con = factory.createConnection();
```

`javax.xml.soap.SOAPMessage.` A `SOAPMessage` is the root class for all messages. It can be created using a `MessageFactory` object. Using a messaging profile with the `MessageFactory`, it can produce SOAP messages conforming to the profile. A `SOAPMessage` object contains a SOAP part and zero or more SOAP attachment parts.

`javax.xml.soap.SOAPPart.` When a `SOAPMessage` is created, it contains a `SOAPPart` object that acts as the MIME part container, including the MIME headers and the `SOAPEnvelope`. To obtain the `SOAPPart` object of a `SOAPMessage` object, call a `getSOAPPart` method:

```
SOAPMessage soapMsg = msgFactory.createMessage();
SOAPPart soapPart = soapMsg.getSOAPPart();
```

`javax.xml.soap.AttachmentPart.` To add application-specific attachments to a `SOAPMessage`, an `AttachmentPart` object can be created using the `SOAPMessage.createAttachmentPart` method. The following sample code snippet creates an attachment to a SOAP message with a string data by name `myContentString` and the MIME type `text/plain`:

```
SOAPMessage soapMsg = msgFactory.createMessage();
AttachmentPart attPart = soapMsg.createAttachmentPart();
attPart.setContent(myContentString, "text/plain");
soapMsg.addAttachmentPart(attPart);
```

To attach non-text or binary data:

```
SOAPMessage soapMsg = msgFactory.createMessage();
AttachmentPart attPart = soapMsg.createAttachmentPart();
attPart.setContent
   (new ByteArrayInputStream(dukeJPG), "image/jpeg");
soapMsg.addAttachmentPart(attPart);
```

`javax.xml.soap.SOAPFactory.` Provides the factory class for creating SOAP element fragments, such as adding child elements of a `SOAPEnvelope`, a `SOAPBodyElement`, or a `SOAPHeaderElement`. To add a `SOAPElement` object, call a `createElement` method:

Exceptions

`javax.xml.soap.SOAPException`. Throws an exception while a SOAP exception is occurring. The exception details the reasons such as failure to obtain a SOAP connection, SOAP message header issues, and so forth.

Basic Programming Steps for Using JAXM

The JAXM 1.1 specification defines two different types of communication scenarios where we can use the JAXM APIs for creating, sending, and receiving messages. These scenarios depend upon using a JAXM provider or directly connecting a SOAP service without using a JAXM provider.

Let's take a look at those scenarios and walk through the programming steps required for handling these scenarios.

Using a JAXM Provider

Figure 9.3 illustrates a JAXM provider-based communication scenario.

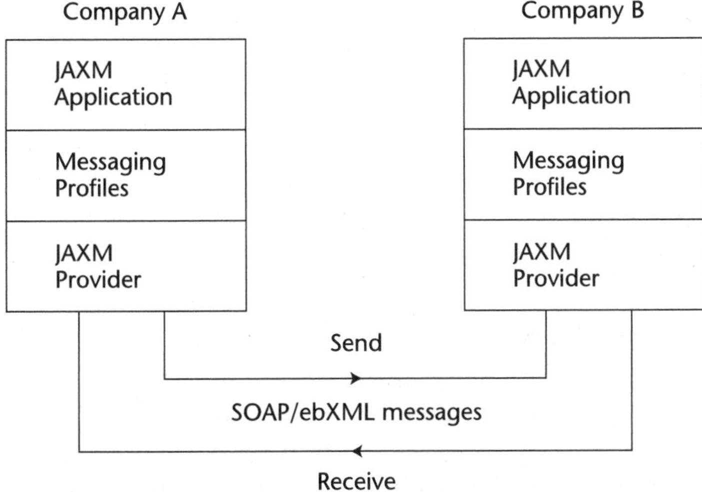

Figure 9.3 JAXM communication using providers.

The key features of using a JAXM provider-based communication are as follows:

- It defines an asynchronous communication model where the sender and receiver do not need to be connected at all times and the receiver does not require blocking of the destination for receiving messages.
- It provides reliability mechanisms to store and forward messages to one-to-many destinations and uses messaging profiles to adopt high-level messaging protocols like ebXML.

If a JAXM messaging provider is used, when a client sends a message, the message goes to the messaging provider and then is forwarded to its recipient. The provider facilitates the transmission to its destination receiving the message on behalf of the application. It is important to note that to run a JAXM application using a messaging provider, we must configure the JAXM client and the messaging provider.

Steps for Sending Messages with a Message Provider

The key programming steps for sending messages using JAXM APIs with a messaging provider are as follows:

1. Create a connection to the provider.
2. Create a message factory.
3. Create a message.
4. Populate the message.
5. Add the attachment parts.
6. Save the message.
7. Send the message.
8. Close the provider connection.

Each of these steps is described in the following paragraphs.

Creating a Connection to the Provider

First, we need to instantiate a `ProviderConnection` object to create an active connection to the messaging provider. To create this connection, we use a JNDI lookup to obtain an instance of the `ProviderConnectionFactory` class. Once we get an instance of the connection factory, we then can create a connection to the messaging provider.

```
//Use a JNDI lookup to create the Initial naming context
 Context ctx = new InitialContext();

// Look up a JAXM provider connection factory
 ProviderConnectionFactory pcf
   = (ProviderConnectionFactory)ctx.lookup(providerURI);

// Create a JAXM provider connection
 ProviderConnection pc = pcf.createConnection();
```

Creating a Message Factory

Use the connection to create a `MessageFactory` object, which is used to create a message. When you create a `MessageFactory` object, the `MessageFactory` returned creates instances of `SOAPMessage` subclasses appropriate to the given messaging profile. Before creating `MessageFactory`, we first must find out the provider-supported profiles from its metadata information and ensure that the provider supports the profile we need to use. In the following snippet, the profile that matches the ebXML profile is passed as a `String` to the method `createMessageFactory`:

```
// Use the Provider connection to obtain provider metadata
 ProviderMetaData metaData = pc.getMetaData();

 // Find out the Provider supported profiles
 String[] supportedProfiles = metaData.getSupportedProfiles();
 String profile = null;

 // find the profile that matches the 'ebxml' profile
 for(int i=0; i < supportedProfiles.length; i++) {
     if(supportedProfiles[i].equals("ebxml")) {
         profile = supportedProfiles[i];
         break;
     }
 }
// Create a message factory from the Connection
// and using profile
 MessageFactory msgFactory = pc.createMessageFactory(profile);
```

Creating a Message

Using the `MessageFactory` object, create a `SOAPMessage` object according to a messaging profile provided with the JAXM 1.1 RI. For instance, using the ebXML profile and its API implementation, the code snippet will be as follows:

```
//Create SOAP message using the ebXML Profile
 EbXMLMessageImpl message =
         (EbXMLMessageImpl)msgFactory.createMessage();

 // Set the sender and receiver destination endpoints
 message.setSender(new Party(senderEndpoint));
 message.setReceiver(new Party(receiverEndpoint));
```

Because ebXML message packaging complies with SOAP 1.1 specifications and SOAP messages with attachments in addition to the ebXML message headers and ebXML specific body elements, it also is possible to use SOAP header elements and SOAP body elements.

Populating the Message

All messages are created with a SOAP part that contains a SOAP envelope, and in turn, the SOAP envelope contains the SOAP header and SOAP body. The SOAP part of the message including its header and body elements can contain only data formatted using XML, whereas a SOAP attachment part can contain any kind of data, including XML, non-XML, and binary data. To populate the message, first do the following:

1. Get the message's `SOAPPart` object, and then get its envelope object:

   ```
   // Get the SOAP Part from the message.
   SOAPPart soapPart = message.getSOAPPart();

   // Get the SOAP Envelope
   SOAPEnvelope soapEnvelope = soapPart.getEnvelope();
   ```

2. Use the `SOAPEnvelope` object to obtain both the `SOAPHeader` object and `SOAPBody` object, which is used for setting the contents of the SOAP part of the message:

   ```
   // Create a soap header from the envelope
   SOAPHeader soapHeader = soapEnvelope.getHeader();

   // Create the SOAPBody
   SOAPBody soapBody = soapEnvelope.getBody();
   ```

3. Add content to the header using a `SOAPHeader` object that contains `SOAPHeaderElement` objects, so a new `SOAPHeaderElement` object is created and added to the header. The new `SOAPHeaderElement` object is initialized with the specified `Name` object.

   ```
   SOAPHeaderElement headerElement =
   soapHeader.addHeaderElement(
   soapEnvelope.createName("BookNo",
   "wiley","http://jws.wiley.com/jws"));
   headerElement.addTextNode("JWS100002");
   ```

4. Add content to the `SOAPBody` using `SOAPBodyElement` objects, so a new `SOAPBodyElement` object is created and initialized with the specified `Name` object.

```
// Create a Name object and add to SOAPBodyElement
Name bodyName = soapEnvelope.createName(
"SubmitPurchaseOrder","wiley",
"http://jws.wiley.com/jws");
SOAPBodyElement sbe =

soapBody.addBodyElement(bodyName);

// Create a Name object and add body child elements
Name elemName = soapEnvelope.createName("BookName");
se.addTextNode("Developing Java Web services");
```

Adding Attachment Parts

Our next step is to add `AttachmentPart` to the message using JavaBeans Activation Framework (JAF) API. To add an attachment to the message, we create an `AttachmentPart` object:

```
// Access the URL of an image attachment
URL url = new URL("http://www.wiley.com/jws/jwsbookcover.jpg");

// Use JAF, and create a JAF DataHandler with this URL
        DataHandler dataHandler = new DataHandler(url);

        // Create and Add an AttachmentPart
        message.addAttachmentPart(
             message.createAttachmentPart(dataHandler));
```

Saving the Message

Update the `SOAPMessage` object with all the additions to the message by calling the `saveChanges()` method:

```
// Save the message
message.saveChanges();
```

Sending the Message

Now that the message has been created and the contents added and it is ready to be sent, the message can be sent asynchronously using the `ProviderConnection` method `send()`:

```
// Send the message
pc.send(message);
```

Closing the Provider Connection

The last step to do is close `ProviderConnection` by calling `ProviderConnection.close()`.

```
// Close the provider connection
pc.close();
```

Receiving Messages

To receive messages, we need to implement a `JAXMServlet` object or a message-driven bean (J2EE 1.4) using a `OneWayListener` interface, and then register it with the endpoint. When the message arrives at its destination, the messaging provider receives the message asynchronously and then calls the registered JAXMServlet or MDB's `onMessage()` method of `OneWayListener` by passing it with the `SOAPMessage` object. The implementation of the `onMessage()` method determines how the message is processed. In the case of receiving messages using request/response-based messaging, we need to use `ReqRespListener`. Using `ReqRespListener` does not require a messaging provider connection because it is bound to use `SOAPConnection` using HTTP.

The key implementation steps for asynchronously receiving messages using a JAXM provider (using `OneWayListener`) are as follows:

1. Create a servlet extending `JAXMServlet` and implementing the `OneWayListener` interface that registers as a listener within the servlet container.
2. Use JNDI to look up and create a JAXM `ProviderConnectionFactory` instance.
3. Create `ProviderConnection` using `ProviderConnectionFactory`.
4. Set `MessageFactory` for the required messaging profile.
5. Implement the `onMessage()` method to receive from the provider and then to process the message.

A typical JAXM-based servlet implementation of receiving messages using `OneWayListener` is shown in Listing 9.1.

```
// Upon receiving messages, the messaging provider
// calls the onMessage method of the OneWayListener,
// and then the SOAPMessage object.

public class ReceivingServlet extends JAXMServlet
                              implements OnewayListener {
//Initialize variables...
  private ProviderConnectionFactory pcf;
  private ProviderConnection pc;

  public void init(ServletConfig servletConfig){

      // lookup connection factory, create a connection and
      // initialize the message factory

      // Using a Local Provider (no URI required)
      ProviderConnectionFactory pcf =
                        ProviderConnectionFactory.newInstance();

      ProviderConnection pc = pcf.createConnection();

      // Set message factory with the required
      // profile API Implementation (ex. ebXML)
      setMessageFactory(new EbXMLMessageFactoryImpl());
  }...

// onMessage() method receives message
  public void onMessage(SOAPMessage message) {
    // process the message
    ....
  }
}
```

Listing 9.1 A code snippet showing a JAXM servlet implementation for a provider-based connection.

Using JAXM without a Provider (Using SOAPConnection)

When using JAXM without a messaging provider, application clients send and receive messages directly with their remote partners via a SOAP connection. The following figure illustrates a JAXM messaging scenario, using `SOAPConnection` without a provider.

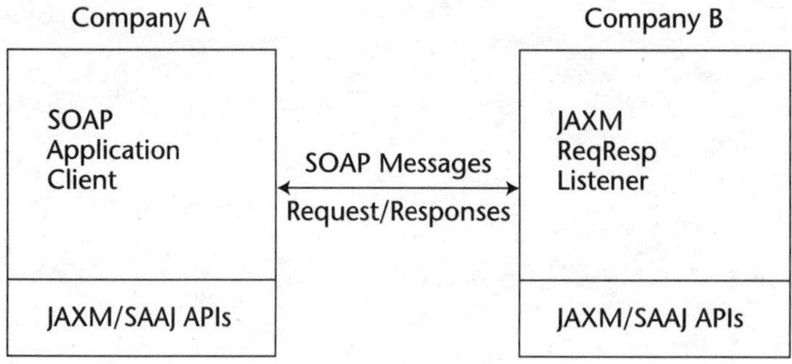

Figure 9.4 A JAXM communication without a provider or using SOAPConnection.

The key features of using JAXM without a provider are as follows:

- The JAXM-without-a-provider scenario defines a point-to-point interaction and synchronous communication model where the sender and receiver exchange messages as requests and responses. The sender sends a message and waits for a response blocking the destination. (See Figure 9-4.)
- The connection between partners is established directly and bound to HTTP.

Steps for Sending a Message without a Message Provider

The key programming steps for sending messages using JAXM APIs without a messaging provider or using a SOAP connection are as follows:

1. Create a SOAP connection.
2. Create a message factory.
3. Create a message.
4. Populate the SOAP message.
5. Add the SOAP attachment parts.
6. Save the SOAP message.
7. Send the message and receive the response.
8. Close the provider connection.

Each of these steps is described in the following paragraphs.

Creating a SOAP Connection

The first step is to create a `SOAPConnection` object for sending messages directly with its partner application. To create this connection, we must obtain an instance from the `SOAPConnectionFactory` class. Once we get an instance of the connection factory, then we can create a `SOAPConnection`:

```
// Create an Instance of SOAP connection factory
SOAPConnectionFactory scf
= SOAPConnectionFactory.newInstance();

// Create a SOAP connection using the factory Instance
SOAPConnection sc = scf.createConnection();
```

Creating a Message Factory

Create an instance of a `MessageFactory` object, which enables the creation of instances of `SOAPMessage`:

```
// Create an instance of the message factory
MessageFactory msgFactory = MessageFactory.newInstance();
```

Creating a Message

Using the `MessageFactory` instance, create `SOAPMessage` objects:

```
SOAPMessage message = msgFactory.createMessage();
```

Populating the SOAP Message

All messages are created with a SOAP part that contains a SOAP envelope, and in turn, it contains the SOAP header and SOAP body. The SOAP part of the message, including its header and body elements, can contain only data formatted using XML, whereas a SOAP attachment part can contain any kind of data, including XML, non-XML, and binary data. This is the same process that we discussed earlier when using the provider.

To populate the message, first we must get the message's `SOAPPart` object and then its envelope object:

```
// Get the SOAP Part from the message.
SOAPPart soapPart = message.getSOAPPart();

// Get the SOAP Envelope
SOAPEnvelope soapEnvelope = soapPart.getEnvelope();
```

Then, we must use the `SOAPEnvelope` object to obtain both the `SOAPHeader` and `SOAPBody` objects used for setting the contents of the SOAP part of the message:

```
// Create a soap header from the envelope
 SOAPHeader soapHeader = soapEnvelope.getHeader();

 // Create the SOAPBody
 SOAPBody soapBody = soapEnvelope.getBody();
```

Then, we add content to the header using a SOAPHeader object that contains SOAPHeaderElement objects. A new SOAPHeaderElement object then is created and added to the header. The new SOAPHeaderElement object is initialized with the specified Name object:

```
SOAPHeaderElement headerElement
        = soapHeader.addHeaderElement(
             soapEnvelope.createName("BookNo", "wiley",
                                   "http://jws.wiley.com/jws"));
 headerElement.addTextNode("JWS100002");
```

Next, we add content to the SOAPBody using SOAPBodyElement objects, and a new SOAPBodyElement object is created and initialized with the specified Name object:

```
// Create a Name object and add to SOAPBodyElement
 Name bodyName = soapEnvelope.createName(
   "SubmitPurchaseOrder","wiley","http://jws.wiley.com/jws");

SOAPBodyElement sbe = body.addBodyElement(bodyName);

// Create a Name object and add body child elements
 Name elemName = soapEnvelope.createName("BookName");

SOAPElement se = body.addChildElement(elemName);
se.addTextNode("Developing Java Web services");
```

Adding SOAP Attachment Parts

Our next step is to add AttachmentPart to the message using the JAF API. This is the same process that we discussed earlier when using the provider.

Now, to add attachments to the message, we create an AttachmentPart object:

```
// Access the URL of an image attachment
URL url = new URL("http://www.wiley.com/jws/jwsbookcover.jpg");

// Use JAF, and create a JAF DataHandler with this URL
DataHandler dataHandler = new DataHandler(url);

// Create and Add an AttachmentPart
```

```
message.addAttachmentPart(
     message.createAttachmentPart(dataHandler));
```

Saving the SOAP Message

Update the `SOAPMessage` object with all the additions to the message by calling the `saveChanges()` method:

```
// Save the message
message.saveChanges();
```

Sending the Message and Receiving a Response

Create a `URLEndpoint`, pass it with the URI of the remote partner, and then send the messages using the `SOAPConnection.call()` method:

```
// Create an Endpoint of the remote partner
URLEndpoint urlEndpoint
           = new URLEndpoint("http://www.coffee.com/purchase");
// Send the message and wait for response
SOAPmessage response = sc.call(message, urlEndpoint);

if (response != null) {
      // do something here...
} else {
      System.err.println("No response received from partner");
}
```

Closing the Provider Connection

The last step is to close the `SOAPConnection` by calling `SOAPConnection.close()`:

```
// Close the SOAP connection
sc.close();
```

Receiving Messages

On the client side, to receive messages synchronously and to send a response message back to the sender, it is required that we use a `JAXMServlet` implementing `ReqRespListener`.

The key implementation steps for synchronously receiving messages using a `ReqRespListener` are as follows:

1. Create a servlet extending `JAXMServlet` and implementing the `ReqRespListener` interface. This registers as a listener within the servlet container.

2. Create a `MessageFactory` instance.
3. Implement the `onMessage()` method to process the incoming message and use the `MessageFactory` instance to create and send a response message.

A typical JAXM-based servlet implementation using `ReqRespListener` for receiving and sending response messages to the sender is shown in Listing 9.2.

```
public class MyReqRespServlet extends JAXMServlet
                                    implements ReqRespListener {
  MessageFactory mf = null;
   // Create a MessageFactory instance
   static {
      try {
         mf = MessageFactory.newInstance();
      } catch (Exception ex) {
         e.printStackTrace();
      }
   };

  public void init(ServletConfig sc) throws ServletException {
     // Initialize servlet config...
  }

  // Upon receiving messages, calls the onMessage method
   // Process the Incoming message and return a response

  public SOAPMessage onMessage(SOAPMessage msg) {

    try {
       System.out.println("The Incoming message: ");
        msg.writeTo(System.out);

     // Create and return a response message
        SOAPMessage resp = mf.createMessage();
        SOAPEnvelope se = resp.getSOAPPart().getEnvelope();
         env.getBody().addChildElement(
              se.createName("ResponseMessage")).addTextNode
                                 ("Received Message, Thanks");

         return resp;
    } catch(Exception e) {
        // ...
  }
  }
}
```

Listing 9.2 A code snippet showing a JAXM servlet implementation for a SOAP-based connection.

This summarizes the JAXM API programming model and the programming steps required to handle the different scenarios defined by the JAXM 1.1 specification.

JAXM Deployment Model

As per the JAXM 1.1 specification, the JAXM-based applications can be packaged and deployed in Java servlet 2.2-compliant or J2EE 1.3-complaint servlet containers. It also is expected that the upcoming J2EE 1.4 specification and reference implementation will address JAXM-specific deployment information and its relationship with message driven Beans.

In the case of the JAXM applications not using a JAXM provider and running as request/response-based SOAP communications, there is no need to follow any packaging or deployment requirements except for the JAXM API and SAAJ API libraries, which are required to be available in its CLASSPATH. In general, it applies to JAXM applications that do not use a servlet/J2EE container environment.

Deploying JAXM-Based Applications in JWSDP 1.0

In a JWSDP 1.0 environment, JAXM applications are implemented as a servlet and are packaged either as a Web Application (WAR) or a J2EE Application (EAR). Typical to servlet deployment, the deployment information is provided using an XML-based deployment descriptor (web.xml).

The key steps in JAXM-based application deployment are as follows:

1. Ensure that the JWSDP environment is up and running. Log onto your JWSDP/Tomcat administration console at http://localhost:8080/admin/index.jsp. Navigate through the sidebar options, Service (Internal Services) Host (jwsdp-services), and check the CONTEXT for `/jaxm-provider` and `/jaxm-provideradmin` available. This ensures that the JAXM provider is deployed and available for use.
2. Create a working directory (for example, d:\jwsdp1_0\mywork\) and build an environment (build.xml), ensuring that the CLASSPATH includes the following JAXM-specific class libraries and application-specific class libraries (JARs).

```
activation.jar
mail.jar
jaxm-api.jar
saaj-api.jar
crimson.jar
dom4j.jar
```

```
commons-logging.jar
servlet.jar
jaxp-api.jar
sax.jar
dom.jar
xercesImpl.jar
xalan.jar
xsltc.jar
```

3. As we discussed earlier in the JAXM programming model, the JAXM-based applications using the provider must be implemented as a servlet extending the `JAXMServlet` interface. In the case of a message-receiving application, it is required that we implement an `onMessage()` method. Create a build script ensuring that the previously listed libraries are included in the CLASSPATH. Compile the application classes.
4. Create a Web application deployment descriptor (`web.xml`), defining the servlet-specific deployment parameters such as class name, mapping, and so forth. For example:

```
<servlet>
      <servlet-name>
          consumerservlet
      </servlet-name>
      <servlet-class>
          ch9.jaxmprovider.WileyConsumerServlet
      </servlet-class>
<load-on-startup>
  1
</load-on-startup>
  </servlet>

<servlet-mapping>
      <servlet-name>
          consumerservlet
      </servlet-name>
      <url-pattern>
          /wileyconsumer
      </url-pattern>
</servlet-mapping>
```

5. Typical to any servlet deployment, ensure that the classes and deployment descriptor reside in a WEB-INF directory. Package the classes, including the deployment descriptor (`web.xml`), as a Web application (`WAR`).

The sample ANT build and deploy script will be shown as follows:

```
<—Compile the source code‡
  <target name="compile">
    <javac srcdir="${work_dir}/src_dir"
           destdir="${build.dir}/${appname}/WEB-INF/classes"
      <classpath >
      <fileset refid="jaxm-appclasspath" />
      <fileset refid="jaxm-classpath" />
      <pathelement location="${servlet.jar}" />
      </classpath>
    </javac>

<—Copy classes and deployment decriptor to  WEB-INF directory‡
    <copy todir="${build.dir}/${appname}/WEB-INF/classes">
      <fileset dir="${work_dir}/src_dir">
      <include name="**/*.xml" />
      </fileset>
    </copy>
  </target>

<—Package the application as WAR‡
<target name="war"
        depends="main"
        description="Creating the WAR file">

    <jar jarfile="webapps/jaxm-${appname}.war"
       basedir="${build.dir}/${appname}" >
       <include name="**"/>
    </jar>
</target>
```

Copy the application WAR file, to the `/webapps` directory in the JWSDP environment and restart the server. Using a Web browser, check to see whether the servlet application is deployed and then test the JAXM services using its clients.

Configuring JAXM Applications Using a JAXM Provider

In the case of JAXM-based applications using a JAXM provider, it is required that we configure the applications with the provider, especially in order to provide information about the mapping endpoint, message retry intervals, logging, and so forth.

Configuring a Client

To configure a client sending messages to a provider, a JAXM provider requires the configuration descriptor file `client.xml`, which defines the `Endpoint`, `CallbackURL`, Provider information, and so forth. The `CallbackURL` defines a message consumer servlet to receive messages in case of callbacks. This `client.xml` must be packaged along with the other classes of the Web/J2EE application during deployment. Listing 9.3 shows a code listing of a sample `client.xml`.

```
<?xml version="1.0" encoding="ISO-8859-1"?>

<!DOCTYPE ClientConfig
    PUBLIC "-//Sun Microsystems, Inc.//DTD JAXM Client//EN"
    "http://java.sun.com/xml/dtds/jaxm_client_1_0.dtd">
<ClientConfig>
    <Endpoint>
      http://jws.wiley.com/jaxmapp/producer
    </Endpoint>
    <CallbackURL>
       http://localhost:8080/jaxm-jaxmapp/messageconsumer
    </CallbackURL>
    <Provider>
      <URI>http://java.sun.com/xml/jaxm/provider</URI>
      <URL>http://localhost:8081/jaxm-provider/sender</URL>
    </Provider>
</ClientConfig>
```

Listing 9.3 Sample `Client.xml`.

Configuring a Provider

The JAXM 1.1 RI provides a JAXM provider administration tool, which enables the configuration of the JAXM provider with the application. It also enables the identification of the JAXM application with the profile used (ebXML, SOAP-RP) and the transport protocol (HTTP(s)), and it also enables the definition of the destination endpoints, parameters required for message retry interval, message logging, and so forth.

In a JWSDP 1.0 environment, the JAXM provider administration console can be accessed via the Web browser at http://localhost:8081/jaxm-provideradmin/index.jsp. In case of provider to provider communication running on different machines, the target provider URL needs to be defined specific to the machine. The provider also can be configured using an XML-based configuration (`provider.xml`). Listing 9.4 is a code listing of a sample `provider.xml`.

```
<?xml version="1.0" encoding="UTF-8"?>
<!DOCTYPE ProviderConfig PUBLIC "-//Sun Microsystems, Inc.//DTD JAXM
Provider//EN" "http://java.sun.com/xml/dtds/jaxm_provider_1_0.dtd">

<ProviderConfig>
  <Profile profileId="ebxml">
    <Transport>
      <Protocol>http</Protocol>
      <Endpoint type="uri">
        <URI>http://www.wiley.com/jaxmebxml/consumer</URI>
        <URL>http://192.168.168.100:8081/jaxm-receiver/ebxml</URL>
      </Endpoint>
      <Endpoint type="uri">
        <URI>http://www.wiley.com/jaxmebxml/producer</URI>
        <URL>http://192.168.168.101:8081/receiver/ebxml</URL>
      </Endpoint>
      <ErrorHandling>
        <Retry>
          <MaxRetries>5</MaxRetries>
          <RetryInterval>2000</RetryInterval>
        </Retry>
      </ErrorHandling>
      <Persistence>
        <Directory>ebxml/wiley</Directory>
        <RecordsPerFile>10</RecordsPerFile>
      </Persistence>
    </Transport>
    <Transport>
      <Protocol>https</Protocol>
      <Persistence>
        <Directory>ebxml-https/</Directory>
        <RecordsPerFile>10</RecordsPerFile>
      </Persistence>
    </Transport>
  </Profile>
  <Profile profileId="soaprp">
    <Transport>
      <Protocol>http</Protocol>
      <Endpoint type="uri">
        <URI>http://www.wiley.com/jaxmsoaprp/producer</URI>
        <URL>http://127.0.0.1:8081/jaxm-provider/receiver/soaprp</URL>
      </Endpoint>
      <ErrorHandling>
```

Listing 9.4 Sample `Provider.xml` for configuring a provider-based communication. *(continues)*

```
        <Retry>
          <MaxRetries>3</MaxRetries>
          <RetryInterval>2000</RetryInterval>
        </Retry>
      </ErrorHandling>
      <Persistence>
        <Directory>soaprp/</Directory>
        <RecordsPerFile>20</RecordsPerFile>
      </Persistence>
    </Transport>
  </Profile>
  <ErrorHandling>
    <Retry>
      <MaxRetries>3</MaxRetries>
      <RetryInterval>2000</RetryInterval>
    </Retry>
  </ErrorHandling>
  <Persistence>
    <Directory>tempdir/</Directory>
    <RecordsPerFile>11</RecordsPerFile>
  </Persistence>
</ProviderConfig>
```

Listing 9.4 Sample `Provider.xml` for configuring a provider-based communication. *(continued)*

The following section discusses how to develop and deploy JAXM-based applications and services in a JWSDP 1.0 environment.

Developing JAXM-Based Web Services

In this section, we illustrate and discuss example scenarios of developing JAXM-based Web services applications using the JAXM 1.1 reference implementation (JAXM RI) provided in the JWSDP 1.0 bundle. In particular, we will be implementing Web services using the following JAXM-based messaging scenarios:

- Point-to-point/Synchronous messaging without using a JAXM provider
- Asynchronous messaging using a JAXM provider

To illustrate the previous scenarios, we implement a purchase order submission process in a B2B connectivity between a seller (service provider) and buyer (service requestor). The buyer sends out an XML message with purchase order information to the service provider, and the service provider receives and acknowledges the message.

Point-to-Point Messaging Using JAXM (SOAPConnection)

In this example scenario, we implement a standalone JAXM application client (service requestor) and a JAXM-based servlet (service provider) running in a JWSDP/Tomcat container environment. Both the service requestor and service provider communicate directly through requests and responses through the same SOAP Connection and without using a JAXM provider. The application client sends a request (purchase order) directly to the JAXM servlet endpoint and passes an XML document, and the JAXM servlet receives the XML document and returns a response.

Creating a Standalone JAXM Client

The JAXM RI provides class libraries to generate SOAP messages using the JAXM/SAAJ APIs and a client-side runtime library to send and receive messages from the remote application partner. We will use these libraries to implement and test them.

Listing 9.5 shows a code listing for a standalone JAXM client (`StandaloneSOAPClient.java`).

```
package jws.ch9.jaxmp2p.sender;

import java.io.*;
import java.net.URL;
import javax.xml.transform.*;
import javax.xml.transform.stream.*;
import org.dom4j.*;

import javax.xml.soap.*;

/*
 *   StandaloneSOAPClient.java
```

Listing 9.5 `StandaloneSOAPClient.java`. *(continues)*

```
*   Usage: StandaloneSOAPClient <endpoint URL> <XML Document>
*/

public class StandaloneSOAPClient {

   // Main method
  public static void main(String args[]) {

    try {
       URL endpoint = null;

       if (args.length != 2) {
           System.err.println("Usage:StandaloneSOAPClient
                                 <endpointURL> <XMLDocument>" );
           System.exit(1);
       }

       // Obtain the endpoint URL of the JAXM receiver as an argument
       endpoint=new URL( args[0] );

       // Create an Instance of SOAP connection factory
        SOAPConnectionFactory scf
              = SOAPConnectionFactory.newInstance();

       // Create a SOAP connection using the factory Instance
        SOAPConnection sc = scf.createConnection();

       // Create an instance of the message factory
        MessageFactory msgFactory = MessageFactory.newInstance();


       // Create a message from the message factory.
        SOAPMessage message = msgFactory.createMessage();

       // Get the SOAP Part from the message.
        SOAPPart soapPart = message.getSOAPPart();

       // Get the SOAP Envelope
        SOAPEnvelope envelope = soapPart.getEnvelope();


       // Get the XML content from the current dir (file)
       //  as a Stream source

        StreamSource ssrc=new StreamSource(
                             new FileInputStream(args[1] ));

       // Set the Content as SOAP part
```

Listing 9.5 StandaloneSOAPClient.java.

```
        soapPart.setContent( ssrc );


        // Save the Message
         message.saveChanges();

         System.out.println("Sending XML message to URL: "+ endpoint);

        // Send the message and obtain the response

         SOAPMessage response = sc.call(message, endpoint);


System.out.println("\n=======================================\n");

         System.err.println("\nMessage sent to :" + endpoint + "
                      \nSent Message logged to file:
P2PMessageSent.txt");

        // Write the sent message to log

         FileOutputStream sentFile =
                    new FileOutputStream("P2PMessageSent.txt");
         message.writeTo(sentFile);
         sentFile.close();


        // Receive the response and display its content as String
         boolean receivedResponse =true;

         if(receivedResponse) {

System.out.println("\n=====================================\n");

           System.out.println("Displaying the response message:");

           // Create an Instance of Transformer factory
            TransformerFactory tFact=TransformerFactory.newInstance();

           // Create a Transformer using the factory Instance
            Transformer transformer = tFact.newTransformer();

           // Obtain the SOAPPart/Content from the SOAP message
            Source content=response.getSOAPPart().getContent();

           // Write the content as String
            StreamResult respMsg=new StreamResult( System.out );
```

Listing 9.5 StandaloneSOAPClient.java. *(continues)*

```
            // Transform the received XML document to String
             transformer.transform(content, respMsg);
           }

           // Close the SOAP connection
           sc.close();

      } catch(Throwable e) {
            e.printStackTrace();
      }
    }
  }
```

Listing 9.5 `StandaloneSOAPClient.java`. ***(continued)***

Ensure that the JAXM RI and other dependent class libraries are available in CLASSPATH. (For CLASSPATH requirement details, refer to the section titled *JAXM Deployment Model* earlier in this chapter.) Then, compile `StandaloneSOAPClient.java` using the Ant build script (`build.xml`). Figure 9.5 shows the output of the compilation.

JAXM Receiver Servlet

Now, let's take a look at the remote partner running as servlet in a JWSDP environment (using a Tomcat servlet container). The servlet extends the JAXM servlet, implements `ReqRespListener`, receives the messages as a SOAP request, and returns a SOAR response message over HTTP. Listing 9.6 shows the code for the JAXM servlet (`JAXMReceiverServlet.java`).

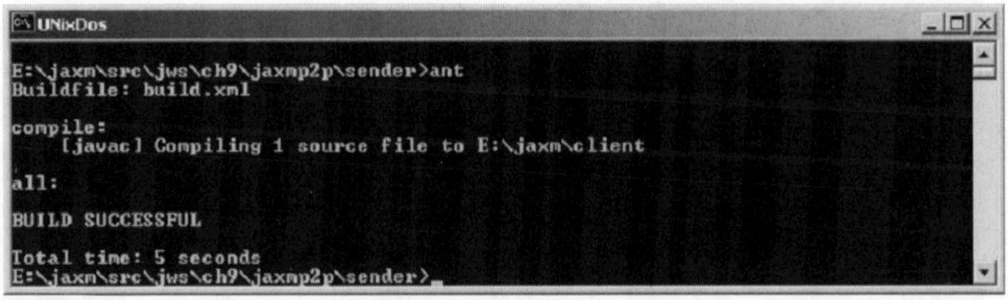

```
UNixDos

E:\jaxm\src\jws\ch9\jaxmp2p\sender>ant
Buildfile: build.xml

compile:
    [javac] Compiling 1 source file to E:\jaxm\client

all:

BUILD SUCCESSFUL

Total time: 5 seconds
E:\jaxm\src\jws\ch9\jaxmp2p\sender>_
```

Figure 9.5 Compiling `StandaloneSOAPClient.java`.

```
package jws.ch9.jaxmp2p.receiver;

import javax.servlet.*;
import javax.servlet.http.*;
import javax.xml.transform.*;
import javax.naming.*;

import javax.xml.soap.*;
import javax.xml.messaging.*;


/**
 * JAXMReceiverServlet.java.
 * Runs as a Servlet in a Servlet container based JWSDP environment
 */

public class JAXMReceiverServlet extends JAXMServlet
                                      implements ReqRespListener
{
    static MessageFactory mf = null;

   // Create an instance of the message factory
    static {
        try {
            mf = MessageFactory.newInstance();
        } catch (Exception e) {
            e.printStackTrace();
        }
    };

    // Initialize servlet config
    public void init(ServletConfig sc) throws ServletException {
        super.init(sc);
    }


   // Upon receiving messages, calls the onMessage method
   // Process the Incoming message and return a response
    public SOAPMessage onMessage(SOAPMessage msg) {

        SOAPMessage message = null;

        System.out.println("Running JAXMReceiverClient");

        try {
```

Listing 9.6 `JAXMReceiverServlet.java`. *(continues)*

```
            System.out.println("Incoming message: ");
            // Write out Incoming message
            msg.writeTo(System.out);

            // Create a SOAP message using message factory instance
            message = mf.createMessage();

           // Get the SOAP Part and create an envelope
           SOAPEnvelope envelope
                   = message.getSOAPPart().getEnvelope();

            // Add elements to the SOAP body
           envelope.getBody()
               .addChildElement(envelope.createName("Response"))
                .addTextNode("Purchase order received successfully");
        } catch(Exception e) {
           e.printStackTrace();

        }
        // Return the response message
        return message;

    }
}
```

Listing 9.6 JAXMReceiverServlet.java. ***(continued)***

Create a Web application deployment descriptor (web.xml) for JAXM-ReceiverServlet. Listing 9.7 shows the code for the deployment descriptor (web.xml).

```
<?xml version="1.0" encoding="ISO-8859-1"?>

<!DOCTYPE web-app
    PUBLIC "-//Sun Microsystems, Inc.//DTD Web Application 2.2//EN"
    "http://java.sun.com/j2ee/dtds/web-app_2_2.dtd">

<web-app>
    <servlet>
        <servlet-name>
            jaxmreceiver
        </servlet-name>
        <servlet-class>
            jws.ch9.jaxmp2p.receiver.JAXMReceiverServlet
        </servlet-class>
```

Listing 9.7 Web deployment descriptor (web.xml).

```
        <load-on-startup>
          2
        </load-on-startup>
      </servlet>

      <servlet-mapping>
          <servlet-name>
              jaxmreceiver
          </servlet-name>
          <url-pattern>
              /jaxmreceiver
          </url-pattern>
      </servlet-mapping>
  </web-app>
```

Listing 9.7 Web deployment descriptor (`web.xml`). *(continued)*

Now, we are all set to compile and deploy the servlet (see Figure 9.6). First, we must ensure that the JAXM RI and other dependent class libraries are available in CLASSPATH as per the CLASSPATH requirement details, provided in the section titled *JAXM Deployment Model*. Navigate to the source directory and run the Ant build script (`build.xml`).

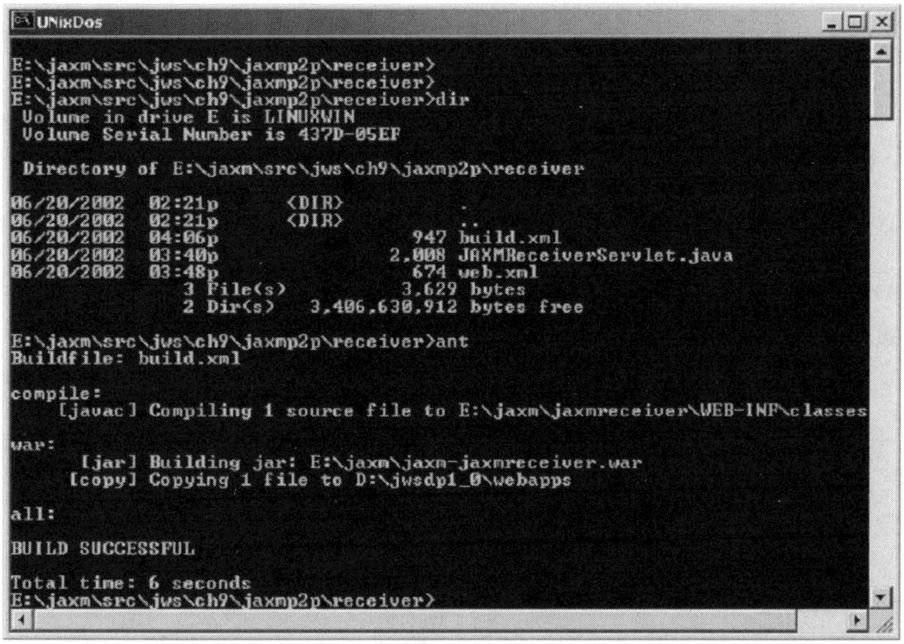

```
UNixDos
E:\jaxm\src\jws\ch9\jaxmp2p\receiver>
E:\jaxm\src\jws\ch9\jaxmp2p\receiver>
E:\jaxm\src\jws\ch9\jaxmp2p\receiver>dir
 Volume in drive E is LINUXWIN
 Volume Serial Number is 437D-05EF

 Directory of E:\jaxm\src\jws\ch9\jaxmp2p\receiver

06/20/2002  02:21p      <DIR>          .
06/20/2002  02:21p      <DIR>          ..
06/20/2002  04:06p                 947 build.xml
06/20/2002  03:40p               2,008 JAXMReceiverServlet.java
06/20/2002  03:48p                 674 web.xml
               3 File(s)          3,629 bytes
               2 Dir(s)   3,406,630,912 bytes free

E:\jaxm\src\jws\ch9\jaxmp2p\receiver>ant
Buildfile: build.xml

compile:
    [javac] Compiling 1 source file to E:\jaxm\jaxmreceiver\WEB-INF\classes

war:
      [jar] Building jar: E:\jaxm\jaxm-jaxmreceiver.war
     [copy] Copying 1 file to D:\jwsdp1_0\webapps

all:

BUILD SUCCESSFUL

Total time: 6 seconds
E:\jaxm\src\jws\ch9\jaxmp2p\receiver>
```

Figure 9.6 Packaging and deploying the `JAXMReceiverServlet`.

The build script will compile and copy the `jaxm-jaxmreceiver.war` file to the Tomcat Webapps directory. Restart the Tomcat server and ensure that the servlet is deployed and `JAXMReceiverServlet` is ready for use. The deployed servlet facilitates a JAXM service endpoint available for use at http://localhost:8080/jaxm-jaxmreceiver/jaxmreceiver.

Testing the Scenario

To test the scenario, ensure that the CLASSPATH is set. Then, run the client program providing the endpoint URL of the receiver and the name of the XML document as parameters for using the following command:

```
java jws.ch9.jaxmp2p.sender.StandaloneSOAPClient
    http://localhost:8080/jaxm-jaxmreceiver/jaxmreceiver
PurchaseOrder.xml
```

If everything works successfully, you should receive the output in Figure 9.7.

As the output shows, the `StandaloneSOAPClient` sends the SOAP message to the endpoint URL of the `JAXMReceiverServlet` as a request. In turn, the `JAXMReceiverServlet` returns a reply message via the same connection, which contains the response "Purchase order received successfully."

Now that you have seen an example of a point-to-point messaging scenario, the following section gives you a look at the asynchronous messaging scenario using the JAXM provider.

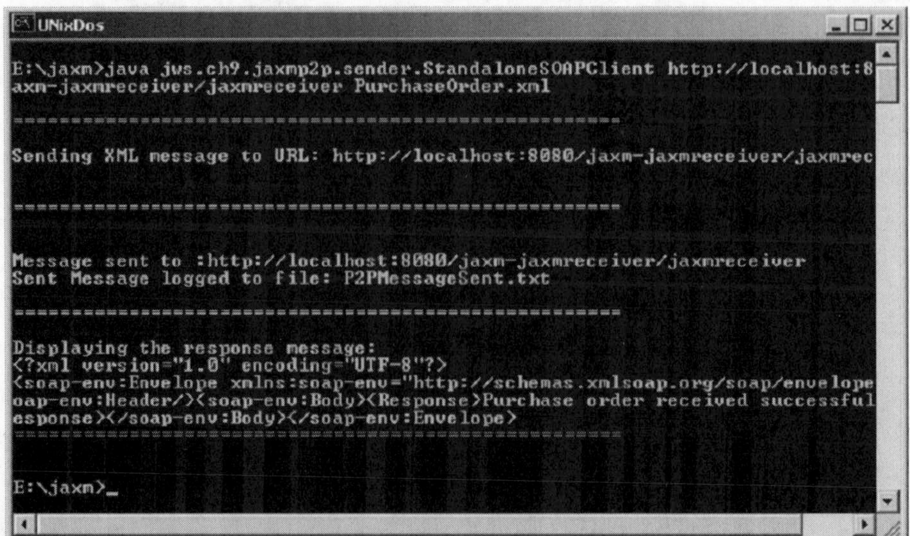

UNixDos
E:\jaxm>java jws.ch9.jaxmp2p.sender.StandaloneSOAPClient http://localhost:8
axm-jaxmreceiver/jaxmreceiver PurchaseOrder.xml
Sending XML message to URL: http://localhost:8080/jaxm-jaxmreceiver/jaxmrec
Message sent to :http://localhost:8080/jaxm-jaxmreceiver/jaxmreceiver
Sent Message logged to file: P2PMessageSent.txt
Displaying the response message:
<?xml version="1.0" encoding="UTF-8"?>
<soap-env:Envelope xmlns:soap-env="http://schemas.xmlsoap.org/soap/envelope
oap-env:Header/><soap-env:Body><Response>Purchase order received successful
esponse></soap-env:Body></soap-env:Envelope>
E:\jaxm>_

Figure 9.7 Output showing the message sent to `JAXMReceiverServlet`.

Asynchronous Messaging Using the JAXM Provider

In this example scenario, we implement both the producer and consumer of messages as servlets using JAXM providers running on a local JWSDP/Tomcat container environment. Both the message producer (service requestor) and message consumer (service provider) communicate asynchronously using the JAXM provider.

We will be using the ebXML messaging profile and its API implementation provided with the JAXM RI. In addition to constructing the basic SOAP message, we also will add ebXML headers in the message, using the APIs provided with JAXM RI. This enables the SOAP message to take advantage of the JAXM provider and the characteristics of ebXML messaging.

The message producer servlet sends a document to its JAXM provider, and in turn, the provider forwards the message to the next destination endpoint. The provider associated with that endpoint receives the message asynchronously and then forwards it to its ultimate destination, which is a message consumer servlet.

ebXML Producer Servlet

Because ebXML is built on SOAP and complies with the SOAP 1.1 specifications and SOAP Messages with Attachments, in this section we will be constructing a SOAP message using the ebXML message profile and its API implementation provided with JAXM 1.1 RI. We will be using a JWSDP 1.0/Tomcat container as our JAXM provider, and both the message producer and consumer servlet will run in the same environment.

The message producer servlet sends a book purchase order (an XML document) to the Wiley Web services provider. As part of the message, it also uses an attachment URL showing the book information.

Listing 9.8 shows the code for the ebXML producer servlet (`ebXMLProducerServlet.java`).

```
package jws.ch9.jaxmebxml.producer;

import java.net.*;
import java.io.*;
import java.util.*;

import javax.servlet.http.*;
import javax.servlet.*;

import javax.xml.messaging.*;
import javax.xml.soap.*;
```

Listing 9.8 `ebXMLProducerServlet.java`. *(continues)*

```
import javax.activation.*;

// Import ebXML profile implementation
import com.sun.xml.messaging.jaxm.ebxml.*;

/**
 * ebXMLProducerServlet.java
 * Uses a provider based connection to send messages
 * Runs as a servlet in a container based environment
 */

public class ebXMLProducerServlet extends HttpServlet {


    private String MessageFrom
            ="http://www.wiley.com/jaxmebxml/producer";
    private String MessageTo =
                       "http://www.wiley.com/jaxmebxml/consumer";

    private String attachmentURL =
          "http://www.wiley.com/cda/product/0,,0471236403,00.html";

    private ProviderConnectionFactory pcf;
    private ProviderConnection pc;
    private MessageFactory mf = null;

    public void init(ServletConfig servletConfig)
                                     throws ServletException {
        super.init( servletConfig );

        try {

         // Creates an instance of ProviderConnectionFactory and
         // establishes Provider connection

         pcf = ProviderConnectionFactory.newInstance();
         pc = pcf.createConnection();
        } catch(Exception e) {
            e.printStackTrace();
        }
    }

    public void doGet(HttpServletRequest req,
                          HttpServletResponse resp)
                      throws ServletException, IOException     {

      PrintWriter out = resp.getWriter();
```

Listing 9.8 ebXMLProducerServlet.java.

```
        resp.setContentType("text/html");

        try {

          if (mf == null) {

           // Get Provider supported messaging profiles
              ProviderMetaData metaData = pc.getMetaData();
              String[] supportedProfiles
                       = metaData.getSupportedProfiles();
              String profile = null;

              for(int i=0; i < supportedProfiles.length; i++) {

              // Find out the ebXML profile by matching ebXML
                 if(supportedProfiles[i].equals("ebxml")) {
                     profile = supportedProfiles[i];
                     break;
                 }
              }

          // Create a Message factory instance using the profile
              mf = pc.createMessageFactory(profile);
          }

          // Create an ebXML message from the message factory.
          EbXMLMessageImpl ebxmlMsg
                          = (EbXMLMessageImpl)mf.createMessage();

          // Set the Message sender and receiver
          ebxmlMsg.setSender(new Party(MessageFrom));
          ebxmlMsg.setReceiver(new Party(MessageTo));



          // Get the SOAP Part from the message.
          SOAPPart soapPart = ebxmlMsg.getSOAPPart();

          // Get the SOAP Envelope
          SOAPEnvelope soapEnvelope = soapPart.getEnvelope();

          // Create the SOAPBody
          SOAPBody soapBody = soapEnvelope.getBody();


          // Create a Name object and add to SOAPBodyElement
          Name bodyName =
```

Listing 9.8 ebXMLProducerServlet.java. *(continues)*

```
        soapEnvelope.createName("SubmitPurchaseOrder",
                      "wiley","http://jws.wiley.com/jws");
SOAPBodyElement sbe = soapBody.addBodyElement(bodyName);

// Create a Name object and add body child elements
Name elemName = soapEnvelope.createName("BookName");
SOAPElement se =  soapBody.addChildElement(elemName);
se.addTextNode("Developing Java Web services");

// Set Attachment URL
URL url = new URL(attachmentURL);

// Add Attachment URL as an attachment
AttachmentPart ap =
        ebxmlMsg.createAttachmentPart(new DataHandler(url));
ap.setContentType("text/html");

// Add the attachment part to the message.
ebxmlMsg.addAttachmentPart(ap);

// Print the message delivery status of Message
out.println("<html><head><title>");
out.println("ebXML Producer Servlet
                         - Status </title></head>");
out.println("<H1> ebXML Producer Servlet
                         - Status </H1></HR>");
out.println("<H3>Message sent to : "
                         + ebxmlMsg.getTo() + "</H3><HR>");

// Write the sent message to a file
out.println("<H3>Sent Message saved to file
           in \"e:\\jaxm\\messages\\ebXMLsent.msg\"</H3>");

FileOutputStream sentFile  =
   new FileOutputStream("e:\\jaxm\\messages\\ebXMLsent.msg");
ebxmlMsg.writeTo(sentFile);
sentFile.close();

// Send the message using the provider connection
pc.send(ebxmlMsg);

out.println("<H3>Message delivered
                    to the provider</H3><HR>");

out.close();

// Close the provider connection
```

Listing 9.8 ebXMLProducerServlet.java.

```
            pc.close();

        } catch(Throwable e) {
            e.printStackTrace();
        }
    }
}
```

Listing 9.8 `ebXMLProducerServlet.java`. *(continued)*

Create a client configuration descriptor (`client.xml`) for the `ebXML-ProducerServlet`, providing the `client endpoint`, `callbackURL`, and its provider URL. Listing 9.9 shows the code for the `Client.xml`.

```
<?xml version="1.0" encoding="ISO-8859-1"?>

<!DOCTYPE ClientConfig
    PUBLIC "-//Sun Microsystems, Inc.//DTD JAXM Client//EN"
    "http://java.sun.com/xml/dtds/jaxm_client_1_0.dtd">
<ClientConfig>
    <Endpoint>
      http://www.wiley.com/jaxmebxml/producer
    </Endpoint>
    <CallbackURL>
       http://localhost:8080/jaxm-jaxmebxml/ebxmlconsumer
    </CallbackURL>
    <Provider>
      <URI>http://java.sun.com/xml/jaxm/provider</URI>
      <URL>http://localhost:8081/jaxm-provider/sender</URL>
    </Provider>
</ClientConfig>
```

Listing 9.9 `Client.xml`.

ebXML Consumer Servlet

Now, let's take a look at the remote partner running as a servlet in a JWSDP environment (using a Tomcat servlet container). The `ebXMLConsumer-Servlet` acts as a service to consume and process incoming JAXM messages. The servlet extends `JAXMServlet` and implements `OneWay-Listener` to receive the messages over HTTP. Listing 9.10 shows a sample code listing for the `ebXMLConsumerServlet.java`.

```
package jws.ch9.jaxmebxml.consumer;

import javax.xml.messaging.*;
import javax.xml.soap.*;
import javax.servlet.*;
import javax.servlet.http.*;

import javax.xml.transform.*;
import java.io.*;
import java.util.*;

// import ebXML profile implementation (JAXM 1.1)
import com.sun.xml.messaging.jaxm.ebxml.*;

/**
 * ebXMLConsumerServlet.java
 * Uses provider based connection to receive messages
 * Runs as a servlet in a container based environment
 */

public class ebXMLConsumerServlet extends JAXMServlet implements
OnewayListener {

    private ProviderConnectionFactory pcf;
    private ProviderConnection pc;

  public void init(ServletConfig sc) throws ServletException {
        super.init(sc);

    try {

       // Creates an intance of ProviderConnectionFactory and
       // ProviderConnection

       pcf = ProviderConnectionFactory.newInstance();
       pc = pcf.createConnection();

       // Sets the Message factory to ebXML profile implementation
       setMessageFactory(new EbXMLMessageFactoryImpl());

    } catch (Exception ex) {
      ex.printStackTrace();
      throw new ServletException("Initialization failed : " +
                                            ex.getMessage());
    }
  }


 // Upon receiving messages, calls the onMessage method
```

Listing 9.10 ebXMLConsumerServlet.java.

```
// processes the Incoming message

public void onMessage(SOAPMessage msg) {

    try {
        System.out.println("Receiving the incoming ebXML message: ");

        // Saves the incoming message
        msg.saveChanges();

        // Writes to a file in a desired location
        FileOutputStream receivedFile
                  = new FileOutputStream\
                        ("e:\\jaxm\\messages\\ebXMLreceived.msg");
        msg.writeTo(receivedFile);
        receivedFile.close();

    } catch(Exception e) {
       e.printStackTrace();
    }
 }
}
```

Listing 9.10 ebXMLConsumerServlet.java. *(continued)*

Deployment

Create a Web application deployment descriptor (web.xml) for both the ebXMLProducerServlet and ebXMLConsumerServlet. The code listing for the deployment descriptor (web.xml) is shown in Listing 9.11.

```
<?xml version="1.0" encoding="ISO-8859-1"?>

<!DOCTYPE web-app
    PUBLIC "-//Sun Microsystems, Inc.//DTD Web Application 2.2//EN"
    "http://java.sun.com/j2ee/dtds/web-app_2_2.dtd">

<web-app>
    <servlet>
        <servlet-name>
            ebxmlproducerservlet
        </servlet-name>
        <servlet-class>
            jws.ch9.jaxmebxml.producer.ebXMLProducerServlet
        </servlet-class>
```

Listing 9.11 Deployment descriptor (web.xml). *(continues)*

```
    <load-on-startup>
      2
    </load-on-startup>
   </servlet>
  <servlet>
       <servlet-name>
           ebxmlconsumerservlet
       </servlet-name>
       <servlet-class>
           jws.ch9.jaxmebxml.consumer.ebXMLConsumerServlet
       </servlet-class>
    <load-on-startup>
      2
    </load-on-startup>
   </servlet>

    <servlet-mapping>
       <servlet-name>
           ebxmlproducerservlet
       </servlet-name>
       <url-pattern>
           /ebxmlproducer
       </url-pattern>
   </servlet-mapping>
       <servlet-mapping>
       <servlet-name>
           ebxmlconsumerservlet
       </servlet-name>
       <url-pattern>
           /ebxmlconsumer
       </url-pattern>
   </servlet-mapping>
  </web-app>
```

Listing 9.11 Deployment descriptor (`web.xml`). *(continued)*

In a JAXM provider-based messaging environment, we need to configure the provider specifying the profile used, the protocol, endpoints for the producer and the consumer of messages, and any other information specific to message retry interval, such as message logging, error handling, and so forth. To accomplish this, use a JAXM 1.1 RI provider configuration tool through a Web browser (for example, http://127.0.0.1:8081/jaxm-provideradmin/index.jsp), and choose Select Profiles → ebXML → HTTP.

Then choose Create a new Endpoint mapping from the Available Action pull-down menu. Then, add the endpoint mappings, as follows:

URI	URL
http://www.wiley.com/jaxmebxml/producer	http://receivermachine:8081/jaxm-provider/receiver/ebxml

Finally, save the changes to the profile. If everything is saved successfully, the JAXM administration console should look like Figure 9.8.

At this point, we are all set to compile and build the Web application. Using an Ant script (build.xml), compile the producer and consumer servlets. Create a Web application (WAR) file containing the `ebXMLProducerServlet` and `ebXMLConsumerServlet` classes, also including the deployment descriptors `Client.xml` and `Web.xml`. Copy the WAR file to the Tomcat/Webapps directory. If everything works successfully, the build process displayed will look like Figure 9.9.

Then, restart the Tomcat server.

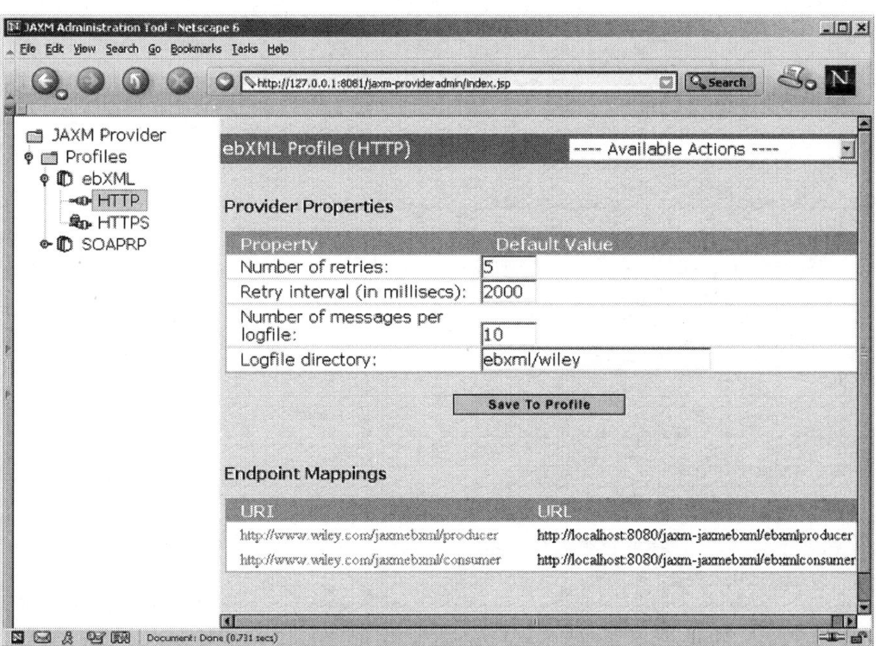

Figure 9.8 Configuring the provider environment.

```
E:\jaxm\src\jws\ch9\jaxmebxml>ant
Buildfile: build.xml

compile:
    [javac] Compiling 1 source file to E:\jaxm\jaxmebxml\WEB-INF\classes
    [javac] Compiling 1 source file to E:\jaxm\jaxmebxml\WEB-INF\classes

war:
      [jar] Building jar: E:\jaxm\jaxm-jaxmebxml.war
     [copy] Copying 1 file to D:\jwsdp1_0\webapps

all:

BUILD SUCCESSFUL

Total time: 8 seconds
E:\jaxm\src\jws\ch9\jaxmebxml>
```

Figure 9.9 Packaging and deploying the ebXMLProducer and Consumer servlets.

Testing the Scenario

To test the scenario, use a Web browser to run the following URL:

```
http://localhost:8080/jaxm-jaxmebxml/ebxmlproducer
```

If everything works successfully, the browser will display the information shown in Figure 9.10.

To ensure the message delivery destination, using a Web browser open the message `ebXMLReceived.msg` that was saved by `ebXMLConsumerServlet`. If everything works successfully, the browser will display the information shown in Figure 9.11.

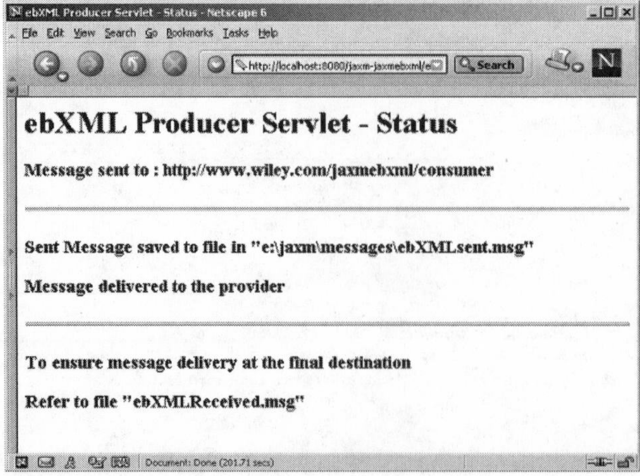

Figure 9.10 Browser showing the status of message sent.

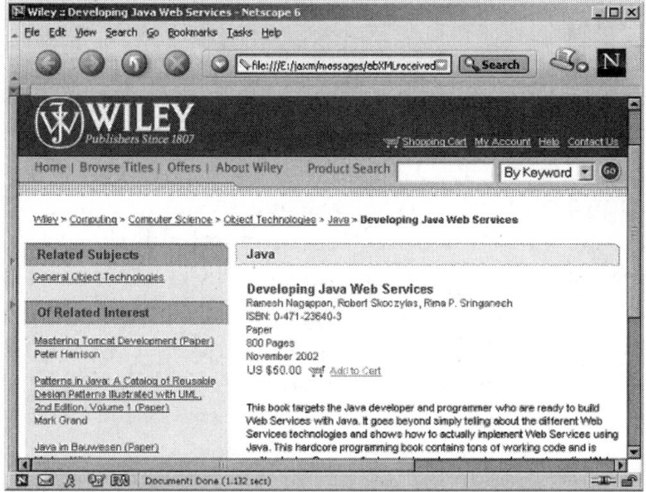

Figure 9.11 Browser showing the contents of attachment in `ebXMLReceived.msg`.

Figure 9.12 shows the messages logged by the JAXM provider during communication. To find out the provider's log of messages, navigate to the JAXM provider logging location, using a Web browser or listing the directory to the following location: %JWSDP_HOME%/work/ServicesEngine /jwsdp-services/jaxm-provider/ebxml/wiley. This applies to the JAXM Reference implementation provided with Sun JWSDP. In case of other JAXM implementations, refer to the provider documentation.

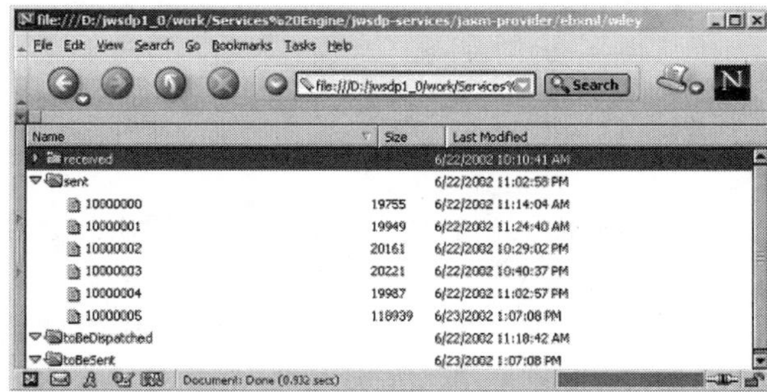

Figure 9.12 Browser showing the JAXM provider message logs.

JAXM Interoperability

A JAXM-based service can interoperate with any SOAP 1.1 provider and its messages with attachments. In an interoperability scenario, the documents exchanged between the JAXM service and the SOAP 1.1-compliant provider have to adopt and agree upon a common message structure, communication protocol, and other supported mechanisms like security, reliability, and so on. In a JAXM provider-based communication model, this is achieved by Messaging profiles. In a SOAP-based communication model without using a JAXM provider, it is important that the SOAP sender and receiver must communicate using a common message structure and protocol bindings.

JAXM in J2EE 1.4

The upcoming release of J2EE 1.4 platform specifications focuses on enabling J2EE components to participate in Web services. As a key requirement, it mandates the implementation of EJB 2.1 specifications that addresses the role of JAXM by enhancing the capabilities of Message-driven beans (MDB) to enable asynchronous processing of JAXM-based messages. In addition to its existing JMS support, the EJB 2.1-compliant MDBs will act as a JAXM message consumer.

In a JAXM-based messaging scenario, the MDBs will implement `java.xml.messaging.ReqRespListener` (for synchronous communication) or `java.xml.messaging.OneWayListener` (for asynchronous communication) as its message listener interfaces. The message destination-specific properties like message type and endpoint will be defined in the EJB deployment descriptor. The key advantages of using MDBs in JAXM communication will allow consuming messages from Web services, enabling J2EE components to participate in Web services.

Summary

In this chapter, we have discussed how to employ JAXM-based XML messaging solutions for enabling Java Web services. We noted that JAXM provides a reliable means of XML-based communication between applications supporting industry standard messaging protocols. In general, we covered the role of JAXM in Web service, JAXM APIs and the programming model, and developing JAXM-based Web services applications.

In the next chapter, we will discuss how to develop Web services applications with remote procedural calls using JAX-RPC.

CHAPTER

10

Building RPC Web Services with JAX-RPC

This chapter discusses the Java API for XML RPC (JAX-RPC), which enables the development of Web services incorporating XML-based remote procedural calls (RPCs).

As we discussed in Chapter 7, "Introduction to the Java Web Services Developer Pack (JWSDP)," JAX-RPC is an integral part of the JWSDP. In a JWSDP-based Web services environment, JAX-RPC provides XML-based RPC functionality between the service requestors and the service provider. JAX-RPC provides standard API mechanisms for creating RPC-based Web services and a runtime services environment for Web services applications. Through these applications, a service requestor client can invoke remote calls to access the services exposed by a service provider. JAX-RPC also defines mappings between WSDL-based service descriptions and Java classes and provides tools to generate WSDL from Java classes and vice-versa. This enables developers to create JAX-RPC clients for Web services that enable interoperability to occur between Web services applications written using different languages and/or running on heterogeneous platforms.

JAX-RPC is quite typical to Java Remote Method Invocation (RMI), which handles RPC mechanisms by passing serialized Java objects between Java applications in a distributed computing environment; whereas JAX-RPC uses SOAP-based RPC and WSDL mechanisms to invoke Web services running on heterogeneous environments. More importantly, JAX-RPC hides all of the complexities of the underlying SOAP packaging and messaging by providing the required mapping between Java and XML/WSDL.

Currently, the JAX-RPC 1.0 is fully compliant with the SOAP 1.1 protocol and WSDL specifications and supports HTTP as its primary transport protocol. This helps the Java Web services developers write JAX-RPC-based Web services applications with minimal effort and little understanding of SOAP RPC. In a Web services business context, using JAX-RPC the service requestor and service provider can execute SOAP-based requests and responses and exchange XML as parameters or return values.

This chapter provides in-depth coverage on the JAX-RPC-based API mechanisms and illustrates its usage scenarios for developing and deploying Web services applications. In particular, we will be focusing on the following:

- The role of JAX-RPC in Web services
- JAX-RPC application architecture
- JAX-RPC implementation model
- JAX-RPC deployment model
- Data type mappings between XML and Java
- Understanding Java to WSDL and WSDL to Java mappings
- Developing JAX-RPC-based Web services.
- JAX-RPC in J2EE 1.4

At the time of this book's writing, JAX-RPC 1.0 has been released as a final specification; its reference implementation and API libraries are available for downloading as part of JWSDP 1.0 at Sun's Web site: http://java.sun.com/xml/download.html.

JAX-RPC was developed by Sun Microsystems as part of its Java Community Process (JCP), backed by J2EE vendors and most Java-based Web services platforms. In this chapter, we will be using the JWSDP 1.0 Reference Implementation (RI) for discussion and also to illustrate the case study examples.

The Role of JAX-RPC in Web Services

In a Web services environment, JAX-RPC defines an API framework and runtime environment for creating and executing XML-based remote procedural calls. The Web service requestors invoke the service provider's methods and transmit parameters and then receive return values as XML-based requests and responses. Typically, the Web service endpoints and the participating application clients use JAX-RPC for defining and executing the RPC-based Web services.

The core features of JAX-RPC are as follows:

- Provides APIs for defining RPC-based Web services, hiding the underlying complexities of SOAP packaging and messaging
- Provides runtime APIs for invoking RPC-based Web services based on
  - Stub and ties
  - Dynamic proxy
  - Dynamic invocation
- Using WSDL, JAX-RPC enables interoperability with any SOAP 1.1-based Web services
- Provides data types mapping between Java and XML
- Supports standard Internet protocols such as HTTP
- Service endpoints and service clients are portable across JAX-RPC implementations

The JAX-RPC-based Web services can be deployed in the Java servlet 2.2- or the J2EE 1.3-compliant server providers. JAX-RPC-based services and clients are developed and deployed as J2EE components.

In a Web services scenario, using JAX-RPC, the service requestor and service provider can communicate and execute SOAP-based requests and responses and exchange XML as parameters or return values. For the service provider, JAX-RPC provides support for exposing business components as Web services; for the service requestor, JAX-RPC defines a mechanism to access and invoke JAX-RPC-based services or any SOAP 1.1-compliant RPC-based Web services. JAX-RPC provides APIs for data type mappings between Java and XML, which enables on-the-fly Java-to-XML and XML-to-Java mappings during communication; that is, when a client invokes a JAX-RPC service, its XML parameters are mapped to Java objects. Similarly, while returning a response, the Java objects are mapped to XML elements as return values. JAX-RPC also enables the development of pluggable serializers and deserializers to support any data type mapping between Java and XML, which can be packaged with a JAX-RPC service. In addition, JAX-RPC defines mappings between WSDL and Java, through which a WSDL document provided by Web services can be mapped to Java classes as client stubs and server-side ties.

Table 10.1 Comparison of JAX-RPC with JAXM

JAX-RPC	JAXM
Synchronous RPC-based service interaction	Asynchronous/synchronous messaging-based service interaction
Message sent as XML-based requests and responses	Message sent as document-driven XML messages
Exposes internals to service requestors	Loosely coupled and does not expose internals to service requestors
Provides a variety of client invocation models	Does not provide a client-specific programming model
No reliability mechanisms	Provides guaranteed message delivery and reliability mechanisms

Comparing JAX-RPC with JAXM

While comparing JAX-RPC with JAXM, both are an integral part of JWSDP but provide different API-based mechanisms for developing Web services. Table 10.1 compares the features of JAX-RPC to JAXM.

JAX-RPC is also a best-fit solution over JAXM especially in request/response communications where high performance, limitations in memory, and maintaining client state are defined as the key requirements.

Now, let's take a closer look at a JAX-RPC-based Web services application and explore its features.

JAX-RPC Application Architecture

Figure 10.1 represents a JAX-RPC-based application architectural model and its core elements.

A typical JAX-RPC application architectural model consists of the following elements:

JAX-RPC service. Represents a business component that can be implemented in Java or generated from existing Java classes or from a WSDL document. In a J2EE environment, it can be implemented as a servlet, stateless session bean, or a message-driven bean. During deployment, the JAX-RPC service is assigned with one or more service endpoints and then is configured to a transport protocol binding. For instance, a JAX-RPC service can be bound to HTTP and all the messages are exchanged as HTTP-based requests and responses using its assigned endpoint. The JAX-RPC services do not dictate that it has to be accessed by a JAX-RPC client and thus a non-Java client running on heterogeneous environments can access it.

JAX-RPC service client. Represents a JAX-RPC-based service client that can access a service. The service client is independent of the target implementation on the service provider. This means that the accessed service can be a service implemented using a Java platform or a SOAP 1.1-compliant service running on a non-Java platform. To support these client scenarios, JAX-RPC defines a variety of client invocation models using different mechanisms, such as stubs-based mechanisms, dynamic proxies, and dynamic invocation. The JAX-RPC service clients can import WSDL exposed by a service provider and can generate Java-based client classes to access the service.

Serialization and deserialization. During communication, JAX-RPC uses serializing and deserializing mechanisms to facilitate Java-to-XML and XML-to-Java mappings, which enables the conversion of the Java primitives and objects to XML-based representations and vice versa. It also is possible to create serializers and deserializers for custom data types.

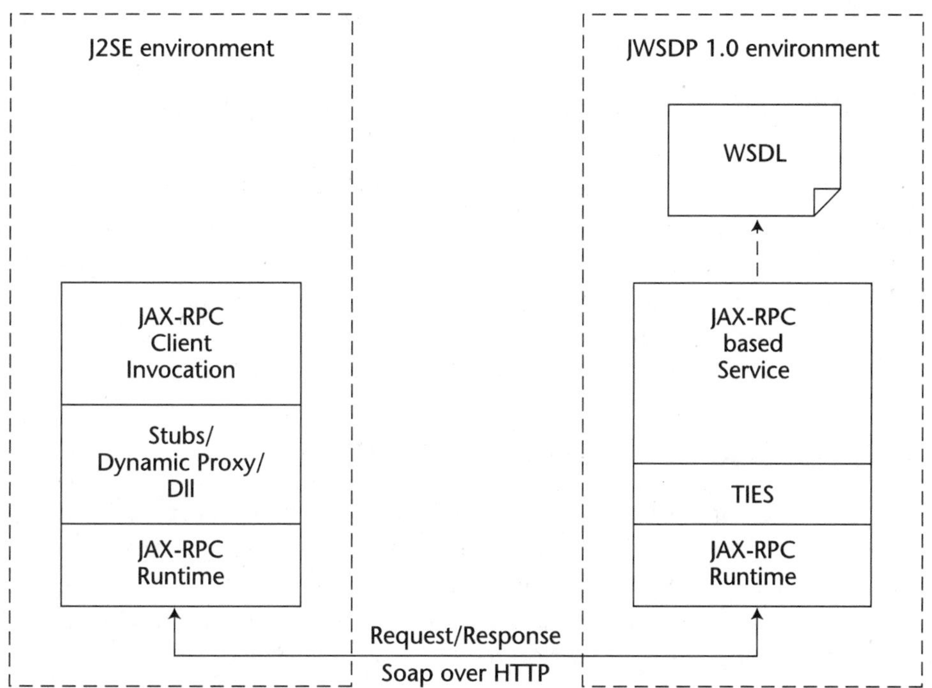

Figure 10.1 JAX-RPC-based Web services application architecture.

xrpcc tool. The JAX-RPC provides the `xrpcc` tool, which enables the generation of the required client and server-side class files and WSDL to enable communication between a service provider and a requestor. In particular, `xrpcc` generates a WSDL document representing the service and the stubs and ties that define the lower-level Java classes. In a service client scenario, `xrpcc` also enables Stub classes to generate using a WSDL exposed by a service provider.

JAX-RPC runtime environment. Defines the runtime mechanisms and execution environment for the JAX-RPC services and service clients by providing the required runtime libraries and system resources. The JAX-RPC 1.0 specification mandates a servlet 2.3 or J2EE 1.3-based servlet container environment for its services and service clients. As per JAX-RPC 1.0, both the JAX-RPC services and service clients using JAX-RPC APIs are required to be implemented as servlets running a servlet 2.2-complaint container. Upcoming J2EE 1.4 specifications will likely provide support for JAX-RPC and enable the creation of JAX-RPC-based services using session beans and message-driven beans. The JAX-RPC 1.0 runtime services also provide support for HTTP-based basic authentication and session management.

Now, let's explore the previous JAX-RPC features and how they are represented using the JAX-RPC APIs and implementation.

JAX-RPC APIs and Implementation Model

As per JAX-RPC 1.0 specifications, JAX-RPC defines both service and client implementation models intending to do RPC-based messaging using a JAX-RPC runtime environment or directly to a SOAP service. The core JAX-RPC APIs are packaged as `javax.xml.rpc`, which provides the runtime mechanisms package and `javax.xml.rpc.handler.*` as its SOAP message handler API package.

JAX-RPC-Based Service Implementation

The JAX-RPC 1.0 specification does not define any APIs for implementing JAX-RPC-based services. JAX-RPC-based services can be implemented using Java classes (similar to writing an RMI application) or by using a WSDL document. In both cases, JAX-RPC does not specify any requirements for its service client implementation to access and use the deployed services.

The following two sections look at those two different ways of services implementation and walk through the programming steps required.

Developing a JAX-RPC Service from Java Classes

As we mentioned earlier, developing a JAX-RPC-based service (also referred to as a JAX-RPC service definition) is quite similar to developing an RMI application. The steps involved are as follows:

1. Define the remote interface (Service Definition).
2. Implement the remote interface (Service Implementation).
3. Configure the service.
4. Generate the stubs and ties.
5. Package and deploy the service.

Now, let's take a look at the previous steps by walking through a sample application.

Defining the Remote Interface (Service Definition)

The service interface defines the set of exposed methods that can be invoked by the service requestor clients. In JAX-RPC, it is referred to as Service Definition. The client stubs and server ties are generated based on this interface. From a programming model's standpoint, the programming rules involved in defining the remote interface are as follows:

- The remote interface of the service definition must be declared as public.
- The remote interface must extend the `java.rmi.Remote` interface and all of the methods must throw a `java.rmi.RemoteException`.
- The remote interface must not contain any declaration as static constants.
- All of the parameters and return values of the methods must be supported as part of JAX-RPC-supported data types. In case of unsupported data types, then it is required to use custom serializers and deserializers to facilitate Java-to-XML and XML-to-Java mappings.

For example, the following is a code listing that defines a remote interface of a service definition (`BookPriceIF.java`):

```
import java.rmi.Remote;
import java.rmi.RemoteException;

public interface BookPriceIF extends Remote {
      public String getBookPrice(String bookName)
                                        throws RemoteException;
 }
```

Implementing the Remote Interface (Service Implementation)

The implementation of the remote interface is the actual class that implements all of the exposed methods defined in the remote interface. In JAX-RPC, it is referred to as Service Implementation. For example, a typical service implementation of a remote interface is as follows:

```
import java.rmi.Remote;
import java.rmi.Remote.*;

public class BookPriceImpl implements BookPriceIF {

  public String getBookPrice (String bookName) {
        System.out.println("The price of the book titled "+ bookName);
        return new String("13.25");
  }
}
```

The service implementation can also implement the `javax.xml.rpc.server.ServiceLifeCycle` interface that allows handling the complete lifecycle of a JAX-RPC service. The `ServiceLifeCycle` interface provides `init()` and `destroy()` methods, which are quite similar to the `init()` and `destroy()` methods in a Servlet lifecycle for initializing and releasing resources. In the case of a service implementation implementing a `ServiceLifeCycle` interface, also allows to set `ServletEndpointContext`, which is quite similar to `SessionContext (in EJBs)` that enables to maintain state information. For example, a typical service implementation of a remote interface implementing `ServiceLifeCycle` is as follows:

```
import java.rmi.Remote;
import java.rmi.Remote.*;
import javax.xml.rpc.server.ServiceLifeCycle;
import javax.xml.rpc.server.ServletEndpointContext;
import javax.xml.rpc.handler.soap.SOAPMessageContext;

public class BookPriceImpl implements BookPriceIF, ServiceLifeCycle {
     private ServletEndpointContext serviceContext;
```

```
public void init(java.lang.Object context){
        serviceContext=(ServletEndpointContext)context;
    }

public String getBookPrice (String bookName) {
SOAPMessageContext soapMsgContext=
          (SOAPMessageContext) (serviceContext.getMessageContext());
      HttpSession session = serviceContext.getHttpSession();
//...Obtain state information here
      System.out.println("The price of the book titled "+ bookName);
       return new String("13.25");
  }
}
```

Configuring the Service

To configure the service, you first need to create a configuration file in an XML format that provides information such as

- The name of the service
- The name of the package containing the stubs and ties
- The target namespace for the generated WSDL and its XML schema and class names of the remote interface and its implementation

The `xrpcc` tool uses this configuration file to generate the stubs and ties of the service.

Listing 10.1 is a code listing of a sample configuration file (`service-config.xml`):

```
<?xml version="1.0" encoding="UTF-8"?>
  <configuration xmlns="http://java.sun.com/xml/ns/jax-rpc/ri/config">
        <service name="WileyBookCatalog"
          targetNamespace="http://www.wiley.com/jws/wsdl"
          typeNamespace="http://www.wiley.com/jws/types"
          packageName="com.wiley.jws.ch10.jaxrpc">
          <interface name="jws.wiley.jaxrpc.BookPriceIF"
            servantName="jws.wiley.jaxrpc.BookPriceImpl"/>
        </service>
    </configuration>
```

Listing 10.1 Sample configuration of a service definition.

To find out the other optional elements of the service configuration file, refer to the JAX-RPC API documents provided with the JWSDP 1.0 bundle.

Generating the Stubs and Ties

Before generating the stubs and ties, ensure that the source code of the remote interface and the implementation is compiled using `javac` and that it is available in CLASSPATH.

Use the `xrpcc` tool to generate the stubs and tie classes, the WSDL document associated with the service, and the property files required by the JAX-RPC runtime environment. In a typical scenario, the `xrpcc` tool can be executed as a command line utility, as follows:

In a Windows environment:

```
xrpcc -classpath %CLASSPATH% -keep
                   -both -d build\classes  serviceconfig.xml
```

In a UNIX environment:

```
xrpcc -classpath $CLASSPATH  -keep
                  -both -d build/classes  serviceconfig.xml
```

In this command, the option `-classpath` refers to the CLASSPATH, including the service interface and implementation classes and JAX-RPC libraries; `-keep` refers to saving the generated source files (.java) and the WSDL documents; `-both` refers to the generating of both the stubs and tie classes; and `-d` refers to the destination directory. To find out more `xrpcc` options, refer to the JAX-RPC implementation documentation for syntax and usage information.

As a result, the preceding command generates the following:

- Client-side stubs and server-side tie classes
- Serialization and deserialization classes representing the data-type mappings between Java primitives and XML data types
- A WSDL document
- Property files associated with the service

Packaging and Deployment

According to JWSDP 1.0, JAX-RPC-based services are specified with only servlet-based service endpoints and the JAX-RPC services are required to be deployed as a servlet in a Java servlet 2.2-based container. This mandates that the JAX-RPC-based services be packaged as a Web application (`WAR`).

To package a JAX-RPC service as a Web application, we need to create a `WAR` file that includes the following classes and other configuration files:

- Remote interface of the service
- Service implementation of the remote interface
- Serializer and deserializer classes
- Server-side (tie) classes created by `xrpcc`
- Property files created by `xrpcc`
- Other supporting classes required by the service implementation
- WSDL document describing the service
- Web application deployment descriptor (`web.xml`)

Except for the deployment descriptor, we have seen the process required for creating those classes and property files using `xrpcc`.

In a JAX-RPC environment, the deployment descriptor is similar to a servlet deployment descriptor (`web.xml`), which provides information about the class name of the JAX-RPC service, its associated property file created by the `xrpcc` tool, the servlet mappings and URL pattern, and so on. Listing 10.2 is a sample code listing of a deployment descriptor (`web.xml`).

```
<?xml version="1.0" encoding="UTF-8"?>

 <!DOCTYPE web-app
     PUBLIC "-//Sun Microsystems, Inc.//DTD Web Application 2.3//EN"
     "http://java.sun.com/j2ee/dtds/web-app_2_3.dtd">

    <web-app>
    <display-name>WileyProductServices</display-name>
    <description>Wiley Web Services Company</description>
    <servlet>
        <servlet-name>JAXRPCEndpoint</servlet-name>
        <display-name>JAXRPCEndpoint</display-name>
        <description>Endpoint for Wiley Book Catalog
Service</description>
        <servlet-class>com.sun.xml.rpc.server.http.JAXRPCServlet
                                      </servlet-class>
        <init-param>
          <param-name>configuration.file</param-name>
          <param-value>/WEB-INF/WileyBookCatalog_Config.properties
                                        </param-value>
        </init-param>
        <load-on-startup>0</load-on-startup>
     </servlet>
```

Listing 10.2 Sample deployment descriptor for a JAX-RPC service definition. *(continues)*

```
    <servlet-mapping>
       <servlet-name>JAXRPCEndpoint</servlet-name>
       <url-pattern>/jaxrpc/wiley/*</url-pattern>
    </servlet-mapping>
    <session-config>
       <session-timeout>60</session-timeout>
   </session-config>
</web-app>
```

Listing 10.2 Sample deployment descriptor for a JAX-RPC service definition. *(continued)*

To package the service as Web application, use the `jar` utility and create a Web application archive (`WAR`). For example,

```
jar cvf wileywebapp.war .
```

Finally, to deploy the service as a Web application running in a JWSDP 1.0/Tomcat environment, just copy the `WAR` file to the servlet engine `/ webapps` directory. For example, to deploy in a Tomcat servlet container in a Windows environment, deploy the following:

```
copy wileywebapp.war %CATALINA%/webapps
```

Then restart the Tomcat server, which automatically deploys the service as an application. To verify the service deployment, use your Web browser and execute the following URL (using the URL pattern defined in the deployment descriptor):

```
http://localhost:8080/bookpriceservice/jaxrpc/wiley
```

If everything has been deployed successfully, the browser will display "A Web Service is installed at this URL" (see Figure 10.2).

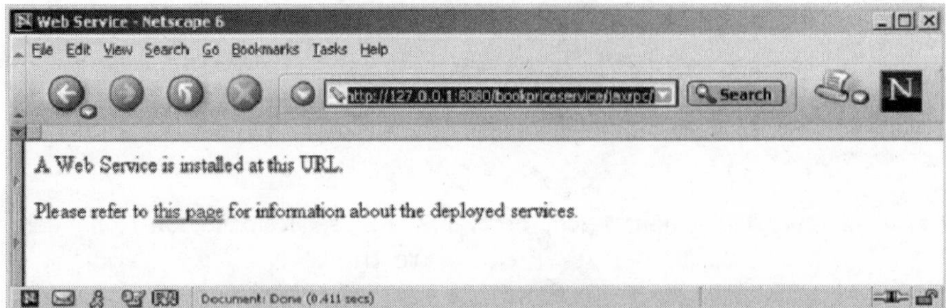

Figure 10.2 Browser showing successful installation of a JAX-RPC-based service.

Developing a JAX-RPC-Based Service from a WSDL Document

In this section, we will look at developing a JAX-RPC-based service using a WSDL document exposed by an existing Web services environment. In this case, by importing a WSDL document from an existing Web service, the `xrpcc` utility generates the JAX-RPC services classes. The key steps involved are as follows:

1. Create a service configuration referring to the WSDL.
2. Generate the client-side stubs and server-side ties using `xrpcc`.
3. Package and deploy the service.

To illustrate the previous steps, read the following sections. For the example, assume that a Web service and its WSDL location are available at the following URL:

```
http://nramesh:80/axis/AcmeProductCatalog.jws?WSDL
```

Create a Service Configuration Using WSDL

To configure the service, you first must create a configuration file in an XML format that provides information about the URL location of the WSDL, including the name of the service and the name of the package for the generated stubs and ties. The `xrpcc` tool uses this configuration file to generate the stubs and ties and the RMI interfaces of the service.

Listing 10.3 is a sample code listing of a sample configuration file (`serviceconfig.xml`).

```
<?xml version="1.0" encoding="UTF-8"?>
<configuration
          xmlns="http://java.sun.com/xml/ns/jax-rpc/ri/config">
<wsdl location=" http://nramesh:80/axis/AcmeProductCatalog.jws?WSDL"
              packageName="com.wiley.jws.ch10.jaxrpc.wsdl">
 </wsdl>
 </configuration>
```

Listing 10.3 Sample service configuration using WSDL.

To find out other optional elements of the service configuration file, refer to the JAX-RPC API documents.

Generating the Stubs and Ties

Before generating the stubs and ties, ensure that the source code of the remote interface and the implementation is compiled using `javac`. Also ensure that the code is available in CLASSPATH.

Use the xrpcc tool to generate the stubs and tie classes, the WSDL document associated with this service, and the property files required by the JAX-RPC runtime environment. In a typical scenario, the xrpcc tool can be executed as a command line utility shown as follows:

In a Windows environment:

```
xrpcc -classpath %CLASSPATH% -keep
                    -both -d build\classes  serviceconfig.xml
```

In a UNIX environment:

```
xrpcc -classpath $CLASSPATH  -keep
                   -both -d build/classes  serviceconfig.xml
```

In the previous command, the option -classpath refers to the CLASSPATH including the service interface and implementation classes and JAX-RPC libraries, -keep refers to saving the generated source files (.java) and the WSDL documents, -both refers to the generating of both the stubs and tie classes, and -d refers to the destination directory. To find out more xrpcc options, refer to the JAX-RPC implementation documentation for syntax and usage information.

As a result, the previous command generates the following:

- Client-side stubs and server-side tie classes
- Serialization and deserialization classes representing the data-type mappings between Java primitives and XML data types
- A WSDL document for the service
- Property files for service configuration

Packaging and Deployment

The packaging and deployment steps are quite similar to those we discussed in the earlier section titled *Developing a JAX-RPC from Service using Java Classes*. Because JWSDP 1.0 specifies only servlet-based service endpoints, the JAX-RPC-based services are packaged as a Web Application (WAR).

JAX-RPC-Based Client Implementation

According to the JAX-RPC 1.0 specification, JAX-RPC-based service clients are independent of target service implementation, and the service client does not depend upon its service provider or its running platform using

Java or non-Java environments. The JAX-RPC provides client-side APIs and defines a client invocation model for accessing and invoking Web services.

Now, let's take a look at the JAX-RPC client-side APIs and the client invocation models.

JAX-RPC Client-Side APIs

The JAX-RPC 1.0 client-side APIs are defined in a single package structure as `javax.xml.rpc`, which provides a set of interfaces and classes that support the JAX-RPC clients intending to invoke RPC-based services, and the JAX-RPC runtime implements them.

The `javax.xml.rpc` package provides a set of interfaces and classes for creating JAX-RPC clients, which support the different JAX-RPC client invocation models. The JAX-RPC API interfaces and classes are as follows:

INTERFACES

`javax.xml.rpc.Stub` Is the base interface for the JAX-RPC stub classes. All JAX-RPC stub classes are required to implement this interface. This interface represents the client-side proxy or an instance of the target endpoint.

```
private static Stub createMyProxy() {
  return (Stub)(new StockPrice_Impl().getStockPriceIFPort());
}
```

`javax.xml.rpc.Service` Acts as a factory class for creating a dynamic proxy of a target service and for creating Call instances for invoking the service.

```
Service service =
        serviceFactory.createService(new QName(qService));

Call call = service.createCall(target_port);
```

`javax.xml.rpc.Call` Provides support for the JAX-RPC client components to dynamically invoke a service. In this case, after a call method is created, we need to use the setter and getter methods to configure the call interface for the parameters and return values.

```
Call call = service.createCall(target_port);
    call.setTargetEndpointAddress(target_endpoint);
    .
    call.setOperationName
        (new QName(BODY_NAMESPACE_VALUE, "getStockPrice"));
```

CLASSES

javax.xml.rpc.ServiceFactory Is an abstract class that provides a factory class for creating instances of javax.xml.rpc.Service services.

```
ServiceFactory sfactory =
        ServiceFactory.newInstance();
Service service =
      serviceFactory.createService(new QName(qService));
```

javax.xml.rpc.ParameterMode Provides a type-safe enumeration of the parameter mode.

```
call.addParameter( "stocksymbol", QNAME_TYPE_STRING,
                                 ParameterMode.IN );
```

javax.xml.rpc.NamespaceConstants Defines the constants used in JAX-RPC for the XML schema namespace prefixes and URIs.

EXCEPTIONS

javax.xml.rpc.JAXRPCException Throws an exception while a JAX-RPC exception is occurring. The exception details the reasons for the failure, which are related to JAX-RPC runtime-specific problems.

javax.xml.rpc.SERVICEException Throws an exception from the methods in the JAVAX.XML.RPC.SERVICE interface and ServiceFactory class.

JAX-RPC Client Invocation Programming Models

The JAX-RPC 1.0 specification defines the implementation of a JAX-RPC-based client using any of the following client invocation programming models:

- Stub-based
- Dynamic proxy
- Dynamic invocation

Now, let's take a look at these different ways of client implementation and walk through the programming steps required for each.

Stub-Based Client

A stub-based model is the simplest client-programming model. This model uses the local stub classes generated by the xrpcc tool. To create the stub-based client invocation, ensure that the stub classes are available in the CLASSPATH.

Listing 10.4 is a sample code listing of a client using stub-based client invocation.

```
// Import the Stub Interface
import javax.xml.rpc.Stub;

public class BookCatalogClient {

// Main method
  public static void main(String[] args) {

    try {
      // Obtain the Instance of the Stub Interface
      BookCatalogIF_Stub stub = (BookCatalogIF_Stub)
                    (new BookCatalog_Impl().getBookCatalogIFPort());

       // Configure the stub setting required properties
      // Setting the target service endpoint
            stub._setProperty(
                javax.xml.rpc.Stub.ENDPOINT_ADDRESS_PROPERTY,
                       "http://www.wiley.com/jws/jaxrpc/bookcatalog");
      // Execute the remote method
      System.out.println (stub.getBookPrice("JAX-RPC in 24 hours"));

    } catch (Exception ex) {
            ex.printStackTrace();
    }
  }
}
```

Listing 10.4 Sample code illustrating a stub-based client invocation.

Dynamic Proxy-Based Client

A dynamic proxy client enables the invocation of a target service endpoint dynamically at runtime, without requiring a local stub class. This type of client uses the dynamic proxy APIs provided by the Java reflection API (`java.lang.reflect.Proxy` class and `java.lang.reflect.InvocationHandler` interface). Particularly, the `getPort` method on the `javax.xml.rpc.Service` interface enables a dynamic proxy to be created. Listing 10.5 is a sample code listing of a client using a dynamic proxy-based client invocation.

```
// Import Service & ServiceFactory

import javax.xml.rpc.Service;
import javax.xml.rpc.ServiceFactory;

import javax.xml.namespace.QName;
import java.net.URL;

public class BookCatalogProxyClient {

  // Main Method
  public static void main(String[] args) {

     try {
      // WSDL location URL
      String wsdlURL =
"http://www.wiley.com/jws/jaxrpc/BookCatalog.wsdl";

      // WSDL namespace URI
      String nameSpaceURI = "http://www.wiley.com/jws/wsdl";

      // Service Name
      String serviceName = "BookCatalogService";

      // Service port Name
       String portName = "BookCatalogIFPort";

       URL bookCatalogWSDL = new URL(wsdlURL);

       // Obtain an Instance of Service factory
       ServiceFactory serviceFactory = ServiceFactory.newInstance();

       // Create a service from Instance using WSDL
       Service bookCatalogService =
                 serviceFactory.createService(bookCatalogWSDL,
                                   new QName(nameSpaceURI,
serviceName));

       // Get the proxy object
       BookCatalogIF bcProxy = (BookCatalogIF)
bookCatalogService.getPort(
             new
QName(nameSpaceURI,portName),proxy.BookCatalogIF.class);

       // Invoke the remote methods
       System.out.println(bcProxy.getBookPrice("JAX-RPC in 24 hours "));

      } catch (Exception ex) {
```

Listing 10.5 Sample code illustrating a client using dynamic proxy.

```
                ex.printStackTrace();
            }
        }
    }
```

Listing 10.5 Sample code illustrating a client using dynamic proxy. *(continued)*

Dynamic Invocation Interface (DII) Client

Using the Dynamic Invocation Interface (DII) enables the client to discover target services dynamically on runtime and then to invoke methods. During runtime, the client uses a set of operations and parameters, establishes a search criterion to discover the target service, and then invokes its methods. This also enables a DII client to invoke a service and its methods without knowing its data types, objects, and its return types.

DII looks up a service, creates a `Call` object by setting the endpoint specific parameters and operations, and finally invokes the call object to execute the remote methods. Listing 10.6 is a sample code listing of a client using DII-based client invocation.

```
// imports
import javax.xml.rpc.Call;
import javax.xml.rpc.Service;
import javax.xml.rpc.JAXRPCException;
import javax.xml.namespace.QName;
import javax.xml.rpc.ServiceFactory;
import javax.xml.rpc.ParameterMode;

public class BookCatalogDIIClient {

    // Service Name
    private static String qService = "BookCatalogService";

    // Port Name
    private static String qPort = "BookCatalogIF";

    // Name space URI
    private static String BODY_NAMESPACE_VALUE =
                              "http://www.wiley.com/jws/wsdl";

    // Encoding style
    private static String ENCODING_STYLE_PROPERTY =
```

Listing 10.6 Sample code illustrating a JAX-RPC client using DII. *(continues)*

```
                                  "javax.xml.rpc.encodingstyle.namespace.uri";

    // XML Schema
     private static String NS_XSD =
                                    "http://www.w3.org/2001/XMLSchema";

     // SOAP encoding URI
     private static String URI_ENCODING =
          "http://schemas.xmlsoap.org/soap/encoding/";


     // Main method
     public static void main(String[] args) {

       try {
             String target_endpoint =
                   "http://www.wiley.com/jws/jaxrpc/bookcatalog";

             // Obtain an Instance of Service factory
             ServiceFactory sFactory =
                                  ServiceFactory.newInstance();
             // Create a Service
            Service service =
                 sFactory.createService(new QName(qService));

            // Define a port
             QName port = new QName(qPort);

             // Create a Call object using the service
             Call call = service.createCall(port);

             // Set the target service endpoint
             call.setTargetEndpointAddress(target_endpoint);

             // Set properties - SOAP URI, Encoding etc.
             call.setProperty(Call.SOAPACTION_USE_PROPERTY,
                                                   new Boolean(true));

             call.setProperty(Call.SOAPACTION_URI_PROPERTY, "");

             call.setProperty(ENCODING_STYLE_PROPERTY, URI_ENCODING);

             // Set Parameter type and Return value type as String
             QName QNAME_TYPE_STRING = new QName(NS_XSD, "string");

             call.setReturnType(QNAME_TYPE_STRING);

             // Set operations
             call.setOperationName(new QName(BODY_NAMESPACE_VALUE,
```

Listing 10.6 Sample code illustrating a JAX-RPC client using DII.

```
                                                        "getBookPrice"));

            // Set Parameters
            call.addParameter("BookName", QNAME_TYPE_STRING,
                                                   ParameterMode.IN);
            String[] BookName = {"JAX-RPC in 24 hours"};

            // Invoke and obtain response object
            Object response = (Object)call.invoke(BookName);

            System.out.println(response.toString());

        } catch (Exception ex) {
            ex.printStackTrace();
        }
    }
}
```

Listing 10.6 Sample code illustrating a JAX-RPC client using DII. *(continued)*

A DII client also can be invoked using one-way RPC mechanisms. In that case, the client does not require setting the return value types, and the call can be invoked as follows:

```
call.invokeOneWay(parameter);
```

Now, let's take a look at the JAX-RPC-supported data types mapping between Java and XML.

JAX-RPC-Supported Java/XML Mappings

JAX-RPC abstracts and hides the complexities of SOAP and XML data types by providing serialization and deserialization features and by performing automatic mapping between Java classes and XML data (and vice versa). To handle these chores, JAX-RPC 1.0 provides APIs and conventions for mappings between the Java data types and XML/WSDL data as per the XML schema 1.0 representation (XSD) and SOAP 1.1 encoding (SOAP-ENC) specifications. The online locations of those specifications are as follows:

```
http://www.w3.org/2001/XMLSchema
http://www.w3.org/2001/XMLSchema-instance
http://schemas.xmlsoap.org/soap/encoding/
```

The xrpcc tool provides these features by automating the tasks of mapping XML to Java classes and also the mapping between WSDL definitions and their mapping Java representations.

In a JAX-RPC-based Web services scenario, when a JAX-RPC service is invoked, the JAX-RPC runtime transforms the XML-based RPC call to its corresponding Java object representation and then executes the required service using them; this process is referred to as *deserialization*. After execution, the service returns the call to its service client by transforming the returning Java objects as an XML-based data representation; this process is referred to as *serialization*.

Now, let's take a look at the standard mappings that are supported by JAX-RPC 1.0.

Java/XML Data Type Mappings

JAX-RPC 1.0 provides support for the following mapping between Java classes and XML data types as defined in XML schema 1.0 (xsd) and SOAP 1.1 encoding (SOAP-ENC). Table 10.2 shows the JAX-RPC-supported Java primitives and their mapping XML data types.

In an example scenario, using a Java primitive, such as

```
float price;
```

is mapped to an XML schema representation as

```
<element name="price" type="xsd:float"/>
```

Table 10.3 shows the JAX-RPC-supported Java classes and their mapping XML data types.

Table 10.2 JAX-RPC-Supported Java Primitives and Mapping XML Data Types

JAVA PRIMITIVES	XML SCHEMA DEFINITION
int	xsd:int
long	xsd:long
float	xsd:float
double	xsd:double
short	xsd:short
boolean	xsd:boolean
byte	xsd:byte

Table 10.3 JAX-RPC-Supported Java Classes and Mapping XML Data Types

JAVA CLASSES	XML SCHEMA DEFINITION
String	xsd:string
BigDecimal	xsd:decimal
BigInteger	xsd:integer
Calendar	xsd:dateTime
Date	xsd:dateTime

Arrays

JAX-RPC supports the mapping of XML-based array types to a Java array. This enables mapping an XML array containing elements of XML data types to corresponding types of the Java array. For example, a Java array, such as

```
int [] employees;
```

is mapped to an XML schema representation as

```
<element name="employees" type="xsd:Array"/>

<employees arrayType="xsd:int[2]">
<employeeID>1001</employeeID>
<employeeID>1002</employeeID>
</employees>
```

Java Classes to XML Structure and Complex Types

JAX-RPC provides support for mapping XML structure and complex value types as JavaBeans with the getter and setter methods. The bean property must be a JAX-RPC-supported Java type, as in the code in the following example.

The following XML schema represents information about a product:

```
<element name="Product"/>
<complexType>
        <all>
             <element name="productID" type="xsd:int"/>
             <element name="productDesc" type="xsd:string"/>
             <element name="price" type="xsd:float"/>
             <element name="color" type="xsd:string"/>
        <all>
</complexType>
```

The preceding schema is mapped to a Java class representation as follows:

```
public class Product implements java.io.Serializable {
      // ...
      public String getProductID() { ... }
      public void setProductID(int productID) { ... }
      public String getProductDesc() { ... }
      public void setProductDesc(String productDesc) { ... }
      public float getPrice() { ... }
      public void setPrice(float price) { ... }
      public String getColor() { ... }
      public void setColor(String color) { ... }
}
```

Java/WSDL Definition Mappings

JAX-RPC specifies the mappings for a JAX-RPC-based service endpoint definition to a WSDL service description and vice versa. The `xrpcc` tool facilitates these mappings by mapping a WSDL document to a Java package, including Java interfaces and classes that provide bindings of a WSDL document in a Java representation.

The Java representation mapping to the abstract WSDL definitions is as follows:

`wsdl:types` Maps the WSDL message types to the Java method parameter types of the target service.

`wsdl:message` Maps the WSDL message to the Java method parameters of the target service.

`wsdl:operation` Maps the WSDL operation to the Java method of the service interface.

`wsdl:portType` Maps the WSDL port type to the service interface.

The following WSDL document represents a service for obtaining a book price from a book catalog service:

```
<message name="GetBookPriceInput">
       <part name="bookName" type="xsd:string"/>
</message>
<message name="GetBookPriceOutput"?
        <part name="price" type="xsd:float"/>
</message>
<portType name="BookCatalogServiceIF">
      <operation name="GetBookPrice"  parameterOrder="bookName">
```

```
            <input message="tns:GetBookPriceInput"/>
            <output message="tns:GetBookPriceOutput"/>
      </operation>
</portType>
```

The preceding document is mapped to a Java class representation (`BookCatalogServiceIF.java`) as

```
public interface BookCatalogServiceIF extends java.rmi.Remote {
         public float getBookPrice(String bookName)
                      throws java.rmi.RemoteException;
}
```

As we discussed earlier, the `xrpcc` tool facilitates the WSDL-to-Java and Java-to-WSDL mappings. In the future, it is expected that JAX-RPC will support Java APIs for XML binding (JAXB) for providing Java-to-XML and XML-to-Java mappings. To find out more information on JAXB, refer to Chapter 8, "XML Processing and Data Binding with Java APIs."

Handling SOAP Attachments in JAX-RPC

As per SOAP 1.1 specifications, a SOAP message may contain zero to many attachment parts using MIME encoding. JAX-RPC allows attaching SOAP attachment parts using JavaBeans Activation Framework (JAF). During runtime, JAX-RPC uses `javax.activation.Datahandler` and `javax.activation.DataContentHandler`, which provide access to the attachments using the `getContent` method of the `DataHandler` class.

Table 10.4 lists the standard Java data type mapping of the attachment parts for certain MIME types.

Table 10.4 Mapping of MIME Types to Java Data Types

MIME TYPE	JAVA DATA TYPE
`image/gif`	`java.awt.Image`
`image/jpeg`	`java.awt.Image`
`text/plain`	`java.lang.String`
`multipart/*`	`javax.mail.internet.MimeMultipart`
`text/xml` or `application/xml`	`javax.xml.transform.Source`

Developing JAX-RPC-Based Web Services

In this section, we illustrate and discuss an example scenario of developing JAX-RPC-based Web services applications and JAX-RPC-based service client invocation models using the JWSDP 1.0 environment.

To demonstrate this, we use a fictitious example implementing a JAX-RPC-based request/response scenario showing how a service requestor (service client) obtains a book price from a JAX-RPC-based Web services provider. The service client makes a request using a book name (string) as a parameter, and the service provider returns a response to the service client with the book price (float).

Creating a JAX-RPC-Based Service (BookPriceService)

The key steps for creating a JAX-RPC-based service (`BookPriceService`) using a JWSDP 1.0/Tomcat-based environment are as follows:

1. Develop the remote interface of the service (`BookPriceServiceIF.java`).
2. Create the implementation class of the remote interface (`BookPriceServiceImpl.java`).
3. Configure the service (`BookPriceService.xml`).
4. Set up the environment and compile the source code.
5. Generate the server-side artifacts (ties) and the WSDL document.
6. Package and deploy the service (`BookPriceService.war`).
7. Test the service deployment and the WSDL.
8. Generate the client stubs and package as a client JAR (`BookPriceServiceStubs.jar`).

The following sections will explore the preceding tasks involved in creating `BookPriceService` and will walk you through them.

Develop the Service's Remote Interface

The service's remote interface defines the remote methods of the `BookPriceService` that are invoked by the service requestor clients. Listing 10.7 is a code listing that defines a service's remote interface.

JAX-RPC in J2EE 1.4

The upcoming release of J2EE 1.4 platform specifications focuses on enabling J2EE components to participate in Web services. As a key requirement, it mandates the implementation of JAX-RPC 1.0 and EJB 2.1 specifications, which address the role of JAX-RPC in J2EE application components including EJBs. This means that all J2EE-compliant application servers will implement JAX-RPC, which allows exposing J2EE components as RPC-based Web services.

In EJB 2.1 specifications, it mandates the Stateless session EJBs to be exposed as Web services using a *Web Services Endpoint Interface*, which follows the same rules as a JAX-RPC service interface. This means the methods defined in the *Web Services Endpoint Interface* must be implemented in the bean implementation class. The EJB 2.1 deployment descriptor also introduces a new `<service-endpoint>` element, which contains the class name of the Web services endpoint interface. In the case of application exceptions, it is the responsibility of the container to map the exceptions to SOAP faults as per SOAP 1.1 specifications. At the time of this writing, the EJB 2.1 public draft specifies Web services endpoint interface for Stateless Session EJBs only.

The introduction of JAX-RPC in J2EE environments enables J2EE components accessed as Web services using heterogeneous clients including both Java and non-Java applications. It also takes advantage of J2EE container services like transactions, application security, and so on.

JAX-RPC Interoperability

A JAX-RPC Service provider can interoperate with any SOAP 1.1/WSDL 1.1-compliant service client and, similarly, a JAX-RPC Service client can interoperate with any SOAP 1.1/WSDL 1.1-compliant service provider.

To ensure JAX-RPC interoperability with other SOAP implementation providers, it is quite important to verify their compliance with specifications such as SOAP 1.1, WSDL 1.1, HTTP 1.1 transport, and XML Schema 1.0. To find out more information on JAX-RPC interoperability with other SOAP implementations, refer to Sun's SOAP Interoperability testing Web site at http://soapinterop.java.sun.com. (For more information on SOAP and WSDL interoperability and developing an interoperability scenario, refer to Chapter 6, "Creating .NET Interoperability.")

```
(BookPriceServiceIF.java):
package jws.ch10.jaxrpc.bookprice;

import java.rmi.Remote;
import java.rmi.RemoteException;

public interface BookPriceServiceIF extends Remote {
    public String getBookPrice(String bookName)
                            throws RemoteException;
}
```

Listing 10.7 BookPriceServiceIF.java.

Create the Service Implementation Class of the Interface

It provides an implementation for all the methods declared in the remote interface. The code in Listing 10.8 implements the methods in a service's remote interface (BookPriceServiceImpl.java).

```
package jws.ch10.jaxrpc.bookprice;

public class BookPriceServiceImpl implements BookPriceServiceIF {

float bookprice = 0;

// Implementation of getBookPrice() method
// creates a fictitious price !

public float getBookPrice( String bookName) {

    for( int i = 0; i < bookName.length(); i++ ) {
      bookprice = bookprice + (int) bookName.charAt( i );
    }
    bookprice = bookprice/3;

    return bookprice;
  }
}
```

Listing 10.8 BookPriceServiceImpl.java.

Configure the Service

To generate the client-side and server-side artifacts (stubs and ties), you must create a configuration file that provides information on the service name, target namespaces of the service, required package and class names, and so forth.

Listing 10.9 is a code listing of the configuration file (`BookPriceService.xml`).

```
<?xml version="1.0" encoding="UTF-8"?>
<configuration xmlns="http://java.sun.com/xml/ns/jax-rpc/ri/config">
   <service name="BookPriceService"
        targetNamespace="http://jws.wiley.com/wsdl"
        typeNamespace="http://jws.wiley.com/types"
        packageName="jws.ch10.jaxrpc.bookprice">
        <interface name="jws.ch10.jaxrpc.bookprice.BookPriceServiceIF"

servantName="jws.ch10.jaxrpc.bookprice.BookPriceServiceImpl"/>
     </service>
</configuration>
```

Listing 10.9 `BookPriceService.xml`.

Set Up the Environment and Compile the Source Code

Next you need to create a CLASSPATH environment that includes the JWSDP 1.0 class libraries for JAX-RPC and its supporting packages. To ensure this, make sure that the class libraries (`*.jar`) in `%JWSDP_HOME%/common/lib/` and `%JWSDP_HOME%/common/endorsed/` are included.

Use `javac` and compile the source code of the remote interface (`BookPriceServiceIF.java`, in this example) and the implementation (`BookPriceServiceImpl.java`). You choose to use an Ant build script. After successful compilation, ensure that the compiled classes are available in the CLASSPATH. Figure 10.3 shows the compilation of the service definition classes.

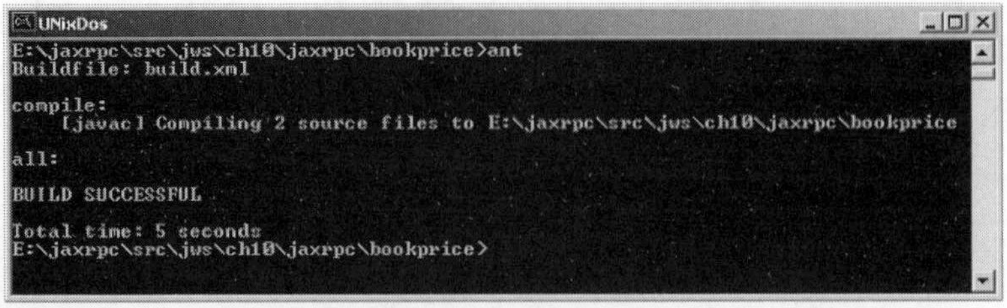

```
UNixDos
E:\jaxrpc\src\jws\ch10\jaxrpc\bookprice>ant
Buildfile: build.xml

compile:
    [javac] Compiling 2 source files to E:\jaxrpc\src\jws\ch10\jaxrpc\bookprice

all:

BUILD SUCCESSFUL

Total time: 5 seconds
E:\jaxrpc\src\jws\ch10\jaxrpc\bookprice>
```

Figure 10.3 Building the services classes using Ant.

Generate Server-Side Artifacts (Ties) and WSDL

Using the xrpcc tool, generate the server-side artifacts and the WSDL document associated with the service. In a JWSDP 1.0 environment, the xrpcc tool requires -server and -keep as options for generating the server-side tie classes and the WSDL document.

Listing 10.10 is a code listing of the Ant script specific to creating server-side tie classes and the WSDL document associated with the service (BookPriceService.xml).

```
<!-- ============== Create Server Ties & WSDL ============ -->

<target name="server-ties">
    <property name="xrpcc" value="${JWSDP_HOME}/bin/xrpcc.bat"/>
     <exec executable="${xrpcc}">
        <arg line="-classpath ." />
        <arg line="-keep" />
        <arg line="-server" />
        <arg line="-d ." />
        <arg line="BookPriceServiceConfig.xml" />
     </exec>
</target>
```

Listing 10.10 Ant script for using 'xrpcc' for generating server ties and WSDL.

To run xrpcc from the command line on Windows, use the following command:

```
xrpcc.bat  -classpath %CLASSPATH% -keep -server
                          -d . BookPriceServiceConfig.xml
```

To run xrpcc from the command line on UNIX, use the following command:

```
xrpcc.sh  -classpath $CLASSPATH -keep -server
                          -d . BookPriceServiceConfig.xml
```

The xrpcc tool generates the following tie classes, including the source files (not listed):

```
BookPriceServiceIF_GetBookPrice_RequestStruct.class
BookPriceServiceIF_GetBookPrice_ResponseStruct.class
BookPriceServiceIF_GetBookPrice_RequestStruct_SOAPSerializer.class
BookPriceServiceIF_GetBookPrice_ResponseStruct_SOAPSerializer.class
BookPriceService_SerializerRegistry.class
BookPriceServiceIF_Tie.class
```

In addition to the previous tie classes, the tool also generates the WSDL document and the configuration properties file associated with the service as follows:

```
BookPriceService.wsdl
BookPriceService_Config.properties
```

The property file will look like the following:

```
# This file is generated by xrpcc.

port0.tie=jws.ch10.jaxrpc.bookprice.BookPriceServiceIF_Tie
port0.servant=jws.ch10.jaxrpc.bookprice.BookPriceServiceImpl
port0.name=BookPriceServiceIF
port0.wsdl.targetNamespace=http://jws.wiley.com/wsdl
port0.wsdl.serviceName=BookPriceService
port0.wsdl.portName=BookPriceServiceIFPort
portcount=1
```

In JWSDP1.0, in order to make the WSDL description accessible through a browser, one manual modification is required for the BookPriceService_Config.properties file to work. Although it is not recommended to modify the configuration properties file, it is possible to do so. Add the following line at the end of BookPriceService_Config.properties:

```
wsdl.location=/WEB-INF/BookPriceService.wsdl
```

With this line enabled, the WSDL now can be referenced by pointing the browser to http://localhost:8080/bookpriceservice/jaxrpc?WSDL.

Package and Deploy the Service

Because JWSDP 1.0 currently enables deployment of the JAX-RPC-based service as a Web application (WAR), create a deployment descriptor (web.xml) and insert BookPriceService_Config.properties as a parameter value for the parameter name configuration.file.

Listing 10.11 is a code listing of the Web deployment descriptor (web.xml) for deploying BookPriceService.

```
<?xml version="1.0" encoding="UTF-8"?>
<!DOCTYPE web-app
    PUBLIC "-//Sun Microsystems, Inc.//DTD Web Application 2.3//EN"
    "http://java.sun.com/j2ee/dtds/web-app_2_3.dtd">
```

Listing 10.11 Deployment descriptor (web.xml) for deploying BookPriceService.

```
<web-app>
 <display-name>BookPriceService</display-name>
 <description>BookPriceService</description>
 <servlet>
    <servlet-name>JAXRPCEndpoint</servlet-name>
    <display-name>JAXRPCEndpoint</display-name>
    <description>Endpoint for Book Price Service</description>
    <servlet-class>com.sun.xml.rpc.server.http.JAXRPCServlet
    </servlet-class>
    <init-param>
       <param-name>configuration.file</param-name>
        <param-value>/WEB-INF/BookPriceService_Config.properties
        </param-value>
    </init-param>
    <load-on-startup>0</load-on-startup>
 </servlet>
 <servlet-mapping>
    <servlet-name>JAXRPCEndpoint</servlet-name>
    <url-pattern>/jaxrpc/*</url-pattern>
 </servlet-mapping>
 <session-config>
    <session-timeout>60</session-timeout>
 </session-config>
</web-app>
```

Listing 10.11 Deployment descriptor (web.xml) for deploying `BookPriceService`. *(continued)*

At this point, we are all set to compile and package the Web application. Create a Web application (`WAR`) file containing the classes including the deployment descriptors `web.xml` and configuration property file `Book-PriceService_Config.properties`.

Listing 10.12 is a sample code listing of an Ant script, which packages and deploys `bookpriceservice.war` in a JWSDP 1.0 environment (that is, a Tomcat `/webapps` directory).

```
<!-- ==================== Package ================== -->
<target name="package">
  <delete dir="./WEB-INF" />
    <copy todir="./WEB-INF">
      <fileset dir=".">
     <include name="*.xml"/>
     <include name="*.wsdl"/>
     <include name="*.properties"/>
```

Listing 10.12 Ant script for packaging `BookPriceService`. *(continues)*

```
        </fileset>
      </copy>
        <copy todir="./WEB-INF/classes">
        <fileset dir=".">
       <include name="**/*.class"/>
        </fileset>
      </copy>
        <jar jarfile="${JAXRPC_WORK_HOME}/bookpriceservice.war">
          <fileset dir="." includes="WEB-INF/**" />
        </jar>
      <copy todir="${JWSDP_HOME}/webapps">
        <fileset dir="${JAXRPC_WORK_HOME}">
       <include name="bookpriceservice.war"/>
        </fileset>
      </copy>
    </target>
```

Listing 10.12 Ant script for packaging `BookPriceService`. *(continued)*

The successful running of the previous Ant script copies the `bookpriceservice.war` to the JWSDP1.0/Tomcat environment `/Webapps` directory and then restarts the Tomcat server. Figure 10.4 shows the successful packaging and deployment of `BookPriceService` in the Tomcat Web container.

Test the Service Deployment and WSDL

To test the successful packaging and deployment of the service, run the following URL using a Web browser:

```
http://127.0.0.1:8080/bookpriceservice/jaxrpc/
```

If everything works successfully, the browser will display the page shown in Figure 10.5.

```
UNixDos
E:\jaxrpc\src\jws\ch10\jaxrpc\bookprice>ant package
Buildfile: build.xml

package:
   [delete] Deleting directory E:\jaxrpc\src\jws\ch10\jaxrpc\bookprice\WEB-INF
     [copy] Copying 5 files to E:\jaxrpc\src\jws\ch10\jaxrpc\bookprice\WEB-INF
     [copy] Copying 8 files to E:\jaxrpc\src\jws\ch10\jaxrpc\bookprice\WEB-INF\c
lasses
      [jar] Building jar: E:\jaxrpc\bookpriceservice.war
     [copy] Copying 1 file to D:\jwsdp1_0\webapps

BUILD SUCCESSFUL

Total time: 3 seconds
E:\jaxrpc\src\jws\ch10\jaxrpc\bookprice>_
```

Figure 10.4 Packaging and deployment of `BookPriceService`.

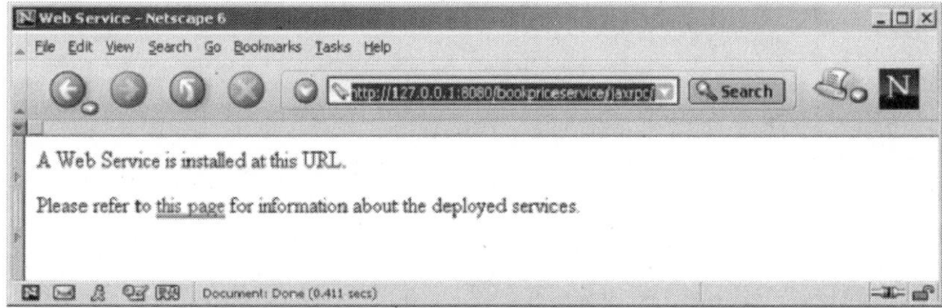

Figure 10.5 Browser displaying the installation of `BookPriceService`.

And, to display the WSDL document, run the following URL using a Web browser:

```
http://127.0.0.1:8080/bookpriceservice/jaxrpc?WSDL
```

If the WSDL generation is successful, the browser will display the page shown in Figure 10.6.

Generating Client-Side Artifacts (Stubs)

Using the `xrpcc` tool, generate the client-side stubs of the service. In a JWSDP 1.0 environment, the `xrpcc` tool requires a `-client` option for generating the client-side stub classes. Ensure that the generated classes are copied to the directory client-stubs, which helps package the client stubs separately.

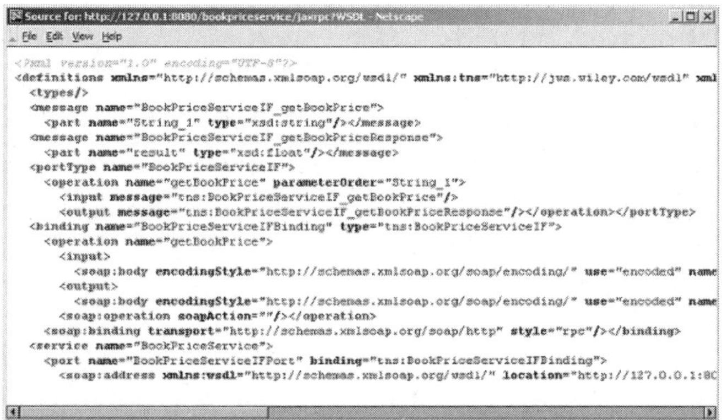

Figure 10.6 Browser showing the WSDL of `BookPriceService`.

The following is a code listing of the Ant script specific to creating client-side stub classes:

```
<!-- ==================== Create Client Stubs ============= -->
 <target name="client-stubs">
     <property name="xrpcc" value="${JWSDP_HOME}/bin/xrpcc.bat"/>
      <exec executable="${xrpcc}">
         <arg line="-classpath ." />
         <arg line="-client" />
         <arg line="-d ./client-stubs" />
         <arg line="BookPriceServiceConfig.xml" />
      </exec>
  </target>
```

This is the tool that generates the following stub classes in the client-stubs directory:

```
BookPriceService.class
BookPriceService_Impl.class
BookPriceService_SerializerRegistry.class
BookPriceServiceIF_GetBookPrice_RequestStruct.class
BookPriceServiceIF_GetBookPrice_ResponseStruct.class
BookPriceServiceIF_GetBookPrice_RequestStruct_SOAPSerializer.class
BookPriceServiceIF_GetBookPrice_ResponseStruct_SOAPSerializer.class
BookPriceServiceIF_Stub.class
```

Now, navigate to the client-stubs directory and, using the `jar` utility, create the `client-stubs.jar` file, including all the stub classes. Additionally, include the remote interface of the service `BookPriceServiceIF.class`. Ensure that the `client-stubs.jar` file is in the CLASSPATH for developing service clients.

Developing JAX-RPC Clients (BookPriceServiceClient)

As we discussed earlier, JAX-RPC 1.0 enables a JAX-RPC-based client to be implemented using three different client invocation models. To illustrate our `BookPriceService` client example, we will implement all three models of client implementation and walk through them in the following sections.

Stub-Based Client

In this client model, we will implement a standalone Java client that uses the stub classes (`client-stubs.jar`), which act as a proxy for invoking remote methods. The client uses the command line argument service `endpoint`, which refers to the target service endpoint.

Listing 10.13 is a code listing of the stub-based service client (`BookPriceServiceClient.java`).

```
package jws.ch10.jaxrpc.bookprice.stubclient;

// Import the Stub Interface
import javax.xml.rpc.Stub;
import jws.ch10.jaxrpc.bookprice.BookPriceServiceIF;

public class BookPriceServiceClient {

// Main method
  public static void main(String[] args) {

    try {

      if(args.length==0) {
        System.out.println("Usage:
         java jws.ch10.bookprice.stubclient.BookPriceServiceClient
                                              SERVICE_ENDPOINT");
        return;
      }

      // Obtain the Instance of the Stub Interface
      BookPriceServiceIF_Stub stub = (BookPriceServiceIF_Stub)
         (new BookPriceService_Impl().getBookPriceServiceIFPort());


      // Configure the stub setting required properties
      // Setting the target service endpoint
      stub._setProperty(
                javax.xml.rpc.Stub.ENDPOINT_ADDRESS_PROPERTY,
                                                     args[0]);


      // Execute the remote method
      System.out.println ("\nThe retail book price in Japanese yen:"
                   + stub.getBookPrice("JAX-RPC in 24 hours"));

    } catch (Exception ex) {
        ex.printStackTrace();
    }
  }
}
```

Listing 10.13 `BookPriceServiceClient.java`.

```
UNixDos
E:\jaxrpc\client>javac -d . *.java

E:\jaxrpc\client>java jws.ch10.jaxrpc.bookprice.stubclient.BookPriceServiceClien
t http://127.0.0.1:8080/bookpriceservice/jaxrpc/BookPriceServiceIF

The retail book price in Japanese yen:739.46063

E:\jaxrpc\client>
E:\jaxrpc\client>
```

Figure 10.7 Output showing stub-based client invocation on `BookPriceService`.

Ensure that the `client-stubs.jar` and JAX-RPC API libraries are available in the CLASSPATH and that the JWSDP 1.0/Tomcat server is up and running. Then, compile the source code using `javac` and execute the client providing the service endpoint as the argument.

If everything works successfully, we see output like that shown in Figure 10.7.

Dynamic Proxy-Based Client

In the dynamic proxy client model, we will implement a standalone Java client that invokes a target service endpoint dynamically at runtime without using the local stub class. The `getPort` method on the `javax.xml.rpc.Service` interface enables a dynamic proxy to be created.

Listing 10.14 is a code listing of the dynamic proxy-based service client (`BookPriceServiceProxyClient.java`).

```
package jws.ch10.jaxrpc.bookprice.proxyclient;

// Import Service & ServiceFactory

import javax.xml.rpc.Service;
import javax.xml.rpc.ServiceFactory;
import jws.ch10.jaxrpc.bookprice.*;

import javax.xml.namespace.QName;
import java.net.URL;


public class BookPriceServiceProxyClient {

// Main method
  public static void main(String[] args) {

    try {
```

Listing 10.14 `BookPriceServiceProxyClient.java`.

```
        // WSDL location of the BookPriceService
        String wsdlURL
            = "http://127.0.0.1:8080/bookpriceservice/jaxrpc?WSDL";


        // WSDL namespace URI
        String nameSpaceURI = "http://jws.wiley.com/wsdl";

        // Service Name
        String serviceName = "BookPriceService";

        // Service port Name
         String portName = "BookPriceServiceIFPort";

         URL serviceWSDL = new URL(wsdlURL);

         // Obtain an Instance of Service factory
         ServiceFactory serviceFactory = ServiceFactory.newInstance();

         // Create a service from Instance using WSDL
         Service bookPriceService =
                   serviceFactory.createService(serviceWSDL,
                              new QName(nameSpaceURI, serviceName));

         // Get the proxy object
         BookPriceServiceIF bpProxy =
           (BookPriceServiceIF) bookPriceService.getPort
         (new QName(nameSpaceURI,portName), BookPriceServiceIF.class);

         // Invoke the remote methods
         System.out.println("\nThe retail book price
                          in Japanese Yen :"
                    + bpProxy.getBookPrice("JAX-RPC in 24 hours"));

      } catch (Exception ex) {
          ex.printStackTrace();
      }
    }
  }
```

Listing 10.14 `BookPriceServiceProxyClient.java`. *(continued)*

Ensure that the JAX-RPC API libraries are available in the CLASSPATH and that the JWSDP 1.0/Tomcat server is up and running and then compile the source code using `javac`.

If everything works successfully, you should see output like that shown in Figure 10.8.

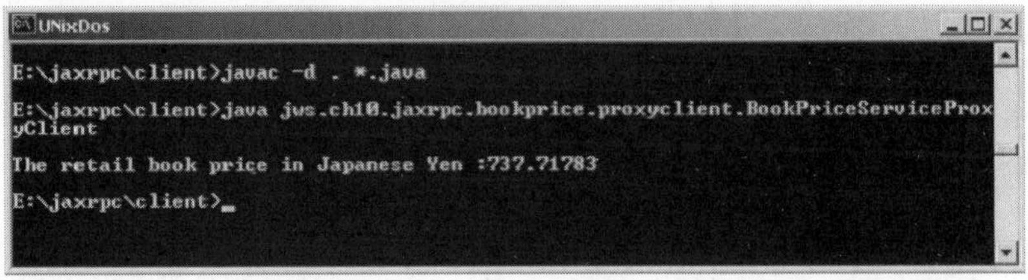

```
E:\jaxrpc\client>javac -d . *.java

E:\jaxrpc\client>java jws.ch10.jaxrpc.bookprice.proxyclient.BookPriceServiceProx
yClient

The retail book price in Japanese Yen :737.71783

E:\jaxrpc\client>_
```

Figure 10.8 Output showing a dynamic proxy-based invocation on `BookPriceService`.

Dynamic Invocation Interface (DII) Client

In the DII client model, the client discovers the target service dynamically at runtime and then invokes its methods. Listing 10.15 is a code listing of a DII client (`BookPriceServiceDIIClient.java`).

```
package jws.ch10.jaxrpc.bookprice.diiclient;

// Imports
import javax.xml.rpc.Call;
import javax.xml.rpc.Service;
import javax.xml.rpc.ServiceFactory;
import javax.xml.rpc.JAXRPCException;
import javax.xml.rpc.ParameterMode;

import javax.xml.namespace.QName;
import java.net.URL;


public class BookPriceServiceDIIClient {

// Main method
  public static void main(String[] args) {


      // Service Name
      String qService = "BookPriceService";

      // Port Name
      String qPort = "BookPriceServiceIF";

      // Name space URI
       String BODY_NAMESPACE_VALUE = "http://jws.wiley.com/wsdl";


      // Encoding style
```

Listing 10.15 `BookPriceServiceDIIClient.java`.

```
    String ENCODING_STYLE_PROPERTY =
                    "javax.xml.rpc.encodingstyle.namespace.uri";


   // XML Schema
     String NS_XSD = "http://www.w3.org/2001/XMLSchema";


    // SOAP encoding URI
    String URI_ENCODING = "http://schemas.xmlsoap.org/soap/encoding/";


   try {
    String target_endpoint =
"http://127.0.0.1:8080/bookpriceservice/jaxrpc/BookPriceServiceIF";

   // Obtain an Instance of Service factory
      ServiceFactory sFactory =
                          ServiceFactory.newInstance();

        // Create a Service
           Service service =
                sFactory.createService(new QName(qService));

           // Define a port
            QName port = new QName(qPort);

            // Create a Call object using the service
            Call call = service.createCall(port);

            // Set the target service endpoint
            call.setTargetEndpointAddress(target_endpoint);

            // Set properties - SOAP URI, Encoding etc.
            call.setProperty(Call.SOAPACTION_USE_PROPERTY,
                                              new Boolean(true));

            call.setProperty(Call.SOAPACTION_URI_PROPERTY, "");

            call.setProperty(ENCODING_STYLE_PROPERTY, URI_ENCODING);

            // Set Parameter In type  as String
             QName QNAME_TYPE_STRING = new QName(NS_XSD, "string");

            // Set Return value type as String
            QName QNAME_TYPE_FLOAT = new QName(NS_XSD, "float");
            call.setReturnType(QNAME_TYPE_FLOAT);
```

Listing 10.15 `BookPriceServiceDIIClient.java`. *(continues)*

```
            // Set operations
            call.setOperationName(new QName(BODY_NAMESPACE_VALUE,
                                                "getBookPrice"));

            // Set Parameters
            call.addParameter("String_1", QNAME_TYPE_STRING,
                                             ParameterMode.IN);

            String[] BookName = {"JAX-RPC in 24 hours"};

            // Invoke and obtain response
            Object respObj = (Object) call.invoke(BookName);


            System.out.println("\nThe retail book price
                         in Japanese Yen:" + respObj.toString());

    } catch (Exception ex) {
            ex.printStackTrace();
    }
   }
}
```

Listing 10.15 `BookPriceServiceDIIClient.java`. *(continued)*

Ensure that the JAX-RPC API libraries are available in the CLASSPATH and that the JWSDP 1.0/Tomcat environment is up and running and then compile the source code using `javac`.

If everything works successfully, you should see output like that shown in Figure 10.9.

```
E:\jaxrpc\client>javac -d . *.java

E:\jaxrpc\client>java jws.ch10.jaxrpc.bookprice.diiclient.BookPriceServiceDIIClient

The retail book price in Japanese Yen:737.5

E:\jaxrpc\client>
```

Figure 10.9 Output showing a DII-based invocation on `BookPriceService`.

Summary

In this chapter, we have discussed how to develop JAX-RPC-based services and service clients for enabling Java Web services. We noted that JAX-RPC provides a RPC-based communication model between applications supporting industry standard messaging protocols. In general, we covered the role of JAX-RPC in Web services, JAX-RPC APIs and its programming model, JAX-RPC-supported mappings for Java and XML/WSDL, and the development of the JAX-RPC-based Web services applications.

In the next chapter, we will discuss how to describe, publish, and discover Web services using JAXR.

CHAPTER

11

Java API for XML Registries

As we discussed in Chapter 5, "Description and Discovery of Web Services," registering and discovering Web services from shared *registries* is an important aspect of the Web services paradigm. These registries should be able to understand XML-based protocols such as SOAP. These registries should ideally be capable of maintaining rich metadata information about registered Web services. This chapter discusses the Java API for XML Registries (JAXR) 1.0, an API for communicating with such XML registries.

The following are the key topics discussed in this chapter:

- Introduction to JAXR
- JAXR architecture
  - JAXR architectural components
  - JAXR capabilities and capability profiles
  - JAXR programming model
  - JAXR information model
  - Classification of registry objects
  - Association of registry objects

- JAXR registry services API
  - Connection management API
  - Life cycle management API
  - Query management API
- Understanding JAXR by examples
  - JAXR support in JWSDP 1.0
  - Publishing using JAXR
  - Querying using JAXR
  - Deleting information using JAXR

Introduction to JAXR

JAXR is a standard Java API for use in registering/publishing and discovering/querying Web services from XML-based registries such as UDDI and ebXML Registry/Repository. JAXR is an integral part of the J2EE 1.4 platform, which is due to be released in early 2003.

JAXR does not define any new registry standard, rather it defines a Java API for performing registry operations over a diverse set of registries. JAXR also performs a unification of diverse information models of various registries, so that regardless of the registry in use, the applications can use the same code for managing registry information. In the next section, we will examine the architecture of JAXR as well as its architectural components.

Visit the following site to download the final JAXR draft specification: http://java.sun.com/xml/downloads/jaxr.html

JAXR Architecture

JAXR Architectural Components

JAXR architecture involves three main components: registry provider, JAXR provider, and JAXR client. Each of these components are discussed in the paragraphs that follow.

Registry Provider

A registry provider actually implements the registry standard such as UDDI, ebXML registry/repository, or OASIS registry. A registry provider may or may not provide implementation for JAXR.

JAXR Provider

JAXR provider implements the JAXR specification. A JAXR application/ JAXR client would access the registry through the JAXR provider. There are three categories of JAXR providers: JAXR pluggable providers, registry-specific providers, and JAXR bridge providers. Each of these is described in the paragraphs that follow.

JAXR Pluggable Provider

The JAXR pluggable provider is implemented so that it can work with any registry. Pluggable providers provide a single abstraction for multiple registry-specific JAXR providers and thereby save JAXR applications from having to deal with multiple registry-specific JAXR providers.

Registry-Specific Provider

Registry-specific provders provide JAXR support for a specific registry. Typically, it plugs into the JAXR pluggable provider and is used by the JAXR pluggable provider in a delegation pattern. Note that the JAXR specification does not define a contract between the pluggable provider and the registry-specific provider. The next version of the JAXR specification will contain a *Services Provider Interface* (SPI) to provide such a contract between the two.

JAXR Bridge Provider

JAXR bridge providers are registry-specific. This kind of provider is strictly based on the registry specification such as a UDDI or ebXML registry/ repository; this is so that the provider can be used to communicate with target registries based on these specifications, regardless of who the registry vendor is. That is, a JAXR bridge provider also is a JAXR registry-specific provider — however, the reverse is not always true. A registry-specific provider may deviate slightly from the underlying registry's specification.

JAXR Application (or JAXR Client)

A JAXR application is a Java program that uses the JAXR API to access the services provided by the registry through a JAXR provider. A JAXR application can be a standalone Java application or an enterprise component hosted in a managed environment, such as an EJB or servlet container. Typically, a JAXR application and a JAXR provider would be located in the same JVM.

Figure 11.1 shows an architecture diagram of JAXR.

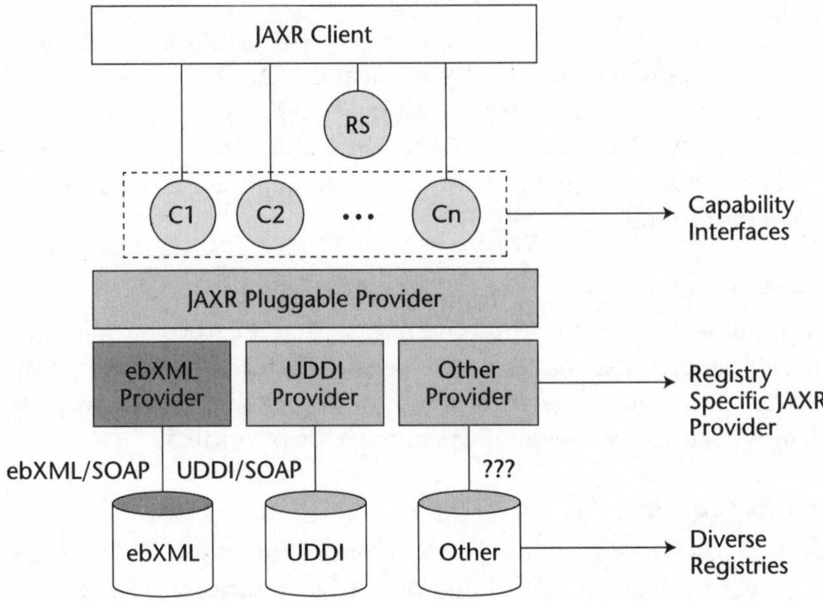

Figure 11.1 JAXR architecture.

In Figure 11.1, you can see the following: RS represents the `Registry-Service` interface, which is the main interface that must be implemented by all the JAXR providers. A JAXR application connects to this interface via the `Connection` object, through which it eventually connects to the JAXR capability interfaces. The `Connection` interface is discussed in the *Connection Management API* section later in this chapter.

C1, C2, through Cn represent JAXR interfaces implemented by the JAXR provider. Each of these interfaces is responsible for providing a specific type of registry functionality, such as querying registry data, adding/modifying/deleting registry data, and so on. In JAXR terminology, these interfaces are referred to as *capability interfaces*. Capabilities are discussed in detail in the next section.

JAXR Capabilities and Capability Profiles

As we mentioned earlier in the chapter, JAXR provides a single, unified API for accessing different registries. Registries vary significantly in their capabilities and the underlying information model.

Typically, if an API is designed to support a diverse set of functionalities, it tends to provide support for only the most common functionalities. A classic example of this observation would be JDBC (Java Database Connectivity). If you look at JDBC, it provides support for only the most common features found in popular databases. The way JDBC is designed makes it incapable of including any features that are not commonly found in all the databases. Due to its architecture, if JDBC did include support for functionality that was specific to a particular database, the rest of the database vendors would have a hard time implementing a JDBC provider because there would be no way that the vendor could ignore the capability, which is required by the JDBC specification but is unsupported by their database. This architecture of the JDBC API does not render it unacceptable because the degree of variation of functionality provided by different databases is comparatively less, and hence, the need for a more flexible architecture is less. However, this is not the case for registries.

The degree of variation of the functionalities that are provided by different registries is quite high; sometimes from the protocol they use to the information model they support. Thus, designing a unified API such as JAXR using a similar approach as JDBC (that is, the aforementioned least common denominator approach) would render JAXR almost useless for one or the other type of registry. One of the main objectives of JAXR is to provide support for diverse registries through an API that is broad in scope and capable rather than a least common denominator API. To be able to offer high functionality while not bloating the API unnecessarily, JAXR introduced the concept of capabilities and their profiles, both of which are discussed in the following sections.

JAXR Capabilities

A *capability* is a group of related features, for example, features related to finding information in the registry. Each capability is represented by a Java interface in JAXR. For example, `BusinessLifeCycleManager` and `LifeCycleManager` are two JAXR interfaces that represent the same kind of capability (that is, life cycle management) but at different functional levels. Similarly, the `BusinessQueryManager` and `DeclarativeQueryManager` JAXR interfaces include capabilities pertaining to query management, again at different levels of functionality.

JAXR Capability Profiles

A JAXR *capability profile* is a group of capability interfaces at the same level. JAXR currently defines two capability profiles for two different functional levels: basic and advanced. They are as follows:

Level 0 Capability Profile

Interfaces that belong to the Level 0 Capability Profile provide basic support of life-cycle management and querying capabilities. Interfaces belonging to the Level 0 Capability Profile also are known as the *Business API*. Capability interfaces belonging to this profile include:

- BusinessLifeCycleManager
- BusinessQueryManager

Level 1 Capability Profile

Interfaces that belong to the Level 1 Capability Profile provide advanced support of life-cycle management and querying capabilities. Support for the Level 1 Capability Profile also implies support for Level 0 capabilities. Interfaces belonging to the Level 1 Capability Profile also are known as the *Generic API*. Capability interfaces belonging to this profile include the following:

- LifeCycleManager
- DeclarativeQueryManager

JAXR providers supporting access to registries that do not provide advanced capabilities required by a Level 1 Profile implementation can choose to not implement this more advanced profile. For example, a JAXR provider for UDDI registry *does not* require implementation of a Level 1 Capability Profile because UDDI registries do not support the advanced functionalities of the Level 1 registries. However, JAXR providers for ebXML registry/repository must be Level 1 compliant.

A JAXR application can discover a given JAXR provider's capability level by using the methods on the `CapabilityProfile` interface.

The JAXR Programming Model

JAXR API is divided into the following two main packages:

javax.xml.registry. This package defines the interfaces responsible for providing usual registry services, for example, connection management, life-cycle management, and querying.

javax.xml.registry.infomodel. This package provides interfaces representing the information model of a JAXR-enabled registry. The JAXR information model is discussed in the next section.

JAXR Information Model

The term information model refers to the *types* of information that are supported by a particular directory or registry. The *information model* is considered to be an important feature for any registry; the richer the information model of a registry is, the more usable the registry becomes. Different registries have different information models. In fact, there is no standard information model in place for XML-based registries. JAXR is the first standard that attempts to provide a unified view of the information model for XML Registries.

The JAXR information model is based on the ebXML registry's information model as defined by the ebXML registry information model (RIM) specification. It has been further extended, in order to support UDDI. EbXML RIM presents a comprehensive model for structuring information compared to the UDDI Data Structure (UDDI-DS), which is why JAXR provides inherent support for ebXML RIM right from the beginning.

The JAXR information model's related interfaces are defined in a separate package called javax.xml.registry.infomodel. These interfaces present a Java binding to the unified information model from two dominant registry specifications: UDDI and ebXML registry. An important point to remember is that the JAXR information model presents a view of how information may be structured in a JAXR-enabled registry and does not represent in any way the structural model of information in the underlying repository.

Classes and Interfaces

The following list discusses some of the important and frequently used classes and interfaces in the JAXR information model:

`RegistryObject`. This is the base class that is extended by most of the objects in the JAXR information model. It provides a minimal set of metadata for these registry objects in terms of associations that the objects may have, classifications that classify these objects, their description, audit trail, external identifiers, external links (URLs, for instance), and so on. Classifications, external identifiers, and associations are discussed later in this chapter.

`RegistryEntry`. The JAXR information model objects that require additional coarse-grained metadata, such as version information, would extend this interface. This interface is the base interface for the interfaces in the model that require additional metadata beyond what is provided by the relatively lighter-weight and more finer-grained `RegistryObject` interface.

`Organization`. The type `Organization` extends `Registry-Object` and is intended to represent information pertaining to any organization in the JAXR-enabled registry. Typically, an `Organization` instance can have different types of relationships with other `Organization` instances, such as a parent-child relationship, for example. An `Organization` can have one or more `Services`.

`Service`. The `Service` type represents information pertaining to the Web services that are published by an organization in a JAXR-enabled registry. Corresponding to each `Service`, zero or more `ServiceBindings` can be present in a registry. This type also extends `RegistryObject`.

`ServiceBinding`. A `ServiceBinding` instance extends `RegistryObject`. This type specifies the technical information related to the `Services` published by an organization. Typically, this information refers to access mechanisms such as a URI; they are provided in order to specify an interface for accessing the Web service.

`SpecificationLink`. A `ServiceBinding` can have a `Specifi-cationLink` establishing a link to one of its technical specifications. This technical specification can consist of information such as how to invoke a SOAP RPC Web service, how the service would behave under different contexts, and so on.

`ClassificationScheme`. This type of JAXR information model can be used to specify the taxonomy that has been used for classifying a particular `RegistryObject`. Some of the common examples of classification schemes include the Dewey Decimal System used in libraries to categorize books. Another common example would be the North American Industry Classification System, or NAICS, used to categorize businesses based on the services they offer, the vertical they belong to, and so on.

The classification functionality of JAXR is discussed in more detail in the section titled *Classification of Registry Objects* later in this chapter. For now, just remember that JAXR enables the classification of `RegistryObjects` through homegrown classification schemes.

`Classification`. `Classification` instances are used to classify a `RegistryObject` instance using `ClassificationScheme`. Classifications are discussed in more detail in a later section.

`Concept`. A `Concept` instance can be used to represent anything virtually. Some of the common uses of `Concept` objects are as follows:

1. They can be used to define hierarchical tree structure and detailed elements of a classification scheme. The root of a classification tree structure is an instance of `ClassificationScheme`, whereas the rest of the descendent nodes of the classification tree are instances of `Concepts`.
2. They can be used to serve as a proxy for content that is externally stored to a Level 0 registry by providing a unique ID for the external content, akin to the UDDI `tModels` when they are used for the purposes of providing a technical fingerprint for content external to the UDDI registry, such as a WSDL document.

`Association`. This type is used to define associations between different objects in the JAXR information model. Associations are discussed later in this chapter.

`ExternalIdentifier`. `ExternalIdentifier` instances are used to provide identification information to a `RegistryObject` apart from the 128-bit UUID Key ID. This identification information may be based on some well-known identification scheme such as a social security number. In order to represent the identification scheme, the JAXR information model reuses the `ClassificationScheme` class.

`ExternalLink`. Instances of this type provide a URI link to the content that is managed outside the registry. Unlike content managed in a repository, such external content may change or be deleted at any time without the knowledge of the registry. A `RegistryObject` may be associated with one or more `ExternalLinks`. The potential use of the `ExternalLink` capability may be in a GUI tool that displays the `ExternalLinks` defined for a `RegistryObject`. The user may click on such links and navigate to an external Web page in order to get further information.

`Slot`. Slot instances provide the capability of adding arbitrary attributes to the `RegistryObject` instances at runtime. This ability to add attributes dynamically enables the extensibility of the information model.

ExtensibleObject. The ExtensibleObject interface consists of methods that enable the addition, deletion, and lookup for Slot instances. Thus, the ExtensibleObject interface provides a dynamic extensibility capability to various objects in a JAXR information model. Several interfaces in the JAXR information model are extended from ExtensibleObject including Organization, RegistryObject, Service, ServiceBinding, Classification, ClassificationScheme, Association, and so on.

ExtrinsicObject. This type is used to provide metadata about the repository item (for example, a WSDL document or an XML Schema document), about which a registry has no knowledge. The ExtrinsicObject provides access to a repository item in a JAXR-enabled registry. An instance of this type is required for each repository item.

AuditableEvent. An AuditableEvent instance is a RegistryObject used to represent audit trail information for a particular RegistryObject.

User. Instances of this type are RegistryObjects used to provide information about registered users within a registry. Each User is affiliated with an Organization. User objects are used in the AuditTrail for a RegistryObject.

PostalAddress. PostalAddress instances represent a postal address for a User and an Organization.

RegistryPackage. This is used to logically group the related RegistryObject instances.

Figure 11.2 shows the inheritance relationships between different objects in the JAXR information model.

Classification of Registry Objects

Classification denotes the categorization of entities based on a well-defined scheme known as a *classification scheme* or *taxonomy*. Classification enables a rapid discovery of registry objects. Thus, the ability to be able to classify objects of a registry is considered to be one of the most significant features. JAXR supports the classification of objects registered with a JAXR-enabled registry in order to support such rapid discovery of objects.

The Classification, ClassificationScheme, and Concept interfaces of the JAXR information model are used to provide classification support in JAXR.

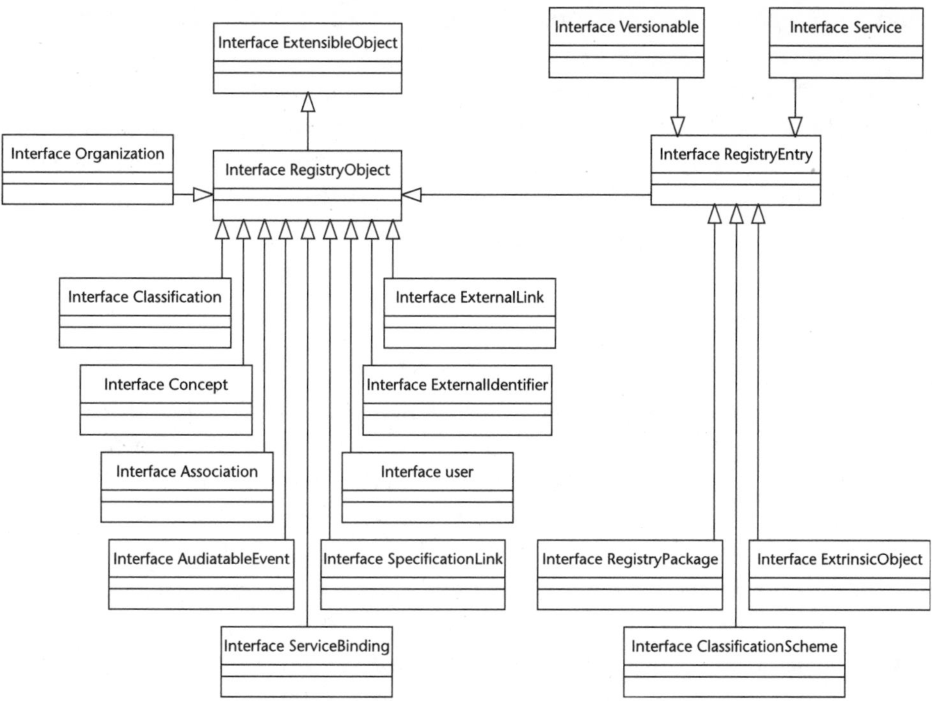

Figure 11.2 The JAXR information model.

The `Classification` interface is used to classify `RegistryObject` instances. A `RegistryObject` may be classified along multiple dimensions by adding zero or more `Classification` instances to the `RegistryObject`. The `RegistryObject` interface provides overloaded `addClassification()` methods, in order to enable a JAXR application to add `Classification` instances to the `RegistryObject`, and thus to classify that particular `RegistryObject`.

The `ClassificationScheme` interface is used to represent taxonomies or schemes that can be used to provide taxonomical data for categorizing `RegistryObject` instances. A `Classification` instance uses a `ClassificationScheme` instance to identify the taxonomy used to classify its `RegistryObject` along that particular dimension. For example, a Geography `ClassificationScheme` can provide a taxonomy system that defines a geography structure with continents, countries within continents, states within countries, and probably even cities and towns within states.

Figure 11.3 shows associations between RegistryObject, Classification, and ClassificationScheme. As you can see in the figure, RegistryObject may be associated with zero or more Classification instances based on the number of dimensions along which it has been classified. In any case, a Classification instance is associated with exactly one ClassificationScheme instance in order to identify the taxonomy used to classify RegistryObject.

Types of Taxonomies

Taxonomy is defined in terms of a structure consisting of elements, known as taxonomy elements, and their relationship with each other. As an example, consider an illustrative geography taxonomy consisting of a country taxonomy element, which in turn would have a containment relationship with the continent taxonomy element. Thus, while a Classification instance uses a ClassificationScheme instance to identify the taxonomy for classification, it also needs some way of identifying a specific taxonomy element used for classifying RegistryObject.

JAXR supports taxonomies in two ways based on the location of taxonomy elements and their structural relationship-related information: internally and externally.

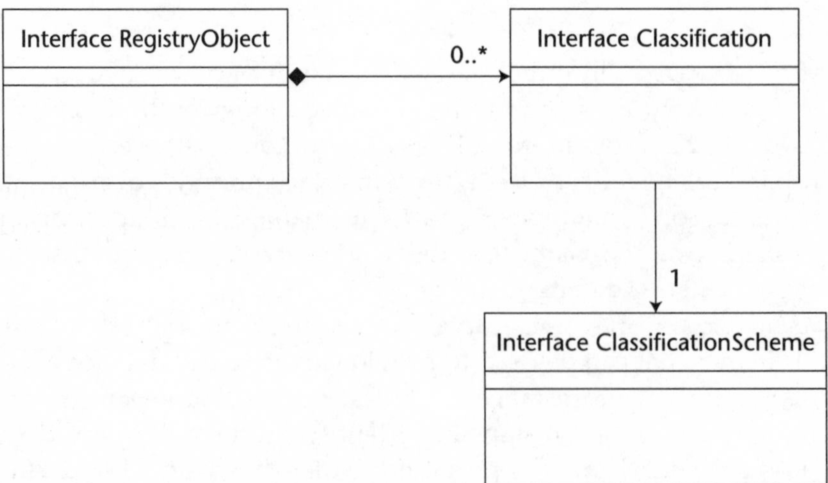

Figure 11.3 Classifying a registry object.

Internal Taxonomy

The information about taxonomy elements and their structural relationships is available internally within a JAXR provider. This type of taxonomy obviously provides more functionality (and thus value) to a JAXR application because a JAXR provider can now validate whether references to taxonomy elements in a classification are meaningful and correct.

However, the internal structure maintained within the JAXR provider needs to be updated whenever the taxonomy evolves. Thus, this added maintenance could be considered a drawback of the internal taxonomies.

JAXR makes use of the concept interface for representing taxonomy elements and their structural relationship with each other in order to describe an internal taxonomy. As mentioned earlier, concept instances can be used to define tree structures where the root of the tree is a `ClassificationScheme` instance and each node in the tree is a concept instance.

External Taxonomy

Information about taxonomy elements and their structural relationships is available externally to the JAXR provider. JAXR applications can use external taxonomies without having to import the complete taxonomy structure. Also, because the structure resides externally to the JAXR provider, there is no need to update the structure whenever taxonomy evolves, thus making taxonomy more flexible to changes.

However, in this case there is no means for a JAXR provider to validate the references to taxonomy elements in a classification.

Types of Classification

In any case, the classification instance would always use `ClassificationScheme` to identify the taxonomy, internal or external. Now, based on the kind of taxonomy used by a classification, a classification can be categorized as one of the following: interal or external.

Internal Classification

If a `Classification` instance is used to classify a `RegistryObject` using an internal taxonomy, the classification is referred to as *internal classification*. In order to use an internal taxonomy, the JAXR application uses the `setConcept()` method on a `Classification` instance to refer to the `Concept` instance representing the taxonomical element. Another point to note is that a JAXR application does not need to call `setClassificationScheme()` on a `Classification` instance when using internal taxonomies because the classifying `Concept` already knows its root `ClassificationScheme`.

Figure 11.4 shows an example of internal classification, in which a `Concept` instance is used to represent the taxonomy element. Here, an organization named ACME Computer Services is classified as a *Custom Computer Programming Services* provider, using the NAICS standard taxonomy made available as an internal taxonomy.

External Classification

If a `Classification` instance is used to classify a `RegistryObject` using an external taxonomy, the classification is referred to as *external classification*. A JAXR application would call the `setClassificationScheme()` method on the `Classification` instance to specify an external taxonomy. Also, in order to refer to the taxonomy element, the application would call the `setValue()` method on the `Classification` instance to define a unique value that represents the taxonomy element within the external taxonomy.

Figure 11.5 shows an example of an external classification, in which the same ACME Computer Services organization is classified using the NAICS standard taxonomy as a *custom computer programming services* provider. However, in this case, the NAICS standard taxonomy is not available internally to the JAXR provider and so a `Concept` instance is not used to identify the taxonomy element. Rather, a name/value pair is used to refer to the externally located taxonomy element, where providing a name is optional but providing a value to the taxonomy element is mandatory.

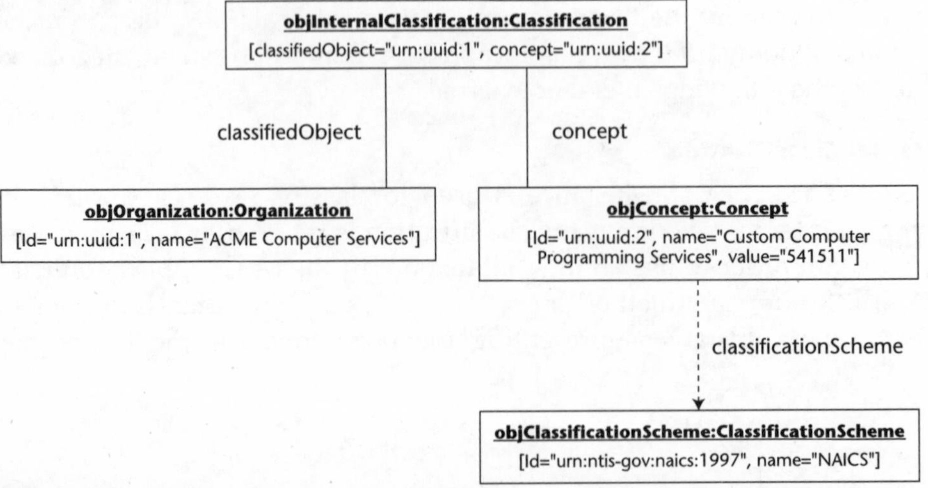

Figure 11.4 An example of internal classification.

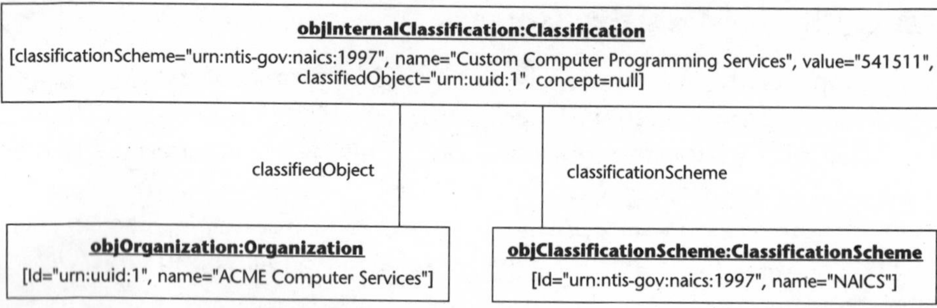

Figure 11.5 An example of internal classification.

Multidimensional Classification

A `RegistryObject` can be classified along multiple dimensions, which means that a `RegistryObject` may be classified by multiple taxonomies or classification schemes. Figure 11.6 depicts an example wherein the ACME Computer Services organization is classified by two internal taxonomies, Industry and Geography. Please note that for brevity, the figure does not show the entire taxonomical structure.

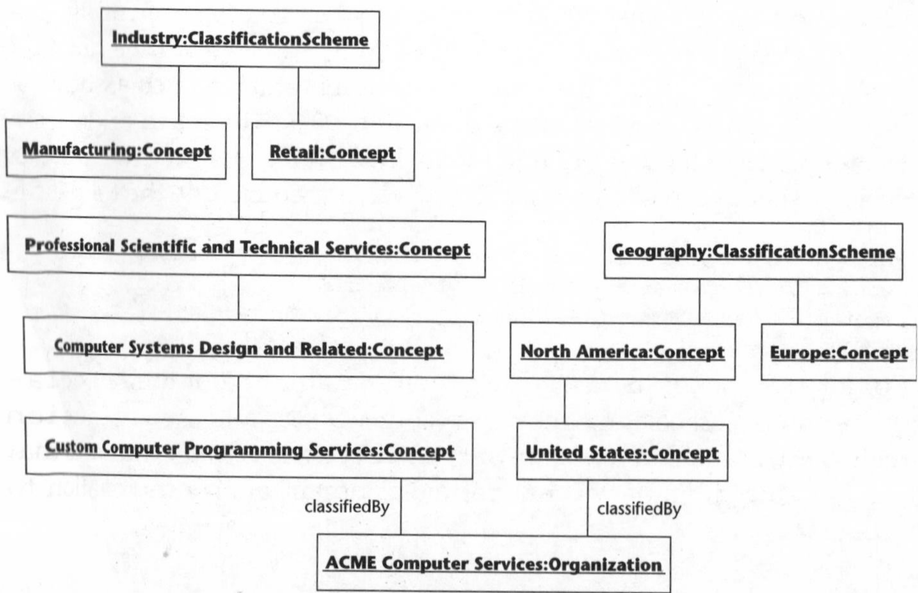

Figure 11.6 An example of a multi-dimensional classification.

Association of Registry Objects

JAXR supports the association between registry objects. A `RegistryObject` may be associated with zero or more `RegistryObject` instances. The JAXR information model defines an `Association` interface, which can be used to associate any two given registry objects. An `Association` instance represents an association between a source `RegistryObject` and a target `RegistryObject`, referred to as *sourceObject* and *targetObject*, respectively.

Figure 11.7 shows an example where two classification schemes are associated with each other. In this example, the newer version of the NAICS classification scheme (NAICS2001) is associated with the older version of the NAICS classification scheme (NAICS1997) so that the newer version supersedes the older version.

In the figure, you can see that the newer version of the NAICS classification scheme is the sourceObject and the older version is the targetObject, because the type of association implies that the sourceObject `Supersedes` the targetObject. Thus, the newer version of the classification scheme has to be the sourceObject in order to supersede the older version of the classification scheme in the registry. So, as can be seen from the figure, it is important which object plays the sourceObject and the targetObject because these objects determine the semantics of an association.

Types of Associations

Each `Association` instance has an `associationType` attribute that identifies the type of that association. In Figure 11.7 you can see one such type: `Supersedes`. JAXR has defined an enumeration of such association types, `AssociationType`, in the form of a `ClassificationScheme`. This enumeration has been defined to include all the well-known forms of associations between two objects. The types defined include the following:

```
RelatedTo    HasMember     HasChild  HasParent         ExternallyLinks
Contains     EquivalentTo  Extends   Implements        InstanceOf
Supersedes   Uses          Replaces  ResponsibleFor    SubmitterOf
```

So, for example, if the `associationType` attribute of the `Associ`-`tion` instance, associating the `User` sourceObject and `Organizat` targetObject, is equal to the value `SubmitterOf`, this clearly indicate the user is the submitter of that particular organization's informa this registry.

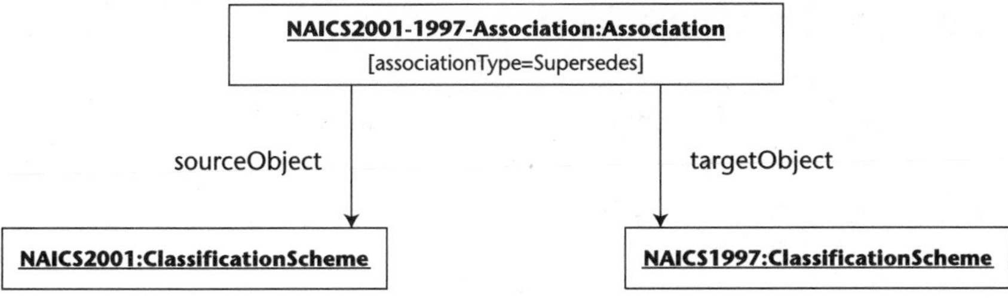

Figure 11.7 An example of a RegistryObject association.

Association Use Cases

Based on the ownership of the objects between whom the association has been created, two common use cases have been identified by JAXR: intramural associations and extramural associations. The following describe each of these cases.

Intramural Associations

Intramural associations are defined when a user creates an association between two registry objects that were created by the same user. Such an association does not need to be confirmed by anybody else because the party that creates the association is the same party that owns the registry objects being associated. Thus, intramural association is implicitly considered to be confirmed by the registry.

Extramural Associations

Extramural associations are a bit more sophisticated than intramural associations; users owning either or both objects being associated are different than the user that created the association.

Extramural association needs to be confirmed explicitly by the parties that own the associating registry objects. Respective parties can use the `confirmAssociation()` method on the `BusinessLifeCycleManager` interface in their JAXR applications to confirm the association in question. Consequently, an association can be unconfirmed by an owner of any of the associating registry objects by using the `unconfirmAssociation()` method on `BusinessLifeCycleManager`. An unconfirmed association would not be visible to the third-party registry users.

Now, let's take a look at the JAXR programming APIs responsible for managing the connections to the JAXR providers, managing life cycles of registry objects, and querying the registry.

JAXR Registry Services API

As mentioned earlier in the chapter, the interfaces pertaining to JAXR registry services are defined in a separate package called `javax.xml.registry`. Programming interfaces can thus be categorized based on the registry services provided as follows:

- Connection Management API
- Life-Cycle Management API
- Query Management API

The following sections explain the APIs involved with managing connections to a JAXR provider.

Connection Management API

JAXR connection management activity can be further broken down into finer grained sub-activities. Each of these sub-activities is discussed in the following sections in the order of the sequence in which they should occur.

Looking Up a ConnectionFactory

A JAXR `ConnectionFactory` object needs to be configured in a provider-specific way before successfully creating connections with a JAXR provider. There are two ways of obtaining a `ConnectionFactory` object, as follows:

- A JAXR application can get hold of the `ConnectionFactory` instance by performing a lookup on the JNDI directory. The registration of a `ConnectionFactory` instance with the JNDI naming service is JAXR provider-specific.
- Another way for a JAXR application to obtain the `ConnectionFactory` instance is by using the `newInstance()` static method on the `ConnectionFactory` abstract class. The JAXR application may indicate which factory class to instantiate when calling the `newInstance()` method by defining the system property `javax.xml.registry.ConnectionFactoryClass`.

The following code shows how to obtain a ConnectionFactory object through a newInstance() method.

```
// Add System property to define which provider-specific
// ConnectionFactoryClass to use.

System.setProperty ("javax.xml.registry.ConnectionFactoryClass",
"com.sun.xml.registry.uddi.ConnectionFactoryImpl");

// Create ConnectionFactory using the class specified in
// the System property and static newInstance method

ConnectionFactory objConnectionFactory =
ConnectionFactory.newInstance();
```

Setting Connection Properties on ConnectionFactory

After a ConnectionFactory instance is available to a JAXR application, that instance then can configure the ConnectionFactory instance with a Properties object by calling the setProperties() method on ConnectionFactory. The properties specified may be either standard or non-standard provider-specific properties. Standard properties are defined by the JAXR specification.

Some of the more important standard connection properties are listed in Table 11.1.

The following code shows how to set the queryManagerURL and lifeCycleManagerURL configuration properties on the ConnectionFactory object.

```
// Setting the Connection configuration properties

Properties objProperties = new Properties();

objProperties.put ("javax.xml.registry.queryManagerURL",
"http://java.sun.com/uddi/inquiry");

objProperties.put ("javax.xml.registry.lifecycleManagerURL",
"http://java.sun.com/uddi/publish");
```

Table 11.1 Standard Connection Properties

PROPERTY	DATA TYPE	DESCRIPTION
`javax.xml.registry.queryManagerURL`	String	URL to the query manager service hosted by the target registry provider. A *query manager* service is responsible for handling all of the query requests.
`javax.xml.registry.lifeCycleManagerURL`	String	URL to the life-cycle manager service hosted by the target registry provider. If this is not explicitly specified, it defaults to the queryManagerURL. A life-cycle manager service is responsible for handling all life-cycle management-related requests.
`javax.xml.registry.security.authenticationMethod`	String	Specifies the authentication method to be used by the JAXR provider when authenticating with the registry provider.
`javax.xml.registry.uddi.maxRows`	Integer	Specifies the maximum number of rows to be returned for find operations. The property is specific to UDDI only.
`javax.xml.registry.postalAddressScheme`	String	Identifies the ID of the default ClassificationScheme used to structure the postal address information. The reason for the JAXR specification to use a ClassificationScheme for a postal address is because in different geographies, the postal addresses are structured in different ways. Hence, using ClassificationScheme in this case offers more flexibility of representing address information.

Creating a JAXR Connection

After configuring connection properties, the JAXR application can create a `Connection` to the JAXR provider and thus to the registry provider. An application can use a `createConnection()` method on the `ConnectionFactory` object to achieve this. This method checks whether all the required connection properties, for instance `javax.xml.registry.queryManagerURL`, are defined properly or not. If a discrepancy is found, then the method will throw a `javax.xml.registry.InvalidRequestException`.

JAXR supports the following two types of connections:

Synchronous connections. The JAXR provider must process each request method call completely in a synchronous manner before returning a non-null `JAXRResponse` containing the response to that request. In this case, the JAXR application thread is blocked until the JAXR provider has processed the request.

Asynchronous connections. For each incoming asynchronous request, the JAXR provider allocates a globally unique request ID. After the unique request ID is allocated, the provider returns a non-null `JAXRResponse` immediately to the JAXR application. The returned `JAXRResponse` does not contain the actual response value. Internally, the provider maintains a mapping between the request ID and its corresponding `JAXRResponse` instance so that as soon as the reply arrives from the underlying registry provider at some time in the future, the JAXR provider can find the corresponding `JAXRResponse` instance and deliver the reply to the instance. This is when the actual response value is available to the JAXR application.

The application should never attempt to read the value directly from the returned `JAXRResponse` instance without first checking whether the value is available to be read, because attempting to read an unavailable response value can cause the JAXR application thread to block. The application can determine the availability of a response value by using `getStatus()` method on a `JAXRResponse` instance. The method then returns STATUS_UNAVAILABLE if the value is not yet available. Also, the `isAvailable()` method of `JAXRResponse` can be used to see whether the response value is available or not.

JAXR applications can use the `setSynchronous()` method on a `Connection` instance to dynamically alter its synchronous or asynchronous connection preference.

The following code shows the creating of a JAXR connection and then the setting of the communication preference to synchronous:

```
Connection objConnection =
objConnectionFactory.createConnection();

objConnection.setSynchronous(true);
```

Security Credentials Specification

JAXR applications can use the `setCredentials()` method to dynamically alter the security credentials on a `Connection` instance. This method provides a way for the JAXR application to specify its identity-related information to the JAXR provider, which in turn submits this information to a registry provider, which then authenticates the JAXR application.

Typically, security credentials need to be provided to the JAXR provider only when performing privileged operations on the registry, such as adding, deleting, and modifying information. Security credentials are not required by the JAXR provider for non-privileged operations, such as the querying of information in the registry.

Using a Connection to Access the Registry

After creating `Connection` through `ConnectionFactory`, the JAXR application can use various capability-specific interfaces. However, in order to get access to these interfaces, the application must first obtain the `RegistryService` instance by calling the `getRegistryService()` method on the `Connection` instance. After this, the JAXR application can use the `RegistryService` interface to:

- Access the life-cycle management functionality of the JAXR provider to create, update, and delete objects in the target registry provider, through the following methods:

  `getBusinessLifeCycleManager()`. Enables the life-cycle management capabilities of a Business API to be accessed

  `getLifeCycleManager()`. Enables the life-cycle management capabilities of a Generic API to be accesssed

- Access the query management functionality of the JAXR provider to find and retrieve objects from the target registry provider, through the following methods:

  getBusinessQueryManager(). Enables the querying capabilities of a Business API to be accessed

  getDeclarativeQueryManager(). Enables the querying capabilities of a Generic API to be accessed

Listing 11.1 shows how to access the `RegistryService` object and eventually, the capability-specific interfaces.

```
// Get access to the RegistryService object

RegistryService objRegistryService =
objConnection.getRegistryService();

// Now get the query management and life cycle management
// capability interfaces of the Business and Generic API.

BusinessQueryManager objBusinessQueryManager =
objRegistryService.getBusinessQueryManager();

BusinessLifeCycleManager objBusinessLifeCycleManager =
objRegistryService.getBusinessLifeCycleManager();

DeclarativeQueryManager objDeclarativeQueryManager =
objRegistryService.getDeclarativeQueryManager();

LifeCycleManager objLifeCycleManager =
objRegistryService.getLifeCycleManager();
```

Listing 11.1 Accessing the RegistryService object.

Closing a JAXR Connection

A JAXR application can close the connection to a JAXR provider by calling the `close()` method on the `Connection` object, as shown in the following code:

```
objConnection.close();
```

Accessing Multiple Registries

JAXR enables multiple registries to be accessed through a federated or nonfederated approach.

Federated Approach

The federated approach is where the JAXR application can create an instance of `FederatedConnection`, a sub-interface of `Connection`. The `FederatedConnection` interface defines a single logical connection to multiple registry providers. This type of connection then can be used to perform distributed or federated queries against target registry providers while making them look as if they were a single logical registry provider. Federated queries are discussed in a later section. It is important to note that it is optional for a JAXR provider to support federated connections in JAXR 1.0.

In order to create a federated connection, JAXR applications can use the `createFederatedConnection()` method on a `ConnectionFactory` instance. This method takes a `Collection` of `Connection` instances to the individual registry providers as an argument. This `Collection` can consist of `FederatedConnection` instance(s) as well.

Nonfederated Approach

JAXR applications can hold multiple connections to multiple registry providers concurrently. However, these connections are non-federated, meaning that each connection uses a single JAXR provider to access a single registry provider.

In the next section, we will take a look at the APIs involved in the life-cycle management of registry objects.

Life-Cycle Management API

As mentioned earlier, the JAXR Life-Cycle Management API consists of the following two interfaces:

`LifeCycleManager`. This interface provides complete support for handling the life cycle of all the objects in the JAXR information model. This interface belongs to the Generic API.

`BusinessLifeCycleManager`. This interface provides support for handling the life cycle of only the key objects in the JAXR information model. This interface belongs to the Business API.

Some life-cycle management operations may be privileged and thus require authentication and authorization.

The following sections look at the life-cycle management capabilities provided by each of the previous two interfaces.

Interface LifeCycleManager

This interface supports four life-cycle operations as follows:

- Creating registry objects
- Modifying registry objects
- Deleting registry objects
- Deprecating/un-deprecating registry objects

We will look at each of the four life-cycle operations in the following sections.

Creating Registry Objects

Creating registry objects using the `LifeCycleManager` interface can be achieved in two steps:

1. First create the specification of the information model object that needs to be created in the registry, using one of the factory create methods of the `LifeCycleManager` interface.

   These factory methods follow the naming pattern `create<Interface>()`, where `<Interface>` represents the name of the interface in JAXR information model package `javax.xml.registry.infomodel`.

   Examples of such factory methods include `createOrganization()`, `createAssociation()`, `createClassification()`, `createClassificationScheme()`, `createConcept()`, `createEmailAddress()`, `createUser()`, `create External-Identifier()`, and so on.

   There also is a generic factory method called `createObject()` available, which enables clients to create any type of information model object.

2. After the specification of the information model object has been created in memory, it then can be saved to the actual registry by using the `saveObjects()` method.

   This method takes `java.util.Collection` as an argument. The Collection consists of heterogeneous instances of `RegistryObject` created using the factory create methods.

The method signature of `saveObjects()` is as follows:

```
public BulkResponse saveObjects(java.util.Collection objects) throws
JAXRException
```

The BulkResponse interface is returned by many methods in the JAXR API in cases where the response needs to include a Collection of objects. The BulkResponse instance returned from the saveObjects() method contains a Collection of keys that are accessed via the getCollection() method on BulkResponse. These are the Key instances identifying those objects that were saved successfully to the registry.

The BulkResponse also may contain a Collection of SaveException instances in case of partial success, where only a subset of objects was saved successfully. SaveException provides information on each error that prevented some objects in the Collection parameter from being saved successfully. The reason SaveException instances are returned as a Collection as part of BulkResponse rather than being thrown as an exception is so that the BulkResponse can be returned to the JAXR application, despite the exception.

The status information on whether the saveObjects() operation was completely successful or otherwise can be obtained by using a getStatus() method on the BulkResponse instance. getStatus() would return JAXRResponse.STATUS_WARNING, in case of partial success.

The semantics of the BulkResponse object remains quite the same for other methods in the API.

Modifying Registry Objects

The LifeCycleManager interface does not provide a separate method for modifying the registry objects. In order to modify an existing registry object, the saveObjects() method can be used. The JAXR application first should create the specification of the information model object with the modified attributes and then it should call the saveObjects() method. The registry provider then would determine whether the given object already exists in the registry. If it does exist in the registry, its state would be replaced in the registry.

Deleting Registry Objects

The LifeCycleManager interface provides a deleteObjects() method for deleting objects that exist in the registry. The method signature of deleteObjects() is as follows:

```
public BulkResponse deleteObjects (java.util.Collection keys)
throws JAXRException
```

The `Key` instances of the registry objects to be deleted are specified within the `Collection` argument to this method. An attempt to remove a registry object that has valid references to other registry objects would result in an `InvalidRequestException`, returned within a `BulkResponse`. However, this is the case only when a registry provider supports such integrity constraints on the registry.

Deprecating/Un-Deprecating Registry Objects

An object that is not required anymore can be deprecated. *Deprecating* a registry object marks it as obsolete and likely to be deleted sometime in the future. JAXR applications can use the `deprecateObjects()` method to deprecate the existing registry objects. The method signature for `deprecateObjects()` is as follows:

```
public BulkResponse deprecateObjects (java.util.Collection keys)
throws JAXRException
```

The `Key` instances of the registry objects to deprecate are specified within the `Collection` argument to this method. A JAXR provider would not enable deprecated registry objects to participate in associations and classifications; however, existing references to deprecated objects would continue to function properly.

A deprecated registry object may be *un-deprecated* using the `unDeprecateObjects()` method of the `LifeCycleManager` interface. The method signature for `unDeprecateObjects()` is as follows:

```
public BulkResponse unDeprecateObjects (java.util.Collection keys)
throws JAXRException
```

Again, the `Key` instances of the registry objects to un-deprecate are specified within the `Collection` argument to this method.

Interface BusinessLifeCycleManager

The `BusinessLifeCycleManager` life-cycle management interface provides a high-level business-level API to add, modify, and delete the key objects in the JAXR information model. These key information model objects are as follows:

- `Organization`
- `Service`
- `ServiceBinding`
- `Concept`
- `Association`
- `ClassificationScheme`

The methods available in the `BusinessLifeCycleManager` interface are as shown in Table 11.2.

Table 11.2 BusinessLifeCycleManager Methods

METHOD	DESCRIPTION
`void confirmAssociation (Association assoc)`	Confirms this `Association` by the respective `User` that owns either of the source/target objects.
`BulkResponse deleteAssociations (java.util.Collection associationKeys)`	Deletes the `Association` objects corresponding to the specified `Key` instances from the registry.
`BulkResponse deleteClassificationSchemes (java.util.Collection schemeKeys)`	Deletes the `ClassificationScheme` objects corresponding to the specified `Key` instances from the registry.
`BulkResponse deleteConcepts (java.util.Collection conceptKeys)`	Deletes the `Concept` objects corresponding to the specified `Key` instances from the registry.
`BulkResponse deleteOrganizations (java.util.Collection organizationKeys)`	Deletes the `Organization` objects corresponding to the specified `Key` instances from the registry.
`BulkResponse deleteServiceBindings (java.util.Collection bindingKeys)`	Deletes the `ServiceBinding` objects corresponding to the specified `Key` instances from the registry.
`BulkResponse deleteServices (java.util.Collection serviceKeys)`	Deletes the `Service` objects corresponding to the specified `Key` instances from the registry.

Table 11.2 *(Continued)*

METHOD	DESCRIPTION
`BulkResponse saveAssociations (java.util.Collection associations, boolean replace)`	Adds/modifies the specified `Association` instances. If the *replace* flag is set to true, the specified `Association` objects replace any existing associations of that `User`. When the *replace* flag is set to false, the specified `Association` instances are saved to the registry, while any existing associations not being updated by this call are preserved.
`BulkResponse saveClassificationSchemes (java.util.Collection schemes)`	Adds/modifies the specified `ClassificationScheme` instances to the registry.
`BulkResponse saveConcepts (java.util.Collection concepts)`	Adds/modifies the specified `Concept` instances to the registry.
`BulkResponse saveOrganizations (java.util.Collection organizations)`	Adds/modifies the specified `Organization` instances to the registry.
`BulkResponse saveServiceBindings (java.util.Collection bindings)`	Adds/modifies the specified `ServiceBinding` instances to the registry.
`BulkResponse saveServices (java.util.Collection services)`	Adds/modifies the specified `Service` instances to the registry.
`void unConfirmAssociation (Association assoc)`	Undoes the previous confirmation of this association by the user associated with this JAXR application.

A Note on Life-Cycle Management and Federated Connections

Life-cycle management operations are not supported over federated connections. If a JAXR application tries to get hold of any of the life-cycle management capability interfaces from `RegistryService` over a federated connection, the JAXR provider throws an `UnsupportedCapabilityException`.

The next section discusses the various querying capabilities supported by JAXR.

Query Management API

The JAXR Query Management API consists of the following two interfaces:

`BusinessQueryManager`. This interface provides the capability to query the key objects in the JAXR information model. This interface belongs to the Business API.

`DeclarativeQueryManager`. This interface provides support for querying any object in the JAXR information model on an ad-hoc basis. This interface belongs to the Generic API.

Any non-privileged registry user can query the capabilities of JAXR. The following sections discuss each of these capability interfaces in more detail.

Interface BusinessQueryManager

This high-level querying interface provides methods for querying the following key objects in the JAXR information model:

- `Organization`
- `Service`
- `ServiceBinding`
- `Concept`
- `Association`
- `ClassificationScheme`
- `RegistryPackage`

Table 11.3 shows the list of all the methods provided by the `BusinessQueryManager` interface and their descriptions. Note that the arguments to these methods are discussed following the table.

Table 11.3 BusinessQueryManager Methods

METHOD	DESCRIPTION
`BulkResponse findAssociations (java.util.Collection findQualifiers, java.lang.String sourceObjectId, java.lang.String targetObjectId, java.lang.Collection associationTypes)`	Finds instances of `Association` that match all of the criteria specified by the parameters of this call.

Table 11.3 BusinessQueryManager Methods *(continued)*

METHOD	DESCRIPTION
`BulkResponse findCallerAssociations (java.util.Collection findQualifiers, java.lang.Boolean confirmedByCaller, java.lang.Boolean confirmedByOtherParty, java.util.Collection associationTypes)`	Finds all of the `Association` instances owned by the user corresponding to the calling JAXR application that match all of the criteria specified by the call parameters.
`ClassificationScheme findClassificationSchemeByName (java.util.Collection findQualifiers, java.lang.String namePattern)`	Finds a `ClassificationScheme` instance by name, based on the specified name pattern and find qualifiers.
`BulkResponse findClassificationSchemes (java.util.Collection findQualifiers, java.util.Collection namePatterns, java.util.Collection classifications, java.util.Collection externalLinks)`	Finds all the instances of `ClassificationScheme` that match the criteria specified by the call parameters.
`Concept findConceptByPath (java.lang.String path)`	Finds the `Concept` instance based on the path specified. If the specified path matches more than one of the `Concept` instances, then the one that is most general (or higher in the `Concept` hierarchy) is returned. The *path,* in this case, is the absolute path leading from `ClassificationScheme` to that `Concept`. For example, the path `/Geography-id/NorthAmerica/United States` represents the `Concept` with the value of `UnitedStates` with a parent `Concept` of the value of `NorthAmerica` under a `ClassificationScheme` with ID `Geography-id`.

(continues)

Table 11.3 BusinessQueryManager Methods *(continued)*

METHOD	DESCRIPTION
`BulkResponse findConcepts (java.util.Collection findQualifiers, java.util.Collection namePatterns, java.util.Collection classifications, java.util.Collection externalIdentifiers, java.util.Collection externalLinks)`	Finds all the `Concept` instances that match all of the criteria specified by the call parameters.
`BulkResponse findOrganizations (java.util.Collection findQualifiers, java.util.Collection namePatterns, java.util.Collection classifications, java.util.Collection specifications, java.util.Collection externalIdentifiers, java.util.Collection externalLinks)`	Finds all the `Organization` instances that match all of the criteria specified by the call parameters.
`BulkResponse findRegistryPackages (java.util.Collection findQualifiers, java.util.Collection namePatterns, java.util.Collection classifications, java.util.Collection externalLinks)`	Finds all the `RegistryPackage` instances that match all of the criteria specified by the call parameters.
`BulkReponse findServiceBindings (Key ServiceKey, java.util.Collection findQualifiers, java.util.Collection classifications, java.util.Collection specifications)`	Finds all the `ServiceBinding` instances that match all of the criteria specified by the call parameters.
`BulkResponse findServices (Key orgKey, java.util.Collection findQualifiers, java.util.Collection namePatterns, java.util.Collection classifications, java.util.Collection specifications)`	Finds all the `Service` instances that match all of the criteria specified by the call parameters.

The common arguments that most of the methods previously discussed take are as follows:

- `namePatterns`
- `findQualifiers`
- `classifications`
- `specifications`
- `externalIdentifiers`
- `externalLinks`

These arguments are discussed in detail in the following sections.

namePatterns

This argument defines the `Collection` consisting of pattern strings. Each pattern string is a partial or full name pattern with wildcard searching as specified in the SQL-92 LIKE specification. By default, this is a logical OR operation of the name patterns specified in the `Collection`.

The following code is a partial listing of code that shows how to search for all of the `Organization` instances whose name begins with the letter *A*.

```
// Specify the name pattern

Collection colNamePatterns = new ArrayList();
colNamePatterns.add ("A%");

// Execute the query

BulkResponse objBulkResponse =
objBusinessQueryManager.findOrganizations (null,
colNamePatterns, null, null, null, null);

// Get hold of the Collection of Organization instances
// returned as search result

Collection colOrganizations = objBulkResponse.getCollection();
```

findQualifiers

This argument defines the `Collection` of find qualifiers as defined by the `FindQualifier` interface. These find qualifiers affect the find operation behavior in terms of string matching, sorting, and so on. Some of the commonly used find qualifiers defined in the `FindQualifier` interface are described in Table 11.4.

Table 11.4 Commonly Used Find Qualifiers

QUALIFIER	DESCRIPTION
`FindQualifier.CASE_SENSITIVE_MATCH`	Marks the find operation to be case sensitive.
`FindQualifier.SORT_BY_DATE_ASC`	Specifies that the result of the find operation should be sorted date-wise in an ascending order.
`FindQualifier.SORT_BY_NAME_ASC`	Specifies that the result of the find operation should be sorted name-wise in an ascending order.

(continues)

Table 11.4 Commonly Used Find Qualifiers *(Continued)*

QUALIFIER	DESCRIPTION
`FindQualifier.SORT_BY_DATE_DESC`	Specifies that the result of the find operation should be sorted date-wise in a descending order.
`FindQualifier.SORT_BY_NAME_DESC`	Specifies that the result of the find operation should be sorted name-wise in a descending order.

The following code is a partial listing of the code that shows how to search for all of the `Organization` instances whose names begin with the letter *A* in a case-sensitive manner. The code also specifies that the result of the find operation be sorted by name in ascending order.

```
// Specify the name pattern

...

// Now specify the find qualifiers for this search
// operation

Collection colFindQualifiers = new ArrayList();

colFindQualifiers.add (FindQualifier.CASE_SENSITIVE_MATCH);

colFindQualifiers.add (FindQualifier.SORT_BY_NAME_ASC);

// Execute the query

BulkResponse objBulkResponse =
objBusinessQueryManager.findOrganizations (colFindQualifiers,
colNamePatterns, null, null, null, null);

// Get hold of the Collection of Organization
// instances returned as search result
```

classifications

This argument is a `Collection` of `Classification` instances that classify the registry objects to look for. This is analogous to `categoryBag` in UDDI. By default, this is a logical AND operation of the classifications specified in the `Collection`, which means that it requires a match on ALL of the `Classification` instances specified in order to qualify as a match to the given criteria.

The following is a partial listing of the code that depicts how to search for all of the `Organization` instances with names that begin with the letter *A* and are classified by the standard NAICS taxonomy as a *Custom Computer Programming Services* provider; in a case-sensitive manner. The code also specifies that the result of the find operation be sorted by name in ascending order.

```
// Specify the name pattern

...

// Specify the find qualifiers for this search
// operation

...

// Specify the classification instances that would be
// used as a criteria to the given find operation

// First get hold of the required ClassificationScheme

ClassificationScheme objNAICSClassificationScheme =
objBusinessQueryManager.findClassificationSchemeByName (null,
"ntis-gov:naics");

// Now create the classification instance that would
// provide the specification of the classification to
// the find operation

Classification objClassification = (Classification)
objBusinessLifeCycleManager.createClassification
(objNAICSClassificationScheme, "Custom Computer Programming
Services", "541511");

// Create the Collection to pass as an argument to
// the find operation

Collection colClassifications = new ArrayList();

colClassifications.add (objClassification);

// Finally execute the query

BulkResponse objBulkResponse =
objBusinessQueryManager.findOrganizations (colFindQualifiers,
colNamePatterns, colClassifications, null, null, null);

// Get hold of the Collection of Organization
// instances returned as search result
```

specifications

This argument is a Collection of RegistryObject instances that present a technical specification analogous to tModelBag in UDDI. This also is a logical AND operation of all the specifications passed in the Collection argument, by default.

The following is a partial listing of the code that shows how to search for all of the Organization objects in the registry that have published services whose technical specifications are defined in a WSDL document.

Note that this example uses the uddi-org:types taxonomy as defined by the UDDI specification (this taxonomy was explained in Chapter 5, "Description and Discovery of Web Services"). The example begins with finding this externally available taxonomy and then constructing the Classification specification based on this taxonomy. This Classification specifies the taxonomy element as wsdlSpec; thus, searching for Concept instances classified by the previous Classification instance would lead toward retrieving all of the Concept instances in the registry that link to the WSDL document managed externally. Eventually, the example searches for the Organization corresponding to these WSDL Concept instances.

```
// Find the Concept instances representing the taxonomy
// element (WSDL document) of the uddi-org:types
// classification scheme

// First get hold of the required ClassificationScheme

ClassificationScheme objUDDIOrgTypesClassificationScheme =
objBusinessQueryManager.findClassificationSchemeByName (null,
"uddi-org:types");

// Now create the Classification instance specifying
// the taxonomy element through a name/value pair,
// since the taxonomy is available externally. This
// classification would serve as the search criteria in
// the findConcepts() operation

Classification objWSDLSpecClassification = (Classification)
objBusinessLifeCycleManager.
createClassification (objUDDIOrgTypesClassificationScheme,
"wsdlSpec", "wsdlSpec");

// Create the Collection to pass as an argument to
// the find operation

Collection colClassifications = new ArrayList();
```

```
colClassifications.add (objWSDLSpecClassification);

// Finally execute the findConcepts() query to get hold
// of all the Concepts that are classified as WSDL
// technical specification documents
BulkResponse objBulkResponse =
objBusinessQueryManager.findConcepts (null, null,
colClassifications, null, null, null);

// Get hold of the Collection of Concept
// instances returned as search result

Collection colSpecificationConcepts =
objBulkResponse.getCollection();

// Iterate through the Collection of Concept instances
// and eventually get hold of Organizations
// corresponding to each of these Concept instances.
// These are the organizations that have published
// their technical specifications as WSDL documents.
// Note that the validation code has been omitted for
// brevity.

Iterator objIterator = colSpecificationConcepts.iterator();

while (objIterator.hasNext())
{
     Concept objWSDLConcept = (Concept)
     objIterator.next();

     String sWSDLConceptName =
     objWSDLConcept.getName().getValue();

     Collection colExternalLinks =
     objWSDLConcept.getExternalLinks();

     Collection colSpecificationConcepts1 = new ArrayList();

     colSpecificationConcepts1.add (objWSDLConcept);

     objBulkResponse = objBusinessQueryManager.findOrganizations
      (null, null, null, colSpecificationConcepts1, null, null);

     Collection colWSDLSpecOrganizations =
     objBulkResponse.getCollection();

     // Now traverse through this Collection of
     // Organization instances

     Iterator objOrganizationIterator =
```

```
        colWSDLSpecOrganizations.iterator();

        while (objOrganizationIterator.hasNext())
        {
            Organization objOrganization = (Organization)
            objOrganizationIterator.next();

            // Retrieve and display information about the
            // this Organization. This code has been
            // omitted for brevity.

            ...
        }

    }
```

externalIdentifiers

This argument is a `Collection` of `ExternalIdentifier` instances that provide an external identifier for the registry object using an external identification scheme such as DUNS, for instance. This argument is analogous to the `identifierBag` in UDDI. By default, this is a logical AND operation of all the external identifiers passed in the `Collection` argument.

externalLinks

This argument is a `Collection` of `ExternalLink` instances that provides an external link that links the registry object to content managed outside the registry. This argument is analogous to `overviewDoc` in UDDI. This is a logical AND operation and requires a match on all specified `ExternalLink` instances in order to qualify as a match for this criteria.

Interface DeclarativeQueryManager

This interface provides a flexible API for querying all of the objects in the JAXR information model. This interface provides the capability of performing ad-hoc queries using declarative language syntax. Presently, the declarative syntaxes supported include SQL-92 and OASIS ebXML registry Filter Queries. Support of the SQL queries is optional for some of the registries (including ebXML registry), which means that if the target registry does not support SQL queries, then method calls on `DeclarativeQueryManager` would throw `UnsupportedCapabilityException`.

The `DeclarativeQueryManager` interface provides the following two methods for performing query operations.

Query createQuery (int queryType, java.lang.String queryString)

A JAXR application should use this method to create a query object based on the given queryType value. The value of queryType can be one of the following:

QUERY_TYPE_SQL In the case of SQL-92 queries.

QUERY_TYPE_XQUERY In the case where XQuery language syntax is used. The current JAXR version does not support XQuery syntax. However, this queryType value is kept for the future use.

QUERY_TYPE_EBXML_FILTER_QUERY In the case of ebXML Filter queries.

The queryString argument takes the query in the syntax corresponding to the type of query language specified by the queryType argument. A JAXR provider can optionally perform a client-side validation of the query string provided through this argument and can throw InvalidRequest-Exception when an invalid query is specified. In cases where the JAXR provider does not support client-side syntax validation, if the query string specified is invalid, the registry provider would detect the error and would return a RegistryException within the BulkResponse.

This method returns an instance of the Query interface, which encapsulates the declarative queries. This interface exposes the following two methods:

int getType() This method returns the type of the query that this Query instance represents.

java.lang.String toString() This method returns the string representation of the encapsulated query.

After the JAXR application has a Query instance, it would execute the query by calling the executeQuery() method.

executeQuery (Query query)

This method executes the declarative query encapsulated by the Query interface. This method returns a BulkResponse consisting of a homogeneous Collection of objects. The type of the objects is defined by the FROM clause in case of an SQL-92 query. For example, "SELECT FROM Service WHERE ...", would return a Collection of Service instances.

Listing 11.2 shows how to use DeclarativeQueryManager for performing an SQL-92 syntax-based ad-hoc query. Upon execution, this query would return all of the Organization objects with names beginning with the letters 'ACM'.

```
// Construct the Query instance that would encapsulate the SQL-
// 92 query

String sQueryString = "SELECT FROM Organization WHERE name LIKE
\'ACM%\'";

Query objQuery = objDeclarativeQueryManager.createQuery
(Query.QUERY_TYPE_SQL, sQueryString);

// Now execute the query

BulkResponse objQueryResponse =
objDeclarativeQueryManager.executeQuery (objQuery);

Collection colQueryResults = objQueryResponse.getCollection();

// Now traverse through this homogeneous Collection of
// Organization instances
```

Listing 11.2 Querying using DelcarativeQueryManager.

In the next section, we will show you how to develop and deploy JAXR applications using JWSDP 1.0.

JAXR Support in JWSDP 1.0

JWSDP 1.0 provides the Reference Implementation (RI) of the JAXR 1.0 specification. There are two main components of JAXR RI: the registry server and the registry browser. See the following sections for details on both of these components.

Registry Server

The JWSDP Registry Server implements a private version 2.0 UDDI registry. The `RegistryServlet` component hosted by the Tomcat Servlet container, also a part of JWSDP, services all of the registry requests. The repository for the JWSDP registry server is a data store based on the native XML database Xindice, which is a part of the Apache XML project.

> **FEDERATED QUERIES**
>
> **A JAXR application can issue a federated query against multiple registry providers in a manner similar to the non-federated query approach, that is, by calling methods on `BusinessQueryManager` and `DeclarativeQueryManager` interfaces. The only difference in this case is that the `RegistryService` instance, through which these query management interfaces are obtained, should be accessed from a `FederatedConnection` instance rather than the regular primitive `Connection` instance.**

The registry server includes a tool named Indri that enables you to inspect this database directly. More information on using the Indri tool can be found online in the Java Web services tutorial version 1.0, available at the following URL: http://java.sun.com/webservices/docs/1.0/tutorial/doc/RegistryServer5.html#64401

Note: This tutorial is a comprehensive resource on various Java APIs for Web services as well as JWSDP. It is bundled along with several examples that provide a good understanding on Java XML technologies. You can download the entire tutorial by visiting the following URL: http://java.sun.com/webservices/downloads/webservicestutorial.html.

Starting the Registry Server

Starting the registry server requires two steps, as listed in the following text. Note that these steps assume that JWSDP 1.0 has been installed and configured properly; for more information on JWSDP configuration, please refer to the online documentation available at the JWSDP download page at the following URL: http://java.sun.com/webservices/downloads/webservicespack.html.

1. Start the Tomcat server process by typing the `startup` command at the command prompt (assuming JWSDP_HOME/bin is set in the system path).
2. Start the Xindice database server process by typing the `xindice-start` command at the command prompt (assuming `JWSDP_HOME/bin` is already set properly in the system path).

Shutting Down the Registry Server

To shut down the Tomcat server process, type the `shutdown` command at the command prompt.

Similarly, in order to shut down the Xindice database server process, type the `xindice-stop` command at the command prompt.

Registry Browser

The second component of the JAXR RI is called the registry browser (it also is sometimes referred to as the JAXR browser). This browser is a GUI tool that performs various registry operations, such as adding, modifying, browsing, and deleting registry data. This tool provides an interface for selecting any registry that we wish to use (and not just the private UDDI registry browser of JWSDP).

Type the `jaxr-browser` command at the command prompt to bring up the Registry Browser. Figure 11.8 shows the registry browser tool.

In order to select the registry, you must select the corresponding appropriate `queryManagerURL` or `lifeCycleManagerURL` from the registry location dropdown box. For example, you could select http://www-3.ibm.com/services/uddi/v2beta/inquiryapi as the registry location in order to use the UDDI public registry hosted by IBM.

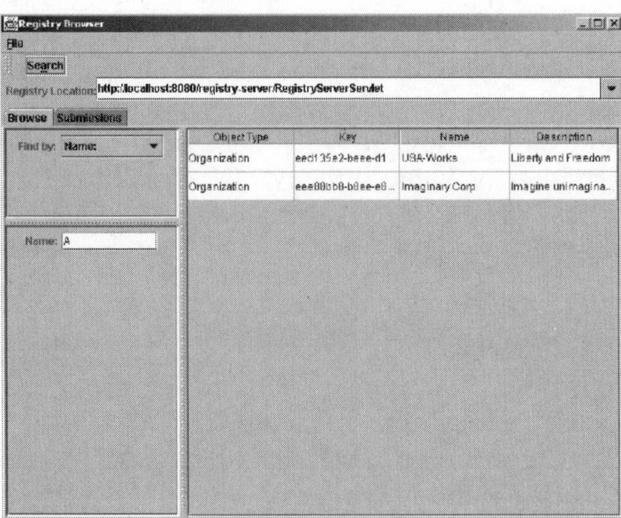

Figure 11.8 The registry browser tool.

In order to use the JWSDP registry server, you could select http://localhost:8080/registry-server/RegistryServerServlet as the registry location. Upon selection, the tool would try to connect to the actual registry. After the tool has successfully connected to the registry, we can start working with the registry.

The registry browser also provides an interface for submitting information on new organizations and their services and service bindings. When submitting an organization and its services and service bindings, we also can classify them using standard and non-standard taxonomies.

Figure 11.9 shows the registry browser tool window that lists the expanded tree of standard industry taxonomy, NAICS. As can be seen in this figure, we are trying to classify the fictional *Imaginary Corp.* as a water, sewer, and pipeline construction company.

More information on the registry browser tool can be obtained from the online Java Web services tutorial at the following URL: http://java.sun.com/webservices/downloads/webservicespack.html

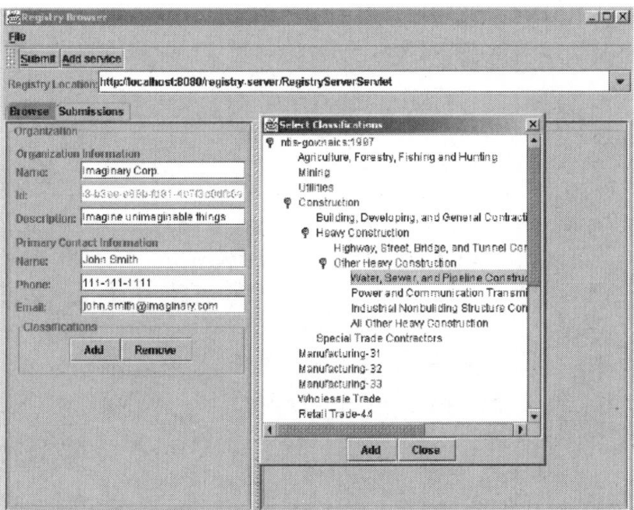

Figure 11.9 Classification using the registry browser.

Understanding JAXR by Examples

This section focuses on providing three JAXR application examples, each focusing on one of the common registry services provided by a JAXR-enabled registry. The source code of these examples is present in the following files:

`Publish.java`. Demonstrates the publishing of an `Organization` and its `Service` to a private UDDI registry using a Level 0 Business API.

`Query.java`. Demonstrates the querying for `Organization` objects based on the criteria specified using a Level 0 Business API.

`Delete.java`. Demonstrates the removing of an `Organization` and thus its published `Service` from the registry using a Level 0 Business API.

We will deploy these JAXR applications on the Java Web Services Developer Pack (JWSDP) 1.0 platform. These examples use the JWSDP registry server to test the JAXR applications.

All three of these examples along with their source code and readme.txt, consisting of setup instructions, can be downloaded from this book's companion Web site at www.wiley.com/compbooks/nagappan.

Note: The reason we chose a private registry rather than a public registry for our examples is due to the successful adoption of registries in private environments compared to public environments.

Publishing Using JAXR

We will begin our examples with `Publish.java`, the JAXR application aimed toward publishing information about an organization. `Publish.java` shows us how to publish an organization named *ACME Computer Services* and its services, and it also demonstrates the classification of ACME Computer Services based on two taxonomies: the standard industry taxonomy NAICS and the standard geography taxonomy ISO-CH 3166. In the following sections, we examine the source code of `Publish.java`, its compilation, and then execution.

Programming Steps for Publishing

The entire publishing logic is provided by a `doPublish()` method of the `jws.ch11.Publish` class, and hence, its implementation is of most interest to us. The following steps outline the inner workings of `doPublish()`.

1. Construct the `Properties` object and populate it with connection-oriented properties.
2. Obtain the `ConnectionFactory` object by calling a `newInstance()` method on the `ConnectionFactory` class, eventually creating the `Connection` object.
3. Obtain the `RegistryService` instance from the `Connection` object in order to get access to the capability interface `BusinessLifeCycleManager`.
4. Set the appropriate security credentials, testuser/testuser as UID/Password in this case, on the `Connection` object. The reason for specifying credentials is because publishing is a privileged registry operation. Thus, the JAXR provider needs to supply proper credentials to the registry provider so that the latter can authenticate the user associated with the JAXR application.
5. Now, instantiate the information model objects corresponding to typical organizational information, such as the contact person in the organization and his/her email addresses and telephone numbers, the service that organization publishes to the registry and its service binding, and finally the organization's classification information.
6. Now, call the `saveOrganizations()` method on `BusinessLifeCycleManager` to save `Organization` information to the registry.
7. Finally, examine the `BulkResponse` object returned from `saveOrganizations()` and check whether the save operation was successful.

Publish.java Source Code

Listing 11.3 contains the complete code listing of `Publish.java`.

```
package jws.ch11;

import javax.xml.registry.*;
import javax.xml.registry.infomodel.*;

import java.io.*;
import java.net.*;
import java.security.*;
import java.net.*;
import java.util.*;

public class Publish
{
     // References to Registry Server URLs for publishing and
     // querying information, respectively

     String sRegistryURLForPublishing;
     String sRegistryURLForQuerying;

     public static void main(String[] args)
     {
          try
          {
               String p_sRegistryURLForPublishing =
               "http://localhost:8080/registry-server/
               RegistryServerServlet";

               String p_sRegistryURLForQuerying =
               "http://localhost:8080/registry-server/
               RegistryServerServlet";

               Publish objPublish = new Publish
               (p_sRegistryURLForPublishing,
               p_sRegistryURLForQuerying);

               objPublish.doPublish();
          }
          catch(JAXRException e)
          {
               System.err.println("JAXRException occurred.
               Exception Message: " + e.getMessage());
          }
```

Listing 11.3 Publish.java.

```
    }

    public Publish(String p_sRegistryURLForPublishing,
    String p_sRegistryURLForQuerying)
    {
        // References to local Registry Server

        sRegistryURLForPublishing =
        p_sRegistryURLForPublishing;

        sRegistryURLForQuerying = p_sRegistryURLForQuerying;
    }

    public void doPublish() throws JAXRException
    {
        Connection objConnection = null;

        try
        {
            // Set the appropriate connection properties

            Properties objProperties = new Properties();

            objProperties.setProperty(
            "javax.xml.registry.queryManagerURL",
            sRegistryURLForQuerying);

            objProperties.setProperty(
            "javax.xml.registry.lifeCycleManagerURL",
            sRegistryURLForPublishing);

            objProperties.setProperty(
            "javax.xml.registry.factoryClass",
            "com.sun.xml.registry.uddi.ConnectionFactoryImpl");

            // Now construct the ConnectionFactory object
            // and initiate the connection to the JAXR
            // registry provider

            ConnectionFactory objConnectionFactory =
            ConnectionFactory.newInstance();
            objConnectionFactory.setProperties(objProperties);
```

Listing 11.3 `Publish.java.` *(continues)*

```
objConnection =
objConnectionFactory.createConnection();

// Construct the JAXR RegistryService object
// and eventually get hold of
// BusinessLifeCycleManager object

RegistryService objRegistryService =
objConnection.getRegistryService();

BusinessLifeCycleManager
objBusinessLifeCycleManager =
objRegistryService.getBusinessLifeCycleManager();

// Initializing username and password to the
// defaults for the local Registry Server
// i.e. testuser and testuser respectively

String sPassword = "testuser";
String sUserName = "testuser";

// Supply the connection with appropriate
// security credentials in the form of JAAS
// PasswordAuthentication type

PasswordAuthentication objPasswordAuthentication
= new PasswordAuthentication(sUserName,
sPassword.toCharArray());

Set setCredentials = new HashSet();

setCredentials.add(objPasswordAuthentication);

objConnection.setCredentials(setCredentials);

// Now it is time to intialize appropriate
// types corresponding to the information that
// we want to publish to JAXR-enabled registry
// (in this case our local Registry Server)

// Information regarding primary contact person
// for this organization

PersonName objPersonName  = (PersonName)
objBusinessLifeCycleManager.createObject
```

Listing 11.3 Publish.java.

```
(LifeCycleManager.PERSON_NAME);

objPersonName.setFullName("John Smith");

// Email address(es) of this primary contact

EmailAddress objEmailAddress1 =
objBusinessLifeCycleManager.createEmailAddress
("john.smith@acmecompserv.com");

objEmailAddress1.setType("Office");

EmailAddress objEmailAddress2 =
objBusinessLifeCycleManager.createEmailAddress
("jsmith99@yahoo.com");

objEmailAddress1.setType("Personal");

Collection colEmailAddresses = new ArrayList();
colEmailAddresses.add(objEmailAddress1);
colEmailAddresses.add(objEmailAddress2);

// Telephone number(s) of this primary contact

TelephoneNumber objTelephoneNumberLine1 =
(TelephoneNumber)

objBusinessLifeCycleManager.createObject
(LifeCycleManager.TELEPHONE_NUMBER);

objTelephoneNumberLine1.setNumber
("800-123-4567");

objTelephoneNumberLine1.setType("Toll-Free");

TelephoneNumber objTelephoneNumberLine2 =
(TelephoneNumber)

objBusinessLifeCycleManager.createObject
(LifeCycleManager.TELEPHONE_NUMBER);

objTelephoneNumberLine2.setNumber
("800-234-5678");

objTelephoneNumberLine2.setType("Toll-Free");
```

Listing 11.3 `Publish.java.` *(continues)*

```
Collection colTelephoneNumbers = new ArrayList();

colTelephoneNumbers.add
(objTelephoneNumberLine1);

colTelephoneNumbers.add
(objTelephoneNumberLine2);

// The User type would refer to this primary
// contact

User objUser =
(User)objBusinessLifeCycleManager.createObject
(LifeCycleManager.USER);

objUser.setPersonName(objPersonName);

objUser.setEmailAddresses(colEmailAddresses);

objUser.setTelephoneNumbers
(colTelephoneNumbers);

// Service(s) published by the organization to
// the registry

Service objService = (Service)
objBusinessLifeCycleManager.createObject
(LifeCycleManager.SERVICE);

objService.setName(objBusinessLifeCycleManager.
createInternationalString("Billing Services"));

objService.setDescription
(objBusinessLifeCycleManager.
createInternationalString("A set of Billing
Management Services for our customers"));

// Create ClassificationSchema and
// Classification instances for NAICS taxonomy

ClassificationScheme
objIndustryClassificationScheme =
(ClassificationScheme)
objBusinessLifeCycleManager.createObject
(LifeCycleManager.CLASSIFICATION_SCHEME);

javax.xml.registry.infomodel.Key objNAICSKey =
```

Listing 11.3 Publish.java.

```
(javax.xml.registry.infomodel.Key)
objBusinessLifeCycleManager.createKey
("uuid:C0B9FE13-179F-413D-8A5B-5004DB8E5BB2");

objIndustryClassificationScheme.setKey
(objNAICSKey);

objIndustryClassificationScheme.setName
(objBusinessLifeCycleManager.
createInternationalString
("ntis-gov:naics:1997"));

Classification objIndustryClassification =
(Classification) objBusinessLifeCycleManager.
createClassification
(objIndustryClassificationScheme, "Custom
Computer Programming Services", "541511");

// Create ClassificationSchema and
// Classification instances for ISO-
// Ch:3166:1999 (Geography based) taxonomy

ClassificationScheme
objGeographyClassificationScheme =
(ClassificationScheme)
objBusinessLifeCycleManager.createObject
(LifeCycleManager.CLASSIFICATION_SCHEME);

javax.xml.registry.infomodel.Key objISOCHKey=
(javax.xml.registry.infomodel.Key)
objBusinessLifeCycleManager.createKey
("uuid:4e49a8d6-d5a2-4fc2-93a0-0411d8d19e88");

objGeographyClassificationScheme.setKey
(objISOCHKey);

objGeographyClassificationScheme.setName
(objBusinessLifeCycleManager.
createInternationalString("iso-ch:3166:1999"));

Classification objGeographyClassification =
(Classification) objBusinessLifeCycleManager.
createClassification
(objGeographyClassificationScheme, "United
States", "US");

// Create Organization object and
```

Listing 11.3 `Publish.java`. *(continues)*

```
// populate it with the above pieces of
// information

Organization objOrganization = (Organization)
objBusinessLifeCycleManager.createObject
(LifeCycleManager.ORGANIZATION);

objOrganization.setName(
objBusinessLifeCycleManager.
createInternationalString("ACME Computer
Services"));

objOrganization.setDescription(
objBusinessLifeCycleManager.
createInternationalString("Provides professional
services in the areas of Computer Software"));

objOrganization.setPrimaryContact(objUser);
objOrganization.addService(objService);

objOrganization.addClassification(
objIndustryClassification);

objOrganization.addClassification(
objGeographyClassification);

Collection colOrganizations = new ArrayList();
colOrganizations.add(objOrganization);

// Now submit the information to the JAXR
// provider, which in turn submits the
// information to the actual registry

BulkResponse objBulkResponse =
objBusinessLifeCycleManager.
saveOrganizations(colOrganizations);

// Check to ensure everything is alright

if (objBulkResponse.getStatus() ==
JAXRResponse.STATUS_SUCCESS)
{
     System.out.println("Organization and related
     services were published successfully.\n");

     // Get hold of the 128-bit UUID of the
     // newly created Organization in the
```

Listing 11.3 Publish.java.

```
        // registry

        Collection colKeys = objBulkResponse
        .getCollection();

        Iterator objKeyIterator =
        colKeys.iterator();

        javax.xml.registry.infomodel.Key
        objOrganizationKey = null;
        if (objKeyIterator.hasNext())
        {
             objOrganizationKey =
              (javax.xml.registry.infomodel.Key)
             objKeyIterator.next();
             String sOrganizationID =
             objOrganizationKey.getId();

             System.out.println("Key
             corresponding to the newly created
             Organization is: \n" +
             sOrganizationID);

             System.out.println("\nSave this key
             for later use.");
        }
    }
    else
    {
        System.err.println("Problem(s) encountered
        during the JAXR save operation. Detailed
        Error Message(s) shown as under :\n");

        Collection colExceptions =
        objBulkResponse.getExceptions();

        Iterator objIterator =
        colExceptions.iterator();

        while (objIterator.hasNext())
        {
            Exception objException = (Exception)
             objIterator.next();

             System.err.println(objException.
             toString());
        }
```

Listing 11.3 `Publish.java`. *(continues)*

```
            }
        }
        catch (JAXRException e)
        {
            System.err.println("JAXRException occurred.
            Exception Message: " + e.getMessage());

            e.printStackTrace();
         }
        finally
        {
            if (objConnection != null)
            {
                try
                {
                    objConnection.close();
                }
                catch(JAXRException e)
                {
                    System.err.println("Exception
                    occured while closing the
                    connection. Exception Message: " +
                    e.getMessage());
                    e.printStackTrace();
                }
            }
        }
    }
}
```

Listing 11.3 Publish.java. *(continued)*

Compiling Publish.java

You should use the ant tool for compiling and executing Publish.java as well as Query.java and Delete.java. The compilation and execution of the ant scripts for all three of these Java files are available in a build.xml file in the same directory as these Java files.

Listing 11.4 shows the partial listing of the ant script for compiling Publish.java.

```
<project name="Java Web Services Book - Ch. 11 Demos"
default="build" basedir=".">

     <target name="init">
          <tstamp/>
     </target>
     <property name="build.home" value="build" />

     <path id="classpath">
          <fileset dir="${jwsdp.home}/common/lib">
               <include name="*.jar" />
          </fileset>

          <fileset dir="${jwsdp.home}/common/endorsed">
               <include name="*.jar" />
          </fileset>
     </path>

     <target name="prepare" depends="init" description="Create
     build directory.">
          <mkdir dir="${build.home}" />
     </target>

     <target name="compile-publish" depends="prepare"
     description="Compiles Publish.java file.">

          <javac srcdir="." destdir="${build.home}">
               <include name="Publish.java" />
               <classpath refid="classpath"/>
          </javac>
     </target>

     ...

</project>
```

Listing 11.4 ANT script for compiling `Publish.java`.

As can be seen from Listing 11.4, the compilation script ensures that the library JAR files in `JWSDP_HOME/common/lib` and `JWSDP_HOME/common/endorsed` are available in the CLASSPATH.

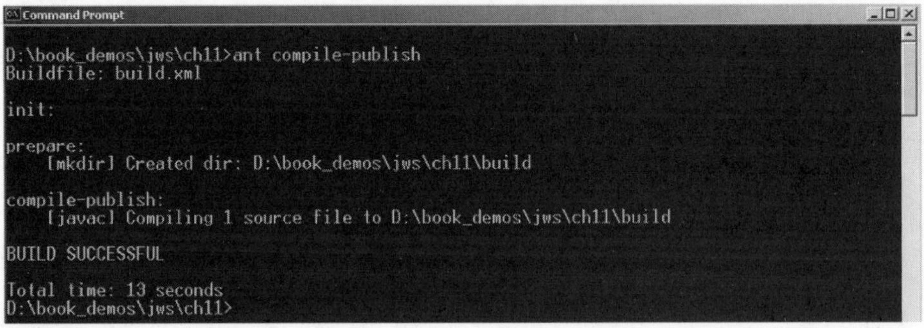

```
D:\book_demos\jws\ch11>ant compile-publish
Buildfile: build.xml

init:

prepare:
    [mkdir] Created dir: D:\book_demos\jws\ch11\build

compile-publish:
    [javac] Compiling 1 source file to D:\book_demos\jws\ch11\build

BUILD SUCCESSFUL

Total time: 13 seconds
D:\book_demos\jws\ch11>
```

Figure 11.10 Compiling `Publish.java`.

In order to compile `Publish.java`, run the `Ant` tool from the command line as shown:

```
> ant compile-publish
```

Figure 11.10 shows the compilation output of `Publish.java`.

Executing Publish.java

The `Ant` script responsible for executing `Publish.java` is shown as follows:

```
<project ...>
     ...
     <target name="run-publish" depends="compile-publish"
     description="Runs Publish.java.">
          <java classname="jws.ch11.Publish" fork="yes">
               <classpath refid="classpath"/>
               <classpath path="${build.home}"/>
          </java>
     </target>
     ...
</project>
```

In order to execute `Publish.java`, run the `Ant` tool from the command line as shown:

```
> ant run-publish
```

Figure 11.11 displays the execution output of `Publish.java`.

```
D:\book_demos\jws\ch11>ant run-publish
Buildfile: build.xml

init:

prepare:

compile-publish:
    [javac] Compiling 1 source file to D:\book_demos\jws\ch11\build

run-publish:
     [java] Organization and related services were published successfully.
     [java]
     [java] Key corresponding to the newly created Organization is:
     [java] eeea9967-fdee-ea99-3171-a6b2b8957092
     [java]
     [java] Save this key for later use.

BUILD SUCCESSFUL

Total time: 2 minutes 55 seconds
D:\book_demos\jws\ch11>_
```

Figure 11.11 Executing `Publish.java`.

You can verify the details of this newly created organization with the help of the registry browser. For example, Figure 11.12 shows the details of ACME Computer Services from the registry browser tool.

Querying Using JAXR

`Query.java` shows us how to search organizations based on the naming patterns provided by the user. In the following sections, we examine the source code of `Query.java`, its compilation, and then its execution.

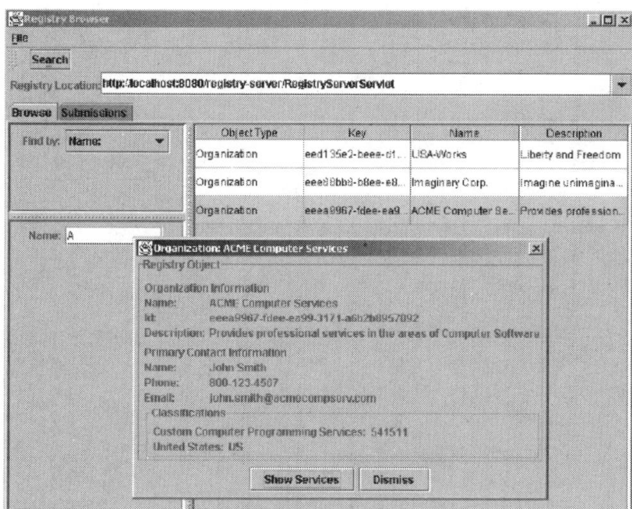

Figure 11.12 Verifying using registry browser.

Programming Steps for Querying

The querying logic for Query.java is provided by the doQuery() method of the jws.ch11.Query class, and hence, its implementation is of most interest to us. Following are the steps outlining the inner workings of doQuery():

1. Construct the Properties object and populate it with connection-oriented properties.
2. Get hold of the ConnectionFactory object by calling a newInstance() method on the ConnectionFactory class and eventually create the Connection object.
3. Obtain the RegistryService instance from the Connection object in order to get access to the capability interface BusinessQueryManager.
4. Initiate the search operation by calling a findOrganizations() method and supplying it with the naming pattern. The end user provided this naming pattern as the command line input.
5. Finally, traverse through the collection of Organization instances received within the BulkResponse object returned from findOrganizations() and display the various details of each organization, such as its name, contact person-related information, and name and description of the services it provides.

Query.java Source Code

Listing 11.5 shows the partial code listing of the doQuery() method. Note that we have omitted the code sections that were redundant to Publish.java from this listing.

```
public void doQuery() throws JAXRException
{
    Connection objConnection = null;

    try
    {
        // Set the appropriate connection properties
        ...

        // Now construct the ConnectionFactory object and
        // initiate the connection to the JAXR registry
```

Listing 11.5 Query.java.

```
        // provider

        ...

        // Construct the JAXR RegistryService object and
        // eventually get hold of BusinessQueryManager object

        ...

        // Specify the name pattern

        Collection colNamePatterns = new ArrayList();
        colNamePatterns.add("%" + sQueryString + "%");

        // Now search all the organizations whose name
        // matches with the name pattern

        BulkResponse objBulkResponse =
        objBusinessQueryManager.findOrganizations(null,
        colNamePatterns, null, null, null, null);

        Collection colOrganizations =
        objBulkResponse.getCollection();

        // Traverse through all the organizations that were
        // found and returned in the BulkResponse object

        Iterator objOrganizationsIterator =
        colOrganizations.iterator();

        if (!(objOrganizationsIterator.hasNext()))
        {
            System.out.println("No organizations were found
            matching the specified query string.");
        }
        else
        {

            while (objOrganizationsIterator.hasNext())
            {
                Organization objOrganization =
                (Organization)
                objOrganizationsIterator.next();

                // Display main Organization-related
                // information
```

Listing 11.5 `Query.java`. *(continues)*

```
            System.out.println("\nORGANIZATION
            INFORMATION\n");

            System.out.println("Name: " +
            objOrganization.getName().getValue());

            System.out.println("Description: " +
            objOrganization.getDescription().
            getValue());

            System.out.println("Key ID: " +
            objOrganization.getKey().getId());

            // Now get hold of Primary Contact for
            // this Organization and display
            // information pertaining to him

            User objPrimaryContact =
            objOrganization.getPrimaryContact();

            if (objPrimaryContact != null)
            {
                 PersonName objPersonName =
                 objPrimaryContact.getPersonName();

                 System.out.println("Primary Contact
                 Information:");

                 System.out.println("\tName: " +
                 objPersonName.getFullName());

                 Collection colTelephoneNumbers =
                 objPrimaryContact.
                 getTelephoneNumbers(null);

                 Iterator objTelephoneNumbersIterator
                 = colTelephoneNumbers.iterator();

                 while (objTelephoneNumbersIterator.
                 hasNext())
                 {
                      TelephoneNumber
                      objTelephoneNumber =
                      (TelephoneNumber)

                      objTelephoneNumbersIterator.
```

Listing 11.5 Query.java.

```
                next();

                System.out.println("\tPhone
                Number: " + objTelephoneNumber.
                getNumber());
            }

            Collection colEmailAddresses =
            objPrimaryContact.
            getEmailAddresses();

            Iterator objEmailAddressesIterator =
            colEmailAddresses.iterator();

            while (objEmailAddressesIterator.
            hasNext())
            {
                EmailAddress objEmailAddress =
                (EmailAddress)
                objEmailAddressesIterator.next();

                System.out.println("\tEmail
                Address: " +
                objEmailAddress.getAddress());
            }
        }

        // Now display Service and ServiceBinding
        // information pertaining to this
        // Organization

        Collection colServices =
        objOrganization.getServices();

        Iterator objServicesIterator =
        colServices.iterator();

        while (objServicesIterator.hasNext())
        {
            Service objService = (Service)
            objServicesIterator.next();
            System.out.println("Service(s)
            Information:");

            System.out.println("\tName: " +
            objService.getName().getValue());
```

Listing 11.5 `Query.java`. *(continues)*

```
                    System.out.println("\tDescription: "
                    + objService.getDescription().getValue());

                    Collection colServiceBindings =
                    objService.getServiceBindings();

                    Iterator objServiceBindingsIterator =
                    colServiceBindings.iterator();

                    while
                    (objServiceBindingsIterator.hasNext())
                    {
                         ServiceBinding objServiceBinding
                         = (ServiceBinding)
                         objServiceBindingsIterator.
                         next();

                         System.out.println("
                         ServiceBinding
                         Information for this
                         Service:");

                         System.out.println("\t\t
                         Description: " + objServiceBinding.
                         getDescription().getValue());

                         System.out.println("\t\tAccess URI: "
                         + objServiceBinding.getAccessURI());
                    }
               }
          }
     }
}
catch (Exception e)
{
     ...
}
finally
{
     ...
}
}
```

Listing 11.5 `Query.java`. *(continued)*

Compiling Query.java

The following is the `Ant` script responsible for compiling `Query.java`:

```
<project ...>
     ...
     <target name="compile-query" depends="prepare"
     description="Compiles Query.java file.">

          <javac srcdir="." destdir="${build.home}">
               <include name="Query.java" />
               <classpath refid="classpath"/>
          </javac>
     </target>
     ...
</project>
```

Again, note that the compilation and execution scripts for all these examples are available in the `build.xml` file.

Now, in order to compile `Query.java`, run the `Ant` tool from the command line as shown:

```
> ant compile-query
```

Executing Query.java

The following is the `Ant` script responsible for executing `Query.java`:

```
<project ...>
     ...
     <target name="run-query" depends="compile-query"
     description="Runs
     Query.java. Argument: -DQueryString &lt;QueryStringValue&gt;">

          <java classname="jws.ch11.Query" fork="yes">
               <arg line="${QueryString}"/>
               <classpath refid="classpath" />
               <classpath path="${build.home}"/>
          </java>
     </target>
     ...
</project>
```

In order to find the organizations with names that match the naming pattern 'ACM', execute `Query.java` using the `Ant` tool from the command line as shown:

```
> ant run-query -DQueryString ACM
```

Figure 11.13 shows the execution output of `Query.java`.

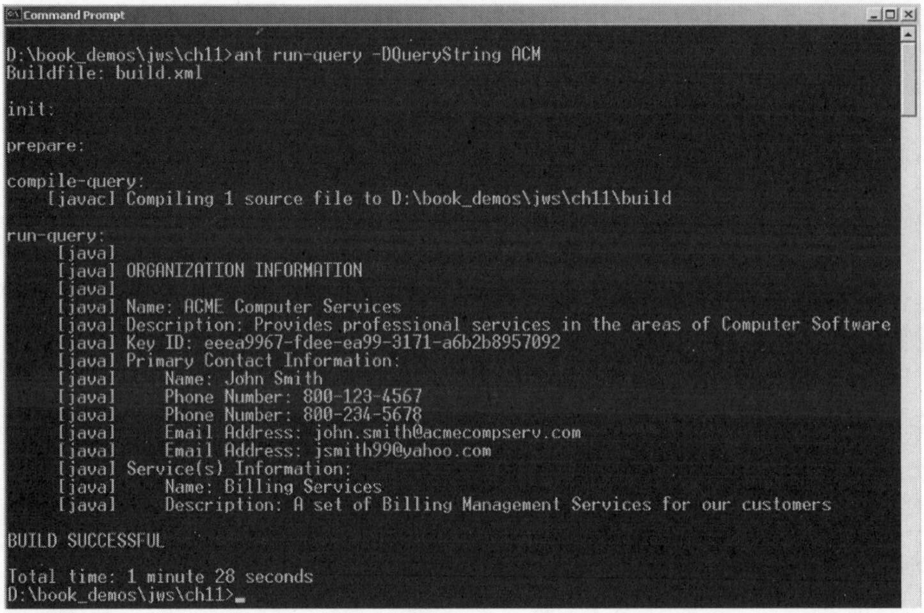

```
D:\book_demos\jws\ch11>ant run-query -DQueryString ACM
Buildfile: build.xml

init:

prepare:

compile-query:
    [javac] Compiling 1 source file to D:\book_demos\jws\ch11\build

run-query:
     [java]
     [java] ORGANIZATION INFORMATION
     [java]
     [java] Name: ACME Computer Services
     [java] Description: Provides professional services in the areas of Computer Software
     [java] Key ID: eeea9967-fdee-ea99-3171-a6b2b8957092
     [java] Primary Contact Information:
     [java]     Name: John Smith
     [java]     Phone Number: 800-123-4567
     [java]     Phone Number: 800-234-5678
     [java]     Email Address: john.smith@acmecompserv.com
     [java]     Email Address: jsmith99@yahoo.com
     [java] Service(s) Information:
     [java]     Name: Billing Services
     [java]     Description: A set of Billing Management Services for our customers

BUILD SUCCESSFUL

Total time: 1 minute 28 seconds
D:\book_demos\jws\ch11>
```

Figure 11.13 Executing `Query.java`.

Deleting Information Using JAXR

`Delete.java` shows us how to delete an `Organization` from a registry based on its key ID. A *key ID* in JAXR RI is a 128-bit UUID. There are numerous ways in which you can obtain a key ID for an `Organization` that you want to delete, one of which is by viewing its details in the registry browser. In the following sections, we will examine the source code of `Delete.java`, its compilation, and execution.

Programming Steps for Deleting

The deletion logic is provided by a `doDelete()` method of the `jws.ch11.Delete` class, and hence, its implementation is of most interest to us. The following steps outline the inner workings of `doDelete()`:

1. Construct the `Properties` object and populate it with connection-oriented properties.
2. Get hold of the `ConnectionFactory` object by calling a `newInstance()` method on the `ConnectionFactory` class and eventually create the `Connection` object.

3. Obtain the `RegistryService` instance from the `Connection` object in order to get access to the capability interface `BusinessLife-CycleManager`.
4. We would need to set the appropriate security credentials (testuser/testuser) on the `Connection` object, because the deletion of information from a registry is a privileged operation.
5. Now, call the `deleteOrganizations()` method, supplying it with the key of the organization to delete. The end user provides this 128-bit UUID, corresponding to the organization to delete, at the command line.
6. Finally, check the status of the delete operation by calling `getStatus()` on the returned `BulkResponse` object.

Delete.java Source Code

Listing 11.6 is the partial code listing of the `doDelete()` method. Again, note that we have omitted the code sections that are redundant to `Publish.java` from this listing.

```
public void doDelete() throws JAXRException
{
     Connection objConnection = null;

     try
     {
          // Set the appropriate connection properties

          ...

          // Now construct the ConnectionFactory object and
          // initiate the connection to the JAXR registry
          // provider

          ...

          // Construct the JAXR RegistryService object and
          // eventually get hold of BusinessLifeCycleManager
          // object

          ...

          // Initializing username and password to the defaults
```

Listing 11.6 `Delete.java`. *(continues)*

```
// for the local registry Server

...

// Supply the connection with appropriate security
// credentials in the form of JAAS PasswordAuthentication
// type.

...

// Now get hold of the Key based on the string
// representation of the UUID of Organization to
// delete

javax.xml.registry.infomodel.Key objOrganizationKey =
objBusinessLifeCycleManager.createKey
 (sOrganizationKey);

// Create a collection and add the Key (s)of
// Organization(s) that need to be deleted from the
// registry

Collection colOrganizationKeys = new ArrayList();

colOrganizationKeys.add (objOrganizationKey);

// Now ask the JAXR provider to delete the
// Organization corresponding to the specified key

BulkResponse objBulkResponse =
objBusinessLifeCycleManager.deleteOrganizations
 (colOrganizationKeys);

// Check to see if the delete operation went okay

if (objBulkResponse.getStatus() ==
JAXRResponse.STATUS_SUCCESS)
{
     System.out.println("Organization and related
     services were deleted successfully.");
}
else
{
     System.err.println("Problem(s) encountered
     during the JAXR delete operation. Detailed
     Error Message(s) shown as under :\n");

     Collection colExceptions =
```

Listing 11.6 Delete.java.

```
                    objBulkResponse.getExceptions();

                    Iterator objIterator =
                    colExceptions.iterator();

                    while (objIterator.hasNext())
                    {
                         Exception objException = (Exception)
                         objIterator.next();

                         System.err.println(objException.toString());
                    }
               }
          }
          catch (JAXRException e)
          {
               ...
          }
          finally
          {
               ...
          }
     }
```

Listing 11.6 `Delete.java`. *(continued)*

Compiling Delete.java

The following is the `Ant` script responsible for compiling `Delete.java`:

```
<project ...>
     ...
     <target name="compile-delete" depends="prepare"
     description="Compiles Delete.java file.">

          <javac srcdir="." destdir="${build.home}">
               <include name="Delete.java" />
               <classpath refid="classpath"/>
          </javac>
     </target>
     ...
</project>
```

To compile `Delete.java`, run the `Ant` tool from command line as shown:

```
> ant compile-delete
```

Executing Delete.java

The `Ant` script responsible for executing `Delete.java` is shown as follows:

```
<project ...>
     ...
     <target name="run-delete" depends="compile-delete"
     description="Runs Delete.java. Argument: -DKey
     &lt;KeyValue&gt;">

          <java classname="jws.ch11.Delete" fork="yes">
               <arg line="${Key}"/>
               <classpath refid="classpath" />
               <classpath path="${build.home}"/>
          </java>
     </target>
     ...
</project>
```

In order to delete the ACME Computer Services organization, execute `Delete.java`, supplying it with the key ID of ACME Computer Services. Use the `Ant` tool to achieve this as shown:

```
> ant run-delete -DKey eeea9967-fdee-ea99-3171-a6b2b8957092
```

Figure 11.14 shows the execution output of `Delete.java`.

Deletion of ACME Computer Services can be verified either by executing `Query.java` or by searching for this organization by using the registry browser tool.

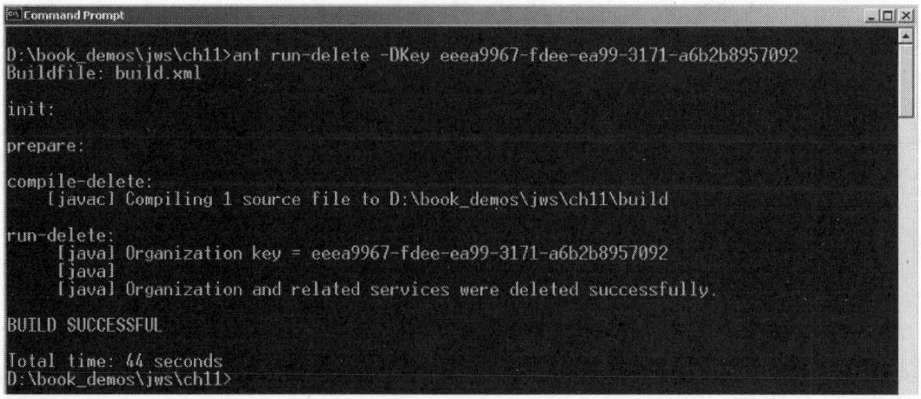

```
D:\book_demos\jws\ch11>ant run-delete -DKey eeea9967-fdee-ea99-3171-a6b2b8957092
Buildfile: build.xml

init:

prepare:

compile-delete:
    [javac] Compiling 1 source file to D:\book_demos\jws\ch11\build

run-delete:
     [java] Organization key = eeea9967-fdee-ea99-3171-a6b2b8957092
     [java]
     [java] Organization and related services were deleted successfully.

BUILD SUCCESSFUL

Total time: 44 seconds
D:\book_demos\jws\ch11>
```

Figure 11.14 Executing `Delete.java`.

Summary

In this chapter, we examined the details of JAXR, a Java specification meant for working with XML registry services. Specifically, we looked at the architectural components, the JAXR information model, the registry services API, and specific examples of JAXR in action.

In the next chapter, we will see how the Java Web Services Developer Pack works, using a case study.

CHAPTER

12

Using the Java Web Services Developer Pack: Case Study

This chapter focuses on implementing a complete Web services solution using the Java Web Services Developer Pack (JWSDP) 1.0. It puts together all the JWSDP-based APIs covered in this book to demonstrate a Web services example. To accomplish the demonstration process, we will use a fictional company named ACME Corporation, a wholesaler providing Web services, as an example. This chapter covers the following key topics:

- An overview of the ACME application
- The architectural model of the ACME Web service in terms of the service provider, service broker, and service requestor
- Step-by-step instructions on how to implement the code using various APIs from JWSDP
- The deployment steps for each environment
- How to run the Web services and client application

Case Study Overview

The ACME Corporation caters various services to its computer retail clients for the ordering of wholesale computer parts. Among the services offered is the catalog and ordering service. The purpose of these services is to automate and facilitate the ordering of products over the Internet for computer retailers. These services will be available to clients all over the world. Through this process, the ACME Corporation will reach out to a much bigger market of computer retailers.

The Roles of Service Provider, Requestor, and Registry

The catalog service will be able to deliver product information to its Web customers by displaying a catalog of available products. The buyers of the product will be able to select the items and quantity from the catalog and submit the orders through the ordering service. The ordering service will parse the incoming order and insert it into the database. It then will notify the respective warehouse with the order information. The company has two different warehouses, depending on the type of product: one warehouse for software orders and the other for hardware orders. At each warehouse, the employee responsible for picking the products will retrieve the order information from the computer and start the order picking process. Once prepared, the order is shipped to the buyer using the address provided during ordering.

These Web services from ACME Corporation are targeted toward online retailers. The Web sites hosted by these retailers will offer two functions to their end users: product catalog browsing and product ordering. In order to provide these functionalities, the retailer Web sites will make use of the catalog and ordering Web services. The retailers thus consume the order and catalog Web services, and hence, play the role of service requestor, whereas ACME Corporation plays the role of service provider. For the course of this case study, consider a fictional retailer of computers named Computer Buy.

Figure 12.1 shows the high-level view of the interaction that takes place between the important components and entities involved in this case study.

In order to put things into perspective, we must understand the roles played by these components and entities in this case study.

Important Components and Entities

The entities that play an important role in the ACME Web services scenario are shown in Figure 12.1. The following sections will describe each of these entities and the roles they play in this scenario.

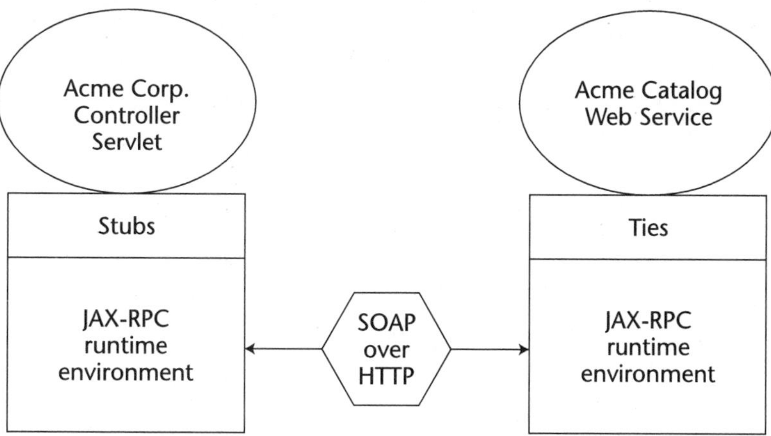

Figure 12.3 ACME catalog communication using JAX-RPC.

The JAX-RPC service design is independent of the type of client that will be accessing the application. The service will expose one service that will extract the catalog information from the database by using a Data Access Object (DAO). The sequence diagram in Figure 12.4 shows what happens when a RPC request is sent from a JAX-RPC client to a service endpoint. The steps in that sequence are as follows:

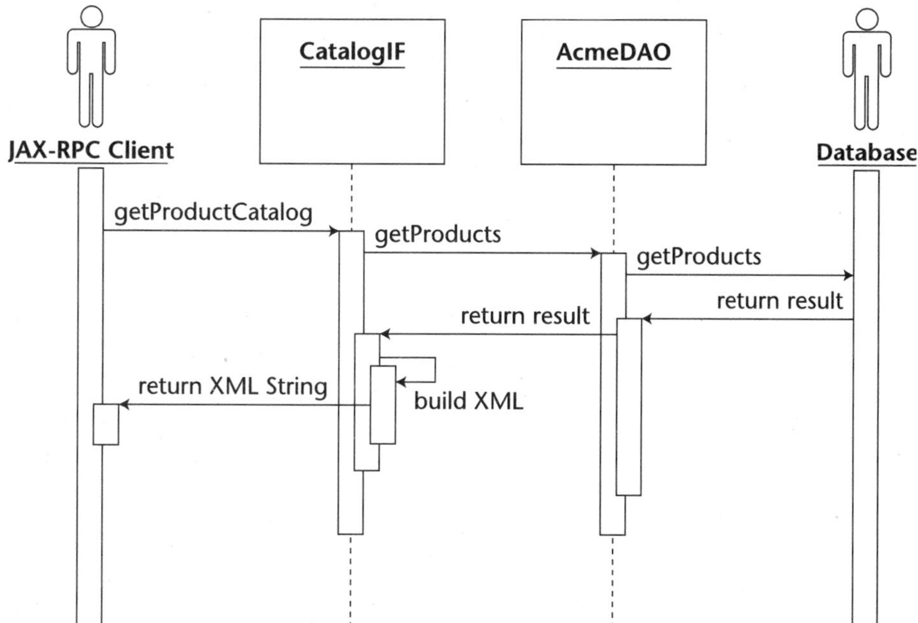

Figure 12.4 Sequence of getting a product catalog.

1. The service requestor sends a `getProductCatalog()` RPC request to the JAX-RPC service endpoint (`CatalogIF`).
2. The service requestor's JAX-RPC runtime environment marshals the request into a SOAP message with RPC semantics and sends it to the remote service.
3. The message arrives at the service provider's side, and is unmarshaled by the provider's JAX-RPC runtime environment that executes the `getProductCatalog()` method with the parameters provided in the request. In this case, no parameters were provided.
4. The service provider calls the `ACMEDAOHelper` class to extract the product information from the database.
5. The service provider creates an XML file representing the catalog and returns it to the remote client.
6. The service requestor receives the XML catalog and displays it to the user.

ACME Ordering Service

The ordering service is implemented using JAXM and SAAJ APIs. The Computer Buy retailer and ACME Corporation services use point-to-point request-response messaging, and therefore, a messaging provider is not needed in this case. The client order will be submitted to a helper class that will establish a `SOAPConnection` with the ACME ordering service. A `SOAPMessage` will be constructed by the requestor based on the order information, and it will be submitted and sent to the ordering service. The service will decompose the `SOAPMessage` and insert the content into the database with the help of an `AcmeDAOHelper` class. Once the database transaction completes, a status message will be returned to the requestor indicating whether the transaction was successful or not.

JWSDP 1.0 includes JAXM and SAAJ APIs that are leveraged in this scenario. The JAXM API requires that a JAXM provider be used. Because the client will connect to the service using a `SOAPConnection`, we will use only the SAAJ part of the API to send SAOP messages (see Figure 12.5). Although this approach is simple, it is not considered reliable. In order to achieve reliability and guaranteed message delivery, it is recommended that a JAXM provider is used. For more information about JAXM and SAAJ, refer to Chapter 9, "XML Messaging Using JAXM and SAAJ."

Figure 12.6 shows what happens when a SOAP message is sent from a client to the service endpoint. The sequence of steps is as follows:

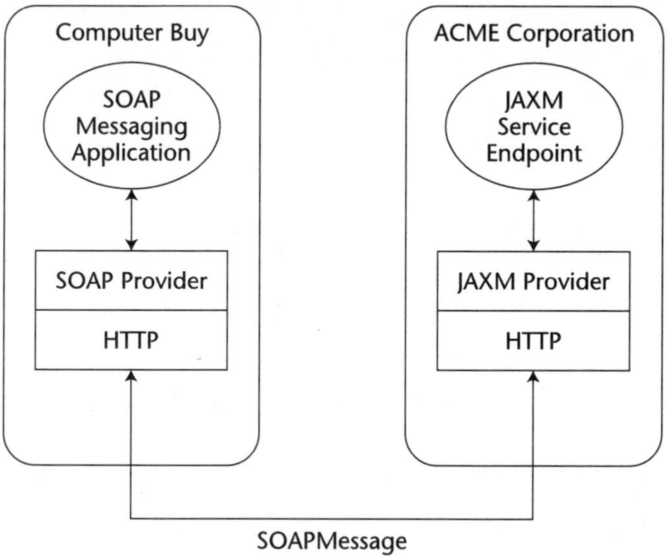

Figure 12.5 ACME order service communication using JAXM.

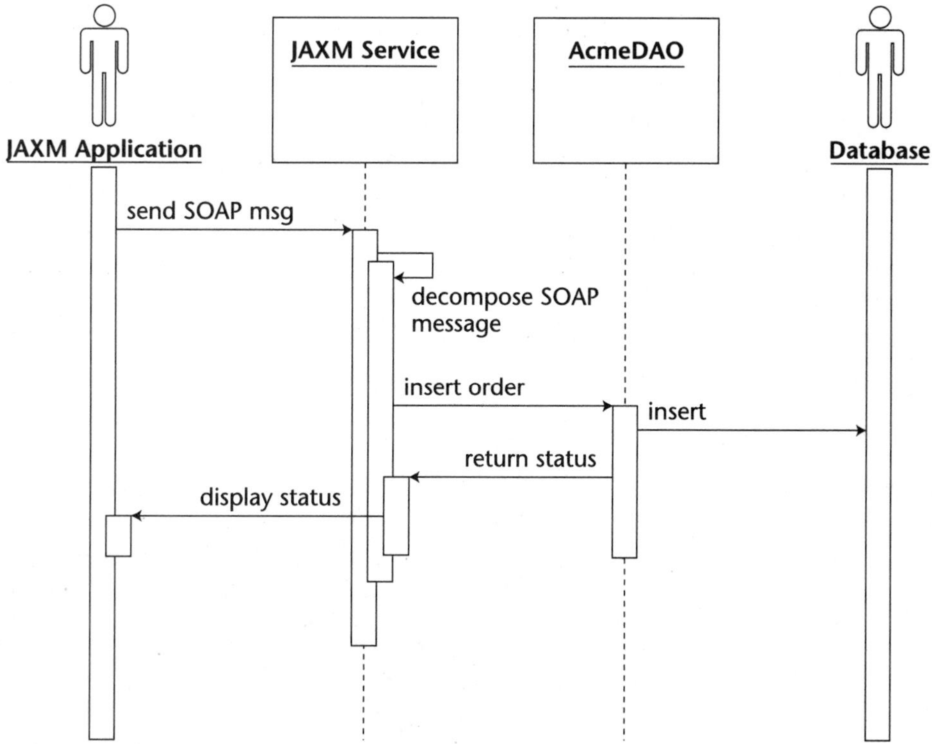

Figure 12.6 Sequence of ordering products.

1. The service requestor establishes a connection with the provider.
2. The service requestor builds a SOAP message based on the input provided by the order form.
3. The service requestor sends the SOAP message to the service provider.
4. The service provider decomposes the SOAP message and calls the `AcmeDAO` to insert the order information into the database.
5. The service provider creates a new SOAP message with the status information about the transaction.
6. The service provider returns the status SOAP message to the JAXM client.
7. The service requestor receives the message and displays it to the user.

Designing the Publishing and Discovery Classes

The following paragraphs examine how the publishing and discovery classes are designed.

JAXR-Based Publish and Discovery Mechanisms

To demonstrate the publishing and discovery of our catalog service, we will use a JAXR API to fetch and store information in the service registry.

The service broker in our case study will use the JWSDP registry server as its private UDDI service registry. The UDDI registry is used for publishing the catalog service by the ACME Corporation (service providers) and for the discovery of the service by the Computer Buy retailer (service requestors).

Registry Parameters for Catalog Service

In the case study, we publish the catalog service with the properties used by the `JAXPublish` class. These properties are shown in Listing 12.1.

```
endpoint=http://acmeservices.org:8080/acme-services/jaxrpc/CatalogIF
query.url=http://acmeservices.org:8080/registry-
server/RegistryServerServlet
publish.url=http://acmeservices.org:8080/registry-
server/RegistryServerServlet
registry.username=testuser
```

Listing 12.1 `CatalogRegistry.properties` used for JAXR publishing.

```
registry.password=testuser
org.name=JAXRPCAcmeProductCatalog
org.description=Acme Catalog Service
person.name=Jane Doe
phone.number=(800) 234-4567
email.address=jane.doe@acmeservices.com
classification.scheme=ntis-gov:naics
classification.name=Computer and Computer Peripheral Equipment and
Software Merchant Wholesalers
classification.value=42343
service.name=JAXRPCAcmeProductCatalog
service.description=Product Catalog offered by the service
service.binding=JAXRPCAcmeProductCatalog Service binding
key.file=orgkey.txt
```

Listing 12.1 `CatalogRegistry.properties` used for JAXR publishing.

The service is stored using a NAICS common classification scheme called Computer and Computer Peripheral Equipment.

Publishing the ACME Catalog Service

The service provider will call an `OrgPublish` utility class that uses `JAXRPublish`. The `JAXRPublish` class relies on the JAXR API for establishing a connection with the registry and for using `RegistryService`, `BusinessLifeCycleManager`, and `BusinessQueryManager` for publishing new services. The configuration parameters used by `OrgPublish` will be retrieved from the `CatalogRegistry.properties` file. This process will be done outside of the service implementation code. In other words, it will have to be executed by the service deployer, once the service has been successfully deployed in the Tomcat Web container. Figure 12.7 is a class diagram that shows the relation between the `OrgPublish` and the `JAXRPublish` classes.

Discovering the ACME Catalog Service

The discovery of the service will be handled differently than publishing, in the sense that it will be used by a Web service client application (computerBuy.com). The catalog service requestor has implemented a helper class that will aid in the discovery of the service. First, it establishes a connection with the registry, then it executes a query that will perform a search based

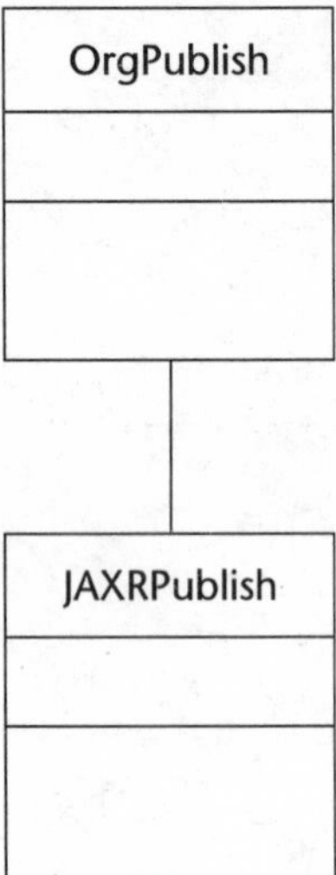

Figure 12.7 Publishing classes.

on a given criteria. The current implementation searches the registry by NAICS common classification schemes. There are various other search possibilities, but we will only list one in this case study.

The service requestor will use `JAXLookupHelper` (see Figure 12.8) in the `CatalogHelper` class to locate the location (URL) of the service endpoint. This search is implemented in a query class called `JAXRQueryByNaicsClassification`. Other query classes can be plugged into the helper to provide different search criteria such as by WSDL, by service name, and so forth.

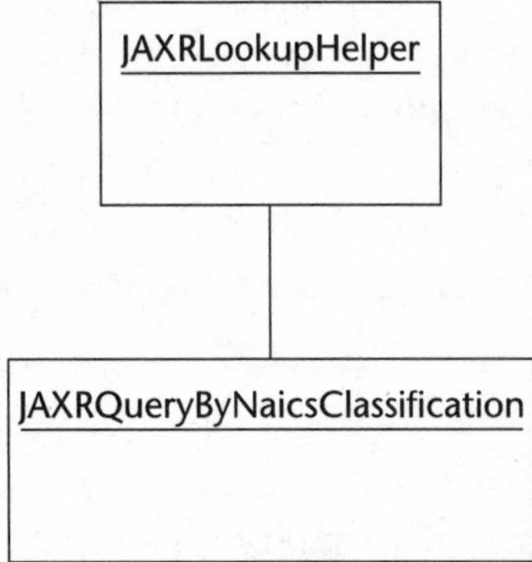

Figure 12.8 Discovery classes using JAXR.

Designing the Service Requestor Environment (computerBuy.com)

The Computer Buy Web site will act as the service delivery layer, providing content to the retailers and aggregation of services offered by the ACME Corporation. The Computer Buy Web site will be composed of various Java Server Pages (JSPs) for content presentation and some Java classes that will provide the functionality to dynamically contact ACME Corporation services to get product catalog information or provide order information.

Content Presentation Using Java Server Pages and JSTL

The presentation part of the computerBuy.com Web application will be done using JSPs and Java Server Pages Standard Tag Libraries (JSTLs). JSTL tags will aid in the conditional processing and parsing of XML data returned from the Web service.

Service Requestor Clients for Catalog and Ordering Service

The service that will be responsible for handling the communication with the Web services is called the service requestor. The service requestor is made up of Web components that reside on the same Web server as the Computer Buy Web site. The requestor consists of a servlet that intercepts all of the incoming HTTP requests from the Computer Buy employees and uses the appropriate Helper classes to invoke the correct Web service. The helpers are implemented as regular Java classes. The catalog service will use a JAX-RPC implementation to make a call to a remote object to retrieve the product information. The ordering service will be implemented as a JAXM messaging service that retrieves the order provided by the employees on the Computer Buy site. Figure 12.9 shows a class diagram of the two service helper classes and the front controller class that is used as the entry point for all of the HTTP requests.

Designing a JAX-RPC DII Client for Catalog Service

When a request to view a product catalog occurs, the service requestor uses helper classes to fetch the service endpoint from the service registry. Figure 12.10 is a class diagram with a description of what role these classes play in getting a list of catalog products from the service provider.

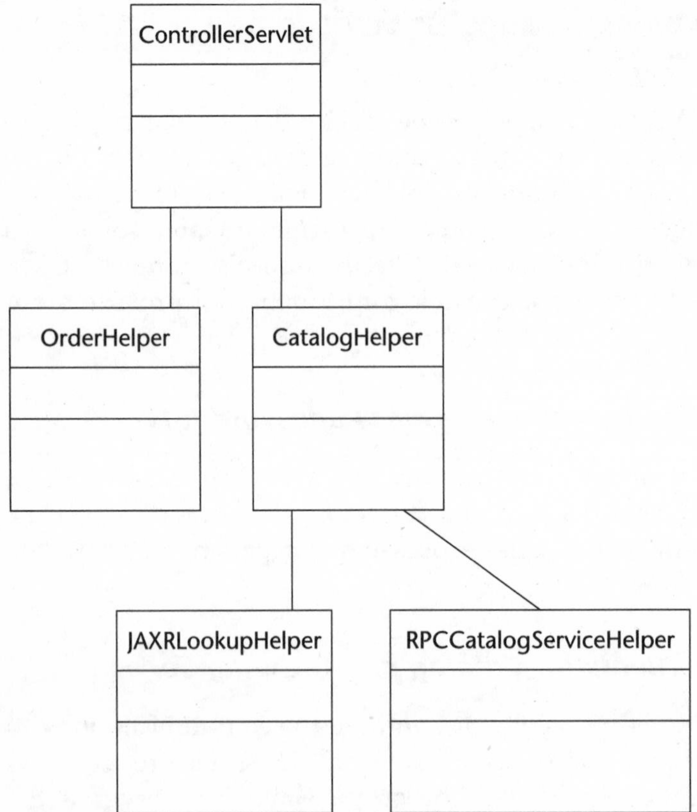

Figure 12.9 Service requestor helper classes.

The following helper classes are used by the requestor when calling the catalog service:

`jws.ch12.helper.CatalogHelper` This helper class encapsulates the registry lookup process and the JAX-RPC call to the catalog service.

`jws.ch12.jaxr.JAXRLookupHelper` This helper class uses JAXR API for the discovery of the services. It calls a query class that makes a `JAXRConnection` to the UDDI registry and queries the registry based on criteria set by the requestor.

`jws.ch12.jaxr.JAXRQueryByNAICSClassification` This JAXR query class is used to search organizations based on a common classification scheme. For more detail on classification schemes, refer to Chapter 11, "Java API for XML Registries."

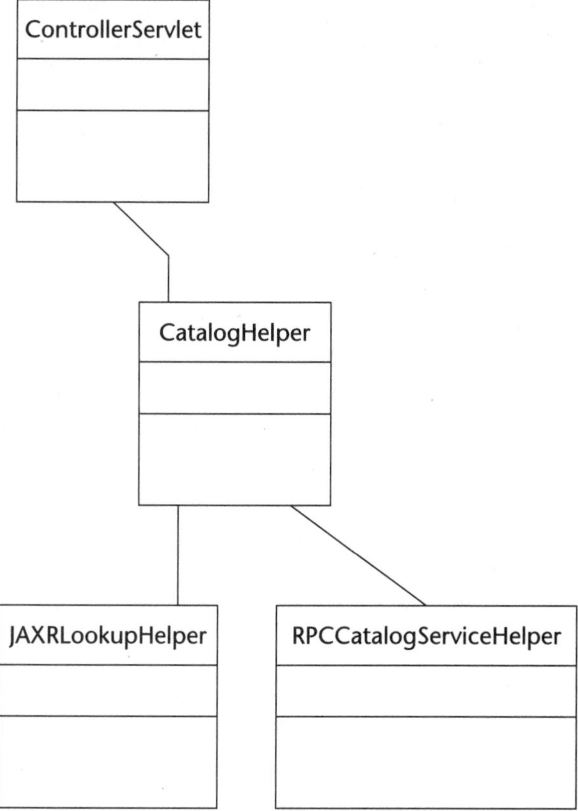

Figure 12.10 Catalog service helper classes.

`jws.ch12.helper.RPCCatalogServiceHelper.java` This helper class uses the endpoint provided by the `JAXRLookupHelper` and uses it to establish a connection to the catalog service. It uses the JAX-RPC API to send an RPC SOAP message to the service endpoint, which requests a catalog as an XML string.

There are a few factors that one may consider when designing a JAX-RPC client:

- Is this Web service going to be exposed in a UDDI?
- Will the client application discover the service in a registry?
- Will the client application know of the services offered by the provider?
- Will the client and service coexist as part of the same network?
- Will the service change the implementation or signature of its methods frequently?

When these factors are taken into consideration, the client implementation may be easier to design. The various possibilities of JAX-RPC clients include the following:

- Static stub implementation
- Dynamic proxy
- Dynamic Invocation Interface (DII)

In this case study, the client of the service will use a Dynamic Invocation Interface (DII) technique as opposed to a more traditional way of using a static stub/skeleton. Because we want to discover and execute the service at runtime, DII is a good alternative. Otherwise, service stubs and ties would have to be created and deployed on every client machine so that the client could execute the service by using its local stub. DII enables us to use other APIs (such as JAXR) to discover the catalog service endpoint in the UDDI service registry and to execute the service dynamically at runtime. Note that the DII implementation only applies to client helper classes, so the service provider has no knowledge of what kind of client (static or dynamic) is calling it.

Figure 12.11 is a sequence diagram that steps through a series of classes that get called when a user selects to view a catalog.

The sequence diagram shows the steps involved in getting a product catalog:

1. From the main JSP, the buyer (a Computer Buy employee) selects the `get Product Catalog` function, which submits a request that gets intercepted by the `ControllerServlet`.
2. The `ControllerServlet` examines the parameters sent and instantiates the `CatalogHelper` class.
3. The `CatalogHelper` class uses the `JAXRLookupHelper` class to discover and call the catalog service endpoint.
4. The catalog service uses the `AcmeDAO` to make a selection of all products from the database and returns the result back to the service.
5. The result is converted into an XML structure and is returned to the client as an XML string.
6. This XML string then is parsed and displayed to the buyer.

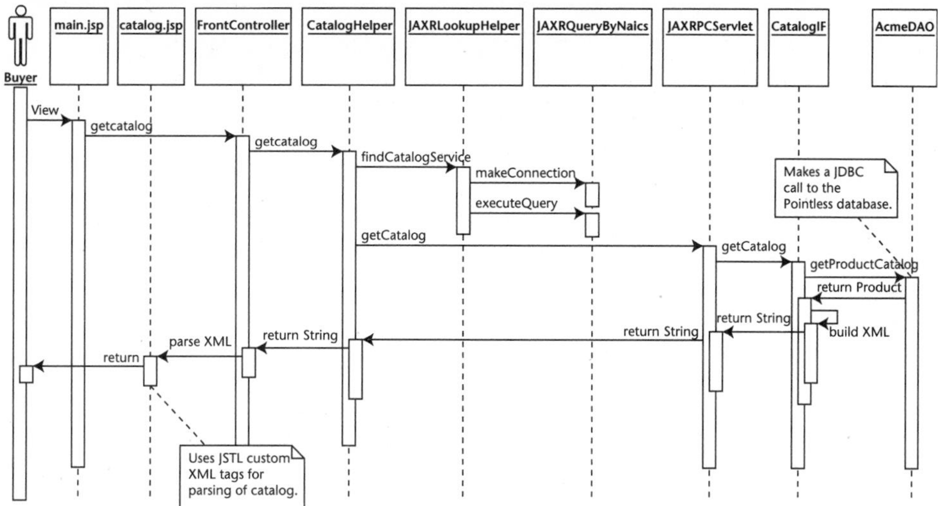

Figure 12.11 View catalog sequence diagram.

JAXM Client for Ordering Service

The ordering service is called using the `OrderHelper` class. The `OrderHelper` class is instantiated in `ControllerServlet`, provides the logic for creating a `SOAPConnection`, then creates and sends a `SOAPMessage` with the order information. In this case study, we are using the SAAJ API instead of JAXM API, because we do not need an intermediary messaging provider. This could be just as easily implemented using a provider, but for this case study we will use a single `SOAPConnection`. Figure 12.12 shows a class diagram of the Computer Buy application (service requestor).

`jws.ch12.helper.OrderHelper` This helper class is used for submitting orders to the ordering service. It uses a JAXM request-response model for sending SOAP messages using SOAP Attachment API for Java (SAAJ). More information on JAXM and SAAJ can be found in Chapter 9.

`jws.ch12.model.CustomerDetails` This class acts as a transport object that is used for holding customer information, such as a name and an address.

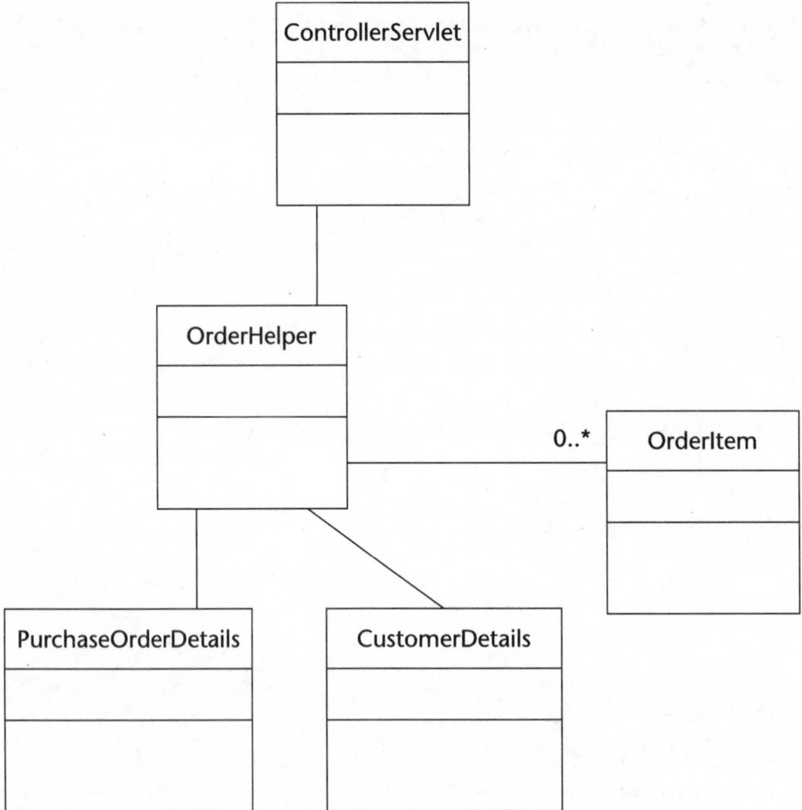

Figure 12.12 Order service helper class.

`jws.ch12.model.OrderItem` This class is a place holder for an item that has a product ID and quantity ordered. The list of ordered items is stored in an array of `OrderItem`.

`jws.ch12.model.PurchaseOrderDetails` This class encapsulates the customer details and order items into one single transfer object that is passed to the `OrderHelper` class, converted into XML, and sent over to the Web service as a SOAP message. Figure 12.13 is a sequence diagram that shows the different steps executed when placing an order.

Figure 12.13 shows the steps involved in getting a product catalog:

1. The first step is used to get the product list so that the user can place an order.
2. From the main JSP, the buyer (a Computer Buy employee) selects the products and quantity, and then submits the request that gets intercepted by the `ControlletServlet`.

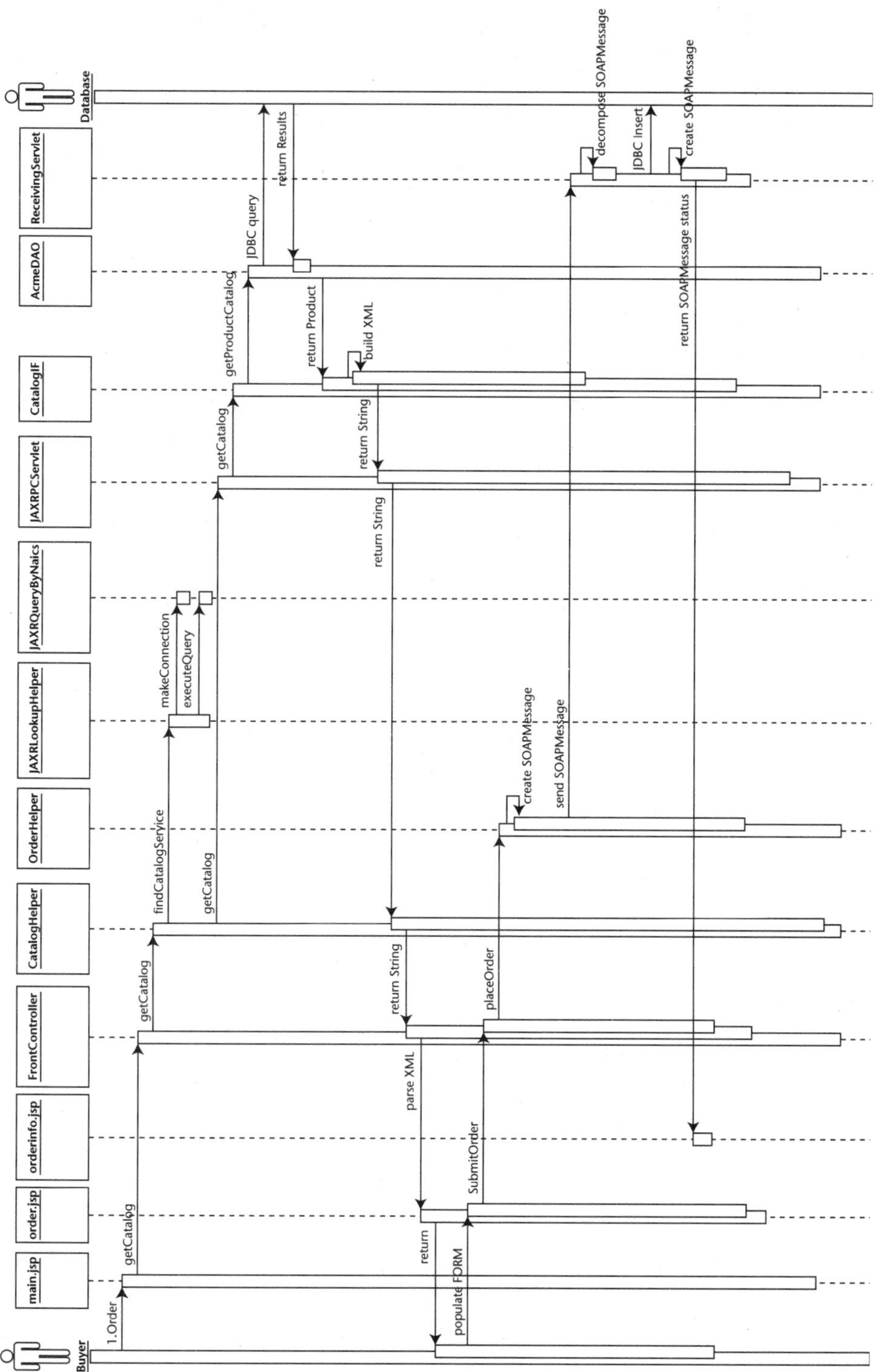

Figure 12.13 Order service sequence diagram.

3. The `ControllerServlet` examines the parameters sent and instantiates the `OrderHelper` class. The service endpoint that it needs to contact is stored in a configuration file (`jaxmendpoint.properties`) on the Computer Buy server.
4. The `OrderHelper` class uses the purchase order details that are gathered from the user request and sent to the service as a SOAP message.
5. The service decomposes the SOAP message and inserts the order into the database.
6. The service returns a SOAP reply to the buyer.

Now that we have discussed the various pieces to this puzzle, let's delve a little deeper and examine how to implement the services and clients.

Implementation

The implementation of this case study consists of three parts:

1. Developing the service provider as the implementation of JAX-RPC and JAXM service endpoints for the catalog and ordering services
2. Creating the service broker, where the services are published
3. Implementing the Computer Buy Web site (service requestor) to enable retailers to view product catalogs and orders online

Each of these parts is discussed in the following sections.

Developing the Service Environment

First, we will look at the catalog service. The implementation of the service uses JAX-RPC APIs to create a service that receives RPC requests from clients using SOAP-encoded messages. The JAX-RPC runtime environment handles the creation of the SOAP message on the client side and the decomposition of the message on the server side.

ACME Catalog Service

The product catalog implementation requires the implementation of one remote interface (`CatalogIF`) and one implementation (`CatalogImpl`) class that implement the business logic defined in the remote interface.

Creating the Service Definition Interface

The service requires an implementation of a remote interface defining methods that can be called by remote clients. The interface must extend a `java.rmi.Remote` interface and each method must throw a `java.rmi.RemoteException`. The following is an example of our `CatalogIF` interface:

```
import java.rmi.Remote;
import java.rmi.RemoteException;

public interface CatalogIF extends Remote {
    public String getProductCatalog() throws RemoteException;
}
```

The following criteria must be satisfied when implementing a service interface:

- The service interface must extend from `java.rmi.Remote`.
- All methods must throw a `java.rmi.RemoteException`.
- No method can be declared static or private.
- Method parameters and return types must be supported by JAX-RPC types. In our case, we will be using primitive and standard Java data types.

Creating the Service Implementation Class

The `CatalogImpl` class is the implementation of the service class that implements the `CatalogIF` interface. In other words, the service implementation class has an implementation method for all business methods defined in the interface. Because we only have one method, `getProductCatalog()`, we will provide only one implementation of this method, which is as follows:

```
public class CatalogImpl implements CatalogIF  {
  public String getProductCatalog() {
   try {
     System.out.println("Provider : Catalog Service called");
     AcmeDAOHelper helper = new AcmeDAOHelper();
     Product [] products =  helper.getProductCatalog();
     StringBuffer xmlStr =
                 new StringBuffer("<?xml version=\"1.0\"?>");
     Product product = null;
     xmlStr.append("<Catalog>");
```

```
        for (int i=0; i < products.length; i++) {
          product = products[i];
          xmlStr.append("\n<Product>");
          xmlStr.append("\n<Number>");
          xmlStr.append(product.getId());
          xmlStr.append("</Number>");

          xmlStr.append("\n<Name>");
          xmlStr.append(product.getName());
          xmlStr.append("</Name>");

          xmlStr.append("\n<Description>");
          xmlStr.append(product.getDesc());
          xmlStr.append("</Description>");

          xmlStr.append("\n<Price>");
          xmlStr.append(product.getPrice());
          xmlStr.append("</Price>");

          xmlStr.append("\n<Currency>");
          xmlStr.append(product.getCurrency());
          xmlStr.append("</Currency>");

          xmlStr.append("\n<Type>");
          xmlStr.append(product.getType());
          xmlStr.append("</Type>");
          xmlStr.append("\n</Product>");

        }
        xmlStr.append("</Catalog>");
       return xmlStr.toString();
      } catch (AcmeDAOException ade) {
          System.out.println("AcmeDAOException occurred :
                                 "+ade.getMessage());
      } catch (Exception e) {
          System.out.println("Exception occurred : "+e.getMessage());
      }
     return null;
     }
```

Figure 12.14 is a class diagram for the service implementation and service interface.

The `getProductCatalog()` method uses a Data Access Object (DAO) to implement all of the database-related work through JDBC calls. The DAO selects products from the products table and returns an array of products to the service. The service then iterates over the array of products and creates an XML file, which then is returned as a string to the remote client (service requestor).

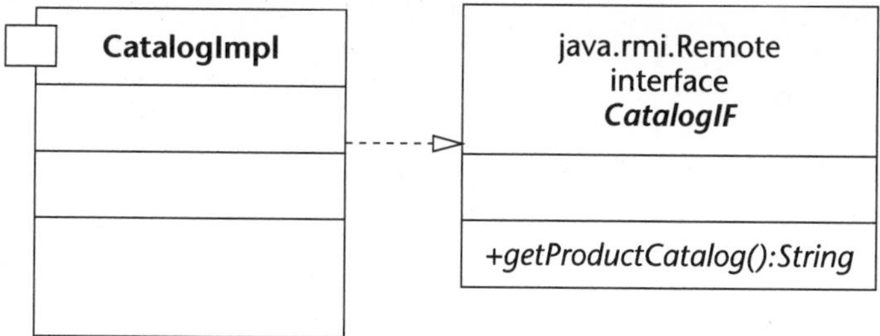

Figure 12.14 Catalog service class diagram.

Before deploying this service, we must specify the JAXRPC endpoint information in the web.xml deployment descriptor. The following is a snippet of code that includes everything you need to put in the web.xml for the service to work correctly:

```
<servlet>
    <servlet-name>JAXRPCEndpoint</servlet-name>
    <display-name>JAXRPCEndpoint</display-name>
    <description>Endpoint for Catalog Web Service</description>
    <servlet-class>
       com.sun.xml.rpc.server.http.JAXRPCServlet
    </servlet-class>
    <init-param>
        <param-name>configuration.file</param-name>
        <param-value>
           /WEB-INF/AcmeProductCatalog_Config.properties
        </param-value>
    </init-param>
    <load-on-startup>0</load-on-startup>
</servlet>
<servlet-mapping>
    <servlet-name>JAXRPCEndpoint</servlet-name>
    <url-pattern>/jaxrpc/*</url-pattern>
</servlet-mapping>
```

When the client invokes the JAXRPC service endpoint (`http://acmeservices.org:8080/acme-services/jaxrpc/CatalogIF`), the `JAXRPCEndpoint` servlet intercepts the request and executes the correct service by looking at the information retrieved from the configuration file (`/WEB-INF/AcmeProductCatalog_Config.properties`). The configuration file is generated at compile time (`xrpcc`) and resides in the WEB-INF directory of the Web application. The following is a sample configuration file:

```
# This file is generated by xrpcc.
port0.tie=jws.ch12.jaxrpc.CatalogIF_Tie
port0.servant=jws.ch12.jaxrpc.CatalogImpl
port0.name=CatalogIF
port0.wsdl.targetNamespace=http://acmeservices.org/wsdl
port0.wsdl.serviceName=AcmeProductCatalog
port0.wsdl.portName=CatalogIFPort
portcount=1
```

Now, let's proceed to the next service implementation using JAXM and SAAJ APIs.

ACME Ordering Service

The product ordering service uses a JAXM request-response communication model by implementing the service using JAXM and SAAJ APIs. The API enables the two communicating parties to exchange SOAP messages by opening a `SOAPConnection` and sending a `SOAPMessage` by calling the call method on the `SOAPConnection`. The call returns a `SOAPMessage` that is used to provide feedback information about the database transaction that was issued from the ordering service.

The ordering service is invoked when the user submits an order from the Web site. The `ControllerServlet` intercepts the request and instantiates an `OrderHelper` with the endpoint URL. The endpoint URL then is fetched from the `WEB-INF/jaxmendpoint.properties` file of the Web site. Because the client uses an ultimate recipient, we will not publish and discover this service in the registry server.

The `ControllerServlet` forwards all of the parameters entered in the form to the `OrderHelper` class by calling its `placeOrder()` method. A string is returned from the method indicating the status of the transaction:

```
OrderHelper helper = new OrderHelper(endpoint);
String status = helper.placeOrder(poDetails);
```

The `OrderHelper` requires an endpoint string as a parameter to the constructor. The endpoint specifies the URL where the JAXM service endpoint resides. The `OrderHelper` acts as the sending client of the SOAP message.

The OrderHelper class creates a SOAPConnection:

```
SOAPConnectionFactory scf =
                      SOAPConnectionFactory.newInstance();
SOAPConnection con = scf.createConnection();
URLEndpoint urlEndpoint = new URLEndpoint(anEndPoint);
```

When the placeOrder() method is called, the helper takes a PurchaseOrderDetails class as a parameter and creates a SOAP message from the information provided. The following is a snippet of code that creates the SOAP message. A detailed explanation is available in Chapter 9.

```
MessageFactory mf = MessageFactory.newInstance();
SOAPMessage msg = mf.createMessage();
SOAPPart sp = msg.getSOAPPart();
SOAPEnvelope envelope = sp.getEnvelope();
SOAPBody body = envelope.getBody();
Name bodyName = envelope.createName("PurchaseOrder", "PO",
              "http://acmeservices.org");

SOAPBodyElement purchaseOrder =
                body.addBodyElement(bodyName);
javax.xml.soap.Name childName = envelope.createName("Info");
SOAPElement info = purchaseOrder.addChildElement(childName);
childName = envelope.createName("Date");
SOAPElement pDate = info.addChildElement(childName);
pDate.addTextNode(poDetails.getPurchaseDate());
childName = envelope.createName("PaymentType");
SOAPElement pType = info.addChildElement(childName);
pType.addTextNode(poDetails.getPaymentType());
```

Figure 12.15 shows the steps involved in sending a JAXM SOAP message. The ControllerServlet and OrderHelper are components that are part of the service requestor (Computer Buy retailer), and JAXMOrderReceivingServlet is the JAXM service endpoint that receives JAXM messages sent from the retailers. AcmeDAOHelper is a class that encapsulates the JDBC code that is used for the database operations. The JAXMOrderReceivingServlet uses the DAO to update the order information in the database.

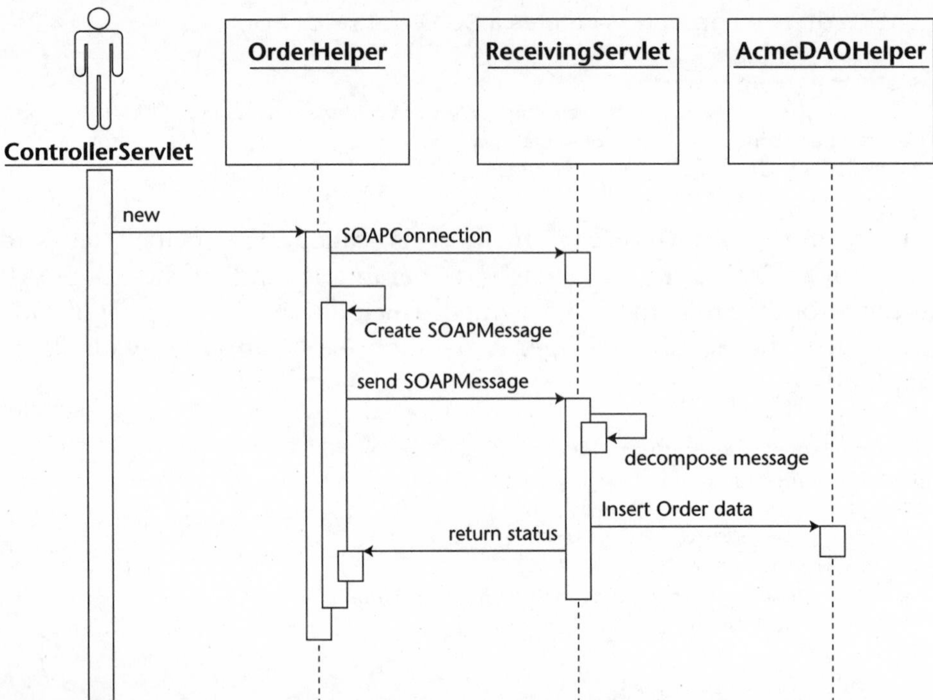

Figure 12.15 `OrderHelper` **and a JAXM-receiving servlet.**

```
<?xml version="1.0" encoding="UTF-8"?>
<soap-env:Envelope
xmlns:soap-env="http://schemas.xmlsoap.org/soap/envelope/">
  <soap-env:Header/>
    <soap-env:Body>
      <PO:PurchaseOrder xmlns:PO="http://acmeservices.org">
        <Info>
         <Date>06/17/2002</Date>
         <PaymentType>Visa</PaymentType>
         <PaymentCardNumber>1234567890123456</PaymentCardNumber>
        </Info>
        <CustomerDetails>
         <Name>Robert Skoczylas</Name>
         <Street>1st Ave</Street>
         <City>Montreal</City>
         <State>QC</State>
         <Zip>H9H 5B3</Zip>
         <Country>Canada</Country>
         <BusinessPhone>514-222-3454</BusinessPhone>
```

```
          <MobilePhone>514-223-5554</MobilePhone>
          <Email>rob@yahoo.com</Email>
        </CustomerDetails>
        <OrderItems>
          <LineItem>
           <ProductNumber>3000</ProductNumber>
<Quantity>100</Quantity>
          </LineItem>
        </OrderItems>
      </PO:PurchaseOrder>
   </soap-env:Body>
</soap-env:Envelope>
```

At the service end, the recipient is implemented as a servlet called `jws.ch12.jaxm.receiver.JAXMOrderReceivingServlet`. The servlet extends a `JAXMServlet` and implements `ReqRespListener` (see Figure 12.16). The `RegRespListener` requires the implementation of an `onMessage()` method, so that when the service is invoked this method is called.

The receiving servlet takes the incoming `SOAPMessage`, decomposes it, and inserts the data in the database using the `AcmeDAOHelper` class. When the DAO completes the transaction, the `JAXMOrderReceivingServlet` builds a new `SOAPMessage`, adds a status message, and returns it to the client. The following is a snippet of code showing the creation of a status `SOAPMessage`. The status then is displayed to the user in the confirmation page.

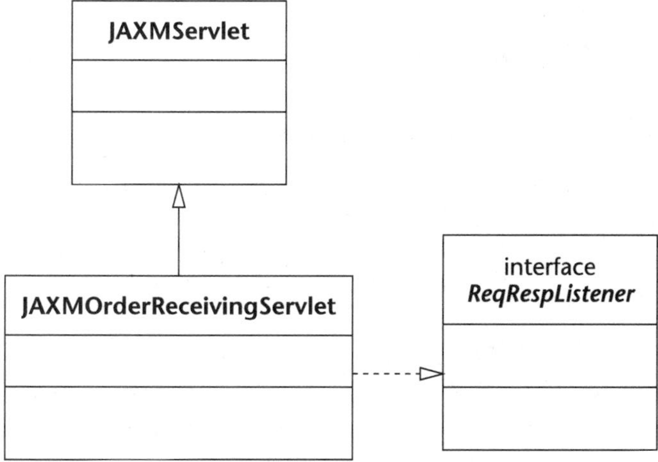

Figure 12.16 `ReceivingServlet` **class diagram.**

```
SOAPMessage msg = fac.createMessage();
SOAPEnvelope envelope = msg.getSOAPPart().getEnvelope();
envelope.getBody()
.addChildElement(envelope.createName("Status"))
.addTextNode(statusMsg);
msg.saveChanges();
return msg;
```

Now that all of the classes are implemented, we must configure the web.xml deployment descriptor to specify the JAXM service endpoint. The following is a snippet of `web.xml` that defines the `JAXMOrder-ReceivingServlet` endpoint:

```
<servlet>
  <servlet-name>JAXMOrderServiceEndpoint</servlet-name>
  <servlet-class>
    jws.ch12.jaxm.receiver.ReceivingServlet
  </servlet-class>
  <load-on-startup>3</load-on-startup>
</servlet>

<servlet-mapping>
  <servlet-name>JAXMOrderServiceEndpoint</servlet-name>
  <url-pattern>/receiver</url-pattern>
</servlet-mapping>
```

When calling the JAXM service endpoint from the `OrderHelper`, we use the following URL found in the `WEB-INF/jaxmendpoint.properties`:

```
to=http://acmeservices.org:8080/acme-services/receiver
```

Publishing the ACME Catalog Service

The publishing of a service is performed by the service provider. Once a service is successfully deployed, it must be published for other clients to discover and use it. The catalog service provider publishes the information about itself into the registry. In this case study, this step is implemented as a standalone class that reads the `CatalogRegistry.properties` file and uses the information from that property file to publish to the registry.

Steps Involved in Publishing a Service

The main class used for populating the registry is called `JAXRPublish`. The steps that are involved in publishing a service are as follows:

1. Connect to the registry provider.

```
ConnectionFactory factory = ConnectionFactory.newInstance();
factory.setProperties(props);
connection = factory.createConnection();
```

2. Obtain authorization for registry updates and provide the information.

```
PasswordAuthentication passwdAuth =
new PasswordAuthentication(username,
password.toCharArray());
Set creds = new HashSet();
creds.add(passwdAuth);
connection.setCredentials(creds);
```

3. Register the service. Once all of the attributes have been set, it is time to register the service using `BusinessLifeCycleManager`.

```
BulkResponse response = blcm.saveOrganizations(orgs);
Collection exceptions = response.getExceptions();
```

The following information was provided to the `JAXPublish` class:

Business Name:	JAXRPCAcmeProductCatalog
Contact Information:	Person name: Jane Doe
	Phone number: (800) 234-4567
	Email: jane.doe@acmeservices.com
Classification Scheme (Classification, Code):	NAICS (Computer and Computer Peripheral Equipment and Software Merchant Wholesalers, 42343)
Service Description:	Product Catalog offered by the service
Service Access Point (endpoint):	JAXRPCAcmeProductCatalog Service binding (http://acmeservices.org:8080/acme-services/jaxrpc/CatalogIF)

`JAXRPublisher` is called by the `OrgPublisher` class that essentially calls `JAXPublisher` with the correct parameters. These parameters are retrieved from the `CatalogRegistry.properties` file. After running the `OrgPublisher`, we should see the output shown in Figure 12.17.

```
MS-DOZE
E:\WS\chapters\12 - Case Study JWSDP\AcmeProvider>d:\jwsdp-1_0\bin\ant.bat run-jaxr-publish
Buildfile: build.xml

run-jaxr-publish:
     [echo] Running OrgPublisher.
     [echo] Note: Remember to start the registry server before running this program.
     [java] queryURL = http://localhost:8080/registry-server/RegistryServerServlet
     [java] publishURL = http://localhost:8080/registry-server/RegistryServerServlet
     [java] username = testuser
     [java] password = testuser
     [java] endpoint = http://localhost:8080/acme-services/jaxrpc/CatalogIF
     [java] keyFile = orgkey.txt
     [java] Created connection to registry
     [java] Got registry service, query manager, and life cycle manager
     [java] Established security credentials
     [java] Organization saved
     [java] Organization key is ee80b844-b4ee-80b8-2f77-6c3b58328e87

BUILD SUCCESSFUL

Total time: 1 minute 28 seconds
E:\WS\chapters\12 - Case Study JWSDP\AcmeProvider>
```

Figure 12.17 `OrgPublisher` output.

The output displays the result of the publishing and writes a unique organization key to the `orgkey.txt` file. Now that the service is published in the registry, the missing step is to implement the service client or service requestor.

Browsing the Service Registry

The service broker uses the JWSDP registry server and provides support for the UDDI version 2.0 registry specification. The registry server provides the capabilities to search our private registry for particular organizations and provides the functionality for publishing an organization or service into the registry. This implementation of the registry serves a great purpose for accessing the information with the JAXR API. The current release of the registry provides the following:

- An XML database (Xindice) from the Apache XML project. It serves the purpose of a repository for data stored in the registry.
- Indri, a graphical user interface (GUI) that enables you to manage the database data.

In the previous section, we published the catalog service in the registry. Let's now open the registry browser provided in the JWSDP and view the content that was published. The browser requires that we specify the registry location. This is the URI that points to the registry server. In our case, we will be using the JWSDP implementation that is installed under `http://localhost:8080/registry-server/RegistryServerServlet`. The search will be performed by name and will contain the string "Catalog".

Figure 12.18 shows the result of our query.

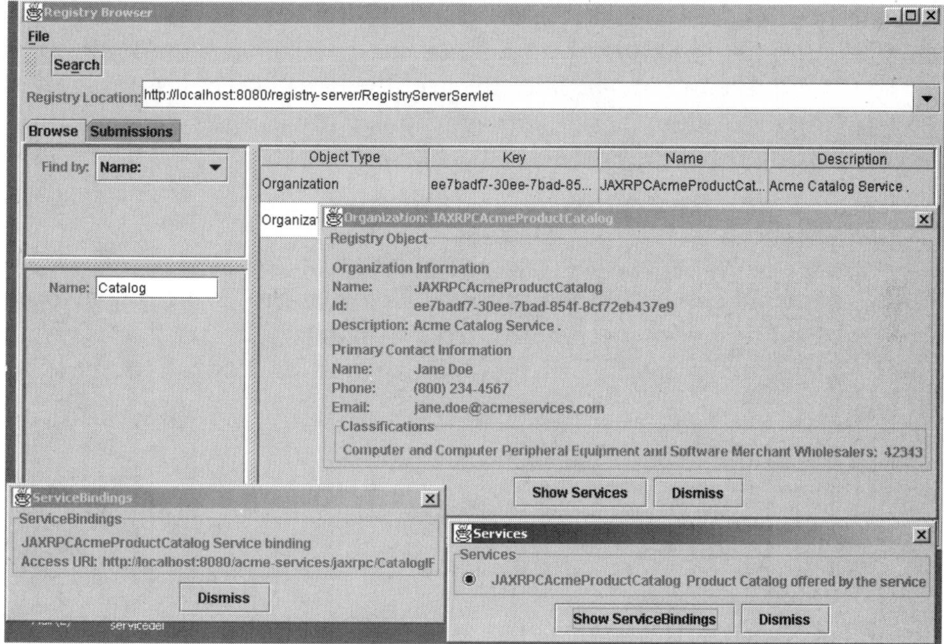

Figure 12.18 Registry browser search results.

The query returned a `JAXRPCAcmeProductCatalog` organization that was previously published. In the detailed windows, we can view the registry object, the services, and service bindings.

The next step is to implement the Computer Buy Web site (service requestor), which will look up the catalog service in the registry server and insert the order information in the database.

Developing the Service Requestor Environment

The Computer Buy Web site components are considered to be the service clients. These components that form the Web site were designed based on design patterns. The intercepting component is a servlet that will act as the `ControllerServlet`. The controller servlet will use one or several helper classes for specific tasks. These helper classes implement different logic, depending upon the type of work that is required (for example, `OrderHelper` for ordering and `CatalogHelper` for getting catalog information).

The Web application consists of a `ControllerServlet` and some helper classes that make interacting with ACME Web services easy. The helper classes encapsulate the plumbing required, such as establishing connections with the services. Figure 12.19 shows the helper classes in relation to the `ControllerServlet`. The `ControllerServlet` determines the type of request and instantiates the appropriate helper class.

The following sections describe the responsibility of each class.

Dispatching of Requests with ControllerServlet

`ControllerServlet` is an implementation of `HttpServlet`. The controller is the main servlet of the Computer Buy site, providing dispatching facilities based on the request submitted by the user. The servlet uses two helper classes to locate the demanded services and forward requests to them.

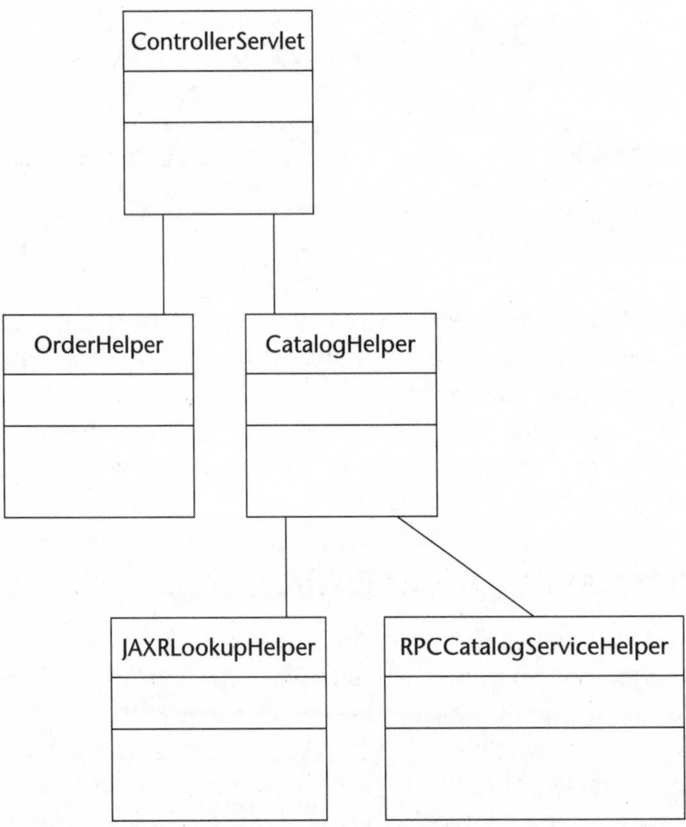

Figure 12.19 Computer Buy Web site class diagram.

In order to dispatch a request, the `ControllerServlet` expects a `sevice_type` and forward parameters in the incoming `HttpServlet Request`. The `service_type` parameter serves to determine whether the service being called is an order or catalog service. The forward parameter indicates whether the response should be forwarded to the catalog or order service. This means that when a user requests to see a catalog, the `service_type=ProductCatalog` and `forward=catalog` are a result. On the other hand, if the user wants to order, then we still need to call the catalog but will forward to order.

The following is a snippet of code that forwards requests to different helper classes and JSPs, depending upon their requested service type and forward page:

```
if (serviceType != null && serviceType.equals("ProductCatalog")) {
  CatalogHelper catalogHelper = new CatalogHelper();
  String catalog = catalogHelper.getCatalog();
  request.setAttribute("xml",catalog);
  RequestDispatcher dispatcher =
                    request.getRequestDispatcher(fwdPage);
  dispatcher.forward(request,response);
}
```

Notice that the catalog service helper returns an XML string representing the product catalog. The string then is saved in an HTTP session attribute. The catalog XML string then is extracted from the session and parsed by the XML custom tag library that's included in the JWSDP 1.0 release under the JSTL 1.0 package. See Chapter 7 for a brief description of the JSTL tag libraries.

The following sections cover the helper classes used by the Controller servlet. The helpers encapsulate the plumbing required to discover and make calls to the remote Web services.

Catalog Service Requestor

A Catalog helper class uses `JAXRLookupHelper` to fetch services from the registry and uses `JAXRPCCatalogHelper` to make JAX-RPC DII calls to the catalog service endpoint.

Example Call to JAXRLookupHelper

The following is a call to JAXRLookupHelper to find services that qualify in the "42343" classification scheme:

```
JAXRLookupHelper helper = new JAXRLookupHelper();
ArrayList services = helper.findCatalogServices("42343","Computer and "+
"Computer Peripheral Equipment and Software Merchant "+
   "Wholesalers");
```

The lookup helper returns an array of services found in the registry with NAICS number = 42343. We then can look at the first service from the array and make a JAX-RPC call to the service. If no services were found, the service uses a local instance:

```
Iterator it = services.iterator();
String endpoint = null;
 if (it.hasNext()) {
    endpoint = (String)it.next();
    System.out.println("Service : "+endpoint);
 } else {
    System.out.println("No service found in the registry, using
default");
    endpoint = "http://localhost:8080/acme-services/jaxrpc/CatalogIF";
 }
```

Now that we have an endpoint string, we pass it to the RPCCatalog ServiceHelper class. RPCCatalogServiceHelper calls the service with a getCatalog() method request. The response consists of an XML string representing the catalog:

```
RPCCatalogServiceHelper csh = new
RPCCatalogServiceHelper(endpoint,"","");
return csh.getProductCatalog();
```

The catalog string then is stored as a request attribute and forwarded to the catalog JSP. The catalog JSP extracts the XML string and displays it to the user.

Dynamic Invocation Interface (DII) Helper

The JAX-RPC DII client implementation was chosen to demonstrate a more dynamic model, where the service is discovered in the UDDI registry at runtime and the client can call a remote procedure without knowing the name of the service or procedure ahead of time. Therefore, the service does not use static stubs to make remote calls, but rather it uses Service and Call interfaces to dynamically call the remote service.

Now, let's look at how this client implements the `getProductCatalog()` method.

The `RPCCatalogServiceHelper` class uses the following interfaces and classes for dynamic invocation:

`Call` Supports the dynamic invocation of a remote operation on a service port

`Service` Is a factory for call objects, dynamic proxies, and stubs; only the generated services are factories for stubs

`Qname` Is a qualified name based on the namespaces in an XML specification

1. Obtain an instance of `ServiceFactory`.

```
ServiceFactory factory =
                 ServiceFactory.newInstance();
Service service =
                 factory.createService(new QName(qnameService));
```

2. Create a `Call` object, and set an endpoint and other properties. The endpoint is retrieved from the `JAXRLookupHelper` class.

```
call.setTargetEndpointAddress(endpoint);

call.setProperty(Call.SOAPACTION_USE_PROPERTY,
                   new Boolean(true));
call.setProperty(Call.SOAPACTION_URI_PROPERTY, "");
call.setProperty(ENCODING_STYLE_PROPERTY, URI_ENCODING);
```

3. Set return type, in our case it will be a `String`:

```
QName QNAME_TYPE_STRING = new QName(NS_XSD, "string");
//the return type will be an XML string
call.setReturnType(QNAME_TYPE_STRING);
```

4. Set a method name to be called on the remote object.

```
call.setOperationName(new QName(BODY_NAMESPACE_VALUE,
                           "getProductCatalog"));
```

5. Call the service. `getProductCatalog()` does not take any parameters, resulting in a null value in the invoke method. The return type is a string; and explicit cast is needed because the invoke method returns an object type:

```
result = (String)call.invoke(null);
```

Ordering a Service Requestor

The OrderHelper class is used for sending SOAP messages to a JAXM service endpoint. It takes a purchase order transfer object and converts it into a SOAP message. This SOAP message then is sent over a SOAPConnection to the receiving servlet.

How a SOAP Message Is Sent

The helper class takes a string representing the JAXM endpoint. It then creates a URLEndpoint object by passing the endpoint string:

```
urlEndpoint = new URLEndpoint(anEndPoint);
```

It creates a SOAPConnection in the constructor and uses this connection for sending SOAP messages:

```
SOAPConnectionFactory scf =
                        SOAPConnectionFactory.newInstance();
con = scf.createConnection();
```

The helper class provides a method called placeOrder() that takes in a PurchaseOrderDetails transfer object. The transfer object is a standard JavaBean object, with accessor methods holding the values entered in the order form. The purchase order object then is used to create the SOAPMessage. The following is a snippet of code that demonstrates the creation of the message:

```
Name bodyName = envelope.createName("PurchaseOrder",
                                    "PO",
                                    "http://acmeservices.org");


SOAPBodyElement purchaseOrder =
                body.addBodyElement(bodyName);

javax.xml.soap.Name childName = envelope.createName("Info");
SOAPElement info = purchaseOrder.addChildElement(childName);
childName = envelope.createName("Date");
SOAPElement pDate = info.addChildElement(childName);
pDate.addTextNode(poDetails.getPurchaseDate());

childName = envelope.createName("PaymentType");
SOAPElement pType = info.addChildElement(childName);
pType.addTextNode(poDetails.getPaymentType());

childName = envelope.createName("PaymentCardNumber");
SOAPElement pNum = info.addChildElement(childName);
pNum.addTextNode(poDetails.getPaymentNumber());
```

The helper sends the SOAPMessage by using the SOAPConnection previously created:

```
SOAPMessage reply = con.call(msg, urlEndpoint);
con.close();
```

The call method of the SOAPConnection takes in the SOAPMessage and the endpoint of the JAXM service. It returns a SOAPMessage that indicates the status of the transaction. The status string is extracted from the SOAPMessage and is returned to the ControllerServlet. ControllerServlet stores the status as a request attribute and forwards it to a confirmation JSP, which displays this status message to the buyer.

Using a JSP Standard Tag Library (JSTL) for Presentation

In order to run the sample, we must include jstl.jar and standard.jar in /WEB-INF/lib of the Computer Buy retail Web application. The JAR files can be found under the <JWSDP_HOME>/tools/jstl and <JWSDP_HOME>/tools/jstl/standard directories. In addition, tld files must be added to the /WEB-INF directory. The case study does not use these tags extensively but rather includes a simple example demonstrating XML parsing. For more information, refer to the JSTL documentation included with JWSDP 1.0 at http://java.sun.com/webservices/docs/1.0/tutorial/doc/JSTL.html.

The web.xml sets the following taglib alias:

```
<taglib>
    <taglib-uri>http://java.sun.com/jstl/xml</taglib-uri>
    <taglib-location>/WEB-INF/x.tld</taglib-location>
</taglib>
```

The order and catalog JSPs then use the following syntax to parse the XML. Looking back a few sections, we called the getProductCatalog() method on the catalog helper class from within ControllerServlet. The helper returned an XML string that we have saved in the HTTP session attribute using key="xml". The XML string is parsed in the following snippet by using the tag lib call to the XML taglib's parse() method:

```
<%@ taglib prefix="x" uri="http://java.sun.com/jstl/xml" %>

<x:parse xml="${xml}" var="cataloglist" scope="application" />
```

Once parsed, the result is saved in the scoped attribute specified by the var parameter. Now that we have the string parsed, let's use the Xpath local expression language to traverse the result. We use the *out* tag to evaluate and display the node value to the JspWriter object:

```
<x:forEach select="$cataloglist//Product">
 <TR>
  <TD>
<x:out select="./Number"/>
  </TD>
</x:forEach>
```

Discovering the ACME Catalog Service Using JAXR

The discovery of the Web services is performed within the catalog service helper. This helper uses a JAXRLookup class in order to call the UDDI registry and to perform a query that will return an array of services that match the search criteria. There are various ways to search the directory: by name, by NAICS classification, and so on. In this case study, we will search by NAICS classification.

The following steps are performed when a lookup of a service takes place:

1. Connect to the UDDI registry provider. Using the JAXRQuery ByNAICSClassification utility class, we will establish a connection with the registry:

   ```
   ConnectionFactory factory =
                       ConnectionFactory.newInstance();
   factory.setProperties(props);
   connection = factory.createConnection();
   System.out.println("Created connection to registry");
   ```

2. Search the registry using a query utility class. The search requirements are NAICS name and value. Because ACME deals with computer wholesale, we will use the following parameters for the search criteria:

   ```
         naicsName=Computer and Computer Peripheral Equipment and
   \     Software
         Merchant Wholesalers
         NaicsValue=42343
   ```

3. The query class first will get the necessary managers to perform the query:

   ```
   RegistryService rs = connectio—-n.getRegistryService();
   BusinessQueryManager bqm = rs.get90
   BusinessQueryManager();
   BusinessLifeCycleManager blcm =
                               rs.getBusinessLifeCycleManager();
   ```

4. Then, it will set the classification scheme to NAICS, indicating that this is the technique used in our query:

```
ClassificationScheme cScheme =
bqm.findClassificationSchemeByName(null,"ntis-gov:naics");
```

5. Finally, the `BusinessQueryManager` is used to find organizations based on the search criteria:

```
Classification classification = (Classification)
blcm.createClassification(cScheme,
                          naicsName,
                          naicsValue);
Collection classifications = new ArrayList();
classifications.add(classification);
BulkResponse response = bqm.findOrganizations(null,
                                                 null,
                                              classifications,
                                                 null,
                                                 null,
                                                 null);
orgs = response.getCollection();
```

6. The result is a collection of `Organization` objects that the helper class will have to go through in order to find the service endpoint. The helper class iterates through the collection and retrieves the end-point values for each organization and stores it in an `ArrayList`:

```
Iterator orgIter = orgs.iterator();
// Display organization information
try {
  while (orgIter.hasNext()) {
    Organization org = (Organization) orgIter.next();
    System.out.println("Org name: " +
                        jQuery.getName(org));
    System.out.println("Org description: "+
                        jQuery.getDescription(org));
    System.out.println("Org key id: " +
                       jQuery.getKey(org));
    // Display service and binding information
    Collection services = org.getServices();
    Iterator svcIter = services.iterator();
    while (svcIter.hasNext()) {
      Service svc = (Service) svcIter.next();
      System.out.println(" Service name: " +
                          jQuery.getName(svc));
      System.out.println(" Service description: " +
                            jQuery.getDescription(svc));
```

```
        Collection serviceBindings =
                  svc.getServiceBindings();
        Iterator sbIter = serviceBindings.iterator();
        while (sbIter.hasNext()) {
          ServiceBinding sb =
                       (ServiceBinding) sbIter.next();
          String endpoint = sb.getAccessURI();
          System.out.println("  Binding Description: " +
                              jQuery.getDescription(sb));
          System.out.println("  Access URI: " + endpoint);
          serviceList.add(endpoint);
        }
      }
    }
```

7. The `ArrayList` containing the endpoint strings is returned and used to call the DII client class.

Now that we have all the pieces implemented, we can start setting up the JWSDP 1.0 environment and start deploying the service requestor and service provider code. Now, let's first look at what is required in terms of the runtime environment and settings.

Setting Up the JWSDP Environment

The following section covers the different settings that are needed to run the service provider (ACME Corporation), service requestor (Computer Buy retailer), and service broker (JWSDP service registry).

Service Provider Runtime Infrastructure (acmeprovider.com)

The following paragraphs show how the service provider runtime is configured, built and deployed, and verified.

JWSDP 1.0 Configuration Requirements

An instance of a Tomcat Web container must be installed for hosting Java Web services components offered by the ACME Corporation.

Database Configuration

The database used for this case study is Pointbase v4.2.

Pointbase Database

The details of how to set up the PointBase database (v4.2) and run the SQL scripts are covered in the JWSDP tutorial. (For more information, refer to the Java Sun Web site at http://java.sun.com/webservices.)

In this case study, we provide the scripts that will facilitate the setup process. The files are included in the source code, which is available for downloading from the Web site at www.wiley.com/compbooks/nagappan under Chapter 12, "Using the Java Web Services Developer Pack: Case Study."

- `Db_create.sql` is a database script that creates new tables and inserts necessary data for the application to run.
- `Build.xml` is an Ant build script that will run the `db_create.sql` script using Pointbase tool classes.

How to Set Up the Database

The following is a summary of steps required for setting up the database (Windows):

- Install the PointBase 4.2 database server.
- Run the PointBase server by executing `$PB_HOME/bin/start_server.exe`.
- Move `pbserver42.jar` and `pbtools42.jar` to `JWSDP_HOME/common/lib`.
- Run `$JWSDP_HOME/bin/ant.bat` from the directory where the `build.xml` file is placed.

The output of the run should be similar to the one shown in Figure 12.20.

The previous steps will install the necessary JAR files in the JWSDP environment as well as create database tables and populate some of the tables with necessary data. The services also require that `java.sql.DataSource` is registered so that the clients can look the `DataSource` up using JNDI API. To register the `DataSource`, open the Admin tool (http://youhost:8080/amin) and configure the data source with the following parameters:

- JNDI name: `jdbc/AcmeDB`
- Driver URI : `jdbc:pointbase:server://localhost/sample`
- Driver class: `com.pointbase.jdbc.jdbcUniversalDriver`
- Username: public
- Password: public

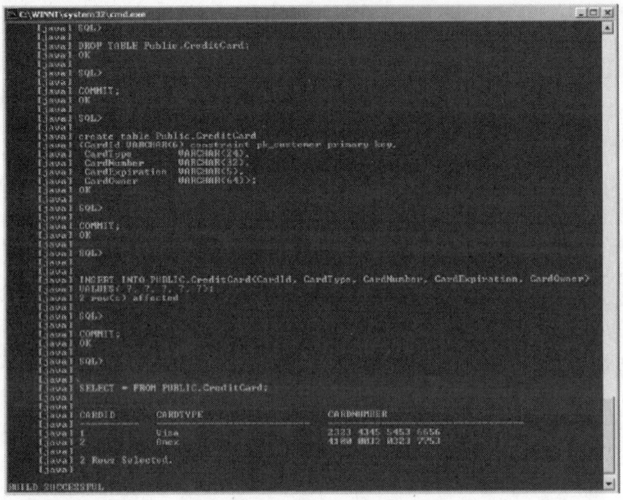

Figure 12.20 The `db_setup.sql` result screen.

For a detailed explanation, refer to the Tomcat Admin tool at the Java Sun Web site: http://java.sun.com/webservices/docs/1.0/tutorial/doc/Admintool5.html#64662.

Once configured and saved, the `server.xml` file should contain a context entry similar to the following:

```
<Resource name="jdbc/AcmeDB" scope="Shareable"
     type="javax.sql.DataSource" auth="Container"/>
<ResourceParams name="jdbc/AcmeDB">
  <parameter>
    <name>user</name>
    <value>public</value>
  </parameter>
  <parameter>
    <name>driverName</name>
    <value>jdbc:pointbase:server://localhost/sample</value>
  </parameter>
  <parameter>
    <name>password</name>
    <value>public</value>
  </parameter>
  <parameter>
    <name>driverClassName</name>
    <value>com.pointbase.jdbc.jdbcUniversalDriver</value>
  </parameter>
</ResourceParams>
```

The data access object of the service provider uses JNDI to look up the registered `DataSource`. The following shows a snippet from the DAO `DataSource` lookup:

```
InitialContext ic = new InitialContext();
DataSource ds = (DataSource) ic.lookup("java:comp/env/jdbc/AcmeDB");
```

Starting the Environment

The following are servers needed for this case study. The order is not important, but for this example to work, we will need all three pieces up and working. We will start with the following servers all running in a Windows environment:

- Tomcat Web container: `$JWSDP_HOME/bin/startup`
- PointBase database server: `$PB_HOME/tools/server/start_server.exe`

Building and Deploying the Service Provider Components

In order to build the service provider, we must go to the `AcmeProvider` directory and execute an Ant build command. The following steps are required for the build to be executed successfully:

1. Open a DOS prompt.
2. Go to the `AcmeProvider` directory.
3. Start Apache Tomcat.
4. Execute `<JWSDP_HOME>/bin/ant.bat` install.

The output shown in Figure 12.21 should appear in the console window.

The build command compiles the Java source and runs the *xrpcc* compiler that generates stubs, ties, and configuration files used by the JAX-RPC implementation. The following are two different ways to generate the stubs and ties:

- Starting with RMI interface and implementation class
- Starting with a WSDL file

In this use case, we will use the first option because we have defined our `CatalogIF` service interface and `CatalogImpl` service implementation class.

```
MS-DOZE
E:\WS\chapters\12 - Case Study JWSDP\AcmeProvider>d:\jwsdp-1_0\bin\ant.bat install
Buildfile: build.xml

clean:
   [delete] Deleting directory E:\WS\chapters\12 - Case Study JWSDP\AcmeProvider\build
   [delete] Deleting directory E:\WS\chapters\12 - Case Study JWSDP\dist

prepare:
     [echo] Creating the required directories....
    [mkdir] Created dir: E:\WS\chapters\12 - Case Study JWSDP\AcmeProvider\build\server
    [mkdir] Created dir: E:\WS\chapters\12 - Case Study JWSDP\AcmeProvider\build\shared
    [mkdir] Created dir: E:\WS\chapters\12 - Case Study JWSDP\dist
    [mkdir] Created dir: E:\WS\chapters\12 - Case Study JWSDP\AcmeProvider\build\WEB-INF\classes

compile-server:
     [echo] Compiling the server-side source code....
    [javac] Compiling 21 source files to E:\WS\chapters\12 - Case Study JWSDP\AcmeProvider\build\sha
red

set-xrpcc:

xrpcc-server:
     [echo] Running xrpcc for the server....

setup-web-inf:
     [echo] Setting up ./AcmeProvider/build//WEB-INF....
   [delete] Deleting directory E:\WS\chapters\12 - Case Study JWSDP\AcmeProvider\build\WEB-INF
     [copy] Copying 28 files to E:\WS\chapters\12 - Case Study JWSDP\AcmeProvider\build\WEB-INF\clas
ses
     [copy] Copying 1 file to E:\WS\chapters\12 - Case Study JWSDP\AcmeProvider\build\WEB-INF
     [copy] Copying 1 file to E:\WS\chapters\12 - Case Study JWSDP\AcmeProvider\build\WEB-INF

build-service:

build:

copy-webapp:
     [echo] Copying to webapps directory
     [copy] Copying 2 files to D:\jwsdp-1_0\webapps\acme-services\WEB-INF
     [copy] Copying 28 files to D:\jwsdp-1_0\webapps\acme-services\WEB-INF\classes

install:
     [echo] Installing the application....
  [install] OK - Installed application at context path /acme-services
  [install]

BUILD SUCCESSFUL

Total time: 21 seconds
E:\WS\chapters\12 - Case Study JWSDP\AcmeProvider>_
```

Figure 12.21 The `AcmeProvider` build output.

The configuration XML file used by the *xrpcc* compiler is used for generating the correct stubs and ties for the service. It contains the names of classes and interfaces used by the service. In addition, the information from `conf.xml` is used to create the `AcmeProductCatalog_Config.properties` used by the `JAXRPCEndpointServlet`.

The following is a sample `config.xml` file, which is included in the source code of this use case:

```
<?xml version="1.0" encoding="UTF-8"?>
 <configuration xmlns="http://java.sun.com/xml/ns/jax-rpc/ri/config">
 <service name="AcmeProductCatalog"
   targetNamespace="http://acmeservices.org/wsdl"
   typeNamespace="http://acmeservices.org/types"
   packageName="jws.ch12.jaxrpc">
   <interface name="jws.ch12.jaxrpc.CatalogIF"
     servantName="jws.ch12.jaxrpc.CatalogImpl"/>
 </service>
 </configuration>
```

After running *xrpcc*, the following `AcmeProductCatalog_Config.properties` configuration file is generated and placed in the WEB-INF directory:

```
# This file is generated by xrpcc.
port0.tie=jws.ch12.jaxrpc.CatalogIF_Tie
port0.servant=jws.ch12.jaxrpc.CatalogImpl
port0.name=CatalogIF
port0.wsdl.targetNamespace=http://acmeservices.org/wsdl
port0.wsdl.serviceName=AcmeProductCatalog
port0.wsdl.portName=CatalogIFPort
portcount=1
```

The *xrpcc* tool also generates the following WSDL. In order to generate this file, the *xrpcc* command should have the `-keep` attribute:

```
<?xml version="1.0" encoding="UTF-8"?>

<definitions name="AcmeProductCatalog"
targetNamespace="http://acmeservices.org/wsdl"
xmlns:tns="http://acmeservices.org/wsdl"
xmlns="http://schemas.xmlsoap.org/wsdl/"
xmlns:xsd="http://www.w3.org/2001/XMLSchema"
xmlns:soap="http://schemas.xmlsoap.org/wsdl/soap/">
  <types/>
  <message name="CatalogIF_getProductCatalog"/>
  <message name="CatalogIF_getProductCatalogResponse">
    <part name="result" type="xsd:string"/></message>
  <portType name="CatalogIF">
    <operation name="getProductCatalog" parameterOrder="">
      <input message="tns:CatalogIF_getProductCatalog"/>
      <output message="tns:CatalogIF_getProductCatalogResponse"/>
    </operation>
  </portType>
  <binding name="CatalogIFBinding" type="tns:CatalogIF">
    <operation name="getProductCatalog">
      <input>
        <soap:body
encodingStyle="http://schemas.xmlsoap.org/soap/encoding/"
                   use="encoded"
namespace="http://acmeservices.org/wsdl"/>
      </input>
      <output>
        <soap:body
encodingStyle="http://schemas.xmlsoap.org/soap/encoding/"
                   use="encoded"
namespace="http://acmeservices.org/wsdl"/>
      </output>
      <soap:operation soapAction=""/>
```

```
    </operation>
    <soap:binding transport="http://schemas.xmlsoap.org/soap/http"
                  style="rpc"/>
  </binding>
  <service name="AcmeProductCatalog">
    <port name="CatalogIFPort" binding="tns:CatalogIFBinding">
      <soap:address location="REPLACE_WITH_ACTUAL_URL"/>
    </port>
  </service>
</definitions>
```

The WSDL file is installed with the service and resides in the WEB-INF directory of the service. To make the WSDL description accessible through a browser, one manual modification must occur to the `AcmeProductCatalog_Config.properties` file for this to work. Although it is not recommended to modify the `config` file, it is possible to do so. Add the following line at the end of `AcmeProductCatalog_Config.properties`:

```
wsdl.location=/WEB-INF/AcmeProductCatalog.wsdl
```

The WSDL can now be referenced by pointing the browser to http://yourhost:8080/acme-service/jaxrpc?WSDL.

Figure 12.22 is a result of this query.

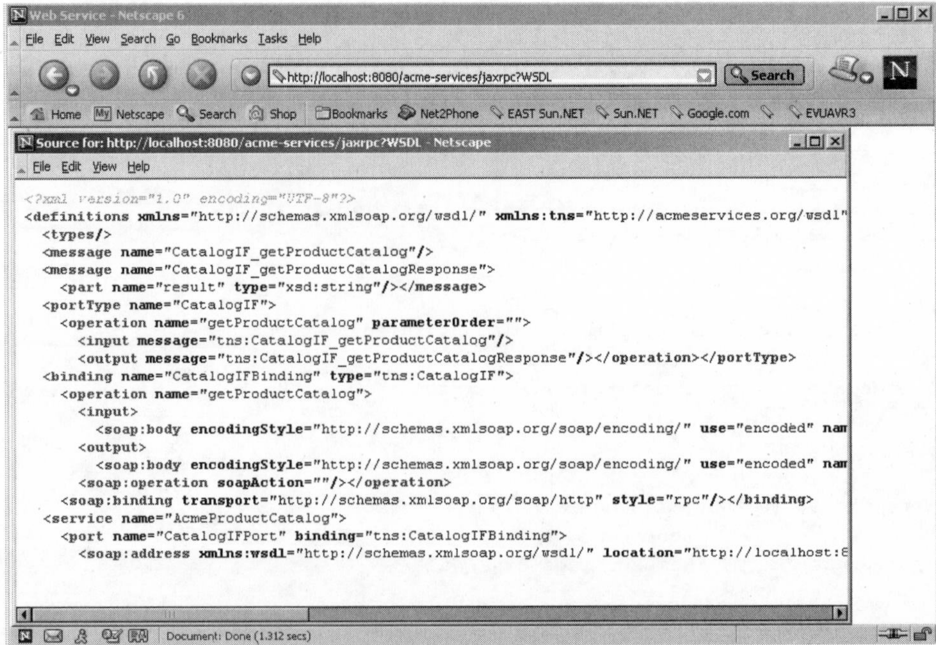

Figure 12.22 WSDL description of the catalog service.

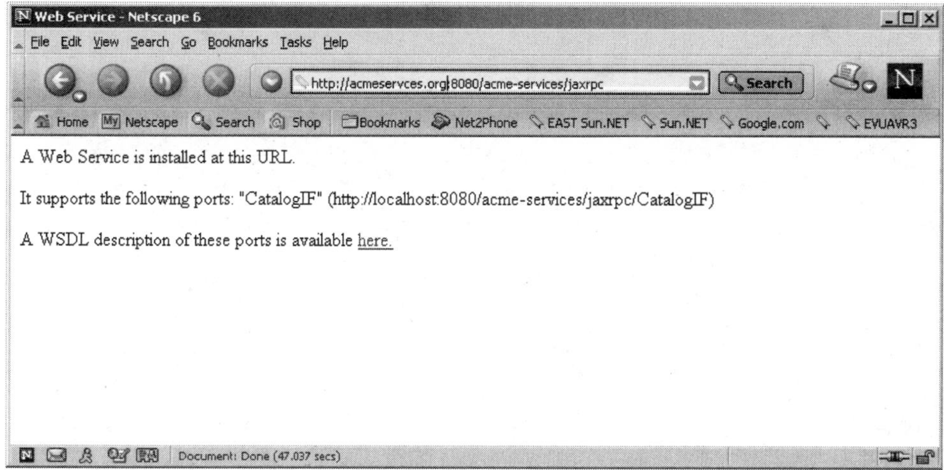

Figure 12.23 Catalog service endpoint test.

To test that the JAX-RPC endpoint is successfully installed and running, go to the following URL: http://<yourhost>:8080/acme-services/jaxrpc. If the service is correctly working, the output should be as displayed in Figure 12.23.

Verifying the Deployment

The build scripts provide the Web application manager tasks that can be called to install, remove, reload, or list Web applications. In order to verify the installed services, run the following command from the `AcmeProvider` directory:

```
<JWSDP_HOME>/bin/ant.bat list
```

Figure 12.24 is an output from this command showing that the `/acme-services` and `/acme applications` are running.

Service Registry Infrastructure

The JWSDP registry server will be used for this case study to demonstrate the publishing and discovery capabilities of our ACME clients and services. The registry will host information about a particular service, and clients of the service will be able to look it up by using a JAXR API. There are no specific configuration requirements to get the registry running. We will not use any graphical registry browsers to browse the registry; instead, we will use command line tools and APIs to access the registry.

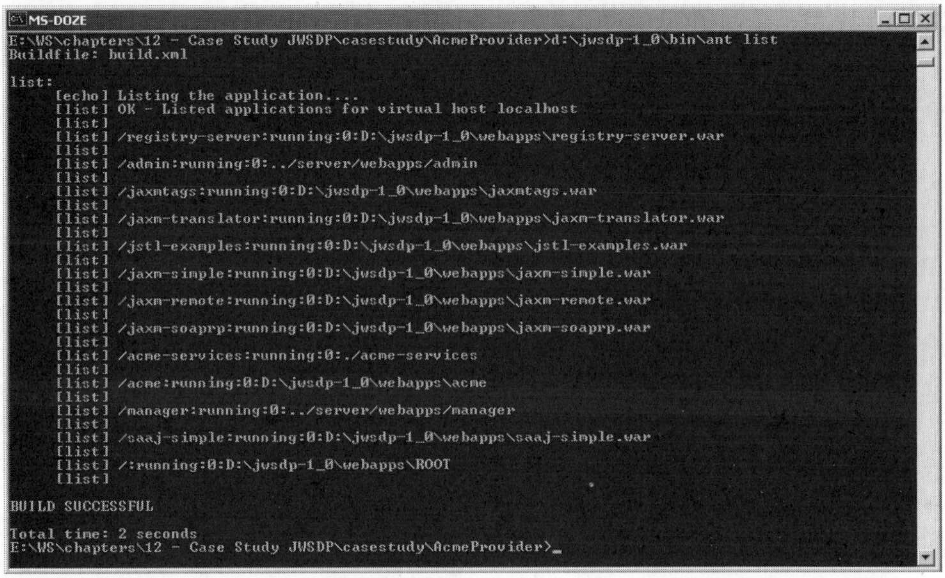

```
MS-DOZE
E:\WS\chapters\12 - Case Study JWSDP\casestudy\AcmeProvider>d:\jwsdp-1_0\bin\ant list
Buildfile: build.xml

list:
     [echo] Listing the application....
     [list] OK - Listed applications for virtual host localhost
     [list]
     [list] /registry-server:running:0:D:\jwsdp-1_0\webapps\registry-server.war
     [list]
     [list] /admin:running:0:../server/webapps/admin
     [list]
     [list] /jaxmtags:running:0:D:\jwsdp-1_0\webapps\jaxmtags.war
     [list]
     [list] /jaxm-translator:running:0:D:\jwsdp-1_0\webapps\jaxm-translator.war
     [list]
     [list] /jstl-examples:running:0:D:\jwsdp-1_0\webapps\jstl-examples.war
     [list]
     [list] /jaxm-simple:running:0:D:\jwsdp-1_0\webapps\jaxm-simple.war
     [list]
     [list] /jaxm-remote:running:0:D:\jwsdp-1_0\webapps\jaxm-remote.war
     [list]
     [list] /jaxm-soaprp:running:0:D:\jwsdp-1_0\webapps\jaxm-soaprp.war
     [list]
     [list] /acme-services:running:0:./acme-services
     [list]
     [list] /acme:running:0:D:\jwsdp-1_0\webapps\acme
     [list]
     [list] /manager:running:0:../server/webapps/manager
     [list]
     [list] /saaj-simple:running:0:D:\jwsdp-1_0\webapps\saaj-simple.war
     [list]
     [list] /:running:0:D:\jwsdp-1_0\webapps\ROOT
     [list]

BUILD SUCCESSFUL

Total time: 2 seconds
E:\WS\chapters\12 - Case Study JWSDP\casestudy\AcmeProvider>_
```

Figure 12.24 Tomcat Web application list.

To start the registry environment, ensure that the Tomcat Web application server is started and running. In order to start the registry environment, the following database has to be started:

Xindice database used by the JWSDP registry server: $JWSDP_HOME/bin /xindice-start

Service Requestor Runtime Infrastructure (computerBuy.com)

The following paragraphs show how the service requestor runtime is configured, started, and built and deployed.

JWSDP 1.0 Configuration Requirements

A Tomcat Web container environment is needed for hosting Computer Buy's Web site. The Web site will have a servlet component that will handle the delegation to various helper classes used to call ACME Corporation's services.

Starting the Environment

The Computer Buy retailer only requires that the Web application server hosting the components be started. The following is an example of how to start the Tomcat server on Windows:

- Tomcat Web container: `$JWSDP_HOME/bin/startup`

Building and Deploying the Service Requestor Components

The process of building the requestor is not much different from the service provider, except that fewer tasks are called. In order to build the service requestor, we must go to the `AcmeRequestor` directory and execute the `ANT` build command. The following steps are required for the build to be executed successfully:

1. Open a DOS prompt.
2. Go to the `AcmeRequestor` directory.
3. Start the Apache Tomcat.
4. Execute the `<JWSDP_HOME>/bin/ant.bat` install.

The output shown Figure 12.25 should appear in the console window.

```
Select MS-DOZE

E:\WS\chapters\12 - Case Study JWSDP\AcmeRequestor>d:\jwsdp-1_0\bin\ant.bat install
Buildfile: build.xml

init:

prepare:
    [mkdir] Created dir: E:\WS\chapters\12 - Case Study JWSDP\AcmeRequestor\build
    [mkdir] Created dir: E:\WS\chapters\12 - Case Study JWSDP\AcmeRequestor\build\WEB-INF
    [mkdir] Created dir: E:\WS\chapters\12 - Case Study JWSDP\AcmeRequestor\build\WEB-INF\classes
    [mkdir] Created dir: E:\WS\chapters\12 - Case Study JWSDP\AcmeRequestor\build\WEB-INF\lib

build:
    [javac] Compiling 16 source files to E:\WS\chapters\12 - Case Study JWSDP\AcmeRequestor\build\WE
B-INF\classes
     [copy] Copying 1 file to E:\WS\chapters\12 - Case Study JWSDP\AcmeRequestor\build\WEB-INF
     [copy] Copying 6 files to E:\WS\chapters\12 - Case Study JWSDP\AcmeRequestor\build\WEB-INF
     [copy] Copying 10 files to E:\WS\chapters\12 - Case Study JWSDP\AcmeRequestor\build\WEB-INF\lib

     [copy] Copying 6 files to E:\WS\chapters\12 - Case Study JWSDP\AcmeRequestor\build

copy-webapp:
     [echo] Copying to webapps directory
    [mkdir] Created dir: D:\jwsdp-1_0\webapps\acme
    [mkdir] Created dir: D:\jwsdp-1_0\webapps\acme\WEB-INF
    [mkdir] Created dir: D:\jwsdp-1_0\webapps\acme\WEB-INF\classes
    [mkdir] Created dir: D:\jwsdp-1_0\webapps\acme\WEB-INF\lib
     [copy] Copying 6 files to D:\jwsdp-1_0\webapps\acme
     [copy] Copying 7 files to D:\jwsdp-1_0\webapps\acme\WEB-INF
     [copy] Copying 10 files to D:\jwsdp-1_0\webapps\acme\WEB-INF\lib
     [copy] Copying 17 files to D:\jwsdp-1_0\webapps\acme\WEB-INF\classes

install:
  [install] OK - Installed application at context path /acme
  [install]

BUILD SUCCESSFUL

Total time: 37 seconds
E:\WS\chapters\12 - Case Study JWSDP\AcmeRequestor>_
```

Figure 12.25 `AcmeRequestor` build output.

The requestor code is now successfully installed under <JWSDP_HOME>/webapps/acme. To access the ACME Web site, open your browser and enter the following URL: http://<yourhost>:8080/acme/main.jsp.

Executing a Scenario

The Computer Buy Web site (computerBuy.com) provides a portal to the various services offered by the ACME Corporation. In order to access the portal, open a favorite Web browser and enter the following URL: http://<yourhost>: 8080/acme/main.jsp.

The page shown in Figure 12.26 should be displayed.

At this stage, the user can call the product catalog Web service or the product ordering Web service. If the user selects to view the product catalog, a JAXRPC message will be sent to the JAXRPC service endpoint. The service will execute the getProductCatalog() method and return an XML string containing catalog information. The catalog then is parsed by the XML taglib and displayed to the end user.

Figure 12.27 shows a sample product catalog retrieved from the Web service.

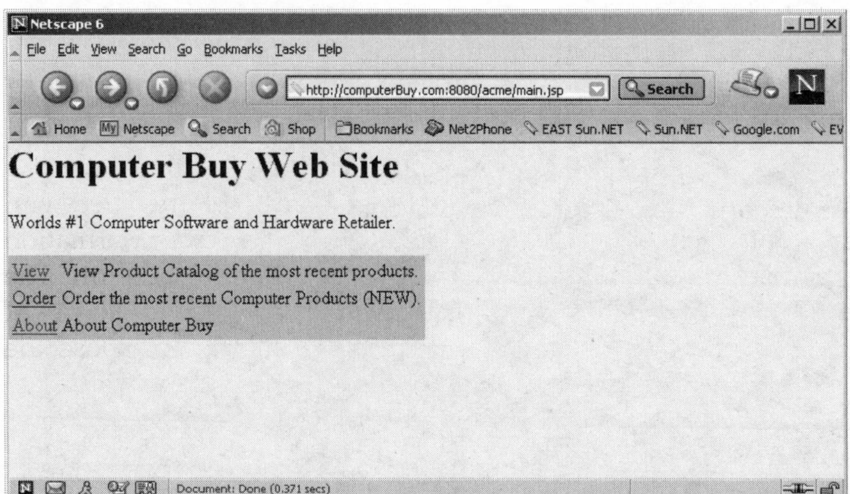

Figure 12.26 ACME Web portal main page.

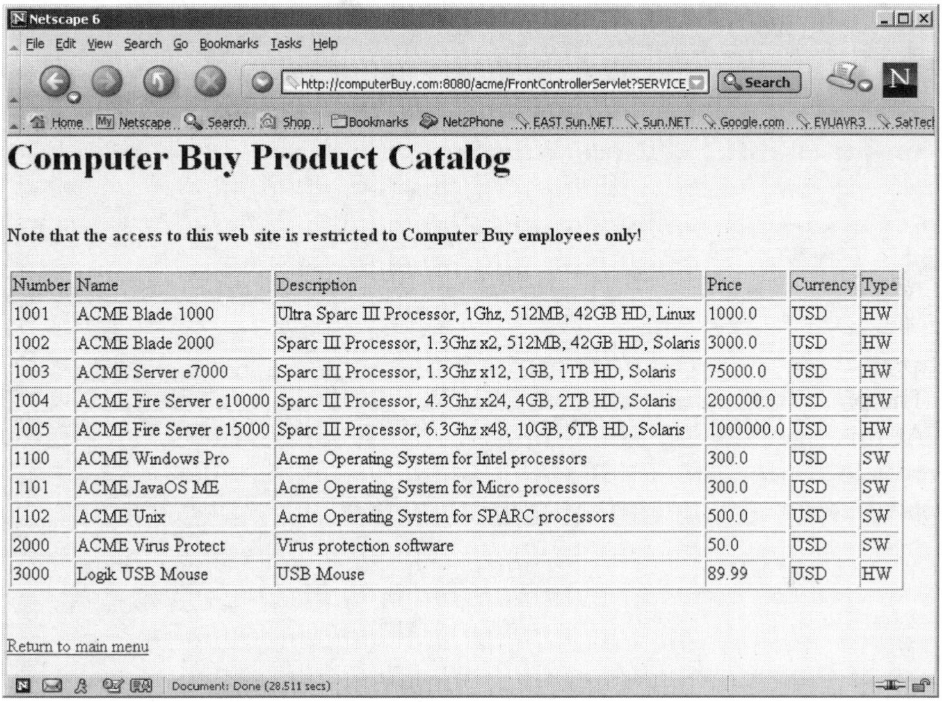

Computer Buy Product Catalog

Note that the access to this web site is restricted to Computer Buy employees only!

Number	Name	Description	Price	Currency	Type
1001	ACME Blade 1000	Ultra Sparc III Processor, 1Ghz, 512MB, 42GB HD, Linux	1000.0	USD	HW
1002	ACME Blade 2000	Sparc III Processor, 1.3Ghz x2, 512MB, 42GB HD, Solaris	3000.0	USD	HW
1003	ACME Server e7000	Sparc III Processor, 1.3Ghz x12, 1GB, 1TB HD, Solaris	75000.0	USD	HW
1004	ACME Fire Server e10000	Sparc III Processor, 4.3Ghz x24, 4GB, 2TB HD, Solaris	200000.0	USD	HW
1005	ACME Fire Server e15000	Sparc III Processor, 6.3Ghz x48, 10GB, 6TB HD, Solaris	1000000.0	USD	HW
1100	ACME Windows Pro	Acme Operating System for Intel processors	300.0	USD	SW
1101	ACME JavaOS ME	Acme Operating System for Micro processors	300.0	USD	SW
1102	ACME Unix	Acme Operating System for SPARC processors	500.0	USD	SW
2000	ACME Virus Protect	Virus protection software	50.0	USD	SW
3000	Logik USB Mouse	USB Mouse	89.99	USD	HW

Return to main menu

Figure 12.27 The ACME product catalog.

The next option enables the user to order some products from the Web site. By selecting the order option, the catalog service is called once again to retrieve the latest catalog information, and then the user is presented with a form that contains the catalog with some more user-specific information entries. The user must fill in the information and submit the form. The form then is converted into a SOAP message and sent over to the JAXM service endpoint. The JAXM service uses SAAJ API to decompose the SOAP message and enters the information provided by the user into the database. The service provider then constructs a new SOAP message, indicating the status of the service transaction.

Figure 12.28 shows a form where the user (buyer) must provide some information.

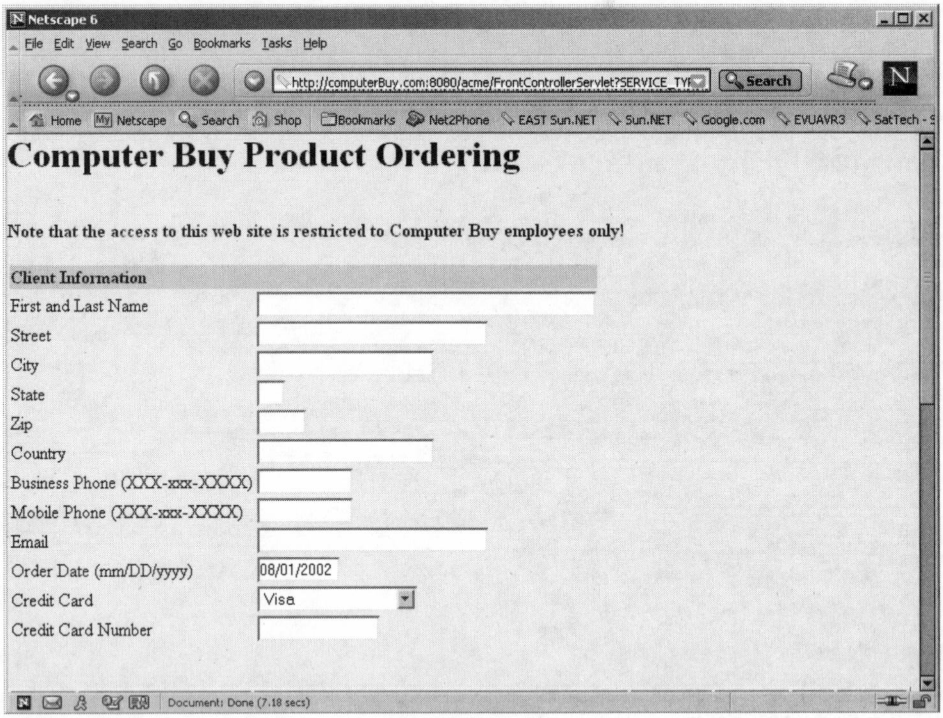

Figure 12.28 Order service user information form.

Right beneath the user information form is the catalog with a quantity column. Figure 12.29 shows a sample form from the ordering page. Here, the Computer Buy employee can specify the amount of product he or she would like to purchase.

This concludes this case study with the JWSDP. This case study has provided many examples but has not taken features, such a JAXM messaging with a provider, Web services security, and Web services using J2EE, into consideration. The majority of these implementations would require additional APIs and containers that are not provided by the package but that could be achieved with minimum efforts.

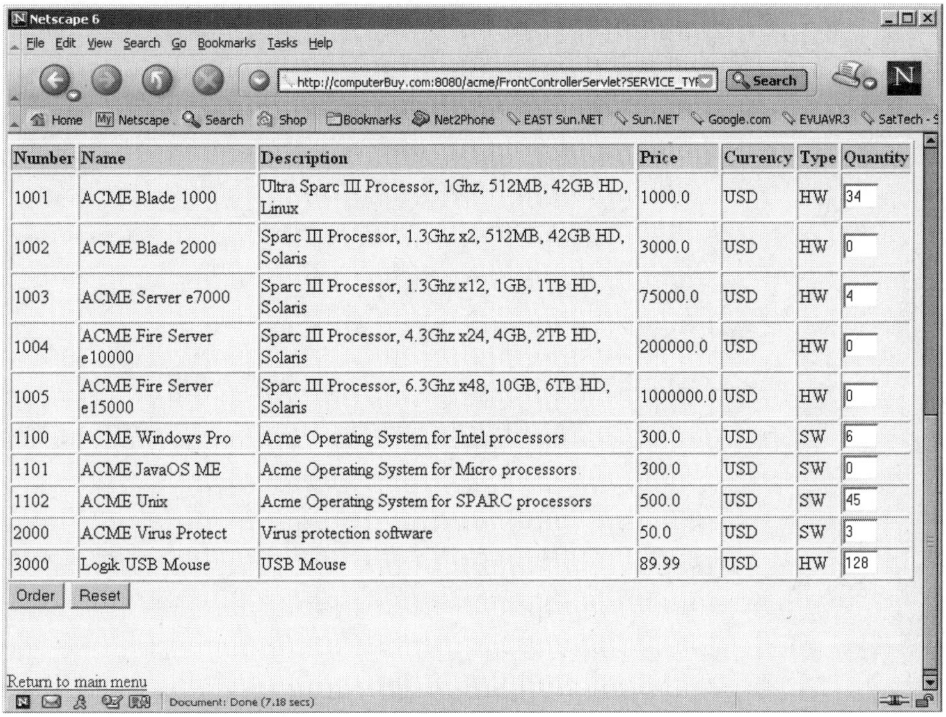
Netscape 6
File Edit View Search Go Bookmarks Tasks Help
http://computerBuy.com:8080/acme/FrontControllerServlet?SERVICE_TY
Search
Home
Netscape
Search
Shop
Bookmarks
Net2Phone
EAST Sun.NET
Sun.NET
Google.com
EVUAVR3
Number Name Description Price Currency Type Quantity
1001 ACME Blade 1000 Ultra Sparc III Processor, 1Ghz, 512MB, 42GB HD, Linux 1000.0 USD HW 34
1002 ACME Blade 2000 Sparc III Processor, 1.3Ghz x2, 512MB, 42GB HD, Solaris 3000.0 USD HW 0
1003 ACME Server e7000 Sparc III Processor, 1.3Ghz x12, 1GB, 1TB HD, Solaris 75000.0 USD HW 4
1004 ACME Fire Server e10000 Sparc III Processor, 4.3Ghz x24, 4GB, 2TB HD, Solaris 200000.0 USD HW 0
1005 ACME Fire Server e15000 Sparc III Processor, 6.3Ghz x48, 10GB, 6TB HD, Solaris 1000000.0 USD HW 0
1100 ACME Windows Pro Acme Operating System for Intel processors 300.0 USD SW 6
1101 ACME JavaOS ME Acme Operating System for Micro processors 300.0 USD SW 0
1102 ACME Unix Acme Operating System for SPARC processors 500.0 USD SW 45
2000 ACME Virus Protect Virus protection software 50.0 USD SW 3
3000 Logik USB Mouse USB Mouse 89.99 USD HW 128
Order
Reset
Return to main menu
Document: Done (7.18 secs)

Figure 12.29 Order service product catalog form.

Summary

This chapter provided us with a case study that brought all of the APIs together in creating a Web service example using the Java Web Services Developer Pack 1.0. This chapter demonstrated how we can implement, deploy, and test a small Web services application by using Java XML APIs. It covered JAXP XML processing, JAX-RPC method invocation, JAXM and SAAJ messagingJSTL, and JAXR publishing and discovery.

The following chapter focuses on Web services security and provides a detailed background on what is required to develop a secure Web services application.

PART

Four

Security in Web Services

CHAPTER 13

Web Services Security

With the explosion of the Web services technologies and its widespread evangelism, the traditional methods of securing your applications are not relevant anymore. Applying the same old mechanisms for establishing trust among Web services or between a Web service and its consumer is no longer appropriate. New challenges have arisen from the very paradigm of Web services, which remain unaddressed by the traditional security methods. Thus, the promoters of Web services needed to figure out some way of securing Web services that can be potentially accessed by a complete stranger over the network. Without the proper security infrastructure in place, the adoption of Web services would not have been possible. This realization gave birth to a plethora of technologies and standards that can be used to secure a Web service.

This chapter provides detailed information on such technologies. Also, this chapter provides in-depth information on how to apply these technologies in order to secure Web services. This chapter is divided into the following sections:

- Challenges of securing Web services
    - Technologies behind securing Web services
    - Rapid-fire cryptography

- XML encryption
- XML signatures
- XML Key Management Specification (XKMS)
- Security Assertions Markup Language (SAML)
- XML Access Control Markup Language (XACML)

Challenges of Securing Web Services

The industry has been talking about Web services for almost three years now. The main benefit of Web services architecture is the ability to deliver integrated, interoperable solutions. Ensuring integrity, confidentiality, and security of a Web service by applying a well-defined security model is important for both the Web services providers and their consumers.

Defining a comprehensive security model for Web services requires the integration of currently available security processes and technologies with the evolving security technologies. It demands the unification of technological concepts relevant to Web services, such as messaging, with process-based concepts, such as policies, trust, and so forth. This unification of technologies and concepts should take place in such a way that it supports the abstraction of functional requirements of application security from the specific implementation mechanisms. For example, a patient viewing his medical records should not be impacted by whether he is using a cell phone or a desktop to do so, as long as the device on which he is viewing his records is able to properly convey security information, such as identity, trust, and so on, to the Web service.

Also, the goal of a Web services security model should be to make it as easy as possible for implementers of Web services to build interoperable security systems based on heterogeneous solutions. For example, the Web services security model should enable the provisioning of authentication services based on any architecture, such as PKI or Kerberos. The idea is to come up with technologies that can leverage upon existing security architectures as well as make them interoperate with one another.

On the other hand, every customer and Web service has its own security requirements based upon their business needs and operational environment. For example, interactions of services and service consumers that take place within an enterprise may focus more on the ease of use, whereas services that are exposed to consumers from outside the enterprise will focus more on the handling of denial-of-service attacks elegantly.

Because the requirements for security architectures is a product of permutations and combinations of various factors, it is all the more sensible to define an approach towards securing Web services where the services can be secured via a set of flexible, interoperable security alternatives, which can be configured, thus enabling a variety of security solutions.

To address these challenges, several initiatives in the area of Web services security are currently underway. Although complete coverage of all the information on security is beyond the scope of this book, this chapter attempts to cover as many of the initiatives as possible, especially the key ones. Keep in mind, though, that there is always more to learn and know!

Technologies behind Securing Web Services

Much work is currently underway on a number of technologies to secure an XML-based Web service. All of these technologies are represented by their respective specifications being developed at several standards bodies, almost in parallel. However, all of these standards efforts are focusing on coming up with a set of specifications that can deliver a complete solution in terms of securing the Web service.

In this chapter, we focus on the following five most prominent technologies in areas of XML security:

- XML Encryption
- XML Signature (XML DSIG)
- Security Assertions Markup Language (SAML, pronounced "sam-el")
- XML Access Control Markup Language (XACML)
- XML Key Management Services (XKMS)

Also, while discussing each of these technologies, we will walk through examples that should give us a good idea on how to use these technologies together in order to secure a real-world Web service.

Before these XML security standards are examined in detail, we need to familiarize ourselves with the important concepts of cryptography that form the foundation of most of these XML security technologies, such as XML Encryption, XML Signature, and XKMS. If you are already well versed with cryptography, you can skip this section.

Rapid-Fire Cryptography

Encryption and digital signatures are a part of a bigger science of cryptography. Cryptography is the art of secret writing, the enciphering and deciphering of messages in secret code or cipher, as many would put it. Usually developers are seen less aware of cryptography. The most common mistake thus made by developers is failing to identify and apply cryptographic techniques to scenarios where they are most required. Cryptography is a huge area, and complete coverage of this topic is beyond the scope of this book; nevertheless, we will examine the basics of cryptography in this section. For those who are interested in further reading on the subject, we recommend Bruce Schneier's book on *Applied Cryptography* (John Wiley & Sons, 1996; see www.counterpane.com/applied.html). This is one of the best books ever written on cryptography.

Four Goals of Cryptography

So why do we need cryptography in software? The answer is to achieve four goals: confidentiality, authentication, integrity, and non-repudiation. The following sections discuss each of these goals.

Confidentiality

Confidentiality deals with ensuring that only authorized parties are able to understand the data. Unauthorized parties may know that the data exists, but they should not be able to understand what the data is. Thus, when the data is transmitted on the wire, unauthorized parties can view the data by sniffing in between, but our data would still remain confidential as long as the sniffers are unable to understand it.

Confidentiality is made possible through encryption. Encryption is the process of converting a particular message into scrambled text, also known as ciphertext, by applying some cryptographic algorithm and secret information. Cryptographic algorithms are known as ciphers, and the pre-encrypted form of the message is known as plaintext. Only people with secret information with which the ciphertext was generated then would be able to unscramble or decrypt the message.

Authentication

Authentication ensures the identity of the party in a given security domain. Usually, this involves having some sort of password or key through which the user would prove his or her identity in a particular security domain. Authentication is extremely important for services to be able to tell to whom all they are providing their services. Likewise, it is very important for consumers of services, so that they know exactly with whom they are interacting. Authentication forms the basis for authorization that deals with managing access to protected resources by an authenticated user based on his or her policies.

Many approaches toward authentication are currently in use. Some of the widely used ones are based on either keys, digital certificates, or passwords.

Integrity

Integrity is about protecting sensitive information from unauthorized modifications. In the case of a message being transmitted on the wire, integrity ensures that the message received by the recipient was the same message that was sent originally by the sender, that the message has not been tampered with since it was sent.

Different hashing algorithms are used to generate a sort of a checksum to guarantee integrity.

Non-repudiation

Repudiation is to refuse to accept something. Non-repudiation is a technique in which one party ensures that another party cannot repudiate, or cannot refuse to accept, a certain act. Non-repudiation forms the basis of electronic commerce. For example, a supplier of raw materials would want to ensure that the customer does not repudiate later its placing of an order for materials!

Digital signatures can be used to provide non-repudiation in computer security systems.

Cryptography Algorithms

Several algorithms can be used to encrypt information. Remember the *secret information* we mentioned earlier that is used to encrypt and decrypt data? That secret information is known as a *key* in cryptography terms. Keys form the basis of many cryptography algorithms. These key-based cryptography algorithms work on the assumption that the security of a crypto- system is resting entirely on the secrecy of a key and not on the secrecy of a algorithm.

Also, the strength of a key against a brute force attack (an attack in which every possible key combination is tried in sequence to decrypt a ciphertext) makes for an important feature of a key. The length of the key indicates the strength of a key. The longer the key length, the more impractical it becomes to successfully carry out a brute force attack because of the sheer number of combinations that are required to get hold of the *right* key to decrypt the data. However, the strength of the key provides for stronger encryption, given the assumption that the key's secrecy has not been compromised. Remember that the key's strength becomes weaker as computing power increases, and the key's length has to keep extending in order to provide the same level of security.

Now, let's take a look at different cryptography algorithms that are used widely.

One-Way Hash Function Algorithms

A one-way hash function computes a fixed-length hash (message digest) for a given message. Hashing is the process of jumbling data, so that the hashed version of the data can be used during transmission/storage processes instead of the clear-text version. The reason it is called one-way is because, given the hash, it is computationally infeasible to find the actual message. Also, one of the characteristics of a one-way hash function is that a slight change in the message would change the resultant hash, thus providing a mechanism akin to checksums in cryptography.

One-way hash algorithms are used widely for hashing passwords and storing their hash rather than storing the passwords in clear text. This way, even if an intruder breaks into the system, he would not get much out of hashed passwords. Finally, at the time of user authentication, the password entered by the user in clear text is hashed and the hash is sent across the network rather than sending the clear text password. So now the receiving end would compare the received hash with the pre-stored hash and see if both these hashes match. If they do, then it is concluded that the user entered a valid password, and hence, should be authenticated. Also, one-way hash functions are used in digital signatures, as we will see later in the chapter.

There are three widely used one-way hash function algorithms: MD4, MD5, and SHA, where MD stands for Message Digest and SHA stands for Secure Hashing Algorithm. MD4 and MD5 produce a 128-bit hash, whereas SHA produces a 160-bit hash.

Symmetric Algorithms (Symmetric Ciphers)

Symmetric ciphers are the simpler of the two classes of key-based cryptography algorithms (the other class is asymmetric ciphers, which we will discuss later). In symmetric ciphers, the same key is used to encrypt and decrypt the message.

Consider this example of Alice and Bob as shown in Figure 13.1, wherein Alice encrypts her message using a key and then sends the message to Bob. Bob would use the same key to decrypt the message. However, in order for Bob to decrypt the message, Alice has to somehow communicate the key to Bob such that the key remains private to them and that nobody else can get their hands on the key. This is the reason why keys used in symmetric ciphers also are known as secret keys.

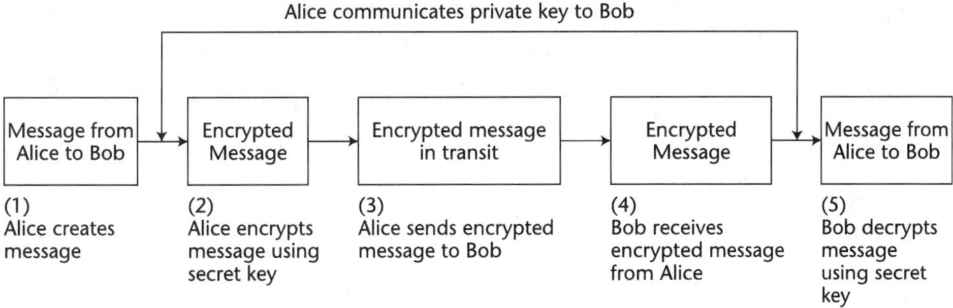

Figure 13.1 Symmetric cryptography.

The most widely deployed algorithm for symmetric encryption until now has been the Data Encryption Standard (DES). DES uses keys that are just 64 bits long. (In reality, only 56 bits are available for storing the actual key bits, because the rest of the eight bits are reserved for parity checks.) The key length that DES encryption supports is an issue, especially taking into consideration the powerful computer resources that are available today if someone intends to break the keys by employing a brute force attack. This shortcoming of DES was identified in 1997 when the efforts to formulate the Advanced Encryption Standard (AES) began. AES (see the National Institute of Standards and Technology [NIST] Web site at http://csrc/nist.gov/encryption/aes) supports three key lengths: 128-bit, 192-bit, and 256-bit. These key lengths have made encryption much more stronger, at least for now.

AES was officially declared a NIST standard in 2001, and hence, is not yet widely adopted. However, until then Triple-DES (3DES) standard serves as an enhanced replacement over DES. Triple-DES uses three 64-bit keys, thus bringing the overall key length to 192 bits. A user provides the entire 192-bit key rather than providing each of the three keys separately to a 3DES algorithm implementation. During the actual encryption of data, the implementation would break the user-given 192-bit key into three subkeys, padding the keys if necessary so that they are 64 bits long. The procedure for encryption is exactly the same as in DES, with the only difference being that encryption is repeated three times (hence the name Triple-DES). The data first is encrypted with the first key, then decrypted with the second key, and then finally encrypted again with the third key. Triple-DES obviously is three times slower than standard DES, but it is much more secure than DES.

Symmetric encryption is quite simple. As is evident from the example illustrated in Figure 13.1, as long as Alice can distribute a key such that the secrecy of the key is maintained, encryption and decryption remain fairly easy. Also, time has shown that symmetric ciphers are faster when it comes to the encryption and decryption of large chunks of data. However, the very simplicity of symmetric ciphers also gives rise to two very common problems:

- How would Alice communicate with large sets of people securely? If Alice has to communicate securely with each of them on an individual basis, she needs to have a corresponding key for each of these parties. This is because no third party can misuse their secret key by tapping into the communication carried between Alice and another of the remaining parties. This leads her to a very difficult management scenario when the number of people communicating securely with her increases.
- Another common problem in symmetric ciphers is the distribution of secret keys. How can Alice and the parties with whom she is communicating exchange secret keys so that their security is not compromised?

These issues are addressed by asymmetric ciphers.

Asymmetric Algorithms (Asymmetric Ciphers)

Asymmetric encryption is different from symmetric encryption in that it uses a pair of keys, instead of a single key, for encryption and decryption. One of the keys in this pair is kept private, known as the *private key*, and the other one is distributed publicly, known as a *public key*. The way asymmetric encryption works is that one of the keys in the Private/Public key pair can *only* decrypt the information encrypted by the other key in the key pair.

Consider again our Alice and Bob example in a new scenario as shown in Figure 13.2. In this example, Alice uses an asymmetric cipher to encrypt the information that she sends to Bob. First, Alice creates a message that she encrypts using Bob's public key. Then, when Bob receives the encrypted message, he uses his secret/private key to decrypt it. As long as Bob's private key has not been compromised, both Bob and Alice can be assured that the message has been communicated securely.

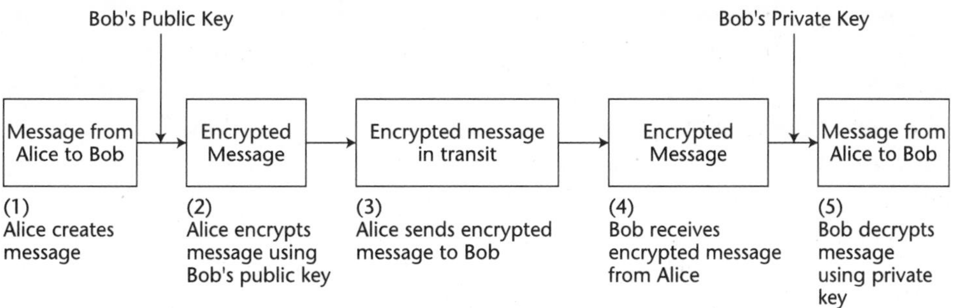

Figure 13.2 Asymmetric cryptography.

This approach towards encryption is definitely more secure and manageable when compared to symmetric ciphers. In asymmetric encryption, Bob does not care whether his public key is available to people whom he does not even know. No one would be able to decrypt the information meant for him (Bob) because they do not have his private key. Similarly, Alice is not worried about somebody else sending her message(s) in the name of Bob, because the moment she is not able to decrypt the message sent by Bob's imposter, she realizes that the person at the other end is not Bob.

Also, for Bob it is much more manageable to carry out secured communication with as many parties as he wants because he does not have to generate separate keys for each of those parties. He simply must give out his public key to everyone interested in encrypting and decrypting the messages sent to/by him. Bob then would use his private key (which is only available to him, unless his private key has been compromised) to encrypt/decrypt the messages at his end. Again, Bob can distribute his public key in anyway he wants, without worrying about the key falling into the wrong hands.

Although, asymmetric ciphers provide a more secured encryption approach, its very complexity results in slow encryption, especially of large data, in practice. Thus, both symmetric and asymmetric encryptions have their own cons: Symmetric encryption is fast especially when encrypting large chunks of data, but then it uses the same key for encrypting and decrypting data. Asymmetric encryption is slow but is much more secure because it uses different keys for encrypting and decrypting data.

Therefore, although using symmetric or asymmetric encryptions alone may sound like a bad idea because of their respective limitations, a hybrid approach actually works much better. According to this hybrid approach, the message first is encrypted using a single-use secret key that has been randomly generated specifically for that particular message. This message-specific key then is encrypted using the recipient's public key, and both the encrypted message and encrypted secret key then are sent to the recipient, who on receipt would use his private key to decrypt the message-specific secret key, thus giving him access to his message. Because the actual message is encrypted using a symmetric cipher, it is much faster. In addition, because the message-specific key is a relatively smaller group of data to encrypt, asymmetric cipher speed limitations are avoided along with the manageability of asymmetric encryption. The Secure Socket Layer (SSL) protocol uses this hybrid approach for encrypting entire sessions between communicating parties, with the only difference being that a single-use secret key (that gets randomly generated) is used for the duration of the entire session instead of for a specific message.

One of the widely used asymmetric algorithms is RSA (Rivest-Shamir-Adelman). Other famously known asymmetric algorithms are Blowfish, Diffie-Helman, and ElGamal (a derivative of Diffie-Helman). Asymmetric ciphers have their applications largely in encryption as well as digital signatures, as we will see in the sections titled *XML Encryption* and *XML Signatures*.

This class of asymmetric ciphers is often referred to as *public key cryptography*. An implementation of public key cryptography along with support for the most-needed management functionalities, such as managing keys, making public keys of users available to others, identity management of users, managing digital certificates (discussed later) of users, and so forth, is known as Public Key Infrastructure (PKI).

Digital Signatures

A user can use a public/private key to sign a message. A digital signature is akin to its physical counterpart, the handwritten signature, in that the sender digitally signs a message so that the recipient can verify that the message really came from the sender. Digital signatures also provide for an integrity check. That is, they ensure that the message has not been tampered with after it was signed.

The process of digitally signing a message involves creating a hash for the message and encrypting this hash using the sender's private key. Finally, the message is sent with the encrypted hash. On receiving the message and the encrypted hash, the recipient would decrypt the hash using the sender's public key. This confirms that the message arrived from the sender and no one else (non-repudiation). Also, by re-computing the hash of the arrived message and then comparing it with the decrypted hash, the recipient can verify that the message has not been changed since it was signed (an integrity check).

Figure 13.3 depicts a scenario where Alice sends her digital signature along with the message that she sends to Bob.

As can be seen from Figure 13.3, a digital signature does not involve encrypting the actual message. The actual message is sent *as is* along with the encrypted hash that serves as the digital signature. Thus, in order to protect the message from eavesdroppers while in transit, anyone can either encrypt the message and then digitally sign it or they can digitally sign the message first and then encrypt it. Either method should be usable. The result is an encrypted message with an encrypted hash that only the intended recipient is able to read. This scenario thus yields confidentiality, non-repudiation, as well as integrity in communication.

Two popular algorithms for digital signatures are RSA and Digital Signature Algorithm (DSA). Support for both of these algorithms is provided in XML Encryption as well as XML Signature specifications.

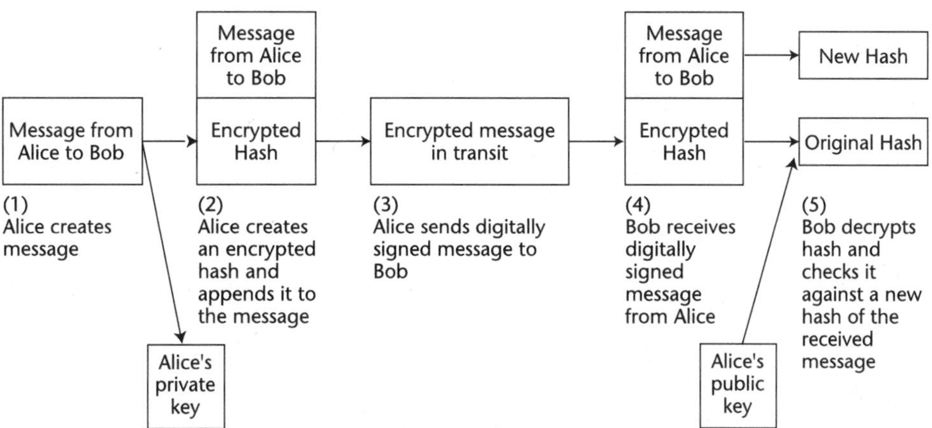

Figure 13.3 Digital signature example.

Digital Certificates

So far we have discussed keys and their role in cryptography. However, a key by itself does not contain any binding information, such as to whom the key belongs to, who issued the key, and the period over which it is valid. Without this supporting information, there is no way that one can link a particular key with its actual owner. Digital certificates provide an exact means to describe this supporting information that binds a user with a specific public key. Putting this into context in our Alice and Bob example, if Alice wanted to get Bob's public key to send him an encrypted message, she would first get hold of Bob's digital certificate that confirms Bob's identity and contains his public key.

Now this raises another issue: How can Alice be sure that she has retrieved Bob's genuine certificate and not that of his imposter? This is when Certificate Authority (CA) comes into picture. The CA acts as a trusted third party for the certificates. A CA is supposed to verify the identity of an individual or business, before it issues a digital certificate. A CA manages the process of certificate creation, issuance, and revocation. At the time of certificate creation, a CA signs the digital certificate with its own private key. So now when Alice receives Bob's digital signature that has been digitally signed by a CA's private key, she takes for granted that the identity of Bob has been verified by that CA and that she is interacting with the genuine Bob and not some imposter.

A few big names in the CA business are Verisign, Thawte, Entrust, and Valicert. Also, the current industry standard for digital certificates is X.509 from CCITT (stands for Commite' Consultatif International de Telecommunications et Telegraphy in French).

XKMS, as we will see later (see *XML Key Management Specification [XKMS]*), deals entirely with the real-time management of certificates and keys.

XML Encryption

The XML Encryption standard is currently been developed at the W3C. W3C officially undertook the XML Encryption activity in late January 2001. At present, XML Encryption is a Candidate Recommendation—that is, it has yet to become a W3C standard. (A specification becomes an official W3C standard once it attains the W3C recommendation status.)

XML Encryption forms the basis of Web services security. This technology is aimed at defining the process of encrypting and decrypting digital content. XML Encryption is so called because it uses XML syntax for representing the content that has been encrypted as well as for representing the information that enables the recipient of the encrypted content to decrypt it. XML Encryption does *not* talk about other security issues such as authentication, authorization, integrity, or trust, although it may form the basis for them. The standard is completely centered on providing confidentiality to the information that has been encrypted.

What XML Encryption Is

The need for an XML Encryption standard was conceived quite some time after the XML Signature Working Group was formed. XML Signature was entirely focused on expressing digital signatures in XML, and hence, precluded any work on Encryption. People soon realized that XML was becoming the language of the Web and that the industry would need mechanisms for not only digitally signing XML entities but also for encrypting them. This realization eventually led to the formation of the W3C XML Encryption Working Group.

Secure Sockets Layer (SSL), developed by Netscape Communications, and Transport Layer Security (TLS), from Internet Engineering Task Force (IETF), are the two protocols that are used typically for transmitting encrypted data apart from providing authentication using digital certificates over TCP/IP. Now XML Encryption is not a replacement to SSL/TLS. Rather, it is focused on providing a feature set that is not provided by SSL/TLS presently. XML Encryption enables the encryption of data at different granularity levels. This means that one can select to encrypt parts of data using XML Encryption. For example, within a particular XML document, one can select to encrypt only a specific XML document element while leaving the rest of the document as it is. This is unlike SSL/TLS, wherein entire groups of data have to be encrypted in order to transport the data through an SSL/TLS channel. This leads us to encrypt even the information that is not security sensitive. Encryption, as it stands, is comparatively an expensive operation and thus should be used judiciously.

Another added value that XML Encryption provides is that it enables the establishment of secure sessions with more than one party. Also, XML Encryption can be used to encrypt both XML as well as non-XML data just like general encryption done using, say, SSL/TLS.

To understand XML Encryption better, let's take a look at the following use case. Consider a transaction that involves three parties: the buyer, the vendor, and the bank. The buyer, Bob, makes a purchase of certain goods at the vendor, Sue Company's Web site, and agrees to pay Sue Company

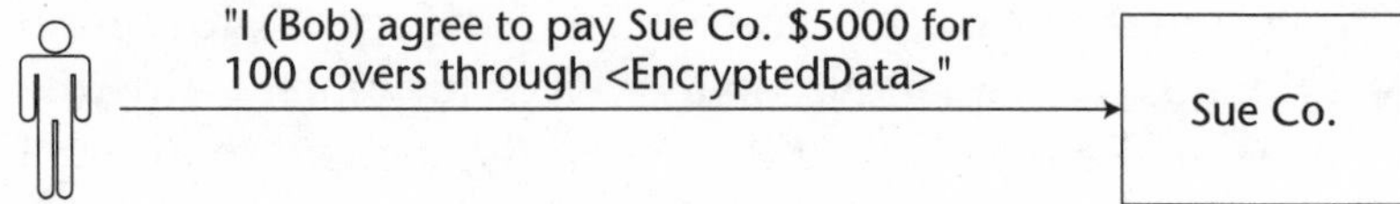

Figure 13.4 Bob encrypts his American Bank account number.

$5,000 in return. In order to make the purchase, Bob supplies all the relevant information to Sue Company. This information also consists of Bob's American Bank account number, which is obviously a sensitive piece of information. As a result, before Bob puts this information on the wire, he needs to ensure that he has encrypted it. Now based on what Bob wants to encrypt, he can either use SSL/TLS or XML Encryption. For example, if Bob wants to encrypt the entire information, he can very well use SSL/TLS. However, if he just wants to keep the account number confidential, then he would want to use XML Encryption to encrypt just that particular piece of information. This use case scenario is illustrated in Figure 13.4.

Once Sue Company had received the purchase order from Bob, it would need to debit the amount for that particular sale from Bob's American Bank account. As a result, Sue Company would need to inform the American Bank to do so. Now, when Sue Company passes this particular information to American Bank, it definitely needs to encrypt the bank account number to keep it confidential from unintended recipients, such that only the American Bank can decrypt it. However, Sue Company also may want to encrypt the information about the specific purchase (that is, that Bob purchased 100 covers), such that American Bank cannot decrypt it. The reason that the Sue Company might want to do this is because of privacy concerns: American Bank does not need to know what specific purchase Bob made. And that is where XML Encryption can play its role. Using XML Encryption technology, the Sue Company can encrypt different pieces of data with different keys so that the recipient can decrypt and thus read only the piece of data that it is supposed to. This scenario is illustrated in Figure 13.5.

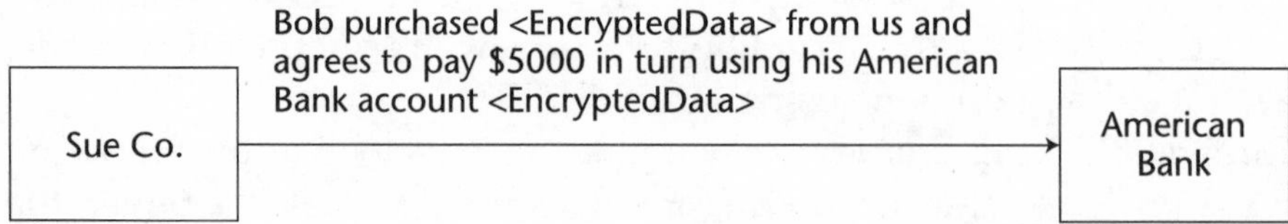

Figure 13.5 Sue Company encrypts purchase information, not to be decrypted by American Bank.

We will discuss the specifics of XML Encryption in the next section, but before that, let's see what implementations of XML Encryption are available out there.

Implementations of XML Encryption

At the time of this book's writing, the following implementations of XML Encryption are available:

XML Security Suite from IBM (www.alphaworks.ibm.com/tech/xmlsecuritysuite). This toolkit consists of implementations for XML Signature, XML Encryption, and XML Access Control Language (now part of the XACML effort).

XML Security Library, Aleksey Sanin (MIT License) (www.aleksey.com/xmlsec/). This is a C library, and hence, practically of no use to Java developers. However, some old C gurus can definitely find this useful. The library has implemented XML Encryption Candidate Recommendation, XML Signature Recommendation, Canonical XML v1.0 W3C Recommendation, and Exclusive XML Canonicalization standards.

Trust Services Integration Kit (TSIK) from Verisign (www.xmltrustcenter.org/developer/verisign/tsik/index.htm). This toolkit provides extensive support for the XKMS standard. However, the support for XML Encryption as well as XML Signatures is quite limited, as of this writing.

Phaos XML (www.phaos.com/e_security/prod_xml.html). This toolkit provides a fairly complete implementation for XML Signature and XML Encryption.

XML Encryption, by Example

With this introduction on XML Encryption, let's take a look at exactly how we could encrypt and decrypt data (XML or non-XML) using the XML Encryption implementation that comes as part of XML Security Suite from IBM. Before we go ahead, please note that at the time of this book's writing, XML Security Suite's implementation of XML Encryption is based on Candidate Recommendation, and hence, if any changes get introduced to the final XML Encryption Recommendation, the implementation would change. Also, the XML Security Suite implementation is not based on standard interfaces for XML Encryption. Java Specification Request (JSR) 106 is supposed to provide a standard Java API for XML Encryption. Follow up on this JSR at www.jcp.org/jsr/detail/106.jsp.

NOTE **You would need to configure XML Security Suite as well as all the software components on which it depends before trying this example on your local system. Further information on configuring XML Security Suite is available as part of the documentation that comes along with its download. XML Security Suite uses Java Cryptography Extension (JCE) as the underlying cryptography framework. Thus, a fair understanding of JCE is required. For beginners, we suggest reading the article written by Raghavan N. Srinivas, a fellow Evangelist at Sun, http://developer.java.sun.com/developer/technical/Articles/Security/optionalpackages/, to get information on JCE and other Java security packages.**

The example we are going to use here deals with encrypting an XML document that is exchanged between two businesses. These two businesses, American Bank and Canadian Bank, collaborate with each other for transferring funds from an account in American Bank to another account in Canadian Bank. American Bank and Canadian Bank achieve a funds transfer with the help of a clearing house, say, ACME Clearing House (ACH, something akin to Automated Clearing House), that coordinates the process of transfer between these two banks. We will not go into details of the funds transfer, however, in order to keep things simple. Figure 13.6 gives a high-level view of the funds transfer process.

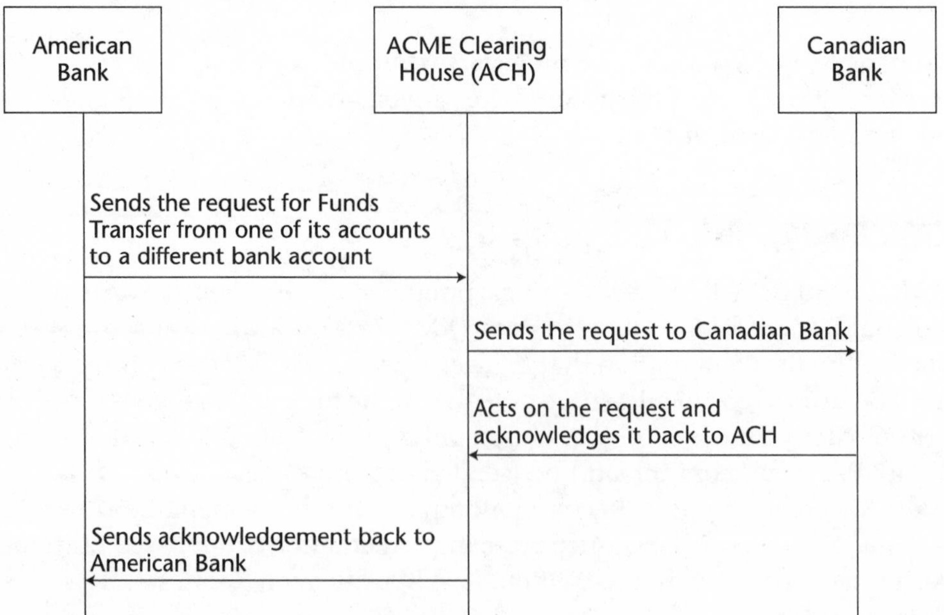

Figure 13.6 High-level view of the funds transfer process.

For accomplishing transfer of funds, we assume that American Bank and Canadian Bank as well as the ACH are hosting Web services and related components at their ends. The following list shows how these Web services would interact with one another as well as with other components of their respective subsystems.

Figure 13.7 depicts an interesting architecture, where we have multiple Web services interacting with one another asynchronously using JAXM. Also within the enterprise, we have Web services interacting with Message Driven Beans (MDBs) by submitting messages to a JMS Destination, say, a queue. The following steps describe the interactions among these Web services:

1. *FT_RequestReceiver_WS* is a JAXM Web service hosted by ACH, which upon receiving a SOAP message about transferring funds from *FT_SubmitRequest_ACH_WS* Web service hosted by American Bank sends a message to an internal JMS queue.
2. *FT_ProcessRequest_MDB* is an MDB that picks up the message from this internal queue. It converts the JMS message to an appropriate SOAP request and submits it to *FT_RequestReceiver_ACH_WS* JAXM Web service hosted by Canadian Bank.
3. On receiving the SOAP request, *FT_RequestReceiver_ACH_WS* posts a JMS message to a queue. This JMS message is received and processed by the fulfillment MDB, *FT_Fullfillment_ACH_MDB*.
4. Once the funds transfer request has been fulfilled, this MDB would send a SOAP message using JAXM APIs to the *FT_Notification_WS* Web service hosted by ACH, which in turn would send a SOAP message to *FT_RequestStatusReceiver_ACH_WS*, hosted by American Bank. This SOAP message notifies American Bank that the requested funds transfer has taken place.

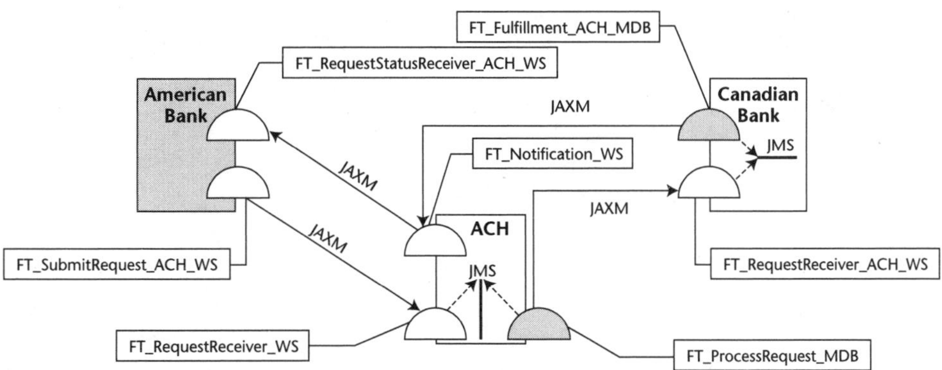

Figure 13.7 Web Services involved in the funds transfer process.

Throughout this book, we will follow up with this example, wherever it makes sense. For now, however, we will limit our scope to just encrypting the XML document that is sent as an attachment to the SOAP request made by Web service *FT_SubmitRequest_ACH_WS*, which is hosted by American Bank. This SOAP request is received by *FT_RequestReceiver_WS* Web service, which is hosted by ACH. The XML document attached to this SOAP request, named `transfer_details.xml`, consists of information about the source and target bank accounts along with other transfer-related details. Listing 13.1 is a simple version of `transfer_details.xml`.

```
<?xml version="1.0" encoding="UTF-8" ?>
<Transfer_Details>
    <Accounts>
        <Source>
            <Holder_Name>
                John Smith
            </Holder_Name>

            <Number>
                1234352 56783341 90234532
            </Number>
        </Source>

        <Target>
            <Holder_Name>
                Mary Smith
            </Holder_Name>

            <Number>
                5332234 32345532 55532158
            </Number>
        </Target>
    </Accounts>

    <Transfer_Amount Currency="USD">
        3000
    </Transfer_Amount>
</Transfer_Details>
```

Listing 13.1 `Transfer_details.xml.`

So now, before putting this XML document on the wire as a payload to a SOAP request message, American Bank needs to encrypt the information pertaining specifically to the source and target bank accounts, represented by the `<Accounts>` element and its subelements. However, before American Bank uses XML Encryption to do so, it needs to ensure that ACH DOES understand the messages that are encrypted using the XML Encryption syntax and that ACH is able to successfully *process* the received the XML document consisting of encrypted data, so that the encrypted data can be decrypted and read successfully.

Taking the given scenario one step further, assume that both American Bank and ACH use a utility class, say `EncryptDecrypt`, to respectively encrypt and decrypt the `<Accounts>` element in `transfer_details.xml`. Thus, both Web services, *FT_SubmitRequest_ACH_WS* hosted by American Bank and *FT_RequestReceiver_WS* hosted by ACH, use `EncryptDecrypt` for performing encryption and decryption functions. Hence now, our interest lies specifically in knowing how `EncryptDecrypt` has been implemented. Because we already know how to implement JAXM Web services by now, to keep this example simple we will not go into the details of how *FT_SubmitRequest_ACH_WS* and *FT_RequestReceiver_WS* Web services have been implemented. Rather we will demonstrate the encryption and decryption of the `<Accounts>` element with the help of a Java main class, say `EncryptionTest.java`. This Java main class in turn uses the `EncryptDecrypt` utility class to perform the actual encryption and decryption. Figure 13.8 shows a UML class diagram depicting the association between the `EncryptionTest` and `EncryptDecrypt` classes.

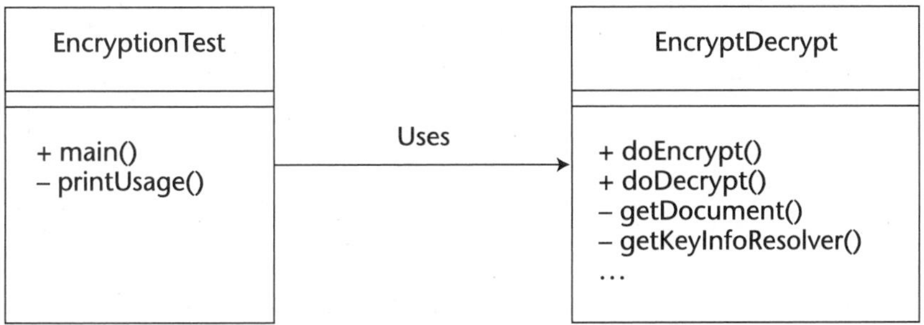

Figure 13.8 EncryptionTest and EncryptDecrypt class diagram.

Now, EncryptionTest takes a couple of arguments as input:

<option> This argument requires the mode in which we want to use EncryptionTest—that is, encrypt or decrypt.

<keyinfo> This argument takes the name of the XML document consisting of information on the key, such as key alias, name of the keystore storing the key(s), password for the keystore, type of keystore (JKS or JCEKS), and private key password. Key(s) specified in a keyinfo XML document would be used to encrypt and decrypt the data. The structure of this XML document is totally specific to IBM XML Security Suite. In our case, this argument would be American_Bank_keyinfo.xml while encrypting and ACH_keyinfo.xml while decrypting. American_Bank_keyinfo.xml is shown in Listing 13.2. It specifies the information of the RSA public key of ACH that American Bank would use to encrypt the <Accounts> element.

```
<?xml version="1.0" encoding="UTF-8"?>
<keyinfo>
     <keystore>
          <name>American_Bank_keystore</name>
          <type>jceks</type>
          <password>keystorepwd</password>
     </keystore>

     <keys>
          <key>
               <alias>ACH</alias>
               <password/>
          </key>
     </keys>
</keyinfo>
```

Listing 13.2 American_Bank_keyinfo.xml.

Note that here we would not be specifying the key password because American Bank uses the public key of ACH to encrypt the data and not the private key, and hence, no password is required. Whereas ACH's ACH_keyinfo.xml would be used to get information about the keys that ACH uses to decrypt and to carry key password information. This is because ACH uses a private key to decrypt the data, and hence, the password is required.

<source> This argument takes the name of the XML document consisting of the element to be encrypted, that is, `transfer_details.xml` in our case.

<Xpath> This argument takes the XPath expression of the element in the `<Source>` XML document that we want to encrypt. For example, because we want to encrypt the `<Accounts>` element in `target_details.xml`, we will give the following XPath expression: `//*[name()='Accounts']`.

<Template> This argument will take the name of the XML document that carries the template for encrypting the data. It will consist of all sorts of information pertaining to encryption, such as the information of the key used for encryption, algorithms used for encrypting data, and so forth. Also, note that using templates for supplying encryption-related information is specific to XML Security Suite only.

Taking a good look at this template document should give us several ideas about XML encryption syntax. For our example, we will pass the encryption template that is present in the `encryption_template.xml` document. Listing 13.3 shows how our encryption template looks.

```
<?xml version="1.0" encoding="UTF-8"?>
<EncryptedData Id="ed1" Type="http://www.w3.org/2001/04/xmlenc#Element"
xmlns="http://www.w3.org/2001/04/xmlenc#">

     <EncryptionMethod
     Algorithm="http://www.w3.org/2001/04/xmlenc#tripledes-cbc"/>

     <ds:KeyInfo xmlns="http://www.w3.org/2000/09/xmldsig#">

          <EncryptedKey xmlns="http://www.w3.org/2001/04/xmlenc#">

               <EncryptionMethod Algorithm=
               "http://www.w3.org/2001/04/xmlenc#rsa-1_5"/>

               <ds:KeyInfo
               xmlns="http://www.w3.org/2000/09/xmldsig#">
                    <KeyName>ACH</KeyName>
               </KeyInfo>

               <CipherData>
                    <CipherValue/>               </CipherData>
          </EncryptedKey>     </KeyInfo>     <CipherData>
<CipherValue/>     </CipherData></EncryptedData>
```

Listing 13.3 `Encryption_template.xml`.

So now let us take a look at what these elements represent:

<EncryptedData> This element is the core element in the XML Encryption syntax. It becomes the document root of the XML document carrying the encryption information.

<EncryptionMethod> This element specifies the algorithm that is used for encrypting the data. This is an optional element. However, when not present, the recipient of an XML encryption document should know the algorithm that was used in advance, to successfully decrypt the encrypted data. In our template, we specify that we will be using a 3DES algorithm for encrypting data.

<ds:KeyInfo> As can be seen from the corresponding namespace, this element belongs to the XML Signature namespace. XML Encryption specification leverages on an XML Signature standard for representing key-related information. The reason is because this work was already done in XML Signature by the time XML Encryption effort began.

<ds:KeyInfo> This element enables recipients to obtain the key needed to decrypt data or to perform any other kind of cryptographic function, such as validating a digital signature, for example. In short, the rest of the XML security specifications use this XML "type" to leverage key identification and exchange semantics. However, the `<ds:KeyInfo>` element does not represent any information that can help the recipient establish trust in this key or that gives hints to the recipient about the validity of the binding information for the key. For these facilities, Web services will have to rely upon technology such as XKMS.

This element can contain names (aliases in JCE terms) of keys, key values, certificates, and related data. This element is optional in the XML Encryption syntax. This means that an XML Encryption document may not carry a `<ds:KeyInfo>` element, in which case, the recipient should have some other means of getting hold of key to the decrypt (/encrypt). The recipient may use XKMS to get key information, or both of the parties can manually exchange keys for encryption and decryption or use some key exchange protocol.

<EncryptedKey> This is an extension to the `<ds:KeyInfo>` element. This element is used to transport encrypted keys from the sender to the recipient(s). In our case, the `<EncryptedKey>` element represents the encrypted 3DES key. It also specifies the algorithm using the 3DES key that was encrypted as RSA 1.5. This means that an RSA key was used to encrypt this key. The child `<ds:KeyInfo>` element further specifies the name of the RSA key that was used to encrypt the 3DES key. Thus, the recipient should have the RSA key in advance to decrypt this encrypted key. Also, the `<CipherData>` element represents the encrypted data as a sequence of base64-encoded octets.

`<CipherData>`. This is a mandatory element, which provides encrypted data. It either contains the encrypted octet sequence as base64-encoded text of the `<CipherValue>` element, or it provides a reference to an external location where an encrypted octet sequence may be present. It references this external location via a `<CipherReference>` element.

These were all the parameters that we needed to specify for running `EncryptionTest`, Java's main application for encrypting and decrypting. Now, we will begin with examining the process for encrypting the `<Accounts>` element, and then we will proceed with decryption.

Encrypting <Accounts> XML Element

The following outlines the steps carried out for executing `EncryptionTest` so as to encrypt the `<Accounts>` element.

Generating a Key Pair

We will need to create a public key that American Bank will use to encrypt the data that eventually gets sent to ACH's Web service. As is specified in `encryption_template.xml`, an RSA key pair is required for both encryption and decryption. We will use Sun's Keytool utility to create this RSA key pair. Keytool is a key and certificate management utility that ships with the J2SE platform. For more information on this utility, refer to http://java.sun.com/j2se/1.3/docs/tooldocs/solaris/keytool.html. The following command is executed to create a public key that would be used by American Bank to encrypt the data it sends to ACH. Note that the private key corresponding to this public key must be available with ACH in order to decrypt data.

```
keytool -genkey -alias ACH -keyalg RSA -dname "CN=ACH_Emp, O=ACH, C=US"
-keypass keypwd -keystore American_Bank_keystore -storepass keystorepwd
```

This command creates an RSA (as specified by the `-keyalg` argument) public key pair with alias ACH. This is the alias that we specified in the `<ds:KeyName>` element in our `encryption_template.xml`. Keytool also will create a certificate containing the newly generated public key with the domain name as specified by `-dname` argument. Also, the command specifies a password for the private key of this key pair. The password we gave it is `keypwd`. Finally, we specify the name of the keystore as `American_Bank_keystore`, wherein the RSA key pair, as well as the certificate, would reside. Note that we also can use IBM's `KeyGenerator` utility that comes along with XML Security Suite to achieve the same results. Upon execution of the previous `Keytool` command, we should be able to see a newly created keystore file named `American_Bank_keystore` in the current directory.

Execute EncryptionTest with the -encrypt Option

The following shows what our command line would look like when running `EncryptionTest`, assuming that all the required JARS are available in the CLASSPATH.

```
> java jws.ch13.EncryptionTest -encrypt American_Bank_keyinfo.xml
transfer_details.xml "//*[name()='Accounts']" encryption_template.xml
```

Upon successful execution of `EncryptionTest`, we should be able to see an encrypted `transfer_details.xml` on the standard output. Figure 13.9 shows the screenshot of a standard output.

As we can see from the output in Figure 13.9, the `<Transfer_Details>` element has not been encrypted and thus appears in clear text. Also, the `<Transfer_Amount>` element has not been encrypted and thus also can be seen in clear text. Only the `<Accounts>` element has been encrypted.

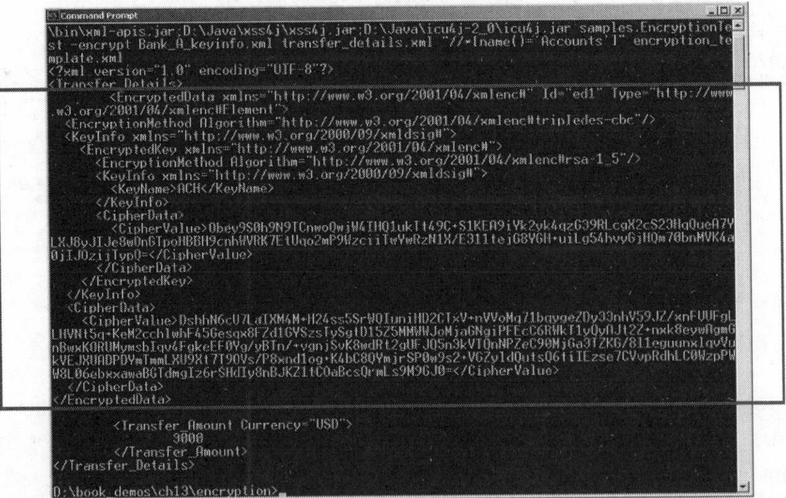

Command Prompt
\bin\xml-apis.jar;D:\Java\xss4j\xss4j.jar;D:\Java\icu4j-2_0\icu4j.jar samples.EncryptionTest -encrypt Bank_A_keyinfo.xml transfer_details.xml "//*[name()='Accounts']" encryption_template.xml
<?xml version="1.0" encoding="UTF-8"?>
<Transfer_Details>
<EncryptedData xmlns="http://www.w3.org/2001/04/xmlenc#" Id="ed1" Type="http://www.w3.org/2001/04/xmlenc#Element">
<EncryptionMethod Algorithm="http://www.w3.org/2001/04/xmlenc#tripledes-cbc"/>
<KeyInfo xmlns="http://www.w3.org/2000/09/xmldsig#">
<EncryptedKey xmlns="http://www.w3.org/2001/04/xmlenc#">
<EncryptionMethod Algorithm="http://www.w3.org/2001/04/xmlenc#rsa-1_5"/>
<KeyInfo xmlns="http://www.w3.org/2000/09/xmldsig#">
<KeyName>ACH</KeyName>
</KeyInfo>
<CipherData>
</CipherData>
</EncryptedKey>
</KeyInfo>
<CipherData>
</CipherData>
</EncryptedData>
<Transfer_Amount Currency="USD">
3000
</Transfer_Amount>
</Transfer_Details>
D:\book_demos\ch13\encryption>

Figure 13.9 EncryptionTest -encrypt output.

The encrypted output would get stored in a file on your system with the name transfer_details_encrypted.xml. The *FT_SubmitRequest_ACH_WS* Web service of American Bank would send this transfer_details_encrypted.xml as a SOAP attachment to the request it sends to the *FT_RequestReceiver_WS* JAXM service of ACH. Once ACH receives the SOAP request and strips out the attachment transfer_details_encrypted.xml, it will have to decrypt the <Accounts> element. To demonstrate this functionality, we will again use the EncryptionTest Java main application with the -decrypt option.

Decrypting the <Accounts> XML Element

The following steps are carried out for executing EncryptionTest so as to decrypt the <Accounts> element.

Generating a Key Pair

We will create the RSA key pair whose private key will be used by ACH for decrypting the document. Again, we will use the Keytool utility to generate an RSA key pair with alias ACH. This time we will store the key pair and the corresponding certificate in a file named ACH_keystore in the local directory. The command line arguments that we pass to Keytool as follows:

```
> keytool -genkey -alias ACH -keyalg RSA -dname "CN=ACH_Emp, O=ACH,
C=US" -keypass keypwd -keystore ACH_keystore -storepass keystorepwd
```

Execute EncryptionTest with the -decrypt Option

Now, we are all set for decryption. The following are the command line arguments that we will pass to EncryptionTest in order to decrypt transfer_details_encrypted.xml:

```
> java jws.ch13.EncryptionTest -decrypt ACH_keyinfo.xml
transfer_details_encrypted.xml "//*[namespace-
uri()='http://www.w3.org/2001/04/xmlenc#' and local-
name()='EncryptedData']"
```

Note that this time we supply ACH_keyinfo.xml as the key information file. Also, the XPath expression now points to <EncryptedData> element(s) in the source-encrypted document, whose name is passed as one of the arguments (transfer_details_encrypted.xml). Output of this execution will be the decrypted <Accounts> element as shown in Figure 13.10.

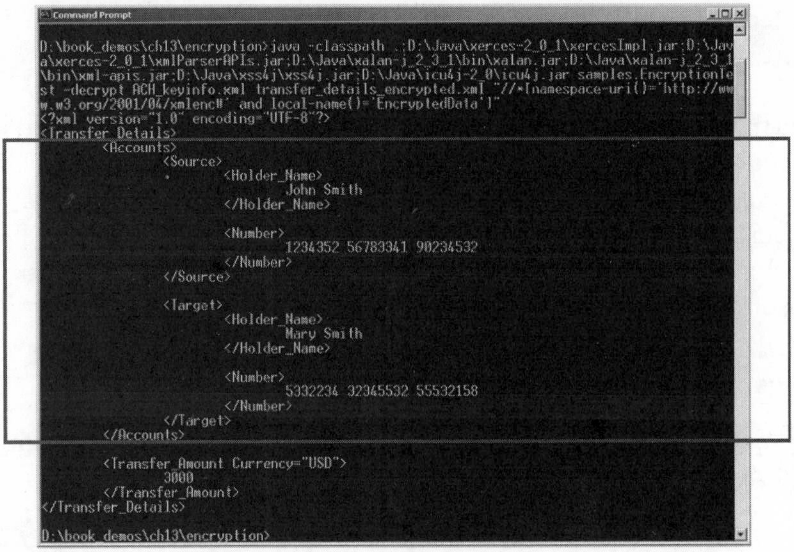

```
Command Prompt

D:\book_demos\ch13\encryption>java -classpath .;D:\Java\xerces-2_0_1\xercesImpl.jar;D:\Jav
a\xerces-2_0_1\xmlParserAPIs.jar;D:\Java\xalan-j_2_3_1\bin\xalan.jar;D:\Java\xalan-j_2_3_1
\bin\xml-apis.jar;D:\Java\xss4j\xss4j.jar;D:\Java\icu4j-2_0\icu4j.jar samples.EncryptionTe
st -decrypt ACH_keyinfo.xml transfer_details_encrypted.xml "//*[namespace-uri()='http://ww
w.w3.org/2001/04/xmlenc#' and local-name()='EncryptedData']"
<?xml version="1.0" encoding="UTF-8"?>
<Transfer_Details>
        <Accounts>
                <Source>
                        <Holder_Name>
                                John Smith
                        </Holder_Name>

                        <Number>
                                1234352 56783341 90234532
                        </Number>
                </Source>

                <Target>
                        <Holder_Name>
                                Mary Smith
                        </Holder_Name>

                        <Number>
                                5332234 32345532 55532158
                        </Number>
                </Target>
        </Accounts>

        <Transfer_Amount Currency="USD">
                3000
        </Transfer_Amount>
</Transfer_Details>

D:\book_demos\ch13\encryption>
```

Figure 13.10 EncryptionTest -decrypt output.

This is how we use `EncryptionTest` and the `EncryptDecrypt` utility. The next section examines the code of both of these Java classes, present in `EncryptionTest.java`.

Programming Steps for Encryption and Decryption

The following shows the required imports in `EncryptionTest.java`:

```
package jws.ch13;

/* Standard Java imports
 */
import java.io.*;
import java.security.*;
import java.security.cert.*;
import java.util.*;

/* JCE, JAXP imports
 */
import javax.crypto.*;
import javax.xml.parsers.*;
import javax.xml.transform.*;

/* IBM XML Security Suite - XML Encryption imports
 */
```

```
import com.ibm.xml.enc.*;
import com.ibm.xml.enc.type.*;
import com.ibm.xml.enc.util.*;
import com.ibm.dom.util.DOMUtil;

/* Apache Xerces, Xalan, XPath, DOM and SAX imports
 */
import org.apache.xerces.parsers.*;
import org.apache.xml.serialize.*;
import org.apache.xpath.*;
import org.w3c.dom.*;
import org.xml.sax.*;
```

Now, `EncryptionTest.java` is the Java main class. This class parses the command line arguments and appropriately calls the `doEncrypt()` or `doDecrypt()` methods on the `EncryptDecrypt` utility class from `main()` as shown:

```
public class EncryptionTest
{
     public static void main(String[] args) throws Exception
     {
          //Check to see if the program is supposed to do encryption
          if (sMode.equals("-encrypt") && args.length == 5)
          {
               EncryptDecrypt objEncryptDecrypt =
               new EncryptDecrypt();

               objEncryptDecrypt.doEncrypt(args[1], args[2],
               args[3], args[4], true);
          }
          else if (sMode.equals("-decrypt") && args.length == 4)
          {
               EncryptDecrypt objEncryptDecrypt =
               new EncryptDecrypt();

               objEncryptDecrypt.doDecrypt(args[1], args[2],
               args[3], true);
          }
          else
          {
               printUsage();
          }
     }
}
```

The real fun is in understanding how the `EncryptDecrypt` class works. More importantly, how do the `doEncrypt()` and `doDecrypt()` methods work? Let's begin by understanding the `doEncrypt()` method first.

The first API call in doEncrypt() is for creating the EncryptionContext object. EncryptionContext is the core API in XML Security Suite's implementation, and it maintains the context object for encryption. This context object manages information about encryption, such as the encryption algorithm used, the encryption key used, the data that needs to be encrypted, and the encryption template that is in use. Once we get the encryption context, we create an algorithm factory instance and set it on the encryption context. This factory object will be used by the context when the actual encryption takes place for creating instances of algorithm objects. These calls are as shown in the following code:

```
public void doEncrypt (String sKeyInformationXMLDocumentName, String
sSourceXMLDocumentName, String sXPathExpressionForNodeToEncrypt,
String sTemplateXMLDocumentName) throws Exception
{
     EncryptionContext objEncryptionContext =
     new EncryptionContext();

     AlgorithmFactoryExtn objAlgorithmFactoryExtn =
     new AlgorithmFactoryExtn();

     objEncryptionContext.setAlgorithmFactory
     (objAlgorithmFactoryExtn);
```

Once we set the factory object, we will have to create the Keyinfo and KeyInfoResolver objects. Keyinfo is the Java type representation of the *_keyinfo.xml document that we pass as a command line argument to EncryptionTest.java. This *_keyinfo.xml document consists of information such as the keystore name where the key is stored, the password for the private key, the key alias, and the type of JCE keystore (JKS or JCEKS). The Keyinfo object then is used to initialize the KeyInfoResolver object.

In order to initialize the KeyInfoResolver object, we make use of getKeyInfoResolver(), which is a user-defined method. This method helps to initialize the KeyInfoResolver object. As the name suggests, the KeyInfoResolver object resolves keys from information that is made available through *_keyinfo.xml. It also ensures that the type of keys match with the type of the encryption algorithm. For example, it checks whether an RSA key pair is available if the specified encryption algorithm is RSA 1.5. Once the KeyInfoResolver object has been initialized, we set it on the EncryptionContext. The code for this API call is as follows:

```
Keyinfo objKeyinfo = getKeyinfo(sKeyInformationXMLDocumentName);

KeyInfoResolver objKeyInfoResolver = getKeyInfoResolver
```

```
(objKeyinfo, objAlgorithmFactoryExtn);

objKeyInfoResolver.setOperationMode
(KeyInfoResolver.ENCRYPT_MODE);

objEncryptionContext.setKeyInfoResolver(objKeyInfoResolver);
```

Now we will get hold of the data that we have to encrypt. As one of the arguments to `EncryptionTest`, the name of the source XML document is already available. What we will now do is to de-serialize this XML document to a DOM tree—that is, we want to undergo DOM parsing. To do this, we will use a user-defined method called `getDocument()` that would basically parse the source XML document into a DOM tree. Once that is done, we will select all of the nodes that match the XPath expression given as an argument to `EncryptionTest`. In our case, this XPath expression will refer to the `<Accounts>` element and its sub-elements:

```
Document objDocument = getDocument(sSourceXMLDocumentName);

NodeList objNodeList = XPathAPI.selectNodeList
(objDocument, sXPathExpressesionForNodeToEncrypt);
```

We also have to get the document element of the encryption template XML document (`encryption_template.xml`) that we passed as an argument:

```
Element objTemplateDocumentElement =
getDocument(sTemplateXMLDocumentName).getDocumentElement();
```

Next, we traverse through all of the nodes in the `NodeList` object and encrypt each of them one by one, as shown in the following code:

```
for (int i = 0, l = objNodeList.getLength(); i < l; i++)
{
     Node objNode = objNodeList.item(i);

     if (objNode.getNodeType() == Node.ELEMENT_NODE)
     {
          objEncryptionContext.setData((Element)objNode);

          objEncryptionContext.setEncryptedType((Element)
          objTemplateDocumentElement.cloneNode
          (true), null, null, null);

          objEncryptionContext.encrypt();
          objEncryptionContext.replace();
     }
}
```

setData() is called on EncryptionContext to set the data for encryption. All the information pertaining to the algorithm and the key is made available from the template by calling setEncryptedType() with a method argument as the document element of the encryption template XML document. Then, we finally encrypt the document by calling encrypt(), and we replace the original element in the DOM tree with the encrypted one by calling replace().

Now, we have to serialize this DOM tree consisting of encrypted nodes back to XML and store it into a file on the local disk—say, transfer_details_encrypted.xml. We achieve this by calling a user-defined method named writeDocumentToFile(). This method uses Xalan's XMLSerializer API to serialize a DOM tree to XML:

```
writeDocumentToFile(objDocument, sEncryptedXMLDocumentName);
```

In addition, we also display the serialized, encrypted document to standard output. For this, we will call a user-defined method named writeDocumentToStandardOutput():

```
writeDocumentToStandardOutput(objDocument);
```

This is all that is required to encrypt an <Accounts> element in a transfer_details.xml document. To take a look at encrypted transfer_details.xml, open transfer_details_encrypted.xml in your local directory.

Now, let's see how we can decrypt transfer_details_encrypted.xml. Again, in order to decrypt, EncryptionTest must call the doDecrypt() method on the EncryptDecrypt utility class, passing it over all of the arguments it received from the command line. Our doDecrypt() method is shown in the following code. The first thing we do in doDecrypt() is to get hold of the DecryptionContext object. This core object maintains the information necessary for making decryption possible:

```
public void doDecrypt (String sKeyInformationXMLDocumentName, String
sEncryptedXMLDocumentName, String  sXPathExpressionForNodeToDecrypt)
throws Exception
{
     DecryptionContext objDecryptionContext =
     new DecryptionContext();
```

Next, we create an instance of `AlgorithmFactory` and set it on the decryption context. Then, we resolve the key information specified by `ACH_keyinfo.xml` to the actual keys by creating a `KeyInfoResolver` object and setting it on the `DecryptionContext`, as shown in the following code.

```
AlgorithmFactoryExtn objAlgorithmFactoryExtn =
new AlgorithmFactoryExtn();

objDecryptionContext.setAlgorithmFactory (objAlgorithmFactoryExtn);

Keyinfo objKeyinfo = getKeyinfo (sKeyInformationXMLDocumentName);

KeyInfoResolver objKeyInfoResolver = getKeyInfoResolver
(objKeyinfo, objAlgorithmFactoryExtn);

objKeyInfoResolver.setOperationMode (KeyInfoResolver.DECRYPT_MODE);

objDecryptionContext.setKeyInfoResolver (objKeyInfoResolver);
```

Now, we de-serialize the encrypted `transfer_details_encrypted.xml` document to the DOM tree, and we finally select all of the nodes into a `NodeList` object by giving the appropriate XPath expression:

```
Document objDocument = getDocument (sEncryptedXMLDocumentName);

NodeList objNodeList = XPathAPI.selectNodeList
(objDocument, sXPathExpressesionForNodeToDecrypt);
```

Now we will traverse through the selected `NodeList` and decrypt all the encrypted elements one by one:

```
for (int i = 0, l = objNodeList.getLength(); i < l; i++)
{
     Node objNode = objNodeList.item(i);

     if (objNode.getNodeType() == Node.ELEMENT_NODE)
     {
          Element objElementToDecrypt = (Element)objNode;

          if (EncryptedData.isOfType(objElementToDecrypt))
          {
               objDecryptionContext.setEncryptedType
```

```
                    (objElementToDecrypt, null, null, null);

                    objDecryptionContext.decrypt();
                    objDecryptionContext.replace();
            }
        }
    }
```

Once we decrypt all the elements, we then would display the decrypted `transfer_details.xml` document on the standard output:

```
writeDocumentToStandardOutput(objDocument);
```

With this, we are finished writing our encryption and decryption code.

This example, along with the source code and readme.txt consisting of setup instructions, can be downloaded from Wiley's Web site at www.wiley.com/compbooks/nagappan.

By now, we should understand the basics of XML Encryption. We still need to cover a few things with respect to XML Encryption, such as canonicalization. However, this feature applies to XML Signatures as well, so we will talk about it in the next section.

XML Signatures

The XML Signature specification, in its very simplest form, provides a mechanism for applying digital signatures to XML documents and other Internet resources and encoding those signatures as XML. The goal behind using XML in digital signatures is to provide strong integrity for message authentication, signer authentication, and non-repudiation services for data of any type, no matter if this data is located within the XML document that bears the digital signature or elsewhere.

The XML Signature specification has been finalized and was developed at W3C. More information on XML Signature and its related specifications can be found at www.w3.org/Signature.

Now, let's begin by looking at the different types of XML Signatures.

Types of XML Signatures

There are three types of signatures supported by the XML Signature specification: enveloped signatures, enveloping signatures, and detached signatures. Each of these types will be discussed in the following sections.

Enveloped Signatures

With enveloped signatures, the signature is over the XML content that contains the signature as an element. The root XML document element provides the content. Obviously, enveloped signatures must take care not to include their own value in the calculation of the signature value. Listing 13.4 shows an example of an enveloped signature.

```
<doc Id="doc0">
     <elem/>
     <Signature>
          ...
          <Reference URI="doc0"/>
          ...
     </Signature>
</doc>
```

Listing 13.4 An enveloped signature structure.

Enveloping Signatures

With enveloping signatures, the signature is over the content found within an `<Object>` element of the signature itself. The `<Object>` or its content is identified via a `<Reference>` element through a URI or a transform, in the signature. Listing 13.5 is an example of an enveloping signature.

```
<Signature>
     ...
     <Reference URI = "#ID0"/>
     ...
     <Object Id="ID0">
          <doc/>
               <elem/>
          </doc>
     </Object>
</Signature>
```

Listing 13.5 An enveloping signature structure.

Detached Signatures

With detached signatures, the signature is over the content external to the `<Signature>` element, and this external content is identified via a URI or transform. Consequently, the signature is "detached" from the content it signs. This definition typically applies to separate data objects, but it also includes the instance where the `Signature` and data object reside within the same XML document but are sibling elements. Listing 13.6 is an example of a detached signature.

```
<doc>
     <Signature>
          ...
          <Reference URI=
          "http://www.ach.com/fundstransfer/fundstransferproc.html"/>
          ...
     </Signature>
     <elem/>
</doc>
```

Listing 13.6 A detached signature structure.

XML Signature Syntax

Now, let's take a look at some of the common elements that comprise the XML Signature syntax in this section.

<Signature> Element

The `<Signature>` element is a parent element of XML Signature. It identifies a complete XML Signature within a given context. It contains the sequence of child elements: `<SignedInfo>`, `<SignatureValue>`, `<KeyInfo>`, and `<Object>`. Also, an optional `Id` attribute can be applied to the `<Signature>` element as an identifier. This is useful in the case of multiple `<Signature>` instances within a single context.

<SignedInfo> Element

The `<SignedInfo>` element is the next element in the sequence and is a complex element of an XML Signature. It encompasses all of the information that is actually signed. The contents of this element include a sequence of elements: `<CanonicalizationMethod>` (see the following *Canonicalization* section), `<SignatureMethod>`, and one or more `<Reference>` elements.

The <CanonicalizationMethod> and <SignatureMethod> elements describe the type of canonicalization algorithm used in the generation of a <SignatureValue>. <Reference> element that defines the actual data that we are signing. They define a data stream that would eventually be hashed and transformed. The actual data stream is referenced by a URI.

<KeyInfo> Element

<KeyInfo> is an optional element. However, it is a very powerful feature of XML Signature that is utilized by the rest of the XML security-related specifications. This element enables the integration of trust semantics within an application that utilizes XML Signatures. The <KeyInfo> element consists of information used to verify XML signatures. This information can be explicit, such as a raw public key or an X.509 certificate, or the information can be indirect, specifying some remote public key information source via a <RetrievalMethod> element. A <KeyInfo> element enables a recipient to verify the signature without having to hunt for the verification key.

An application receiving a <KeyInfo> element must decide whether to trust the information presented by this element or not. This decision-making must done by the application and is out of the scope of an XML Signature specification. One way to manage trust in the application that relies on XML Signatures is to delegate it to a trust engine that takes as an input a <KeyInfo> element, which makes a trust decision based on that and informs the requestor about that trust decision. Such a trust engine can very well be implemented using XKMS, as we will see when we talk about it in a later section.

Figure 13.11 shows how an XML document, containing a <Signature> element, is given as an input to a parser to get hold of the <KeyInfo> element. This element contains an X.509 certificate that is subsequently passed to a trust engine that conveys the trust decision to the signature validation component of an XML Signature implementation.

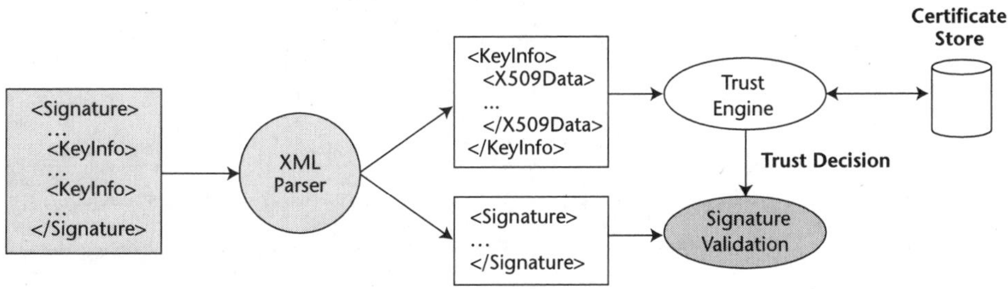

Figure 13.11 An XML signature validation.

ASN.1 AND BER/DER

ASN.1 is OSI's notation for specifying abstract types and values. ASN.1 does not specify how these objects are encoded into bits. This is specified by a set of encoding rules. Two are in common use: the Basic Encoding Rules (BER) and the Distinguished Encoding Rules (DER). BER specifies more than one way to encode some values, while using DER results in a unique encoding for each ASN.1 value. The X.509 certificate specification is specified with ASN.1. Kerberos 5 uses ASN.1 and DER to encode its protocol messages.

The `<KeyInfo>` element can consist of a child element named `<KeyValue>`. The `<KeyValue>` element is designed to hold a raw RSA or DSA public key with child elements `<RSAKeyValue>` and `<DSAKeyValue>`, respectively. Public keys inside the `<KeyValue>` element are represented in base64 encoding rather than by using the already defined standard public key format encoded in the Basic Encoding Rules (BER). The reason for the XML Signature specification writers to not leverage upon the already defined X.509 public key format is because in order to decode the standard X.509 public key format, a rather heavyweight Abstract Syntax Notation One (ASN.1) parser must be used. However, this is not the case with an XML markup because any XML parser can be used to successfully parse the `<KeyValue>` element even without an implementation of the XML Signature available on that system.

Table 13.1 shows the `<KeyInfo>` child elements.

Table 13.1 <KeyInfo> Child Elements

ELEMENT NAME	DESCRIPTION
`<KeyName>`	A simple text-identifier for a key name
`<KeyValue>`	Either an RSA or DSA public key
`<RetrievalMethod>`	Enables remote referencing of the key information
`<X509Data>`	X.509 certificates, names, or other related data
`<PGPData>`	PGP-related keys and identifiers
`<SPKIData>`	SPKI keys, certificates, or other SPKI-related data
`<MgmtData>`	Key agreement parameters, such as Diffie-Helman parameters

<Object> Element

`<Object>` is an optional element. When present, it can contain data of any type. The `<Object>` element can carry optional `MimeType`, `ID`, or `Encoding` attributes. The following describes the use of each of these attributes:

Encoding. This attribute provides a URI that identifies the method by which the object is encoded.

MimeType. This attribute describes data within the `<Object>` element. For example, if the `<Object>` element contains a base64-encoded JPG, the `Encoding` may be specified as `'base64'` and the `MimeType` as `'image/jpg'`.

ID. This attribute is commonly referenced from a `<Reference>` element in `<SignedInfo>`. This element is typically used for enveloping signatures where the object being signed is to be included in the `<Signature>` element.

Canonicalization

The XML 1.0 recommendation defines the syntax of a class of objects called XML documents. However, it is possible for two "logically" equivalent XML documents to physically differ. Consider the following two different XML elements:

```
<Patient weight="120" height="5.5"/>
<Patient height="5.5" weight="120"/>
```

If we do a byte-by-byte string comparison on these two elements, they are different. But from an XML processing perspective, they are equivalent. Two equivalent XML documents may differ on issues such as physical structure, attribute ordering, character encoding, or insignificant placing of white spaces.

However, proving the equivalence of XML documents is extremely important especially in domains such as digital signatures, checksums, version control, and conformance testing. Also, as is obvious from the previous discussion, equivalence testing cannot be done on a byte-by-byte basis without taking into consideration the physical structure of an XML document and not the syntactic equivalence.

To solve this problem, W3C started work on the Canonical XML specification in 1999. It is currently a W3C Recommendation. The Canonical XML specification defines an XML Canonicalization algorithm for taking an

XML document and generating a so-called *canonical form* of it that can be correctly compared, byte-by-byte, to canonical forms of other documents. The canonical forms of any two logically equivalent XML documents will always be byte-by-byte identical. If a comparison of the canonical forms of two documents shows that they are not byte-by-byte identical, it indicates that the information content of the two documents is not logically equivalent.

XML Digital Signatures supports two canonicalization algorithms: Canonical XML (omits comments) and Canonical XML with Comments. Again, canonicalization algorithms can be specified through the `<CanonicalizationMethod>` child element of the `<SignedInfo>` element.

Implementations of XML Signature

At the time of this book's writing, the implementations of XML Signature, shown in Table 13.2, are available.

Table 13.2 Implementations of XML Signature

IBM's XML Security Suite	www.alphaworks.ibm.com/tech/xmlsecuritysuite
IAIK XML Signature Library	http://jcewww.iaik.tu-graz.ac.at/products/ixsil/index.php
HP Web Services Platform 2.0	www.hpmiddleware.com/SaISAPI.dll/SaServletEngine.class/products/hp_web_services/default.jsp
Infomosaic SecureXML Digital Signature	www.infomosaic.net/
NEC Solutions' XML Digital Signature Software Library	www.sw.nec.co/jp/soft/xml_s/appform_e.html
Phaos XML	www.phaos.com/e_security/dl_xml.html
RSA BSAFE Cert-J	www.rasecurity.com/products/bsafe/certj.html
Verisign's XML Signature SDK (Part of Verisign's Trust Services Integration Kit)	www.xmltrustcenter.org/xmlsig/developer/verisign.index.htm

For the example on XML Signature that follows, we will use IBM's XML Security Suite library.

XML Signature: An Example

So now that we know about what XML Signature is and its syntax, let's see how to sign a document and then verify the signature on this document. For demonstrating this, we will refer to the Funds Transfer example again.

In this example, Web service *FT_SubmitRequest_ACH_WS,* hosted by American Bank, submits the request for transferring funds to ACH, hosted by *FT_RequestReceiver_WS.* As part of this SOAP interaction, *FT_Submit-Request_ACH_WS* sends `transfer_details.xml` as a payload to the SOAP request. As we know, `transfer_details.xml` consists of all the details pertaining to a funds transfer. Thus, it is obvious on the part of ACH to be able to authenticate the identity of American Bank by demanding a signed `transfer_details.xml` document from American Bank. Also, ACH can use this signed information for confronting any potential repudiation claims made by American Bank in the future.

American Bank, therefore, signs `transfer_details.xml` with its private key and sends the signed XML document to *FT_RequestReceiver_WS* of ACH. Upon receiving this SOAP message, *FT_RequestReceiver_WS* extracts the signed `transfer_details.xml` payload and verifies the XML digital signature, thus reaching the conclusion that a funds transfer request is really being made by American Bank.

Again, our main focus is to understand the core logic for signature generation and validation, and hence, for the scope of this example we will not bother implementing the actual *FT_SubmitRequest_ACH_WS* and *FT_RequestReceiver_WS* services. Our example demonstrates signing `transfer_details.xml` and verifying the signed contents of `transfer_details.xml`, with the help of a Java main class `SignatureTest`, which in turn uses a `GenerateValidateSignature` utility class that implements the actual signature functionality. In a real-life scenario, both *FT_SubmitRequest_ACH_WS* and *FT_RequestReceiver_WS* Web services would use the `GenerateValidateSignature` utility class, for performing these signature functions. Figure 13.12 shows the UML class diagram depicting an association between the `SignatureTest` and `GenerateValidateSignature` classes.

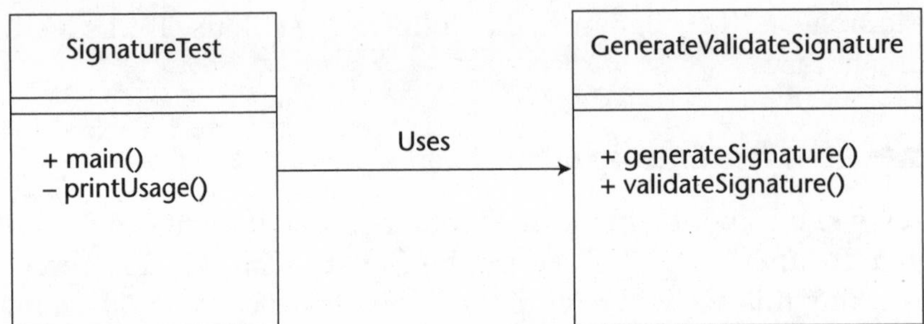

Figure 13.12 SignatureTest and GenerateValidateSignature class diagram.

Now, `SignatureTest` takes a couple of arguments as input:

`<option>` This argument requires the mode in which we want to use `SignatureTest`: generate or validate.

`<your-key-alias>` This argument takes the alias of the public key that we (and assumingly American Bank) would use for signing the `transfer_details.xml`. We will generate a key pair with the alias `American_Bank`, using the `Keytool` utility previously discussed. The following is the command we need to use in order to achieve this:

```
> keytool -genkey -dname "CN=American_Bank_Emp, O=American Bank, C=US"
-alias American_Bank -storepass keystorepwd -keypass keypwd
```

`<storepassword>` This takes a keystore password as an argument. In this case, it would be `keystorepwd`.

`<keypassword>` This argument takes a private key password, which we use to sign the `transfer_details.xml`. In this case, it would be `keypwd`.

`<source-xml-document URL>` This argument takes the URL of the XML document that we want to sign. For this example, we specify the URL of `transfer_details.xml`, which is locally stored.

Now, let's see how to sign `transfer_details.xml` and validate the signed `transfer_details.xml` document in the following sections.

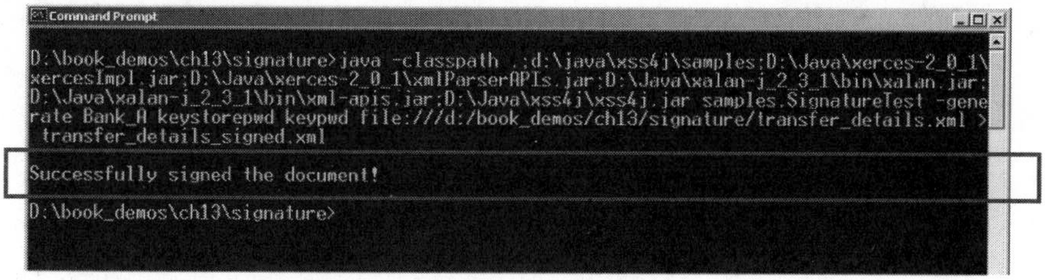

```
Command Prompt

D:\book_demos\ch13\signature>java -classpath .;d:\java\xss4j\samples;D:\Java\xerces-2_0_1\
xercesImpl.jar;D:\Java\xerces-2_0_1\xmlParserAPIs.jar;D:\Java\xalan-j_2_3_1\bin\xalan.jar;
D:\Java\xalan-j_2_3_1\bin\xml-apis.jar;D:\Java\xss4j\xss4j.jar samples.SignatureTest -gene
rate Bank_A keystorepwd keypwd file:///d:/book_demos/ch13/signature/transfer_details.xml >
 transfer_details_signed.xml

Successfully signed the document!

D:\book_demos\ch13\signature>
```

Figure 13.13 The SignatureTest -generate screenshot.

Signing transfer_details.xml

In order to sign `transfer_details.xml`, the following is the command line usage of `SignatureTest`, assuming that all of the required JAR files are available in the CLASSPATH:

```
> java jws.ch13.SignatureTest -generate American_Bank keystorepwd keypwd
file:///d:/book_demos/ch13/signature/transfer_details.xml >
transfer_details_signed.xml
```

As is clear from the previous command, the output of this execution is redirected to `transfer_details_signed.xml`, which now consists of the `<Signature>` document element containing the *detached* digital signature for `transfer_details.xml`.

Upon successful execution of `SignatureTest`, we should be able to see a message on standard output as shown in the screenshot in Figure 13.13.

The actual signature XML document is stored in `transfer_details_signed.xml`, which is shown in Listing 13.7.

```
<Signature xmlns="http://www.w3.org/2000/09/xmldsig#">
     <SignedInfo>
          <CanonicalizationMethod Algorithm=
          "http://www.w3.org/TR/2001/REC-xml-c14n-20010315">
          </CanonicalizationMethod>
```

Listing 13.7 `Transfer_details_signed.xml.` *(continues)*

```
        <SignatureMethod Algorithm=
        "http://www.w3.org/2000/09/xmldsig#dsa-sha1">
        </SignatureMethod>

        <Reference URI = "file:///
        d:/book_demos/ch13/signature/transfer_details.xml">

             <DigestMethod Algorithm =
             "http://www.w3.org/2000/09/xmldsig#sha1">
             </DigestMethod>

             <DigestValue>
                  zYL4sRVOsp6sZNcEx9EMF84nXYQ=
             </DigestValue>
        </Reference>
   </SignedInfo>

   <SignatureValue>
   Mm4lZx25UPj2bvq4cbnf7gyt368F5sbz9gVZmypZBKMHlt0+4Irykg==
   </SignatureValue>

   <KeyInfo>
        <KeyValue>
             <DSAKeyValue>
                  ...
             </DSAKeyValue>
        </KeyValue>

        <X509Data>
             <X509IssuerSerial>
                  <X509IssuerName>
                       CN=American_Bank_Emp,O=American Bank,C=US
                  </X509IssuerName>

                  <X509SerialNumber>
                       1021226821
                  </X509SerialNumber>
             </X509IssuerSerial>

             <X509SubjectName>
                  CN=American_Bank_Emp,O=American Bank,C=US
             </X509SubjectName>

             <X509Certificate>
                  ...
             </X509Certificate>
        </X509Data>
   </KeyInfo>
</Signature>
```

Listing 13.7 `Transfer_details_signed.xml`. *(continued)*

Listing 13.7 is an example of a detached signature that references the actual data through a URI. The listing shows the following elements:

`<CanonicalizationMethod>` This element specifies the canonical XML algorithm used to get the canonical form of the `transfer_details.xml` document.

`<SignatureMethod>` This element specifies the algorithm that is used when the hash of the data was calculated. This hash then gets encrypted using the key that we specify.

`<KeyInfo>` This element contains all of the trust related information of the DSA key that was used to sign the document.

Validating the Signed transfer_details.xml

For verifying the detached `<Signature>` element containing the signing information of `transfer_details.xml` placed in `transfer_details_signed.xml`, the following command line must be given:

```
> java jws.ch13.SignatureTest -validate < transfer_details_signed.xml
```

As can be seen from the standard output, the `<Signature>` in `transfer_details_signed.xml` is validated in two ways. First is the validation of the actual `<SignedInfo>` element to see if it has been tampered since its creation, and second is checking of the actual data by dereferencing the reference to see if the data has changed since it was signed.

And, the output to this validation operation is shown in Figure 13.14.

This is how we use `SignatureTest` and thus, the `GenerateValidateSignature` utility class. The next section examines the code of both of these Java classes, present in `SignatureTest.java`.

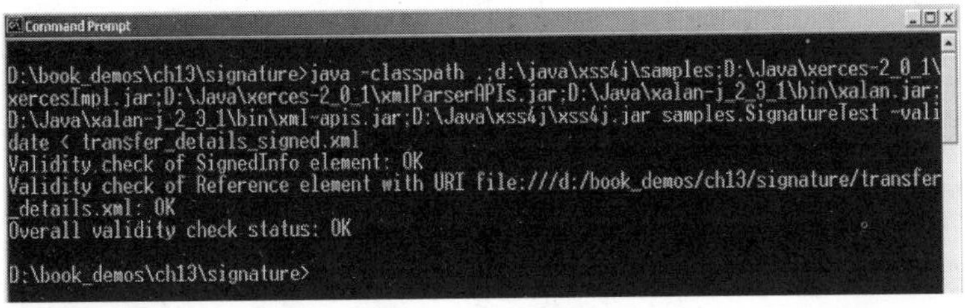

```
Command Prompt

D:\book_demos\ch13\signature>java -classpath .;d:\java\xss4j\samples;D:\Java\xerces-2_0_1\
xercesImpl.jar;D:\Java\xerces-2_0_1\xmlParserAPIs.jar;D:\Java\xalan-j_2_3_1\bin\xalan.jar;
D:\Java\xalan-j_2_3_1\bin\xml-apis.jar;D:\Java\xss4j\xss4j.jar samples.SignatureTest -vali
date < transfer_details_signed.xml
Validity check of SignedInfo element: OK
Validity check of Reference element with URI file:///d:/book_demos/ch13/signature/transfer
_details.xml: OK
Overall validity check status: OK

D:\book_demos\ch13\signature>
```

Figure 13.14 `SignatureTest -validate.`

Programming Steps for Generating and Validating XML Signature

The following shows the required imports in SignatureTest.java:

```
package jws.ch13;

/* Standard Java imports
 */
import java.io.*;
import java.net.URL;
import java.security.*;
import java.security.cert.*;

/* IBM XML Security Suite related imports
 */
import com.ibm.xml.dsig.*;
import com.ibm.xml.dsig.util.*;
import com.ibm.dom.util.*;

/* JAXP, DOM, SAX related imports
 */
import javax.xml.parsers.*;
import org.w3c.dom.*;
import org.xml.sax.*;
```

Now, the SignatureTest.java main class parses the command line arguments and appropriately calls the generateSignature() or validateSignature() methods on the GenerateValidate-Signature utility class as shown in the following code:

```
public class SignatureTest
{
     public static void main(String[] args) throws Exception
     {
          if (args[0].equals("-generate") && args.length == 5)
          {
               String sAlias = args[1];
               char [] caStorePassword = args[2].toCharArray();
               char [] caKeyPassword = args[3].toCharArray();
               String sSourceURL = args[4];

               GenerateValidateSignature
               objGenerateValidateSignature =
               new GenerateValidateSignature();

               objGenerateValidateSignature.generateSignature
```

```
                (sAlias, caStorePassword, caKeyPassword,
                sSourceURL);
            }
            else if (args[0].equals ("-validate")
            && args.length == 1)
            {
                GenerateValidateSignature
                objGenerateValidateSignature =
                new GenerateValidateSignature();

                objGenerateValidateSignature.validateSignature();
            }
            else
            {
                printUsage();
            }
        }
    }
```

The core signature functionality is performed by the `generateSignature()` and `validateSignature()` methods on the `GenerateValidateSignature` class. Let's begin with the signature generation functionality by understanding the `generateSignature()` method first.

`generateSignature()` starts with creating a new DOM tree instance. This DOM tree instance then is passed to the constructor of the `TemplateGenerator` class. The `TemplateGenerator` object uses a template of an XML signature in order to create the actual signature document. Constructor also takes the appropriate signing and XML canonicalization algorithms as arguments. This is shown in the following:

```
public void generateSignature
(
    String sAlias, char [] caStorePassword, char [] caKeyPassword,
    String sSourceURL
) throws XSignatureException, IOException, KeyStoreException,
SignatureStructureException, NoSuchAlgorithmException,
CertificateException, UnrecoverableKeyException,
ParserConfigurationException, SAXException
{
    Document objDocument =
    DOMParserNS.createBuilder().newDocument();

    TemplateGenerator objTemplateGenerator = new TemplateGenerator
    (objDocument, XSignature.SHA1, Canonicalizer.W3C2,
    SignatureMethod.DSA);
```

Then, a reference to the actual data (that is, to the transfer_details.xml document stored locally) is created using the TemplateGenerator object. Eventually, this reference is added to the TemplateGenerator object as shown in the following code:

```
Reference objReference = objTemplateGenerator.createReference
(sSourceURL);

objTemplateGenerator.addReference(objReference);
```

Now, we get hold of the keystore file from the default keystore location (that is, a *.keystore file stored under the user's home directory) and load the keystore file in the memory. Subsequently, we also get hold of the private key with which we use to sign the XML document:

```
String sKeyStorePath = System.getProperty("user.home") +
File.separator + ".keystore";

KeyStore objKeyStore = KeyStore.getInstance("JKS");

objKeyStore.load (new FileInputStream(sKeyStorePath),
caStorePassword);

Key objPrivateKey = objKeyStore.getKey(sAlias, caKeyPassword);

if (objPrivateKey == null)
{
     System.err.println("Could not get hold of the private key for
     alias: " + sAlias);

     System.exit(1);
}
```

In addition, we also get hold of the X.509 certificate from the default keystore, which we use to sign the transfer_details.xml document, as the following code shows:

```
X509Certificate objX509Certificate =
(X509Certificate)objKeyStore.getCertificate(sAlias);

KeyInfo.X509Data objX509Data = new KeyInfo.X509Data();

objX509Data.setCertificate(objX509Certificate);
objX509Data.setParameters(objX509Certificate, true, true, true);

KeyInfo.X509Data[] objX509DataArray = new KeyInfo.X509Data[]
{ objX509Data };
```

A KeyInfo object also is created. This KeyInfo object represents the <KeyInfo> element in the actual signature document. It carries the public key and the X.509 certificate of the signer:

```
KeyInfo objKeyInfo = new KeyInfo();

objKeyInfo.setX509Data(objX509DataArray);
objKeyInfo.setKeyValue(objX509Certificate.getPublicKey());
```

We now get hold of the SignatureElement, representing <Signature>, and set it to KeyInfo object:

```
Element objSignatureElement =
objTemplateGenerator.getSignatureElement();

objKeyInfo.insertTo(objSignatureElement);
```

By now, we have already set a reference to data that we need to sign, which is specified by the keys to use for signing and the certificate information of the signer. Next, we will perform the actual signing operation. However, to do so we will need to create the SignatureContext object first:

```
SignatureContext objSignatureContext = new SignatureContext();
objSignatureContext.sign(objSignatureElement, objPrivateKey);

System.err.println("\nSuccessfully signed the document!");
```

After the signing is performed, we finally will add the SignatureElement instance (representing <Signature>) to the newly created DOM tree. After appending the <Signature> element to the DOM tree, also serialize the DOM tree to the standard output as XML. We will use XPath's XPathCanonicalizer API to achieve this serialization:

```
objDocument.appendChild(objSignatureElement);

Writer objWriter = new OutputStreamWriter(System.out, "UTF-8");

XPathCanonicalizer.serializeAll(objDocument, true, objWriter);

objWriter.flush();
```

This is all that is required to sign transfer_details.xml. The newly generated detached signature of transfer_details.xml is stored in transfer_details_signed.xml in your local directory.

Now, let's see how to validate the detached signature present in transfer_details_signed.xml. In order to validate, SignatureTest will call the validateSignature() method on the GenerateValidate-Signature utility class. Our validateSignature() method is shown in the following code. The first thing we do in this method is to get hold of the SignatureContext object. This core object maintains the information necessary for validating signatures:

```
public void validateSignature() throws IOException, SAXException,
ParserConfigurationException, XSignatureException
{
     SignatureContext objSignatureContext = new SignatureContext();
```

Now, we read the signature XML document from the standard input. In addition, we parse this signature document and create the DOM tree, as the following code shows:

```
InputStream objInputStream = System.in;
InputSource objInputSource = new InputSource (objInputStream);

Document objDocument = DOMParserNS.createBuilder().parse
(objInputSource);
```

Now, we get hold of the <Signature> from the DOM tree. Eventually, we also get the <KeyInfo> element:

```
NodeList objNodeList = objDocument.getElementsByTagNameNS
(XSignature.XMLDSIG_NAMESPACE, "Signature");

if (objNodeList.getLength() == 0)
{
     System.err.println("\nERROR: Invalid Signature document
     specified. The given document has no <Signature> element.");

     System.exit(1);
}

Element objSignatureElement = (Element)objNodeList.item(0);

Element objKeyInfoElement = KeyInfo.searchForKeyInfo
(objSignatureElement);
```

Now, we retrieve the public key using the signature to be validated:

```
Key objPublicKey = null;

KeyInfo objKeyInfo = new KeyInfo (objKeyInfoElement);
```

```
Key objKeyFromKeyValue = objKeyInfo.getKeyValue();

if (objKeyFromKeyValue != null)
{
     objPublicKey = objKeyFromKeyValue;
}
```

And finally, we verify the digital signature:

```
Validity objValidity = objSignatureContext.verify
(objSignatureElement, objPublicKey);
```

Then, we check the status of the signature verification and print the appropriate messages to the standard output:

```
if (objValidity.getSignedInfoValidity())
{
     System.err.println("Validity Check of SignedInfo element: OK");
}
else
{
     System.err.println("Validity check of SignedInfo element: FAILED");
}

if (objValidity.getReferenceValidity(0))
{
     System.err.println("Validity check of Reference element with URI "
+
     objValidity.getReferenceURI(0) + ": OK");
}
else
{
     System.err.println("Validity check of Reference element with URI "
+
     objValidity.getReferenceURI(0) + ": FAILED");
}

if (objValidity.getCoreValidity())
{
     System.err.println("Overall validity check status: OK");
}
else
{
     System.err.println("Overall validity check status: FAILED");
}
```

The `getSignedInfoValidity()` method checks for the validity of the `<SignedInfo>` element; `getReferenceValidity()` checks the validity of data referenced in order to see if the data has changed since it was signed. The `getCoreValidity()` validity check method returns true if both `getSignedInfoValidity()` and `getReferenceValidity()` return true.

This entire example, along with the complete source code and `readme.txt` consisting of setup instructions, can be downloaded from Wiley's Web site at www.wiley.com/compbooks/nagappan.

We just discussed how digitally signing helps to provide strong signer authentication, and thus, non-repudiation in Web services. What now is important to know is how can trust be established in the key that is used in cryptographic functions, such as encryption or signing. This is the area on which XKMS, which is discussed in the next section, is focused.

XML Key Management Specification (XKMS)

XML Key Management Specification is the next step in the evolution of the Public Key Infrastructure (PKI). PKI has long been used to mitigate the risks of automated electronic business environments. However, PKI has proven to be quite difficult to implement effectively. Interoperability is another problem that has almost always existed in the PKI world. However, these problems are small enough to stop us from using PKI when we take into consideration the huge promise of PKI, that is, the establishment of trust in the electronic world, which is key to the success of e-commerce and Web services. XKMS is positioned exactly to solve these issues of PKI, making it even more easy to deploy and ubiquitous. XKMS combines the interoperability of XML with the security of PKI to provide an easy method of securing PKI-based applications. XKMS presents a model wherein applications using PKI do not have to deploy the infrastructure locally. Rather, they can send XML requests to PKI components hosted by a trust services provider, who would actually execute those PKI requests. These requests may be for issuing a certificate or retrieving/creating a certificate, key, or revocation of a certificate. Thus, XKMS provides a very good opportunity for moving the complexity of a PKI to trust processing centers, such as Verisign, Entrust, and so forth. This means that applications and Web services relying on XKMS do not have to deploy any PKI software on their systems, rather they would issue XML requests to the Web services hosted by trust services providers. In fact, Verisign happens to be one of the first such trust services providers. They have hosted Web services that can service XKMS requests. These XKMS Web services have been hosted at http://xkms.verisign.com.

Thus, XML-based Web services developers can take advantage of XKMS to integrate authentication, digital signatures, and encryption that involves complex procedures such as certificate processing, certificate revocation status checking, and so forth, without having to deal with the hassles of proprietary PKI softwares. With XKMS, developers can delegate all or part of the processing of digital signatures and encrypted elements to an XKMS trust services provider, thus shielding the application from the complexities of an underlying PKI. By doing this, the resultant XML client becomes much simpler and lighter.

This is a very powerful concept, especially when thought of in the context of devices. XKMS presents a possibility for a thin device, such as a PDA, to register its certificate by consuming the Web services of a trust services provider, with nothing more than support for a plain XML parser and minimal footprint for XML Encryption and XML Signature implementations present on the device. No implementation of client-side PKI services needs to be present in this scenario.

Figure 13.15 shows the overall picture of how people actually use XKMS. In this figure, different Web services issue different XKMS requests to the trust services providers, either for registering a key pair, for retrieving public keys, or for validating them. The trust services provider would then, in turn, talk to the underlying PKI implementation to actually perform these PKI operations.

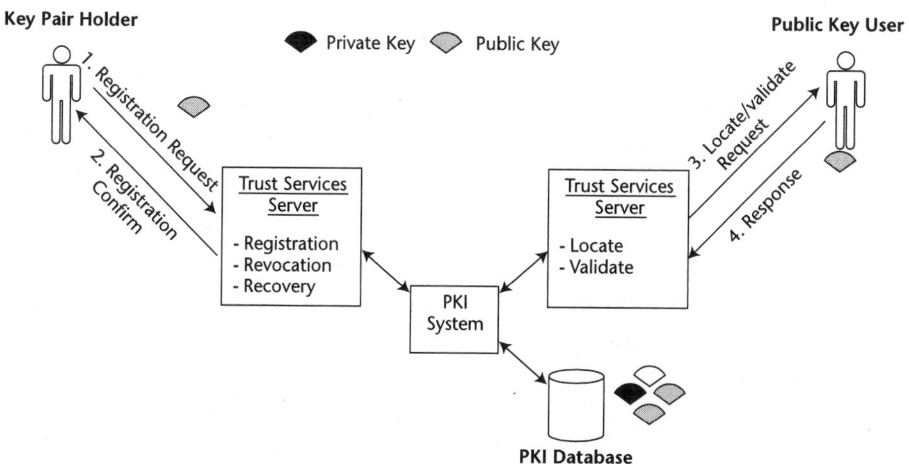

Figure 13.15 XKMS usage diagram.

Verisign, Microsoft, and webMethods first initiated the XKMS 1.0 effort. In early 2001, these companies submitted the XKMS 1.0 specification to W3C as a note. W3C has based its XML Key Management Working Group (WG) on this XKMS note. Currently, this WG is working on the next version of XKMS: XKMS 2.0. Further information on the XML Key Management WG and specifically XKMS 2.0 can be found at www.w3.org/2001/XKMS/.

The XML Key Management WG also defines another specification called the XML Key Management Specification - Bulk Operation (X-BULK). Its first working draft can be found at www.w3.org/TR/xkms2-xbulk/. X-BULK extends XKMS protocols to encompass the bulk registration operations necessary for interfacing with systems such as smart card management systems. X-BULK specifies structures containing this bulk registration information using XML Schema Definitions and WSDL. We will take a look at X-BULK in the following text.

XKMS Components

The XML Key Management Specification relies upon the other two XML security standards from W3C: XML Encryption and XML Signatures. Now, XKMS has been designed to come up with mechanisms through which Web services can leverage upon the PKI support provided by other Web services. Also, the main objective of XKMS has always been to enable a user using a public key to verify a digital signature, to encrypt data, or to locate that public key as well as other information pertaining to the holder of the corresponding private key. To meet these objectives, core XKMS functionalities have been divided into two sub-specifications:

XML Key Information Service Specification (X-KISS). X-KISS defines a protocol that Web services can use to delegate the processing of key information associated with an XML signature, XML encryption, or any other public key, to a trust services provider Web service. Its functions mainly include locating a required public key and describing the information that binds, such as a key to the owner of its corresponding private key.

XML Key Registration Service Specification (X-KRSS). X-KRSS defines a protocol that a Web service can use to register a key pair supplying the proper information pertaining to the holder of that key pair. That key pair then would be used in the subsequent requests made using an X-KISS protocol.

Both of these protocols utilize SOAP and WSDL. To find more information on SOAP, please refer to Chapter 4, "Developing Web Services Using SOAP," and to find more information on WSDL, please refer to Chapter 5, "Description and Discovery of Web Services." These protocols are designed so that they are compatible with all of the major PKI specifications, such as Pretty Good Privacy (PGP), Public Key Infrastructure X.509 (PKIX), and Simple Public Key Infrastructure (SPKI).

NOTE **Any XKMS requests and responses can be enveloped within SOAP requests/responses or they also can be sent as an attachment to the SOAP requests. However, the key thing to note here is that there is no standard defined currently that deals with what a SOAP envelope should look like when it is carrying an X-BULK request. This problem introduces interoperability issues among Web services that work with X-BULK or even XKMS, for that matter.**

Also, the schemas for different XKMS (X-KISS, X-KRSS, and X-BULK) requests and responses, which we saw in this section, are not the final ones. Specification work is still in progress and currently a lot of things are being added and modified. Thus, the schemas may change at a later phase. However, such concepts pretty much will remain the same.

XKMS Implementations

Two implementations of XKMS are available for the Java platform as of this writing:

- Verisign XKMS Toolkit (also a part of Verisign's Trust Services Integration Kit 1.0) (www.xmltrustcenter.org/xkms/index.htm)
- Entrust XKMS Toolkit (http://xkms.entrust.com/xkms/index.htm)

Note that there is no standard API for XKMS in a Java platform. Java Specification Request (JSR) 104, titled XML Trust Service APIs, is working toward creating standard APIs for XKMS. More information on this can be found at www.jcp.org/jsr/detail/104.jsp.

Knowing this, let's now go into the details on the specific components of XML Key Management Specification, namely X-KISS, X-KRSS, and X-BULK.

XML Key Information Service Specification (X-KISS)

In the context of an XML signature, the `<ds:KeyInfo>` element enables the service to verify a digital signature, and in the context of XML encryption,

<ds:KeyInfo> specifies key information that was used to encrypt the document. Thus, <ds:KeyInfo> forms the basis of both of these cryptographic functions: signing and encryption.

By design, the XML signature and XML encryption specifications do not mandate the use of a particular trust policy. This implies that the signer, encryptor, or both are not required to include any key-related information in the XML document. Thus, XML encryption or signature may or may not include the <ds:KeyInfo> element. Even if it includes <ds:KeyInfo>, it may specify either a PGP key or X.509 data or may simplify the key name or a URL where the entire <ds:KeyInfo> information can be found. The information provided by a signer or an encryptor therefore may be insufficient by itself to decide whether or not to place trust in the key and perform a cryptographic operation, such as signing.

Let's go a step further and imagine that the sender of an XML signature or encryption document provides relevant key information encoded in the form of an X.509 certificate. But even then, the client (who can be running on a device) may not be able to parse the X.509 certificate. Consider the usual case of encryption wherein the client is required to know the public key of the recipient that it would be using to encrypt the information. In this situation, it is almost logical for the client to have some means of discovering information pertaining to keys from some external Web service offered by a trusted Web service provider.

This is where X-KISS comes into play. X-KISS enables a client, a Web service, to delegate part or all of the tasks required to process the Trust element, <ds:KeyInfo>, to a *Trust Service.*

X-KISS Locate Service

X-KISS can be used to create trust services that can locate key information by resolving the <ds:KeyInfo> element. A trust service may resolve the <ds:KeyInfo> element using some locally available data (for example, keys that are previously registered with this particular trust services provider), or by resolving the <ds:RetrievalMethod> element (more information can be found on this element in the *XML Signature* section), or by acting as a gateway to an underlying PKI based on non-XML syntax.

Figure 13.16 illustrates a scenario wherein a trust service locates a key'd information by acting as a gateway between an XML client and a non-XML based server-side PKI system.

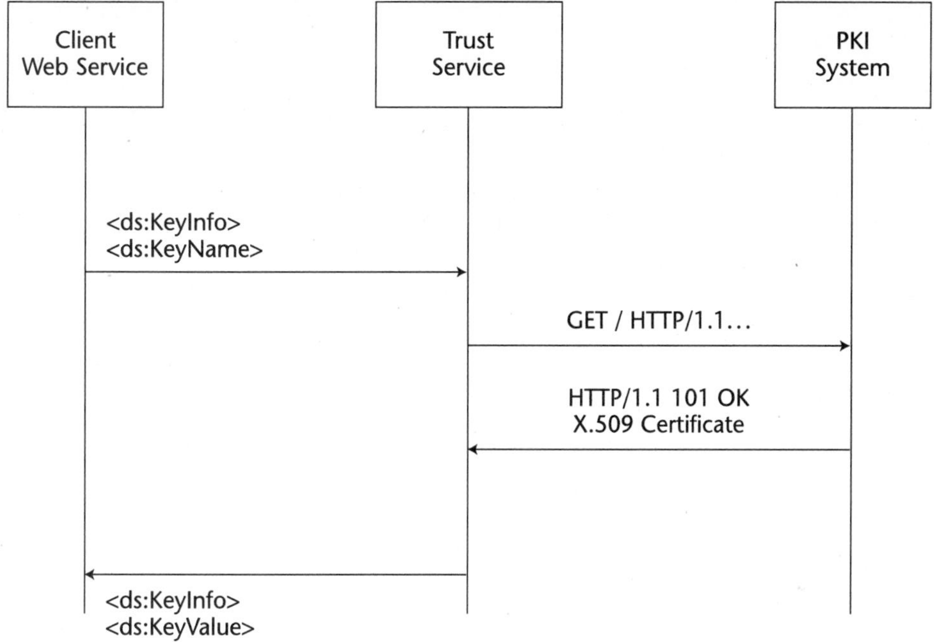

Figure 13.16 XKMS locate service.

Now, let's go back to our Funds Transfer example, where ACH's *FT_RequestReceiver_WS* receives a signed XML document from American Bank. In this example, American Bank *may* not send the value of the RSA public key whose corresponding private key is used to sign the `transfer_details.xml` document. Rather, imagine that the `<ds:KeyInfo>` element sent consists of only the `<ds:KeyName>` of the key used to sign the document. Therefore, in order to retrieve the corresponding public key to validate the signature, ACH's *FT_RequestReceiver_WS* Web service would have to send a query request to the trust services provider's (for example, Verisign) *Locate* Web service. ACH Web service sends the `<ds:KeyInfo>` element to the Locate service requesting the `<KeyName>` and `<KeyValue>` elements, which correspond to the public key of American Bank to be returned.

Listing 13.8 is a sample XKMS request that ACH's Web service would send to retrieve the public key of American Bank.

```
<Locate>
     <Query>
          <ds:KeyInfo>
               <ds:KeyName>American Bank</ds:KeyName>
          </ds:KeyInfo>
     </Query>
     <Respond>
          <string>KeyName</string>
          <string>KeyValue</string>
     </Respond>
</Locate>
```

Listing 13.8 X-KISS locate key request.

The XKMS request in Listing 13.8 has the following elements:

<Locate> This element consists of the query for locating the key or certificate.

<Query> This element consist of the `<ds:KeyInfo>` element, which may consist of any information that can help the Locate service get hold of the actual key (for example, a key name or the `<ds:RetrievalMethod>` element).

<Respond> This element specifies the type of information that the requestor is looking for from the Locate service. In our example, it is name of the key and its value.

The response that is received for the query shown in Listing 13.8 is shown in Listing 13.9.

```
<LocateResult>
     <Result>Success</Result>
     <Answer>
          <ds:KeyInfo>
               <ds:KeyName>
                    O=American Bank, CN="American_Bank_Emp"
               </ds:KeyName>
               <ds:KeyValue>...</ds:KeyValue>
          </ds:KeyInfo>
     </Answer>
</LocateResult>
```

Listing 13.9 X-KISS locate key response.

The XKMS response in Listing 13.9 has the following elements:

<LocateResult> This element consists of the response given by the Locate service in response to the query.

<Result> This element consists of the status of the response in terms of the original query. The status can be either success, failure, or pending depending upon if the operation was queued or not for future processing.

<Answer> This element carries the actual query response. In our example, it consists of the name of the key and the corresponding key value of the public key for American Bank. However, it also can consist of either an X.509 certificate or a key name based on the information asked for in the original request's `<Respond>` element.

The following code shows most of the important API calls a client Web service would make to interact with an X-KISS Locate service. These calls are made using Verisign's Trust Services Integration Toolkit (TSIK). For simplicity reasons, the following is only a fraction of the code:

```
public void Locate (string[] args) throws Exception
{
     String sKeyName = args[0];

     String responses[] =
     {XKMSLocate.KeyName, XKMSLocate.KeyValue};

     XKMSLocate objLocate = new XKMSLocate
     (sKeyName, responses);

     XKMSLocateResponse objLocateResponse =
     objLocate.sendRequest(transport);

     System.out.println("Response status: " +
     objLocateResponse.getStatus());
}
```

For the complete source code, please refer to the examples that come along with Verisign's TSIK.

An important thing to note here is that such a Locate service does not report revocation status for a certificate or the trustworthiness of a key. A client Web service (such as ACH's *FT_RequestReceiver_WS*) is responsible for verifying the trustworthiness of a key by receiving an assertion from the trust services provider itself or a third party about the validity status of the binding (holder <-> key) of the key in question. In order to get these benefits, one must query the Validate service of an XKMS trust services provider.

X-KISS Validate Service

An X-KISS Validate service provides everything that a Locate service can provide. In addition, it also is capable of providing an assertion to the client Web service about the validity of the binding status between the public key and the rest of the data about the holder of that key. The way the *Validate* trust service works is that the client Web service sends a prototype containing all or some of the elements for which the status of binding is required. Once the validity of this key binding has been determined, the Trust service returns the status result to the client in the form of a `<KeyBinding>` structure.

To understand this better, consider the Funds Transfer example again where ACH's *FT_RequestReceiver_WS* Web service calls the Locate Web service in order to get hold of the public key of the signer of the `transfer_details.xml` document, upon receiving `transfer_details_signed.xml` and `transfer_details.xml` from American Bank. In this example, *FT_RequestReceiver_WS* also wants to ensure that the key used for signing `transfer_details.xml` has a valid binding—that is, it belongs to American Bank and has not been revoked. Thus, *FT_RequestReceiver_WS* sends a request to the X-KISS Validate service to assert the validity of this key's binding.

Listing 13.10 is what the XKMS request to such a Validity service would look like.

```
<Validate>
     <Query>
          <ds:KeyInfo>
               <ds:KeyName>...</ds:KeyName>
               <ds:KeyValue>...</ds:KeyValue>
          </ds:KeyInfo>
     </Query>
</Validate>
```

Listing 13.10 X-KISS validate key request.

The response received would consist of the `<KeyBinding>` structure that would carry the status of the validity of the binding, as well as the interval through which the validity holds (`<ValidityInterval>`) (see Listing 13.11).

```
<ValidateResult>
    <Result>Success</Result>

    <Answer>
        <KeyBinding>
            <Status>Valid</Status>
            <KeyID>
                http://www.xmltrustcenter.org/assert/200
            </KeyID>

            <ds:KeyInfo>
                <ds:KeyName>...</ds:KeyName>
                <ds:KeyValue>...</ds:KeyValue>
            </ds:KeyInfo>

            <ValidityInterval>
                <NotBefore>
                    2000-09-20T12:00:00
                </NotBefore>

                <NotAfter>
                    2000-10-20T12:00:00
                </NotAfter>
            </ValidityInterval>
        </KeyBinding>
    </Answer>
</ValidateResult>
```

Listing 13.11 X-KISS validate key response.

Knowing this information, let's talk about key lifecycle services that are made possible with X-KRSS.

XML Key Registration Service Specification (X-KRSS)

Existing certificate management protocols, such as those defined by PKIX, support only a single part of the key life cycle (typically, certificate issuance). In addition, they are too complex to deal with for the lightweight Web services of today.

The goal of the X-KRSS specification is to respond to this need for a complete and simpler key life cycle management protocol that focuses on applications, such as Web services, to be their clients.

X-KRSS supports the entire key life cycle in a single specification. X-KRSS handles the following functions:

- Key registration
- Key revocation
- Key recovery

Let's take a look at each of these operations.

X-KRSS Registration Service

Client Web services use a registration service implemented by an XKMS trust services provider to register a key pair and the associated binding information. The key pair also may be generated by the registration service as well, if one is not supplied along with the registration request. At the time of registration, the service may require the client Web service to provide a key pair along with additional information pertaining to authentication. Upon receipt of a registration request, the service verifies the authentication and Possession of Private (POP) key information provided (if any) by the requestor and registers the key and associated binding information with itself.

Let's understand this in context of our funds transfer example. In our example, both American Bank and ACH can use a X-KRSS registration service to register their respective key pairs and bindings. The XKMS request shown in Listing 13.12 considers a request for registration that is sent by ACH, along with an RSA key pair for its Web site www.ach.com/fundstransfer. Assuming that ACH has previously received a pass code (say, "ABCD") from its trust services provider, a hash (SHA [password]) also is sent along with this request for authentication purposes.

```
<Register>
    <Prototype Id="keybinding">
        <Status>Valid</Status>
        <KeyID>http://www.ach.com/fundstransfer</KeyID>
        <ds:KeyInfo>
            <ds:KeyValue>
                <ds:RSAKeyValue>
                    <ds:Modulus>...</ds:Modulus>
                    <ds:Exponent>...</ds:Exponent>
                </ds:RSAKeyValue>
```

Listing 13.12 X-KRSS register key request.

```
            </ds:KeyValue>
            <ds:KeyName>
                http://www.ach.com/fundstransfer
            </ds:KeyName>
        </ds:KeyInfo>
    </Prototype>

    <AuthInfo>
        <AuthUserInfo>
            <ProofOfPossession>
                <ds:Signature URI="#keybinding" [RSA-Sign
                (KeyBinding, Private)] />
            </ProofOfPossession>

            <KeyBindingAuth>
                <ds:Signature  URI="#keybinding" [HMAC-
                SHA1 (KeyBinding, Auth)] />
            </KeyBindingAuth>
        </AuthUserInfo>
    </AuthInfo>

    <Respond>
        <string>KeyName<string>
        <string>KeyValue</string>
        <string>RetrievalMethod</string>
    </Respond>
</Register>
```

Listing 13.12 X-KRSS register key request. *(continued)*

The XKMS request for registration in Listing 13.12 has the following elements:

<Prototype> This element represents the prototype of the key and binding information that ACH wants to register.

<AuthInfo> This element presents two things:

- Proof of Possession of Private (POP) key by providing the `<ds:Signature>` element
- Authentication to the registration service in the form of a `<KeyBindingAuth>` element

Listing 13.13 shows the response received.

```
<RegisterResult>
     <Result>
          Success
     </Result>

     <Answer>
          <Status>
               Valid
          </Status>

          <KeyID>...</KeyID>

          <ds:KeyInfo>

               <ds:RetrievalMethod URI=
               "http://www.PKeyDir.test/Certificates/12"
               Type = http://www.w3.org/2000/09/xmldsig#X509Data"/>

               <ds:KeyValue>
                    <ds:RSAKeyValue>...</ds:RSAKeyValue>
               </ds:KeyValue>

               <ds:KeyName>...</ds:KeyName>
          </ds:KeyInfo>
     </Answer>
</RegisterResult>
```

Listing 13.13 X-KRSS register key response.

An important thing to note in the response to the registration request is that the service returns a <ds:RetrievalMethod> element that gives the URI where it was stored the actual X.509 certificate data. Thus, subsequent locate or validate requests for a key corresponding to www.ach.com/fundstransfer ACH should point toward this particular URI.

X-KRSS Revocation Service

A registration service may permit client Web services to revoke previously issued assertions about the validity of their keys. A revocation request is created in the same manner as the initial registration request for the key, except that the status of the prototype is now Invalid.

The sample X-KRSS revocation request is shown in Listing 13.14, wherein ACH is trying to revoke the binding for the public key associated with resource www.ach.com/fundstransfer. Note that ACH again will have to authenticate itself to the trust services provider using the same password that it used before for registration. Also note that the sample revocation request shown in Listing 13.14 has omitted a lot of the repeat elements.

```
<Register>
     <Prototype Id="keybinding">
          <Status>Invalid</Status>
          <KeyID>http://www.ach.com/fundstransfer/</KeyID>
          <ds:KeyInfo>...</ds:KeyInfo>
     </Prototype>

     <AuthInfo>...</AuthInfo>

     <Respond>
          <string>KeyName<string>
          <string>KeyValue</string>
     </Respond>
</Register>
```

Listing 13.14 X-KRSS key revocation request.

The response to this revocation request is pretty much the same as that to the registration request, with the only difference being that the status of the binding registered is now changed to Invalid.

X-KRSS Key Recovery Service

A key recovery is required when the holder of the key pair loses the private key. Following up with our example, if ACH somehow loses the private key it registered earlier, it must contact the administrator of the trust services provider about this loss. This communication between the client and the administrator is out of the scope of XKMS. However, the assumption is that during this communication, the administrator will provide ACH with some sort of recovery operation authorization code. ACH then would make the actual X-KRSS recovery request, wherein it would supply this authorization code.

The X-KRSS recovery request is the same as that of the X-KRSS revocation request, with the only difference being that the `<AuthInfo>` element now carries the hash of the authorization code. In addition, the response received is exactly the same as the one in the case of key revocation. The reason this is so is because whenever a key recovery operation is performed, the policy of the trust service provider is to revoke the private key and binding with the public key.

Now, let's see what X-BULK provides in addition to X-KRSS and X-KISS.

X-BULK

XKMS currently addresses key registration, information, and validation services on a one-by-one basis. However, it also has been recognized that the standard needs to address scenarios that require bulk operations, such as the issuance of multiple certificates. This example is the kind of operation for which the X-BULK specification was created.

X-BULK defines top-level batch elements, such as <BulkRegister>, <BulkResponse>, <BulkStatusRequest>, and <BulkStatus-Response>, representing registration requests/responses and status requests/responses. Each of these single batch request/response structures consists of independently referenceable requests/responses. Batches are produced both from a requestor and responder. A responder will process an entire batch, formulate a batch response, and then send that response to the original requestor.

Listing 13.15 is an example of an X-BULK request made by a client Web service for the bulk registration of certificates. Please note that some parts of the request have been omitted for brevity reasons.

```
<BulkRegister xmlns="http://www.w3.org/2002/03/xkms-xbulk">
     <SignedPart Id="id-0">

          <BatchHeader>
               <BatchID>batch-0</BatchID>
               <BatchTime>...</BatchTime>
               <NumberOfRequests>2</NumberOfRequests>
          </BatchHeader>

          <xkms:Respond>
               <string xmlns="">X509Cert</string>
          </xkms:Respond>

          <Requests number="2">
               <Request>
                    <xkms:KeyID>
                         mailto:somebody@ach.com
                    </xkms:KeyID>

                    <dsig:KeyInfo>
                         <dsig:X509Data>
                              <dsig:X509SubjectName>
                                   CN=FirstName LastName
                              </dsig:X509SubjectName>
```

Listing 13.15 X-BULK key registration request.

```
                    </dsig:X509Data>

                    <dsig:KeyValue>
                         <dsig:RSAKeyValue>
                              ...
                         </dsig:RSAKeyValue>
                    </dsig:KeyValue>
               </dsig:KeyInfo>

               <ClientInfo>
                    <EmployeeID
                    xmlns="urn:ach">
                         12345
                    </EmployeeID>
               </ClientInfo>
          </Request>

          <Request>...</Request>
     </Requests>
</SignedPart>

<dsig:Signature>...</dsig:Signature>

</BulkRegister>
```

Listing 13.15 X-BULK key registration request. *(continued)*

To understand the request shown in Listing 13.15, let's focus on the following important elements:

<BulkRegister> This is the top element in a bulk request message that carries information such as the batch ID, the type of response it is expecting from X-BULK service, the actual sequence of the requests, and the signature used to sign the given bulk request.

<BatchHeader> This consists of general batch-related information such as the batch ID, batch creation date, number of requests included in that given batch, and so on.

<Request> This is the element that carries the related information pertaining to individual requests, such as the `<KeyID>` and `<ds:KeyInfo>` elements, for those requests.

<ClientInfo> This specifies information about each request that can be used by the trust services provider for its usual bookkeeping. In our example, `<ClientInfo>` consists of the employee ID of the holder of the keys in the ACH domain.

`<dsig:Signature>` This provides information about the digital signature that was used to sign the X-BULK message.

Listing 13.16 is the X-BULK response received by the requesting Web service.

```
<BulkRegisterResult
xmlns="http://www.w3.org/2002/03/xkms-xbulk">

     <SignedPart Id="id-0">
          <BatchHeader>
               <BatchID>batch-0</BatchID>
               ...
               <NumberOfRequests>2</NumberOfRequests>
          </BatchHeader>

          <RegisterResults number="2">
               <xkms:RegisterResult>
                    <xkms:Result>
                         Success
                    </xkms:Result>

                    <xkms:Answer>
                         <xkms:Status>
                              Valid
                         </xkms:Status>

                         <xkms:KeyID>...</xkms:KeyID>

                         <dsig:KeyInfo>
                              ...
                         </dsig:KeyInfo>
                    </xkms:Answer>
               </xkms:RegisterResult>

               <xkms:RegisterResult>
                    ...
               </xkms:RegisterResult>
          </RegisterResults>
     </SignedPart>

     <dsig:Signature>...</dsig:Signature>

</BulkRegisterResult>
```

Listing 13.16 X-BULK key registration response.

- Netegrity JSAML Toolkit (http://members.netegrity.com/access/downloads.cfm)
- Baltimore SelectAccess 5.0 (www.baltimore.com/selectaccess/saml/)
- Systinet WASP Card (www.systinet.com/eap/wasp_card/download/license.html)

This is a Web service that can be consumed by Web services intending to provide SSO functionality based on SAML.

Apart from these implementations, quite a few organizations have declared their ability to support SAML in their platforms:

- Entrust in their New Web Services Trust Framework
- Internet 2
- Verisign in their Trust Services Integration Kit (TSIK)
- Entegrity
- Securant

As can be seen from the previous list, SAML has gained a lot of industry traction. In addition, Java Specification Request (JSR-155), titled "Web Services Security Assertions," is aiming toward providing a standard set of APIs, exchange patterns, and implementation for exchanging assertions between different Web services based upon SAML. These exchange patterns define patterns for exchanging assertions using request/response, synchronous and asynchronous patterns, and fire and forget mechanisms, and they are based on JAX-RPC and JAXM APIs. To find out more information on JSR 155, visit the Java Community Process Web site at www.jcp.org/jsr/detail/155.jsp.

What SAML Defines

SAML specification consists of the following set of documents:

Assertions and protocol. This document defines the syntax and semantics for XML-encoded SAML assertions, protocol requests, and protocol responses.

Bindings and profiles. This document specification defines the frameworks for embedding and transporting SAML assertion requests and responses.

Security and privacy considerations. This document intends to provide information to implementers of SAML systems about possible threats, and thus security risks, to which a SAML-based system is subjected. Also, the document provides guidelines on mitigating

To understand the bulk response shown in Listing 13.16, let's take a look at some of the main elements:

`<BulkRegisterResult>` This is the top element in a bulk response message that carries information such as the batch ID, the number of results included, the actual sequence of the results pertaining to registration requests, and the signature used to sign the given bulk response.

`<BatchID>` This element acts as a co-relation identifier between the bulk request and bulk response.

`<RegisterResults>` This element consists of individual `<xkms:RegisterResult>` elements.

Security Assertions Markup Language (SAML)

The whole vision of Web services was conceived with the notion of interoperability between different applications running on disparate systems. As the plumbing of the Web services was being figured out, a major development also was taking place that supported the idea of making disparate security systems interoperate with each other. Two main standards, Security Services Markup Language (S2ML) and Authentication Markup Language (AuthML), were committed toward making different security systems talk to each other meaningfully—the latter was mainly focused on making security systems exchange authentication-related information among themselves. SAML was the result of merging these two parallel efforts into a single technology. This merging took place when both of these specifications were submitted to the Organization for the Advancement of Structured Information Standards (OASIS) by respective organizations: S2ML from Netegrity and AuthML from Securant Technologies. In order to refer to the SAML specification page hosted by the OASIS Security Services Technical Committee, visit the OASIS Web site at www.oasis-open.org/committees/security/. As of this book's writing, the SAML specification set has already reached the committee specification level.

SAML is a technology resulting from the increased trend toward sharing information among different organizations. Although the base technologies behind Web services facilitate this trend of inter-organization distributed computing, there had been no standard way of sharing information pertaining to the security domain of an organization with its partner businesses, customers, and the like. Even though this sharing of security-related information such as the credentials of one domain's users or policy information of another domain's users was made possible, it was highly proprietary and required the security system at each end to tightly couple one with the other. Thus, the cross-domain sharing of security information was not easy and standard, which is exactly the problem that is addressed by the SAML standard.

SAML allows the development of federated systems, enabling seamless integration and the exchange of information among different security systems. This capability, in turn, enables a variety of solutions to be designed that deal with specific uses ranging from Single Sign-On (SSO) to authorization services to back-office transactions. SSO represents a user's ability to authenticate in one security domain and to use the protected resources of another security domain *without* re-authenticating. Figure 13.17 depicts a scenario wherein an authenticated employee of GoodsCompany.com is capable of changing his benefits information using HR services provided by an outsourced benefits services provider BenefitsProvider.com, without having to re-authenticate himself again to BenefitsProvider.com's security domain.

The assumption in the scenario shown in Figure 13.17 is that GoodsCompany.com and BenefitsProvider.com somehow exchanged information related to the user's authentication (whether the user was authenticated or not), with each other, thus enabling the user to change his benefits information.

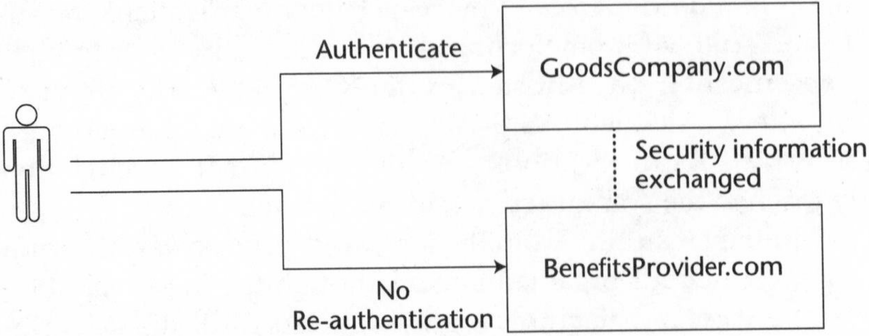

Figure 13.17 A SAML Single Sign-On (SSO) scenario.

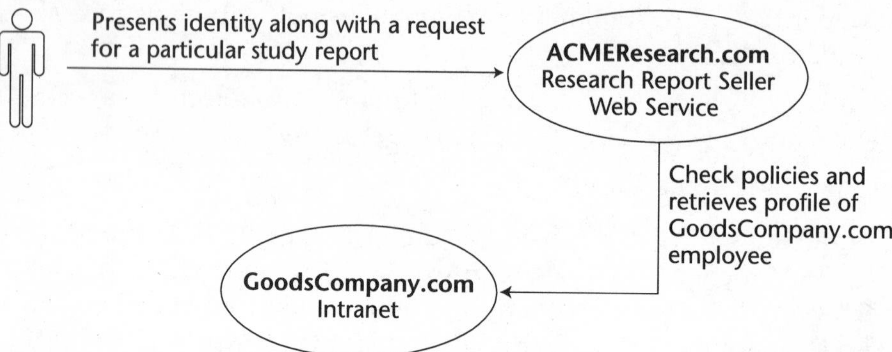

Figure 13.18 A SAML back-office transaction scenario.

Figure 13.18 provides another scenario wherein an authenticated employee of GoodsCompany.com uses the company intranet for ordering a research report hosted by another partner organization—say, ACME Research. In this case, before enabling the employee to make the purchase of a specific research report, ACMEResearch.com makes sure to check that employee's policies to see whether he is allowed to take a credit for that given amount by his company. In addition, ACMEResearch.com's Web service also can pull out profile information on this employee, such as his shipping address, from GoodsCompany.com's databases. Nevertheless, this back-office transaction scenario is made possible by SAML.

SAML provides an XML-based framework for exchanging security-related information over networks, and thus over the Internet. One important thing to understand is that SAML in no way defines new mechanisms for authentication and/or authorization. It merely defines XML structures in which to represent information pertaining to authentication and authorization, so that these structures can be marshaled across the system boundaries and can be understood by the recipient's security systems.

SAML Implementations

At the time of this book's writing, the following implementations of SAML are available:

- Sun ONE Identity Server (part of the Sun ONE Platform for Network Identity) (www.sun.com/software/sunone/tour/identity/)

those security risks. Hence, this document must be read by anyone who will work with SAML on future projects.

Conformance program specification. This document defines a SAML conformance system that is aimed toward achieving compatibility and interoperability among all of the applications that implement SAML.

Now, let's look at the architecture of SAML.

SAML Architecture

SAML is an XML-based framework for exchanging security information. This security information is exchanged in the form of an *assertion* or facts about subjects. A *subject* is an entity that has an identity in some security domain. A typical example of a subject is a person identified by his or her email address in a particular Internet domain. So in this case, the email address becomes the identity of this particular user in the given Internet domain. However, the subject also can very well be some code, in which an assertion may be required so that the code can be allowed to execute on a system.

A *SAML authority,* also known as an *issuing authority,* issues the assertions. Any given business can assume the role of an issuing authority as long as it can issue assertions that can be relied upon by the consuming party. Typically, the role of an issuing authority is played by one of the following parties:

- Third-party security service providers, such as Microsoft through its Passport initiative, XNSORG through its Web Identity platform, or DotGNU through its Virtual Identity Platform.
- Individual businesses "acting as" security services providers within *Federations*. For example, businesses such as AOL, AMEX, VISA, and American Airlines would issue assertions about security information for their respective sets of users within the federations in which they participate.

There are three types of core assertions defined by the SAML specification: authentication assertion, authorization assertion, and attribute assertion. Based on the type of the assertion issued, the issuing authority is known as the authentication authority, authorization authority, or attribute authority. Assertions also can be digitally signed using XML Signature as specified by the SAML profile of XML Digital Signature, which is still a security services committee working draft, as of this writing.

Figure 13.19 depicts the architecture of a typical SAML system. In this figure, a relying party, a party that consumes SAML assertions, sends a request for some kind of SAML assertion to the issuing authority, which in turn creates a SAML assertion and returns it back to the relying party in a SAML response. This request/response protocol is bound to the actual transport or application protocol, such as HTTP or SOAP, respectively.

All assertions, no matter what type, have some of the following elements in common:

- Issuer and Issuance timestamp.
- Assertion ID.
- Subject, for which the assertion has been requested/issued. The subject's information includes the name and security domain to which the subject belongs. Optionally, subject information also can consist of some sort of data that can be used for authenticating the subject.
- Advice element consisting of any additional information that the issuing authority may wish to provide to the relying party in regards to how the assertion was made. For example, the issuer can use an advice element to present some evidence that backs the decision of the assertion on the issuing authority's part so that the evidence can be used for citation purposes in the future. Also, an advice element can be used to present the proof of assertion claims. Another possible use of an advice element can be to specify distribution information for getting timely updates on an assertion. Advice is an optional element.

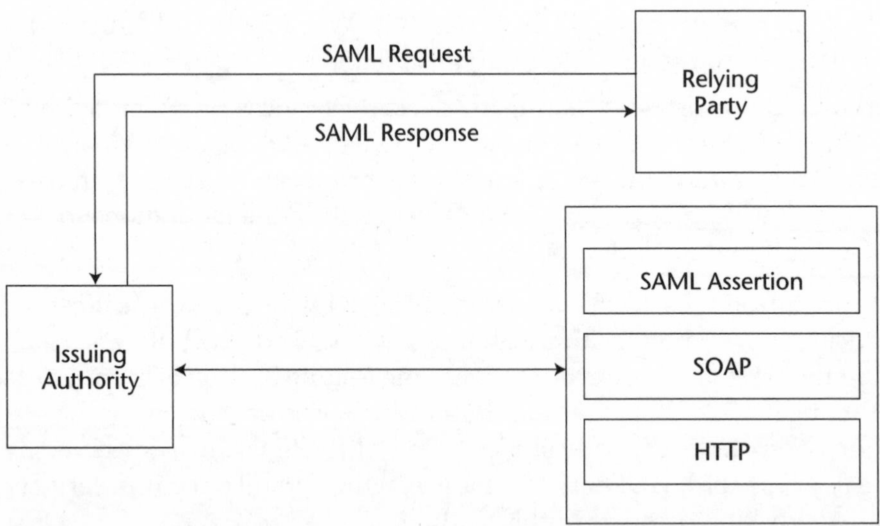

Figure 13.19 SAML architecture.

- Conditions element, also an optional element. However, if an assertion consists of a conditions element, then its validity is dependent upon the evaluation of the conditions provided. If any of the conditions fail, the relying party must reject the assertion. Conditions can include the following:
  - Validity period within which the assertion would remain valid and after which the assertion would expire.
  - Audience restrictions information, which includes relying parties to whom the issuer of this assertion is liable. By including this condition, the issuer declares that it should not be held accountable for the accuracy or trustworthiness of this assertion by parties who do not belong to intended audiences.
  - Target restrictions information, which includes targeting relying parties for which the authority has issued this assertion. If the consuming party is not one of the target parties, then it must reject such assertion and should not use it. Conditions can be user-defined as well, apart from those defined in the SAML specification.

So what does each of these assertions look like? How are assertions exchanged between an issuing authority and a relying party? These are precisely the questions that next few sections will answer. Let's begin with authentication assertion. Note that in the rest of this section on SAML, we will refer to the example scenario of GoodsCompany.com and BenefitsProvider.com as depicted in Figure 13.17.

Authentication Assertion

A relying party sends a request to an issuing authority to assert that a certain subject, 'S', was authenticated. Listing 13.17 shows how the request for the authentication assertion would look.

```
<samlp:Request
MajorVersion="1" MinorVersion="0"
RequestID="123.45.678.90.12345678">

     <samlp:AuthenticationQuery>
          <saml:Subject>
               <saml:NameIdentifier SecurityDomain =
               "GoodsCompany.com" Name="jsmith"/>
          </saml:Subject>

     </samlp:AuthenticationQuery>
</samlp:Request>
```

Listing 13.17 SAML request for authentication assertion.

As we can see from Listing 13.17, the relying party requests that the issuing authority issue an assertion for a subject whose name is "jsmith" in security domain "GoodsCompany.com". The relying party in this case can be anyone with enough privileges to issue assertion requests. The SAML response to this request is an assertion containing authentication statements for the given subject as shown in Listing 13.18.

```
<samlp:Response
MajorVersion="1" MinorVersion="0"
RequestID="128.14.234.20.90123456"
InResponseTo="123.45.678.90.12345678"
StatusCode="Success">

     <saml:Assertion
     MajorVersion="1" MinorVersion="0"
     AssertionID="123.45.678.90.12345678"
     Issuer="GoodsCompany, Inc."
     IssueInstant="2002-01-14T10:00:23Z">

          <saml:Conditions
          NotBefore="2002-01-14T10:00:30Z"
          NotAfter="2002-01-14T10:15:00Z"/>

          <saml:AuthenticationStatement
          AuthenticationMethod="Password"
          AuthenticationInstant="2001-01-14T10:00:20Z">

               <saml:Subject>
                    <saml:NameIdentifier
                    SecurityDomain="GoodsCompany.com"
                    Name="jsmith" />
               </saml:Subject>

          </saml:AuthenticationStatement>
     </saml:Assertion>
</samlp:Response>
```

Listing 13.18 SAML response consisting of an authentication assertion.

The returned assertion contains a <saml:Conditions> element defining the conditions that determine the validity of this assertion. In this example, the <saml:Conditions> element states that this assertion is valid only during a certain time period.

The <saml:AuthenticationStatement> element specifies the authentication method in which the act of authentication was carried out.

In our example, subject "jsmith" in the security domain "Goods Company.com" was authenticated using password authentication. However, any authentication mechanism can be used with SAML. Again, <saml:AuthenticationStatement> also specifies the time instant during which the act of authentication was performed.

NOTE The actual act of authentication or authorization is out of the scope of the SAML specification, which implies that SAML does not specify or mandate the act of authentication or authorization. This means that issuers can make assertions about acts of authentication or authorization that already have occurred. Thus, there is a disconnect between the actual act of authentication or authorization and the issuance of an assertion about it. Therefore, a malicious authority *may* abuse its power and issue the relying parties a valid but wrongful authentication or authorization assertion, and there is no way for the relying party to know that the issuing authority lied to it about actually authenticating or authorizing the subject. This brings up a significant point that the SAML applications should not be consuming assertions from any and every issuing authority. In fact, the SAML applications should rely upon assertions issued by trusted authorities only and under well defined "Trust Agreements" and "Security Breach" contracts.

Attribute Assertion

A SAML request for attribute assertion is sent by a relying party to an issuing authority to assert the value of certain attributes, 'A', 'B', . . . for a certain subject, 'S'. Listing 13.19 shows an example of the request for an attribute assertion.

```
<samlp:Request ...>
     <samlp:AttributeQuery>
          <saml:Subject>
               <saml:NameIdentifier
               SecurityDomain="GoodsCompany.com"
               Name="jsmith"/>
          </saml:Subject>

          <saml:AttributeDesignator
          AttributeName="Employee_ID"
          AttributeNamespace="GoodsCompany.com"/>

     </samlp:AttributeQuery>
</samlp:Request>
```

Listing 13.19 SAML request for an attribute assertion.

As we can see from Listing 13.19, the relying party requests the issuing authority to issue an assertion stating the value of the attribute "Employee_ID" for a subject named "jsmith" in the security domain "GoodsCompany.com". The SAML response to this request is shown in Listing 13.20.

```
<samlp:Response ...>
    <saml:Assertion ...>

        <saml:Conditions .../>

        <saml:AttributeStatement>
            <saml:Subject>
                <saml:NameIdentifier
                SecurityDomain="GoodsCompany.com"
                Name="jsmith"/>
            </saml:Subject>

            <saml:Attribute
            AttributeName="Employee_ID"
            AttributeNamespace="GoodsCompany.com">

                <saml:AttributeValue>
                    123456
                </saml:AttributeValue>

            </saml:Attribute>
        </saml:AttributeStatement>
    </saml:Assertion>
</samlp:Response>
```

Listing 13.20 SAML response consisting of an attribute assertion.

The returned SAML response asserts that the value of the attribute "Employee ID" for the subject "jsmith" in the security domain "GoodsCompany.com" is "123456".

Authorization (Decision) Assertion

A SAML request for an authorization assertion is sent by the relying party to the issuing authority to assert whether the subject 'S' is allowed the access of type 'D' to resource 'R', given certain evidence 'E' (if any). Evidence is an assertion upon which an issuing party can rely upon while making an authorization decision.

An example of a SAML request for authorization assertion in the following code requests the issuing authority to assert whether the subject `"jsmith"` can be allowed access of type `"Read"` and `"Change"` (defined in the `"GoodsCompany.com"` namespace) to resource `"http://www.BenefitsProvider.com/GoodsCompany/benefits"`. This resource represents the Benefits Management Web service hosted by GoodsCompany.com's outsourced benefits services provider: BenefitsProvider.com, as shown in Listing 13.21.

```
<samlp:Request ...>
     <samlp:AuthorizationDecisionQuery
     Resource = "http://www.BenefitsProvider.com/
     GoodsCompany/benefits">

          <saml:Subject>
               <saml:NameIdentifier
               SecurityDomain="GoodsCompany.com"
               Name="jsmith"/>
          </saml:Subject>

          <saml:Actions Namespace="GoodsCompany.com">
               <saml:Action>Read</saml:Action>
               <saml:Action>Change</saml:Action>
          </saml:Actions>

          <saml:Evidence>
               <saml:Assertion>
                    ...Some assertion...
               </saml:Assertion>
          </saml:Evidence>

     </samlp:AuthorizationQuery>
</samlp:Request>
```

Listing 13.21 SAML request for authorization decision assertion.

The SAML response to this request is an assertion containing an authorization decision statement as shown in Listing 13.22.

```
<saml:Response ...>
     <saml:Assertion ...>
          <saml:Conditions .../>
```

Listing 13.22 SAML response consisting of an authorization decision assertion. *(continues)*

```
            <saml:AuthorizationDecisionStatement
            Decision="Permit"
            Resource="http://www.BenefitsProvider.com/
            GoodsCompany/benefits">
                 <saml:Subject>
                      <saml:NameIdentifier
                      SecurityDomain="GoodsCompany.com"
                      Name="jsmith"/>
                 </saml:Subject>
            </saml:AuthorizationStatement>

      </saml:Assertion>
 </samlp:Response>
```

Listing 13.22 SAML response consisting of an authorization decision assertion. *(continued)*

The returned assertion contains a `<saml:AuthorizationDecision-Statement>` saying that subject "`rimap`" is permitted the requested type of access on the given resource.

NOTE **Applications working with SAML can define their own specific assertions. In fact, they can also define their own protocol for exchanging these assertions. However, this extensibility comes at the cost of interoperability. Hence, in such scenarios, one must ensure that all of the participating parties do agree to the syntax and semantics of the user-defined assertions being exchanged. Also, they must agree to a common protocol. More importantly, SAML implementations of all parties must interoperate with each other.**

SAML Bindings and Protocols

A SAML binding is a way to transport SAML request and response messages. A binding is achieved by mapping a SAML message exchange to a particular communication or messaging protocol. For example, an HTTP binding for SAML describes how SAML request and response message exchanges are mapped into HTTP message exchanges. A SAML SOAP binding describes how SAML request and response message exchanges are mapped into SOAP message exchanges. So far, the SAML specification has already defined the SOAP-over-HTTP binding. This binding specifies how to carry a SAML request or response within a SOAP body element.

A SAML profile is the way to embed and extract SAML assertions into a framework or protocol. A profile describes how the SAML assertions are embedded into or combined with other objects (for example, files of various types or headers of communication protocol, such as HTTP) by an originating party, and then are sent by the originating party to a destination, and subsequently processed at the destination. For example, a SAML profile for SOAP defines how SAML assertions can be added to SOAP messages and how SOAP headers are affected by SAML assertions. Currently, the SAML Web browser profile for Single Sign-On (SSO) has been defined.

SAML Web Browser SSO profiles support SSO scenarios in Web services delivered through browsers. There are two SSO profiles defined for Web browser-based Web services:

Browser/Artifact profile. This profile supports SSO scenarios where a user accesses a secured resource on a destination site, and an artifact (reference) is sent along with the request. The destination site uses this artifact or reference to de-reference the actual assertion and to finally get hold of this assertion. In fact, the SSO use case that we will see in the following section uses this profile.

Browser/POST profile. This profile supports SSO scenarios where assertions are exchanged as part of the HTML form that gets POST-ed to destination site upon the submittal of a request to a resource on the destination site.

Work also is currently in progress to define a SAML profile for XML Signature.

Model of Producers and Consumers of SAML Assertions

Figure 13.20 provides a view of most of the elements in the SAML problem space. The diagram does not describe message flow; instead, it only describes the entities producing and consuming assertions. This model is required for understanding the interactions of a SAML system with the rest of the security domain.

To understand this model, let's begin with the system entity. It is a part of an application functionality that initiates some action that would ultimately be rejected or permitted. An application user may request functionality that requires authentication. In this case, the system entity requests the service from another entity, called the credentials collector, whose job is to collect credentials from the application user.

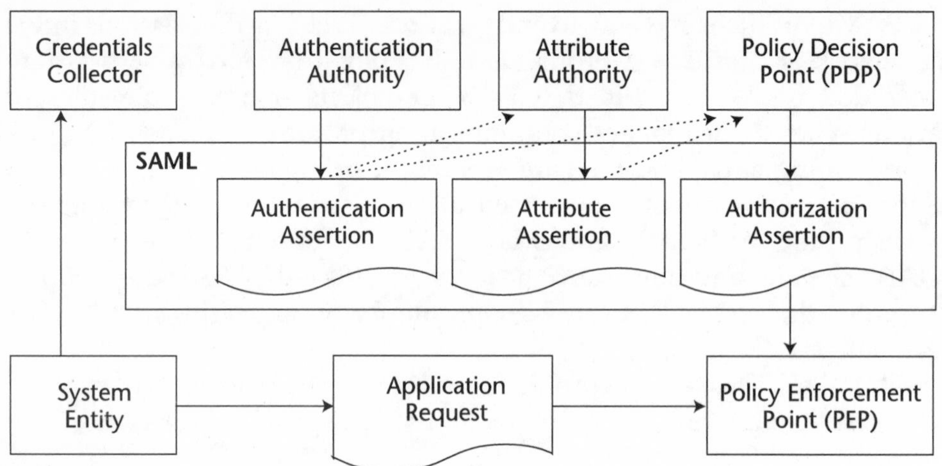

Figure 13.20 Producers and consumers model for SAML assertions.

After collecting credentials, the credentials collector requests the authentication authority to issue an assertion containing an authentication statement about the application user. Attribute Authority and Authorization Decision Authority then can use this authentication assertion to further issue an attribute assertion and authorization assertion, respectively. Authorization authority also is known as Policy Decision Point (PDP) because the decisions on authorizing the access to any resource of a given system are made by this entity.

A PDP is requested to make an authorization decision typically by Policy Enforcement Point (PEP). PEP does not define policies of its own; rather, it acts on the authorization decisions made by PDP.

Knowing this, we will now proceed to an example that illustrates implementing Single Sign-On using SAML.

Single Sign-On Using SAML

In this section, we will see how to implement a SSO use case using SAML technology. The use case expands the SSO scenario depicted in Figure 13.21, wherein a GoodsCompany employee wishes to make changes to his benefits information while browsing through GoodsCompany intranet portal http://GoodsCompany.intranet. Hence, the employee selects a link on http://GoodsCompany.intranet, which leads him to Benefits Management

Service, hosted by an outsourced HR benefits provider, BenefitsProvider.com, at www.BenefitsProvider.com/GoodsCompany/benefits.

The focus of this example is to use the browser/artifact profile to achieve SSO whenever an authenticated GoodsCompany employee changes the domain from http://GoodsCompany.intranet to www.BenefitsProvider.com /GoodsCompany/benefits.

Figure 13.21 shows the sequence of interactions that takes place between the GoodsCompany.com employee, the GoodsCompany's intranet portal, and BenefitsProvider.com. Let's examine each of these interactions one-by-one.

1. In this first interaction, the employee authenticates himself to the GoodsCompany's security domain.

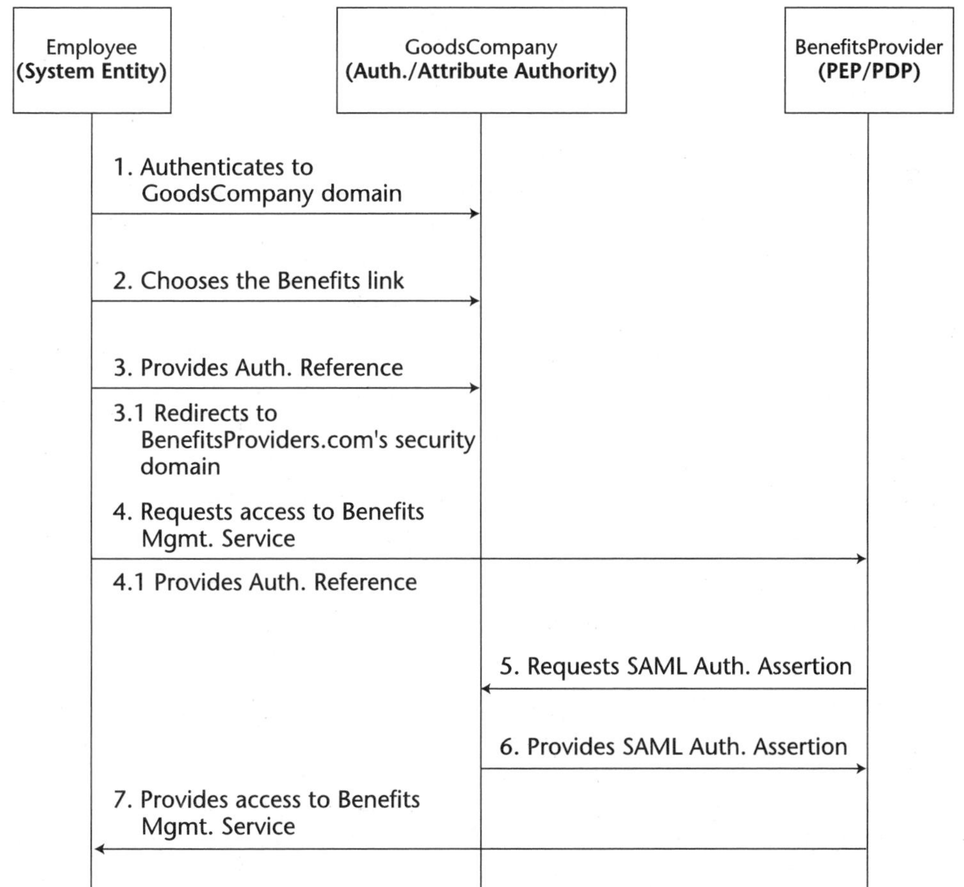

Figure 13.21 Interactions between an employee, the GoodsCompany intranet portal, and BenefitsProvider.

2. Next, the employee browses through GoodsCompany's intranet portal (that is, http://GoodsCompany.intranet) and selects a URL that leads him to a service that assists employees with their personal needs. The employee uses this service's interface to select a link that will eventually lead him to manage his HR benefits.
3. When the employee selects the benefits link, a service hosted by GoodsCompany.com generates an authentication assertion for this employee and creates a reference (artifact) to this assertion. This service then stores the assertion and redirects the employee to the BenefitsProvider.com domain. While redirecting, the service also appends the assertion reference to the HTTP request.
4. Next, the employee sends an HTTP GET request to the BenefitsProvider.com domain. This request contains the assertion reference created in Step 3.
5. BenefitsProvider.com receives the request from the GoodsCompany's employee. The request carries a reference to an authentication assertion issued by GoodsCompany, Inc. Now, BenefitsProvider will want to de-reference this assertion to get the actual authentication assertion. To do so, it requests that a particular service, hosted by GoodsCompany.com, returns the referenced SAML assertion.
6. The GoodsCompany.com domain then provides BenefitsProvider.com with the requested authentication assertion.
7. BenefitsProvider.com then gets the assertion from GoodsCompany stating that the given employee is authenticated. Based on this assertion, BenefitsProvider.com makes a decision to permit access by this employee to its Benefits Management Service, and therefore eventually redirects the employee to Benefits Management Service (that is, www.BenefitsProvider.com/GoodsCompany/benefits).

These are all of the steps involved in this SSO scenario. Now, let's see how this entire scenario has been implemented. First, we must identify all of the software components to be used to implement this scenario.

Figure 13.22 shows all the components to be used in this implementation. Later, we will take a look at the code of some of the very interesting components in this design—that is, `ForwardToBenefitsProvider`, `BenefitsProviderEntry`, and `GoodsCompanyAssert`. The rest of the components are regular JSPs/Servlets, and hence, not of much interest to us.

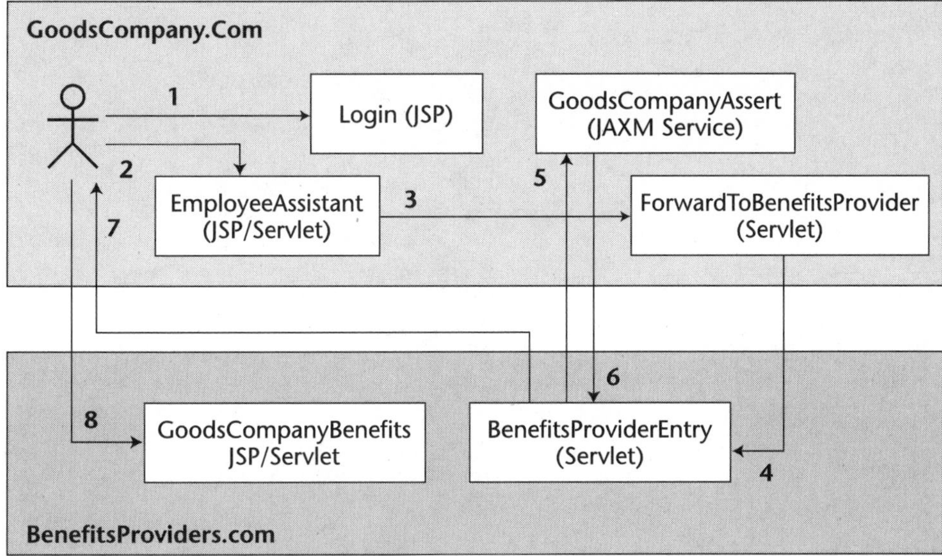

Figure 13.22 Implementation components.

For this code sample, we will be using the SAML implementation that comes as part of iPlanet Directory Server Access Management Product (iDSAME) that, in turn, is now a part of the Sun ONE Platform for Network Identity. For more information on this product, please read the section titled *SAML Implementations*.

In addition, please note that the code shown herewith is merely a skeleton of the code used in implementing the presented use case. In other words, a complete source code for this particular example is not available.

Implementing ForwardToBenefitsProvider

`ForwardToBenefitsProvider` is a servlet component whose main job is to generate an assertion containing authentication statements about the employee in question and to store this generated assertion to some disk storage. The `EmployeeAssistant` (JSP/Servlet) component calls this servlet whenever it needs to redirect the user to the Benefits Management Service hosted by BenefitsProvider.com.

Listing 13.23 is the sample implementation of the `doGet()` method of the `ForwardToBenefitsProvider` servlet.

```
public void doGet (...)
{
     //Generate the assertion for this user
     Assertion objAssertion = getAssertion(request.getRemoteUser());

     //Writes the assertion to a store (a filesystem, say) and
     //returns a reference (a random number) to this assertion.
     AssertionArtifact objArtifact = createAssertionArtifact
     (objAssertion, "GoodsCompany.Com", "BenefitsProvider.Com");

     String sReference = objArtifact.getAssertionArtifact();

     //Now time for redirecting the user to
     //BenefitsProviderEntry servlet, with assertion reference
     Response.sendRedirect
     ("http://www.BenefitsProvider.com/BenefitsProviderEntry
     ?SAMLart = " + sReference);
}
```

Listing 13.23 ForwardToBenefitsProvider component—`doGet()` method.

`doGet()` gets hold of an assertion for the employee through a user-defined method `getAssertion()` (sample implementation follows). `doGet()` then creates an assertion artifact (reference) and finally redirects the user to the `BenefitsProviderEntry` servlet.

`getAssertion()` is an interesting method. It creates an assertion and populates it with authentication and attribute statements. In addition, it also puts in conditions and audience restrictions in the newly created assertion. Listing 13.24 shows its implementation.

```
public Assertion getAssertion (...)
{
     //Create SAML Conditions under which this assertion is valid
     Conditions objConditions = new Conditions (StartDate, EndDate);

     //Add Audience Restriction Condition, if any
     objConditions.addAudienceRestrictionCondition (objAudience);

     //Add Target Restricton Condition, if any
     objConditions.addTargetRestrictionCondition (objTarget)

     //Create the Subject relevant to this assertion
```

Listing 13.24 ForwardToBenefitsProvider component—`getAssertion()` method.

```
    NameIdentifier nameIdentifier =
    new NameIdentifier(sSecurityDomain, sUserName);

    //Now make an Authentication Statement
    AuthenticationStatement objAuthStmt =
    new AuthenticationStatement
    ("Password", new Date(), objSubject);

    //Now build Attribute Assertion
    Attribute attribute = new Attribute
    ("Department", "GoodsCompany.com", DepartmentValue);

    List attributeList = new HashList();
    attributeList.add(attribute);

    AttributeStatement objAttrStmt = new AttributeStatement
    (attributeList, objSubject);

    //Now build an Assertion containing above
    //AssertionStatements
    String sIssuer = "GoodsCompany, Inc.";

    Set objStmts = new HashSet();
    objStmts.add(objAuthStmt);
    objStmts.add(objAttrStmt);

    Assertion objAssertion = new Assertion
    (AssertionID,sIssuer, new Data(), objConditions, objStmts);

    //Finally return the newly created Assertion
    return objAssertion;
}
```

Listing 13.24 ForwardToBenefitsProvider component—`getAssertion()` method. *(continued)*

Implementing BenefitsProviderEntry

`BenefitsProviderEntry` is a servlet component that gets called whenever a user from another domain tries to enter BenefitsProvider.com's security domain. This is the servlet that receives requests from the employee when the employee is redirected from the GoodsCompany.com's domain. `BenefitsProviderEntry` extracts the assertion reference from the HTTP request parameters and then calls back the `GoodsCompanyAssert` Web service that is implemented as a JAXM service. Thus, in order to communicate with `GoodsCompanyAssert`, `BenefitsProviderEntry` uses JAXM SOAP APIs for making a SOAP RPC call.

GoodsCompanyAssert returns the <Assertion> element within the response SOAP message. BenefitsProviderEntry extracts the <Assertion> element from the SOAP message and checks its validity using a user-defined function, isAssertionValid(). Once the validity of assertion is confirmed, the employee's request is redirected to the actual Benefits Management Service—that is, to www.BenefitsProvider.com/GoodsCompany/benefits.

Listing 13.25 is a partial sample code for the BenefitsProviderEntry servlet.

```
public void doGet(...)
{
     //Extract the value of request parameter "SAMLart"
     String sReference = request.getParameters("SAMLart");

     //Now populate a SOAP message consisting of this reference
     //and send it synchronously to GoodsCompanyAssert JAXM
     //Service (GoodsCompany.com/partners/GoodsCompanyAssert)
     //in order to get the actual assertion

     ...

     SOAPMessage objAssertionSOAPMsg = objSOAPConnection.call
     (objRequestSOAPMessage, objURLEndpoint);

     //Now the returned AssertionSOAPMsg consist of Assertions.
     //So get hold of the Assertion element from the SOAP
     //message body and populate the SAML Assertion

     ...

     Assertion objAssertion = new Assertion
     (objSOAPAssertionListElement);

     //Once we have Assertion, check for its validity
     boolean bValid = isAssertionValid(sPartner,objAssertion);

     //If everything is okay then redirect the user to Benefits
     //(http://www.BenefitsProvider.com/GoodsCompany/benefits)

     response.sendRedirect
     ("http://www.BenefitsProvider.com/GoodsCompany/benefits");
}
```

Listing 13.25 BenefitsProviderEntry component–doGet() method.

A validity check of an assertion consists of checking that the assertion has been issued by a valid party, the period through which the assertion will remain valid, whether this assertion is supposed to be consumed by parties *including* us, and so forth. These are the types of checks that the `isAssertionValid()` method would perform and return the result based on the evaluation of all the checks. Listing 13.26 shows the sample code for this method.

```
public boolean isAssertionValid (String FromPartner,
Assertion objAssertion)
{
     //Make sure that the assertion is coming from a valid
     //partner
     ...

     //Check the period through which assertion will remain
     //valid
     Conditions objConditions = objAssertion.getConditions();

     boolean bValid = objConditions.checkDateValidity
     (new Date());

     //Now check whether we are one of the intended audiences
     boolean bValid = objConditions.checkAudience (Audience);

     //Finally return the result of validity check
     return bValid;
}
```

Listing 13.26 BenefitsProviderEntry component—`isAssertionValid()` method.

Implementing GoodsCompanyAssert

The `GoodsCompanyAssert` component of this implementation is a JAXM service that receives requests from various partners of GoodsCompany (in a federation, for example) to assert various things about GoodsCompany personnel, of course with proper privileges. In our scenario, this service receives SOAP requests consisting of assertion references. `GoodsCompanyAssert` de-references these assertion references by retrieving the corresponding assertions from the store and returning them back to the requestor within a SOAP response message. The implementation of this service is shown in Listing 13.27. For more information on implementing JAXM services, refer back to Chapter 9, "XML Messaging Using JAXM and SAAJ."

```
public SOAPMessage onMessage (SOAPMessage objIncomingSOAPMsg)
{
     //Extract the SOAP Body first and then extract the assertion
     //reference from the incoming SOAP message's body
     SOAPElement objReference = extractElement
     (objIncomingSOAPBody, "AssertionArtifact");

     //Now retrieve the Assertion corresponding to this reference
     //from the assertion store (A filesystem, say)
     ...

     //Now populate response SOAP message's body with this
     //assertion
     objResponseSOAPBody.addBodyElement
     (objResponseSOAPEnv.createName("Assertion", null, null));
     ...

     //Now time to send the response SOAP message to the caller
     return objResponseSOAPMsg;
}
```

Listing 13.27 GoodsCompanyAssert component—`onMessage()` method.

These components form most of the portion of implementing a SAML-based SSO system that uses the browser/artifact profile. Knowing this, we will conclude our discussion on SAML and move on to XACML, a complementary technology standard of SAML.

XML Access Control Markup Language (XACML)

XACML is a technology that enables access control policies to be expressed in XML. XACML aims to provide XML documents with a sophisticated access control model and fine-grained access control specification language. With this specification, the access control policies regulate how an XML document appears to the end user. In addition, the updates to the document also can be governed by the policies. XACML should enable one to specify and execute fine-grained and complex authorization policies.

Common ACLs use a three-tuple format like <Object, Subject, Action>. XACML extends this to the <Object, Subject, Action, Condition>-oriented policy in the context of a particular XML document. The notion of a subject comprises the concepts of identity, group, and role. The granularity of an object can be as fine as single elements within the document. Currently, there are four possible actions: read, write, create, and delete, however, the language can be extended to more actions.

XACML is based on a *Provisional Authorization* model wherein we can specify provisional actions (conditions) associated with primitive actions such as read, write, create, and delete. Most of the access control systems are based on the following model:

User A makes a request to access Resource R on a system in some context, and the system either authorizes the request and grants access or denies it.

XACML goes one step further and tells the user not only that his request was granted or denied but also that his request would be authorized provided he takes certain actions or that his request is denied but the system must still take certain actions. A classic example of such a provisional action is auditing. Encryption, signature verification, and XSLT transformations also are examples of some other provisional actions apart from the basic read, write, create, and delete examples.

Let's consider an example of a provisional authorization model. Such a model would enable us to define fine-grained policies such as the following:

- Authorized access to a resource, for example, www.BenefitsProvider.com/GoodsCompany/benefits, must be logged.
- A user should be authorized to change the previous resource only if a valid digital signature is provided with each change request.
- If an unauthorized access is detected, the system administrator will be alerted by a warning message.

To implement all of these policies in our system using existing access control mechanisms, we would need to hard-code all of the policy control logic in our application. However, in a provisional authorization system such as the one defined by XACML, all of these policies can be processed by the Policy Enforcement Point (PEP) and do not have to be written by application developers. The XACML standard began as a submission of the XML Access Control Language (XACL) to OASIS by IBM. XACML activity began in April 2001 and there is still not much out there in terms of a concrete specification, as of this writing. In order to keep track of ongoing specification activity, visit the OASIS Web site at www.oasis-open.org/committees/xacml/.

Architecture of an XML Access Control System

Figure 13.23 shows the architecture for an XML access control system. Here, PEP manages the access to target resources represented in XML. The target resource may be originally written for XML or it may be converted to an XML format from another data structure using XSLT transformations. Policy Decision Point (PDP) receives an access request issued by PEP and makes an access decision using information from Policy Information Point (PIP), which provides information such as current time, and Policy Repository Point (PRP), which manages a set of access control policies. Note that a requestor could be a human user (using a browser) or another Web service.

SAML and XACML

SAML enables a PEP to make a request to a remote PDP asking for an authorization assertion. Essentially the request says that given the following policy inputs, assert whether the access is or is not allowed. Presently, SAML has no generalized way of specifying the policy inputs. A small fixed set of policy inputs is allowed, but PDP's authorization decision also could have been based upon input from other policies (and not just the ones defined by a SAML assertion request), which do not appear in either a SAML assertion request or response. Even if PEP is not aware of the inputs that the PDP requires to make an authorization decision, the PDP should specify in the response all of the inputs it used to make the authorization decision. This specification is not a policy language requirement. But, given that XACML is general enough to specify policies based on all of the inputs and provisional actions, XACML would be a natural fit for defining a syntax that SAML can leverage for expressing current values of the inputs used by the policies. This is where XACML can complement SAML.

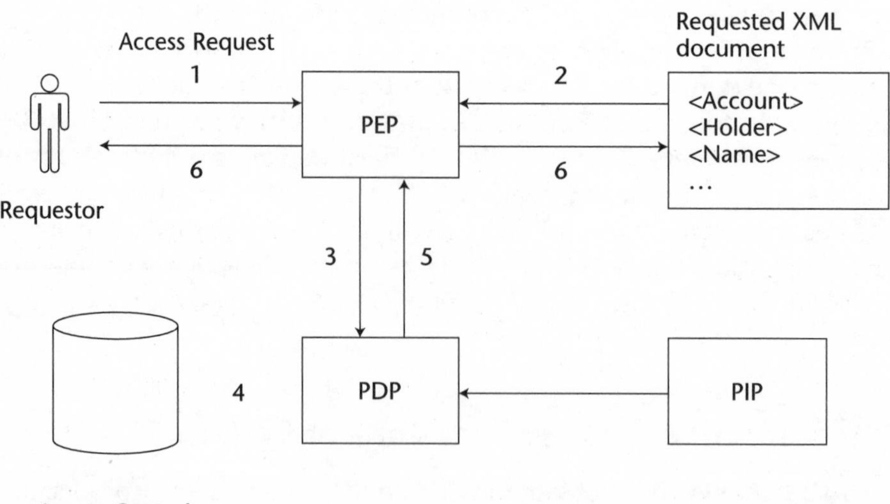

Figure 13.23 XML Access Control System architecture.

Sample XACML Policy

The XACML policy example in Listing 13.28 illustrates the connection between XACML and SAML. This policy assumes that a SAML `AuthorizationDecisionQuery` has been received by a SAML PDP, requesting that an authorization assertion is issued to the GoodsCompany employee so that he can read/modify his benefits information. The policy here specifies a rule that the so-called employee of Goods-Company, Inc. should be granted read/modify access to his benefits information, that is, all the resources under `www.BenefitsProvider.com/GoodsCompany/`, only if his identity information as specified by Xlink address`samlp:AuthorizationDecisionQuery/Subject/NameIdentifier/Name` is found in the online personnel database hosted by GoodsCompanyat `www.BenefitsProvider.com/GoodsCompany/database/personnel/empdb`.

```
<?xml version="1.0"/>
<rule>
     <target>
          <subject>

samlp:AuthorizationDecisionQuery/Subject/NameIdentifier/Name
          </subject>

          <resource>
               <patternMatch>
                    <attributeRef>
                         samlp:AuthorizationDecisionQuery/Resource
                    </attributeRef>

                    <attibuteValue>
                         http://www.BenefitsProvider.com/
                         GoodsCompany/*
                    </attibuteValue>
               </patternMatch>
          </resource>

          <actions>
               <saml:Actions>
                    <saml:Action>
                         read
                    <saml:Action>

                    <saml:Action>
                         change
                    <saml:Action>
```

Listing 13.28 XACML policy. *(continues)*

```
            </saml:Actions>
        </actions>
    </target>

    <condition>
        <equal>
            <attributeRef>
                samlp:AuthorizationDecisionQuery/Subject/
                NameIdentifier/Name
            </attributeRef>

            <attributeRef>

http://www.GoodsCompany.com/database/personnel/empdb/
            </attributeRef>
        </equal>
    </condition>

    <effect>
        Permit
    </effect>
</rule>
```

Listing 13.28 XACML policy. *(continued)*

Conclusion

All of the security standards for Web services mentioned in this chapter sound very promising. We do have standards in almost every area of security handling trust, policies, interoperability between security systems, fine-grained access control policies for XML documents, and so on. However, one of the issues with these XML security standards is that there is no standard that currently ties these standards to Web services and especially SOAP. We need a standard that specifies how to sign all or a part of a SOAP message, how to pass credentials in a SOAP message, how to encrypt all or part(s) of a SOAP message, and so on, so that the interoperability promise of Web services is maintained.

At the time of this book's writing, WS-Security, a new OASIS specification effort, is aimed toward providing a standard syntax for incorporating XML Encryption, XML Signature, and XKMS Requests/Responses within SOAP Signatures. You can find more information on WS-Security at www.oasis-open.org/committees/wss/.

Summary

In this chapter, we have examined challenges that are posed by Web services and have discussed all of the technologies and standards that are available to meet those challenges. In addition, we also have taken a look at some of the basic concepts of cryptography in this chapter. By now, we have gained a good understanding on the positioning, application, and usage of the following Web services security-related standards:

- XML Encryption
- XML Signature
- XML Key Management Specification
- Security Assertions Markup Language
- XML Access Control Markup Language

In the next chapter, we will take a look at Sun ONE, Sun Microsystems' vision of Web services and more.

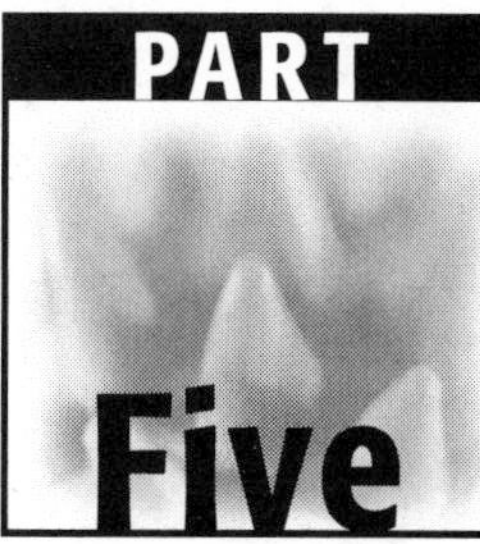

Web Services Strategies and Solutions

CHAPTER

14

Introduction to Sun ONE

By the late 1990s, almost the entire industry felt the need for a single, coherent architecture that was capable of providing an across-the-board solution from operating platforms to application servers. This urgent need formed the basis of the two important architectures that were introduced almost simultaneously by rival companies Microsoft and Sun Microsystems. These architectures, .NET and Sun Open Net Environment (Sun ONE), from Microsoft and Sun Microsystems, respectively, provide an end-to-end solution that an organization can adopt mainly in order to reduce the complexity and cost of investments of IT projects. This chapter introduces and provides key information about one of these visions—that is, Sun ONE.

In this chapter, we will examine the core of the Sun Open Net Environment in terms of the following:

- The vision behind Sun ONE
- Delivering Services on Demand
- Sun ONE Architecture

The Vision behind Sun ONE

The key mantra behind Sun ONE is *Services on Demand*. A Service on Demand (SoD) is a service that can be delivered to the consumer, when the consumer needs it, on any device in which the consumer needs it. Therefore, it is basically an anytime, anywhere, any device computing paradigm. The SoD vision enables a business to leverage its enterprise information assets to perform its business operations and to communicate with others—anywhere, anytime, and on any device. Sun ONE uses the term Services on Demand to encompass a service built using any of the following software methods:

Local applications. Defined as a monolithic application running on PCs/workstations

Client/Server applications. Applications structured so that the presentation layer and business layer run on a heavy client, such as a desktop with the required client runtime installed where the data is stored in the backend in the database layer

Web applications. Applications that can service requests and send responses over the Web protocols, mainly HTTP

Web services. Applications that use XML-based protocols, usually on top of Web protocols

Web clients. Applications that are delivered over the Web to Java technology-enabled devices, such as personal digital assistants (PDAs), cellular phones, and personal computers

Sun ONE thus represents a vision that is more of an evolution of network computing than a revolution. It presents a continuum to the previous computing approaches. Table 14.1 presents a table describing different waves of computing and their schematics, in an evolutionary manner.

We understand that the first three phases of computing have already taken place. The fourth phase is what we are living in right now—the phase of Web services. This is the phase in which services are delivered over the Web protocols, mainly HTTP. The services in this phase are described using XML-based languages, such as WSDL, and can be registered with service registries (for example, UDDI). Also, these services can be consumed using request/response or messaging protocols based on SOAP. We know, by now, how to write such simple Web services using basic Web services protocols such as SOAP, WSDL, and UDDI. Interestingly, Sun ONE takes that effort a step further by supporting a framework that enables Web services to be created, which can be stateful and complex so that they can be used for performing business functions. These Web services also are termed as *Business Web services* in Sun ONE. Such Web services are discussed in the next section titled *Delivering Services on Demand*. Sun ONE also envisions another phase of Web services, known as *Federated Web services*, which again are discussed in the next section.

Table 14.1 Evolution of Computing

COMPUTING METHOD	PERIOD	PROTOCOLS	SCHEMATIC
Local applications	Until late 1980s	None	
Client/server	Late 1980s–1994/1995	None	
Web applications	1995–1999/2000	HTTP	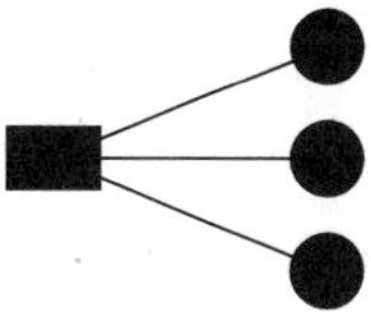
Web services (Simple, Business, Federated)	2001–???	HTTP, XML	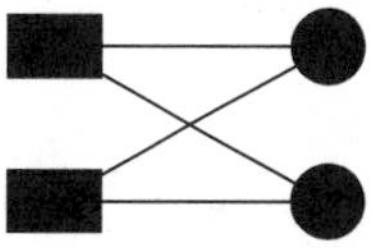
??? (Includes Web services, peer services, Jini services)	2003/2004 onward	XML, RDF, JXTA, Jini, and so forth	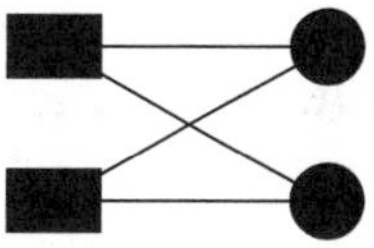

No term has been coined yet for the fifth phase of computing shown in Table 14.1. The idea here is to come up with a framework and underlying infrastructure required for enabling true Services on Demand such that the consumer should be able to use any device to consume a particular service, using *any transport mechanism,* such as Web (HTTP), JXTA, or Jini.

JXTA technology, open sourced by Sun Microsystems, provides a standard framework for building peer-to-peer (P2P) services. JXTA defines a set of open protocols that enables building P2P applications in any language, including Java. Currently, the JXTA community has provided JXTA runtime implemented for Java language. For more information on JXTA, visit the JXTA community Web site at www.jxta.org.

Jini is a distributed computing technology, originally from Sun Microsystems, that enables networked devices and software services to interconnect with each other *dynamically.* These networked devices and software services can form communities on an ad-hoc basis without any a priori knowledge or configuration. This enables the creation of network services (software or hardware) that are highly adaptive to change. Jini technology enables the building of such adaptive networks that can be evolved over time and space. For more information on Jini, visit the Jini official Web site at wwws.sun.com/software/jini.

This phase is supposed to have begun and should gain full momentum by mid-2003 or 2004.

Delivering Services on Demand (SoD)

Currently, the Sun ONE architecture can deliver *Services on Demand over the Web*. Later on, Sun may include other mechanisms such as JXTA or Jini, say, for delivering SoD using Sun ONE architecture. The Web-based mechanisms for delivering SoD consist of the following:

- Web applications
- Web services
- Web clients

Web Applications

A Web application is a traditional way of delivering a service wherein the markup generated by the service is sent back as part of the service response to the consumer. Most of the time, the consumer simply uses a Web browser as a client application that renders the markup received as part of the service response. Eventually, the consumer uses this rendered markup as a visual interface in order to interact with the service. Sun expects most of the SoD prior to year-end 2002 to be delivered as Web applications. Sun ONE architecture includes a variety of standards and products that can be used for developing and deploying Web applications. We will discuss these in the section titled *Sun ONE Architecture.*

Web Services

A Web service is a newly conceived method of delivering a SoD such that all communication between the service and the consumer takes place through XML-based RPC or XML-based messaging mechanisms. A Web service can be described such that its interfaces and semantics are readable by other applications. This gives a Web service the unique capability of being used by other services as a component. Similarly, a Web service also can be registered to a public or private registry such that another application can locate it and decide whether to use it or not, by studying its registration metadata. Web service metadata also can convey information required for consuming the Web service as part of a certain choreography or flow. A Web service thus is a componentization of an application's services.

Web services adoption, according to Sun and other industry experts, will take place in three phases. These are simple Web services, business Web services, and federated Web services, described in the following sections.

Simple Web Services

A simple Web service is typically based upon the SOAP, UDDI, and WSDL stack of protocols. It also is typically stateless with limited metadata capabilities. Also, a simple Web service is less reliable, owing to the limitations of the underlying SOAP protocol. The reason it is called simple is because it cannot be used for delivering complex "business" type functionality due to the limited availability of metadata and reliability. Most of the Web services pilots we see today are of such a type. In fact, all the information presented in this book pertains to creating such a type of simple Web services.

Business Web Services

A business Web service has the ability to participate in horizontal business functions such as Enterprise Application Integration (EAI) with internal business applications as well as with business partners (B2B). Also, a business Web service has the ability to provide vertical-oriented business functions such as supply chain or customer relationship management.

Sun ONE architecture implements such a business Web service using an electronic business Extensible Markup Language (ebXML) stack of technologies. The next section provides an introduction to ebXML architecture.

EbXML Technical Architecture

The ebXML standard was developed as a joint effort between OASIS and UN CEFACT. OASIS is a non-profit consortium that drives the development, convergence, and adoption of e-business standards in the areas of security, Web services, XML conformance, business transactions, electronic publishing, and interoperability. For more information on the OASIS charter and activities, visit www.oasis-open.org. The UN CEFACT mission is to contribute to the growth of global commerce by facilitating international transactions through the simplification and harmonization of procedures and information flows. More information on UN CEFACT can be obtained from www.unece.org.

The first version of the ebXML specification stack was released in May 2001. In itself, ebXML is a huge area and has been developed by the very same people involved in developing and adopting the Electronic Data Interchange (EDI) standard almost 20 years ago. More information on ebXML can be found at the ebXML Web site (see www.ebXML.org).

The ebXML standard represents a technical architecture consisting of several pieces that when combined together would allow a Web service to be created that could be used for business process driven integration with trading partners and customers. The ebXML technology stack consists of the following specifications:

- Messaging Service
- Business Process Specification Schema (BPSS)
- Registry/Repository
- Collaborative Protocol Profile (CPP)/Collaborative Protocol Agreement (CPA)
- Core components

EbXML has been designed so that these specifications can be used independent of each other. So, for example, a business environment can implement ebXML Messaging Service only and choose not to implement the rest of the stack. Figure 14.1 represents a scenario wherein two companies, Company A and Company B, are enabled for performing business-to-business collaboration and integration using ebXML architecture.

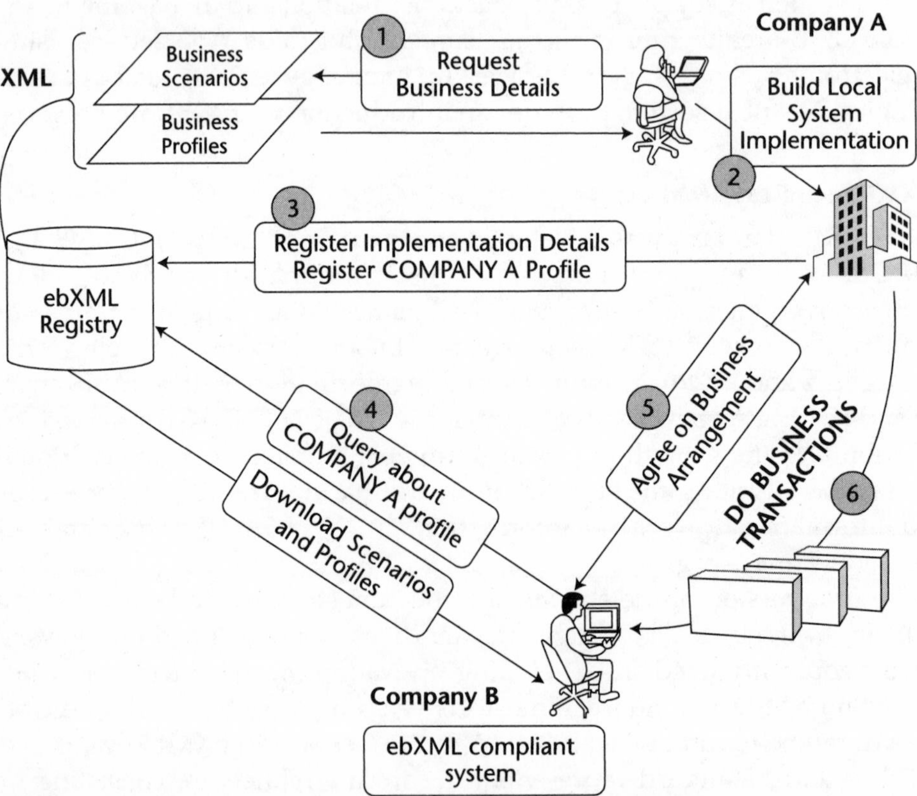

Figure 14.1 ebXML-enabled business-to-business commerce.

The following provides a brief explanation of the steps presented in Figure 14.1:

1. A Company A that intends to ebXML-enable its business begins with getting hold of its business processes and business documents that it needs for conducting collaboration with its business partner. There are two ways in which Company A can get these. One way is where Company A creates its own homegrown business process and business document models and registers them eventually to the ebXML Registry/Repository, so that its prospective business partner can share them. Another way is where Company A uses a vertical standard business process and document models. So, for example, if Company A happens to be in a high-tech manufacturing domain, it can leverage upon the standard business processes, aligned for the high-tech vertical, defined within the Rosettanet standards organization. In this case, Company A would retrieve the business process models from a public ebXML Registry/Repository hosted by, say, Rosettanet.

   These business processes are described using the ebXML Business Process Specification Schema (BPSS) standard. Business documents exchanged with partners and/or customers can be built using the ebXML Core Components specification.

2. After determining the business processes and business documents to use for business-to-business collaboration, Company A then ebXML-enables its local systems. It configures the runtime so that communication can be carried out securely and reliably with the prospective business partners. Also, it configures its Business Process Management Systems so that they understand ebXML BPSS and act according to the business process defined therein.

3. After configuring its local system to support ebXML, Company A then registers its profile information in the form of ebXML Collaborative Protocol Profile (CPP), to an ebXML Registry/Repository such that a partner can discover its CPP. A CPP typically consists of technical metadata information about business systems of a particular organization. For example, the CPP of Company A specifies information such as the level of security supported by its business systems, the level of reliability supported by its business systems, the messaging service supported by its business systems, and so on. Also, CPP is capable of specifying functional metadata information about a particular organization such as its supported business processes (standard or non-standard), the business documents it

uses, a URI specifying the location or identifying these business processes and document models, and so on.

Thus, ebXML CPP provides rich metadata, which is a must for conducting serious business-to-business collaborations.

4. Eventually Company B, which then may be looking for a prospective business partner, discovers the CPP of Company A. Company B then studies the CPP to gain an understanding of the technical and functional aspects of Company A's business systems.
5. Then at some point in time, Company B will somehow communicate to Company A its interest in making it a business partner. Both Company A and B then would work out details of this collaborative partnership offline and finally negotiate a contract representing the terms of doing business. In the ebXML world, this contract is manifested as a Collaborative Protocol Agreement (CPA). A CPA typically specifies the technical and functional nature of the collaboration. It specifies the business process these collaborating organizations are to adhere to, the level of reliability and security supported by the information systems of the collaborating organizations, and so on.

   Once a CPA is negotiated, it then is stored at some location such that both Company A and B can access it.
6. Now, both these companies will tune their business information systems so that they can begin conducting electronic business with each other in accordance with the technical and functional specification and details defined in the CPA and BPSS. The runtime communication is carried out using ebXML Messaging Service. ebXML Messaging Service is designed to provide the necessary security and reliability features required for performing real-world electronic business.

Mainstream adoption of such business Web services is expected to begin sometime in 2003 or 2004. Several vendors have already started providing complete or partial implementation of an ebXML technology stack. Sun ONE will provide support for ebXML in its standard APIs as well as in its products. JAX-R and JAX-M APIs provide support for ebXML Messaging Service and ebXML Registry/Repository standards. This book does not cover ebXML-related specifics when discussing the previously mentioned APIs. Sun ONE products supporting ebXML will start emerging sometime during 2003.

Federated Web Services

Federated Web services will be based on the vision and technologies formed within the Liberty Alliance. Sun and member companies from technology as well as other industry sectors formed the Liberty Alliance to formulate a network identity solution for the Internet that enables advanced services such as single sign-on for consumers as well as business users in an open, federated way. A federated network identity model will enable every business or user to manage their own data, and to ensure that the use of critical personal information is managed and distributed by the appropriate parties chosen by the user or business, rather than a central authority.

Liberty Alliance will roll out Liberty technology in phases. However, the ultimate goal of this alliance is to enable federated commerce. The specifications for the first phase of Liberty technologies were released in July 2002. These specifications can be obtained from www.projectliberty.org/.

Web Clients

Web clients is another mechanism for delivering Services on Demand. This mechanism enables the services to be downloaded as Java applications on the client's devices, such as desktop computers, handheld devices, set-top boxes, and so forth. Sun ONE architecture provides multiple technologies for achieving this. Java 2 Platform Mobile Edition (J2ME) is one such technology that is used for writing applications that will be eventually downloaded to resource-constrained devices such as cellular phones or PDAs.

Another technology provided by Sun ONE for delivering Services on Demand is Java Web Start. Java Web Start enables a full-featured Java application to be launched from within a Web browser by clicking a Web page link. Java Web Start caches all the application files necessary on the local client machine and directs the subsequent requests to the cached copy of the application. More information on Java Web Start can be found at http://java.sun.com/products/javawebstart/.

Besides these, Sun ONE provides other Web clients APIs for delivering Services on Demand. Further information on Sun ONE Web client models can be found at wwws.sun.com/software/sunone/docs/arch/chapter10.pdf.

Sun ONE Architecture

Sun ONE Architecture basically factors a Service on Demand into separate layers, each of which handles a specific aspect, such as identity management, integration, or application services, of the service. We will begin with examining these different layers of a Sun ONE SoD, and then we will see the standards/technologies and products that can fit into these different layers.

Sun ONE Service Layers

Figure 14.2 shows the architecture of a Sun ONE SoD composed of different layers, each handling or providing a specific functionality.

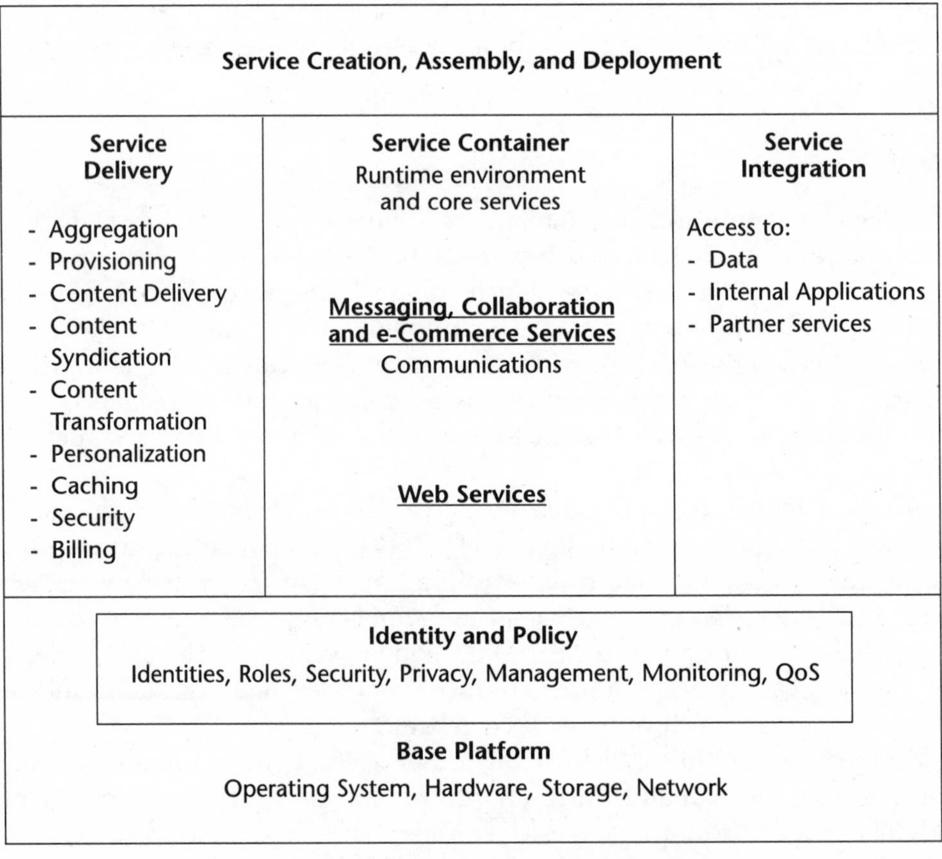

Primary source: Sun ONE Architecture Guide

Figure 14.2 Sun ONE architecture: Service layers.

The various layers of the architecture are as follows:

- The topmost layer in Figure 14.2 deals with creating and deploying a SoD. This layer focuses on tools that can be used for building the service.
- The bottom layer in Figure 14.2 talks about providing platform services such as those provided by the operating system. Also, this layer represents the extended services provided by operating environments such as storage and networking. Identity and policy services also can be a part of platform services in Sun ONE architecture.
- The Service Delivery layer deals with the functionalities required for provisioning the SoD. These functionalities include content caching, content transformation, content aggregation, personalization, and so forth. This layer also may manage other advanced service provisioning features such as content syndication, billing, single sign-on, and so on.
- The Service Container layer provides the runtime services needed by application services hosted by the container. Container provides middleware services such as persistence, state management, transaction management, and monitoring to the hosted application components. These hosted application components may very well be part of packaged application software, such as office communications software, e-commerce software, CRM software, and so on. Web services are hosted within such a service container in Sun ONE architecture.
- The Service Integration layer of a Sun ONE SoD deals with accessing data applications within the organizational boundaries (EAI) or application services hosted by business partners of an organization (B2B).

Sun ONE Standards and Technologies

Knowing this, let's now take a look at the standards and technologies that form the basis of these different layers of a Sun ONE SoD. Figure 14.3 shows the Sun ONE service layers populated with relevant standards and technologies in that space.

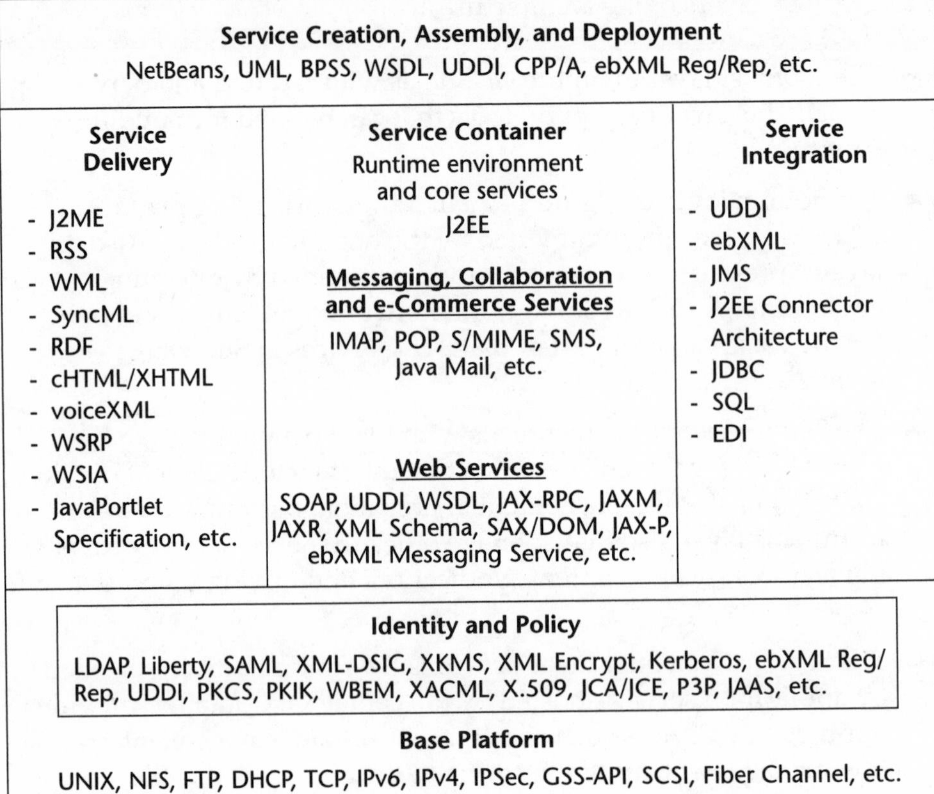

Primary source: Sun ONE Architecture Guide

Figure 14.3 Sun ONE architecture: Standards and technologies.

As can be seen from Figure 14.3, the Sun ONE platform is significantly based upon either ongoing or already developed standards:

- For service creation, assembly, and deployment, we will use the NetBeans, WSDL, and UDDI standards mainly. For creating a business SoD, we can use the CPP/CPA, ebXML BPSS, and ebXML Registry/Repository standards.
- The base platform in Sun ONE architecture can be based on standards such as UNIX, NIS, IPv6, and IPv4. Also, the extended platform services in the areas of storage can be based on standards such as SCSI and Fiber Channel.

- The Service Delivery layer again can be based on a plethora of standards and technologies in content transformation, formatting, and provisioning space mainly. Various standards such as XHTML, VoiceXML, and cHTML represent the formatted content as markup. Also, the J2ME technology platform can be used for provisioning services as Java applications on resource-constrained hand-held client devices.
- The Service Container layer is based on the industry standard J2EE platform. Also, Sun ONE supports standards for packaged application components such as Java Mail, S/MIME, POP, IMAP, and SMS in the areas of messaging and collaboration. The Sun ONE service container can support hosting Web services built upon the standard SOAP/UDDI/WSDL standards. In addition, it also can support hosting Web services built using ebXML technology specifications.
- Sun ONE architecture enables the integration with backend data, internal applications, as well partner services by leveraging standards and technologies such as J2EE Connector Architecture, JMS, JDBC, SQL, EDI, UDDI, ebXML Registry/Repository, and so on.

Now, let's see which products can be used for providing infrastructure to the Sun ONE SoD.

Sun ONE Product Stack: Integrated versus Integrate-able

Currently, Sun ONE is an architecture that is based upon industry standards encompassing different areas of a SoD. As a result, although Sun ONE is the branded vision and architecture from Sun Microsystems, a Sun ONE implementation can quite possibly be based upon products adhering to these standards, from companies other than Sun Microsystems. This scenario presents what is known as an "Integrate-able" product stack wherein Sun ONE architecture is realized using infrastructure products from different companies. For example, anyone can implement a Sun ONE SoD using Sun's Sun ONE Portal server along with BEA's WebLogic Application Server.

An "Integrated" product stack to build and deploy SoD using all the Sun ONE branded products also is provided by Sun Microsystems. Sun thus presents alternatives for implementing Sun ONE architecture-based services. Figure 14.4 shows the Sun ONE integrated product stack consisting of the Sun ONE-branded products from Sun Microsystems.

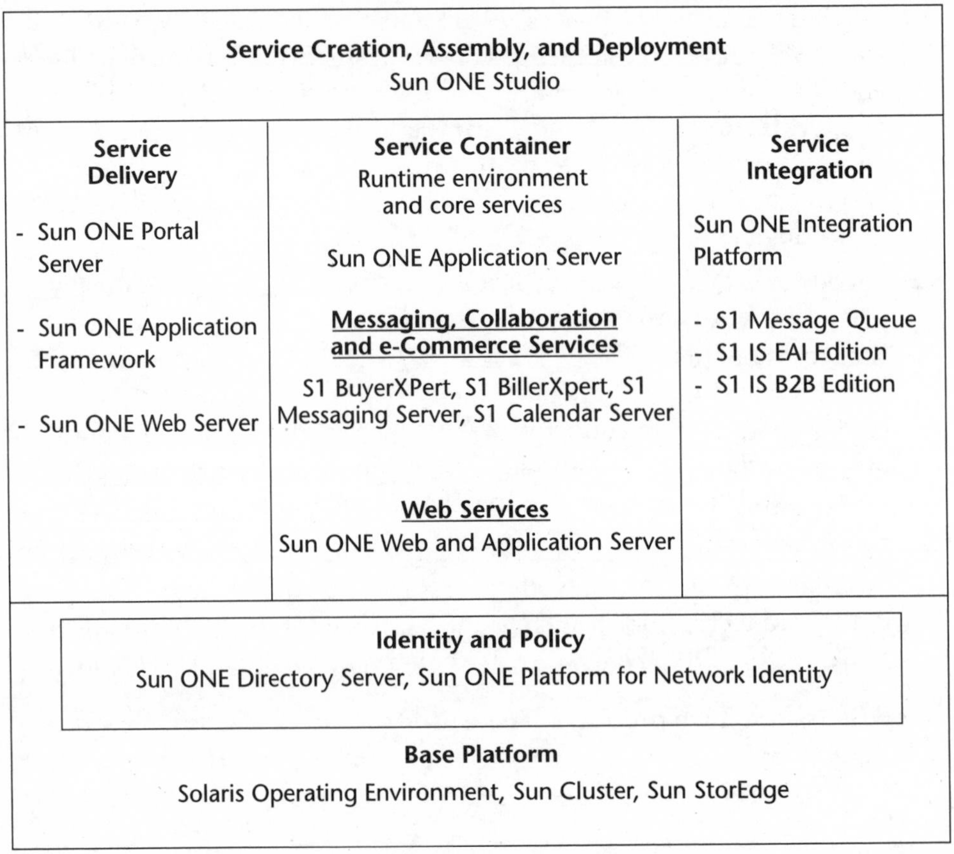

Service Creation, Assembly, and Deployment Sun ONE Studio		
Service Delivery - Sun ONE Portal Server - Sun ONE Application Framework - Sun ONE Web Server	**Service Container** Runtime environment and core services Sun ONE Application Server **Messaging, Collaboration and e-Commerce Services** S1 BuyerXPert, S1 BillerXpert, S1 Messaging Server, S1 Calendar Server **Web Services** Sun ONE Web and Application Server	**Service Integration** Sun ONE Integration Platform - S1 Message Queue - S1 IS EAI Edition - S1 IS B2B Edition
Identity and Policy Sun ONE Directory Server, Sun ONE Platform for Network Identity		
Base Platform Solaris Operating Environment, Sun Cluster, Sun StorEdge		

Primary source: Sun ONE Architecture Guide

Figure 14.4 Sun ONE architecture: Integrated product stack.

Now, Let's briefly discuss the functionalities provided by some of the major Sun ONE products shown in Figure 14.4.

Sun ONE Studio

Sun ONE Studio comes in two flavors: Sun ONE Studio 4 (formerly Forte for Java) and Sun ONE Studio 7, Compiler Collection (formerly Forte Compiler Collection).

Sun ONE Studio 4 is an IDE for the Java language system. It is based on the open source NetBeans Tools platform. NetBeans has a modular design—it defines a framework that can be used to develop modules focusing on a specific set of functionalities (UML modeling or performance monitoring, for example), such that these modules can be plugged in on any NetBeans-based IDE to use the specific functionality that it provides. Also, because NetBeans is written using Java technology, this IDE is available on most of the platforms. Sun ONE Studio 4 is available in three editions: Enterprise Edition, Community Edition, and Mobile Edition.

Enterprise Edition. It provides an environment to develop J2EE 1.3 applications and deploy them to a wide range of application servers, such as Sun ONE's Application Server, BEA's WebLogic Application Server, or Oracle's 9iAS. Also, Sun ONE Studio 4 provides built-in support for creating and deploying Web services based on WSDL, UDDI, and SOAP technologies. It also supports Web services creation using the Java APIs for XML. In order to develop J2EE 1.2 platform applications, Sun ONE Studio 3.0 also has been made available.

Community Edition. It provides an IDE for developing stand-alone applications, Java applets, Java Bean components, and database aware 2-tier Web applications using JavaServer Pages/Servlets/JDBC technologies.

Mobile Edition. It enables the development of J2ME MIDlet applications. It provides a debugger for debugging the source code of the MIDlets. Also, the support for mounting emulators as well as SDKs from third parties has been made available.

Sun ONE Studio 7, Compiler Collection provides tools for the rapid development of applications using the language systems of C, C++, and Fortran. This IDE is targeted toward ISVs and corporate developers involved heavily in maintaining and developing legacy applications.

Solaris Operating Environment

The newest version of Solaris Operating Environment is 9.0, which was launched by Sun in the summer of 2002. Interestingly, this new version of Solaris provides traditional OS functionality plus application and directory management services, that is, Sun bundles the Sun ONE Application Server and Sun ONE Directory Server along with Solaris 9.0. Apart from this, Solaris 9 OE also carries enhancements in the areas of scalability, availability, manageability, and security. Also, the earlier versions of Solaris OE are available.

Sun Cluster

Sun Cluster software is designed to deliver high availability application services to a data center or an enterprise. It basically extends the Solaris operating environment to enable the use of its core services, such as devices, file systems, and networks in a seamless manner across a tightly coupled cluster. Thus, it helps increase the service levels of software.

Sun ONE Portal Server

The Sun ONE Portal Server (formerly iPlanet Portal Server) is a platform for deploying business-to-business, business-to-consumer, and business-to-employee portals. It provides the services required to build portal sites, including user and community management, personalization, content aggregation, integration, security, and search functionalities. It also provides support for the access of services by wireless clients, secure remote access, and knowledge management.

Sun ONE Web Server

The product is an environment for deploying Web applications. It supports the JavaServer pages and Servlet technologies to generate personalized and dynamic content. The Sun ONE Web Server is bundled with the Sun ONE Directory Server to enable centralized server management and user authentication.

Sun ONE Messaging Server

Formerly known as iPlanet Messaging Server, this product provides a solution for communication and messaging. For example, it enables the deployment of unified communication services, bringing together telephone services with e-mail notification, faxing, paging, and other technologies. This provides a single entry point to retrieve voice mails, e-mails, address books, and calendar information.

Sun ONE Directory Server

The Sun ONE Directory Server (formerly iPlanet Directory Server) offers a central repository for storing and managing identity profiles, access privileges, and application and network resource information. Information stored in the Sun ONE Directory Server can be used to provide services such as authentication, authorization, access management, and single sign-on to the users.

Sun ONE Identity Server

Formerly known as iPlanet Directory Server Access Management Edition, the Sun ONE Identity Server is designed to help organizations manage secure access to Web-based resources. The product provides an identity system that includes access management, identity administration, and directory services. It supports the policy-driven administration of identities.

Sun ONE Application Server

Sun ONE Application Server (formerly known as iPlanet Application Server) provides a J2EE-based platform for the development, deployment, and management of middleware application components. The product provides a broad range of middleware services such as persistence, state management, load balancing, transaction management, security, and so forth, to the components hosted within.

Sun ONE Integration Server

Two editions of the Sun ONE Integration Server (formerly iPlanet Integration Server) are available: Sun ONE Integration Server EAI Edition and Sun ONE Integration Server B2B edition. The former is focused on providing data- and process-based integration of internal applications using XML-based technologies such as SOAP, while the latter provides a platform for integrating with customers and trading partners of an organization.

Sun ONE Message Queue

This product (known formerly as iPlanet Message Queue) is message-oriented middleware (MOM) software. It implements the JMS specification.

The integrated Sun ONE product stack from Sun is obviously quite complete, covering almost all areas of software infrastructure and tools. Further information on Sun ONE products can be obtained from wwws .sun.com/software/sunone/.

Summary

In this chapter, we introduced Sun ONE, Sun's vision of a standards-based software, architecture, and platform for building Services on Demand (SoD). The main components of Sun ONE have been examined: The vision behind Sun ONE; delivering Services on Demand; Sun ONE architecture, service layers, standards, and technologies; and the Sun ONE Integrated Product Stack.

Further Reading

Chapter 1

Java Remote Method Invocation (RMI) home	http://java.sun.com/products/jdk/rmi/
Java RMI tutorial	http://java.sun.com/docs/books/tutorial/rmi/
Java RMI over IIOP	http://java.sun.com/products/rmi-iiop
Java 2 Platform, Enterprise Edition (J2EE)	http://java.sun.com/j2ee/
Java Web services home	http://java.sun.com/webservices/
Microsoft DCOM home	www.microsoft.com/com/tech/DCOM.asp
Object Management Group (OMG) homepage	www.omg.org/
Web services zone home	www.ibm.com/developerworks/webservices/

Chapter 2

DSML homepage	www.dsml.org
ebXML homepage	www.ebxml.org
ebXML messaging specifications	www.ebxml.org/specs/index.htm
IBM WSFL page	www.ibm.com/software/solutions/webservices /pdf/WSFL.pdf
OASIS BTP activity home	www.oasis-open.org/committees /business-transactions/
OASIS UDDI activity home	www.oasis-open.org/cover/uddi.html
Sun WSCI information page	www.sun.com/software/xml
W3C SOAP activity home	www.w3.org/TR/SOAP/
W3C WSDL activity home	www.w3.org/TR/wsdl12
W3C XML activity home	www.w3.org/XML

Chapter 3

Apache Axis information	http://xml.apache.org/axis
BEA Weblogic information	www.bea.com
J2EE design patterns	http://java.sun.com/blueprints/patterns /j2ee_patterns
Server-side.com J2EE patterns	www.theserverside.com/patterns/index.jsp
SJC J2EE patterns	http://developer.java.sun.com/developer /technicalArticles/J2EE/patterns/
Sun Java Web services blueprints	http://java.sun.com/blueprints/webservices/
Sun Java Web services pages	http://java.sun.com/webservices/
W3C Web services activity home	www.w3.org/2002/ws/

Chapter 4

Apache Axis project	http://xml.apache.org/axis/
Apache SOAP project	http://xml.apache.org/soap/
ebXML messaging service specifications	www.ebxml.org/specs/ebMS2.pdf
W3C SOAP 1.2 adjuncts	www.w3.org/TR/soap12-part2/
W3C SOAP 1.2 messaging framework primer	www.w3.org/TR/soap12-part1/
W3C SOAP 1.2 primer	www.w3.org/TR/soap12-part0/
W3C XML protocol activity home	www.w3.org/2000/xp/Group/

Chapter 5

UDDI community portal	www.uddi.org
UDDI cover pages	www.oasis-open.org/cover/uddi.html
UDDI, ebXML and XML/EDI (paper)	www.xml.org/feature_articles/2000_1107_miller.shtml
UDDI and WS-inspection (paper)	www-106.ibm.com/developerworks/webservices/library/ws-wsiluddi.html
UDDI Web site (unofficial)	www.uddicentral.com
WSDL, compilation of low-level issues	http://wsdl.soapware.org/
WSDL cover pages	http://xml.coverpages.org/wsdl.html
WSDL, a paper on using WSDL with SOAP	www-106.ibm.com/developerworks/webservices/library/ws-soap/
WSDL tools, a compilation	http://pocketsoap.com/wsdl/
WSDL W3C note	www.w3.org/TR/wsdl
Yahoo group for discussion on UDDI issues	www.oasis-open.org/cover/uddi.html
Yahoo group for discussion on WSDL issues	http://groups.yahoo.com/group/wsdl/

Chapter 6

Microsoft SOAP interoperability page	www.mssoapinterop.org/
SOAP builders interoperability homepage	www.xmethods.com/ilab/
SOAP builders interoperability results page	www.whitemesa.com/interop.htm
Web service interoperability organization home	www.ws-i.org

Chapter 7

Document Object Model (DOM) home	www.w3.org/DOM/
Java API for XML-based RPC (JAX-RPC) home	http://java.sun.com/xml/jaxrpc/
Java API for XML Messaging (JAXM) home	http://java.sun.com/xml/jaxm/
Java API for XML Processing (JAXP) home	http://java.sun.com/xml/jaxp/
Java API for XML Registries (JAXR) home	http://java.sun.com/xml/jaxr/
Java Architecture for XML Binding (JAXB) home	http://java.sun.com/xml/jaxb/
Java technology and XML	http://java.sun.com/xml/index.html
Java XML pack home	http://java.sun.com/xml/downloads /javaxmlpack.html
JWSDP home	http://java.sun.com/webservices /webservicespack.html
SAX home	www.saxproject.org/

Chapter 8

Java API for XML Processing (JAXP) home	http://java.sun.com/xml/jaxp/
Java Architecture for XML Binding (JAXB) home	http://java.sun.com/xml/jaxb/
The CASTOR project home	http://castor.exolab.org/
Crimson JAXP parser home	http://xml.apache.org/crimson/index.html
Document Type Definition (DTD) home	www.w3.org/TR/html4/sgml/dtd.html
Extensible Stylesheet Language (XSL) home	www.w3.org/Style/XSL/
OASIS home	www.oasis-open.org/
O'Reilly XML.com home	www.xml.com
World Wide Web Consortium (W3C) home	www.w3c.org
W3C XML schema home	www.w3.org/XML/Schema
Xalan Java transformer home	http://xml.apache.org/xalan-j/index.html
Xerces2 Java parser home	http://xml.apache.org/xerces2-j/index.html
XML Industry portal home	www.xml.org
XML Path Language (XPATH) home	www.w3.org/TR/xpath
XSLT specification home	www.w3.org/TR/xslt

Chapter 9

JAXM home page	http://java.sun.com/xml/jaxm/
JWSDP download information	http:java.sun.com/webservices /webservicespack.html
JWSDP tutorial	http://java.sun.com/webservices/docs/1.0 /tutorial/index.html
SAAJ home page	http://java.sun.com/xml/saaj/index.html
Sun JAXM/SAAJ tutorial	http://java.sun.com/webservices/docs/1.0 /tutorial/doc/JAXM.html

Chapter 10

JAX-RPC home page	http:java.sun.com/xml/jaxrpc/
JWSDP download information	http://java.sun.com/webservices/webservicespack.html
JWSDP tutorial	http://java.sun.com/webservices/docs/1.0/tutorial/index.html
Sun JAX-RPC tutorial	http://java.sun.com/webservices/docs/1.0/tutorial/doc/JAXRPC.html

Chapter 11

Yahoo group for discussion on JAXR issues	http://groups.yahoo.com/group/jaxr-discussion/
An article on JAXR at onjava.com	http://www.onjava.com/pub/a/onjava/2002/02/27/uddi.html
Articles on JAXR at Javaworld.com	http://www.javaworld.com/javaworld/jw-06-2002/jw-0614-jaxr.html http://www.javaworld.com/javaworld/jw-05-2002/jw-0517-webservices.html
An article on registration and discovery of Web services to UDDI and ebXML registries using JAXR	http://developer.java.sun.com/developer/technicalArticles/WebServices/jaxrws/
Java.sun.com chat with JAXR spec. lead	http://developer.java.sun.com/developer/community/chat/JavaLive/2002/jl0507.html
JAXR cover pages	http://xml.coverpages.org/jaxr.html
Presentation on JAXR	http://fr.sun.com/developpeurs/sdc/webservices/pres/jaxr_v5.pdf

Chapter 12

Java Web services developer pack home	http://java.sun.com/webservices /webservicespack.html
Java Web services tutorial home	http://java.sun.com/webservices/docs/1.0 /tutorial/index.html

Chapter 13

Liberty Alliance, official Web site	www.projectlibert.org
Securing Web services, articles on issues	www.line56.com/articles/default .asp?ArticleID=3779 http://zdnet.com.com/2100-1107-867689.html
Sun Dot Com builder Web services best practices	http://dcb.sun.com/practices/webservices/
Web Services Security forum at Webservices.org	www.webservices.org/index.php/article /archive/5/
Web services security forum at XWSS	www.xwss.org/index.jsp
Web services security at Theserverside.com (paper)	www.theserverside.com/resources/article .jsp?l=Systinet-web-services-part-3
WS-security, paper introducing	www-106.ibm.com/developerworks/library /ws-secure/

Chapter 14

Sun ONE architecture guide	http://wwws.sun.com/software/sunone/docs /arch/index.html
Sun ONE official Web site	http://wwws.sun.com/software/sunone/

Index

A

Abstract Syntax Notation One, 654
actor attribute, 127
addBusinessKey ( ) method, 265
addHeader ( ) method, 410
addName ( ) method, 261
<add_publisherAssertions> function, 227, 252
AdminClient utility, 158
Advanced Encryption Standard, 625
<Answer> element, 675
Ant utility, 62, 69, 77, 83, 89–92, 310
Apache
  Tomcat server, 147–149, 165–166, 172–173, 309
  Xalan, 166
  Xerces, 148, 166, 342, 345
  See also Ant utility; Axis
Applied Cryptography (Bruce Schneier), 622
architectural models, 6–15
arrays, 119, 121–123, 473
<Assertion> element, 704
<assertionStatusReport> data structure, 253
Association class, 501, 508–509
asymmetric algorithms, 626–628
asynchronous connections, 513–514
AttachmentPart object, 417, 422
attachments, SOAP, 109–110, 116–117
attribute assertion, SAML, 693–694
attributes, 320, 335–336
AuditableEvent instance, 502
authentication, 622–623
authentication assertion, SAML, 691–693
<AuthInfo> element, 679, 681
authorization, 143–144, 622
authorization assertion, SAML, 694–696
<authToken> data structure, 250
Axis (Apache)
  downloading, 62, 147, 165
  features, 62, 146–147
  infrastructure and components, 150–154, 158–159
  installing, 147–149
  .NET client, building
    infrastructure, 279–280
    overview, 278–279
    service provider, 282–284
    service requestor, 284–289
  remote administration, 152

Axis (Apache) *(continued)*
service requester setup, 98–99
Tomcat server, 147–149
Web service creation, example
DAO classes, use of, 180–187
database creation, 167–173
infrastructure, building, 161–165
service provider, 165–173, 175–176, 191–194
service requestor, 173, 176–178, 194–196
testing services, 179–180, 196–198
XML Helper classes, use of, 187–191
Web services programming model, 155–160
WSDL tools, 215

B

B2B. *See* business-to-business (B2B) communication
Basic Encoding Rules, 654
`<BatchHeader>` element, 683
`<BatchID>` element, 685
BEA, 15, 61. *See also* WebLogic
`<beanMapping>` tag, 152
BEEP (Blocks Extensible Exchange Protocol), 137–138
binding, 302–304, 385, 395–396, 696. *See also* Java Architecture for XML Binding
`<bindingDetail>` data structure, 241, 245, 252
`<binding>` element, 205, 210
`<bindingTemplate>` data structure, 230–231, 241, 242, 244, 251
Blocks Extensible Exchange Protocol (BEEP), 137–138
`Body` element, 112, 213, 228
browser, registry, 535–537
`build.xml` script, 69, 77–78, 83–84, 89–91
`<BulkRegister>` element, 682, 683
`<BulkRegisterResult>` element, 685
`BulkResponse` interface, 518–521, 682
`<BulkStatusRequest>` element, 682
`<BulkStatusResponse>` element, 682
`<businessDetail>` data structure, 244, 246, 251, 257
`<businessEntity>` data structure, 229–230, 237, 239, 244, 251, 257
`<businessInfo>` data structure, 235–237, 261
`BusinessLifeCycleManager` interface, 516, 519–521
`<businessList>` data structure, 235–238, 261
`BusinessQueryManager` interface, 523–531
`<businessService>` data structure, 230, 238, 241, 244, 247, 251
business-to-business (B2B) communication, 17, 19–21, 24–25, 30–32, 720

C

`Call` object, 469
canonicalization, XML, 655–656
`<CanonicalizationMethod>` element, 652, 653, 661
capabilities, JAXR, 497
capability interfaces, 496
capability profiles, JAXR, 497–498
Cape Clear, 35
cascading style sheets, 364
CASTOR (Exolab), 384–385
categorization, 233–236
`<categoryBag>` data structure, 232, 233, 236, 248
Certificate Authority, 630
`characters ( )` method, 348
`<CipherData>` element, 641

Classification interface, 501, 503–506, 527–528
ClassificationScheme interface, 500, 503–508
clientgen utility, 62, 92
<ClientInfo> element, 683
client/server application, 6–10
close ( ) method, 515
Collaborative Protocol Agreement, 722
comment, XML, 318
Common Language Runtime (CLR), 275, 276
Common Object Request Broker Architecture (CORBA), 6–10
communication models, 14–15, 50–51, 57
complexType, 335, 336
Component Object Model (COM), 13
Concept instances, 501, 505
conditional processing, 370
confidentiality, 622
confirmAssociation ( ) method, 509
ConnectionFactory object, 510–511, 513–514, 516
Connection interface, 496
connection management API, 510–516
connection pool, creating, 65
Content-ID reference, 116–117
Content-Location reference, 116–117
ControllerServlet, 593–595
CORBA. *See* Common Object Request Broker Architecture
CPP/CPA, ebXML, 30, 49
createConnection ( ) method, 408, 513
createMessageFactory method, 415
createObject ( ) method, 517
Crimson parser, 339, 342, 345
cryptography, 621–628

D

DAO classes, 70–78, 180–187, 280–283
database server, 6
database tables, 65–70
Data Encryption Standard, 625
DataHandler class, 475
data source, creating, 65
data structures, UDDI, 229–232
data types, 331, 333, 472–475
DCOM (Distributed Common Object Model), 13–14
DeclarativeQueryManager interface, 531–533
decryption, 643–650
DecryptionContext ( ) object, 648–650
DefaultHandler class, 344, 346–347, 349
<definitions> element, 205, 208
<delete_binding> function, 228, 252
<delete_business> function, 227, 251, 265
deleteObjects ( ) method, 518
<delete_publisherAssertions> function, 227
<delete_service> function, 228, 252
<delete_tModel> function, 228, 252
deployment descriptor, 88–89, 445–447, 461–462, 480–481
deprecateObjects ( ) method, 519
deserialization, 124, 152, 455, 472
destroy ( ) method, 458
detached signatures, 652
<detail> element, 113, 250, 410
digital certificate, 630
digital signature, 33, 142–143, 628–629, 667

Digital Signature Algorithm (DSA), 629
DII. *See* Dynamic Invocation Interface
Directory Services Markup Language, 31–32
<discard_authToken> function, 228, 250
<dispositionReport> data structure, 238, 250, 251, 252
Distinguished Encoding Rules, 654
Distributed Common Object Model (DCOM), 13–14
distributed computing
  advantages, 5–6
  challenges in, 16–17
  core technologies, 6–14
  definition, 4–5
  importance, 5–6
  J2EE role in, 17–19
  service-oriented architecture, 22, 41
  XML role in, 19
DLL. *See* Dynamic Link Library
Document Builder, JAXP, 340
DocumentBuilderFactory class, 340, 342, 355–357
Document object, 357–359
Document Object Model (DOM), 300, 647, 648
Document Type Definition (DTD), 299, 325–329
doDecrypt ( ) method, 648
doDelete ( ) method, 265, 557–558
doEncrypt ( ) method, 645–648
doGET ( ) method, 702
doPublish ( ) method, 538
doQuery ( ) method, 551
doSearch ( ) method, 261
doSubmit ( ) method, 257
DSA (Digital Signature Algorithm), 629
<DSAKeyValue> element, 654
<ds:CanonicalizationMethod> element, 143
<ds:KeyInfo> element, 640, 671–674
<ds:KeyName> element, 673
<ds:Reference> element, 143
<ds:RetrievalMethod> element, 672, 680
<ds:Signature> element, 679, 684
<ds:SignatureMethod> element, 143
DTD. *See* Document Type Definition
Dynamic Invocation Interface (DII), 469–471, 488–490, 578, 596
Dynamic Link Library (DLL), 277–278, 286–287

E

electronic business Extensible Markup Language (ebXML)
  Business Process Specification Schema (BPSS), 721, 722
  Collaborative Protocol Profile (CPP), 721–722
  components of, 30, 49
  consumer servlet, 443–445
  development of, 719
  Messaging Service, 720, 722
  producer servlet, 439–443
  Registry/Repository, 46, 721, 722
  technical architecture, 719–723
  Web services implementation, 53
  WUST technologies, 45
element, XML
  attributes, 320, 335–336
  collision, 323
  complex, 332
  declaration, 325
  description, 319–320
  explicit and implicit types, 333
  local and global definitions, 334
  multi-attribute, 327

prefixes, use of, 323
XML Schema, 330–335
encodingStyle attribute, 111, 112, 213–214
EncryptDecrypt class, 637, 645, 648
<EncryptedData> element, 640
<EncryptedKey> element, 640–641
encryption, 140–142, 622, 641–643, 644–650
EncryptionContext object, 646
<EncryptionMethod> element, 640
EncryptionTest class, 637–641
endDocument ( ) method, 347
endElement ( ) method, 348
Entegrity, 688
entities, XML, 320–322, 327–328
Entrust, 630, 668, 671
enumeration data type, 118–119
enveloped signatures, 651
Envelope element, 108, 110–111
enveloping signatures, 651
ErrorListener interface, 375
executeQuery ( ) method, 532
Exolab, 384–385
extensibility elements, 211
Extensible Markup Language. *See* XML
ExtensibleObject interface, 502
Extensible Stylesheet Language. *See* XSL
Extensible Stylesheet Language Transformation. *See* XSLT
ExternalIdentifier instances, 501, 532
ExternalLink class, 501, 532
ExtrinsicObject class, 502

F

FactoryConfigurationError message, 340, 345
FactoryConfiguration Exception message, 348, 359
faultactor element, 113
faultcode element, 113
<fault> element, 112–115, 209, 210
faultstring element, 113
FederatedConnection interface, 516, 534
federated Web services, 723
<find_binding> function, 227, 241–243
<find_business> function, 227, 234, 261
FindBusiness object, 261
<findQualifiers> element, 236, 239, 241, 242, 248
FindQualifiers interface, 526–527
<find_relatedBusinesses> function, 227, 238–240
<find_service> function, 227, 240–241
<find_tModel> function, 227, 243–244

G

generateSignature ( ) method, 662–663
GenerateValidateSignature class, 657, 661–663, 666
getAssertion ( ) method, 702
<get_assertionStatusReport> function, 253
get_authToken method, 228, 250, 257, 265
<get_bindingDetail> function, 227, 245
<get_businessDetailExt> function, 227
<get_businessDetail> function, 227, 244, 245
getCatalog ( ) method, 596

getCoreValidity ( ) method, 668
getDocument ( ) method, 647
getFeature ( ) method, 346
getKeyInfoResolver ( ) method, 646
getPort method, 467, 486
getProductCatalog ( ) method, 583–584, 597, 599, 612
<get_publisherAssertions> function, 252
getReferenceValidity ( ) method, 667–668
<get_registeredInfo> function, 253
getRegistryService ( ) method, 514
<get_serviceDetail> function, 227, 245
getSignedInfoValidity ( ) method, 667–668
getStatus ( ) method, 513
<get_tModelDetail> function, 227, 245
getXMLReader ( ) method, 349

H

HandlerBase class, 344, 346–347, 349
handlers, Axis, 150
hashing, 624, 629
Header attribute, 111
HTML tags, 314
HTTP (Hyper Text Transfer Protocol), 17, 131–134, 137, 290

I

IBM
  e-Business, 37
  Key Generator utility, 642
  MQSeries, 15
  Network Accessible Services Specification Language (NASSL), 202
  products, 35
  UDDI access point URLs, 228
  Web Services Toolkit, 215, 254
  WebSphere Application Server 4.5, 35
  XML Security Suite, 656
<identifierBag> data structure, 231, 236
init ( ) method, 458
<input> element, 209, 210
integrity, 623, 629
interface class, 70
intermediaries, SOAP, 125–128
interoperability
  challenges, 290
  importance of, 271
  Java API for XML Messaging (JAXM), 450
  Java API for XML RPC (JAX-RPC), 491
  means of ensuring, 272–273
  SOAP proxies, 273
  testing, 274, 292
  W3C XML Schema Definitions (XSD), defining, 273
  of Web services, 26
  Web Services Interoperability Organization, 291–292
  WSDL and, 273
invoke ( ) method, 157
IOPSIS, 35
iPlanet products, 36, 701, 730, 731
isAssertionValid ( ) method, 704, 705
isAvailable ( ) method, 513
isNamespaceAware ( ) method, 356–357
ISO 3166 categorization system, 234, 248
issuing authority, SAML, 689–695
isValidating ( ) method, 357
isValid ( ) method, 395

J

J2EE architecture, 17–19
JABBER, 105
Java2WSDL utility, 153, 215–220
Java API for XML Messaging (JAXM)
  application architecture, 403–406
  asynchronous messaging
    deployment, 445–448
    ebXML consumer servlet, 443–445
    ebXML producer servlet, 439–443
    testing, 448–449
  communication using provider, 414–419
  communication without a provider, 420–424
  deployment, 425–430
  description, 58, 304–306, 722
  interoperability, 450
  in J2EE 1.4 platform, 450
  java.xml.messaging, 407–408
  java.xml.soap, 409–413
  JAX-RPC compared, 454
  message interaction patterns, 406
  point-to-point messaging, 431, 434–438
  role in Web services, 402–403
Java API for XML Processing (JAXP)
  API model, 339
  classes and interfaces, list of, 340–341
  description, 58, 298, 337–338
  DOM
    description, 300, 353
    document builder, 357–358
    namespaces, 356–357
    processing model, 354
    sample source code, 360–364
    tree, 359
    validation, 357
  implementations, 342
  parser, 339
  pluggable interface, 301–302, 338–339
  reference implementation, 303
  SAX
    default handler, creating, 346–348
    description, 299, 342–343
    features, setting, 346
    namespaces, setting, 345–346
    processing model, 343
    reading and writing XML, 349
    sample source code, 350–353
    SAX parser, 344–349
    validation, setting, 346
  threading, 383
  uses for, 338
  version, 314, 338
  XSLT
    description, 300–301, 373–377
    sample code, 377–383
Java API for XML Registries (JAXR)
  architecture components, 494–496
  association of registry objects, 508–509
  capabilities, 497
  capability profiles, 497–498
  classes and interfaces, 499
  classification of registry objects, 502–507
  deleting information, 557–561
  description, 58, 308, 494, 722
  information model, 499, 503
  programming model, 498
  publishing
    compiling, 547–549
    executing, 549–550
    programming steps, 538
    source code, 539–547
  querying, 551–557
  Registry Browser, 535–537
  Registry Server, JWSDP, 533–535
  registry services API
    connection management API, 510–516

Java API for XML Registries (JAXR) *(continued)*
  life cycle management API, 516–521
  query management API, 522–533
Java API for XML Remote Procedure Calls (JAX-RPC)
  application architecture, 454–456
  client
    classes, 466
    description, 455
    Dynamic Invocation Interface (DII), 469–471, 488–490
    dynamic proxy-based, 467–469, 486–488
    exception, 466
    interfaces, 465
    stub-based, 466–467, 484–486
  description, 58, 306–308
  example Web service, 307–308
  interoperability, 491
  in J2EE 1.4 platform, 491
  JAXM compared, 454
  mapping, 472–475
  role in Web services, 452–453
  service
    configuring, 459, 463, 478
    definition, 457–458, 476–477
    description, 454–455
    developing from Java classes, 457–462
    developing from WSDL document, 463–464
    implementation, 458–459, 477
    packaging and development, 460–462, 464, 480–482
    testing, 482–483
  stubs and ties, generation of, 460, 479–480, 483–484
Java Architecture for XML Binding (JAXB)
  data binding generation, 386–392
  description, 58, 302–304, 383–385
  marshalling XML, 392–394
  sample code, 395–399
  services provided, 303
  unmarshalling Java, 394–395
Java Database Connectivity (JDBC), 59, 497
Java for WSDL (JWSDL), 202
Java Messaging Service (JMS), 15, 137, 305
Java RMI (Remote Method Invocation), 10–13
Java Server Pages (JSP), 59
Java Server Pages Standard Tag Library (JSTL), 58, 309, 599–600
Java Web Services Developer Pack (JWSDP)
  Ant build tool, 311
  Apache Tomcat container, 309
  case study
    architecture, 567–568
    discovery of Web services, 600–602
    execution, 612–615
    overview, 563–567
    publishing and discovery classes, 572–574
    service provider, designing, 568–572
    service provider, developing, 582–593
    service provider, runtime infrastructure, 602–609
    service registry, browsing, 592–593
    service registry infrastructure, 609–610
    service requestor, designing, 575–582
    service requestor, developing, 593–602
    service requestor, runtime infrastructure, 610–612
  components, 58

description, 36, 311–312
document-oriented APIs, 297–298
downloading, 311
Java XML Pack, 297
JAXB, 302–304
JAXM, 304–306
JAXP, 298–303
JAXR, 308
JAX-RPC, 306–308
JSTL, 309
procedure-oriented APIs, 298
registry server, 59, 310
UDDI implementation, 254
Java Web Start, 723
java.xml.messaging, 407–408
Java XML Pack, 297
java.xml.soap, 409–413
JAXB. *See* Java Architecture for XML Binding
JAXM. *See* Java API for XML Messaging
JAXP. *See* Java API for XML Processing
JAXR. *See* Java API for XML Registries
JAX-RPC. *See* Java API for XML Remote Procedure Calls
JDBC (Java Database Connectivity), 59, 497
Jini, 717
JMS (Java Messaging Service), 15, 137, 305
JSP (Java Server Pages), 59
JSTL (Java Server Pages Standard Tag Library), 58, 309, 599–600
JWSDL (Java for WSDL), 202
JWSDP. *See* Java Web Services Developer Pack

K

key
in asymmetric algorithms, 626–628
definition, 623
key pair creation, 641–643
length, 623, 625
private, 626–628
public, 626–628
secret, 624, 626
in symmetric algorithms, 624–626
See also Cryptography
`<KeyBindingAuth>` element, 679
`<KeyBinding>` element, 676
`<keyedReference>` element, 239, 248
`Key Generator` utility (IBM), 642
`<KeyInfo>` element, 638, 646, 652–654, 661, 665–666
`KeyInfoResolver` object, 646, 649
`<KeyName>` element, 673
key recovery service, X-KRSS, 681–685
key registration request, X-BULK, 682–683
key registration response, X-BULK, 684
key revocation request, X-KRSS, 681
keystore file, 664
Keytool utility (Sun), 641–643
`<KeyValue>` element, 673

L

Liberty Alliance, 723
Life Cycle Management API, 516–521
`LifeCycleManager` interface, 516, 517–519
`<Locate>` element, 674
`<LocateResult>` element, 675
locate service, XKMS, 672–675

M

marshalling, 303, 392–394
`maxOccurs` attribute, 331–333
Message Driven Beans, 407, 635
`<message>` element, 205, 208

MessageFactory object, 412, 415, 418, 421, 424
Message-Oriented Middleware (MOM), 14–15
messaging-based communication model, 51, 155, 157–158
Microsoft Corporation. *See specific applications*
Microsoft Intermediate Language (MSIL), 274–275
Microsoft Messaging Queue, 15
minOccurs attribute, 331–333, 336
misUnderstood attribute, 115
mustUnderstand attribute, 111, 113, 115–116

N

NAICS categorization system, 234, 248, 508
namespace, XML
  default, 322, 323
  description, 322–323
  DOM and, 356–357
  setting, 345–346
  XML Schema declaration, 329
  XSL, 367
naming conventions, XML, 316–317
.NET (Microsoft)
  class library, 275–276
  client development
    compiling client application, 278, 288
    compiling SOAP proxy as a DLL, 277–278, 286–287
    environment setup, 282
    executing client from Windows environment, 278, 289
    infrastructure, building, 279–281
    proxy, generating, 277, 285
    service provider, creating, 282–283
    service provider, implementing, 283–284
    service requestor, creating, 284–289
    testing the client, 289
    WSDL, obtaining, 277, 284
  Common Language Runtime, 275
  compilers, 275
  description, 37, 274–275
  Web site, 276
NetBeans, 728–729
Netegrity, 685, 688
newDocumentBuilder ( ) static method, 355
newInstance ( ) method, 344, 355, 374–375, 510
newSAXParser ( ) static method, 344
newTransformerFactory ( ) method, 374–375
non-repudiation, 623, 629
North American Industry Classification System (NAICS), 234, 248, 508
not ( ) function, 370

O

<Object> element, 652, 655
Object Request Broker (ORB), 8, 9
one-way hash function algorithms, 624
OneWayListener interface, 407–408, 418
onMessage ( ) method, 407–408, 418, 424
onMethod ( ) method, 706
Oracle, 35–36
Organization for the Advancement of Structured Information Standards (OASIS), 30, 32–34, 685, 707, 719
Organization instance, 500
<output> element, 209, 210

P

parse ( ) method, 349
ParserConfiguationException message, 345, 348, 357, 359
Parser Configuration, JAXP, 340
parsing, 298
<part> element, 205, 208–209, 213–214
password, 624
Phaos XML, 633
placeOrder ( ) method, 587, 598
PointBase database, 62, 65, 69, 78, 84, 166, 603
Point-to-Point message model, 15
Policy Decision Point (PDP), 698, 708
Policy Enforcement Point (PEP), 698, 707
Policy Information Point (PIP), 708
Policy Repository Point (PRP), 708
polymorphic accessor, 119
<port> element, 205
<portType> element, 205, 208, 209, 210
Possession of Private (POP) key, 678, 679
PostalAddress instances, 502
processing instruction, XML, 318
prolog, XML, 317
<Prototype> element, 679
ProviderConnectionFactory object, 408, 414, 418
ProviderConnection object, 414, 417–418
proxy, 277, 285
Public Key Infrastructure, 32–33, 628, 668–670
<publisherAssertion> data structure, 230, 251, 252, 253
Publish/Subscribe message model, 15

Q

qname attribute, 115
<Query> element, 674
querying, using JAXR, 551–557
Query interface, 532
Query Management API
  BusinessQueryManager interface, 522–531
  DeclarativeQueryManager interface, 531–533

R

<Reference> element, 652, 653
<registeredInfo> data structure, 253
<RegisterResults> element, 685
registration service, X-KRSS, 678–680
registry browser, 535–537
RegistryEntry interface, 499–500
RegistryObject class, 499–505
RegistryPackage class, 502
Registry Server, JWSDP, 310, 533–535
RegistryService interface, 496, 514
<relatedBusinessesList> data structure, 238, 240
<relatedBusinessInfo> data structure, 238–239
remote interface, session bean, 85–86
remote procedure call (RPC)
  communication model, RPC-based, 50–51, 155–158
  Web services, RPC-based, 174–180
  See also Java API for XML Remote Procedure Calls
replace ( ) method, 648
ReqRespListener interface, 408, 418, 423–424
<Request> element, 683
<Respond> element, 674
<Result> element, 675

<RetrievalMethod> element, 653
revocation service, X-KRSS, 680–681
RMI-IIOP protocol, 12–13, 56
root, 317–318, 366
RSA (Rivest-Shamir-Adelman) algorithm, 628, 629, 641–643
<RSAKeyValue> element, 654

S

SAML. *See* Security Assertions Markup Language
<save_binding> function, 227, 252
<save_business> function, 227, 233, 251, 257
SaveBusiness object, 257
saveChanges ( ) method, 417, 423
saveObjects ( ) method, 517–518
<save_service> function, 227, 233, 251
<save_tModel> function, 227, 233, 252
SAX. *See* Simple Access for XML
SAXParser class, 340, 344, 348–349
SAXParserFactory class, 340, 344, 345
scalability, 6, 10, 14
Schneier, Bruce *(Applied Cryptography)*, 622
SearchBusiness function, 260
searching, information in a UDDI registry, 260–264
Securant Technologies, 685, 688
Secure Socket Layer (SSL), 137, 628, 631, 632
security
- authorization, 143–144
- challenges of, 620–621
- cryptography, 621–628
- description, 140
- digital certificates, 630
- digital signatures, 142–143, 629–630
- encryption, 140–142
- goal of, 620
- JAXR, 514
- XACML, 706–710
- XKMS, 668–675
- XML Encryption, 630–638
- XML Signature, 651–657
- *See also* Security Assertions Markup Language (SAML); *specific protocols and technologies*

Security Assertions Markup Language (SAML)
- architecture, 689–691
- attribute assertion, 693–694
- authentication assertion, 691–693
- authorization (decision) assertion, 694–696
- back-office transaction scenario, 687
- bindings and protocols, 696–697
- description, 33–34, 685–687
- documents, 688–689
- implementation, 687–689
- model of producers and consumers, 697–698
- Single Sign-On, 686, 698–706
- XACML and, 708

serialization, 124, 152, 455, 472
ServiceBinding instance, 500
Service class, 500
service container, 43, 52
Service Container layer, Sun ONE, 724, 725, 727
Service Delivery layer, Sun ONE, 724, 725, 727
service description, WSDL-based, 52, 55
<serviceDetail> data structure, 245, 251
<service> element, 205, 210
servicegen utility, 62, 91
Service Integration layer, Sun ONE, 724, 725

ServiceLifeCycle interface, 458
<serviceList> data structure, 240, 241, 242
service-oriented architecture (SOA), 22
service provider development
  application design, 63–64
  class diagram, 64
  client creation, 92–93
  DAO classes, building, 70–78
  database tables, creating, 65–70
  development environment, setting up, 65
  generating Web services, 91–94
  implementing J2EE components, 70
  sequence diagram, 64
  session bean, building, 85–91
  steps, 62–63
  testing service provider, 95–98
  XML Helper classes, building, 79–84
service requester, 27, 98–101
session bean, 70, 85–91
SetConcept ( ) method, 505
setCredentials ( ) method, 514
setData ( ) method, 648
setEncryptedType ( ) method, 648
setErrorListener ( ) method, 375
setFeature ( ) method, 346
setNamespaceAware ( ) method, 346
setProperties ( ) method, 511
<set_publisherAssertions> function, 227, 253
setURIResolver ( ) method, 376
setValidating ( ) method, 346
SignatureContext object, 665
<Signature> element, 652, 653, 655, 659, 665, 666
<SignatureMethod> element, 652, 653, 661
SignatureTest class, 657–662, 666
<SignatureValue> element, 143, 652
<SignedInfo> element, 143, 652, 655, 661, 667
Simple Access for XML (SAX)
  default handler, creating, 346–348
  description, 299, 342–343
  features, setting, 346
  namespaces, setting, 345–346
  processing model, 343
  reading and writing XML, 349
  sample source code, 350–353
  SAX parser, 344–349
  validation, setting, 346
Simple Mail Transport Protocol (SMTP), 134–136
Simple Object Access Protocol (SOAP)
  binding, WSDL, 212–214
  communication models, 128–130
  components, 46
  description, 28, 103–104
  emergence of, 105–106
  encoding, 109, 118–124
  interoperability and, 272–274
  JAXM messaging, 305–306
  JAX-RPC and, 307–308
  limitations, 199
  message anatomy
    attachments, 109–110, 116–117
  envelope, 109, 110–111
    Fault element, 112–115
    header, 111
    mustUnderstand attribute, 115–116
    request message, 107
    response message, 108
  message exchange model, 124–127
  message exchange patterns, 138–140

Simple Object Access Protocol
(continued)
proxies, 273, 277
security, 140–144
SOAP over BEEP, 137–138
SOAP over HTTP, 131–134, 137
SOAP over HTTP/SSL, 137
SOAP over JMS, 137
SOAP over SMTP, 134–136
specifications, 106
versions, 47, 104
in Web services architecture, 45, 46–47
Web services development using Apache Axis
Axis infrastructure, 149–154, 161–165
Axis programming model, 154–160
example, 160
implementation of messaging-based services, 180–198
implementation of RPC-based services, 174–180
installing Axis, 147–149
service provider environment, creating, 165–173
service requestor environment, creating, 173
XML-based protocols, 104
XML message discontinuities, 290
Single Sign-On (SSO), 686, 698–706
Slot class, 501
SMTP (Simple Mail Transport Protocol), 134–136
SOA (service-oriented architecture), 22
SOAP. *See* Simple Object Access Protocol
soapAction attribute, 150, 213, 290
<soap:address> element, 210, 214
SOAP Attachments API for Java, 306
<soap:binding> element, 212–213
<soap:body> element, 213–214
SOAPBodyElement object, 417, 422
SOAPBody object, 290, 409–410, 416–417, 421–422
SOAPConnectionFactory class, 421
SOAPConnection object, 411–412, 418–423, 431
SOAPElement object, 412
SOAP Encoding, 46
SOAPEnvelope object, 46, 108, 110, 410, 412, 416, 421
SOAPFaultElement object, 410
SOAPFault object, 290, 410
SOAPHeaderElement object, 416, 422
SOAPHeader object, 111, 409–410, 416, 421–422
SOAPMessage object, 411, 415, 417–418, 421, 423
SOAP Messaging, 128, 130
<soap:operation> element, 213
SOAPPart object, 409, 412, 416
SOAP RPC, 46, 128–130
SOAP Transport, 46
Solaris Operating Environment, 729
SpecificationLink class, 500
SSL (Secure Socket Layer), 137, 628, 631, 632
SSO (Single Sign-On), 686, 698–706
startDocument ( ) method, 347
startElement ( ) method, 348
Structure data type, 120–121
Sun
Cluster software, 729–730
Crimson parser, 339, 342
Keytool utility, 641–643
products, 36
Sun ONE (Open Net Environment) architecture
product stack, 727–731
service layers, 724–725

Solaris Operating Environment, 729
standards and technologies, 725–727
Sun Cluster, 729–730
Sun ONE Application Server, 36, 731
Sun ONE Directory Server, 730
Sun ONE Identity Server, 687, 730–731
Sun ONE Integration Server, 731
Sun ONE Message Queue, 15, 731
Sun ONE Messaging Server, 730
Sun ONE Portal Server, 730
Sun ONE Studio, 215, 728–729
Sun ONE Web Server, 730
description, 36, 37
ebXML, 719–723
Platform for Network Identity, 701
Services on Demand, 715–718, 724–725
vision behind, 715–717
Web applications, 718
Web clients, 723
Web services, 718–723
symmetric algorithms, 624–626
synchronous connections, 513–514
Systinet
products, 36
UDDI Registry, 224, 255–256
WASP, 36, 215–221, 254–255, 688

T

tag, HTML, 314
tag, XML, 309, 314–319, 335
targetNamespace attribute
tcpmon utility, 153–154, 179–180, 198
TemplateGenerator class, 663–664
templates, XSL, 368–369
TLS (Transport Layer Security), 631, 632
<tModel> data structure, 231, 233–235, 237, 243, 244
<tModelDetail> data structure, 245, 252
<tModelInstanceDetails> data structure, 237
<tModelList> data structure, 243
Transformer, JAXP, 340
TransformerFactory class, 340, 342, 374
Transformer Factory Configuration Error, JAXP, 340
transparency, 9
Transport Layer Security (TLS), 631, 632
Triple-DES standard, 625
trust service provider, 675
Trust Services Integration Kit (Verisign), 633
trust services providers, 668–670, 678
two-tier architecture model, 6
<typeMapping> tag, 152
<types> element, 205, 208, 209

U

UDDIApiInquiry object, 261
UDDIApiPublishing object, 257, 265
UDDI Business Registry (UBR), 223–224
unDeprecateObjects ( ) method, 519
Universal Description, Discovery, and Integration (UDDI)
categorization, 233–236
data structures, 229–232
description, 29, 222–223
implementations, 254–255
inquiry API functions
find_xx functions, 235–244
get_xx functions, 244–248
search qualifiers, 248–249

Universal Description, Discovery, and Integration (UDDI) *(continued)*
limitations, 269
programming API, 226–229
publishing API functions, 249–253
publishing information to a UDDI registry, 257–260
registering as Systinet UDDI registry user, 255–256
registries
business uses of, 225
categorization in, 233–235
deleting information from, 264–268
description, 49
interfaces, 224, 225
private and public, 223
searching information in, 260–264
specifications, 225–226
UBR (UDDI Business Registry), 223
in Web services implementation, 52
in Web services architecture, 46, 49
unmarshalling, 303, 394–395
`URIResolver` interface, 376
`URLEndpoint` object, 423, 598
`User` objects, 502

V

`ValidateException` message, 395
`validate ( )` method, 395
validate service, X-KISS, 676–677
`validateSignature ( )` method, 662–663, 666
validation
Document Type Definition, 325–328
DOM and, 357
importance of, 324
JAXB services for, 303
parser configuration for, 346
SAX support for, 343
XML Schema, 328–336
`<ValidityInterval>` element, 676
Verisign, 630, 656, 668, 671, 675, 688
`VersionMismatch` attribute, 113

W

WASP (Systinet), 36, 215–221, 254–255, 688
WDDX (Web Distributed Data Exchange), 105
WebLogic
`clientgen` utility, 62, 92
database table creation, 65–69
deployment descriptor, 88–89
description, 34–35, 61–62, 215, 254
home page generation, 95–96
`servicegen` utility, 62, 91
Workshop, 61
Web service deployment descriptor (WSDD) file, 151–152, 158–159, 176
Web services
architecture
communication models, 50–51
core building blocks, 43–45
design requirements, 43
service-oriented architecture, 41
standards and technologies, 45–50
W3C working group on, 42
benefits, 38, 620
challenges in, 34
characteristics of, 25–26
definition, 22
description, 21–22
emergence of, 20
example scenario, 22–24
implementation steps, 52–53
life cycle, 203–204
motivation for, 24–25
operational model, 26–27
reasons for choosing over Web applications, 26